Exploring Criminal Justice

An Introduction

Don M. Gottfredson

Rutgers University

Roxbury Publishing Company
Los Angeles, California

Library of Congress Cataloging-in-Publication Data

Gottfredson, Don M.
  Exploring Criminal Justice: An Introduction
  Don M. Gottfredson
    p. cm.
    Includes bibliographical references and index.
    ISBN 1-891487-03-5
    1. Criminal justice, Administration of—United States. 2. Crime—United States. 3. Criminal law—United States. I. Title.
HV9950.G676 1999
364—dc21   97-29836
                                                                          CIP

Exploring Criminal Justice: An Introduction

Publisher and Editor: Claude Teweles
Copy Editors: Elsa Van Bergen and Robert Watrous
Assistant Editors: Carla Max-Ryan, Jim Ballinger, Christine Daley, and Sacha Howells
Production Editors: Renee Burkhammer and Dawn VanDercreek
Typography: Synergistic Data Systems
Cover Design: Marnie Deacon Kenney

Printed on acid-free paper in the United States of America. This paper meets the standards for recycling of the Environmental Protection Agency.

ISBN 1-891487-03-5

A Comprehensive Instructor's Resource Testing Program and Free Study Guide are available.

Roxbury Publishing Company
P.O. Box 491044
Los Angeles, California 90049-9044
Tel: (310) 473-3312 • Fax: (310) 473-4490
Email: roxbury@crl.com

Table of Contents

CHAPTER THREE:
Crime and the Law 45

CHAPTER FOUR:
The Nature and Extent of Crime 67

Preface

Here is my reason for writing this book, an explanation of why it turned out as it did, and how I think it should be evaluated.

I have written *Exploring Criminal Justice: An Introduction* for students in introductory criminal justice courses. This book would be useful reading for practitioners, particularly leaders in law enforcement, the courts, and corrections. I would like legislators, prosecutors, judges, governors, corrections administrators, others who make criminal justice policy, and members of the press, to read this book, but I do not expect them to. My intent therefore is to catch future criminal justice leaders and decision makers while they are still in college.

An author's preferences shape a book. I prefer to examine criminal justice from a rational viewpoint, although much of criminal justice is not rational. I choose to focus on decision making, though emphasis on structures and functions is more common. I favor an emphasis on potential contributions of science, even though the criminal justice system, appropriately, is embedded in a world of values. I select a focus on the most common, mundane, everyday crimes that clog the system, rather than on more dramatic, newsworthy but rare events. I emphasize how the criminal justice system responds to these most ordinary and routine crimes, rather than exceptional ones, and how offenders are processed in the criminal justice system. I believe that changes are needed toward more rationality, better decisions, increased knowledge, greater fairness, and improved effectiveness.

Nearly 350 years ago, Thomas Hobbes wrote his book *Leviathan*, which still stimulates thought on the topic of criminal justice. He wrote out of fear and a yearning for safety, though he valued liberty. He sought justice but thought it necessary to give up some freedom in order to obtain protection by the state. He sought to find the solution to this dilemma entirely by rational thought, and remarkably he anticipated many issues of contention in the criminal justice system that are discussed in this book. Hobbes relied chiefly on his own deductions, to the neglect of observation and fact. At the end of his great work, he nevertheless imposed an empirical test for its acceptance in these words:

> To conclude, there is nothing in this whole discourse . . . contrary either to the Word of God, or to good manners; or to the disturbance of the public tranquillity. Therefore I think it may be profitably printed, and more profitably taught in the Universities, in case they also think so, to whom the judgment belongeth.[1]

A test of the value of this book will be in whether it is found useful in the colleges and universities, "to whom the judgment belongeth."

Note

1. Hobbes, T. (1962) [1651]. *Leviathan*, Michael Oakeshott, (ed.), New York: Macmillan, 510.

Acknowledgements

Substantial parts of this book are a result of collaboration in research with Michael R. Gottfredson, University of Arizona, and Stephen D. Gottfredson, Virginia Commonwealth University. Gary D. Gottfredson of Gottfredson Associates, carefully reviewed a draft of the manuscript and suggested many substantial improvements. They cannot fairly be blamed for the book's shortcomings, but the better parts are probably due to them. Scott H. Decker, University of Missouri-St. Louis also read the manuscript and provided improvements. I am grateful also for additional intellectual debts due many friends and colleagues too numerous to list.

The project was conceived by Claude Teweles, President of Roxbury Publishing Company, whose help, support, and sage advice always were valued.

Appreciation and thanks are due to the people who read the first-draft manuscript for the publisher, offered many helpful suggestions, and thereby improved it. They included: Dean J. Champion, Minot State University; Ellen G. Cohn, Florida International University; Chris W. Eskridge, University of Nebraska at Omaha; Dennis M. Giever, Indiana University of Pennsylvania; William P. Heck, Northeastern State University, Oklahoma; Dennis Hoffman, University of Nebraska at Omaha; Lawrence Travis III, University of Cincinnati; Gennaro F. Vito, University of Louisville; and Richard A. Wright, State University of Arkansas. Comments on the earlier proposal for the book, which also provided beneficial guidance, were provided by: Paul Cromwell, Wichita State University; Scott H. Decker, University of Missouri, St. Louis; Thomas McAninch, Scott Community College; Frank Scarpitti, University of Delaware; and Kevin Thompson, North Dakota State University.

Tips for Students

Use the Glossary

The terms used in criminal justice often have specialized meanings that are not always clear to the general public. For example, newspaper and television reporters often confuse jails with prisons and probation with parole. Such terms are defined in the glossary at the end of this book.

Explore Criminal Justice on the World Wide Web

Informative reports, articles, and data about many aspects of crime and the criminal justice system are available increasingly on the internet. Here are some starting points:

The Criminal Justice Links by Cecil E. Greek at the School of Criminology and Criminal Justice at the Florida State University is an excellent place to start exploring (http://www.fsu.edu/~crimdo/cj.html). Follow your interests to many criminal justice topics and internet sites, often with keyword search engines. Another starting point is the National Criminal Justice Reference Service (http://www.ncjrs.org) which is one of the most extensive sources available on criminal and juvenile justice topics. Another site with links to criminal justice resources is (http://www.ojp.usdoj.gov/BJA/). For criminal justice data, start with the Bureau of Justice Statistics (http://ojp.usdoj.gov./bjs/) or the Sourcebook of Criminal Justice Statistics Online (http://www.albany.edu/sourcebook/). More recent data for many of the charts and tables in this book might be updated at the sourcebook site.

CHAPTER ONE

Introduction

Themis, Goddess of Justice The Museum Company.

Chapter One

This chapter explains the main themes of this book and provides an overview of the criminal justice system "in a nutshell." The system is explained as a series of decisions in the processing of accused persons and offenders through law enforcement, the courts, and corrections agencies, with all these decisions related to one another.

Noone can avoid the topic of crime and justice. It greets us with the morning news. It pervades our everyday lives. It stimulates debates in every part of society—from national to local levels.

Everyone has opinions about what should be done about crime. Many people hold strong and even passionate beliefs. Some ideas are based on solid facts, others on mere guesswork. Some are backed by thoughtful analyses, while others are shot from the hip. Some people emphasize the need for community safety and others stress individual freedom, but everyone wants both.

This book is an introduction to law enforcement, the criminal courts, and corrections in America. Together, these make up the U.S. criminal justice system. This book is meant as an invitation to further study about our criminal justice system.

The Main Themes of This Book

Four themes are critical to understanding the criminal justice system and how it can be improved. The first is the conflict between our desires for both personal liberty and community safety. This conflict is reflected in the everyday decisions made throughout the criminal justice system. The second theme is the idea that the agencies of criminal justice—law enforcement, the courts, jails, prisons, and probation and parole boards—are all parts of one system of criminal justice. These agencies all interact with one another and are, in turn, effected by the others. The third theme is an emphasis on the decision making of all those who work in the criminal justice system—police, prosecutors, judges, and corrections personnel. Their decisions ought to be made within a framework of legal requirements and ethical constraints. Nevertheless, the decision-making process typically allows much latitude and choice. The fourth theme is that a reliance on scientifically gathered and evaluated information should be the main resource for both decision making in the criminal justice system and the further development of the system itself. In this chapter, these themes will be explored. They are central to this book.

Personal Liberty and Community Safety

We all value both freedom and safety. It may not be immediately obvious that these values must lead to conflict, but they do, throughout our society and the criminal justice system. The behavior of some people must be controlled for the safety of others. But too much constraint by government infringes on the freedom we enjoy. Constraint is a necessary cost of civilization and the safety it provides.

> *Liberty must be limited in order to be possessed.*
> *—Edmund Burke*

Consider the decision that must be made soon after a person is arrested and taken into custody: will the accused remain in jail while awaiting trial or be released? This decision is the responsibility of a magistrate, who is a judge, when an accused person presumed innocent is first brought into court. At the heart of every such decision is a delicate balance between the goal of preserving individual freedom and the equally important goal of protecting the community. This difficult problem, arising from our values of both liberty and safety, was described by a Presidential Commission 30 years ago. Except for the reference only to males, the statement is still apt.

> The importance of this decision to any defendant is obvious. A released defendant is one who can live with and support his family, maintain his ties to his community, and busy himself with his own defense by searching for witnesses and evidence and by keeping in close touch with his lawyer. An imprisoned defendant is subjected to the squalor, idleness, and possible criminalizing effect of jail. He may be confined while presumed innocent only to be freed when found guilty; many jailed defendants, after they have been convicted, are placed on probation rather than imprisoned. The community also relies on the magistrate for protection when he makes his decision about releasing a defendant. If a released defendant fails to appear for trial, the law is flouted. If a released defendant commits crimes, the community is endangered.[1]

The strain between the desired rights of both persons and community—rights to both freedom and safety—also affects the integrity of the criminal justice process and perceptions of it. The conflict is drawn sharply, and legal scholars—even judges of the highest court in the land, the Supreme Court of the United States—often disagree. Consider the question, frequently in the news, whether evidence illegally seized by the police should be allowed into evidence at trial. In defense of allowing the use of such evidence, Appellate Court Justice Benjamin Cordozo said, "The criminal is to go free because the constable has blundered."[2]

In a landmark case, Supreme Court Justice Tom Clark delivered an opposing opinion, referring to Justice Cordozo's statement:

> In some cases this undoubtedly will be the result. . . . The criminal goes free, if he must, but it is the law that sets [that person] free. Nothing can destroy a government more quickly than a failure to observe its own laws, or worse, its disregard of the charter of its own existence.[3]

Supreme Court Justice Oliver Wendell Holmes expressed a similar view much earlier in his classic statement:

> We must consider the two objects of desire, both of which we cannot have, and make up our minds which to choose. It is desirable that criminals should be detected, and to that end that all available evidence should be used. It also is desirable that the Government should not itself foster and pay for other crimes, when they are the means by which the evidence is to be obtained. . . . We have to choose, and for my part I think it a less evil that some criminals should escape than that the Government should play an ignoble part.[4]

In delivering these opinions, Justices Holmes and Clark recognized the relation between maintaining the integrity of the criminal justice system and the search for both personal freedom and public safety. They echoed an admirable statement made by Cicero 2,000 years ago: "We are servants of the law in order to be able to be free."[5] Fundamental issues of liberty and safety are at stake, and they are essentially at odds with one another.

> *Everyone who receives the protection of society owes a return for the benefit.*
> *—John Stuart Mill*

Overview of the Criminal Justice System

The continuing strain between desire for individual freedom and needs for community protection is reflected at each stage in the processing of offenders. The main parts of the criminal justice system are summarized in Figure 1.1.[6] This chart shows the typical flow of cases through the system as a sequence of events. The process starts when a crime is committed, followed by an investigation and arrest by the police. The system is then divided into two related "subsystems"—one for juveniles and one for adults. Of course, not all persons accused of a crime go through the whole system. Many drop out at some point along the way and do not proceed to full processing.

If the accused person is an adult, the next main step is prosecution. It is up to a prosecutor—a lawyer for the state—to charge the individual with committing a crime. Another important early step in the process is the first appearance of the accused man or woman in court before a magistrate. Another step, often combined with this first appearance, is a preliminary hearing in court. At any of these and later points, a judge or a prosecutor may decide to drop the case. Also, at any point in the process, the accused person may be kept in jail or released.

The next main steps are different for cases involving more serious offenses, called felonies, and less serious ones, called misdemeanors. In either case, the person who is accused is formally charged in court. This step is called an arraignment.

The procedures of the criminal justice system usually are triggered by a call to the police. These officers have responded to a complaint of a break in and are deciding on their next steps. What they decide to do next will be critical to the rest of the criminal justice process. What should be their main concerns?

Figure 1.1 Overview of the Criminal Justice System

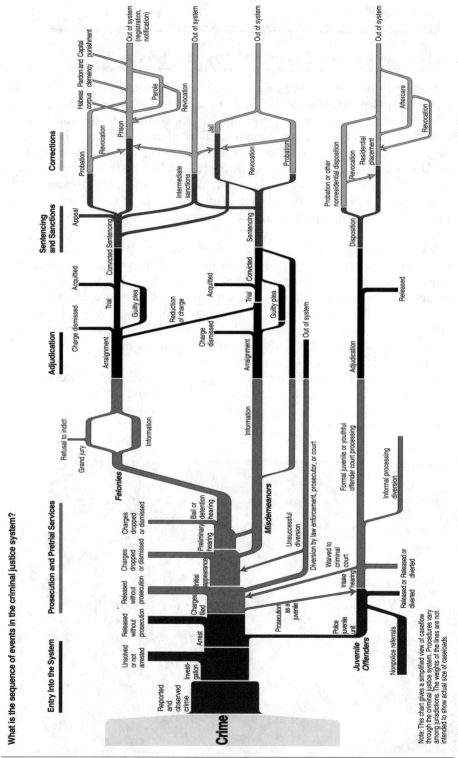

What is the sequence of events in the criminal justice system?

Note: This chart gives a simplified view of caseflow through the criminal justice system. Procedures vary among jurisdictions. The weights of the lines are not intended to show actual size of caseloads.

Source: Chaiken, J. (1998). "Revision for the Symposium on the 30th Anniversary of the President's Commission on Law Enforcement and Administration of Justice," Washington, D.C.: Bureau of Justice Statistics, U.S. Department of Justice, http://www.ojp.usdoj.gov.bjs.

If the case still has not been dropped by either the prosecutor or a judge, it may or may not go to trial. If there is a trial, there may or may not be a jury. Most cases do not go to trial because the accused person, now called a defendant, pleads guilty. This is often a result of an important process not shown on the chart, called plea negotiation or plea bargaining. It is a negotiation between the prosecutor and the lawyer for the defendant. If they reach an agreement, it must also be approved by the court.

If the defendant is convicted, the next step is sentencing by the court. Depending on the crime, the law, and court rules, penalties are decided by the judge. It is then up to the correctional agencies to carry them out. The penalties most often used are jail, prison, and probation—or a combination of them. Probation often requires that specified conditions or other punishments, including confinement, must be met.

As the chart shows, the process is different for juveniles. Some juveniles are sent to the adult courts, but many youths that remain in the juvenile court are handled informally; others proceed to judgment, called adjudication, by a judge. Even if the case is processed informally, the youth still may be confined and may participate in various programs in order to avoid potentially more severe consequences. When a youth's case is processed formally through adjudication, the decisions made usually involve probation and residential placement. Probation may include a variety of required penalties and programs. Residential placement may be in the community or confinement in a state institution.

Both youths and adults who are confined later may go through a process known as release consideration, conducted by a parole board. Whether or not there is a parole board, most offenders are supervised in the community after their release. This supervision usually is called parole, even if there is no parole board.

No single description of the criminal justice process is applicable to all jurisdictions (areas of legal authority), or individual legal systems. Specific procedural steps vary, depending especially on whether an accused person is processed for a felony (a more serious crime) or misdemeanor (less serious) charge. For example, procedures vary among jurisdictions in the use of a grand jury, a body of citizens who determine if there is sufficient evidence to bring the accused to trial. Most often, a grand jury is not involved, and the prosecutor proceeds on the basis of a document called an information. Procedures also differ among jurisdictions in the use of a preliminary hearing, when a decision regarding bail or arraignment may be made.

Not all suspects proceed through this process in the same fashion. Accused individuals may confess, waive (give up) their right to have an attorney or a trial, or plead guilty. Other defendants may contest the procedures at every step by challenging the state to prove its case. Also, there are opportunities for appeal at various stages. Specific procedures at each step are determined partly by local laws and customs. Nevertheless, Figure 1.1 summarizes the usual steps from arrest to final release in state systems.

Procedures in the federal system are similar to those in the states. Here the role of the prosecutor is served by the U.S. Attorney. An investigation often begins with a report or detection of an offense by federal officials, or by a referral from state or local prosecutors. A grand jury investigation may come before an arrest. The process continues through the federal courts, the Federal Bureau of Prisons, and the federal probation and parole system.

Criminal Justice as a System

The procedures for the punishment and control of crime should be regarded as one system. Yet, criminal justice in the U.S. is composed of a collection of agencies that were never designed as an integrated system with a single, coordinated set of objectives and programs. Instead, each of the major agencies of criminal justice—law enforcement, courts, and corrections—has developed separately. Each agency has developed within different governmental structures, each has different sources of support and different budgets, and each has different objectives. Each has developed its own requirements for staffing, drawing on different resource pools for personnel and requiring different programs of training and education. Usually, legal education is required for judges, prosecutors, and defense attorneys; in-service training is required for police and correctional officers; and college degrees are required for correctional personnel such as probation or parole officers and prison counselors. Nevertheless, all of these agencies are expected to function together in seeking justice and controlling crime.

Although these agencies are regulated by various rules and procedures, it is the people who work within these organizations who make decisions about suspects, accused persons, defendants, inmates, probationers, and parolees. Like people everywhere, those in the criminal justice system have their own personal goals, obligations, hopes, and characteristics. Some of the differences in processing cases in the criminal justice system are the result of individual differences in the people who make the decisions.

Some of the variability in criminal justice processing is because of differences in emphasis on objectives, in choices of available resources, and in information. Some is due to differences among agencies with differing organizational objectives. Each agency has a somewhat different mission. Some variability is due to differences in individual beliefs and attitudes. The result is variability in decision making, with both some predictability and some uncertainty.

Because their objectives often conflict, the various parts of the criminal justice system are not organized and operated in an orderly fashion as a single unit. There is much inefficiency in criminal justice organizations, and agencies or individuals often work at cross-purposes. They may be opposed by design, as with the positions of the defense attorney and the prosecutor. As a result, some criminal justice scholars and practitioners have suggested that because the word "system" implies a degree of organization and coordination that is far from an apt description of criminal processing, they believe it properly should be called a "non-system." That assertion is, however, merely a criticism of the lack of coordination and efficiency by the collection of agencies that make up the criminal justice system. It is best regarded as one system, despite the justifications for such objections, for several reasons (Box 1.1).

First, although the agencies of criminal justice have different obligations and objectives, the public (the "consumers" of criminal justice) expects them to be united in the ultimate purpose of seeking justice. This general goal should be of utmost importance to them all. The public is disenchanted with the system when justice is not seen to be served.

Second, the whole is more than the sum of its parts. Whatever happens in one part affects all the other parts. For example, changes in policies about arrest, bail setting, or sentencing affect populations of jails and prisons, as

Box 1.1

Criminal Justice Is Best Regarded as a System Because:

- All criminal justice agencies are expected to do justice and reduce crime;
- What happens in one part affects all the other parts;
- All workers in the criminal justice process make decisions about offenders;
- It helps understand how the parts are related.

do policies of the prosecutor. Sentencing policies set by judges or by a state agency may become less effective when a prosecutor who has a different agenda changes policies about plea bargaining decides not to prosecute on some charges, or determines to vigorously pursue others.

All parts of the system are affected by the other parts. U.S. Supreme Court decisions may change police policies, behavior, and practices. In turn, these may affect how a prosecutor handles charges—thus influencing conviction and sentencing rates. As another example, prison overcrowding may lead to the development of alternatives to confinement. This may result in changing programs in probation or parole agencies—such as house arrest, restitution (payment to victims for loss or damage), or community service. Political agendas that influence legislation may increase criminal penalties, adding substantially and quickly to the workloads of all agencies of the system. A dramatic event, such as a violent crime that is committed by a parolee, may radically affect not only the decisions of a parole board but also those of correctional management about such prison programs as furloughs (a permitted absence from prison) or work release.

Decisions made by police, prosecutors, and judges interact. Decisions by judges affect the behavior of both police and prosecutors and determine, in part, who will be confined in jails and prisons and for how long. Decisions by police affect judges, as when the seizure of improperly obtained evidence must be excluded from a trial. When police fail to make arrests on warrants (court orders) that they consider trivial the judges may stop issuing the warrants, while improperly drawn requests for warrants may not be approved by judges.

Administrators of jails and prisons must make decisions about inmate placements, which affect security in both the correctional institutions and the larger community. Decisions made by legislators, judges, and parole boards affect corrections administration. The critical workload requirements of jails and prisons are determined by the decisions of legislatures, judges, and parole boards. Their decisions are determined largely by public perceptions of crime and by the fear of crime that is influenced by the press, and, in turn, by the beliefs and aspirations of politicians. The entire system is influenced by political views, which are shaped in part by public opinion. Decisions by politicians may be based on their perceptions of what the public wants.

Third, one feature of criminal justice processing ties all the parts together. That is the passage of an offender through the agencies of government that carry out procedures for dealing with persons accused of crime. Police officers, prosecutors, judges, wardens, parole board members, and probation and parole officers *all* make decisions about alleged offenders against the law. This sequence of criminal justice decisions was described 20 years ago by one scholar as follows:

> . . . the glue which cements distant and often disparate agencies, offices and courts is the criminal justice *process* which cycles individuals from free citizens to suspects, to defendants, to convicted offenders, to probationers, inmates or parolees, and, in most instances, to eventual discharge and return to society.[7]

Fourth, for purposes of analysis, it is necessary to form a concept of criminal justice as an entire system in order to view its complexity, the interdependence of its participants, and the relationship of its functions. Examining only one part at a time—for example, police or prosecutors or judges—without regard to their effects on other parts of the system has only limited values. Decisions taken at one stage of processing are linked to those at other stages, and a change at any one point influences all others. Therefore, students of criminal justice must view the system as a whole.

Decisions in the Criminal Justice System

The flow chart of Figure 1.1 shows not only a series of episodes that make up the criminal justice process, but also the sequence of decisions that are made about offenders. Examining that series of decisions provides a different kind of overview of the system. The following case will provide an example.

Some Results of a Decision to Burgle

A man entered a house through an unlocked window at 10pm, demanded money from a woman alone in her home, and threatened her with a loaded pistol. When she did not turn over the money immediately, he shook her violently and threw her to the floor. He grabbed her purse, took $30 from it, and ran out of the house.

He was arrested after a citizen decided to call the police to report a suspicious-looking man running from his neighbor's home. A police car was sent to the scene because a dispatcher decided to do so. Two police officers in a patrol car happened to be nearby and responded. On arriving at the scene, they saw a man apparently trying to enter a nearby house through a window. He saw the officers, jumped into a car, and sped away. The officers decided to follow him. The car sped erratically down the street and crashed into a light pole. The officers decided to take the suspect into custody. When he ran, the officers decided that he was resisting arrest. One officer decided to tackle him and the other decided to hit him twice with a nightstick. They decided to search for weapons, and they found a pistol and a small plastic bag containing a white powder. They then decided that there was probable cause to arrest the driver, which they decided to do, and they decided to handcuff him, to take him to the station, and to "read him his rights."

He was interviewed in prison five months later, and part of the conversation is reported in Box 1.2. Actually, when the police arrested that prison inmate as a suspect, they triggered an elaborate—but fairly predictable—series of events that resulted in the man's incarceration. The process that landed him in prison involved many people, including the victim, a neighbor, the police, the prosecutor, the public defender, a magistrate, a judge, a pro-

Box 1.2

Chapter 1

▲ ▲ ▲ ▲ ▲ ▲

Interview in Prison

Prison Counselor (PC): "What are you doing here?"

Inmate (I): "Ten years."

PC: "Yes, but why?"

I: "Because the criminal justice system is a farce."

PC: "What do you mean?"

I: "They don't protect your rights, man. I didn't even have a trial."

PC: "You had a lawyer, didn't you?"

I: "No, I had a public defender."

PC: "What was the charge?"

I: "Robbery"

PC: "You didn't do it?"

I: "Oh, I did it. But they didn't *prove* it. They call it the criminal justice system because it's criminal, man, the way they mess you around."

bation officer, various sheriff's deputies in the county jail, and interviewers prior to a bail hearing. It might have also involved bail bondsagents, jurors, and others. The events the offender could expect were not yet over and would involve many others in the criminal justice arena. They would include various correctional workers—custodial and treatment staff—a parole board, parole officers, and others.

Much earlier, when the accused man was still in the county jail, not yet convicted and sent to the state prison, he had been interviewed by a worker from a non-profit justice assistance agency. The interviewer discovered that the man had no family ties in the city, no permanent residence, and no employment. The worker decided not to recommend ROR—that he be released on his own recognizance, that is, on his own promise to appear later when required.

At an initial appearance in court, a magistrate decided not to release the defendant without bail and set it at $50,000. Lacking funds, the accused stayed in jail. He was interviewed by a sheriff's deputy, who decided that he was not a threat to others in the general population of the jail, not an escape or suicide risk, and not in need of any immediate medical treatment. The deputy decided to assign him to the general population with a medium security classification.

At a preliminary hearing, the magistrate decided that there was probable cause to believe that the accused man had committed a felony and decided also on a date for the trial. At the same time, noting the defendant's lack of resources, the judge decided to appoint a public defender to represent him.

The county assistant prosecutor decided to investigate the circumstances of the alleged offense and decided that the evidence indicated that the accused had committed the following crimes: breaking and entering, burglary, assault with intent to rob, aggravated assault, armed robbery, robbery with force or threat, petty theft, reckless driving, carrying a concealed weapon, resisting arrest, and possession of a controlled substance (cocaine). The prosecutor knew that the maximum sentences for these offenses, if the accused were to be convicted of them all, could total as much as 70 years. She decided that the evidence was not strong for the more serious charges of robbery, assault, and burglary, because the victim failed to identify the accused in a line-up that the police had decided to conduct. The strongest evidence was that for the weapon, possession, and driving charges.

The public defender, the suspect's defense attorney, knew the possible penalties as well. He knew also that there was a probable desire on the part of the assistant prosecutor to avoid a lengthy trial but also to obtain a conviction, especially for the violent crimes. He made his own evaluation of the strength of the evidence. They jointly decided that a guilty plea to the robbery charge and dropping the other charges would be in the best interests of the defendant and the state.

After discussion with the public defender, the defendant, seeking to minimize the expected prison term, decided to plead guilty to the charge of robbery. The judge decided to accept the plea and to dismiss the other charges. The judge knew that the offender could be placed on probation or sent to either the county jail or the state prison. If the judge decided on prison, the defendant could be sentenced, under the laws of the state, to between one and 20 years. If the judge decided on jail, the defendant could be confined for up to a year; and this could be, if the judge so decided, combined with a term of probation. The judge decided on the sentence of 10 years in the state prison. Under the laws of the state, if the judge decided to execute, or carry out, the sentence, the convicted man would be required to spend one-third of that time in prison before being eligible to be considered for parole by the state parole board.

At a sentencing hearing, the judge read a presentence report that had been prepared by a probation officer and provided details of the offense and the defendant's social history. This was required in this state for felony cases, as decided by the chief justice of the supreme court of the state. The probation officer had decided to recommend against probation because of the offender's extensive criminal history.

The judge decided to execute the sentence, instead of granting a suspended sentence, and the convicted offender was delivered by the sheriff's officers to the custody of the Director of Corrections. A correctional officer decided that restraints were not necessary while moving the prisoner. After he was taken to a reception center for the state prison system, the correctional staff decided that the inmate did not require maximum, close, or protective custody and that he could be placed in the general population.

The man was interviewed the next day as part of a series of procedures used for inmate classification that would guide others in deciding on the choices of institutional assignments for custody and treatment. These procedures would determine, for example, the particular prison to which he would be sent, how closely he would be guarded, and his placement in work, school, or vocational programs. These choices would structure much of the inmate's life for the next several years—at least until the parole board decided to parole him or his term expired.

The inmate's term, however, was shortened somewhat when institutional staff decided to award him "good time" (time off for good behavior). Since the inmate had no alleged rule infractions in prison, the correctional staff did not have to decide on either guilt or penalty for any rule violations. However, at reclassification (the review of a prisoner's status after two years) they did decide to reduce his custody classification from medium to minimum. This made the inmate eligible for consideration for assignment to a work release program, which the correctional staff decided against. At his next parole board hearing, the board would decide whether to parole him or not.

If they did decide on parole, they would decide also on any special conditions of release, and the parole division of the state department of corrections would begin a process of decisions concerning his supervision and program placements. If conditions of parole were alleged to have been violated, a parole officer would decide whether to recommend that parole be revoked (withdrawn). If so, the parole board would decide whether the parolee would be returned to prison to finish his term or continued on parole, with or without changed conditions.

The Nature of Criminal Justice Decisions

Decisions are the stuff of the criminal justice system. The decisions noted in this hypothetical example are but a few of the many made at every step in the criminal justice process. Many are of extreme importance to the individuals directly affected, to crime control, and to justice. They deal with issues of liberty or the loss of it and with other serious intrusions into individual lives. They concern also the community's desire and need for protection. They are critical to the efficient, effective, and humane functioning of the criminal justice system.

In examining decisions, the concept of *rational* decision making is useful.[8] A *rational* decision is the choice, among those possible for the decision maker, that makes it most likely that the objectives of the decision will be achieved. It requires examination, at each step in the criminal justice process, of the goals, choices, and information needs of decision makers. The concept is simple but important. You can apply it to your own decisions. For any decision you make, you can identify your goals, your possible choices, and the information you have. Then you can select what seems at the time to be the best decision. You probably want to choose the option most likely to achieve your goals.

A similar analysis can be applied to both individual (or case) decisions and institutional (or management) decisions in criminal justice. For example, police officers decide on a case-by-case basis to make an arrest or not. Police managers make policy decisions that may involve programs or patterns of enforcement—such as an emphasis on enforcement of handgun laws, "crackdowns" in high crime areas, curfew enforcement, or targeting repetitive offenders for surveillance.

Criminal justice decisions ordinarily are made within wide areas of choice. The aims of the decisions are not always clear, and often their purposes are the subject of heated controversy and debate. Usually they are not guided by clear decision policies. Often the participants are not able to tell us the basis for the decisions they make. Adequate information for the decisions is often not available. Rarely can we demonstrate that the decisions are rational.

Rational Decisions

The definition of a rational decision points to the three parts of any decision, as suggested in Box 1.3.

First, there is a *goal*, or a set of goals or purposes, to be achieved in making the decision. If it is not known what is intended to be achieved in making a decision, then it is not possible to assess the rationality of that decision.

Box 1.3

Rational Decision Making

A rational decision is a decision that, on the basis of the information available, selects the alternative action that maximizes the likelihood of achievement of specified goals and objectives. Thus, for any decision, it is necessary to specify the **goals** of the decision, to identify the available **alternatives**, and to have confidence that the data available provide **information** that reduces uncertainty about the outcomes of the decision.

Second, the decision maker has some choices, some *alternatives*. If there is no choice, there is no decision to be made. Usually there is a choice, but the only alternative may be to decide not to decide. The choice not to decide may have profound consequences. Choosing to do nothing has its impact: a victim decides not to report a crime, and the criminal justice system is not invoked; a police officer decides not to arrest, and the criminal justice system is not invoked; a prosecutor determines that charges will not be filed, and the criminal justice system is no longer involved. The prison inmate whose case is "continued" after his parole hearing with "no decision" rightly regards this as a denial of parole.

Third, some *information* is available and may be used in reaching the decision. This means that the decision maker has some data that are related to the objectives of the decision.

Information does not mean mere data, no matter how carefully collected or how reliable the facts and figures. Information is data that are *related* to the aims of the decision. Data must be organized and sifted out in order to be useful to the decision maker. As described by Peter Drucker,

> A "database," no matter how copious, is not information. It is information's ore. For raw material to become information, it must be organized for a task, directed toward specific performance, applied to a decision. Raw material cannot do that itself. . . . Computer people still are concerned with greater speed and bigger memories. But the challenges increasingly will be not technical, but to convert data into usable information that is actually being used.[9]

Consider again the magistrate at the bail hearing. An accused person's height or shoe size are data, but they are not related to the likelihood of his or her appearance for trial. Age and the accused person's criminal history may be related to the magistrate's goals for the decision and therefore provide information helpful to reaching it rationally. Unfortunately, knowledge of the relation of the data available for decisions to their objectives is often lacking, and decisions may be based on invalid information. Modern technology can quickly provide a great deal of data to individuals making decisions. In order to be useful, however, the data must be studied and turned into helpful information.

If the victim of a crime, or a police officer, or a judge is unclear about the objectives of a decision, we cannot expect that person to make rational decisions. Of course, people do have objectives in making such decisions, but often they are only vaguely felt and difficult to express. Moreover, the objectives of such decisions often conflict. The decisions made in the criminal justice system are expected to serve many masters. The judge whose sentences are expected to exact punishment, as well as control crime by warning others, rehabilitate the offender, keep the culprit off the streets, and foster the perception that justice is being done experiences such conflicts because these purposes often conflict with each other. The police officer whose arrests are expected to serve interests of both public protection and individual rights is well aware of similar conflicting aims—at least when the opportunity for calm reflection arrives.

So it goes throughout the criminal justice system. Each step in the process requires decisions having profound effects on persons and groups. And at each step, fundamental conflicts may arise. The decision of the victim about reporting a crime to the police is so critical that the victim may be regarded as the principal gatekeeper for the criminal justice system. Decisions made by police are also central. If a crime is reported to or discovered by police officers, it is those officers who ordinarily must decide what to do next. Generally, they must decide whether to invoke the law. This involves first a decision about whether a crime has occurred. It may require deciding legal issues that determine whether an arrest may be made. In deciding whether to arrest, the police may have alternatives such as issuing a citation, referring to a social agency, offering counseling, or doing nothing.

The decisions made by prosecutors are less in the public eye than those of police officers or judges. Nevertheless, the discretion of prosecutors is very broad, and their decisions have profound consequences for the rest of the criminal justice system. They too must decide whether to invoke the law: Should the accused person be charged with a crime? What crime or crimes should be charged? Will the accused be brought to trial, or should a plea of guilty to a lesser offense be negotiated? What resources of the prosecutor's office should be brought to bear on the investigation? Again, the prosecutor may have various goals, some of which may be in conflict. Such goals may include increasing convictions, winning cases, cracking down on specific crimes, changing the behavior of defendants, seeing the guilty punished, or ensuring that the innocent are not.

A plea bargain is a result of negotiation by the defendant—usually, the defense lawyer—and the prosecutor (another lawyer). If the judge accepts the agreement and the defendant pleads guilty, as here, the penalty imposed by the judge may be less severe. Do you believe this practice should be permitted? —*Photo courtesy of www. photostogo.com.*

The judge must follow the law but traditionally has considerable authority and discretion. In analyzing the judge's decisions, the information available, the judge's goals, and available choices must be considered. The judge must depend on the police officer, the prosecutor, the probation officer, and others for information. The sentencing goals of individual judges reflect the often conflicting aims of the entire criminal justice system and seek to provide both deserved punishment and crime control. After guilt has been decided, the judge must consider alternative sentencing choices. The judge must select sentences within legal boundaries that vary among jurisdictions. Thus, sentencing decisions, like those of other criminal justice personnel, involve complex goals, information, various alternatives, and much discretion. Sentencing decisions seriously affect every part of the criminal justice system. Yet, it is a striking fact that they are made without any clear agreement on the aims of sentencing within a coherent, consistent theory of justice.

The administrator of a prison or jail may be compared to someone trying to run a type of hotel without the benefit of a reservation service. Most prisons and jails in the United States are overcrowded. The number of Americans in jail or prison is at an all-time high. The administrator has little to say about who comes to stay or for how long, but within the institution he or she must make many decisions. These decisions, like those of the police, prosecutors, and courts, are of two types: policy decisions and individual case decisions. Policy decisions are broad, involving appropriate levels of development of security and treatment. Individual decisions may be urgently required, such as assigning a prisoner to suicide watch or placing him or her in protective custody, or may be less pressing but still important for the whole program, e.g., selecting the housing unit and work assignment. They may be critical to rehabilitative aims, such as placing an inmate in an educational program, or assigning the person to counseling. The aims, like those elsewhere in the criminal justice system, are complex, and they may be in conflict, as when concerns for security and custody and those of treatment are at odds.

Probation, although typically a part of court supervision, is also a part of community corrections and control. Probation decisions do not end with the judge's selection of a sentencing disposition. Rather, the judge's assignment starts a series of decisions by probation personnel. Similarly, the decision of a paroling authority to release a prisoner under supervision begins a series of decisions by parole personnel. Their objectives, alternatives, and information needs are similar to those of others working in the criminal justice system.

Paroling decisions are highly visible and much debated. Goals of parole board members, like those of judges, reflect differing perspectives: to apply appropriate sanctions or penalties, to provide treatment, to be fair, to represent the general public, and to control prison populations. Like judges, parole boards have been much criticized for arbitrary decision making, for unwarranted disparity (inequality) in granting or denying parole, and for ineffectiveness. Like other criminal justice decision makers, they face complex and often ill-defined aims, many alternative choices, and the problem of having to rely on others in the criminal justice system for information to assist in making the decisions. As always, the goals of societal protection and individual liberty conflict.

Emphasis on Science

The fourth theme of this book is a stress on the use of empirical data — that is, on observable evidence — to permit rational decisions in both

Jail administrators must quickly make many decisions affecting the safety and welfare of defendants, other inmates and staff, as well as those affecting secure custody and the safety of the community. This accused woman awaits trial, isolated from others in protective custody. Under what circumstances would an inmate require such protection? —*Photo courtesy of Erwing Galloway by permission of www. photostogo.com.*

policy and individual decisions in criminal justice. This is an emphasis on science. The power of science can be exercised safely only in a context of values, beyond the scope of this book, but it can be harnessed within ethical constraints to improve our criminal justice system.

The application of scientific methods to criminal justice decision making offers hope for the improvement of our system of criminal justice. A central role for knowledge in a criminal justice world of emotionally charged values may be seen as naive, or an embarrassingly optimistic faith in a potential for rational change. Yet the use of a scientific attitude can avoid unspecified goals, presumptions taken as facts, and untested hunches acted upon with vigor and confidence. We should seek the ideal of well-defined aims and the improvement of methods to attain them, informed by systematic study and based on the evidence.

A questioning attitude, a healthy skepticism, and an insistent demand for the evidence are hallmarks of the scientific perspective. That is a valuable orientation for examining the decisions of the criminal justice system. Still, we have to choose the right questions to ask, and we should ask them in the right way. The best questions are often those that can be answered by looking at the evidence, at the observable facts. This is an attitude that sets the scientific orientation apart from others.

> *The important thing is not to stop questioning.*
> —*Albert Einstein*

Not all good questions about criminal justice are empirical questions, answered by examining the evidence. Some are questions of morality and ethics. In criminal justice, these questions often are interwoven. Both are important, but it is important also not to confuse the two.

The Appearance of Justice

A goal of the criminal justice system, not always prominent but surely desirable, is that justice not only be done but be perceived as being done. A related desire—not the same, but also welcome—is that the criminal justice system be perceived to be effective in crime control. Perceptions of justice and of effectiveness of the system may or may not square with reality, but it is important to ask whether people in general have confidence in the criminal justice system.

That is just what was asked in a recent national public opinion survey reported by Flanagan and Longmire.[10] Figure 1.2 shows the question and the national estimates of answers by persons 18 or older in the United States. Flanagan suggests that these survey results be considered in the context of people's attitudes about crime and criminal justice, on which he comments in Box 1.4.[11] The police, as in earlier surveys, fare the best, (although only 60 percent of those surveyed expressing a lot of confidence may be thought rather discouraging). Only a third of respondents expressed a lot of confidence in the courts, and only a quarter did so for the probation and prison systems—or for the criminal justice system as a whole.

It is easy to speculate about what might keep the confidence ratings down. For example, the police do not always follow the laws they are expected to enforce. Only one televised unlawful beating by police officers can destroy a lot of confidence. Yet, the police have the highest ratings. What about the other parts of the system?

If we examine the stages of the criminal justice system, we may discover features that could reduce public confidence. Victims of crime very often are not advised of any results of their report of a crime. Witnesses, and sometimes victims, may perceive that they themselves have been treated like criminals. Bail may be set in what some may regard as an arbitrary manner, with little thought for the safety of the community. Prosecutors and defense attorneys sometimes are perceived to be so intent on winning that they lose respect for the truth and for the fairness of the court system that they are sworn to protect. Judicial rulings may be seen as biased toward one side or the other. The sentences by judges may be perceived as unpredictable and

---

Figure 1.2 American's Confidence in the Criminal Justice System, 1996

Question: 'First of all, I am going to read you a list of institutions in American society. Please tell me how much confidence you have in each one':

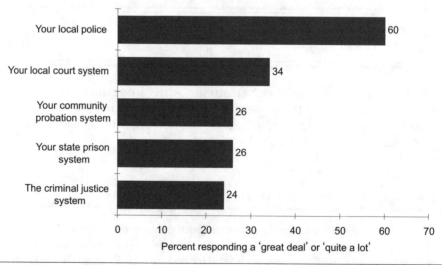

Source: Flanagan, T. (1996). "Community Corrections in the Public Mind," *Federal Probation* 60, 3, 5.

Box 1.4

Chapter 1

▲ ▲ ▲ ▲ ▲ ▲

Timothy Flanagan: In His Own Words

The first dimension is fear of crime. Survey researchers operationalize this dimension as fear, worry, concern, and other terms, but the basic outlines are clear. Americans express a fairly high degree of concern about personal safety and have done so for many years. They worry about their homes being burglarized when they are away and about break-ins when they are at home; they worry about robbery on the streets and in parking lots; they worry about carjackings and drive-by shootings; women worry about sexual assault; and adults worry not only about themselves but about the safety of their children and their elderly parents. Fear of crime is largely unrelated to the objective risk of victimization (older Americans have the lowest victimization rates but the highest fear rates), and fear has remained constant as reported crime rates have gone up and down. There is a rich literature about the factors that produce these high fear levels, especially about the role of the media. . . .

The second primary dimension of Americans' views about crime and justice is exasperation with and loss of confidence in the official criminal justice system. This loss of confidence varies across the criminal justice system—the police are much more highly respected and enjoy more public confidence and support than other components of the criminal justice system—and this has been so for decades. However, this dimension is best summarized in the view that public confidence in the ability of collective security mechanisms to protect them from crime and victimization has declined. And make no mistake about it—social defense, or protecting citizens from criminal victimization, is widely seen by Americans as the superordinate function of the criminal justice system. Efficiency is important, fairness is valued, integrity of justice system officials is expected, but these goals pale in comparison to the expectation that the criminal justice system exists to protect us from crime.

The third dimension is that attributions about criminals have changed. Offenders are no longer seen (if they ever were) as products of poor social settings or as unfortunate victims or "boys gone bad." Instead the view of the criminal in the public mind has transformed into a more volitional, more willful actor—undoubtedly the rise in weapon use, drug use, and gangs has fostered this transformation [citation omitted]. Of course, an important consequence of this attributional shift has been greater willingness to support punitive responses to crime that focus on incapacitation. If offenders choose crime, after all, then rehabilitation as a response seems less appropriate than severe sanctions designed to tilt the equation in favor of choosing a legitimate alternative.

—Timothy Flanagan,
Sam Houston State University

made without due care. Sentences may be seen as unfair—either as too much or too little or as out of line with other similar offenders.

Parole decisions may be seen as biased or careless. Keeping punishment in proportion to crime and equal treatment are important issues. Perceptions of too little or too much time for the crime, or not as much as or more than others guilty of the same crime, frequently lead to complaints. The prison system may be seen as neither punishing enough nor correcting the offender successfully. If escapes from custody occur, prisons do not protect society. Placing prison inmates on work furlough programs or in community halfway houses may be perceived as a foolhardy risk to the safety of the community. Crimes committed by parolees may be seen as obvious evidence of the failure of the entire system.

Police, judges, juries, and corrections administrators often are soundly criticized as the result of a relatively rare event. Thousands of police officers may daily go about their tasks of responding to interpersonal crises in a deliberate, professional manner and of taking care to assure the rights of the accused; but an illegal, brutal beating of a suspect by officers may make headline news and markedly affect the perceptions of the community about the police as a whole. The vast majority of persons released on bail return to court when ordered to do so; but when one bailed suspect is arrested for a crime, calls come from the press for tightening up the bail process to keep more accused persons locked up. When one jury acquits a defendant in a highly publicized trial, during which many television viewers had already reached a verdict of guilty, some persons see this as clear evidence of system failure and call for changing the rules. Thousands of furloughed prisoners complete their terms in the community without incident; but a crime by one furloughed prisoner, widely publicized in a political campaign, may reduce the use in corrections of a wide variety of promising community programs. Most crime is mundane, unpleasant, annoying, and relatively minor; but when a relatively small number of extreme, outrageous, and shocking criminal acts are highly publicized, calls for more severe punishment abound. Longer prison terms are seen as deserved and needed for crime control. Demands for more frequent and longer confinement of both accused and convicted persons increase.

Widespread perceptions of bias—particularly racial bias—no doubt lower the ratings of the justice system and its parts. Whether there is racial bias at a given decision point in the system, or in a given place, or at a given time are questions that can be answered empirically. The evidence is that such bias does affect decisions throughout the system, at some times, in some places, and to some degree. It is clear that some groups of Americans *expect* racial bias in dealings with the criminal justice system.

> *For the urban poor the police are those who arrest you.*
> —*Michael Harrington*

From their review of the evidence on drug policy, Mauer and Huling commented:

> Drug policies constitute the single most significant factor contributing to the rise in criminal justice populations in recent years, with the number of in-carcerated drug offenders having risen by 510 percent from 1983 to 1993. . . . Racial disproportions are worst for drug possession offenses. . . . [B]lacks make up 12–13 percent of the national population and of monthly drug users but 35 percent of drug possession arrestees, 55 percent of convictions, and 74 percent of prisoners sentenced for drug possession. . . . While debate will continue on the degree to which the criminal justice system overall contributes to racial disparities, there is increasing evidence that the policies and practices of the "war on drugs" have been an unmitigated disaster for young blacks and members of other minorities. Whether these policies were consciously or unconsciously designed to incarcerate more members of minority races is a question that may be debated. Those policy choices have, however, not only failed to reduce drug trafficking or use, but have seriously eroded the life prospects of disadvantaged minority Americans. [12]

> *Where justice is denied, where poverty is enforced, where ignorance prevails, and where one class is made to feel that society is an organized conspiracy to oppress, rob, and degrade them, neither persons nor property will be safe.*
> —Frederick Douglass

Justice With Eyes Open

The classic figure of Justice is a symbol with several meanings. Her blindfold represents fair, evenhanded justice; her scales represent a weighing of the evidence and seriousness of the crime; and her sword represents certain punishment for wrongdoers. Much of the criticism of the criminal justice system concerns a perceived lack of fairness and evenhandedness in decisions about accused and convicted offenders. The blindfold makes a good point, but it should be removed.

With eyes open, Justicia can examine justice, including fairness, in the context of a society that changes but nevertheless has enduring ideals. She can better weigh the moral and ethical concerns that provide the basis for the criminal justice system. She can make better use of the evidence that now comes from scientific study. With eyes open, she can acknowledge the importance of observation and can examine the evidence. Then she can make decisions that are more ethically sound, fair, and effective, better protecting both safety and liberty.

Summary

The criminal justice system reflects an enduring conflict between our desires for safety and freedom. We demand both, but this often gives rise to conflict and difficult decisions.

In brief, the process is composed of arrest, charging, conviction, sentencing, and corrections. The three main components are law enforcement, the courts, and corrections.

The collection of agencies that compose criminal justice are best viewed as parts of one system because:

- All have the ultimate purpose of seeking justice.

- Whatever happens in one part affects all the other parts.

- All offenders who do not drop out of the system along the way pass through a succession of criminal justice decision points, and all actors in the criminal justice process have in common that they all make decisions about offenders.

- It is necessary for purposes of analyses of the criminal justice process to conceptualize the whole system and the interdependence of its parts.

The best questions to ask about the criminal justice system are often empirical. These are questions that can be answered by observation—that is, by looking at the evidence. This is an important part of the scientific perspective.

Justice should be done, and justice should be seen to be done. Overall, the public does not now have a great deal of confidence in the criminal justice system.

There is a need for examination of the criminal justice system in the context of our changing society and our enduring ideals of justice while making better use of evidence from scientific study. Rational decisions are required within the framework of the moral, ethical, and legal concerns that are needed to support the criminal justice system.

Notes

1. President's Commission on Law Enforcement and Administration of Justice. (1967). *The Challenge of Crime in a Free Society*. Washington, D.C.: GPO, 31.

2. *People v. De Fore* (1926). Court of Appeals of New York. 242 N.Y. 13, 150 N.E. 587, as cited by Kaplan, J., J. H. Skolnick, and M. M. Feeley. (1991). *Criminal Justice: Introductory Cases and Materials*, 5th ed. Westbury, NY: The Foundation Press, 262–263.

3. *Mapp v. Ohio* (1961). 376 U.S. 643.

4. *Olmstead v. United States* (1928). 277 U.S. 438, 469.

5. As cited in Friedrich, C. J. (1963). *The Philosophy of Law in Historical Perspective*, 2nd ed. Chicago: University of Chicago Press, 34.

6. Chaiken, J. (1998). "Revision for the Symposium on the 30th Anniversary of the President's Commission on Law Enforcement and Administration of Justice," Washington, D.C.: Bureau of Justice Statistics, U.S. Department of Justice, fttp://www.ojp.usdoj.gov/bjs.

7. Newman, D. J. (1978). *Introduction to Criminal Justice*, 2nd ed. New York: Lippincott, 105.

8. Gottfredson, M. R. and D. M. Gottfredson. (1988). *Decision Making in Criminal Justice: Toward the Rational Exercise of Discretion*, 2nd ed. New York: Plenum Press.

9. Drucker, P. F. (1992). "Be Data Literate—Know What to Know." *The Wall Street Journal*, Tuesday, December 1, 1992.

10. Flanagan, T. and D. Longmire. (eds.). (1996). *Americans View Crime and Justice: A National Public Opinion Survey*. Thousand Oaks, CA: Sage, as cited in Flanagan, T. (1996). "Community Corrections in the Public Mind," *Federal Probation* 60, 3, 3–9.

11. Ibid., 4–5.

12. Mauer, M. and T. Huling. (1995). "One in Three Young Black Men Ensnared in Justice System." *Overcrowded Times* 6, 6, 1–10.

CHAPTER TWO

The Criminal Justice System

Photo courtesy of the New Jersey Department of Corrections.

Chapter Two

The overview of the criminal justice system and its decisions presented in Chapter One left out several important steps and concepts. To fill in the blanks, this chapter provides a closer look at criminal justice decision making and the main steps in the criminal justice process.

❑ Questions to Think About
❑ The Criminal Justice System and Its Decision Processes
❑ A Closer Look at the System
❑ Accusation
    Report or Observation of a Crime
    Investigation
    Arrest
    Initial Appearance
    Preliminary Hearing
❑ Prosecution
    Determination of Charges
    Arraignment on Indictment or Information
    Competency
    Plea Bargaining
❑ Conviction
    Trial
    Appeal of the Convictions
    Sentencing
    Presentence Investigation and Report
    Appeal of the Sentence
❑ Punishment
    Discharge
❑ Summary

What are the main parts of the criminal justice system?

Do we have a *system* of criminal justice?

Who makes decisions in the criminal justice system?

What is a *rational* decision?

What are the differences between case and management decisions?

What information is needed for management decisions?

What choices do prosecutors have?

Must the judge sentence a convicted offender to a specific punishment?

Can a judge set aside a jury's verdict?

Can a parole officer revoke a parole and return the offender to prison?

Can you define these terms?

arrest

grand jury

arraignment

jail

probable cause

reasonable doubt

probation

The Criminal Justice System and Its Decision Processes

Criminal justice decisions are made within limits established by the U.S. Constitution, state constitutions, and the statutes and precedents of the criminal law. Despite these restrictions, however, wide areas of discretion remain.

Rational decisions are those most likely to achieve objectives of the decision makers. To get a rational decision, it is necessary to identify what the goals of the decision are, what choices exist, and what information is available for making the decision. This is often more difficult than one might suppose. The purpose of a decision is not always clear. It may even be the subject of heated debate. There may be several objectives, and they may conflict with each other. Few decision makers in the criminal justice system—police, prosecutors, judges, correctional workers—have been trained specifically in making decisions. In many cases they are unable to tell us the basis for their selection of a particular decision alternative. They may say that they had a hunch or chose the alternative that felt best, or they may offer some other vague explanation. They may or may not be aware of all the alternatives available to them. They may or may not invent new alternatives. They may have personal preferences for some choices. Because adequate information for making decisions is usually not available, these decision makers must rely mainly on their own experience and judgment. Their interpretation of that experience may be biased and the judgments they make often are highly subjective. Whether the decisions are rational may be examined at each step in the criminal justice process.

Consider the following examples of typical decisions made on a regular basis throughout the criminal justice system. A police officer, for instance, wants to make "good arrests" that will not be dismissed immediately in court, for example, for lack of evidence. The officer has some information—about the circumstances and evidence of the crime, the offender, and the rules and practices of the police department and of the court—on which to base the decision whether or not to arrest a particular suspect. Similarly, the prosecutor wants to maximize the likelihood of obtaining a conviction on the charges. He or she has some information to go on, such as the strength of the evidence, in deciding whether or not to press charges in a particular case.

In contrast to the prosecutor, who wants to ensure a conviction, the defense lawyer may seek to obtain an acquittal or minimize the prison term. The goal of the judge at sentencing may be to exact the punishment deserved, to protect society by keeping offenders off the streets, to warn others not to commit crimes, to teach offenders a lesson, or to place offenders in rehabilitative programs. The judge may also seek to demonstrate to the public that justice is done, thereby increasing confidence in the criminal justice system.

Criminal justice decisions are complex, but it is helpful, nevertheless, to remember the three main parts of any decision—goals, alternatives, and information. To make a rational decision, one needs to understand what the specific objectives are, identify the alternative decision choices and use the information available to decision makers in achieving their objectives.

When a criminal act occurs, the event may or may not be noticed or observed. If a victim or other observer does not report an offense to the police or other law enforcement officials, the criminal justice system is not involved. But when an offense is reported or alleged, a complex sequence of decisions typically follows.

Recall that the decisions made in the criminal justice system are of two general kinds. *Individual* or case decisions are made about persons. Examples could include decisions to take a person into custody, to release an accused before trial, to sentence a convicted defendant to a specific prison term, to assign an inmate to maximum custody, or to require a special condition of parole. *Institutional* or management decisions deal with questions of general policy. Examples could include decisions to stop arresting persons for possession of marijuana, to prosecute violent crimes vigorously and devote more resources to that endeavor, to develop a house arrest program, to avoid jail before trial for anyone not an immediate threat, to develop a prison industries program, or to form a special unit for intensive supervision.

In both case and management decisions, the general nature of the decision process is the same. A problem exists that requires choices to be made on the basis of information, according to some strategy. These choices have consequences that are critical to the efficient and effective working of the criminal justice system.

Take a specified action: A police officer may decide to arrest a husband who assaults his wife, or a judge may dispose of a case after conviction by suspending the imposed sentence, placing the offender on probation, and requiring a condition of weekly drug testing. These are examples of case decisions. A management decision would be a chief probation officer's de - termination to develop an intensive supervision program that involves reas - signing some officers to smaller caseloads for this purpose.

Decide not to decide: Failing to take action or postponing it may be helpful or costly; but like other alternatives, a decision "not to decide," or to delay the decision, has its own consequences and outcomes.

Investigate further: It might be decided in a particular case that a psycho - logical evaluation is required or that the family situation of a suspect should be further investigated. A chief probation officer might determine that re - search should be done on how well an intensive supervision program works.

An outcome (or, more typically, multiple outcomes) is associated with any decision. The outcome consists of all the consequences of a given decision that concern the person making the decision (or the institution represented).[1] The outcomes have different probabilities and may be valued differently. Also, different "stakeholders," or interested parties, value the outcomes differently.

Looking at decisions in this way makes it obvious that the ability to estimate outcomes—that is, to know what should be expected—is critical to making good decisions. Therefore, it is necessary to keep track of the out-comes associated with the selection of the various alternatives and to keep score. The recording and analysis of past experience is needed to confidently estimate the outcomes to be expected from new decisions.

The required knowledge of decision outcomes is different for the two kinds of decisions. Individual case decisions are based on expected behavior outcomes with information about the person used to arrive at this estimate. Management decisions are based on knowledge or belief in the effects of programs on outcomes.

Testing beliefs about the effectiveness of programs is the basis for pro-gram evaluations. For example, a police chief may devote increased patrol resources to a particular area, based on the belief that this will reduce crime in that area. A legislature may increase prison terms for a particular classi-fication of convicted offenders, based on the belief that this will reduce crimes of a certain kind. A state agency may develop guidelines that define the general policy within which judges must carry out their sentencing, based on the belief that sentences will be made more fair or effective.

Our discussion of rational decision making in criminal justice is not meant to imply that all, or even most, criminal justice decisions are now made rationally. Besides the problems that goals and objectives are not al-ways clear, alternatives are lacking or could be improved, and information is wanting, there is another large obstacle to rational decision making: crime is a topic highly laden with emotion.

Because we value freedom, we react strongly to violations or threats of violation of our persons or property. We resist any threat to our liberty by agencies of the government. Because we value safety, we expect the criminal justice system to protect us. We want both protection for ourselves and for our own liberty.

Because criminal justice decisions, both policy and individual, are made by humans, all human reactions may come into the decision-making process. Decisions in criminal justice may be based more on anger, prejudice, wishful thinking, or impulse than on a rational problem-solving design.

A Closer Look at the System

Consider the criminal justice system as composed of three phases. A person may be:

(1) Accused of a crime.

(2) Prosecuted and convicted.

(3) Punished.

The sequence of major decisions in each of these three phases, as they occur in most states, is depicted in Figures 2.1, 2.2, and 2.3. Put together, these three charts provide a detailed summary of decisions typically made in the entire system.

Accusation

Report or Observation of a Crime

When an apparent crime is *observed* by the police or the prosecutor, who together represent law enforcement, or when a crime is *reported* to either of these agencies, the criminal justice system is invoked.

A crime that is not observed or reported to law enforcement officials, no matter how important it may be, does not prompt a response from the system. This is true whether a crime is not reported because it is not observed by anyone or because it is not regarded as a crime. An example of the latter situation would be an assault upon one spouse by the other that the victim does not realize is a violation of the criminal law.

Even when an event is recognized as a crime, initiation of the criminal justice process is not triggered unless the event is observed by law enforcement officials or reported to them. For instance, if the victim of a spouse's assault acknowledges that the assault is a crime but still refuses to call the police, the system takes no action. If a person is raped but declines to report the attack for fear of retaliation, the system does not become involved. If a theft is not reported because the victim believes that nothing can be done about it, the criminal justice system is not invoked.

This has important consequences. One result is that although there are some useful means for measuring crime (described in Chapter Four), it is impossible to know precisely how much crime there is or whether there is any increase or decrease in it. Another result is that, to the extent that the criminal justice system can be effective in controlling crime, opportunities for crime control are missed.

In the typical course of events, a citizen reports an alleged crime to the police, and an investigation results. Of course, a police officer may observe a crime in progress, or a prosecutor may allege that a crime has occurred. Both police and prosecutors conduct their own investigations to uncover crimes, and sometimes these trigger the sequence of events that we call the criminal justice process.

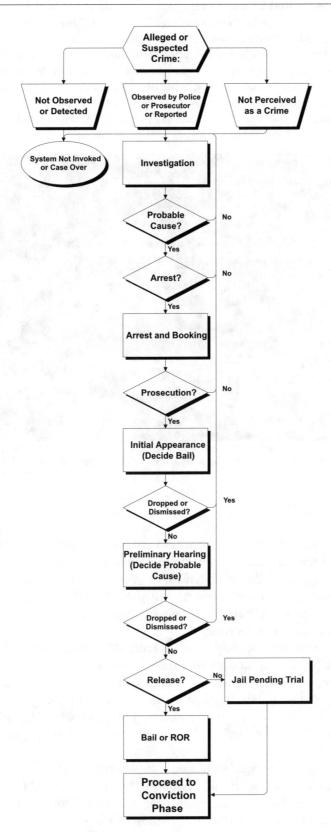

It is the police who typically decide whether to invoke (apply) the law. Usually, it is activated by a call to the police. In his study of the police, Egon Bittner asserted that police officers have "a greater degree of discretionary freedom in proceeding against offenders than any other public official."[2] Ordinarily, the police decide whether a crime has occurred; whether to take a person into custody, make an arrest, or issue a citation; whether to refer a person to another social agency; whether to press for the invoking of the criminal law, or to do nothing about an incident. The police do not merely apply and enforce the law. To a great extent, they exercise discretion in deciding whether to invoke the criminal justice system.[3]

Detectives begin an investigation of the crime scene, collecting and preserving evidence for use in court. If they were to break the law while doing so, should the evidence be allowed to be used in court?

Investigation

Typically, the investigative process is triggered by a victim or witness calling the police, but it might be set in motion by police observation, reports from informers, surveillance activities, or even demands by legislators. An investigation does not usually begin until after the police have decided that a crime has been committed, but it may be started earlier—providing information for making that decision.

The police are not the only ones who might begin an investigation. The process may be started, and carried out completely, by the prosecutor. Investigative reporting may draw the attention of law enforcement to particular individuals or activities. Sometimes, individuals or their families request intervention by the criminal justice system. For example, a drug addict may turn to a special "drug court" as the best or only option for obtaining treatment.

An investigation is needed not only to determine whether a crime has occurred and if an arrest should be made. It is also essential for gathering and preserving the information needed for the prosecutor's decisions about pressing charges and the actual prosecution of a case.

Arrest

Although a person is sometimes charged and summoned to answer in court without being arrested, criminal justice processing usually begins with an arrest. To make an arrest, the police must first determine that there is "probable cause," based on evidence acquired by direct observation or investigation. Probable cause means that, on the basis of the information available, it is reasonable to believe that a crime has been committed by a particular person. An arrest takes a person into custody—depriving the person of liberty—to be called to answer for a crime he or she is suspected of committing. After being arrested, a suspect is then usually taken to the police station where the arrest is registered or "booked."

To arrest a suspect for a misdemeanor (a relatively minor) crime that has not been observed by the arresting officer, an arrest warrant is usually required. This is a written order prepared by a court or some other agency or official authorizing the arrest. Generally, an officer is permitted to make an arrest for a more serious felony crime without an arrest warrant if he or she has probable cause. In this situation, probable cause is more strictly interpreted, meaning that the police officer must have knowledge of sufficient facts and circumstances that would allow a person of reasonable caution to believe that a crime has been committed by the person arrested. A warrant may be needed to arrest a suspect at home, but most arrests on the street take place without one. By law, a police officer is permitted to use only as much force as needed to make an arrest.

At the time of booking for felony charges and some misdemeanors, the suspect's fingerprints are usually taken. (The routine fingerprinting of people arrested provides the basis for most police statistics.) The arresting officer should already have informed the suspect of the rights to remain silent and be assisted by counsel, but at this point, the same information is typically gone over again.

The next steps in the process after booking—the initial appearance, the preliminary appearance, and the arraignment—are sometimes combined or partly so, although they have different purposes. The purpose of the initial appearance before the court is the setting of bail. The preliminary hearing is required so that the judge may determine if there is sufficient probable cause for the case to go to trial. At the arraignment, the defendant is formally charged and required to enter a plea.

Initial Appearance

Within a "reasonable time" after arrest, the suspect must by brought before a magistrate who will decide whether he or she should be granted bail. This is called the initial appearance. Suspects are eligible for release on reasonable bail unless statutes prohibit it, which is often the case for certain serious crimes such as murder and kidnapping.

Traditionally, the purpose of the bail hearing has been to ensure the presence of the suspect at further proceedings. Now, protecting community safety may also be a goal.

In most jurisdictions, certain suspects may be released on ROR—on their own recognizance—that is, on their own promise to appear in court at a later date. In many jurisdictions, it is policy to promptly release everyone arrested for certain minor offenses such as prostitution or drunk and disorderly offenses.

For some minor violations such as traffic offenses, magistrates are commonly permitted to try a case or accept a guilty plea. In felony cases, however, a suspect does not have to enter any plea at this stage, and the magistrate does not investigate the validity of the arrest.

Although the main function of the first appearance is to determine whether the suspect will be released until further processing or held in jail, it also provides an opportunity to notify the accused of his or her legal rights. In some cases the magistrate may decide that the evidence in the case does not warrant further action and dismiss it at that initial appearance.

The initial appearance is often confused with the arraignment — when the accused person is requested to plead to formal charges — because in some jurisdictions this step is actually called the "arraignment" or "first arraignment." It may also be called a "presentment," which distinguishes it from the arraignment where a plea is taken. It may be combined with the preliminary hearing. Often, accused persons have the choice of proceeding after arrest directly to the preliminary hearing.

Preliminary Hearing

The purpose of the preliminary hearing is to determine whether probable cause for the arrest of the accused person existed and whether there is enough evidence to establish probable cause justifying the detention or continued detention of the accused. It is intended to protect the accused from unnecessary prosecution. The magistrate must decide:

- Whether a crime has been committed.
- Whether there is probable cause to believe that the accused person did it.
- Whether there was probable cause for the warrant for the arrest.
- Whether the arrest and any search was reasonable and complied with requirements of the warrant.
- Whether to fix, deny, or continue bail or set other release conditions.

This process may be altered in important ways in some jurisdictions. For example, in the interest of "speedy trials," preliminary steps may be combined into a single hearing. In this case, the suspect may quickly be charged and then appear in court at arraignment. Or, a negotiation among judge, prosecutor, and defense attorney may result in a postponement of possible prosecution while the suspect agrees voluntarily to treatment conditions—as in a currently popular "drug court" model.

Prosecution

Determination of Charges

In most cases, if the suspect is not released outright by the police, the available evidence is given to the prosecutor. This constitutes the basis for the decision whether to prosecute, and, if so, on what charges and specific counts. The prosecutor is in a position of great influence on liberty and reputations,[4] and on needs for community protection.

The prosecutor must decide whether the evidence available or likely to be obtained is sufficient to prove at trial beyond a reasonable doubt the required elements of the offense or offenses charged. The standard of evidence that is required is "probable cause to believe" that a crime has been committed and that the accused person committed it (the same as for the police in making an arrest). The prosecutor, however, must look forward also to the higher standard of "beyond a reasonable doubt," because that is the standard of proof required should the case go to trial.

> *A State's attorney potentially has more control over the liberty and future of an individual than any other public official or public body. His discretion and authority are vast and vest him with powers which are unparalleled by those of any other single person.[5]*
> —R. Mills

Charges are brought formally by the prosecutor in one of two main ways, as seen in Figure 2.2. These differ somewhat among jurisdictions. The first is through an *indictment*, a formal accusation, by a grand jury. The prosecutor presents information that might enable the jury to determine, by majority vote in a closed session without the presence of the defendant(s) or defense attorney, that there is sufficient cause for a trial. If the grand jury decides that this is the case, an indictment is prepared, giving the details of the alleged offense and of the defendant or defendants, in a "true bill." If the grand jury does not reach agreement by majority vote that any defendant should be bound over for trial, it refuses the indictment and returns "no bill." In that case, if the accused person is in custody, he or she is released.

The second, more common way of formally bringing charges is by means of an *information*, a documentation of the charges similar to that issued by a grand jury. The charges and some evidence are presented in open court, where the prosecutor seeks a decision by the judge that the defendant should be brought to trial.

Arraignment on Indictment or Information

If the accused is indicted by a Grand Jury or charged by an information, that person must appear in court to hear the charges and answer a request that he or she plead to those charges. This is an arraignment, which may be called the "arraignment on the warrant" or "arraignment on the complaint." The choices for pleading are usually "not guilty," "not guilty by reason of insanity," "guilty," *nolo contendere*, or "standing mute." The plea of *nolo contendere* means "I will not contend, fight, or maintain a defense," and in a criminal case, it is the same thing as a plea of guilty—for purposes of those criminal proceedings only. Like other pleas, it must be accepted by the court. (A plea of *nolo contendere* cannot be used in a civil proceeding to investigate a private or property matter as proof that the defendant committed the act in question.) "Standing mute" means refusing to plead and is equivalent to a plea of not guilty.

Figure 2.2 The Criminal Justice System: II. Prosecution and Conviction

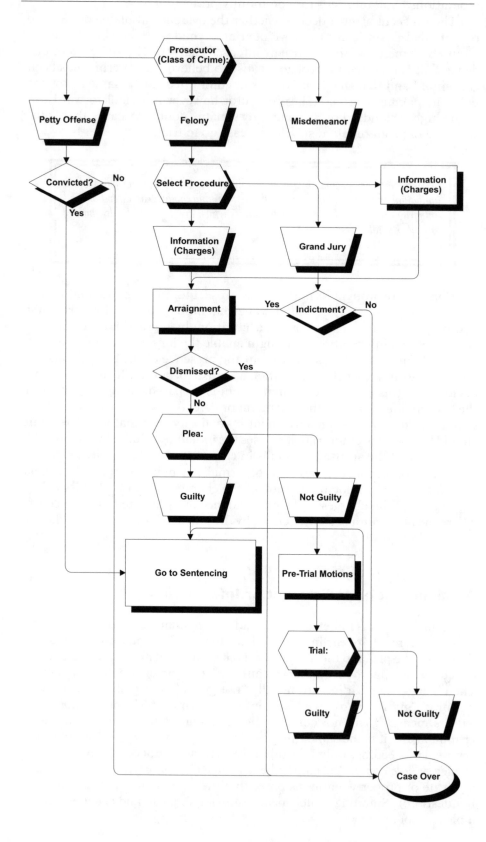

Before accepting a guilty plea, the judge ordinarily explains to the accused person the right to trial and representation by counsel and warns him or her of the possible consequences of the plea. The judge seeks to be assured of the accused person's competence and understanding in making the guilty plea. If the judge is not satisfied that the plea has been made voluntarily and with an understanding of its consequences, or for other reasons, he or she can decide not to accept it.

If the plea is not guilty, the defendant is notified of his or her rights, counsel is appointed if the accused person cannot afford an attorney, and a decision is made as to the competency of the defendant to stand trial.

Competency

The decision about a defendant's competency is based on a legal definition. A criminal defendant is competent to stand trial if he or she understands the charges and proceedings against him or her and is able to consult with a defense attorney with a reasonable degree of understanding. Psychological evaluations may be influential, but the decision is up to the judge alone.

Plea Bargaining

Plea bargaining is a common practice in most jurisdictions. This is a process of negotiation between the prosecuting and defense attorneys. If agreement is reached, the accused person enters a plea of guilty in exchange for a reduction in charges or promises concerning sentencing recommendations.

Conviction

The next steps in the process usually depend on the class or type of crime for which the accused person is charged. If it is a petty offense, conviction upon a plea of guilty or a finding by a court may follow immediately, with sentencing at the same session. For felony cases, as shown in Figure 2.2, a date for trial normally is set, if charges have not been dismissed at arraignment.

Before a trial begins, there may be hearings on pretrial motions. Frequently the defendant will ask the court to suppress evidence claimed to have been obtained illegally. There may be a motion for a "change of venue," that is, a relocation of the trial. There may be motions to "discover" evidence not disclosed to the defense by the prosecutor. There may be motions to postpone the trial. If such motions are not granted by the court, that denial may later be a basis for an appeal to a higher court.

Trial

For defendants pleading other than guilty (or *nolo contendre*) to charges in the indictment or information, the trial is an examination before the appropriate court of the facts or the law at issue in order to hear and settle the case.

In most jurisdictions, a defendant may choose between a jury trial or a bench trial—a trial before a judge, without a jury. In the case of a felony charge or charges, the defendant has the right to a jury trial. In cases of lesser charges, the rules are different in different jurisdictions. Commonly, the right to a jury trial does not extend to lesser charges such as public intoxication, disorderly conduct, or traffic offenses.

The procedures followed at trials are defined by constitutions, statutes, court rules, and appellate court decisions. In all cases the standard of proof—the degree of certainty required to establish guilt—is "beyond a reasonable doubt." Moreover, a conviction must be based only upon properly obtained, presented, and interpreted evidence. The prosecution presents evidence to show culpability—blameworthiness and intentional wrongdoing. The prosecutor tries to establish that all the elements of the crime or crimes charged were present, while the defense contests, refutes, disputes, and seeks to show that the elements of the crime were not present. The defense must raise a reasonable doubt, but it need not do more.

In closing arguments, both the prosecution and the defense may argue for their positions. The judge explains to the jury the applicable provisions of the law and provides other instructions about the meaning of the evidence. While explaining his or her judicial role as the interpreter of the law, the judge also points out that the jury is the finder or determiner of the facts. After all this is done in open court, the jury retires to a closed session to determine whether the defendant is guilty of the crimes charged or of lesser ones. Most state constitutions require that jury verdicts be unanimous.

In all criminal trials defendants have a right to counsel the advice of an attorney. A defendant may waive that right and represent himself or herself, but only at the discretion of the court; defendants are warned against it.

A judge can set aside or reject a jury verdict to convict a defendant if he or she believes that the evidence presented at trial was not sufficient to support that verdict. Or the judge may not wait for a jury finding of not guilty but may direct a verdict of acquittal.

On the other hand, the judge cannot set aside a verdict of not guilty. Such a finding would violate the prohibition of the Fifth Amendment of the U.S. Constitution against "double jeopardy," which provides that ". . . No person . . . shall . . . be subject for the same offense to be twice put in jeopardy of life or limb." The double jeopardy clause generally prevents a second prosecution, regardless of the outcome of a first trial. It also prevents a second punishment. It applies only to criminal settings and does not do away with punitive damages assigned in a civil suit.

Appeal of the Convictions

A defendant who is convicted may appeal the conviction to a higher court, usually only within a specified time after conviction and only if the appellate court decides to consider it. Defendants may seek other remedies, such as making allegations or claims of improper sentences or treatment in confinement. Appeals may eventually involve all courts in the state and federal hierarchy, although state remedies generally must be exhausted before a case can rise to federal review and possibly to the U.S. Supreme Court. Some states, under some conditions, allow appeals by the prosecution. The state usually cannot appeal a finding of not guilty, however, because of the prohibition of double jeopardy.

The Supreme Court of the United States building is a symbol of the balance of needs for public safety and individual freedom. The U.S. Constitution, the supreme law of the land, places the judicial power of the United States in one supreme court and inferior courts established by the Congress. What crimes do you believe should be federal ones? —*Photo courtesy of www.digitalriver.com.*

Sentencing

A conviction means that a person has been publicly, authoritatively, decisively, and enduringly determined beyond a reasonable doubt to have intentionally committed, without excuse or justification, an illegal act causing harm to an innocent victim. This is rarely regarded as punishment enough, and the next step in the criminal justice process is the imposition of a sentence. Most commonly, the sentence is imposed (handed down) by the trial judge. In some states, the jury decides the sentence in noncapital cases. In some jurisdictions, sentencing councils of several judges confer to decide upon a sentence. In some places, juries recommend sentences.

A judge must fix sentences within the boundaries set by statutes passed by legislatures. Sentencing structures differ considerably among the states. In some jurisdictions, for some crimes, sentences set by legislators allow the judge no discretion as to the type of sentence, requiring a "flat" time sentence of a determined period of incarceration. Other laws require a minimum length of time of incarceration before parole may be considered. In other structures, sentences must be fixed within rather narrow bounds but may be increased or decreased by aggravating or mitigating factors. These increase or decrease the blameworthiness of the offender and therefore increase or decrease the severity of the penalty. Such variations may be at the discretion of the judge or may be required to be "plead and proved."

In still another common structure, sentences are indeterminate, that is no fully established, at the time of their imposition, with the exact penalty to be determined later by a paroling authority. In such cases, the offender may be sentenced "to the term prescribed by law," which may include a wide range of possible terms such as "from five years to life."

For some offenses, incarceration may be required. That is, sentences may not be suspended with probation assigned. In many states, sentencing structures are determined by sentencing commissions, which set expected terms for various crimes. Nevertheless, these typically allow some discretion to the sentencing judge. In other places, sentencing guidelines are not provided by a sentencing commission but are used voluntarily by judges. Some of these complexities will be discussed later in this book. For now it is enough to say that in most jurisdictions, for most offenses, the sentencing judge may exercise considerable discretion in imposing a sentence.

In current practice, the major sentencing alternatives are limited—usually probation, confinement, or death. "Alternatives to confinement," "alternative sanctions," or "indetermediate punishments" will be discussed in a later section. Many are used as special conditions of probation.

Types of sentences are commonly set by state statutes and differ among the states. Fines are often a sentencing choice, but in practice are rarely the sole sentence except for minor offenses. In some jurisdictions, other alternatives to confinement, such as required community service or restitution (payment to the victim by the offender), could be the only sentences required. For most sentences, the judge has the choice of sending the offender to jail or prison or placing that person on probation.

When probation is granted, it ordinarily means that the execution of an imposed sentence has been suspended but can be executed if the conditions required by the court are violated. In some jurisdictions, however, the judge may place the defendant on probation before conviction when this is agreed to by the defendant. This process sometimes is called "informal probation" or probation before judgment.

When probation is selected, the offender is subject to the rules and conditions set by the court. If it is later determined by the court that the rules have been broken or the conditions have not been met, the original sentence may be executed. If it is decided to confine an offender to jail or prison, the judge often has the discretion to fix the minimum and maximum terms. (Sentences to jail are usually for a fixed period of time.) "Split sentences" are also common. For a split sentence, the judge specifies a period of time to be served in jail along with a period of probation. In some jurisdictions, this has been called "shock probation" or shock incarceration.

Various conditions may be included with probation. These may include house arrest, intensive supervision, restitution, community service, drug testing, attendance at alcoholics anonymous, narcotics anonymous, or other treatment programs, and electronic monitoring. Some statutes provide that some of these may be "stand alone" sentences, but they rarely are used that way.

If a convicted person is sentenced to a prison term and the sentence is not suspended, the judge usually has little or no control over the specific prison in which the offender will serve the sentence. The sentence commonly includes a phrase such as ". . . be delivered to the custody of the Director of Corrections. . . ." and the specific program, including the place of confinement, is decided by the correctional staff.

Presentence Investigation and Report

Before sentencing, the probation department prepares a presentence report, typically for felons, but sometimes for misdemeanants. This is based on an investigation by the probation officer and is intended to assist the court in determining the appropriate sentence. It later becomes an important source of information for both institutional and community corrections. There is a wide variation among jurisdictions as to whether these reports are required and their quality.

Appeal of the Sentence

Procedures for appeals of sentences differ also among jurisdictions. Often, sentences to death are automatically reviewed. Generally, procedures for review of sentences are similar to those for review of convictions.

Punishment

The sequence of events after sentencing is depicted in Figure 2.3. It shows that the sentencing judge, restricted by the statutes defining the crime or crimes of conviction and specifying the punishment, may have choices of prison, jail, intermediate sanctions, or probation. If the sentence is to prison, but not to death, and the state structure includes a paroling authority, the prisoner may be paroled at the discretion of that authority after a specified time, with or without special conditions. If not paroled, he or she will be released upon the expiration of the sentence, without any supervision or other conditions. In some jurisdictions, prisoners leave as a result of a conditional release, which usually means that the prisoner is released without supervision but is subject to re-imprisonment if conditions—including no new offenses—are not met. An exception would be release by executive pardon or clemency (by a governor, for example) which is rare. If a sentence is to jail, usually for a year or less, the time specified generally must be served before release, although some jurisdictions have procedures for parole from jail. If a sentence is a split sentence, a combination of jail and probation, usually the time set must be served in confinement, followed by community supervision on probation.

A person might be sentenced to any or all of the intermediatee sanctions shown as examples in Figure 2.3, usually imposed as conditions of probation. If probation is the sentence, the court commonly sets special conditions defining the program of supervision. Otherwise, this may be done by probation staff after assigning the probationer to a certain level of supervision and services.

Thus, probation usually refers to a process of community supervision *instead* of incarceration. Parole is a process of community supervision *after* confinement, usually as a result of release by a parole board. Typically, parole is administered by the state, rather than county. Organizational structures differ; the parole service may report to the director of corrections or the parole board.

It is not possible to describe one structure that fits all cases. For example, a unique program in New Jersey allows an inmate (after a screening program in the Department of Corrections) to be considered by a panel of judges (other than the original sentencing judge) for intensive probation supervision operated by the Administrative Office of the Courts of the State, rather than by the counties, as is usual in most states. Although this may sound like "early parole," it is actually a resentencing by judges rather than a discretionary release by a paroling authority. It was

Figure 2.3 The Criminal Justice System: III. Punishment

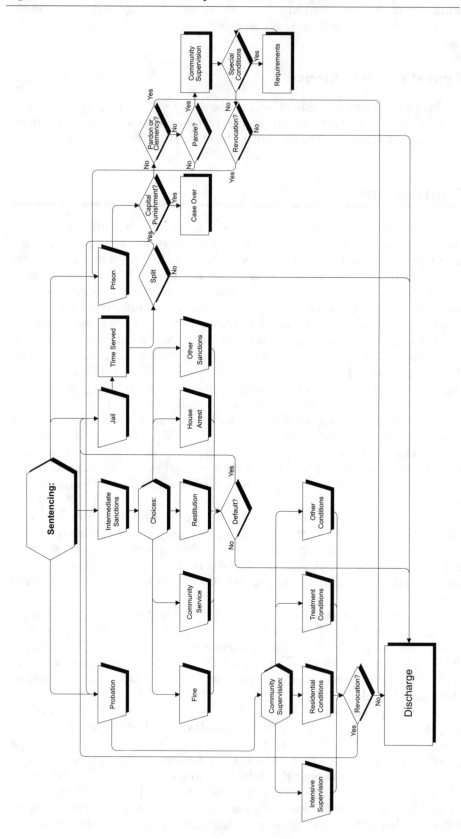

established not by legislation but by a memorandum by the Chief Justice of the Supreme Court of New Jersey.

Chapter 2
▲ ▲ ▲ ▲ ▲ ▲

Although they may have a duty to do so, probation officers usually have some discretion in returning to court a probationer believed to have violated the rules of probation. These may include "technical" violations, including breaking the ordinary rules or not abiding by the special conditions of probation, such as regular reporting to the probation officer, not changing residence or not leaving the county without permission, not possessing firearms, not using drugs, or not committing new offenses. It is up to the court to determine whether probation will be revoked. If so, the sentence previously suspended is executed and the person is sent to jail or prison according to the original sentence. The judge may, alternatively, change the conditions of probation, ordering, for example, a brief stay in jail or requiring participation in a drug-testing program. Probation officers may initiate revocation procedures, but only judges may revoke probation.

Parole officers similarly have some discretion to initiate parole revocation proceedings, but parole can be actually revoked only by the parole board. Parole may be revoked for technical rules violations or for new offenses.

Release from prison may come about in various ways, again depending on procedures in particular jurisdictions. Generally, there are four ways:

1. **Expiration of sentence:** If the maximum sentence has been served in prison, the prisoner must be released, without supervision.

2. **Parole:** If the required time before consideration for parole has been served and the paroling authority decides to parole the prisoner, he or she will leave under parole supervision.

3. **Mandatory release or conditional release:** If the jurisdiction has statutes specifying time off for good behavior or for time spent in work release or similar programs, the prisoner will be released after serving the maximum sentence minus the time credited for these programs, often called "good time." Supervision in the community may or may not be required, depending on the jurisdiction, up to the date of the maximum sentence; and the release may be revoked for violations.

4. **Pardon or commutation:** The President of the United States and all state governors may pardon prisoners or commute sentences. A pardon wipes out any penalty. A commutation reduces a sentence, which could result in release or in an earlier eligibility for parole.

Discharge

When the sentence of a convicted offender has been completed, whether in jail or prison or on probation, he or she is discharged regardless of the mode of release from confinement. Some jurisdictions have procedures for shortening the period of probation or parole, allowing an earlier discharge based on successful completion of a period of community supervision.

Summary

Important decisions are made at every step in the criminal justice process. They are made in the context of the conflict between desires for personal liberty and community safety and community expectations that justice ought to be done. If we seek to make these decisions rationally, the goals, alternatives, and information needed must be examined for both case and management decisions.

The criminal justice system is made up of agencies and procedures that come into play when a person is accused of a crime, convicted, and punished. A report or observation of a crime may lead to arrest, investigation, bail, a preliminary hearing to determine whether there is probable cause to continue the process, and an arraignment. Formal charges issue from a grand jury indictment or an information. The accused, who has a right to counsel, must be charged and requested to offer a plea at an arraignment. Meanwhile or thereafter, a "plea bargain" agreement may be reached, reducing the charges or expected penalty upon a plea of guilty.

If the case goes to trial—an examination of facts or of law before a court of competent jurisdiction—defendants usually may choose a bench or jury trial. Trial procedures are determined by constitutions, statutes, court rules, and appellate decisions. The prosecution must prove the charge(s) beyond a reasonable doubt. The defense seeks to show that at least that much doubt exists in relation to the elements of the crime(s) alleged. In a jury trial, the judge interprets the law but the jury decides on the facts. Convictions, and also punishments, may be appealed to a higher court, but only if that court agrees to consider it.

A conviction means that an accused person has been publicly, authoritatively, decisively, and enduringly determined beyond any reasonable doubt to have intentionally committed, without excuse or justification, an illegal act causing harm to an innocent victim.

The sentence is imposed by the trial court judge informed by a presentence report prepared by a probation officer (usually for felonies, sometimes for misdemeanors). The choices available and the amount of discretion the judge has differs among jurisdictions and types of crime. Typical choices are jail, prison, probation, and alternative punishments. Jail sentences are usually fixed for less than a year in a county facility. Prison sentences typically are for a year or longer in a state institution. Sentences to jail or prison usually may be suspended in whole or in part while the offender serves a period of probationary supervision in the community, which may include a variety of required programs. If the probation rules are violated, the court may execute the sentence originally imposed. Probation supervision often is combined with other community corrections programs or required — in a split sentence — after a stay in jail.

Modes of release from prison commonly include expiration of sentence, parole, and conditional release. The latter two include community supervision and the possible return to prison for rule or law violations.

Notes

1. Cronbach, L. J. and G. C. Gleser. (1957). *Psychological Tests and Personnel Decisions*. Urbana, IL: University of Illinois Press.

2. Bittner, E. (1970). *The Functions of the Police in a Modern Society*. Chevy Chase, MD: Center for Studies in Crime and Delinquency, Public Health Service Publication No. 2059, 107.

3. Goldstein, J. (1960). "Police Discretion Not to Invoke the Criminal Process: Low Visibility Decisions in the Administration of Justice," *Yale Law Journal* 69, 543; Packer, H. (1964). "Two Models of the Criminal Process," *University of Pennsylvania Law Review* 113:1; Kadish, S. (1962). "Legal Norm and Discretion in the Police and Sentencing Process," *Harvard Law Review* 75, 904.

4. Jackson, R. (1940). "The Federal Prosecutor," *Journal of American Judicature Society* 24, 18.

5. Mills, R. (1966). "The Prosecutor: Charging and 'Bargaining'," *Illinois Criminal Procedure*, 511.

CHAPTER THREE

Crime and the Law

Chapter Three

The law defines crimes and establishes the rules that are the basis for the criminal justice system. In this chapter we will explore how our criminal laws came about and how the most common crimes are defined. We will examine the elements of these common crimes and the main defenses available to a person accused of them. We will examine the amendments to the Constitution of the United States that are called the "Bill of Rights" and are of fundamental importance to the workings of criminal justice.

❑ Questions to Think About

❑ What is Crime?

❑ Legal Definition

❑ Where Did We Get Our Criminal Law?

    The Common Law

    Codification

    Current Law

❑ Criminal Law

❑ Elements of a Crime

❑ Defenses

❑ Justifications

❑ Kinds of Crimes

❑ Common Felonies

    Criminal Homicide

    Assault

    Rape

    Robbery

    Burglary

    Larceny

    Fraud

    Arson

    Other Crimes

❑ Crime Seriousness

❑ Summary

What is a crime?

Is crime the same as sin?

Where did we get our criminal laws?

What is the Bill of Rights? Does it apply to the states or only the federal government?

What is the criminal law?

Who decides what the law is?

What defenses does a person have when accused of a crime?

Is intoxication an excuse for crime?

What is the difference between a felony and a misdemeanor? Between a robbery and a burglary?

Who has the burden of proof in a criminal trial when the defendant pleads insanity?

The law is not an alternative to force, as often is thought. Instead, it is a way of transferring force from individuals to groups and from small groups to larger ones. As civilized societies developed, it came to be believed that force should be used not by private persons but only by the state, under certain rules. These rules are the law.[1]

The law is both an engine of government and a brake which restrains government. Force is required to ensure safety, but constraint is required to preserve liberty.

The criminal justice system is made up of the criminal law, law enforcement, the courts, and corrections. The law defines crime and provides the rules and procedures that are the basis for criminal justice. It ought to be reflected in every aspect of decision making throughout the criminal justice process. Central features of the criminal law must be understood before embarking upon an examination of the agencies, structures, people, procedures, and decision processes that compose the criminal justice system.

What Is Crime?

Ask the average citizen to define crime, and you are apt to get a reasonably clear answer expressed with confidence. Ask an expert and expect a more complex and qualified answer spoken with less assurance. Part of the problem lies in an overlapping of two ideas of crime: a "natural" concept and a "legalistic" or "procedural" one. Most people view crime as an act that is fundamentally wrong, strongly disapproved, and deserving of punishment. This is somewhat akin to the idea of sin, but it implies also that there are certain "natural wrongs"—behaviors that should be considered wrong whether or not any law forbids them. From a legal standpoint, the concept of crime originates in the enactments of a particular legal system and is connected with specific procedures, officials, courts, rules of evidence, and avenues of appeal.[2]

Legal Definition

The body of law defining crime is called the criminal, or penal, law. The word "penal" derives from the Latin word for punishment. A possible outcome of the procedures defined in the criminal law is always the imposition of some penalty to a defendant for a prohibited act. There is no crime unless the law specifies a punishment for its violation. Also, there can be no crime and no punishment unless it is forbidden by law.

There is a difference between crimes and "torts." Torts are civil wrongs for which punishments are not prescribed but for which an injured person may have a right to recover damages. A crime may also be a tort, so a person might be sued in a civil court as well as charged in a criminal court. In the United States, the classification of a legal proceeding as criminal takes on a special significance for the study of criminal justice because the U.S. Constitution requires protections of specific defendants' rights in criminal prosecutions.

Besides laws forbidding acts readily thought of as natural crimes, the criminal law includes a wide range of regulatory provisions. The law reflects an ancient contrast between *mala in se*, meaning evil in themselves, and *mala prohibita*, meaning acts that are wrong because they are prohibited.

Murder, assault, burglary, robbery, and theft usually are regarded as natural wrongs, *mala in se*, because they would be thought to be wrong by the community even without a specific prohibition in the criminal law. *Malum prohibitum* acts are those made unlawful by statute. Driving on the left side of the road is an example: it is prohibited not because it is bad in itself (*malum in se*) but because legislators in some places have determined that it is to be prohibited. Reckless driving, on the other hand, would be considered bad in itself. *Malum prohibitum* acts may be just as serious as those inflicted by some traditional crimes, often because large numbers of people are victimized, as in consumer fraud or environmental crimes.

Crime may be defined in many different ways. We might offer, if we wished, social, psychological, or moralistic definitions. But, as Humpty Dumpty said, "When I use a word . . . it means exactly what I choose it to mean—neither more nor less."[3] For the purposes of this book, we will use the following legalistic definition of crime:

> A crime is an intentional act committed without excuse or justification, caus-
> ing a harm that a government has determined to be injurious to the public
> and prosecutable in a criminal proceeding that may result in punishment.

This definition must be discussed in detail. First we will take a brief look at the origins of the criminal law, which will show where some of the elements of the definition came from.

Where Did We Get Our Criminal Law?

The Common Law

When America began, the colonies based their laws mainly on those of England. Nevertheless, the colonists expressed somewhat different values. A long list of capital offenses (crimes for which a death penalty—capital punishment—might be imposed) in England had included most serious offenses, but also many less serious ones and even some not now always considered crimes. Along with murder and rape, the crimes of assault, robbery, burglary, theft, arson, and sodomy called for death. The Plymouth Code of 1636 limited the death penalty to treason, murder, and arson, although some morals offenses still were included. The code was greatly influenced by the Old Testament. Massachusetts also, in 1648, reduced the number of capital crimes and prohibited "cruel and barbarous" punishments, fashioning the criminal law from the Old Testament and English "common law."[4]

The common law refers to the laws that developed in England and then in the United States. They were not written down but were based on customs and traditions reflected in court decisions. These decisions are called judicial precedents, not enacted into law by legislatures or the U.S. Constitution. The common law emphasized general principles to guide judges rather than strict written rules, although eventually court decisions were recorded and made available to the court. Judicial precedents—previously decided cases recognized as authority for deciding later cases—are still an important part of how criminal cases are resolved by the courts, and the general principles of the common law still influence decisions throughout the courts.

The importance of the common law to our present-day criminal law is profound. Some of its important doctrines now are entrenched in the federal and state constitutions. These include the concepts of:

- The supremacy of law.

- The inviolability of person and property.

- The local nature of the criminal jurisdiction.

- Due process of law.

- The rule that no one should be compelled in any criminal prosecution to be a witness against himself.

- The right to trial by jury.[5]

Massachusetts and other colonies began to organize the loose body of law that had evolved. By 1682, William Penn and other Quaker leaders of Pennsylvania had developed a complete code of criminal laws. As described by McClain,

> The Quaker founders of the colony were opposed in principle to cruelty, to gratuitous bloodshed, and, barring the most unusual conditions, the taking of human life. They were repelled by the existing English system of penal sanctions and felt compelled to look for alternatives. The alternative they found was the prison. In their code, imprisonment at hard labor or imprisonment coupled with a fine was the prescribed penalty for all crimes save willful and premeditated murder, the length of imprisonment varying according to the offense and the circumstances surrounding its commission. The terms of confinement were in general not severe. Thus, burglary was punishable by three month's imprisonment and quadruple restitution to the victim. Arson merited a year at hard labor and corporal punishment (usually whipping) according to the discretion of the court. Assault on a magistrate was punishable by a month's confinement. Common assault and battery, as well as manslaughter, were to be punished according to the nature and circumstances of the acts in question. In contrast to the rather mild sanctions accruing to these crimes, sex offenses were sternly dealt with in the Quaker code.[6]

The penalties for bigamy and rape provide examples of how the strict moral views of the Quakers led to relatively harsh punishments. Rape was punishable by life imprisonment upon second conviction. Bigamy was punishable by life imprisonment on first conviction.

In the next several decades, penalties became somewhat more severe, and then the English law returned. After negotiation with the Crown, the colony leaders agreed to substitute English law for their own, and their grand attempt to develop a penal code came to an end.

In part it was dissatisfaction with the administration of English law that led the colonists to revolt. The Declaration of Independence of July 4, 1776, listed, among other grievances against the King of Great Britain, the "abuses and usurpations" of a failure to permit the passing of necessary laws and a protecting of soldiers "by mock trials" from punishment for murders. They criticized the King for "depriving us in many cases, of the benefits of trial by jury," and chastised their "British brethren" for being "deaf to the voice of justice."

We need only to look at the Declaration of Independence to realize the importance of the perception of justice by the people. It is important that people see that justice is done—that they *believe* justice is done. This is, or ought to be, a major aim of the criminal justice system. Failure to meet that requirement, when people do not see justice done, becomes a substantial problem for society. When the law is not seen as being just, the people may feel justified in taking it "into their own hands." Some groups of Americans no longer expect justice from the state.

"Justice" in this context often means "retribution" imposed fairly. Throughout history, social groups have demanded that a legitimate authority (monarch, state, or criminal justice system) exact retribution—that they obtain punishment— for harms done to others. The idea that offenders ought to be punished can be traced back for thousands of years. The concept that punishment should be imposed *because* it is *deserved* is still central to our system of criminal justice. This is the rationale for punishment called "just desert." In this view, punishment does not require any further justification, such as what other outcomes the punishment might achieve.

"Justice" may mean, however, dealing with offenders in a way that will ensure future safety. The rationale of deserved punishment conflicts with other ancient explanations of what should be done with offenders. These ideas stress a quite different rationale—that some good must come from what we do. This theory, in contrast to the view of deserved punishment, is called "utilitarianism." Often, these ideas emphasize that we ought to seek the greatest good for the greatest number.

Codification

Soon after the Declaration of Independence was published, Thomas Jefferson drafted a bill for the General Assembly of Virginia that proposed a new system of criminal penalties. He was influenced greatly by the now-famous essay *On Crimes and Punishments* by the Italian criminologist Cesare Beccaria, who urged a utilitarian, rather than retributive, criminal law.[7] In his view, the purpose of punishment was to achieve some future good, rather than to provide a punishment as retribution, that is, because it was deserved (Box 3.1).

Box 3.1

Cesare Beccaria

Beccaria (1738–1794) believed that in order to be effective as a deterrent to crime, punishment should be prompt, certain, and inevitable, applied to all equally for similar crimes. The severity of punishment, he thought, is less important as a deterrent than its certainty. He wrote:

The certainty of punishment, even though it [punishment] be moderate, will always make a stronger impression than the fear of one more severe if it is accompanied by the hope that one may escape that punishment, because men are more frightened by an evil which is inevitable even though minor in nature. Further, if the punishment be too severe for a crime, men will be led to commit further crimes in order to escape punishment for the crime. . . . It is essential that [punishment] be public, prompt, necessary, minimal in severity as possible under given circumstances, proportional to the crime, and prescribed by the laws.

Thus, Jefferson urged that the only goal of the penal law is the deterrence or prevention of crime; that severe penalties such as death often will not be enforced, and the criminal will go free; that when punishments are proportional to the harm done, the public is more apt to see that the laws are enforced; and that the reform of criminals should be sought.

> *I like the dreams of the future better than the history of the past.*
> —*Thomas Jefferson*

Although these ideas have a contemporary ring, Jefferson's proposals for punishments for some offenses were seen as bizarre and were not passed by the legislature. Fascinated by the idea that the punishment should fit the crime, Jefferson proposed poisoning as the punishment for murder by poison, castration as the sentence for rape, infliction of maiming for mayhem, and burial alive for treason.

After the American Revolution, the movement toward reform of the penal laws picked up steam. In Pennsylvania, the 1776 state constitution required the legislature to reform the penal laws and to make punishments more proportional to the harm done by the crime. That is, penalties should be graded in severity in relation to the seriousness of the crime. Within a short time, the death penalty was eliminated for robbery, burglary, sodomy, and witchcraft. Branding for adultery and fornication was also ended.[8]

> *No free man shall be taken, or imprisoned, or outlawed, or exiled, or in any way harmed, nor will we go upon him nor will we send upon him, except by the legal judgment of his peers or by the law of the land.*
> —*Magna Carta*

Other sources of American criminal law are found in the Babylonian Code of Hammurabi inscribed on stone tablets as long ago as 1760 B.C., in Roman law, in the Magna Carta (1215), and in writings of philosophy, political science, and religion. For example, in 1651 Thomas Hobbes justified and defined punishment as "an evil inflicted by public authority, on him that hath done, or omitted that which is judged by the same authority to be a transgression of the law; to the end that the will of men may thereby the better be disposed to obedience." Thus he, like Jefferson, justified punishment by the idea that it could accomplish a future good—a greater disposition to abide by the law. Hobbes urged that "in punishing men look not at the greatness of the evil past, but the greatness of the good to follow. Whereby we are forbidden to inflict punishment with any other design, than for the correction of the offender, or direction of others."[9] Hobbes argued also that safeguards of liberty are necessary. Punishment was not to be inflicted without a public hearing, nor for an act done before there was a law that forbade it.

In a similar way, seeking a future gain to be served by the imposition of punishment, Edward Livingston, a prominent New Yorker who moved to New Orleans, drafted a criminal code for Louisiana in 1826. It reflected the utilitarian principles of the English philosopher Jeremy Bentham, who, like Jefferson, was influenced by Beccaria. He proposed a graded series of penalties, ranging from fines to imprisonment. The harshness of prison conditions also was ordered in severity according to the seriousness of the offense. Prisons had for him two purposes: the rehabilitation of the offender and the deterrence of crime by example.[10] Livingston's code was rejected by the legislature, but efforts such as these had their effect as other codes were drafted.

American law may be traced from the Old Testament, Plato, and Aristotle, and developments in religious thought right down to present-day writings in the philosophy of law.[11] The views of Hobbes and of Jefferson echoed those of Plato (circa 428–348 B.C.), for whom punishment was a means to correction and a warning to others—both a specific deterrent to crime for the person punished and also a general deterrent: "Not that he is punished because he did wrong, for that which has been done can never be undone, but in order that in future times, he, and those who see him corrected, may utterly hate injustice, or at any rate abate much of their evil doing."[12]

In contrast, the German philosopher Immanuel Kant (1724–1804), who continues to have a strong influence on contemporary philosophy of law and criminal justice, believed that desert alone is a legitimate, indeed required,

Figures on the Los Angeles County Courthouse depict sources of law, including the Old Testament, the Magna Carta, and the Declaration of Independence. —*Photo courtesy of the California History Section, California State Library.*

basis for punishment. Persons ought to be punished strictly according to that deserved for the harm done, not in order to achieve some future good. When a person is punished in order to prevent future crime or achieve some other good in the future, the individual is punished not for what he or she did but as a means to another end. Kant believed that the use of persons as means to some other ends is never justified and never should be permitted. He wrote:

> Even if a civil society resolved to dissolve itself with the consent of all its members—as might be supposed in the case of a people inhabiting an island resolving to separate and scatter themselves throughout the whole world— the last murderer lying in prison ought to be executed before the resolution was carried out. This ought to be done in order that everyone may realize the desert of his deeds.[13]

These contrasting views about the purposes of the criminal law—whether the aims ought to be forward-looking to a future good (deterrence of crime, reform of the offender, keeping the culprit off the streets) or retributive, looking back at the amount of harm done and punishing according to that deserved, are still very much with us.

Current Law

We have seen that English common law—affected by the law that developed earlier elsewhere and by a heritage in literature, philosophy, and other social change—provided the foundation for American criminal law. Now our criminal codes reflect the provisions of the U.S. Constitution, the constitutions of the 50 states, the federal statutes enacted by the U.S. Congress, state statutes enacted by the state legislatures, administrative law dealing with the powers and duties of government agencies, and local laws and regulations.

The U.S. Constitution provides that the Constitution itself is the "supreme law of the land" (Article VI) and requires that ". . . the judges in every State shall be bound thereby, anything in the Constitution or laws of any State to the contrary notwithstanding." The Constitution prohibits suspension of the writ of *habeas corpus* (a court procedure for preventing illegal confinement), bills of attainders (laws inflicting punishment without a trial), and *ex post facto* laws (retroactive laws about punishments or rules of evidence). It provides for the Supreme Court of the United States and spells out its jurisdiction. It specifies that "the trial of all crimes, except in cases of impeachment, shall be by jury, and such trial shall be held in the State where the said crimes shall have been committed . . ." (Article III). The Constitution, including its amendments, provides the basic foundation of our criminal laws (Box 3.2).

We will have many occasions, as we examine the criminal justice system, to refer back to the first ten constitutional amendments—the Bill of Rights— and to the Fourteenth Amendment. At its origin in 1791, the Bill of Rights provided protections effective against the federal government alone. The provisions were not directed at the states. The Fourteenth Amendment (1868) provided the basis for requirements that the states follow the law according to interpretations of the Constitution by the U.S. Supreme Court. The Fourteenth Amendment provided that no state

> . . . shall make or enforce any law which shall abridge the privileges and immunities of citizens of the United States; nor shall any State deprive any person of life, liberty, or property without due process of law; nor deny to any person within its jurisdiction the equal protection of its laws.

Don't interfere with anything in the Constitution. That must be maintained, for it is the only safeguard of our liberties.
—*Abraham Lincoln*

In the early part of the present century, the U.S. Supreme Court began a process of requiring states to provide the protections of the Bill of Rights. By

---

Box 3.2

The Bill of Rights:
The First 10 Amendments to the U.S. Constitution

I.
Congress shall make no law respecting an establishment of religion, or prohibiting the free exercise thereof; or abridging the freedom of speech, or of the press; or the right of the people peaceably to assemble, and to petition the Government for a redress of grievances.

II.
A well regulated Militia, being necessary to the security of a free State, the right of the people to keep and bear Arms, shall not be infringed.

III.
No Soldier shall, in time of peace be quartered in any house, without the consent of the Owner, nor in time of war, but in a manner to be prescribed by law.

IV.
The right of the people to be secure in their persons, houses, papers, and effects, against unreasonable searches and seizures, shall not be violated, and no Warrants shall issue, but upon probable cause, supported by Oath or affirmation, and particularly describing the place to be searched, and the persons or things to be seized.

V.
No person shall be held to answer for a capital, or otherwise infamous crime, unless on a presentment or indictment of a Grand Jury, except in cases arising in the land or naval forces, or in the Militia, when in actual service in time of War or public danger; nor shall any person be subject for the same offence to be twice put in jeopardy of life or limb; nor shall be compelled in any criminal case to be a witness against himself, nor be deprived of life, liberty, or property, without due process of law; nor shall private property be taken for public use, without just compensation.

VI.
In all criminal prosecutions, the accused shall enjoy the right to a speedy and public trial, by an impartial jury of the State and district wherein the crime shall have been committed, which district shall have been previously ascertained by law, and to be informed of the nature and cause of the accusation; to be confronted with the witnesses against him; to have compulsory process for obtaining witnesses in his favor, and to have the Assistance of Counsel for his defence.

VII.
In Suits at common law, where the value in controversy shall exceed twenty dollars, the right to a trial by jury shall be preserved, and no fact tried by jury, shall be otherwise re-examined in any Court of the United States, than according to the rules of the common law.

VIII.
Excessive bail shall not be required, nor excessive fines imposed, nor cruel and unusual punishments inflicted.

IX.
The enumeration in the Constitution, of certain rights, shall not be construed to deny or disparage others retained by the people.

X.
The powers not delegated to the United States by the Constitution, nor prohibited by it to the States, are reserved to the States respectively, or to the people.

this process, which has been called "selective absorption" or "selective incorporation," most of the provisions of the Bill of Rights have been determined to apply not only to the federal government but to the states as well.

This was a gradual process in a series of court cases, first requiring the freedom of speech and of the press. Later, it required such protections as these:

- The right to counsel in felony cases.

- The right to a public trial.

- The right to protection against unreasonable searches and seizures.

The process gained momentum during the term of Chief Justice Earl Warren (1953–1969). The Warren Court extended the guarantees of the Bill of Rights to affect the states in the following ways:

- By excluding evidence in a criminal trial when it had been seized illegally by the police.

- By assuring other rights:

    against self-incrimination
    to confront witnesses
    to a speedy trial
    to a jury trial for all serious crimes
    to protection against double jeopardy (being tried or punished twice for the same crime)
    to counsel in misdemeanant cases.

As a result, all states now must conform in most respects to the Bill of Rights. This has had profound effects on the procedures and practices of the criminal justice system.

Just as federal and state statutes must conform to the provisions of the U.S. Constitution, state statutes must not conflict with the constitution of the particular state.

Criminal Law

The rules governing what behavior is criminal and defining the procedures of the criminal justice system are found in constitutions, statutes, court decisions, and administrative regulations. Basic principles and procedural rights are found in the constitutions and guide the actions of legislators, judges, and administrators. Statutory laws are specific enactments of legislatures and provide the substantive criminal laws of the states, while court decisions set precedents that guide judges in later cases. The law is written by legislators, interpreted and shaped by judges, guided by precedents, and influenced by public argument, sentiment, and personal dispositions.

We can look at the criminal codes to find what has been declared to be illegal and to see what punishments have been prescribed for these acts. But we can obtain a more complete understanding by considering the principles that contribute to the definitions of crimes. As noted by Jerome Hall, "The harm forbidden in a penal law must be imputed to any normal adult who voluntarily commits it with criminal intent, and such a person must be subjected to the legally prescribed punishment."[14] That statement includes seven requirements of crime and suggests some defenses against accusations of crime. If any requirement is absent, there is no crime. There must be an act, forbidden in a penal law, together with a guilty mind of a normal adult who voluntarily causes harm for which a legal punishment is prescribed (Box 3.3).

Box 3.3

Seven Requirements of a Crime

1. *Actus reus*: an act
2. **Illegality**: against the law
3. **Concurrence**: an evil intention and an unlawful act must occur at the same time
4. *Mens rea*: a guilty mind
5. **Cause**: the harm was brought about by the act
6. **Harm**: injury or damage
7. **Punishment**: a penalty may be inflicted

Elements of a Crime

Recall the definition of crime offered previously: a crime is an intentional act committed without excuse or justification, causing a harm that a government has determined to be injurious to the public and prosecutable in a criminal proceeding that may result in punishment. The words "intentional act" are meant to reflect the legal concepts of *actus reas* and *mens rea*. Moreover, there must be a harm caused by the concurrence of the *actus reas* and *mens rea*, and the act must be an illegal one for which punishment may be imposed.

Actus reus, meaning "the guilty act" or "the deed of crime," implies some degree of voluntariness to do something. It differs from crime to crime. For example, in murder, it is homicide, which is the killing of a person by another person. Homicide is not necessarily a crime: the other requisites may be absent, and the killing may be justifiable, for example, in self defense. In burglary, it usually is breaking into another's home or building. In forgery, it is offering as good a document such as a check which is actually false. There is no crime without an act, although the act may be a failure, or omission, to do something required. For example, a parent has a duty to protect a child, and failure to do so may be neglect — a criminal act.

Mens rea, meaning "the guilty mind," refers to the mental state accompanying a forbidden act. It also differs from crime to crime. In murder, it is malice aforethought. Malice means a state of mind that accompanies doing a wrongful act intentionally without justification or excuse; and it refers to an intent to cause harm. Malice aforethought is required for an unlawful homicide to be murder rather than manslaughter. Murder has a premeditated or planned nature that is lacking in manslaughter. In burglary, it is intent to commit a felony, and in forgery, it is intent to defraud or cheat, knowing that the document is false.

Mens rea may be general or specific. There may be a general intent to do the prohibited act, or a special mental element may be required for an offense. An example of the latter is "assault with intent to rape." In a criminal prosecution, the prosecutor must prove beyond a reasonable doubt that the required mental state existed at the same time as the act. There may be exceptions. For example, defenses of insanity, intoxication, and mistake may reduce or remove the effect of a specific *mens rea*. And, some *malum prohibitum* crimes, those designated by the government as unlawful, do not require any specific *mens rea*. These are called crimes of "strict liability" and are usually limited to minor offenses or regulatory offenses such as parking violations. In some jurisdictions, these are considered "violations" and not criminal offenses.

The unlawful action and the evil intent must concur; that is, they must occur at the same time in order for the act to be a crime. The criminal act must be accompanied by a guilty mind.

In felony murder, however, the requisite *mens rea* is inferred from the person's intent to commit a felony, even if there is no intent to take a life. Felony murder is an unlawful homicide that occurs in the commision or attempted commision of a felony. For example, the driver of a getaway car who waited outside of a convenience store during an attempted robbery in which the clerk was shot is guilty of felony murder even though he was not present at the homicide.

All harms are not crimes, but all crimes are acts that have been determined by law to be harmful—to be injurious or damaging. The harm may include physical injury or taking of life, or it might involve a loss of property. In any case, an act is not a crime unless it has been determined to cause harm and therefore has been prohibited by law. The harm must be caused by the act in order for it to be a crime. This is implied by the concurrence of the *actus reas* and the *mens rea*. The act must be against the law, and a punishment must be specified in the law.

> *This is what has to be remembered about the law: Beneath that cold, harsh, impersonal exterior there beats a cold, harsh, impersonal heart.*
> —*David Frost and Anthony Jay*

Defenses

Defenses available to an accused person negate either the existence of a crime, due to an absence of *actus reus* concurring with *mens rea*, or illegality, because the act is not prohibited. The first type of defense is a set of excuses; the second, of justifications.

Infancy is a defense stemming from the common law. Children under the age of 7 were conclusively presumed, at common law, to be without criminal capacity, while those who were 14 were responsible. A "conclusive presumption" seems self-contradictory, but there's the criminal law for you. It means that as a rule of law there is no argument or evidence that can overcome taking the point as a fact. For children between 7 and 14, the common law prescribed a "rebuttable presumption" of criminal incapacity. A rebuttable presumption is an assumption of fact which may be overcome (rebutted) by contrary evidence but which, if not overcome, becomes conclusive. Many states, by statute, have changed the upper age of criminal responsibility for children; and all states have enacted legislation providing for juvenile courts, where criminal conduct by youths of specified ages must or may be dealt with in a juvenile, rather than criminal, proceeding.

Insanity is a legal term meaning a mental disorder that relieves the person of criminal responsibility for his or her actions. The legal concept of insanity has little to do with psychological or psychiatric conceptions of behavior disorders or mental illness. Various tests have been used in the courts to determine legal insanity. The insanity defense is based originally on the common law test called the M'Naghten rule. That test is from an 1843 ruling by the English judges to the House of Lords after the acquittal of Daniel M'Naghten, who wanted to assassinate the Prime Minister, Sir Robert Peel. By mistake, he killed Sir Peel's secretary. M'Naghten's lawyers argued that he did not know what he was doing, and medical testimony supported their contentions of delusions of persecution by the Tories.

The rule was that a person was not responsible for criminal acts and therefore entitled to an acquittal by reason of insanity if, as a result of mental disease or defect, he did not understand what he did or that it was wrong or if he was acting under a delusion which, if true, would have provided a good defense. If the person did not understand at all what he was doing, or if he did not know it was wrong, he was excused—there was no crime. Or, he was excused if he thought, due to a delusion, he was acting in self-defense.

The M'Naghten test has been much criticized, and other tests have replaced it in many, but not all, jurisdictions. The federal rule, passed by the U.S. Congress[15] requires acquittal by reason of insanity if "at the time of the commission of the act the defendant, as a result of a severe mental disease or defect, was unable to appreciate the nature and quality or wrongfulness of his act." Most states have displaced the M'Naghten rule with the test of the American Law Institute's Model Penal Code. This rule states, "A person is not responsible for criminal conduct if at the time of such conduct as a result of mental disease or defect he lacks substantial capacity either to appreciate the criminality (or alternatively, wrongfulness) of his conduct or to conform his conduct to the requirements of law."[16]

You might think it insane to repeatedly do criminal acts that result, as prison inmates often say, in "doing life on the installment plan," but the terms "mental disease or defect" do not include an abnormality shown only by repeated criminal or antisocial conduct.[17] In some states, a defense of "irresistible impulse" may be used. This means that although the person knew what he or she was doing and that it was wrong, the person could not help doing it. In other states, a finding of "guilty but insane" or "guilty but mentally ill" is possible.[18] With this verdict, the judge may sentence to punishment as the law prescribes, but usually with required psychiatric treatment. After treatment, the offender still must serve any remaining sentence.

Defendants are presumed innocent at the start of a criminal proceeding, but they are also presumed sane. The burden of proof is on the prosecution to establish guilt, but the burden to prove insanity is on the defense.

Intoxication from alcohol or drugs, if voluntary, is no defense but it may reduce the seriousness of the crime. More precisely, it is not a defense against crimes of general intent but may refute the existence of *mens rea* necessary to crimes of specific intent. Involuntary intoxication, as when a person is tricked or forced, makes the person's conduct involuntary and thereby allows that person to avoid criminal liability.

A mistake is an act or omission arising from ignorance or misconception which may also exonerate a defendant from criminal liability. The law recognizes two types of mistakes: mistakes of law and mistakes of fact. When it comes to mistakes of law, reliance traditionally has been placed on the maxim, "Ignorance of the law is no excuse." Now, however, the rule is that either kind of mistake provides a valid defense if it denies the presence of the mental state—*mens rea*—required for the crime in question. No *mens rea*, no crime.

Justifications

Self-defense, defense of others, or defense of property may be valid justifications because the law permits the behavior in question. That is, the illegality requirement is not met. In the case of self-defense against an immediate threat of harm, several essential elements must be present. The defendant must be free from fault and nonprovoking. He or she must have no convenient way to escape or avoid a threatened unlawful harm believed to be forthcoming immediately. There must be a genuine belief that force is necessary. The force used must not be more than necessary under the circumstances, and it must be reasonable in relation to the degree of perceived threat. Self-defense may extend to the defense of others or to one's home.

Duress is an action by one person that compels another to do something he or she otherwise need not do. It is a defense against a criminal charge when the act in question was "coerced by use of, or threat to use, unlawful force which a person of reasonable firmness could not resist."[19]

Necessity as a defense excuses the defendant from an act that would otherwise be a crime when he or she has been forced to choose "between two evils." In other words, the defendant has violated the law, but only in the reasonable belief that the act was necessary in order to avoid an imminent greater harm.

Perhaps the most controversial defense, usually called simply "justification" is the legitimate killing of another person by an individual acting properly in the course of his or her duty as a law enforcement officer. Disagreements abound about the proper use of deadly force. One point is clear: although police officers may use whatever force is necessary to arrest, they may use no more than that without committing a crime.

Box 3.4

The SODDI Defense

A popular defense on the television series *Matlock* is the SODDI defense, which obliterates both the *actus reus* and *mens rea* components of crime. SODDI stands for "Some Other Dude Did It."

Kinds of Crimes

Contemporary legal classifications of crimes, like the criminal law generally, owe much to their common law origins. The original common law felonies were "felonious homicide, mayhem, arson, rape, robbery, burglary, larceny, prison breach [escape], and rescue of a felon."[20] (Rescue of a felon meant using force to help a felon escape from legal custody.) Originally, all were capital crimes, punishable by death, except mayhem, punishable by mutilation.

It still is the custom to reserve the term "felony" for generally more serious crimes, typically *mala in se*. Now, criminal codes generally make distinctions between felonies, misdemeanors, and more minor offenses usually called violations or infractions. It is common also to roughly grade offenses within these categories according to classifications of seriousness, with a corresponding gradation of the severity of penalties. Typically, a felony is a crime that may be punished by death or a state prison sentence of a year or more. In some jurisdictions, these crimes are called "high misdemeanors." A misdemeanor is typically punishable by a sentence of less than a year, usually in a county jail. These are mere rules of thumb, because exceptions to these usual designations are common.

The designation as felony or misdemeanor may have important implications, depending upon the jurisdiction. It is common that a person convicted of a felony loses certain civil rights, such as the right to vote or hold public office, or the person may suffer a loss of licenses. An accused felon may have to be tried in a state court rather than a municipal court, and may have to be indicted by a grand jury.

Common Felonies

Usually, state criminal codes define various degrees of common crimes, with harsher penalties assigned or permitted for crimes generally thought to be more serious. Crimes often are graduated in the law in terms of degrees of seriousness. There is no single classification of crimes and penalties that is applied in all jurisdictions, but for most offenses some elements defining crimes are typical.

Criminal Homicide

Homicide means a killing of one person by another. Criminal homicide is such killing when it is not justified or excused. The degree of the crime often is determined by the intent of the person committing the act, which, of course, must be inferred from his or her behavior. Thus, criminal homicide usually is divided into three degrees: murder, manslaughter, and negligent homicide. The classification of criminal homicides depends upon evidence of the mental state of the actor—the *mens rea*—that is, the extent to which the killing was intended and willful.

Murder often is divided into two degrees. Murder in the first degree generally is a premeditated, deliberate, willful killing with malice aforethought. The designation of murder in the first degree, in some jurisdictions, may also be charged, however, in the killing of law enforcement or correctional officers or killing by a prisoner serving a life sentence even when premeditation is absent. A conviction for murder in the second degree means that premeditation and deliberation have not been proved beyond a reasonable doubt, although the intent was to cause death. In this instance there was no malice aforethought.

Voluntary manslaughter is an intentional killing, but one without malice, as "in the heat of unreasonable passion," or else it is a killing which, although unintentional, resulted from unreasonable and grossly reckless conduct. Involuntary manslaughter means that the death was caused unintentionally but resulted from the offender's reckless disregard of a substantial risk to the victim's life.

Felony murder is a criminal homicide caused unintentionally by intentional participation in a felony. If a person kills another while intending only to do him or her serious bodily harm, that also may be felony murder. Felony murder is usually a category of first degree murder.

Assault

An assault is an attempt to inflict bodily injury on another person when there is an apparent ability to cause injury if the attempt is not prevented. A threat combined with the ability to carry it out may be an assault. If an assault results in touching, it may be called battery. Physical injury need not be proved in establishing an assault. An aggravated assault means that the person inflicted serious bodily injury on the victim, or the act was particularly fierce or atrocious, or it was committed with a dangerous or deadly weapon, or it was done intentionally along with another crime. Simple assault usually means one that caused little or no bodily harm.

Rape

In common law, rape meant sexual intercourse (the term "carnal knowledge" was used) forced by a man on a woman not his wife, by use of force or fear, with lack of consent. Penetration was an element of the crime. Otherwise, the offense was at most an attempt. In many jurisdictions, the definition of this crime now has changed, as have the rules of evidence for its prosecution, and often it is called sexual assault. In some jurisdictions, a wife may now charge her husband with rape. There are marked variations among states, but the general trend is toward gender-neutral provisions and elimination of any marital exemption.

Statutory rape is the crime of sexual intercourse with a female younger than an age set by statute, regardless of consent. The age varies among the states ranging from 11 to 18 years.

Robbery

Robbery is forcible stealing. It means taking another's property by violence or putting the victim in fear by threat. A larceny becomes a robbery when force or threat is used. Typically, statutes define a theft as a robbery if: serious bodily injury is inflicted, fear of immediate serious bodily injury or threats of such injury are made, or if the offender commits or threatens to commit any serious felony. Armed robbery is robbery aggravated by a dangerous weapon, whether or not it is used.

Burglary

The common law definition of burglary was a breaking into a dwelling at night with intent to commit a felony. Now it generally means entering a building (not necessarily a dwelling) at night with intent to steal property. It may mean unlawfully remaining in a building with intent to commit any crime, and not only at night. In some jurisdictions, burglary is divided into degrees, depending, for example, whether it takes place at night, in an occupied dwelling, or with possession of a weapon.

Can you tell if this person is committing a crime? What elements of a crime are present?

Larceny

Although larceny means essentially "stealing," there are several classifications of this common crime. A larceny is a taking and carrying away of another's personal property unlawfully with the intent to deprive the owner of it. Larceny requires an absence of permission or authority for the taking, and it may be required that it be a permanent removal — that is, not returned. Early statutes distinguished between *grand larceny* and *petit larceny* (usually now called petty larceny). In 1275 in England, if the value of the property taken was not more than 12 pence, it was classified as petit larceny and did not call for the death penalty. Modern penal codes usually continue to make a distinction based on the value of the property taken (such values varying over time and place), and there may be different degrees of grand larceny. Typically, grand larceny is a felony, petty larceny is a misdemeanor. But, petty theft with a prior petty theft (or with a prior felony conviction) may be a felony. Stealing includes such "taking and carrying away" as car thefts, "confidence games," embezzlement, worthless check offenses, and shoplifting, but these offenses usually are classified by separate codes and penalties.

Fraud

Fraud is an intentional deception resulting in an injury — usually loss of property — to another person. It can include all manner of misrepresentations, tricks, artifice, cunning, deceit, craftiness, misleading conduct, concealment, or nondisclosure. There are many ways to unfairly cheat another person, which is fraud. Crimes of deception include confidence games, forgery, and other illegal transactions, such as credit card offenses, computer crimes, and other kinds of bank trickery or illegal transactions. Some of these often are classified as separate crimes.

Arson

The common law definition of arson was the willful and malicious burning of the dwelling house of another. Now, it commonly includes other structures, public buildings, motor vehicles, or aircraft. Arson may be divided into degrees, according to the extent of harm.

Other Crimes

Crime takes a variety of additional forms. Besides diverse "white-collar" or "corporate" crimes, there are organized crimes and conspiracies. Among the most common are "crimes against the public morality," which include offenses dealing with drugs, alcohol, and vice.

Not all serious harms are themselves crimes, but they may involve crimes. Kidnapping, which is a crime, is seizing and holding a person, by force or threat, for ransom or reward. Terrorism, however, is not itself a crime, although it may of course involve crimes such as kidnapping or other crimes of violence.

The term "conspiracy" means an agreement by two or more persons to commit a specific crime. When a criminal act has been shown to be "in furtherance of a conspiracy," then the culprits are guilty also of the crime of conspiracy. All those who conspired are guilty of the crimes committed by any of the others. The ability to charge the crime of conspiracy along with other accusations is a powerful tool for prosecutors. The charge of conspiracy may be added to the list of alleged offenses either as an attempt to obtain more severe sanctions or as a potential weapon in plea bargaining.

Crime Seriousness

Criminal codes generally are based on legislators' perceptions of the seriousness of the harms done by the crime, and this is reflected in the gradations of punishments provided for in an overall ranking of offenses and for degrees within categories. In a rough way, these gradations agree with most people's perceptions of seriousness. Murder, rape, and kidnapping provide extremes, as do minor thefts and other misdemeanors. But crimes, and persons who commit them, are complex; and the problem of measuring seriousness is not so simple. It may be said that:

> Every crime is, in some respects,
>> like all other crimes,
>> like some other crimes, and
>> like no other crime.

Every crime is like all other crimes because each includes the seven requirements for a crime: *actus reas*, illegality, concurrence, *mens rea*, cause, harm, and provision for punishment.

Every crime is like some other crimes because for a given legal classification of a crime, necessary elements must be present in order that the crime may be classified into that category. Every criminal homicide is a killing of one human being by another that is not justified or excused. And so it goes: every robbery is a stealing by force or threat, each fraud is another way of taking property by cheating.

The fact that every crime is like some other crimes provides the basis for any classification of crimes. That is the case whether the aim is that of the legislator in writing laws or that of the social scientist in classifying criminal behaviors for some other purpose. It is very useful to classify crimes, either based on legal definitions or other criteria. There always is a price, however, for this usefulness. The price is always the loss of some information about the offense and its circumstances.

Every crime is like no other crime because no criminal code can capture entirely the diversity of persons and events that constitute crimes. Since people are all different and circumstances are variable, each crime is in some respects unique, even if all elements defining a particular crime are present.

Perceptions of the seriousness of crimes are based not only upon the perceived harm done, but also the apparent culpability of the offender. Consider the following crimes, and rate the seriousness of each, compared with each other, on a scale of one to 10:

A man robbed another man.

A man robbed a man of $20.00.

A man robbed a blind man of $20.00.

A blind man robbed a blind man of $20.00.

A young sighted man robbed an old blind man of $200.00.

Did your ratings differ? If so, you might want to note that they differed not only with the circumstances of the crime but also with the amount of information you had. And you may have wanted more information before making any rating.

Nearly 70 years ago, L. L. Thurstone invented ways to measure the seriousness of crime as seen by most people.[21] The resulting comparative judgments remain remarkably stable over time.[22] Others, using similar methods, have developed more comprehensive measures.[23] Measuring the seriousness of crimes may involve complex relations between the harm done and the blameworthiness or culpability of the offender, and the various aspects to each of these concepts may not be measured adequately by any single scale. There may be different "kinds" or dimensions of crime; and it may be useful to measure each on a separate scale.

In a study based on this reasoning, S. Gottfredson found that six dimensions underlie people's judgments of crimes (Box 3.5).[24] He found that people tend to see these categories of offenses (based on judgments of behavioral acts rather than legal classifications) as similar in some ways:

Box 3.5

People Recognize Six Kinds of Crimes

Nuisance crimes	Serious **drug** crimes
Personal crimes	
Property crimes	*Average seriousness ratings of crimes in*
Crimes against the **public order**	*these groups differ, but the distributions of*
Fraud crimes	*ratings overlap among categories.*

Nuisance offenses include such crimes as prostitution, gambling, use and possession of marijuana, adultery, disorderly conduct, homosexual acts, exposures, technical violations of parole and probation rules, and drunk driving. In general, people view crimes in this classification as relatively nonserious.

Personal offenses include physical assault, personal harm, interpersonal confrontations, including robbery with physical harm or assault. These generally are seen as the most serious.

Property offenses include crimes involving theft, property damage, and other offenses usually classified as property crimes (but including robbery without serious physical harm or assault).

Crimes against the social order include offenses either committed by an agent or agency in power (an employer, a real estate agent, a police officer, a manufacturer, a doctor, a public official), social crimes (for example, racism, polluting a water supply, marketing contaminated products, price fixing, false advertising), or both.

Serious drug offenses include selling or manufacturing heroin, hallucinogens, cocaine, barbiturates, and amphetamines.

Fraud includes the usual offenses of fraud and deception.

Although these classifications of offenses differ in general in how serious they are considered to be, there is substantial overlap in judged seriousness among the groups. For example, an offense classified as "property crime" may have a higher seriousness value than one classed as a "personal crime," even though personal offenses in general are scored as more serious. A theft of a large amount of money may be seen as more serious than a robbery attempt resulting in a slight physical injury.

Summary

A crime is an intentional act committed without excuse or justification, causing harm that a government has determined to be injurious to the public and prosecutable in a criminal proceeding that may result in punishment. Our criminal laws developed mainly from English common law. Now, they are based on the U.S. Constitution (the supreme law of the land), the constitutions of the 50 states, and statutes enacted by the U.S. Congress or state legislatures. Laws are written by legislators and interpreted and shaped by judges, who are guided also by precedents. They are influenced by public sentiment and personal dispositions.

A crime requires an illegal act, together with a "guilty mind," causing an injury or damage, for which the actor may be punished. Defenses against accusations are excuses and justifications that seek to remove one or more of these requirements of a crime.

Crimes may be classified, for example, as felonies (generally more serious) or misdemeanors (usually less serious) and according to specific offenses with different elements. Offenses often are classified according to degrees of seriousness. People generally see common crimes as falling into six groups that differ in overall seriousness but are made up of crimes that may differ in degrees of seriousness within the groups as well.

Notes

1. Russell, B. (1951). *New Hope for a Changing World*. New York: Simon and Schuster, 74.

2. Hughes, G. (1983). "The Concept of Crime" in S. H. Kadish, (ed.). *Encyclopedia of Crime and Justice*, Vol. 1. New York: The Free Press, 294–301.

3. Dodgson, C. L. (1916). *Alice's Adventures in Wonderland and Through the Looking Glass*. New York: Rand McNally, 186.

4. McClain, C. (1983). "Historical Development in the United States," in S. H. Kadish, (ed.). *Encyclopedia of Crime and Justice* Vol. 1, p. 501. New York: The Free Press.

5. Pound, R. "Do We Need a Philosophy of Law," in Association of the Bar of the City of New York (eds.). (1953). *Jurisprudence in Action*. New York: Baker, Voorhis and Company, 393–396.

6. McClain, C. (1983). "Historical Development in the United States," in S. H. Kadish, (ed.). *Encyclopedia of Crime and Justice* Vol. 1, p. 502. New York: The Free Press.

7. Beccaria, C. [1776]. *Dei delitti e della pena*. (6th ed.) Harlem, An Essay on Crime and Punishments. (Translated from the Italian with the commentary by Voltaire.) (5th ed.), London, 1804, as cited in Monechesi, E., (1973) "Cesare Beccaria" in *Pioneers in Criminology*, 2nd ed., Mannheim, H., (ed.). Montclair, NJ: Patterson Smith Publishing, 45–48.

8. McClain, C. (1983). "Historical Development in the United States," in S. H. Kadish, (ed.). *Encyclopedia of Crime and Justice* Vol. 1, pp. 503–504. New York: The Free Press.

9. Hobbes, T. [1651]. *Leviathan*. Oakeshott, M. (ed.). (1962). New York: Macmillan, 229–231.

10. McClain, C. (1983). "Historical Development in the United States," in S. H. Kadish, (ed.). *Encyclopedia of Crime and Justice* Vol. 1, pp. 505–506. New York: The Free Press.

11. Friedrich, C. J. (1963). *The Philosophy of Law in Historical Perspective*, 2nd ed. Chicago: University of Chicago Press.

12. Plato, *Laws II 934*, as cited in Newman, G. (1978). *The Punishment Response*. New York: Lippencott, 201.

13. Kant, I. [1887]. *The Philosophy of Law* trans. W. Hastie (Edinburgh: T. T. Clear, 1887), as cited by Weiler, P. C. (1974). "The Reform of Punishment," in *Law Reform of Canada Studies in Sentencing*. Ottawa: Information Canada.

14. Hall, J. (1947). *General Principles of Criminal Law*, 2nd ed. Indianapolis: Bobbs-Merril, 18.

15. 18 U.S.C. P17.

16. American Law Institute. (1985). *Model Penal Code*. sec 4.01–4.02. Philadelphia: American Law Institute.

17. Gifis, S. H. (1975). *Law Dictionary* Woodbury, NY: Barron's Educational Series, 106.

18. Klofas, J. and R. Weischeit. (1987). "Guilty but Mentally Ill: Reform of the Insanity Defense in Illinois," *Justice Quarterly*, Vol. 4, 1, 40–50.

19. Gifis, S. H. (1975). *Law Dictionary* Woodbury, NY: Barron's Educational Series, 66–67.

20. Perkins, R. M. (1969). *Criminal Law*, 2nd ed. The Foundation Press, as cited by Gifis, S. H. (1975), 82.

21. Thurstone, L. L. (1927). "The Method of Paired Comparisons for Social Values," *Journal of Abnormal and Social Psychology*. 21, 384–400.

22. Coombs, C. H. (1967). "Thurstone's Measurement of Social Values Revisited, Forty Years Later," *Journal of Personality and Social Psychology,* 6, 91–92; Krus, J., J. L. Sherman, and P. H. Krus. (1977). "Changing Values Over the Last Half Century: The Story of Thurstone's Crime Scales," *Psychological Reports*, 40, 207–211.

23. Sellin, M. E. and M. E. Wolfgang. (1964). *The Measurement of Delinquency*. New York: Wiley; Rossi, P. H., E. Waite, C. E. Bose, and R. Berk. (1974). "The Seriousness of Crime: Normative Structure and Individual Differences," *American Sociological Review* 39, 224–237.

24. Gottfredson, S. D. (1981). *Measuring Offense Seriousness: A Dimensional Approach*. Baltimore: Center for Metropolitan Planning and Research, The Johns Hopkins University.

CHAPTER FOUR

The Nature and Extent of Crime

Chapter Four

We have seen that the criminal justice system is a sequence of decisions and procedures in law enforcement, courts, and corrections, operating within the framework provided by the law. Next we will examine crime and the tendency to commit crime, more closely, including some early, still influential views and a more modern one. How we can measure crime will be discussed, and the main methods used will be compared. This will set the stage for examining each of the main parts of the system in more detail in the chapters that follow.

- ❏ Questions to Think About
- ❏ Concern with Crime
- ❏ Understanding Crime
- ❏ Early Views on Crime and Crime Control
- ❏ The Nature of Crime
    - The General Nature of Crimes
- ❏ How Can Crime Be Measured?
- ❏ Requirements of Measurement
- ❏ The Uniform Crime Reports
- ❏ Crimes Known to the Police
    - Common Crimes
    - Conditions Necessary for Crimes in General
    - Murder
    - Burglary
    - Robbery
    - Auto Theft
    - Other Offenses
- ❏ Self-Control
- ❏ Arrests
    - Crimes Cleared by Arrest
    - Crime Trends
- ❏ National Incident Based Reporting System (NIBRS)
- ❏ Age and Crime
- ❏ The National Crime Victimization Survey
- ❏ Uniform Crime Reports and Victim Surveys Compared
- ❏ Self-Reports of Delinquency and Crime
- ❏ The Regularity and Costs of Crime
- ❏ Summary

Why do some people commit crimes? Why doesn't everybody obey the law?

Why do some people *not* commit crimes? Why doesn't everybody commit crimes?

Are some people more prone to crime than others? Why?

What is a "criminal"?

Can an understanding of the causes of crime help to control crime?

How much crime is there?

How can crime be measured?

Who are the victims of crime? Who is more at risk of being a victim?

What are the most common crimes?

At what ages are people most likely to get into trouble with the law?

Is crime going up or down? Among males? Among females?

How can we know?

Can surveys of victims include all kinds of crime?

Concern with Crime

Fear of criminal violence in America as described nearly 20 years ago still rings true:

> All over the United States, people worry about criminal violence. According to public opinion polls, two Americans in five—in large cities, one in two—are afraid to go out alone at night. Fear is more intense among black Ameri-cans than among whites, and among women than among men. The elderly are the most fearful of all; barricaded behind multiple locks, they often go hungry rather than risk the peril of a walk to the market and back. [1]

In public perceptions crime ranks along with concerns about health care and the nation's economy as a national problem. In a June 1997 poll of a national sample representative of the country's civilian population 18 years old and older, people were asked to name the two most important issues for government to address. Crime and the federal deficit were most often men-tioned (Figure 4.1).

Much of this concern is based on fear—fear for personal safety. Respon-dents in a similar poll of a national sample were asked, "Is there any area right around here—that is, within a mile—where you would be afraid to walk alone at night?" Two out of five persons said yes (Figure 4.2).

Some degree of such fear is realistic, yet it sometimes is out of propor-tion to the real danger. A person is much more likely to die of natural causes than as a victim of crime. The chances of being injured by a criminal act are less than those of being hurt in a car accident. Yet, the threat is there: the odds of being the victim of an assault are far greater than those of death by heart disease, cancer, or accident.

The chances of being the victim of various life events, according to data gathered by the Bureau of Justice Statistics, are shown in Table 4.1. Better estimates might be made by taking account of factors such as age, sex, race,

Figure 4.1 Issues Thought Important for the Government to Address, 1997

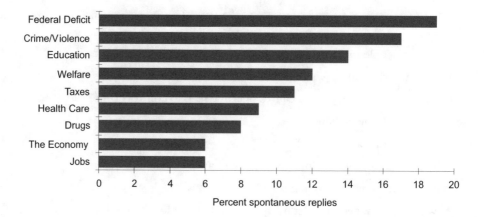

Source: data from Maguire, K. and Pastore, A. L., (eds.) (1997). *Sourcebook of Criminal Justice Statistics*, www.albany.edu.sourcebok (adapted from data from Harris, L., The Harris Poll. Los Angeles: Creators Syndicate, Inc., June 16, 1997).

Figure 4.2 Persons Reporting They Are Afraid to Walk Alone at Night, 1996

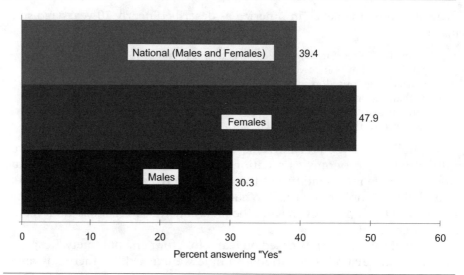

Source: data from Maguire, K. and Pastore, A. L., (eds.) (1997). *Sourcebook of Criminal Justice Statistics* www.albany.edu.sourcebook (from data provided by Princeton Survey Research Center for The Pew Research Center for The People & The Press).

place of residence, and lifestyle, because the chances of victimization are different for various groups. For example, men are more often victims than are women. The elderly are much less often victims than are youths. Victimization rates are highest for those who live in the cities. When it comes to violent victimizations, the risk is greater for African Americans, for young males, for persons in lower-income families, and for the unemployed. Elderly females may be extremely fearful of being a victim of a violent crime, but elderly women have the lowest violent victimization rates.

Table 4.1 Crime Rates and Rates of Other Life Adversities

How Do Crime Rates Compare With the Rates of Other Life Events?

Events	Rate per 1,000 Adults per Year
Accidental injury, all circumstances	242
Accidental injury at home	79
Personal theft	72
Accidental injury at work	58
Violent victimization	31
Assault (aggravated and simple)	24
Injury in motor vehicle accident	17
Death, all causes	11
Victimization with injury	10
Serious (aggravated) assault	9
Robbery	6
Heart disease death	4
Cancer death	2
Rape (women only)	2
Accidental death, all circumstances	0.5
Pneumonia/influenza death	0.3
Motor vehicle accident death	0.2
Suicide	0.1
Injury from fire	0.1
Homicide/"legal intervention" death	0.1
Death from fire	0.03

Source: *Report to the Nation on Crime and Justice*, 2nd ed., 24.

This comparison of the annual incident rates of being a victim of crime and of other life adversities raises the question, "How do we know?" It is widely believed that crime rates are going up and that violent crimes in particular are increasing. Most people's image of crime, shaped in part by newspapers and television, may be the fearful prospect of murder and assault, street robberies, drive-by shootings, and home invasion robberies. Is that an accurate picture of most crime? In order to get the facts about crime, it is necessary to figure out how to measure it. Let us first consider what we wish to measure, that is, the nature of most crime—including murder and assault, robberies, shootings, and home invasions, but also many less dramatic forms of stealing.

Understanding Crime

There is no crime unless a person does something. Since a crime is an act, the study of behavior is relevant to an understanding of crime. Partly because the concept of crime includes not only acts against the law but also a response by society, much of sociology (the study of social groups) and of political science (the study of principles, organization, and methods of government) are, along with psychology, involved in a search for explanations. This does not exhaust the list of disciplines that have contributed to understandings of crime. Biological, economic, and statistical perspectives, as well as theories from moral and legal philosophy, all have contributed to criminology—the study of crime.

It is common to refer to some persons as "delinquents" or "criminals." These terms, however, do not refer aptly to any state of the person, as would be expected in the case of diagnosis of physical or mental disorder. We refer to some state of the person when we say she has diabetes, has a broken leg, or is a person with psychotic disorder. A term such as "criminal," however, refers only in part to an offender's behavior; and it may in fact be called into use by a single act. The word "criminal" relates also to the state of the social system with which the person is involved because of his or her acts. A "crime" refers to a combination of a person's behavior and society's response. As a result, it is not a very helpful description of any person and just about useless for the purposes of this book.

Yet, some people have a greater likelihood than do others of coming into conflict with the law. Some persons have a greater *propensity* or inclination to commit crimes than do others. We would like to understand crime, and also we would like to understand criminality (understood as a propensity to crime). Besides explaining, if we can, why the crime rate goes up or down, or why behavior that is illegal at one time and place is not a crime at another, we would like to explain individual differences in the propensity to commit crimes.

Early Views on Crime and Crime Control

The ideas of deterring crime by punishment or by correction of the offender are based on beliefs about the nature of crime. Some views expressed in the writings of the early Greeks still hold sway. More recently, but still centuries ago, the philosophers known as the British empiricists were concerned with deterrence and correction. Their arguments provided the groundwork for what came to be known as the classical school of criminology. This school is represented by Jeremy Bentham (1748–1832) and Cesare Beccaria (1734–1794).

These early criminologists maintained that man is rational, endowed with free will, and—because he seeks pleasure and avoids pain—can be deterred from crime by punishment. In Bentham's words, "Nature has placed mankind under the governance of two sovereign masters, pain and pleasure."[2] People, Bentham believed, are basically self-interested, and crimes are simply acts committed when the pleasure received as a result of the act is greater than the pain caused. Thus, crime is to be prevented and is caused by the consequences of the act—whether pleasurable or painful. The sources of pleasure and pain, Bentham argued, are physical, political, moral, and religious. Each of these are sources of "sanctions" that naturally restrain behavior, including crime. Eating is a pleasure, but eating too much results in pain. You might briefly hold the upper hand in an argument by clubbing your adversary; but, because you might yourself be injured in the process, you might restrain yourself. Similarly, religious and moral sanctions may operate to deter criminal behavior. Moral sanctions included, for Bentham, the actions of the community that provide pleasure or pain to the person.

Because he sought reforms in the criminal law, he wrote mainly about political sanctions. In order to prevent crime, Bentham thought, the punishment imposed must be just greater than the pleasure derived from it. Punishment was to be justified on the basis of seeking the greatest pleasure for the greatest number. Bentham discussed the importance of the certainty, severity (duration or intensity) and celerity (swiftness) of punishment in reducing crime. To reduce crime, punishment should be certain, just severe enough but no more so, and swift.

Cesare Beccaria (1738-1794) found the punishments used in his time cruel. He was also influenced by British philosophers who emphasized the importance of the association of ideas for understanding why people think and act as they do. He argued that the certainty and swiftness of punishment are more important than severity for crime control, stating:

> The more immediately after the commission of a crime a punishment is inflicted, the more just and useful it will be. . . . An immediate punishment is more useful; because the smaller the interval of time between the punish - ment and the crime, the stronger and more lasting will be the association of the two ideas of crime and punishment.[3]

In contrast to the classical school of criminology, a "positivist" school emerged, associated with the name of Cesare Lombroso (1836–1909) in which investigators sought to identify individuals likely to engage in crime. These workers are best known for seeking mainly biological causes for criminality, particularly in abnormal brain structures, and physiological differences between "criminals" (thought inferior) and others. Their more important contribution, however, was their focus on a scientific, empirical approach to the study of crime and on individual differences. The classical criminologists contributed theory and the positivists contributed ways to test it.

Since these beginnings, the main streams of theoretical development in criminology (hence in criminal justice) have been influenced heavily by both the classical and positivist schools. The arguments of Bentham and Beccaria affect criminal justice policy today. The administration of criminal justice is increasingly informed by applications of the scientific method, which have included some tests of these early writers.

The Nature of Crime

Theories of crime are not the same as theories of criminality. One seeks to explain crime, and the other tries to explain individual differences in the propensity to commit crimes. That is, we may try to explain crime in general, how it affects society, how the level of crime changes from time to time or differs from place to place. Or, we may try to explain why some persons are more likely to commit crimes than are others. Both kinds of theories are an important part of criminology, but their critical examination is beyond the scope of this book. For discussions of common crimes, we will rely on a general theory of crime. It is aimed at explaining the inclination of people to commit ordinary crime—the common crimes that occupy, day after day with tedious repetition, the workers in the criminal justice system and that are the focus of this book. The authors of a general theory of crime, Michael Gottfredson and Travis Hirschi, based their theory in part on the nature of crimes as seen typically in the criminal justice system.[4]

The General Nature of Crimes

Common crimes are called less to our attention than are a small number of much less prevalent ones. Among crimes known to the police, some kind of stealing is by far the most frequent crime, and among arrests made by the police, driving under the influence, vehicle-theft, drug abuse violations, and simple assaults also are exceedingly common. The crimes typically portrayed in the news and in television dramas are the more unusual, hence "newsworthy," or bizarre, or involve well-known persons. If a wife cuts off her husband's penis, that is news partly because it is a sensational but fortunately rare event. If two brothers murder their parents, or a mother pushes her children into the water to drown, or a celebrity is accused of a vicious double murder, we can hardly escape the attention given to these dramatic but unusual events.

Fictional drama may also influence our picture of crime. Fictional accounts often summon an image of crime involving careful planning, impressive foresight, skill, and success. Highly organized gangs gain enormous profits from drugs. Criminal gangs rob banks of millions while calmly killing innocent bystanders. Multiple murderers are rampant, while huge sums of money are laundered by organized crime. The "Pink Panther" burglar gets away with expensive jewelry by imaginative stealth and tricks; and huge stock swindles are commonplace.

These images do not accurately portray the bulk of crime dealt with in the criminal justice system. Michael Gottfredson described the reality in this way:

> [F]or every drive-by shooting in Southern California there are thousands of petty larcenies, and countless truancies, acts of graffiti, joy-rides, fist fights, attempted burglaries and acts of sheer destruction for the hell of it. . . . We are, in reality, dealing with the population and with the state-run system of control so vividly described by the novelist Tom Wolfe:[5]

> > [The Bronx criminal justice system consists of] forty thousand people, forty thousand incompetents, dimwits, alcoholics, psychopaths, knockabouts, good souls driven to some terrible terminal anger, and people who could only be described as stone evil. . . . [Despite the efforts of] fifty judges, thirty-five law clerks, 245 assistant district attorneys, one D.A., and Christ knew how many criminal lawyers, Legal Aid lawyers, court reporters, court clerks, court officers, correction officers, probation officers, social workers, bail bondsmen, special investigators, case clerks, court psychiatrists, the same stupid, dismal, pathetic horrifying crimes [are] committed day in and day out, all the same.[6]

From the nature of crime, Gottfredson and Hirschi infer the nature of the tendency to engage in it. Most crime is unglamorous, unplanned, promising fleeting satisfaction, and entails "acts of force or fraud undertaken in the pursuit of self-interest."[7]

How Can Crime Be Measured?

Government efforts to measure crime have slowly gained ground over the last 100 years. When Edison had invented the phonograph and the first public telephones were being installed, Rutherford B. Hayes was elected President of the United States. When President Hayes, a former President of the American Corrections Association, wanted to know how much crime there was in our country, he sent U.S. marshals off on horseback to the various states and territories to count the numbers of prisoners locked up. It is reported that they never came back.[8]

It is important to know how many prisoners are confined, but that is a poor measure of the extent of crime. In order to become a prisoner, a person who committed a crime must be caught, arrested, prosecuted, convicted, and sentenced to confinement. Although we still cannot know the answer to President Hayes's question with precision, we do now have some useful ways of estimating the extent of crime.

There are three commonly used ways to measure crime:

1. Count crimes known to the police and reported by them;

2. Count crimes reported by victims;

3. Count crimes admitted by those who say they did them.

Much of our knowledge about the extent of crime comes from the first two methods, using procedures known as the Uniform Crime Reports and the National Crime Victimization Survey.

> *Statistics are the only tools by which an opening can be cut through the formidable thicket of difficulties that bars the path of those who pursue the Science of Man.*
> —Sir Francis Galton

If we wish to understand the meaning of data on the extent of crime from any method, we must first know how the data are collected. Unless the meanings of the counts are clear, we will be easily misled. Also, there are two simple principles of classification and measurement that we must understand if we are to appreciate the usefulness and limitations of counts of crime data. Based on these principles, the main strengths and limitations of our measures of crime become apparent.

Requirements of Measurement

All measures of crime require classification. Examples of classifications are offense groups, offender "types," prior record counts, or probation or parole categories. A main requirement of classification is *inclusivity* — that the classes include all the elements of the population of interest. In other words, there must be some appropriate category for all the cases. A second requirement is that the categories used must be mutually exclusive, meaning that any particular case belongs only in one group and cannot be put into more than one. A moment's reflection will show that these two principles are important to an understanding of crime statistics.

If the requirement of *inclusivity* is not met, as is typical in measures of crime, then generalizations about the full extent of crime will be flawed. If some crimes are not included in a data collection system, the results of the effort, no matter how carefully done, cannot enable us to generalize about all crime. Neither of the two main methods used to measure crime includes all crimes. Both the Uniform Crime Reports and the victim survey leave out some crimes. For this reason alone, neither method can tell us comprehensively how much crime there is.

The requirement of *exclusivity* often means that some information is lost in the classification process. For example, if a person is convicted of both robbery and burglary and is classified into the robbery category only, the burglary is not counted. If both robbery and burglary are counted, this will show up as two crimes, although it may have involved only one person and one event. If the crime-counting process counts only the most serious crime, as usually is the case, then not all crimes are counted.

There is another important way that information is lost in the classification and counting process. If Walter enters a convenience store, pulls out a .38 caliber revolver, fires a shot into the air, points the weapon at the clerk and loudly demands, "Put all the money in the bag or I'll blow your head off!" the petrified clerk and six customers may well consider this a very serious offense. They will not think kindly of Tom, waiting in the getaway car, but perhaps their anger will be focused on Walter, who posed the real and immediate threat. Suppose, in another case, that Clem is waiting in line behind six customers. He puts on a ski mask, pulls out a toy pistol, and continues patiently waiting his turn in order to rob the store. When he finally reaches the counter and demands money, he is promptly arrested. The victims may be outraged but think it rather humorous. Or, consider the case of George, drinking with Bill. He wants the rest of Bill's bottle and takes it by force. Bill may be more angry than frightened. If Walter, Tom, Clem, and George each are arrested for robbery or its attempt (of which each is guilty), the quality of the differences among the crimes will be lost when robbery arrests are counted.

The methods of measuring crime are useful for many purposes, but it must be remembered that all methods of measurement are subject to error. This is true in physics, carpentry, and criminal justice. That errors must be expected does not mean the measures are not useful. It does mean that we should be aware of possible sources of error that might mislead us. In order to understand the possible sources of error, we must first be acquainted with how the data are collected.

Errors in data collection systems such as those that provide measures of crime may be sorted into two parts. There is random error, as is the case with all measurements. These are considered "chance" variations. Statistical methods are available to measure this type of error, and it may be possible to rule it out. But there is also the possibility—or maybe the probability—of systematic error, which is a bias in one direction or another, associated with the observer, the method of observing and recording, or both. This is a form of invalidity—it means that the measures include assessment of something other than what was intended. Data are merely *relatively* reliable, and *relatively* valid. They are apt to have some bias, in one way or another.

Thus, we seek criminal justice measures, including measures of crime, that are sufficiently reliable and valid for the specific purposes to which they will be put. Reliability refers to the degree of consistency in measurement, for example, to how much agreement there is in repeated measures using the same procedures. Validity refers to the degree to which *what* is measured is that which is *intended* to be measured. In every case it must be remembered just how the data were collected if we are to understand their meaning, their reliability and validity, and how they might be biased.

> *The greater the number of laws and enactments, the more thieves and robbers there will be.*
> —*Lao Tze, (circa 604–531 B.C.)*

The Uniform Crime Reports

In *Crime in the United States,* each year the Federal Bureau of Investigation reports data submitted voluntarily by law enforcement agencies across the country. The FBI reports the number of offenses known to those agencies, the number of arrests, the number of reported crimes that have been cleared by arrest, the number of law enforcement officers killed, and the value of property stolen and recovered. The amount, trends, rates, and descriptions of selected offenses are reported also. Offenses known to the police and arrests are tabulated by state, region, size of place, and degree of urbanization. The data collection system also includes data about the number of law enforcement personnel and other useful information.

The Uniform Crime Reports (UCR) program was started by a Committee of the International Association of Chiefs of Police in the 1920s. By 1929 they completed the plan that became the foundation for this remarkable data collection program still maintained by the FBI.

The most extensive data are presented for a group of crimes to provide a measure known as the crime index. Data on four categories of crimes against persons (murder and nonnegligent manslaughter, forcible rape, robbery, and aggravated assault) and four property crimes (burglary, larceny-theft, motor vehicle theft, and, added by congressional mandate in 1979, arson) make up the index (Box 4.1). The crime index is the simple sum of these offenses. This means that the crimes are given equal weight in the index. For the crime index, a motor vehicle theft counts as much as a murder or robbery. Both completed and attempted offenses are included. Detailed data are collected about murder, for which a special data collection form is solicited by the FBI. Various detailed data are available also about law enforcement officers killed and about bombing incidents.

Data about offenses known to the police and about arrests of persons accused of crime can be useful for addressing many criminal justice problems. Their usefulness, however, as with all such data, depends on the purposes they are to serve and depends also on a clear understanding of how the data are collected.

The UCR data represent events reported to the police or discovered by them, recorded by the police, and transmitted to the FBI as crimes. Note that the counts from this data collection system are of *events*—for example, of known offenses and arrests—and not counts of offenders or of separate crime incidents. Thus, in order to be counted, an event must be noticed by someone, defined by that person as a crime, reported to the police (if not discovered by them), recorded as a crime by the police, and submitted to the FBI (Box 4.2).

One main limitation of these useful measures of crime is apparent from the first principle of classification already mentioned—inclusivity.[9] Not all crimes are included in the tabulations. If the crime index is taken as a measure of "serious crime," it should be noted that many offenses that may be thought quite serious are not included—for example, kidnapping, child molestation,

Box 4.1

Index Offenses in Uniform Crime Reports

Uniform definitions of offenses have been established for the UCR Program. Abbreviated definitions of crimes called Part I offenses and included in the crime index are as follows:

Criminal homicide—murder and nonnegligent manslaughter: the willful killing of one human being by another;

Forcible rape—the carnal knowledge of a female forcibly and against her will;

Robbery—the taking or attempting to take anything of value from the care, custody, or control of a person or persons by force or threat of force or violence or by putting the victim in fear;

Aggravated assault—an unlawful attack by one person upon another for the purpose of inflicting severe or aggra-

vated bodily injury (usually by a weapon or by means likely to produce death or great bodily harm);

Burglary-breaking or entering—the unlawful entry of a structure to commit a felony or a theft;

Larceny-theft (except motor vehicle theft)—the unlawful taking, carrying, leading, or riding away of property from the possession or constructive possession of another;

Motor vehicle theft—the theft or attempted theft of a motor vehicle;

Arson—any willful or malicious burning or attempt to burn a dwelling house, public building, motor vehicle or aircraft, or personal property of another.

Box 4.2

U.C.R. Requirements

To Be Counted as a Crime in the Uniform Crime Reports, an Event Must Be:

- Noticed by someone.
- Defined by the observer as a crime.
- Discovered by the police or reported to them.
- Defined by the police as a crime.
- Recorded by the police.
- Classified as a crime included in the Uniform Crime Reports.
- Submitted to the FBI.
- Counted by the FBI.

simple assault, extortion, civil rights violations, corporate crimes, or simple weapons offenses. Some nonindex crimes such as fraud, embezzlement, or consumer frauds may produce serious dollar losses to victims. In addition, much crime probably goes unnoticed, and much is never reported to the police.[10] If it is reported to the police, the police may decide not to report it as a crime.[11] Moreover, police recording and reporting practices may change over time.

Thirty years ago, the 1967 President's Commission on Law Enforcement and Administration of Justice concluded that

[O]ne change of importance in the amount of crime that is reported in our society is the change in expectations of the poor and members of minority groups about civil rights and social protection. Not long ago there was a tendency to dismiss reports of all but the most serious offenses in slum areas and segregated minority group districts. . . . Crimes that were once unknown to the police, or ignored when complaints were received, are now much more likely to be reported and recorded."[12]

Other changes in police practices may be reflected in the recording and reporting of crime. If police become more inclined toward formal (e.g. arrest) than informal (e.g., taking a drunk home or counseling and releasing a suspect) handling of cases, reported crime will tend to increase. If police are successful in their efforts to resolve disputes or complaints without making an arrest, the crime rate (as measured by recorded arrests) will go down. If police are more proactive and efficient in discovery of offenses, reported crime will tend to increase. If police are successful in encouraging citizen cooperation in reporting crime, crimes known to the police will go up. If rape victims are treated more sympathetically, more rapes may be reported. If clerical and statistical staff increase or are more efficient, reported crime may go up. If the FBI is successful in encouraging more complete and accurate reporting, then reported crime may go up. If there is political pressure for reported crime to go down, it may; and if the pressure is on to demonstrate a rising crime rate, that too might occur.[13]

Because reporting is voluntary, the reporting rate is pertinent also, but most law enforcement agencies do report to the FBI. For the 1996 report on crimes in 1995, data were collected in 44 states and the District of Columbia by state UCR programs, then forwarded to the FBI. In other states, the data were contributed directly to the FBI. The data came from more than 16,000 law enforcement agencies represesenting nearly 251 million U.S. inhabitants or 95 percent of the total population.[14]

Some conventions adopted by the FBI for the UCR program are important for understanding measures of crime from this source of information. Box 4.3 shows some of them.

The Uniform Crime Reports provide a measure of crime, but it is best regarded as "crimes known to the police." Such a measure can be very useful, and the extent of crime according to these counts is informative.

Box 4.3

Some UCR Conventions

Part I offenses are generally more serious crimes, and their incidence is compiled from crimes and arrests reported to the police.

Part II offenses are generally less serious crimes, and their incidence is compiled from reports of arrests. The offenses included are listed in Table 2, along with the Part I offenses.

The **total crime index** is the sum of all the Part I offenses, that is, the crimes known to the police.

Violent crime is defined as the sum of the Part I offenses classified as homicide, forcible rape, robbery, and aggravated assault.

Property crime is the sum of the Part I offenses burglary, larceny-theft, motor vehicle theft, and arson.

The **crime rate** is the number of offenses for every 100,000 inhabitants, or Total crime index / population X 100,000.

Crimes Known to the Police

Common Crimes

The distribution of index crimes reported to the FBI is shown in Figure 4.3. We can see that theft is by far the most popular form of reported crime

Figure 4.3 Percent Distribution Crime Index Offenses, 1995

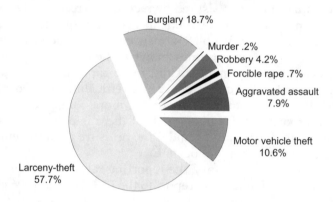

Burglary 18.7%

Murder .2%
Robbery 4.2%
Forcible rape .7%
Aggravated assault 7.9%

Motor vehicle theft 10.6%

Larceny-theft 57.7%

Source: adapted from *Crime in the United States, 1995,* Uniform Crime Reports, Federal Bureau of Investigation, U.S. Department of Justice, October 13, 1996 (Data not available for arson).

among these offenses—more than half. Fortunately, the more shocking crimes of murder, rape, robbery, and assault are relatively much less common. Burglary and taking cars are popular means of thefts, even if not classified into that category.

If the larceny-theft, burglary, and vehicle theft categories are combined into one called "stealing," then we may say that in 1995 stealing accounted for a whopping 87 percent of index crimes. If robbery were to be included as theft also, then "stealing" would account for more than 90 percent of the crimes reported. Most crime, by far, is the illegal taking of someone else's property. The stealing that is classified as larceny-theft is, in fact, the most frequent property crime, accounting for about two-thirds of all, as shown in Figure 4.4.

Shoplifting accounts for about 15 percent of reported thefts. Some kind of stealing, including robbery, accounts for 9 out of 10 reported crimes. Do you expect that most shoplifting and thefts are reported? Why or why not? —*Photo courtesy of www. photostogo.com.*

Figure 4.4 Property Crimes, 1995

Chapter 4
▲ ▲ ▲ ▲ ▲ ▲

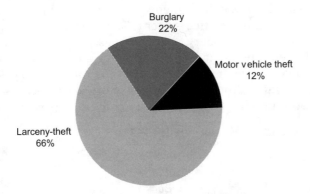

Source: data from *Crime in the United States, 1995*, Uniform Crime Reports, Federal Bureau of Investigation, U.S. Department of Justice, October 13, 1996 (does not include arson).

Most ordinary crime does not require planning, involve foresight, or rely on skill. None of these are necessities for stealing, nor are they required for assaults. The typical burglar selects targets conveniently near home and forces entry or just walks in. The typical robber chooses targets on the spur of the moment and impulsively seeks to take property by force or threat. Thieves steal from the cash drawer when no one is looking or spot a car with a purse on the seat and smash a window to get it. A car thief may cruise a parking lot looking for a car with the keys left in the ignition. Assaults, too, are usually unplanned, erupting in an argument in a bar or a family dispute.

Some crimes do involve huge sums of money and may be carefully planned. Some assaults and murders are done after deliberation. These, however, are exceptions that may distort usual perceptions of crime from the realities. Most crimes, if completed, bring only immediate and brief gratification to the offender.

Figure 4.5 Larceny-theft: Percent Distribution by Type of Theft, 1995

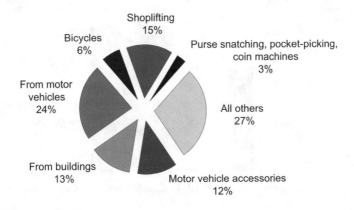

Source: data from *Crime in the United States, 1995*, Uniform Crime Reports, Federal Bureau of Investigation, U.S. Department of Justice, October 13, 1996.

Much data on common crimes are reported in the Uniform Crime Reports. Detailed data on crimes called "Part I" offenses are included, much of which are useful to law enforcement agencies and for policy and planning throughout the criminal justice system. The Part I offenses are criminal homicide, forcible rape, robbery, aggravated assault, burglary and breaking or entering, larceny-theft (except vehicle theft), motor vehicle theft, and arson. For example, it may help to know that the most popular kind of theft is stealing from cars, although taking parts of cars or accessories, taking things from buildings, and shoplifting are common also (Figure 4.5). Or, it

Figure 4.6 Where Robberies Occured, 1995

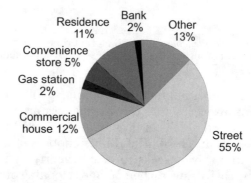

Source: data from *Crime in the United States, 1995*, Uniform Crime Reports, Federal Bureau of Investigation, U.S. Department of Justice, October 13, 1996.

may be useful to know where robberies occurred: are robberies more common on the street, in homes, or at convenience stores? Examine Figure 4.6 for the answer.

Data are presented in the Uniform Crime Reports also about race and gender in relation to known crimes. For example, although whites far outnumber blacks in the population, there are about as many blacks murdered in a year as there are whites who are murdered. Moreover, blacks are more

Figure 4.7 Relation of Race of Murder Victim to Race of Offender (single victim, single offender), 1995

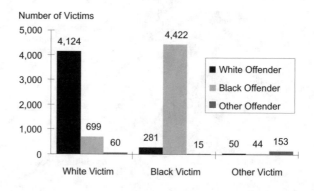

Source: data from *Crime in the United States, 1995*, Uniform Crime Reports, Federal Bureau of Investigation, U.S. Department of Justice, October 13, 1996 (based on 10,032 incidents, with missing data excluded).

Figure 4.8 Relation of Sex of Murder Victim to Sex of Offender (single victim, single offender), 1995

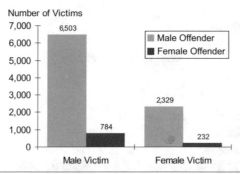

Source: data from *Crime in the United States, 1995,* Uniform Crime Reports, Federal Bureau of Investigation, U.S. Department of Justice, October 13, 1996 (based on 10,032 victims, with missing data excluded).

often murdered by black offenders, just as whites are more often victims of murder by whites (Figure 4.7). Males tend to be murder victims of males, but so do females (Figure 4.8).

Conditions Necessary for Crimes in General

> *It is not enough that a man may merely have the intention to do evil, he must also have the opportunity and the means.*
> —*Lambert A.J. Quetelet*

Crime requires, according to Cohen and Felson, a motivated offender, the absence of a suitable guardian, and a suitable target (Box 4.4).[15] Hirschi and Gottfredson would say "an insufficiently restrained" offender rather than a "motivated" offender, since they prefer to ask why people do *not* commit crimes rather than why they do.

This suggests a way to analyze any type of crime, as does the phrase familiar to police "means, motive, and opportunity." When we consider different kinds of crimes in this way, it often suggests how these crimes might be prevented. Also, it provides some insight about the nature of the specific type of crime.

Box 4.4
Crime Requires:
1. A motivated offender. 2. The absence of a suitable guardian. 3. A suitable target.

Murder

Detailed data are provided by the Uniform Crime Reports on the crime of murder. We see, for example, in Figure 4.9, that by far the most commonly

Figure 4.9 Types of Weapons Used in Murders, 1995

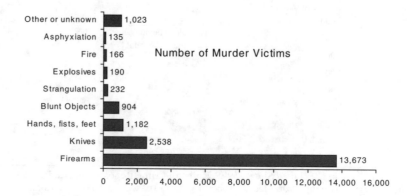

Source: data from *Crime in the United States, 1995,* Uniform Crime Reports, Federal Bureau of Investigation, U.S. Department of Justice, October 13, 1996.

used weapon in 1995, for murders and attempted murders, was a firearm. Most murders (two-thirds) were committed with firearms, although a knife was used in more than one in ten. More than 1,000 persons were killed in 1995 with nothing more than hands, fists, and feet.

Several conditions are required for a murder. There must be a suitable target: the offender and victim must be engaged in interaction with each other. The offender must have the means of taking the life of the other and must be insufficiently restrained from doing so. The victim must lack the opportunity or inclination to get away, and no "suitable guardian" to intervene is available to the victim.

Murder offenders are usually young males (17 to 29 years of age), disproportionately nonwhite (with disproportionately nonwhite victims). Nearly half of murder victims are either related to or acquainted with their assailants. Most violent crimes other than murder are committed by strangers.

In about a fourth of murders in which the circumstances are known, the killing was a result of some other felony. Of these, robbery is the most common. Perhaps due to resistance, perhaps to the offender's anxiety, or maybe as a result of pure hostility, a robbery attempt results in murder. The next most common felony involved in murder is some violation of narcotic drug laws. Less often, murder involves burglary, arson, rape, or other felonies.

Most murders, however, do not involve other felonies. Half result from arguments. The rest are associated with juvenile gangs (one in ten in 1995), romantic triangles, brawls involving alcohol or drugs, or other circumstances. Among female murder victims, a fourth are killed by husbands or boyfriends.

Burglary

A typical burglary suspect arrested in 1995 was a white (two-thirds) male (9 out of 10) in his late teens or early 20s, who broke into a home. About half the burglaries took place in the daytime, half at night. Chances are good that the offender was arrested near his home, found it easy to enter, and stole cash, liquor, stereos, televisions, or other items that could be taken away quickly.

Three conditions must be present for a burglary to occur. First, there must be a suitable target—a building or dwelling capable of entry by someone without permission. It must have contents attractive to the offender and capable of being removed. Second, it must not be monitored by someone able to interfere. Third, there must be an actor who is not sufficiently restrained from taking the available advantage. These elements not only suggest how burglaries occur but also how they can be prevented.

Robbery

Robbery is especially frequent in the cities. Two-thirds of reported robberies in the United States in one year occurred in 32 cities that housed only 16 percent of the nation's population.[16] More than half the robberies take place on the street, but in 1995 1 out of 10 was in a residence. More than half involve weapons, typically a firearm.

Robbery offenders tend to be young (in their late teens). The majority have prior arrests for a variety of offenses—not necessarily robbery. They do not tend to specialize in robbery, and, although they are likely to report money was their motive, many robberies seem incidental to other activities. Many report alcohol and drug use prior to or during the offense, and there is little evidence of planning or fear of getting caught.[17]

The typical robbery thus involves a young man (or young men) with a weapon or other threat who demands money or other valuables, most often of persons on the street but sometimes in a store or residence. After getting the property, he runs away.

Again there must be an attractive target—such as a person with a purse or a business with cash or expensive, portable goods. The offender must have an advantage over the target, in terms of power or force. Again, the offender must be insufficiently restrained. These features suggest how robberies occur and also how they might be reduced.

Auto Theft

The risk of car theft varies with the type of car, its age, brand, accessibility, and fleeting popularity among young persons with a propensity to steal them, often only for a "joyride." The person who drives an older, huge station wagon which most teenagers would not be caught dead driving is not likely to have it stolen.

The typical car thief is young. Most are teenagers (13 to 19), and a fourth of all car thieves are 17 or younger. Cars with antitheft devices are less likely to be stolen. Unlocked cars with keys in the ignition, or unattended with the motor running, are more likely to be taken. Most car thefts are at night.

A popular misconception is that cars are most often stolen by professional car thieves for parts or resale, with large numbers going to "chop shops" or shipment for sale overseas. A relatively small proportion of car thefts do fall into these categories. These relatively rare thefts are more apt to be highly publicized when discovered, with the result of the public being misled. In a typical car theft, a teenager or group of teenagers in a large city take a car left unlocked or unattended with keys available. After driving around for a while, the car is abandoned. The stolen vehicle is often recovered (three times out of five), but an arrest for the crime is unlikely (14 percent).

There must be a suitable target—a car that is accessible, attractive, and capable of being driven. A suitable guardian must be absent. An insufficiently restrained person capable of driving is the other ingredient.

Other Offenses

Gottfredson and Hirschi provide similar analyses for the typical rape, for white-collar crimes, such as embezzlement, and for alcohol and drug offenses. In every case, they argue that from the nature of delinquency and crime, it is easy to see that offenders must be persons who are especially attracted to pleasures of the moment, to short-term problem solutions, who fail to consider the longer-term consequences of their actions.

Moreover, little skill is required. The "burglar" enters likely targets near his home, with

More than half of all robberies known to the police take place on the street, and more than half involve a weapon, usually a firearm. —*Photo courtesy of www. photostogo.com.*

an unlocked door and no one apparently at home. The "robber" victimizes likely targets on the street. The "embezzler" steals from an employer by altering the books, the "car thief" drives away the unattended car with the keys in the ignition; and the "sneak thief" takes money from an unguarded cash drawer. The main requirement for completing personal crimes of assault, rape, or murder is neither brains nor skill but superior strength or force—apparent or real.

In short, criminal behavior is very often petty, usually not completed, rarely brings any lasting benefit to the offender, requires little skill, and always puts long range interests aside for the interests of the moment. The most important offender characteristic is a lack of adequate self-control.[18]

Self-Control

According to the general theory of crime, low self-control is a component of all criminal acts, and it is developed early in life, primarily through the actions of parents (Box 4.5). M. Gottfredson has summarized this point of view as follows:

> In families in which parents care about their children's behavior, in which they monitor their children's actions, in which they recognize deviant behavior and in which they sanction [punish] the use of force and fraud to obtain pleasures of the moment without regard to the long term negative consequences, self-control will become a stable characteristic of the child. To some degree, the school plays a role in the development of self-control, in concert with the family. In such environments, the child learns to care about the wishes of the parents and the school, develops a commitment

to the future and a strong set of values conducive to the denial of self-serving impulses that are costly to others. But in the absence of such early training by the family backed up by the school, the individual will be relatively low on self-control and will as a consequence be unusually yielding to the pleasures of the moment.[19]

Box 4.5

Travis Hirschi: In His Own Words

Research on the connection between child-rearing practices and delinquency has produced consistent results. The nature of these results was anticipated by Sheldon and Eleanor Gleuck in their famous *Unraveling Juvenile Delinquency*, published in 1950. The Gleucks reported that they were able to predict delinquency from an early age using five factors of family background: discipline of the boy by the father, supervision of the boy by the mother, affection of the father for the boy, affection of the mother for the boy, and cohesiveness of the family [reference cited].

More than 30 years later, coming at the child-rearing question from a very different angle, Gerald Patterson and his colleagues at the Oregon Social Learning Center reached conclusions remarkably similar to those reached by the Gleucks. Asking themselves what parents must do to teach the child not to use force and fraud, Patterson and his colleagues came up with a simple scheme. To rear a nondelinquent child, parents must (1) monitor the child's behavior; (2) recognize deviant behavior when it occurs; and (3) punish such behavior. All that is required to activate this system is affection for or invest-

ment in the child. The parent who cares for the child will watch his behavior, see him doing things he should not do, and correct him. Presto! A socialized, decent human being.

Where might this simple system go wrong? Obviously, it can go wrong at any one of four places. The parents may not care for the child (in which case none of the other conditions would be met); the parents, even if they care, may not have the time or energy to monitor the child's behavior; the parents, even if they care and monitor, may not see anything wrong with the child's behavior; finally, even if everything else is in place, the parents may not have the means or inclination to punish the child. So, what may appear at first glance to be nonproblematic turns out to be problematic indeed. Many things can go wrong. According to the Oregon group, in the homes of problem children many things have gone wrong: "Parents of stealers" do not interpret stealing as "deviant"; they "do not track; they do not punish; and they do not care" [references cited].[20]

—Travis Hirschi, University of Arizona

Arrests

One view of the extent of crime—and, more particularly, the workload of the police—is given by the number of arrests reported. There were an estimated 15 million arrests in 1995 (Table 4.2). (Note that these are arrest events, not persons; some persons were arrested more than once.) In 1995, the number of arrests for drug abuse violations (more than 1.4 million) was second in frequency only to larceny-theft. When the offense of aggravated assault is combined with the offense "other assaults," however, there were more than 1.8 million arrests for assault.

Table 4.2 Total Estimated Arrests in the United States, 1995, in Order of Frequency

Larceny-theft	**1,530,200**
Drug abuse violations	1,476,100
Driving under the influence	1,436,000
Assaults (other than aggravated)	1,290,400
Disorderly conduct	748,600
Drunkenness	708,100
Liquor laws	594,900
Aggravated assault	**568,480**
Fraud	436,400
Burglary	**386,500**
Vandalism	311,100
Runaways	249,500
Weapons	243,900
Motor vehicle theft	**191,900**
Robbery	**171,870**
Stolen property	166,500
Curfew and loitering law violations	149,800
Offenses against family and children	142,900
Forgery and counterfeiting	122,300
Prostitution and vice	97,700
Sex offenses (except forcible rape or prostitution)	94,500
Forcible rape	**34,650**
Vagrancy	25,900
Murder and nonnegligent manslaughter	**21,230**
Arson	**20,000**
Gambling	19,500
Embezzlement	15,200
Suspicion	12,100
All other offenses	3,865,400
Total Estimated Arrests, 1995	**15,119,800**

Source: data from *Crime in the United States, 1995*, Federal Bureau of Investigation, U.S. Department of Justice, October 13. 1996.
Note: Index offenses in bold type.

Crimes Cleared by Arrest

Another informative product from the Uniform Crime Reports is the tabulation of index crimes cleared by arrest. Crimes are counted as "cleared" when at least one person is arrested, charged, and turned over for prosecution. (They are considered cleared also, by "exceptional means," when a law enforcement agency is somehow precluded from arrest of an offender—for example, by death.) The crimes classed as violent are more often cleared, and burglary, larceny-theft and motor vehicle theft much less often (Figure 4.10).

Crime Trends

Is crime going up, or is crime going down, or is the crime rate fairly stable? The answer most often given relies on the Uniform Crime Reports data for the index crimes (Figure 4.11) for men and women combined and without any other classification of persons. By this measure, we can see that

Figure 4.10 Percent of Known Crimes Cleared by Arrest, 1995

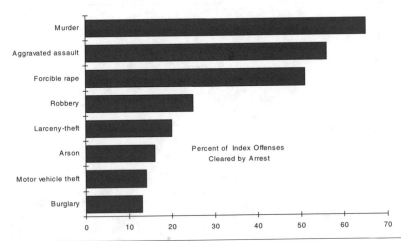

Source: data from *Crime in the United States, 1995*, Uniform Crime Reports, Federal Bureau of Investigation, U.S. Department of Justice, October 13, 1996.

Figure 4.11 Crime Rates Index Offenses, 1974–1995

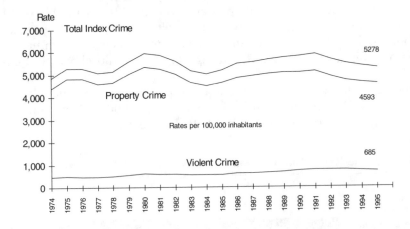

Source: data from *Crime in the United States, 1993*, Uniform Crime Reports, Federal Bureau of Investigation, U.S. Department of Justice, December 4, 1994; *Crime in the United States, 1995*, (October 13, 1996).

the crime rate began rising in the 1970s, peaking in 1980, then declined, but began rising again about the middle of that decade. The increase continued until about 1991 and has been dropping since. Now it is about the same as 20 years ago. These trends are due mainly to changes in the rates of property crimes, which contribute the most to the index, because they are so much more common. The rates of index crimes classed as violent crimes increased steadily after 1974, then leveled off and declined in recent years.

When we examine another decade and a half in advance of the mid-1970s, as in Figure 4.12, we can see that the index crime rate rose markedly throughout the 1960s as well as the 1970s, then declined, increased again

Figure 4.12   Estimated Rates of Offenses Known to the Police, United States, 1960–1995, by Type of Offense

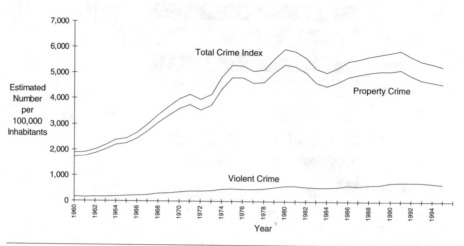

Source: data from Maguire, K. and Pastore, A. L., (eds.). *Sourcebook of Criminal Justice Statistics, 1995*, 324 (adapted by Sourcebook staff from U.S. Department of Justice, Federal Bureau of Investigation, *Crime in the United States, 1975, 1994*. Washington, D.C.: USGPO); *Crime in the United States, 1995*, 1996.

after 1984, then went down more recently. The steady increase in the violent crimes category, however, is again apparent over the 30-year period 1960–1990, leveling off and dropping only in the most recent years. These rates are for both males and females, of all ages, combined. A closer examination of males and females and of different age groups would show different trends.

Crime rates differ markedly among the common offenses included in the crime index. The rate for murder is about 1 in 10,000 persons, but it is more than 3 in 100 persons for larceny/theft (Figure 4.13).

Figure 4.13   Crime Rates, Index Offenses Known to the Police, 1995

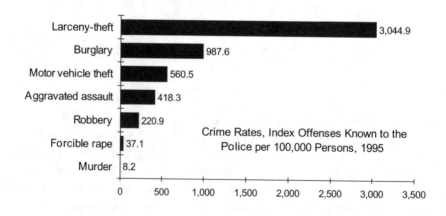

Source: data from *Crime in the United States, 1995,* (Uniform Crime Reports, Federal Bureau of Investigation, U.S. Department of Justice, October 13. 1996).

National Incident Based Reporting System (NIBRS)

In the early 1980s, a substantial program for the improvement and enhancement of the UCR program was begun by the Federal Bureau of Investigation and the Bureau of Justice Statistics.[21] The new program provides all the data of the present UCR program but also includes much more detail about each criminal incident. More information is included about the place of the event, about the weapons used, the extent of property damage, characteristics of both the offender and victim, and the disposition of the complaint. The most serious offense for each individual victim also is counted, rather than only one as in the present UCR program.

The new system will improve this data collection system for determining the extent of crime as known to the police. It has a richer potential than does the existing system for both research and police operational needs. Involving the many law enforcement agencies of the country in the new program is, however, a long and painstaking process. The NIBRS program, like the Uniform Crime Reports, is a voluntary one, and the process of changing police agency procedures is often complex and difficult. By 1996, 9 states were providing data to the FBI according to the new procedures, 21 states were submitting test data, and all but 7 states had plans for development or testing.[22]

Age and Crime

The relation of age to crime, however measured, is nothing short of astonishing. Among the first to document this relation was Lambert A. J. Quetelet, a Belgian mathematician and statistician. More than 150 years ago he commented, "Of all the causes which influence the development of the propensity to crime, or which diminish that propensity, age is unquestionably the most energetic."[23] It still is true that the crime rate increases rapidly in early adolescence and peaks at late adolescence and early adulthood. Then it declines with age, continuing to fall over the life span. Although there are some exceptions (for example, for embezzlement, where opportunities are restricted by age), this is essentially true for all offenses. Rates for property crimes such as vehicle theft, burglary, robbery, theft, and shoplifting peak in middle or late adolescence, when they begin to fall. Violent crime rates peak in late adolescence and early adulthood, then fall.

The well-known fact of the relation of age to crime is consistent with two additional characteristics of crime that are important for an understanding of crime and for criminal justice policies. One is that a propensity to commit offenses continues even as, with age, the frequency with which adults commit offenses decreases. This means that people tend to maintain their rank order in offending frequency even though offending *rates* of adults decrease with age. Consider this analogy: When Michael Jordan reaches old age, he will still make many more baskets than others his age.

The other established fact is that, contrary to usual public opinion, offenders tend more to be "generalists" than "specialists" in a given type of crime. Offenders tend to engage in a broad range of crimes and other forms of deviant behaviors, with no strong pattern of specialization in any particu-

Figure 4.14 Degrees of Propensity to Crime According to Quetelet, 1835

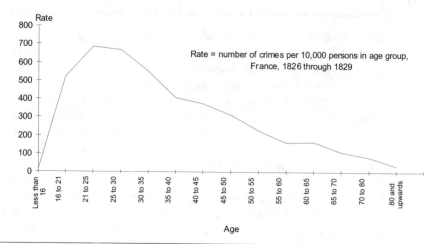

Rate = number of crimes per 10,000 persons in age group,
France, 1826 through 1829

Age

Source: data from Quetelet, L. A. J. (1835). *A Treatise on Man and the Development of His Faculties*. Facsimile reproduction of the English translation of 1842 by S. Diamond. Gainesville, Florida: Scholars' Facsimiles & Reprints, 93.
Note: number of crimes is similar in meaning to "number of convictions" since these were counts of persons "condemned," that is, punished.

lar type of crime.[24] There is some tendency to specialize, but the main picture is that offenders are generalists.

Quetelet plotted the number of known crimes in France according to the ages of the offenders. He adjusted the number of crimes for each age group according to the proportions of persons of that age in the whole population, and plotted the result. Then he portrayed the relation of age to the "degrees of propensity to crime" by smoothing the line graph into a curve. A plotting of the line graph is shown in Figure 4.14, based on his data for the years 1826–1829. In his data, known crimes rise sharply until the early 20s, declining with age thereafter.[25] Similar curves have been found in different cultures, at different times, for males and females, and for different types of crime.[26]

One of the most important facts about crime is that most crimes are done by young persons—those who are in their late teens or 20s. Some crime, of course, is done by the middle-aged or even by the elderly; but the younger have a greater "propensity to crime."

We can see the age distribution for crime in the most recently available arrest data. A method similar to Quetelet's was used to produce Figure 4.15. The number of persons arrested for all offenses in 1995 was divided, for each age group, by the number of that group in the U.S. resident population. The result, Quetelet's old but still informative measure of the "degrees of propensity to crime," was plotted. You can see the similarity of the shape of the line graph to that based on Quetelet's data a century and a half ago.

The age distribution of crime described by Quetelet is shown again when crime rates, measured by arrests, are examined for males and females and for different classifications of crime. It is even seen when the overall rate of crime goes up or down. When crime rates change, the general shape of the age-crime curve stays much the same. The violent crime index for males of different ages is shown in Figure 4.16 for 1992 and 10 years earlier. The peak

Figure 4.15 Arrest Rates per 10,000 Persons, by Age Group, 1995

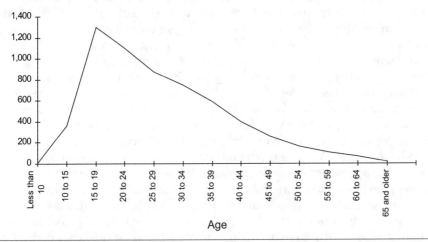

Source: data from *Crime in the United States, 1995*, Uniform Crime Reports, Federal Bureau of Investigation, U.S. Department of Justice, October 13. 1996; U.S. Bureau of the Census (http://www.census.gov.population/estimates/state/stats/96age795.txt).
Note: counts here are numbers of persons arrested, not, as in Quetelet's data, convictions.

Figure 4.16 Violent Crime Index by Age for Males, 1983 and 1992

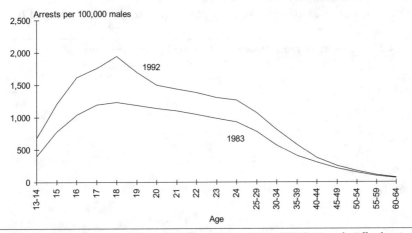

Source: based on data from Poe-Yamagata, E. and Butts, J. A. (1996). *Female Offenders in the Juvenile Justice System*. Washington, D.C.: Office of Juvenile Justice and Delinquency Prevention, 9, using data from Federal Bureau of Investigation (1965–1992) *Age–Specific and Race–Specific Arrest Rates for Selected Offenses*.
Note: arrest rates are arrests per 100,000 population in each age group. Note also that the long tail of the distribution on the right is shortened by grouping ages.

ages are late teens and early 20s. Although the general shapes of the curves for 1983 and 1992 are the familiar ones, that for 1992 is markedly elevated over that for 1983. This reflects an increase in violent crimes, as measured by arrests, for that decade. The *relation* of age to violent crime is similar, but there were more arrests for violent crime in the later year.

Because age is so important a factor in crime rates, changes in rates of crime may be due to changes in the age distributions in the general population. If there are more persons in the crime-prone age groups, as when baby boomers reached adolescence, then an increase in the crime rate may be expected from this source of variation alone. If the proportion of the crime-prone age group in the population goes up, the crime rate may be expected to go up, too. Therefore, it is important to take account of the age-crime relation in seeking to discover why the rate is up or down.

Changes in the crime rate, either up or down, often are the subject of much debate and attention in the press. Frequently, they are attributed to politically popular programs or changes in the number of police, in sentencing laws, or in prison populations. Politicians frequently take credit for drops in the crime rate, claiming they are due to new laws they have supported. This often is done without first considering whether the changes in the crime rate are due instead to changes in the proportions of persons of crime-prone ages. This is a mistake because age is so influential that differences in the age structure of the population should be one of the first explanations considered in trying to account for changes in crime rates.

When we examine the age distribution for property crimes, as in Figure 4.17, we can see similarly that arrests decline with age. In this case, however, there has been little change in the overall rate between the years compared.

There have been recent differences in the changes in crime rates for males and females. Similar pictures are found for the general decline of arrests with age among females. The property crime rates, however, are substantially higher for females in the more recent year, though not for males (Figure 4.18). More striking is that the violent crime index for women is markedly higher (Figure 4.19). This increase is due to a large increase in the number of arrests of females for aggravated assault.[27]

The index crime rates for a given year indicate the likelihood of being a

Figure 4.17 Property Crime Index by Age for Males, 1983 and 1992

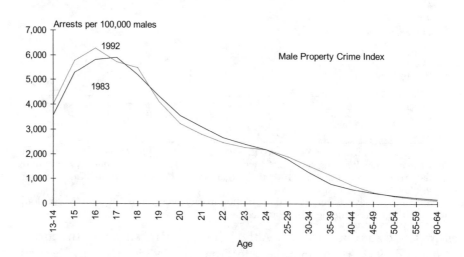

Source: based on data from Poe-Yamagata, E. and Butts, J. A. (1996). *Female Offenders in the Juvenile Justice System.* Washington, D.C.: Office of Juvenile Justice and Delinquency Prevention, 9, using data from Federal Bureau of Investigation (1965–1992) *Age–Specific and Race–Specific Arrest Rates for Selected Offenses.*
Note: arrest rates are arrests per 100,000 population in each age group. Note also that the long tail of the distribution on the right is shortened by grouping ages.

Figure 4.18 Property Crime Index by Age for Females, 1983 and 1992

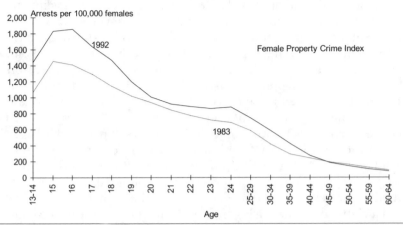

Source: based on data from Poe-Yamagata, E. and Butts, J. A. (1996). *Female Offenders in the Juvenile Justice System*. Washington, D.C.: Office of Juvenile Justice and Delinquency Prevention, 9, using data from Federal Bureau of Investigation (1965–1992) *Age–Specific and Race-n-Specific Arrest Rates for Selected Offenses*.
Note: arrest rates are arrests per 100,000 population in each age group. Note also that the long tail of the distribution on the right is shortened by grouping ages.

Figure 4.19 Violent Crime Index by Age for Females, 1983 and 1992

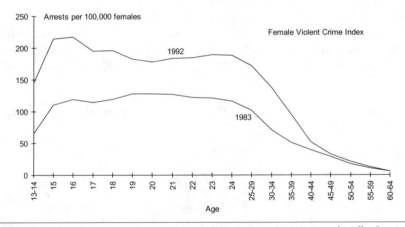

Source: based on data from Poe-Yamagata, E. and Butts, J. A. (1996). *Female Offenders in the Juvenile Justice System*. Washington, D.C.: Office of Juvenile Justice and Delinquency Prevention, 9, using data from Federal Bureau of Investigation (1965–1992) *Age–Specific and Race–Specific Arrest Rates for Selected Offenses*.
Note: arrest rates are arrests per 100,000 population in each age group. Note also that the long tail of the distribution on the right is shortened by grouping ages.

victim of a given type of crime (all else, of course, being equal). Thus, as we saw in Figure 4.13, in 1995 there were eight murders known to the police per 100,000 inhabitants, or fewer than one out of 10,000. On the other hand, the police recorded 304 larceny-theft crimes per 10,000 persons. Except for homicide, however, estimates of victimization rates may be better made from data based on the second method for determining the extent of crime—asking victims of crime about harms done to them.

The National Crime Victimization Survey

The second major method available for counting crimes—asking potential victims about their victimizations—has been pursued vigorously for 30 years in a remarkable program of victim surveys. Police statistics on crimes known to them do not reflect the total extent of crime. Even if all citizens reported all events they considered to be crimes to police or prosecutors, all would not be included in police statistics. Even if all were reported to police, not all could be expected to be reported further to the FBI. What is more critical is that many crimes are not reported to *any* authorities, and that the tendency to report varies with, among other things, types of offenses.

For the 1967 President's Commission of Law Enforcement and Administration of Justice, the National Opinion Research Center of the University of Chicago completed a national survey by sampling 10,000 households to ask "whether the person questioned, or any member of his or her household, had been a victim of crime during the past year, whether the crime had been reported, and, if not, the reasons for not reporting."[28] The commission concluded from the results, "The actual amount of crime . . . is several times that reported in the UCR," with the difference between reported and unreported crime varying over the crime categories. According to the commission, for example, the proportions of victimizations reported to the survey staff and not reported to the police were highest for consumer fraud (90 percent) and lowest for auto theft (11 percent). Reasons given by victims for not reporting also varied over offense classifications. Overall, the most frequent reason given for not notifying the police was that "police could not be effective or would not want to be bothered."

Since 1972, the Bureau of Justice Statistics has collected detailed information from its National Crime Victimization Survey, including data on the frequency and nature of the common crimes of rape, personal robbery, aggravated and simple assault, household burglary, personal and household

Figure 4.20 Estimated Percents of Personal and Property Victimizations, 1994

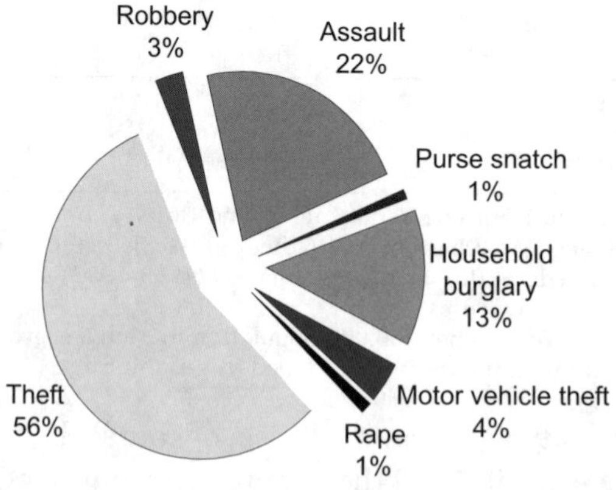

Source: data from Maguire, K. and Pastore, A. L., (eds.). *Sourcebook of Criminal Justice Statistics, 1995* p. 230. (from U.S. Department of Justice, Bureau of Justice Statistics, *Criminal Victimization in the United States, 1994,* (Washington, D.C.: U.S. Department of Justice).
Note: rape includes rape and sexual assault; purse snatch includes purse snatching and pocket picking.

theft, and motor vehicle theft. It does not now include commercial crimes, although surveys of businesses have been done. In the household surveys, interviews are now conducted with all household members at least 12 years old. U.S. Census Bureau personnel conduct interviews with those persons in large, nationally representative samples of households.[29]

This extensive, well-planned survey includes various data about victims, such as their ages, sex, ethnic group membership, marital status, income, and education. It seeks also data on the offender—such as approximate age, sex, race, income level—the relationship of the victim and offender, and data on the circumstances of the victimization—such as the time and place of occurrence, the use of weapons, and the nature of injury or loss.

There are some advantages of the victim surveys for estimating the extent of crime. It is possible to measure both crimes reported to the police and not reported. The method permits crime estimation by methods independent of police agencies, and this may be important if measures are affected by police practices. Because the surveys are based on samples, they permit the inclusion of much more detailed data about crime incidents and victims than that possible with complete counting of all crimes.

There are some disadvantages also. Since they are based on surveys of past events, these data may be influenced by memory effects. There may be omission due to forgetting. Or there may be inaccuracy by "telescoping" a remembered earlier victimization into the time frame asked about. They depend also on the respondent's truthfulness in answering the questions. For some crimes—rape, for example—or some situations—such as events within a family—the victim may be reluctant to report victimizations to interviewers. Some evidence suggests that the method is prone to less accurate measurement of assault and rape victimizations, particularly those among nonstrangers.[30] The survey does not measure commercial crimes, such as burglaries of stores. And of course it does not include homicide.

As with the Uniform Crime Reports, the victim survey shows theft to be by far the most frequent of crimes (Figure 4.20). Taking property illegally—by theft, robbery, burglary, or purse snatching, including vehicle theft—accounts for about three out of four victimizations reported. The rest are assaults.

Two ways of examining the extent of crime from the victim survey results are shown in Figures 4.21 and 4.22. The first shows the numbers of the crimes commonly reported, and the second shows rates. For personal crimes, the rate is based on the number of reported crimes per 1,000 *residents* age 12 or older. For the household crimes, the victimization rates are based on the number of incidents per 1,000 *households*.

Uniform Crime Reports and Victim Surveys Compared

Both statistical programs of the Department of Justice are aimed at measuring the amount and nature of crime. The methods used and crimes covered differ. As a result, the data from the two systems are not strictly comparable. By providing data with different meanings, however, the information provided is complementary. Together, the programs provide a more complete picture of crime. Neither program covers all crime.

Figure 4.21 Estimated Numbers of Personal and Property Victimizations, 1994

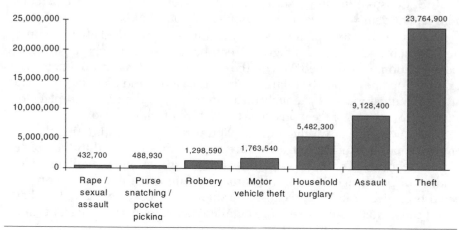

Source: data from Maguire, K. and Pastore, A. L., (eds.) (1996). *Sourcebook of Criminal Justice Statistics, 1995* p. 230. (from U.S. Department of Justice, Bureau of Justice Statistics, *Criminal Victimization in the United States, 1994*, NCJ-151657 (Washington, D.C.: U.S. Department of Justice).

Figure 4.22 Estimated Rates of Personal and Property Victimizations, 1994 (Rates per 1,000 persons or households)

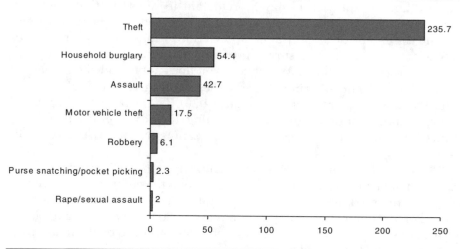

Source: data from Maguire, K. and Pastore, A. L., (eds.) (1996) *Sourcebook of Criminal Justice Statistics, 1995* p. 230. (from U.S. Department of Justice, Bureau of Justice Statistics, *Criminal Victimization in the United States, 1994*, NCJ-151657 (Washington, D.C.: U.S. Department of Justice).

The victim surveys include crimes reported and also not reported to law enforcement. Besides obviously excluding homicide, several other crimes included in the Uniform Crime Reports are not counted. These include arson, commercial crimes, and crimes against children under 12. Even when the same crimes are included in both programs, the definitions vary.

It may not be possible to identify parallel trends using the data from the two programs. Rate measures are calculated differently for the two measures for crimes. The Uniform Crime Reports rates show the number of crimes reported in relation to 100,000 *persons*. The victim survey rates show the numbers per 1,000 *households* or their residents.

The victim survey data are based on samples drawn in such a way as to provide good estimates for the nation, with careful procedures for estimating the amount of error likely in the estimates. On the other hand, the Uniform Crime Reports data are based on the actual counts of reports by participating law enforcement agencies.[31, 32] The Department of Justice compared its two programs as shown in Box 4.6.

Box 4.6

How do UCR and NCS compare?

	Uniform Crime Reports	National Crime Survey
Offenses measured:	Homicide Rape Robbery (personal and commercial) Assault (aggravated) Burglary (commercial and household) Larceny (commercial and household) Motor vehicle theft Arson	Rape Robbery (personal) Assault (aggravated and simple) Household burglary Larceny (personal and household) Motor vehicle theft
Scope:	Crimes reported to the police in most jurisdictions; considerable flexibility in developing small-area data	Crimes both reported and not reported to police; all data are available for a few large geographic areas
Collection method:	Police department reports to FBI or to centralized State agencies that then report to FBI	Survey interviews; periodically measures the total number of crimes committed by asking a national sample or 49,000 households encompassing 101,000 persons age 12 and over about their experiences as victims of crime during a specified period
Kinds of information:	In addition to offense counts, provides information on crime clearances, persons arrested, persons charged, law enforcement officers killed and assaulted, and characteristics of homicide victims	Provides details about victims (such as age, race, sex, education, income, and whether the victim and offender were related to one another) and about crimes (such as time and place of occurrence, whether or not reported to the police, use of weapons, occurrence of injury, and economic consequences)
Sponsor:	Department of Justice Federal Bureau of Investigation	Department of Justice Bureau of Justice Statistics

Source: U.S. Department of Justice. (1988). *Report to the Nation of Crime and Justice*, 2nd ed. Washington, D.C: Bureau of Justice Statistics, 11.

Figure 4.23 Trends in Motor Vehicle Theft Rates, 1980–1995

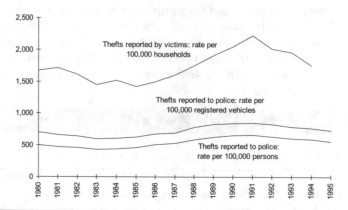

Source: data from Bureau of Justice Statistics (1993). *Highlights from 20 Years of Surveying Crime Victims*. Washington, D.C: U.S. Department of Justice, 14; Maguire, K. and Pastore, A. L. (Eds.), (1996) *Sourcebook of Criminal Justice Statistics–1995*. U.S. Department of Justice, Bureau of Justice Statistics. Washington, D.C.: U.S. Government Printing Office; (1996). Federal Bureau of Investigation, U. S. Department of Justice *Crime in the United States, 1995*; U. S. Department of Transportation, http://www.bts.gov.btsprod/nts/
Note: data not available for 1995 from the National Victimization Survey.

Rates of crime, whether based on crimes known to the police or reported in victim surveys, tell the number of crimes in relation to some other number, such as persons or households. In examining a rate, it is important to remember the nature of the denominator used for calculation.

Consider, for example, the denominators used in calculating the rate of vehicle theft. Victim surveys report it in relation to the number of households; police statistics report it in relation to the number of persons. Why not report it in relation to the number of vehicles available to be stolen? We would expect that the number of thefts of horses and buggies has declined over this century, while the theft of television sets has increased.

The trends in motor vehicle thefts in relation to the number of vehicles registered are shown in Figure 4.23, along with those for the victim surveys and police data. Since 1968, the trends have about the same shape for reported vehicle thefts in relation to the numbers of either vehicles or persons. The trend for reported victimizations—vehicle thefts in relation to the numbers of households—is somewhat similar in shape but gives rather different results.

Self-Reports of Delinquency and Crime

The third general way to measure the extent of crime, besides counting crimes known to the police or reported by victims, is to ask people about the offenses they themselves have committed. Offhand, it may seem that this would not likely be a very helpful method, because people may be reluctant to report their own offenses. Surprisingly, it is very useful for many purposes. Surveys using self-report methods can illuminate what has been called the "dark figure" of crime—crimes unknown from official reporting methods and statistics. They may also help assess the extent of offenses committed by persons in the general population, rather than by selected groups of known offenders. Data obtained by these methods also may provide useful measures of the effectiveness of criminal justice programs, particularly when used together with official statistics.

Table 4.3 Reported Prevalence of Delinquent Behavior
Percent Reporting One or More Offenses

Offense (partial list of included behaviors)	1979 Ages 14 to 20 N=1,543	1986 Ages 21 to 27 N=1,383	1992 Ages 27 to 33 N=1,338
Felony Assault			
Aggravated assault	4	3	2
Sexual assault	0	1	0
Gang fights	6	1	NA
Battery	NA	NA	2
Minor Assault			
Hit teacher	3	NA	NA
Hit parent	2	0	0
Hit student	18	NA	NA
Hit anyone else	0	13	7
Robbery			
Strongarmed students	1	NA	NA
Strongarmed others	2	NA	NA
Strongarmed anyone	NA	0	
Felony Theft			
Stole motor vehicle	1	0	0
Stole something over $500	3	2	1
Broke into building or vehicle	3	1	0
Bought stolen goods	6	4	3
Minor Theft			
Stole something under $50	15	11	7
Joyriding	5	1	1
Illegal Services			
Sold marijuana	10	6	4
Sold hard drugs	2	2	1
White-collar Crime			
Credit card fraud	1	0	0
Used checks illegally	1	1	2
Fraud	3	2	1

Source: data from Maguire, K. and Pastore, A. L. (Eds.) (1996). *Sourcebook of Criminal Justice Statistics–1995*. Washington, D.C.: Bureau of Justice Statistics, from data based on the National Youth Survey Project of Huizinga, and D., Elliott, D.S., Institute of Behavioral Science, University of Colorado.

Note: this is a partial list of offenses used in the sample survey. The table shows only three of nine waves of interviews. Percents are prevalence rates. NA may mean the item was not included because it was not appropriate or because comparable data were not available for successive interviews.

The National Youth Survey, using self-report to measure delinquency, provides an example. The study was based on a sample of adolescents who were ages 11 to 17 in 1976. The sample was designed to be representative of youths born in 1959 through 1965. In the first survey, 1,725 youths who agreed to participate (about three-fourths of those selected for the sample) were interviewed. In eight follow-up surveys, the investigators tried to recontact and interview each person. Some cases were lost each year, but careful comparisons of samples led the investigators to conclude that the representativeness of the samples was not seriously affected by that.

Confidential interviews were completed face to face or by telephone, usually in the home. The full range of delinquent acts reported in the Uniform Crime Reports was included, and additional items were included for some of the later interview waves.[33] Table 4.3 shows a sampling of the results, for three of the surveys. The numbers shown are prevalence rates, showing the percentages of the population that reported engaging in particular offenses within the calendar year shown.

The Regularity and Costs of Crime

Crime rates, however measured, show some variation in crime from time to time, but their consistency is striking. When, more than a century and a half ago, Quetelet began collecting data of the sort reported in this chapter, he was struck particularly by the regularity of crime and its predictability of occurrence rather than by its variation. He wrote,

> [T]here is a *budget* which we pay with frightful regularity—it is that of prisons, dungeons, and scaffolds. Now, it is this budget which, above all, we ought to endeavor to reduce; and every year, the numbers have confirmed [that] there is a tribute which man pays with more regularity than that which he owes to nature, or to the treasure of the state, namely, that which he pays to crime. We might even predict annually how many individuals will stain their hands with the blood of their fellow-men, how many will be forgers, how many will deal in poison, pretty much in the same way as we may foretell the annual births and deaths.[34]

The cost of crime is at best aggravation, loss of property, lessened feelings of security and safety, and at worst, suffering and erosion of the social order. The dollar loss of property crimes can be estimated; and high, though arbitrary, values can be placed also on loss of life and injury. Any such numbers, however, cannot adequately capture the cost in human misery.

The cost of a purse snatching—a relatively minor crime—is not limited to the amount of money in the purse, or to that sum plus the purse. A purse snatching is not counted as an assault; yet, the victim may feel violated, her person invaded, her safety and freedom threatened. Similarly, the cost of a burglary is not limited to the dollar value of the property stolen. Typically, a home has been invaded, privacy violated, and personal security challenged.

> . . . *for the land is full of bloody crimes, and the city is full of violence.*
> —*Ezekial 7:23 (report of a crime wave, about 600 B.C.)*

The costs of personal crimes—homicide, assault, rape—are in part pain and misery. We have a justifiable and admirable reluctance to place a value

**Figure 4.24 Justice System Expenditures, 1992 Fiscal Year,
by Level of Government**

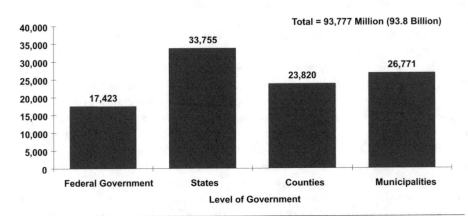

Justice System Expenditures in Millions of Dollars, 1992

Source: data from Maguire, K. and Pastore, A. L. (Eds.) (1996). *Sourcebook of Criminal Justice Statistics–1995*. Washington D.C.: Bureau of Justice Statistics, 2 (based on data provided by the Bureau of the Census to the Bureau of Justice Statistics).

on human life; and although numbers can be attached to criminal homicides to portray associated economic losses, these can be but feeble attempts to measure the losses. Some victims of personal assaults never recover from the trauma.

The costs of crime due to society's efforts to deal with the problem of crime, on the other hand, can be assessed with relative precision, because government agencies must have budgets. The enormous financial cost of the criminal justice system is summarized for a recent year in Figure 4.24. A fair estimate of the total cost of the justice system by the time you read this might be $100 billion a year.

Summary

Both crime and the fear of crime are important national problems. Establishing the facts about crime requires development of methods of measurement. The two main methods of measuring crime are the Uniform Crime Reports of the FBI (counting crimes known to the police) and the Victim Surveys of the Bureau of Justice Statistics (counting crimes reported by victims). Another method uses self-reports.

Understanding the meanings of the statistics reported by these programs requires knowing how the data are collected and appreciating the importance of principles of classification and measurement. This knowledge makes clear both the major strengths and weaknesses of these valuable programs for measuring the extent of crime.

The UCR crime index is based on eight kinds of crime known to the police. These are four categories of crimes against persons (murder and nonnegligent manslaughter, forcible rape, robbery, and aggravated assault) and four property crimes (burglary, larceny-theft, motor vehicle theft, and arson). Detailed data are collected and reported also for nonindex offenses, arrests, crimes cleared by arrest, murder, bombings, and other criminal events. This system provides a thorough picture of crimes known to the police and crime trends in the United States. The most common measure of a crime rate is given by the index crimes per 100,000 inhabitants. The crime rate rose markedly in the 1960s and 1970s, then declined, increased again after 1984, and has declined recently.

Theories to explain why some persons have a greater propensity to crime than others have developed over centuries, but the last 200 years especially have shaped modern conceptions. The classical school of criminology was based on the idea that man is rational, has free will, is basically self-interested, and seeks pleasure and avoidance of pain. Crime can be reduced by making punishment certain, and swift, and just severe enough to outweigh the pleasure to be gained by crime. The positivist school focused on an empirical, scientific approach to understanding crime. These developments helped lay a groundwork for a scientific study of crime. Many disciplines have contributed to criminology, the study of crime. The critical examination of these theories is an important subject, but it is beyond the scope of this book. One theory, called the general theory of crime, provides a framework for discussions in this book.

The general theory of crime emphasizes the age distribution of crime, the tendency of an individual's propensity for delinquent and criminal acts to persist over a lifetime, and the lack of specialization in crimes by offenders. Most crimes are mundane affairs, requiring little effort, planning, or skill, reflecting a lack of foresight and a seeking of short-term or immediate gratification. Low self-control is a component of all criminal acts. It develops when families do not care about their children's behavior, do not monitor it, and do not provide necessary sanctions for unwanted behavior. The school plays a role together with the family. Crime requires an insufficiently restrained offender, the absence of a suitable guardian, and a suitable target. An analysis of crimes according to these components helps explain them and also may provide clues for their prevention.

The age distribution of crime has a remarkably stable shape, found over different times and places, for males and females and for different types of crime. The peak years for doing crimes are the late teens and early 20s. Then, crime declines with age. Although males account for most crime, there have been recent increases in crime by women, particularly assaults. Changes in crime rates may be due to changes in the numbers of persons in the "crime-prone" age groups.

Victim surveys give another picture of crime in America, by asking victims of crimes about their experiences. Crimes not reported to the police, as well as reported crimes, are counted.

The Uniform Crime Reports and victim surveys provide complementary information about the extent of crime in the United States. Both are useful for assessing the extent of the problems of crime in America. They differ markedly in estimates of the total amount of crime known but give similar information in some ways—such as showing theft to be such a common crime.

Self-reports of delinquency and crime are another source of information. Methods based on these reports provide a further way of examining the extent of crime.

The cost of crime ranges from aggravation to misery and erosion of the social order. The economic costs can be estimated but do not portray the losses adequately. The financial cost of the criminal justice system—society's response to crime—is nearly $100 billion a year.

Notes

1. Silberman, C. E. (1980). *Criminal Violence, Criminal Justice*. New York: Vintage Books, 3.

2. Bentham, J. (1970) [1789]. *An Introduction to the Principles of Morals and Legislation*. London: The Athlone Press, 11.

3. Beccaria, C. (1963) [1764]. *On Crimes and Punishments*. Indianapolis: Bobbs-Merrill.

4. Gottfredson, M. R. and T. Hirschi. (1990). *A General Theory of Crime*. Stanford, CA: Stanford University Press.

5. Gottfredson, M. R. (1991). "A General Theory of Crime," in Boendermaker, L., and van der Laan, P.H. (eds.). *L'avenir du systeme penal des mineurs (The Future of the Juvenile Justice System)*. Leuven, Belgium: Academic Publishing.

6. Wolfe, T. Reference as quoted by M. Gottfredson (1991).

7. Gottfredson and Hirschi (1990), 15. Descriptions of common crimes in this chapter are based on the descriptions by Gottfredson and Hirschi (1990), 16–44 and Federal Bureau of Investigation, U.S. Department of Justice (1996). *Crime in the United States, 1995* October 13, 1996.

8. Friel, C. M. (1976). "Zeitgeist: A Perspective on Criminal Justice Information and Statistical Systems," 23–29 in SEARCH Group, Inc., *Third International Symposium*. Sacramento, CA: SEARCH Group.

9. See, for discussions of the limitations of the Uniform Crime Reports, Gottfredson, D. M. and M. R. Gottfredson. (1980). "Data for Criminal Justice Evaluations," in Klein, M. W. and K. S. Teilman (eds.), *Handbook of Criminal Justice Evaluation*. Beverly Hills, CA: Sage; Nettler, G. (1978). *Explaining Crime*. New York: McGraw-Hill; Sutherland, E. and D. Cressey. (1970). *Criminology*. Philadelphia: J. B. Lippencott; President's Commission on Law Enforcement and Administration of Justice. (1967). *The Challenge of Crime in a Free Society*. Washington, D.C.: U.S. GPO; Blumstein, A. (1975). "Seriousness Weights in an Index of Crime." *American Sociological Review* 39: 854–864; Doleschal, E. and L. T. Wilkins. (1972). *Criminal Statistics*. Rockville, MD: National Institute of Mental Health; Hindelang, M. (1974). The Uniform Crime Reports Revisited," *Journal of Criminal Justice* 2: 1–7; and Wolfgang, M. (1963). "Uniform Crime Reports: A Critical Appraisal," *University of Pennsylvania Law Review* 111:708.

10. Hindelang, M. and M. R. Gottfredson. (1976). "The Victim's Decision Not to Invoke the Criminal Process," in McDonald (ed.) *The Victim and the Criminal Justice System*. Beverly Hills, CA: Sage.

11. Black, D. (1970). "Production of Crime Rates." *American Sociological Review* 35: 733–748; Black, D., and Reiss, A. (1967). "Patterns of Behavior in Police and Citizen Transactions," in *Studies of Crime and Law Enforcement in Major Metropolitan Areas*, Vol. II. Washington, D.C.: U.S. GPO; Lundman, R., R. Sykes, and J. Clark. (1978), "Police Control of Juveniles: A Replication," *Journal of Research in Crime and Delinquency* 15: 74–91.

12. President's Commission on Law Enforcement and Administration of Justice. (1967). *The Challenge of Crime in a Free Society*. Washington, D.C.: U.S. GPO, 25.

13. Presidents Commission on Law Enforcement and Administration of Justice (1967); Seidman, D., and Couzens, M. (1974). "Getting the Crime Rate Down: Political Pressure and Crime Reporting," *Law and Society Review* 8: 457–493.

14. Federal Bureau of Investigation, U.S. Department of Justice (1994). *Crime in the United States, 1995*, October 13, 1996.

15. Cohen, L. E. and M. Felson. (1979). "Social Change and Crime Rate Trends: A Routine Activity Approach," *American Sociological Review*, 44, 588–608.

16. Skogan, W. (1979). "Crime in Contemporary America," in Graham, H. and T. Gurr (eds.). *Violence in America*. Beverly Hills, CA: Sage, 375–391, as cited in Gottfredson and Hirschi, (1990), 29.

17. Gottfredson, M. R. and T. Hirschi. (1990). *A General Theory of Crime*, 29–30. Stanford, CA: Stanford University Press.

18. Ibid.

19. Gottfredson, M. R. (1991). "A General Theory of Crime," in Boendermaker, L., and van der Laan, P.H. (eds.),p. 98. *L'avenir du systeme penal des mineurs (The Future of the Juvenile Justice System)*. Leuven, Belgium: Academic Publishing.

20. Hirschi, T. (1995). "The Family," in Wilson, J.Q. and J. Petersilia (eds.), *Crime*. San Francisco: Institute for Contemporary Studies, 124-125.

21. Poggio, E., S. Kennedy, J. Chaiken, and K. Carlson. (1985). *Blueprint for the Future of the Uniform Crime Reporting Program: Final Report of the UCR Study*. Washington, D.C.: U. S. Department of Justice.

22. Roberts, D. J. (1997). Personal communication, SEARCH Group. Sacramento, CA.

23. Quetelet, L. A. J. [1835]. *A Treatise on Man and the Development of His Faculties*. Facsimile reproduction of the English translation of 1842 by S. Diamond. Gainesville, FL: Scholars' Facsimiles & Reprints, 93.

24. Gottfredson, S. D. and D. M. Gottfredson. (1994) "Behavioral Prediction and the Problem of Incapacitation," *Criminology* 32, 3, 441–474.

25. Quetelet, L. A. J. [1835].*A Treatise on Man and the Development of His Faculties*. Facsimile reproduction of the English translation of 1842 by S. Diamond. Gainesville, FL: Scholars' Facsimiles & Reprints, 93.

26. Gottfredson, M. R. and T. Hirschi. (1990). *A General Theory of Crime*, 124–130. Stanford, CA: Stanford University Press.

27. Poe-Yamagata, E. and J. A. Butts. (1996). *Female Offenders in the Juvenile Justice System*. Washington, D.C.: Office of Juvenile Justice and Delinquency Prevention, 2.

28. Ennis, P. (1967) "Criminal Victimization in the United States: A Report of a National Survey. Field Surveys II," Washington, D.C.: President's Commission on Law Enforcement and Administration of Justice; Hindelang, M. (1976). *Criminal Victimization in Eight American Cities*. Cambridge, MA: Ballinger.

29. Maguire, K., and A. L. Pastore. (eds.). (1996). *Sourcebook of Criminal Justice Statistics–1995*. Appendices, 642–643. U.S. Department of Justice, Bureau of Justice Statistics. Washington, D.C.: U.S. GPO.

30. Law Enforcement Assistance Administration. (1972). *San Jose Methods Test of Known Crime Victims, Statistical Report No. 1*. Washington, D.C.: U.S. GPO.

31. Federal Bureau of Investigation, U.S. Department of Justice.(1994). *Crime in the United States, 1993*. December 4, 1994, Appendix IV, 385–386.

32. U.S. Department of Justice. (1988). *Report to the Nation on Crime and Justice*. 2nd ed. Washington, D.C.: Bureau of Justice Statistics, 11.

33. Maguire, K. and A. L. Pastore. (eds.). (1996). Based on Huizinga, D., and Elliott, D. S. (1996). *Prevalence and Offense Rates of Delinquent Behavior 1976–1992 Adjusted and Unadjusted for Triviality and Inappropriateness*. National Youth Survey Report No. 60, Institute of Behavioral Science, University of Colorado.

34. Quetelet, L. A. J. [1835]. *A Treatise on Man and the Development of His Faculties*. Facsimile reproduction of the English translation of 1842 by S. Diamond. Gainesville, FL: Scholars' Facsimiles & Reprints, 6.

CHAPTER FIVE

The Victims

Photo courtesy of www.photostogo.com.

Chapter Five

In the next chapters, each of the main parts of the criminal justice system will be discussed with a closer look at structures, procedures, and decisions. This chapter describes the victims of crime and victims' decisions because it is a victim who usually reports a crime to the police. This is the trigger event for the criminal justice process. We will consider also the role of the victim in the process, some consequences of being a victim of crime, and some ways victims can be assisted by the criminal justice system.

❑ Questions to Think About
❑ The Victims
❑ The Victims Movement
❑ Victim as Gatekeeper to the Criminal Justice System
❑ Victims' Decisions to Report a Crime
❑ The Decision to Report a Crime to the Police
❑ Reasons for Not Calling the Police
❑ The Victim's Goals in Decision Making
❑ Reporting Decisions for Other Crimes
    Shoplifting
    Consumer Frauds
    Victim Participation
    Dark Areas of Crime
❑ Is Victim Screening Desirable?
❑ Victim Alternatives and Information
❑ Trends in Victimizations
❑ Costs of Crime Victimizations
❑ Who Are the Victims?
❑ Psychological Harms
    Burglary
    Robbery
    Rape
    Crime in General
❑ Victim and Witness Assistance Programs
    Victim Compensation
    Restitution
    Restorative Justice
❑ Victimless Crimes?
❑ Summary

What is the role of the victim in the criminal justice system?

How do victim decisions affect the criminal justice process?

How does victim *discretion* in decisions affect the criminal justice system?

What determines whether victims call the police?

What reasons do people give for calling or not calling the police?

Would it be a good thing if all victims reported all crimes?

How is the "crime rate" dependent on reporting by victims?

Is the rate of reporting of crimes by victims going down?

Are some people more at risk of being victims than others?

What are the psychological harms of victimization?

Are there any victimless crimes?

What programs to assist victims are available in the criminal justice system?

The Victims

The justification for the criminal law, and so the criminal justice system, is that someone has been intentionally injured or harmed by someone else's illegal act—someone has been a victim of a crime. Although the system exists for the purpose of preventing or reducing victimization, or else for exacting the punishment deserved because of it, victims traditionally have had a minimal role in the process of criminal justice except for reporting crimes and acting as witnesses (see Box 5.1). Even with severe violations of personal liberty, freedom, and rights, even with resulting physical damage, property loss, and stress, the role of victims is small.

This is a result of a shift over time from individual to collective, or group, responsibility for righting a wrong. In ancient times, the victimized person may have individually chosen the punishment of the perceived offender and possibly inflicted it, with revenge as the driving force. As complex social structures developed, responsibilities for vengeance were transferred from the individual to the group. Tribal needs for safety may have led to raids on behalf of the whole community, aimed at both retaliation and prevention by deterrence—warning others not to do the same thing. Concepts of group responsibilities evolved along with rules and government structures. The

---

Box 5.1

The Role of the Victim in the Criminal Justice Process

- Note behavior that may be criminal and define it as a crime.

- Report crimes to law enforcement.

- Testify in court.

- Testify at sentencing or parole hearings in some jurisdictions.

- Receive victim assistance, restitution, victim compensation, counseling, or shelter, in some jurisdictions.

interests of victims became less important than those claimed by governments as guardians of the community's larger concerns. Crimes became defined as offenses against the King's peace. As a result, the role of victims became that of witnesses whose participation serves not their own interests but those of the state.[1]

A criminal act now is considered to be a crime against the state. The prosecutor in a criminal trial represents the government. The victim typically has little or nothing to do with the criminal justice process other than testifying and otherwise has little or no control over the outcome. This focus on the crime and the offender rather than on victims has drawn attention away from the needs of victims. This focus is changing a little, with some increased attention to victims' needs.

The Victims Movement

The social movement toward greater attention to the consequences of victimization has resulted in changes in public attitudes and policy and increased concern for the needs of victims. Three main themes of this movement have been the following arguments:

1. The difficulties experienced by victims have been ignored by research workers, criminal justice system practitioners, and the public;

2. These difficulties are increased by others, including personnel of the criminal justice system. Victims, victim assistance organizations, and criminal justice practitioners have complained about a neglect of and insensitivity to victims' problems and a callous handling of victims' problems by the criminal justice system;

3. The safeguards and precedents that protect or serve suspects and offenders outweigh those that protect or serve victims.[2]

Before considering further some of the consequences of being a victim of crime and some avenues toward more assistance to victims in the criminal justice system, the traditional role of victims in reporting crimes should be examined. The decisions of victims affect the entire process of criminal justice.

In many jurisdictions, testimony by victims is no longer limited to that given at the trial as to the finding of guilt. Opportunities for testimony at sentencing or parole hearings have been provided. There is increased opportunity for victims to inform the court of the losses they have suffered. There has been some growth of programs to assist victims as witnesses and to compensate them for losses. The "victims' rights" movement has gained momentum since the 1970s, which has included a seemingly unlikely involvement of groups of both politically conservative and liberal points of view.[3] As a result, many state and local governments have passed laws intended to help victims.

Many of these laws, however, are not directly related to victim assistance. Rather, they often are of the "get tougher on crime" variety, increasing penalties and requiring mandatory minimum sentences. Such changes often are urged by victims groups. The intent is to increase the safety of *potential* victims, or else to increase the scale of retribution or revenge. The cry, "What about the victim?" often means "That's not enough punishment." Other changes, however, do provide increased services to actual rather than poten-

The traditional role of the victim in the criminal justice process has been merely to testify in court. Now, the role of the victim is expanding and more attention is being paid to victims' needs. What do you believe the rights of a victim should be? —*Photo courtesy of www.photostogo.com.*

tial victims, including counseling, financial assistance, and—in the case of abused women—shelters and protection. Mainly, however, the victims' role in the criminal justice system still is largely that of reporting to the police and testifying in court.

> *A conservative is a liberal who was mugged the night before.*
> —*Frank L. Rizzo*

Victim as Gatekeeper to the Criminal Justice System

The role of reporting crimes is extremely important to the workings of the criminal justice system. Although a crime occurrence itself signals the *potential* involvement of the criminal justice system, criminal justice agencies and personnel most often become involved only after that crime is reported by a victim. Note the series of decisions that must take place before the criminal justice system becomes involved:

1. The behavior in question must be noticed and the decision to define it as a crime must be made. This discovery and definition may be made by a citizen (victim or witness) or by the police or prosecutor. Usually, it is first made by a victim.

2. Someone must decide that a crime has occurred—that the behavior in question is properly within the scope of the criminal law and the criminal justice system. This too is usually a victim.

3. A decision to enter the event into the criminal justice process ordinarily requires that the event be reported to the police, and in any case, it requires that the law enforcement establishment decide not only that a crime has occurred but also that the criminal justice process should be continued.

The victim is a principal "gatekeeper" of the entire criminal justice process, because it is he or she who ordinarily decides whether to report a crime to the police. This is especially true of the common crimes of theft and assault. (It is less common for some other types of crime, such as consumer frauds and "victimless" crimes such as those involving gambling, narcotics, and prostitution.) In most cases, if the victim does not report the crime to the police, the criminal justice system will not become involved.

Victims' Decisions to Report a Crime

Most known crimes are not discovered by the police. Rather, they are reported to them.[4] In early victimization surveys, only 3 percent of victimizations reported as known to the police came to the attention of law enforcement because the police were on the scene.[5]

The criminal justice system is a kind of filtering process. Cases may drop out of the system all along the way. Events reported to the police as crimes may not be considered to be crimes by law enforcement personnel, who then drop the case. Cases may be dropped by the police for lack of evidence to present to the prosecutor. The prosecutor may decide for various reasons not to file charges. The evidence may be seen as weak, the likelihood of winning the case may be perceived as low, or the prosecutor may decide that

If a victim of a crime does not report it, the criminal justice process usually will not be involved at all. Many victims of domestic violence do not report the abuse they have suffered. What factors operate to decrease reporting of this offense? What could help increase reporting? —*Photo courtesy of www.photostogo.com.*

the accused has a valid defense or excuse. Cases may be dismissed at pre-liminary hearings for lack of probable cause. Persons at trial may be found not guilty. And so it goes, throughout the system. In this sifting process, the victim is the first filter, at least for the common crimes of assault and theft. If victims report to the police, the case *may* proceed through the system, although this is by no means certain. If the case is not reported by a victim to the police, there is very little chance that it will proceed through the process.

The victim's decision whether to report a crime thus has a very substantial impact on the likelihood that the goals of the criminal justice system will be met. That the criminal justice process will not be involved at all is of course the most striking result, but there are other significant consequences as well.

Consider the criminal justice system aims of punishing offenders, achieving fairness, deterring crime, incapacitating offenders, rehabilitating them, and providing a public perception that justice is done. If the criminal justice system is not invoked because a crime was not reported, the offender will not be punished. If some types of offenders are more or less likely to be brought to the attention of the police by victims than are other types, then—since all future decisions of arrest, conviction, and punishment would be initiated only by the victim's action—the goal of equal treatment under the law is obstructed. Offenders can be neither confined for the purpose of pre-venting further crimes nor provided with rehabilitation programs if the criminal justice system is not involved. General deterrence typically is believed by its supporters to be determined by the certainty and severity of punishment. If the victim decides not to report a crime, the chance of any punishment ever being imposed is nearly zero. And, since no one is arrested, convicted, or punished for the crime, the public may not see justice as having been done.

Until recently, victims' decisions concerning the reporting of a crime were not regarded widely as a central step in the criminal justice process. Rather, it usually was supposed that the police were the initiators of the system. The victims' role in triggering the system now is more generally recognized, but nevertheless little is known about how victims make these critical decisions.

The decision has obvious importance not only to the system as a whole but also to the victim individually. A report to the police clearly indicates that a situation has arisen in the life of the victim that he or she believes deserves official state recognition and action. The decision is not necessarily unchangeable, since the victim may later decide not to press charges (someone else in the law enforcement organization still may do so). Perhaps the victim wants to "get even." Or, the victim may hope for restitution—maybe some of the property lost can be recovered or restored. Perhaps the report is motivated by a more general sense of social obligation. It may be seen as a duty to report offenses against the law. For many victims, the report of a crime to the police may be simply perceived as a way to end an immediate crisis—a way out of a difficult situation. A call to the police may be a way to end a victimization in which the victim's only wish is to find a peaceable resolution to a dispute (as, for example, in a domestic assault). Rather than seeking the full weight of the criminal justice process, the victim may be seeking only an escape and an end to the victimization. For other victims, there may be practical concerns such as meeting insurance requirements.

Thus, a report to the police may result from a feeling of social obligation, from anger and a desire to retaliate, from an attempt to deal with a crisis, from an assessment of potential financial gain, or many other reasons.

Victims' decisions to call the police may be motivated by a need to support their belief that a harm or wrong has been done. Police and prosecutors are in positions to validate victims' perceptions if they are taken seriously, or to invalidate them if they are ignored or trivialized. Whether victims report crimes may be influenced by victims' expectations of the law enforcement response.

The Decision to Report a Crime to the Police

Until the development of the victimization surveys already described, no systematic data on either the extent or characteristics of crime unknown to the police were available. These surveys, however, have revealed that a very large proportion of the victimizations reported to interviewers had not been reported to the police. For many kinds of crime, over half were not reported. For whatever reasons, vast numbers of victims of crimes of theft and assault—the most popular forms of crime—decided not to invoke the criminal justice process.

Results of collecting data on the reporting of crimes by victims over a 20-year period from the National Crime Victimization Survey are shown for three major kinds of crimes in Figure 5.1. (More recent data may not be comparable because of changes that have been made in the survey procedures.)

Figure 5.1 Trends in the Percentage of Crimes Reported to the Police, 1972–1992

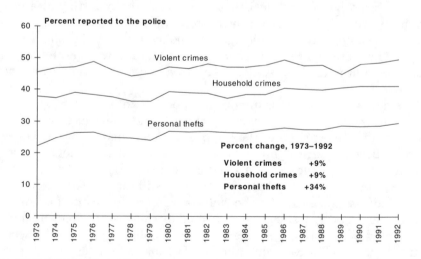

Source: adapted from Bureau of Justice Statistics. 1993. *Highlights from 20 Years of Surveying Crime Victims*. Washington, D.C.: U.S. Department of Justice, 32.

Note: violent crimes include rape, robbery, aggravated assault, and simple assault. For rape and assault, the reason for reporting most often given was to prevent further crimes by the offender. For robbery, it was to recover property. Household crimes include burglary, household larceny, and motor vehicle theft. For each, the most commonly given reason for reporting was to recover property. Personal thefts include personal larcenies with and without contact. The reason for reporting was most commonly to recover property.

Box 5.2

Crime Reporting

Most crimes are not reported to the police.
More likely to be reported are crimes that:
     involve violence,
     victimize businesses,
     are completed,
     injured a victim physically,
     involve female victims.

These data show the proportions of victimizations, by types of crimes, that victims said were reported to the police. Three important facts are shown by these data:

1. Large numbers of crimes are unreported each year. Most crimes are not reported to the police.

2. Different kinds of crimes are reported at different rates. For example, violent crimes are more often reported than are household crimes such as burglary and theft, and the latter are more often reported than are personal thefts. Although not shown in this figure, there are differences between kinds of crimes within these general groups. For example, vehicle theft is much more likely to be reported than is larceny.

3. Rates of reporting or not reporting are fairly stable from year to year, but the proportion of victimizations that are reported is generally increasing.

Other facts are that victimizations of businesses are more likely to be reported than are personal or household victimizations, completed crimes are more likely to be reported than are those only attempted, and crimes are more often reported when the victim has been injured. As Figure 5.2 shows, completed robberies with injury to the victim are reported two-thirds of the time, but attempted robberies without injury are reported less than a third of the time.

Rates of reporting of violent crimes are associated with age and sex. Victims of violent crimes who are age 12 to 19 are less likely to report them. Female victims of violent crimes are more likely to report them than are male victims.[6]

Two methods have been used to try to determine what influences victims' decisions whether to call the police. The first is to ask victims about it directly. The other is to analyze characteristics of the victim, offender, and event in terms of whether or not the police were called.

Crime prevention and punishment aims of the criminal justice system are represented prominently in victims' reasons for calling the police. In 1994, more than a third said the reason they reported personal crimes was to catch or punish the offender. About one person in five said they reported the victimization "because it was a crime." Victims of property crimes more often reported property recovery or insurance as a reason, but a fourth of these victims also said "because it was a crime." Reasons given by victims for calling the police to report personal and property victimizations are shown in Figures 5.3 and 5.4.

Figure 5.2   Percent of Crimes Reported to the Police, According to Whether or Not Injured

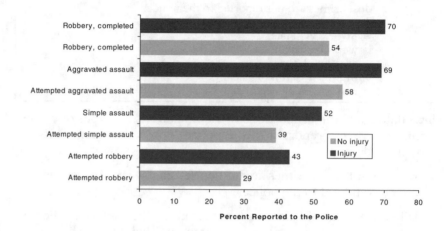

Source: data from Bureau of Justice Statistics. (1993). *Highlights from 20 Years of Surveying Crime Victims*. Washington, D.C: U.S. Department of Justice, 31.

Economic loss is related to reporting also (Figure 5.5). The dollar loss from motor vehicle thefts is very high compared with that due to other thefts (Figure 5.6).

Figure 5.3   Estimated Percentage of Reasons for Reporting Property Victimizations, 1994

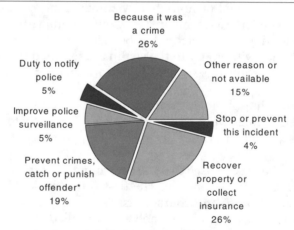

*   "Prevent crimes, catch or punish the offender" includes:
     to prevent further crimes by offender against victim (7 percent),
     to prevent crime by offender against anyone (4 percent),
     to punish offender (3 percent),
     to catch or find offender (5 percent).

Source: data from Maguire, K., and Pastore, A. L. (eds.) (1996). *Sourcebook of Criminal Justice Statistics, 1995*. Washington, D.C: U.S. GPO, table 3.33, p. 246 adapted from *Criminal Victimization in the United States, 1994*, Washington, D.C: U.S. Department of Justice, Table 101. Note: property victimizations include household burglary, motor vehicle theft, and theft.

Figure 5.4 Estimated Percentage of Reasons for Reporting Personal Victimizations, 1994

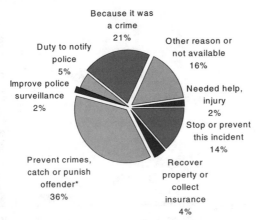

* "Prevent crimes, catch or punish the offender" includes:
   to prevent further crimes by offender against victim (16 percent),
   to prevent crime by offender against anyone (8 percent),
   to punish offender (7 percent),
   to catch or find offender (5 percent).

Source: data from Maguire, K., and Pastore, A. L. (eds.) (1996). *Sourcebook of Criminal Justice Statistics, 1995.* Washington, D.C: U.S. GPO, table 3.33, p. 246 adapted from *Criminal Victimization in the United States,* 1994, Washington, D.C: U.S. Department of Justice, Table 101. Note: personal victimizations include robbery and assault.

Figure 5.5 Percent of Crimes with Economic Loss Reported to the Police

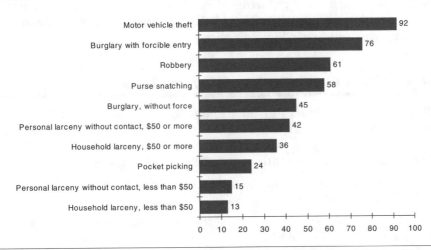

Source: adapted from Bureau of Justice Statistics. (1993). *Highlights from 20 Years of Surveying Crime Victims.* Washington, D.C: U.S. Department of Justice, 31.

Reasons for Not Calling the Police

Reasons most often given for *not* reporting a crime to the police are that the crime was a private or personal matter, the loss was recovered, or the attempted crime was unsuccessful. Many crimes were not reported because "the police would not want to be bothered" or the crime was "not important

Figure 5.6 Average Dollar Loss of Thefts

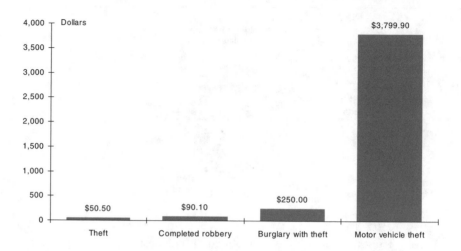

Source: data from Bureau of Justice Statistics. (1993). *Highlights from 20 Years of Surveying Crime Victims*. Washington, D.C: U.S. Department of Justice, 17.

enough." In typical surveys, about one-fifth of the rapes reported (to the interviewers), nearly two-fifths of the robberies, three-fifths of the larcenies, and one-half of the household burglaries that were not reported (to the police) were not reported because the victims believed that "nothing could be done" or that it was "not important enough."

For rapes and assaults, a large share of victims who did not report the event to the police typically explained that the victimization was "a private matter." As a reason for not reporting a crime to the police, "fear of reprisal" usually is not given; but it is reported in victim surveys for nearly one in six rapes that were not reported to the police.

The Victim's Goals in Decision Making

It would be easy to infer too much about how victims arrive at decisions to call or not call the police from these data from the National Crime Victimization Survey. They are subject to the various limitations of the survey method used. The main limitations may be due to the following:

1. Sampling (whether the interviewees adequately represent the whole nation).

2. Accuracy of memory (how well the respondents remember the details of the incident).

3. Willingness of respondents to participate.

4. Sensitivity of the subject matter.

5. Financial benefit to reporting.

6. Respondents' perceptions of the seriousness of the crime.

The categories of reasons used are rather broad and ambiguous. For example, the response "nothing could be done" might mean that after an assault the victim believes that the physical harm done cannot be corrected. Or, the victim may believe that an unknown assailant could not be caught. Or it could mean that the victim believes the criminal justice system to be powerless to prevent a recurrence of an attack. The response "police would not want to be bothered" could mean that the victim thought the harm was very minor or that the police would simply not be interested in any case.

In any event, these data are informative about the victims' exercise of discretion. Many victim's apparently believed that the crime was not worthy of official state action because it was seen as not important or because the police would not be interested. This may represent a diversion of what are seen as relatively minor crimes from the criminal justice system. The fact that completed crimes are more often reported than are those merely attempted is consistent with this interpretation.

Many of those who did report crimes to the police gave utilitarian aims as their reason for reporting. Reasons such as "to catch the person," "to recover property," or for "personal protection" are examples. The many who say they did so because it was a crime is consistent with the idea that they sought validation of their perceptions and feelings. The general purpose of crime prevention is prominent as a reason. Other reasons reflect the aim of retribution (to punish the offender).

Many victims report a crime to the police for personal utilitarian reasons. The relation between the victim's insurance status and reporting to the police, and the relatively high rate of reporting stolen automobiles, are examples. The decision to report a crime may be influenced by a personal cost-benefit analysis more than a social obligation. Often, insurance companies will not refund victims until an official police report is made; and there is a strong association between reporting to the police and whether the victim was covered by theft insurance. In one study, 85 percent of robbery victims with theft insurance reported it to the police, compared with only 51 percent of those without insurance.[7]

A major characteristic of crime which affects reporting to the police is that of the nature of the offense suffered by the victim. The more serious the crime—in terms of physical injury or financial loss—the more likely the crime is to be reported. Victims are more likely to call the police for completed crimes than for attempts, for aggravated rather than simple assault, for crimes involving weapons (particularly guns), for crimes causing injuries (particularly serious ones), and for crimes involving financial loss (particularly great loss). Factors associated with the seriousness of the harm done by a crime are good predictors of whether the police are called. Regardless of the type of crime, more serious harms are more likely to be reported to the police.[8]

Judging from the data provided by victimization surveys, the characteristics of the victims appear to play only a small role in victims' decisions about calling the police. After an extensive review of the evidence, Skogan noted the importance of the seriousness of the crime and stated:

> A consistent finding of victim surveys is that crime reporting is relatively independent of the personal attributes of victims. Within major crime categories there are few impressive differences between blacks and whites, men and women, or high- or low-income families, in the extent to which they mobilize the police when victimized. Non-reporting also is not particularly related to the size or type of community in which victims live. One might expect crime reporting to be higher in urban areas, where informal mechanisms of social control are weaker and the police are often relied upon to regulate conflict and resolve disputes. [But there have been found] no impor-

tant differences between reporting rates by type of crime in urban, suburban, and rural jurisdictions.[9]

One might suppose that attitudes toward the police could substantially influence whether they are called to report crimes, but studies have shown consistently that this depends on the nature of the crime experienced by the victim. Generally, when the harm done to the victim is severe, attitudes toward the police do not play an influential role. The main determinant is the seriousness of the harm done. Only when the crime is not very serious does the victim's attitude toward the police influence reporting.[10]

Reporting Decisions for Other Crimes

Although victimization surveys provide the best available data about the reporting of crimes by victims, many kinds of criminal activity are not included. It is not possible to uncover victimizations of some kinds by the survey method, and for some kinds of crimes (such as consumer fraud) the victim may be unaware of the victimization. Thus, for many crimes, little is known about the critical decision that either brings the offender into the arms of the criminal justice system or does not.

Shoplifting

Shoplifting is a crime of low visibility committed against an organization rather than an individual. In the organization, the staff often do not know whether inventory losses are due to shoplifting, employee theft, delivery fraud, or poor inventory control. It might be thought that since an organization is the victim, less discretion would be exercised about calling the police. Some clever research has been done that shows this not to be so.

Hindelang studied the records of a security firm that kept track of persons caught shoplifting in retail stores.[11] Store staff filled out a form including information about each alleged shoplifter, the type and value of goods stolen, and whether a referral to the police was made. From the records of more than 6,000 incidents over three years, he found that only 26 percent had been reported to the police. Thus, the store personnel exercised much discretion in invoking the criminal justice system process.

Many attributes of the alleged shoplifters (such as age, sex, race) and the stolen merchandise (for example, type and retail value) were available to Hindelang, who therefore was able to determine those attributes that made store employees more likely to call the police after catching a suspect. The value of the stolen property was by far the most influential. What was stolen, who stole it, and how it was stolen also were important. For example, stealing liquor was reported more often, men and older persons were more likely to be reported, and calls were more often made when items were placed under the clothes.

Hindelang showed that shoplifters who stole articles of small value (not liquor and worth less than $1.90) were referred to the police only 10 percent of the time, although those who tried to steal expensive fresh meat by hiding it under their clothes were referred 85 percent of the time. Hindelang suggested that the interpretation of the act of theft by the store personnel may play an important role in moderating the likelihood of referral.

For example, if the items stolen are those which the store personnel believe are to be resold [by the thief]—liquor, cigarettes, and perhaps fresh meat—they may take a firmer position in favor of referral [than they would take] if the items stolen are viewed . . . as essential to survival.

The method of shoplifting may be considered by store personnel in determining intent. One may absentmindedly put a small object in a coat pocket, but putting an object under one's clothes or into another bag is unlikely to be an accident.

In a similar study of records completed by detectives in a large department store, Cohen and Stark also found that the private security guards exercised a large amount of discretion.[12] More than half the shoplifters apprehended were not reported to the police. The investigators also found that the value of the merchandise stolen was strongly associated with the decision whether to call the police. When goods valued at less than $30 were stolen, the shoplifters were referred to the police a third of the time, but those who had stolen merchandise worth more than that were referred three-fourths of the time.

The retail value of goods stolen was associated substantially with the decision to call the police in yet another study.[13] Although it was found that older persons and nonwhites were more likely to be referred to the police than were younger persons and whites, the conclusion was that

[A]lthough offender characteristics are important, the seriousness of the alleged offense is clearly the most critical determinant of whether or not an apprehended shoplifter is referred to the police. Whatever the exact magnitude of the contributions of offender characteristics to the decision to refer, they occur within limits imposed by the seriousness of the offense.

Consumer Frauds

Knowledge about how victims of crimes other than those included in the Uniform Crime Reports or National Crime Victimization Surveys decide to invoke the law is scarce. An example is given by consumer frauds, about which we are unable to even reliably define the extent of the problem. Consumers may complain about suspected frauds to various authorities including the police, but also to better business bureaus, newspaper columns, consumer complaint offices, or attorneys general. Another problem is that victims may not be able to tell the difference between fraud and aggressive business practices, and therefore may have trouble deciding whether an event is indeed a crime that should be reported. There is some evidence that those who do report consumer frauds are more often motivated by a desire for restitution rather than punishment of the offender. They want their money back or the product repaired. [14]

Victim Participation

Perhaps the least likely crimes to be reported to the police are those in which the victim is a participant. Police do receive complaints of robberies and assaults from customers of prostitutes or from prostitutes themselves, but no doubt most such offenses go unreported because of the victim's fear of embarrassment or prosecution.

Dark Areas of Crime

Given the importance of the victim's decision whether to invoke the law, thereby triggering the criminal justice process, the limitations of our knowledge about these decisions must be stressed. Crimes between people known or related to one another, such as child abuse and spouse assault, probably are undercounted by victim surveys. Crimes in which the victim is a participant undoubtedly are underreported. Although some events reported as crimes may not in fact be crimes, a larger gap in knowledge is that crimes other than common theft and assault that are not reported to anyone. Another is whether and to what extent, after calling the police, victims were satisfied with the results of their decisions.

Is Victim Screening Desirable?

Individuals acting for themselves and persons acting as members of organizations appear to decide to call the police partly on the basis of the seriousness of the crime—on the gravity of their loss. Thus, victims are a first filter for the entire criminal justice process, tending to screen out the less serious crimes from further processing.

The large extent to which victims do *not* report crimes raises the question whether or to what extent a criminal justice system can achieve the goals set for it, including fairness, when it can process only those cases selected for it by individual citizens. It is obvious that for a large share of crimes, the offenders never will be held accountable by the criminal justice system. It may be thought that a full reporting by victims is necessary for an efficient and equitable justice system. Yet, there may be advantages to the present citizen-based discretionary system for invoking the criminal justice process. Full reporting, more than doubling the number of offenses now reported, would be imposed on an already overtaxed system. Involvement of the full machinery of the criminal justice system in every victimization would overwhelm the limited resources of the system. It would then be less able to deal efficiently, fairly, and effectively with the more serious cases.

Perhaps many of the less serious offenses may best be resolved by the parties involved, and involving the criminal justice system would be wasteful, or even prevent a friendly settlement of the dispute. If so, this is consistent with the repeated finding that the seriousness of the crime is an important determinant of whether victims decide to report it to law enforcement.

Victim Alternatives and Information

In the criminal justice system, victims have two main choices: to call the police or to do nothing. If the police are notified, victims usually lose control over the process and its outcomes. The disposition of the case is taken out of the victim's hands. Consider the similar circumstance of the police officer. If the main concern of the officer is with justice, then in using discretion not to arrest a suspect the police may believe, on the basis of the available information, that justice has been served. If the decision is to arrest, then control over what happens next is in the hands of the prosecutor, judge, or both. If the decision of the prosecutor or judge is to not proceed further and to drop the case, then the officer may believe that his or her judgment has been ignored and justice has not been served. Victims also may believe that justice is better served by their decision not to notify the police of a crime. On the other hand, victims may believe that justice has not been served when a prosecutor decides not to prosecute.

The large share of crimes that are not reported may have important implications for the development or further expansion of decision alternatives for victims. If a victim fails to report a crime, for example, because it is a personal matter or because of fear of reprisal, the injured person might benefit from other dispute resolution mechanisms such as neighborhood mediation centers. These programs, which leave much more control with victims, may be appropriate for resolving a wide variety of crimes.

Victim-offender mediation programs have been developed slowly during the past 20 years. In these programs, meetings are set up between victims and offenders, along with mediators, or "go-betweens." The purpose is to negotiate an agreement, often involving restitution. By 1992, it was reported that about 100 such programs were operating in the United States. A survey report of programs in four cities—Albuquerque, Austin, Minneapolis-St. Paul, and San Francisco—indicated that four out of five victims and 87 percent of offenders who participated expressed satisfaction with the process. Also, restitution was more often paid after mediation than it was with court orders without mediation. Moreover, victims reported a reduction in anxiety and fear.[15]

Trends in Victimizations

When measured by reported victimizations, the *number* of crimes rose in the 1970s and has declined since 1981. In 1992, compared with 1973, the number of all crimes counted in the surveys was down 6 percent. Household crimes reported by victims were down 3 percent, and personal thefts were down 18 percent. The trend was different for the violent crimes of rape,

Figure 5.7 Trends in Personal Crime Rates, 1973–1992

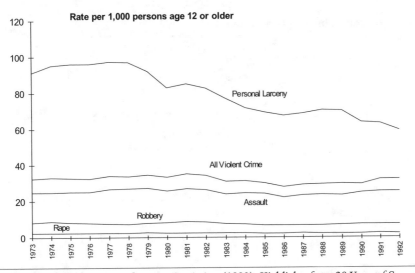

Source: adapted from Bureau of Justice Statistics. (1993). *Highlights from 20 Years of Surveying Crime Victims.* Washington, D.C: U.S. Department of Justice, 31.

robbery, and assault, up by 24 percent.

Since the population continues to increase, the *rates* of crime are of course more informative than are the sheer numbers of victimizations. Major trends in rates of personal crimes over the 20 year period are shown in Figure 5.7. A fairly steady, marked decline in personal larcenies since the 1970s is notable.

Household larceny and burglary have declined over the last dozen years, as shown in Figures 5.8 and 5.9. This is the case with burglaries whether or not force was used to unlawfully enter the building.

The rates of motor vehicle theft reported by victims, shown in Figure 5.10, were quite variable during the 20 year span of 1973-1992. They tended to decrease until 1985, then started increasing. The denominator for calculating the rate is the number of households, not vehicles.

The trends for reporting the violent crimes of rape, robbery, and assault, shown in Figure 5.11, are mixed. There are complex statistical methods for analyzing such trends, but a simple way is to lay a transparent ruler on the

Figure 5.8 Trends in Household Crime Rates, 1973–1992

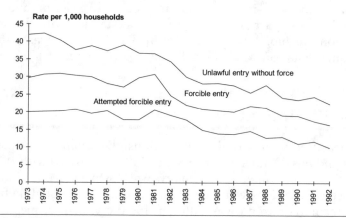

Source: adapted from Bureau of Justice Statistics. (1993). *Highlights from 20 Years of Surveying Crime Victims*. Washington, D.C: U.S. Department of Justice, 31.

Figure 5.9 Trends in Burglary Rates, 1973–1992

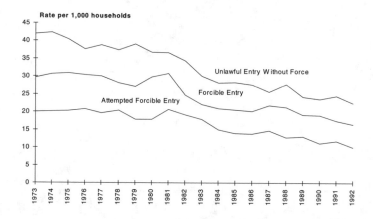

Source: adapted from Bureau of Justice Statistics. (1993). *Highlights from 20 Years of Surveying Crime Victims*. Washington, D.C: U.S. Department of Justice, 12.

Figure 5.10 Trends in Motor Vehicle Theft Rates, 1973–1992

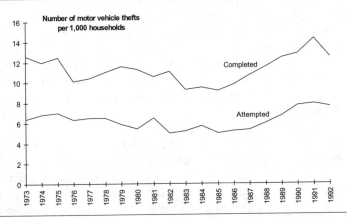

Source: adapted from Bureau of Justice Statistics. (1993). *Highlights from 20 Years of Surveying Crime Victims*. Washington, D.C: U.S. Department of Justice, 14.
Note: compare with Figure 4.23, with rate shown in relation to registered motor vehicles.

Figure 5.11 Trends in Rates for Rape, Robbery, and Assault, 1973–1992

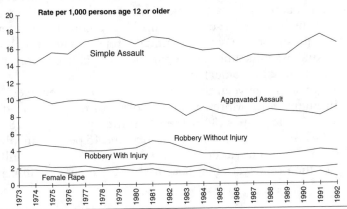

Source: adapted from Bureau of Justice Statistics. (1993). *Highlights from 20 Years of Surveying Crime Victims*. Washington, D.C: U.S. Department of Justice, 9–11.

Figure 5.12 Trends in Female Rape Rates, 1973–1992

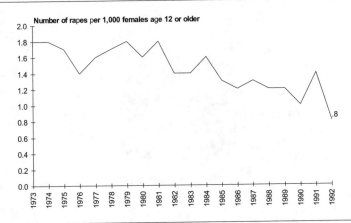

Source: adapted from Bureau of Justice Statistics. (1993). *Highlights from 20 Years of Surveying Crime Victims*. Washington, D.C: U.S. Department of Justice, 9.

trend line, trying to approximate the straight line that fits the data best. If we do that, we will see that the line has an upward slope (that is, an increasing rate) for simple assaults reported by victims. We will find a downward slope for aggravated assault and a fairly stable, somewhat decreasing, rate for robbery. Simple assaults reported were 11 percent more in 1992 than in 1973, and aggravated assaults were down 9 percent. Rates of reporting robberies, particularly those without injury, decreased somewhat over the period. When the scale is changed to show the changes over time better, as in Figure 5.12, we can see that rates of reporting of female victimizations decreased over the years shown.

How the victim survey questions are asked is important, and they have been changed. By the time data from a redesigned survey were available for 1992–1993, the rate of sexual assaults as measured was much higher. A new questionnaire was used after an extensive 10-year project to redesign the methods used in collecting the data. One goal of the project was to produce more accurate and complete reporting of rapes and sexual assaults. Adding questions encouraged the reporting of incidents, and new methods of cueing respondents to report victimizations were used. The wording of questions also was changed in an effort to make them easier to understand. The new questionnaire asks respondents whether they have been victims of forced or unwanted sexual activity. Detailed questions are asked about any forced or coerced intercourse or sexual activity of any kind, completed or attempted.[16] With the new questionnaire, women annually reported about half a million rapes and sexual assaults, and the Department of Justice reported the rate per 1,000 females (12 and older) at 4.6.

The relationships between the victims and the offenders were reported as shown in Figure 5.13. More than 6 out of 10 of these reported assaults were either completed rapes (34 percent) or attempted rapes (28 percent). Nine percent were sexual assaults with injury, and 15 percent involved some injury. Thirteen percent were verbal threats of rape or sexual assault. (Sexual assaults other than rape were not measured in the earlier victimization surveys).

Figure 5.13   Relationship of Lone Offenders to Female Victims of Rape and Sexual Assault (Redesigned Victim Survey) 1992–1993 (Average Annual Percent of Victimizations)

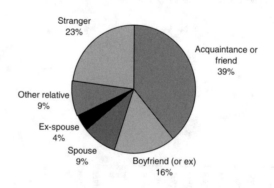

Source: adapted from Bachman, R. and L. E. Saltzman. 1995. *Violence Against Women: Estimates from the Redesigned Survey.* Bureau of Justice Statistics Special Report, Washington, D.C: 1955, 3.

In the earlier victimization surveys, other facts about female rapes reported included the following:

- About half the rapes were done or attempted by someone known to the victim.

- The offender was armed in about a fifth of the cases.

- Stranger rapists were more often armed (29 percent) than were non-stranger rapists (17 percent).

- Among victims who tried to protect themselves, such as by fighting back and yelling and screaming, most reported that it helped rather than made things worse.

- A little over half the victims reported the crime to the police.

- Victims were more likely to report the crime if the rapist was armed, if additional injuries were sustained, and if they received medical attention.

- The relationship of the victim and the offender was not related to reporting to the police.

Costs of Crime Victimizations

The costs of crime—to victims and to society at large—of course cannot be estimated with precision. We could add up a dollar amount of property losses, medical bills, and the like. The huge monetary costs of operating the criminal justice system also can be summed for cities and towns, counties, states, and the federal government. It is much more difficult to assign cost values to pain, suffering, death, the risk of death, and lowered confidence in the social order, the *intangible* costs.

A recent study focused on victim-related costs (excluding costs of the criminal justice system). The research workers tried to estimate intangible as well as measurable actual costs. They tried to assign dollar values to the emotional and psychological effects that can have such serious consequences for victims, translating these into dollar figures using methods of civil law damage suits. They estimated the numbers of crimes of various types and also the average costs of each type. Then they multiplied the costs by crime occurrences to get total costs. They reported that "for the most part, only street crime and domestic crime were counted and their costs calculated." Crimes such as those against business and governments, personal frauds, white collar crimes, child neglect, and most "victimless" crimes were excluded.[17]

They reported that the intangible costs as they estimated them for 1987–1990 generally exceeded all tangible losses combined. The tangible losses were calculated at $105 billion annually, and the intangible ones were much higher—$345 billion. Because of its relative frequency, they reported that, overall, "rape is the costliest crime: With annual victim costs at $127 billion, it exacts a higher price than murder."

Who Are the Victims?

Not everyone has the same risk of being a victim of crime. People in different social circumstances and lifestyles have different risks. Hindelang,

Gottfredson, and Garafalo, for example, listed 18 different groups with very different risks. At the extremes, males aged 16 to 19 who were not in school were nearly five times more likely to be victims of crime in a six-month period than were divorced or separated women 65 or older.[18] Personal characteristics that best distinguished between victims and others were age, marital status, employment status, and sex. These items, along with race and family income, were used to classify persons with different risks of victimization, which the authors explained in terms of "lifestyle" differences. For example, persons who often come into contact with or associate with persons with a high rate of offending are apt to be disproportionately victimized. On the other hand, older, unmarried women, who spend more time at home, less often place themselves at risk. Generally, victims tend to be adolescents or young adults—just as do offenders.

Some persons are at risk of being victimized over and over again. A survey in London indicated that 6 percent of persons accounted for 40 percent of the victimizations.[19] Some persons have an extremely high risk of being victims. Silbert described, from a sample of 200 female prostitutes, that 70 percent reported having been raped by clients (usually many times). Two-thirds reported physical beatings by customers; two-thirds reported beatings by pimps; and 79 percent reported being victims of rape and attempted rape outside their work context. Only 7 percent of the rapes were reported to the police, and only 7 percent reported seeking any kind of assistance.[20]

Rates of victimization are higher in cities than in suburbs or in the country. Typically, victimization rates for central city dwellers are nearly twice as high as are those for people living outside the city.

Psychological Harms

The psychological harm suffered by victims of crime often is substantial and long lasting. This is especially true of personal crimes such as assaults, rapes, and robberies; but serious harm may result from property crimes as well.

Burglary

In interviews with residential burglary victims in London, 60 percent of the victims described intrusion of privacy or emotional upset as the worst thing about the burglary. The victims saw the emotional effects as more important than the financial loss. A third of the victims were not satisfied with how the police handled the burglary, mainly because of an implied lack of importance of the crime. Victim satisfaction was not related to whether the burglar was caught.[21] In another survey of burglary victims in Toronto, Waller found that

> a large portion of respondents who were victimized, especially women, suffered from minor but long-term psychological effects as a result of victimization; the most frequent effect was a general increase in suspicion or distrust, followed by fear of being alone or fear of entering the residence or rooms within the residence.[22]

Robbery

"Mugging" is one kind of robbery. It is a personal confrontation between the victim and offender, who uses force or threat to take property from the victim. It may result in severe shock, anger, shame, self-blame, and an increased sense of vulnerability and distrust. [23]

Rape

Most of what is known about the responses of rape victims to the crime has come from interviews and clinical work with victims. The immediate responses and longer-term reactions both have been described.

The immediate responses were described by Symonds as shock, disbelief, and extreme fright:

> When a victim experiences fright bordering on panic there is a heightened distortion of perceptive thinking and judgment. All behavior is directed at self-preservation. Most learned behavior seems to evaporate, and the victim responds with the . . . patterns of childhood. [24]

According to Symonds, most women during a rape display behavior that may look like cooperation but has its roots in profound terror, with the victim submitting to avoid being killed. This lays a groundwork for long-lasting guilt and shame, to which society, the family, and the criminal justice system may contribute.

The short-term response to rape is an alarm reaction.[25] This is a response of extreme anxiety and disorganization with strong feelings of fear, helplessness, humiliation, depression, anger, and guilt. Many victims have physical symptoms of muscle spasms, nausea, sleep disorders, fear of injury or death, and changes in sexual behavior.

Most observers describe a period of reorganization, such that after a few months the victim is much less disturbed; but negative effects may be long-lasting—for months and even years.[26]

The tendency of rape victims to blame themselves is a special problem of this crime. It is a problem that is often made worse by others—lovers, family members, or criminal justice system personnel—but which also can be helped by support and assistance.

Crime in General

Crime, defined as harm, includes not only the harms of physical damage or property loss, but the harm of stress. The more intrusive the crime, the greater the stress, and the greater the psychological harm. The more supportive victims' resources—friends, family, social service workers, and criminal justice system personnel—the more rapid the recovery.

Victim and Witness Assistance Programs

Since the 1960s, there has been a substantial growth in programs designed to assist victims and witnesses. Most are run by small staffs, many with a larger group of volunteers. Services typically offered are crisis counseling of victims and referral to agencies for specialized services. Attempts often are made to reduce the frustrations of victims and other witnesses in waiting for hearings and trials by monitoring the court process and keeping in touch with witnesses to be of help. They often seek to protect the victim or witness in other ways, such as providing waiting rooms separated from the defendant and the general public. Often, they seek to help in the return of stolen property or evidence. They often provide public education programs that try to inform the public about the plight of victims of crime and the need for greater assistance.

Another frequent aim is to encourage the reporting of crimes to the police by making involvement with the criminal justice system less unattractive. This includes not only help with such information as where to park and providing other courtesies but help with frequent problems such as intimidation. Some procedures that have been recommended or used have been informing victims and witnesses when defendants are released from custody, seeking to speed up the court process when threats are reported, and helping victims or witnesses who have been threatened by escorting them in and out of the courthouse.[27]

Many such programs provide "victim impact" statements to the prosecutor and the judge. Some states have required such statements in criminal cases, and others have passed laws giving victims a right to present them. All states and the District of Columbia now have some provision for these statements. A victim impact statement typically permits a victim to express to the court an account of the losses—economic, physical, or psychological—suffered as a result of the crime. Often, the statement is incorporated into the presentence report prepared by a probation officer, which may include sentencing recommendations to the court. In some jurisdictions, the victim may testify at the time of sentencing, but victims rarely take advantage of the opportunity.

We might think that having victim impact statements would increase victims' perceptions of involvement and satisfaction with the criminal justice system, but that may not be the case. An experiment in a Bronx, New York, court was designed to test this question. Victims were assigned randomly to three groups: (1) interviewed, with no written statement; (2) interviewed, with impact statements written; and (3) not interviewed. No effects on victims' perceptions were found.[28]

We might think that victim impact statements would result in harsher sentences. The investigators also found this not to be the case.[29]

In jurisdictions with active victim-witness programs based in prosecutors' offices, victims do report more satisfaction than those in sites without such programs. Also, they express more satisfaction and more favorable attitudes toward the criminal justice system if they learned the outcome of the case and believed that they had influenced it.[30]

As the criminal case is processed through the system, victims usually have less and less contact with the decision makers involved. They have the most contact with the police, may have some contact with the prosecutor, and have less with the judges and probation officers. The victim is more and more isolated from the process as it proceeds from one stage to the next in the criminal justice system.[31]

Victim Compensation

The idea of using public money to aid crime victims is not a new one. It goes back at least to the (circa) 1750 B.C. code of Hammurabi, which asserted a communal responsibility when individual blame for a crime could not be established. If, for example, a life was lost, the city of the crime was obligated to pay a sum in silver to the heirs of the victim. Compensation was characteristic of Anglo-Saxon law, but by the fourteenth century, fines went to the rulers. Nineteenth-century reformers advocated victim compensation, but the idea did not pick up steam until the 1960s.[32] After New Zealand and Great Britain started victim compensation programs in 1964, the United States began this development also, and now all states have such a program in some form.[33]

Typically, a maximum amount that a victim may receive is set, and often emphasis is placed on compensation for medical expenses and loss of income. Programs may be operated by independent state boards or by other state agencies. A few states place responsibility with the court for awarding victims' claims. Most crime victims do not take advantage of the usually quite limited opportunities for compensation, perhaps because they are unaware of the programs or do not want to be bothered.

Restitution

Restitution programs, usually restricted to property offenses, involve an order of payment by the offender to the victim as a condition of probation or parole, or, in some jurisdictions, a sole sentence (although rarely used as such). Restitution is often a prominent part of assignments for juvenile offenders, but also fairly common in the sentencing of adults, usually as a probation condition. Some jurisdictions have developed residential restitution centers. Convicted persons sentenced to such centers sometimes work outside the center, with earnings placed into an account used for victim restitution.[34]

Restorative Justice

Increased interest has been shown recently by the federal government and some states in concepts of "restorative" rather than "retributive" justice. As described by advocates, "While retributive justice is focused on public vengeance, deterrence, and punishment through an adversarial process, restorative justice is concerned with repairing the harm done to victims and the community through a process of negotiation, mediation, victim empowerment and reparation."[35]

Programs based on the restorative justice concept could be expected to emphasize victim-offender mediation, restitution, community service, and a broad range of community sanctions other than confinement. Rather than advocating specific programs, however, proponents are apt to stress the concept as a new or different way of thinking about how to respond to crime, a way of thinking that can affect decisions throughout the criminal justice system. See Box 5.3 for an example.[36]

Victimless Crimes?

Whether any crimes are "victimless" is a controversial subject. It often is suggested that some crimes have no real victims and also that statutes defining them should be repealed or restricted substantially. Although defi-

Box 5.3

Kay Pranis: In Her Own Words

Restorative justice is not a specific program or set of programs; it is a way of thinking about how to respond to crime, a set of values which can guide decisions on policy, programs, and practice. Restorative justice is based on a reconceptualization of crime as injury to the victim and the community rather than as an affront to the state. The primary purpose of the justice system in the restorative model is to repair the harm resulting from the crime to the degree possible. Victim involvement or perspective (through surrogate victims or advocates when a victim does not wish to participate) is essential to define harms and to identify how they might be repaired.

A comprehensive restorative response engages the community as a resource for reintegration of victims and offenders, and for monitoring and enforcing community standards of behavior. Restorative justice defies traditional liberal and conservative labels but embraces values of both perspectives. A restorative response to crime is a community-building response. Restorative justice prioritizes support to victims, opportunities for victim input, offender understanding of the human harm of the behavior, offender involvement in repairing the harm where possible, and community involvement in all aspects of resolving a criminal incident.

—Kay Pranis, supporting a restorative justice program in Minnesota.

---

nitions vary, offenses such as public drunkenness, sexual acts involving consenting adults, obscenity, pornography, drug offenses, gambling, and juvenile status offenses (offenses by children or youths that would not be crimes if done by an adult) all have been included.

There are two kinds of arguments for the repeal of laws against such acts. Some persons argue that, as a matter of principle, conduct that harms only the actor or actors should not be prohibited by law. Others argue also that in any case it is unwise to punish these acts. Arguments are that, first, for most of these acts, no one complains except the police; second, many of these acts involve the exchange of goods or services desired by the participants; and third, the harms that are sought to be prevented are relatively less serious than those due to crimes with clear victims, and enforcing the laws places an unnecessary heavy burden on the criminal justice system.

Critics of the "victimless crime" concept assert that there is no such thing, because most of these offenses do have victims, or potential victims. The taxpayer must support the treatment of the drug addict and of the addicted person's dependents. Citizens may be harassed or offended by public drunks. The spouse of an adulterer or bigamist is a victim. If there are degrees of victimization, there may be no clear line to draw between criminal and noncriminal behavior.[37]

Summary

Victims generally are ignored in criminal justice system processing except in their roles in reporting crimes, which are offenses against the state, and acting as witnesses. It usually is a report of a crime by a victim, however, that initiates the criminal justice process. Victims may be regarded as the most influential decision makers in the criminal justice system, despite their limited roles after processing has begun, since it is usually the victim who decides whether to call the police. Most crimes are not discovered by the police, but by victims. Yet, victims do not report most of the crimes they suffer.

Different kinds of crimes are reported by victims at different rates. Violent crimes tend to be reported more often than property crimes. The more serious the crime, the more likely it is that it will be reported to the police. Reasons given by victims for not reporting crimes to law enforcement often are that the event was a personal matter (a reason often given for rapes and other assaults), or that the crime attempt was not successful, or that the police would not want to be bothered, or that the crime was not important, or that nothing could be done. Victims often express goals of crime prevention when reporting why they did or did not report a crime.

Regardless of the type of crime, elements of the event that reflect the seriousness of the harm done are good predictors of whether the police will be called: the more serious the harm, the more likely it is that the crime will be reported. As a result, many of what are seen as relatively minor crimes are never reported, but are diverted by victims from processing by the criminal justice system.

Given the centrality of the victim's decision whether to call the police, thereby invoking the criminal justice process, many more questions about how victims make this decision should be answered.

Over the last 20 years, there has been some increase in the proportions of crimes that victims have reported to the police. Victims have more often chosen to call the police to report crimes of violence, household crimes, and especially personal thefts.

Measured by victimizations, crime rates show recent declines in personal larcenies, household larcenies, and burglaries. The violent crimes of rape, robbery, and assault show different trends. Rates for aggravated assault, robberies without injury, and female rape show decreases, but increases are found for simple assaults. Results of a recently redesigned National Crime Victimization Survey, using different methods of questioning so that results are not comparable with the earlier survey data, show higher rates for female rapes and sexual assaults.

Costs of crime to victims cannot be calculated with precision, since there are many intangible consequences to victims that are difficult to measure. Evidence shows, however, that when attempts are made to measure them, the intangible costs may be much higher than the dollar costs.

The more intrusive the crime, the greater is the psychological harm. The stress of victimization has serious, often long-lasting effects. Recovery from the psychological harms of victimization can be assisted by support of family, friends and others, including those involved in the criminal justice system.

Although victims and other witnesses typically have been neglected by the criminal justice system, programs have been developed in most states to assist them and to provide compensation or restitution for losses. An emerging concept of restorative justice emphasizes the repair of harm caused by crimes.

Notes

1. Viano, E. (1983). "Victimology," in Kadish, S. H. (ed.). *Encyclopedia of Crime and Justice*, Vol. 4. New York: The Free Press, 1611–1616.

2. Gottfredson, G. D. (1989). "The Experiences of Violent and Serious Victimization," in Weiner, N. A. and M. E. Wolfgang (eds.). *Pathways to Criminal Violence*. Newbury Park, CA: Sage, 1989.

3. Walker, S. (1994). *Sense and Nonsense about Crime and Drugs*. Belmont, CA: Wadsworth, 168–169.

4. Reiss, A. (1971). *The Police and the Public*. New Haven: Yale University Press.

5. Hindelang, M. and M. R. Gottfredson. (1976). "The Victim's Decision Not to Invoke the Criminal Process," in McDonald, W. (ed.). *Criminal Justice and the Victim*. Beverly Hills: Sage.

6. Zawitz, Marianne W., P. A. Klaus, R. Bachman, L. Bastian, M. W. DeBerry,Jr., M. R. Rand, and B. M. Taylor. (1993). *Highlights from 20 Years of Surveying Crime Victims: The National Crime Victimization Survey, 1973–92*. Washington, D.C.: Bureau of Justice Statistics, U.S. Department of Justice, October, 32.

7. Gottfredson, M. R. and D. M. Gottfredson. (1988). *Decision Making in Criminal Justice: Toward the Rational Exercise of Discretion*. New York: Plenum Press, 25.

8. ——. (1988), 26–29.

9. Skogan, W. (1984). "Reporting Crimes to the Police: The Status of World Research," *Journal of Research in Crime and Delinquency*. 21:2:124.

10. Garofalo, J. (1977). *The Police and Public Opinion*. National Criminal Justice Information and Statistics Service. Washington, D.C.: U.S. GPO.

11. Hindelang M. J. (1974). "Decisions of Shoplifting Victims to Invoke the Criminal Justice Process," *Social Problems* 21: 580.

12. Cohen, L. and R. Stark. (1974). "Discriminatory Labeling and the Five-Finger Discount," *Journal of Research in Crime and Delinquency* 11:25.

13. Lundman, R. (1978). "Shoplifting and Police Referral: A Re-examination," *Journal of Criminal Law and Criminology* 69:395–400.

14. Steel, E. (1975). "Fraud, Dispute, and the Consumer: Responding to Consumer Complaints," *University of Pennsylvania Law Review* 173:1107.

15. Umbreit, M. (1994). "Victim Empowerment Through Mediation: The Impact of Victim-Offender Mediation in Four Cities," *Perspectives* 18, 3, as cited in DiMasco, W. M. (1995). *Seeking Justice: Crime and Punishment in America*. New York: The Edna McConnell Clark Foundation.

16. Bachman, R. and L. E. Saltzman. (1995). *Violence against Women: Estimates from the Redesigned Survey*. Washington, D.C.: Bureau of Justice Statistics, U.S. Department of Justice.

17. National Institute of Justice. (1996).*The Extent and Costs of Crime Victimization: A New Look*. Washington, D.C.: National Institute of Justice, U.S. Department of Justice. (Summary of a report by T. R. Miller, M. A. Cohen, and F. Wierseman titled *Victim Costs and Consequences: A New Look*).

18. Hindelang, M. J., M. R. Gottfredson, and J. Garafalo. (1978). *Victims of Personal Crime: An Empirical Foundation for a Theory of Personal Victimization*. Cambridge, MA: Ballinger.

19. Sparks, R. F. (1982). *Research on Victims of Crime: Accomplishments, Issues, and New Directions*. Rockville, MD: U.S. Department of Health and Human Services.

20. Silbert, M. H. (1984). "Treatment of Prostitute Victims of Sexual Assault," 251–282 in Stuart, I. R., and Greer, J. G. (eds.) *Victims of Sexual Aggression: Treatment of Children, Women, and Men*. New York: Van Nostrand Reinhold.

21. Maguire, M. (1980). "The Impact of Burglary upon Victims," *British Journal of Criminology* 20: 261–275, as cited by Gottfredson, G. D., (1989), 214–215.

22. Waller, I. (1976). "Victim Research, Public Policy and Criminal Justice," *Victimology* 1: 240–252, 247, as cited by Gottfredson, G. D. (1989), 215.

23. Lejeune, R. and N. Alex. (1973). "On Being Mugged: The Event and Its Aftermath," *Urban Life and Culture* 2:259–287, as cited in Gottfredson, G. D. (1989) 216–217.

24. Symonds, M. (1976). "The Rape Victim: Psychological Patterns of Response." *The American Journal of Psychoanalysis* 36: 27–34, as cited in Gottfreson, G. D. (1989), 217.

25. Burgess, A. W. and L. L. Holstrom. (1974). "Rape Trauma Syndrome," *American Journal of Psychiatry* 131: 981–986; Burgess, A. W., and Holstrom, L. L. (1976). "Coping Behavior and the Rape Victim," *American Journal of Psychiatry* 133: 413–418; Arnanat, E. (1984). "Rape Trauma Syndrome: Developmental Variations," 36–53 in Stuart, I. R. and J. G. Greer (eds.). *Victims of Sexual Aggression: Treatment of Children, Women, and Men.* New York: Van Nostrand Reinhold.

26. Gottfredson, G. D. (1989). "The Experiences of Violent and Serious Victimization," in Weiner, N. A. and M. E. Wolfgang (eds.), p. 219. *Pathways to Criminal Violence.* Newbury Park, CA: Sage Publications.

27. Geis, G. (1983). "Victim and Witness Assistance Programs," in Kadish, S. H. (ed.). *Encyclopedia of Crime and Justice.* Vol. 4. New York: The Free Press, 1600–1608.

28. Davis, R. C. and B. E. Smith. (1994). "Victim Impact Statements and Victim Satisfaction: An Unfulfilled Promise?" *Journal of Criminal Justice* 22, 1, 1–12.

29. ——. (1994). "The Effects of Victim Impact Statements on Sentencing Decisions: A Test in an Urban Setting." *Justice Quarterly* 11, 3, 453–512.

30. Herman, J. C. and B. B. Forst. (1984). *The Criminal Justice System Response to Victim Harm.* Washington, D.C.: U.S. GPO.

31. ——. (1994).

32. Geis, G. (1983). "Victim Compensation and Restitution," in Kadish, S. H. (ed.). *Encyclopedia of Crime and Justice,* Vol. 4. New York: The Free Press, 1605–1608.

33. ——. (1983), 1606.

34. ——. (1983), 1607–1608.

35. The Restorative Justice Project, http://www.arastar.net/org/uujj/trjp.htm.

36. Pranis, K. (1966). "Restorative Justice Catching on in Minnesota Corrections," *Overcrowded Times* 7, 2, 9.

37. Frase, R. S. (1983). "Victimless Crime," in Kadish, S. H. (ed.). *Encyclopedia of Crime and Justice.* Vol. 4. New York: The Free Press, 1608–1611.

CHAPTER SIX

The Police

Chapter Six

After victims, the police provide the next filter for the criminal justice system—screening out some minor offenders who will not be subject to full processing. The more serious the crime, the more likely is an arrest. In this decision and in others, the police exercise discretion but are constrained by the law. These topics, the origins of our modern police, what police do, and current trends in policing are the subjects of this chapter.

- ❏ Questions to Think About
- ❏ The Role of the Police
- ❏ Origins of Modern Police
- ❏ Modern Police
- ❏ Police and the Power of Arrest
- ❏ Police Decisions to Arrest
- ❏ Is Police Discretion Necessary?
- ❏ Goals and Alternatives of Arrest Decisions
- ❏ Police Discretion and Arrest Decisions
- ❏ The Police Filter
- ❏ Police Diversion
- ❏ Experimental Study of Arrests
- ❏ Standards for Arrest
    - The Common Law Standard
    - The Probable Cause Standard
    - Exceptions to the Standard
- ❏ Constraints on Searches
- ❏ The Exclusionary Rule
- ❏ Fifth, Fourteenth, and Sixth Amendment Rights
- ❏ Facts About Arrests
- ❏ Some Information Needs
- ❏ Police Management Decisions
    - Information for Management Decisions
    - Police Strikes
    - Hot Spots and Crackdowns
    - Policing Goals and Management Decisions
    - Community Policing
    - Community Policing as Action Research
    - Management Information Systems
- ❏ Summary

Questions to Think About

What do the police do?

How did organized police agencies get started?

How is the strain between desires for freedom and safety reflected in the police function?

Can a police officer:

Search a citizen anytime the officer wishes?
Use force to make an arrest?
Arrest a person without a warrant?
Question a suspect without a lawyer present?

Should a police officer always enforce the law?

Are police more likely to make arrests for minor offenses or for more serious ones?

Has the scope of federal law enforcement increased or decreased in the last 50 years?

Can experiments be done in order to learn about police work?

Is evidence seized illegally by the police allowed to be presented at trial?

Why do police read suspects their rights when making an arrest?

Do police "crackdowns" reduce crime?

How can police administrators improve police effectiveness?

The Role of the Police

The police can both maintain safety and threaten freedom. As described by Herbert Packer:

> The criminal sanction is at once prime guarantor and prime threatener of human freedom. Used providently and humanely it is guarantor; used indis-criminately and coercively, it is threatener. The tensions that inhere in the criminal sanction can never be wholly resolved in favor of guaranty and against threat. But we can begin to try.[1]

No one has expressed the role of the police, their special competence, and our expectations of them better than Egon Bittner in explaining that:

> [T]he police are empowered and required to impose, or, as the case may be, coerce, a provisional solution upon emergent problems without having to brook or defer to opposition of any kind, and that, further, their competence to intervene extends to every kind of emergency, without any exceptions whatever.[2]

As Bittner says, the police are responsible for events in which "something-that-ought-not-to-be-happening-is-happening-and-about-which-someone-had-better-do-something-now!" They can intervene, and they can use force in doing so. Others may not interfere. And, their authority extends to all kinds of emergencies.

We expect the police to intervene in all manner of problem or crisis situations and to compel resolutions. We expect them to maintain order and, when doing so, to follow the law and to enforce it—though not always. We expect them to provide many kinds of services. In terms of usual activities or time spent, law enforcement is a small, but critically important, slice.

> *When one looks at what policemen actually do, one finds that criminal law enforcement is something that most of them do with the frequency located somewhere between virtually never and very rarely.*
> —Egon Bittner

Origins of Modern Police[3]

Ancient Rome had its public police. As early as 27 BC Augustus appointed an officer who had executive and judicial power to maintain public order. Soon the *vigiles* were created—a police force to patrol Rome's streets. After the collapse of the Roman Empire, however, the orderly progression of police development stopped.

In England, the source of so much of our law and criminal justice system, Norman kings in the twelfth century appointed shire-reeves (sheriffs) who could impose fines on persons who broke the law. Earlier, non-landowning households had been grouped into tens and hundreds for self-defense, and the *posse comitatus* of men over 15 years old could be called out to capture offenders. Soon, each 100 households was required to appoint two constables to assist the sheriff, who governed groups of hundreds (shires) by royal authority. Then, kings began appointing justices of the peace as judges from among local landowners. By the end of the thirteenth century, there was a system that persisted for the next 500 years. Magistrates and sheriffs appointed by the king were assisted by a substantial body of constables.

The colonies that became the United States had public police, but they were not much like those in modern law enforcement agencies. Watches were created in Boston in 1631 and in New York (then New Amsterdam) in 1643. A variety of police officials came into existence, variously called constables, marshals, or sheriffs, either elected or appointed. For the next 200 years, policing was done by persons typically described as unorganized, untrained, otherwise unemployable incompetents. Some were paid, as in New Amsterdam, from the beginning. Others worked for fees paid by private persons, obviously a situation that favored those who could pay.

Present-day policing in the United States is indebted for much of its development to the establishment in 1829 of the London Metropolitan Police and its forerunners. The bobbies still owe their nickname to their creator, Sir Robert Peel, the Home Secretary. For the first time, England had, at least in London, a paid, full-time, uniformed police force, organized after a military model that persists today. Constables of many parishes (originally a church district, now similar to a county) had long been seen as inept objects of contempt and ridicule. Standards now were established for bobbies, for height, weight, character, and literacy. Some training was given them, along with a helmet and uniform, and London had an organized police force:

> The creation of the Metropolitan Police capped almost a century of searching for a system to replace the discredited, uncoordinated parish constables. In the mid-eighteenth century, the London magistrates John Fielding and Henry Fielding had created the Bow Street Runners to investigate crime and arrest criminals. Selected from constables with one year's experience, the Runners

were given rudimentary training and paid a portion of all fines resulting from successful prosecution. Prompted by an increasing concern with safety and security in rapidly growing London, six parliamentary commissions examined the problem of policing between 1770 and 1828. The debate raged over the need for safety and the desire for liberty—the conflict pervasive in the history of criminal justice. Prime Minister William Pitt tried to create a metropolitan force in 1785, but the attempt foundered on the opposition of commercial interests. Patrick Colquhoun . . . anticipated later reforms [and] established the Thames River Police in 1798. Nevertheless, by 1829 London still had a bewildering variety of police forces, some voluntary and some paid, organized by parishes, courts, and municipalities.[4]

Patrick Colquhoun gave his 1796 book a title that explains, in the manner of the time, its contents: *A Treatise on the Police of the Metropolis, Containing a Detail of the Various Crimes and Misdemeanors by Which Public and Private Property and Security Are, at Present, Injured and Endangered; and Suggesting Remedies for Their Prevention*. The public was injured and endangered by crime; and an organized police force was needed for crime prevention.

Slowly, the police reform initiated in London spread throughout England. By 1856, Parliament required reforms and gave the government authority to inspect local forces and, if minimum standards were met, to pay a fourth of their costs.

The changes in America followed, with establishment in cities of unified police forces with full-time, paid officers, who even had some training. Boston (1837), New York (1844), and Philadelphia (1854) developed municipal police forces; and most American cities soon had them. The municipal police were supplemented by sheriffs in rural areas, then, as now.

Police development in other areas of what now is the United States was similar to that in the original states but it depended on local circumstances at the start. For example, in the first Spanish settlements in California in 1769, the government was divided between the *Padres*, who exercised control over the missions, and *commendantes* who, besides having control over the military, had responsibilities for controlling crime. When Mexico became independent of Spain in 1821, a new constitution was established, with executive, legislative, and judicial departments. The judicial system adopted by the Constitution of California (1849) and included in the state's application for admission into the Union was already in place under the laws of Mexico. It had the same structure as the California court system today.

Under Mexico, the *alcades* were municipal officers who had local judicial functions, as did justices of the peace, but also they were responsible for order and tranquillity, a police function. In exercising it, they were authorized to ask for assistance from the military *commendante*.

When the Anglo-Americans migrated to California, they generally had no knowledge of the Spanish system. In the northern part, there was no government at all anyway. Some settlers first came for farming; many later came for gold. Whenever a group collected, as for gold mining, they elected an alcade. If a judge was not available, the miners often tried the cases by a jury nevertheless, quickly and finally disposing of the case, often with the aid of a rope and a tree. It was doubtful that the former Mexican laws were in effect. Any law that was applied was the English common law, although it is clear that there was no authorization for that either.

The municipal police in California, the State police, and county sheriffs departments all have developed from these lawless beginnings of miners' and settlers' courts. Such courts were sometimes supported by the military serving a police function. More often, the accused were required to answer to informal "vigilante" groups.

> Vigilance Committees were no rarity in the mining camp sections of Califor-nia. In these rough and ready communities they settled everything from horse stealing to claim jumping and cheating at cards by the economical method of throwing a rope over a convenient limb of a tree and stretching the neck of the accused without too much inquiry into his possible innocence. Often they hanged the right man.[5]

The first constitution drafted for California in 1879 was intended to put more order into law enforcement. It empowered the legislature to "provide for the election by the people of a district attorney, sheriffs, and other neces-sary officers."[6]

Typically, as other territories became states, sheriffs were designated as peace officers for the counties. In the latter part of the nineteenth century, municipal police forces were formed in the manner that they had developed in the eastern states. Earlier, private police organizations sometimes were used.

At about the same time, state police and federal law enforcement agen-cies were started. The Texas Rangers were established in 1835, before Texas became a state.[7] (See Box 6.1.) After Pennsylvania formed a state police force in 1905, most other states followed quickly. Federal marshals were organ-ized by the still new federal government in 1789 and became the principal law enforcement officers of the territories. During the Civil War, the Secret Service was established to combat counterfeiters. Later, the Post Office De-partment and the Immigration and Naturalization Service added inspectors as law enforcement officers. The Federal Bureau of Investigation, so named in 1935, grew out of the Bureau of Investigation that was created in the Department of Justice in 1908 (See Box 6.2).[8]

Box 6.1

Origin of the Texas Rangers

Mexico allowed Stephen Austin to move 300 families into a section of what now is part of Texas. He hired 10 men, who came to be called rangers, to pro-tect the people. Twelve years later, the Revolutionary Government of Texas formed a larger force to guard its bor-der. They enforced the law as they saw fit, under the command of the com-mander in chief of the regular army of Texas. After Texas became a state, the Texas Rangers were kept as the first state-supported police force in the United States, with duties mainly of protecting the Mexican border. With ex-panded state level police functions in Texas, the Rangers became a division of a department of public safety.

Modern Police

We now have several kinds of police that are funded and administered by different governments: municipal, county, state, and federal. From its beginnings in a context of distrust of strong central authority, the police function has been mainly decentralized, with primary responsibility resting on local governments, merely supplemented, for the most part, by state and federal police. Despite this continuing tendency toward decentralization—toward local rather than federal authority—changes in federal laws increas-ingly have extended the federal jurisdiction. For examples, see Box 6.3.[9]

Box 6.2

Origins of the Federal Bureau of Investigation

The United States Department of Justice, established in 1870, did not immediately create an investigative service, although it was authorized to do so. Traditionally, law enforcement had been a local affair. For the next 30 years, U.S. Attorneys General borrowed staff from the Secret Service or else hired the Pinkerton Detective Agency. Pinkerton's, a private company, was a national investigative organization, operating freely across state lines. After the 1906 indictment of two members of Congress for federal land fraud, based on investigation by the Justice Department using the Secret Service, the Congress prohibited the further employment of Secret Service operatives by other departments of the federal government. President Theodore Roosevelt, formerly the Police Commissioner of New York City, remarked that this prohibition ". . . has been a benefit only to the criminal classes. . . . The chief argument in favor [of it] was that the congressmen did not themselves want to be investigated by Secret Service men." He directed the Attorney General to develop an investigative capability within the Department of Justice. The new service, with 38 full- and part-time investigators, was called the Bureau of Investigation. In 1935 it was renamed by Congress the Federal Bureau of Investigation, and J. Edgar Hoover was named as its first Director.

Many services that at some time in some place have been assigned to the police, mainly for administrative convenience, have dropped out of the list of tasks required. Police no longer must inspect boilers, weights and measures, and fire escapes; no more are they required to conduct elections or provide food for the needy; they are not expected now to regulate markets and manufacturing, ensure food supplies, or license newspapers; and they are no longer responsible for street cleaning, lighting, and paving. These

Box 6.3

The Growth in the Reach of Federal Law Enforcement

Years	Extended Reach
1789	Office of Attorney General of the United States created, with United States Attorneys for each federal judicial district.
1789	The Revenue Cutter Service, the first federal police agency, established to deal with smuggling.
1868	Federal detective force of 25 authorized by Congress.
1870	Department of Justice established.
1872	Mail fraud statute enacted—first federal criminal statute used extensively.
1910	White-Slave Traffic (Mann) Act prohibited interstate transport of females for immoral purposes.
1914	Harrison Act imposed tax on those who deal in narcotic drugs.
1919	Dyer Act prohibited interstate transport of stolen vehicles.
1919	Criminal Division established in the Department of Justice.
1932	Fugitive Felon Act made flight from a state to avoid justice a crime.
1932	Kidnapping Act made kidnapping a federal crime.
1934	Anti-Racketeering Act made racketeering a federal crime.
1934	Bank Robbery Act added to the list of 13 major criminal statutes and to Title 18 of the United States code between 1932 and 1935.
1935	Federal Bureau of Investigation established. ☞

☞ Years	Extended Reach
1950s–1960s	Federal laws greatly expanded, covering: gambling (1953), embezzlement of labor union funds (1959), employee benefit plans (1962), gun control, illegal manufacture and distribution of explosives, traveling across state lines to incite a riot (1968), civil rights (1969) consumer protection, occupational safety, traffic in contraband loan sharking, and organized crime. Increased efforts to prosecute organized crime and reduce political corruption and drug trafficking.
1970	Racketeer Influenced and Corrupt Organization (RICO) Act enacted, aimed at crime as a business, incorporating major categories of state crimes and most federal offenses. War declared on white-collar crime.
1971	The Travel Act prohibited interstate travel to promote violations concerning gambling, liquor, narcotics, prostitution, bribery, extortion, or arson.
1972	The Bureau of Alcohol, Tobacco, and Firearms, part of the Bureau of Internal Revenue of the Treasury Department, was upgraded to a separate bureau.
1973	The Bureau of Narcotics of the Treasury Department was renamed the Drug Enforcement Agency (DEA) and moved to the Department of Justice.
1978	Sexual exploitation of children prohibited.
1980s	Fighting violent crime and combating drug trafficking emphasized. Various crimes previously left to the states made federal crimes, in order to increase penalties.
1970s–1990s	Federal Laws continued to expand to cover more crimes previously left to the province of the States

functions now are performed by many different regulatory enforcement officers.

Many services remain, and more have been added. The police still must; search for lost children, settle arguments, direct traffic, enforce parking and traffic laws, investigate accidents, respond to alarms, try to find fugitives, serve warrants and subpoenas, make arrests, seize illegal weapons, contraband, and drugs, preserve evidence, protect witnesses, maintain vehicles, write reports, testify in court, process fingerprints, operate jails (most often sheriffs, sometimes municipal police) and lockups (often municipal police), provide court security (usually sheriffs), conduct laboratory tests, operate emergency telephone services, escort people to ensure their safety, run training programs, give directions, provide first aid, handle

Investigation remains as a central role of the police. This includes the collection and preservation of evidence that may be used later in court. What mistakes could this detective make in collecting this evidence? —Photo courtesy of www.photostogo.com.

demonstrations and control crowds, protect visiting dignitaries, make referrals to social service agencies, and fulfill many other duties. Now they also often operate programs for youth, fix computers and write programs for them, maintain statistical systems, organize neighborhood watch programs, testify before fiscal control agencies, conduct financial audits, conduct investigations of many other kinds, operate store front police offices, collaborate with other community agency personnel and citizen groups in solving problems of concern to the community, and appear on television.

In this context of multiple responsibilities and public expectations, two roles remain as key elements of the criminal justice system. These are the traditionally linked roles of investigation and patrol aimed at maintaining order. In addition to these two central roles, there is the service function.

The publicly funded police agencies that have developed from the American beginnings modeled after those of the London Metropolitan Police now number more than 17,000. Local police departments operated by municipal governments make up 72 percent of these agencies.[10]

Local police departments had an estimated 474,072 full-time employees in the year of the last Justice Department survey (1993). These included 373,554 sworn officers, among whom were 230,000 uniformed officers. There were about a quarter of a million sheriffs' deputies and 77,000 state police officers. These numbers do not include federal agents, or police in transit systems, public housing, state university systems, or other specialized police forces. They do not include part-time or civilian personnel. For 1995, the FBI reported that the police community, including city, county, and state police agencies, employed well over half a million officers and a quarter of a million civilians. The average rate per 1,000 inhabitants was 2.4 full-time officers. The rate is higher for large cities, lower for rural and suburban county law enforcement agencies.[11]

Over recent years, the percentages of females and minorities among police officers have gradually increased overall, although there still is much variability among jurisdictions. In 1993, women composed about 9 percent of full-time officers, although the figure for 1987 was 8 percent. Black officers accounted for 11 percent, compared with 9 percent in 1987. Hispanic officers were reported at 6 percent, an increase from 4 percent in 1987.

What do local police cost? Total operating expenditures for local police departments were reported in the 1993 survey as $24.3 billion. That is a large amount that seems even larger when written out: $24,300,000,000.00. We can more easily comprehend the average operating cost per sworn officer; it was $62,500. The cost per employee was $48,200.[12]

There are now more than 3,000 state and local law enforcement agencies. Of these, 854 have 100 or more officers. The data shown in Figure 6.1 are based on the 661 of these large agencies that responded to the Bureau of Justice Statistics survey. They show that most policing is done by municipal police or, in more rural areas, by sheriff's departments. (This excludes policing done by private security agencies.) There are various "special police," including transit police, park police, airport police, university and college campus police, and public housing police. Some of these are large departments—such as the New York–New Jersey Port Authority Police—but in total they make up only 4 percent of all law enforcement agencies.

Data from the same survey show that most policing is done by men (Figure 6.2) who are white (Figure 6.3) and who had some training (Figure 6.4). Trends are toward more female officers, more minority group mem-

**Figure 6.1 Types of State and Local Law Enforcement Agencies, 1993
(Agencies with 100 or more officers)**

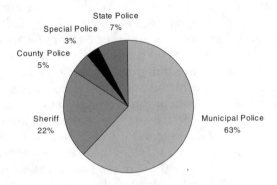

Source: data from Reaves, B. A., and Smith, P. Z. (1995). *Law Enforcement Management and
Administrative Statistics, 1993: Data for Individual State and Local Agencies with 100 or More
Officers,* Washington, D.C.: Bureau of Justice Statistics, *ix.*

**Figure 6.2 Percent of Men and Women in State and Local Law Enforcement
Agencies with 100 or More Officers, by Type of Agency, 1993**

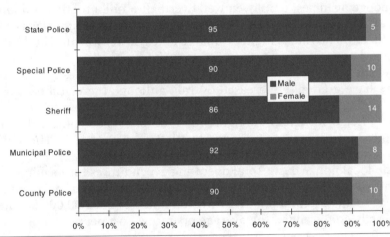

Source: data from Reaves, B. A., and Smith, P. Z. (1995). *Law Enforcement Management and
Administrative Statistics, 1993: Data for Individual State and Local Agencies with 100 or More
Officers*, Washington, D.C.: Bureau of Justice Statistics, *ix.*

bers, and more training, so more recent data, if available, might reflect those
trends. Most new officers had been hired after drug testing (about two-
thirds). Most had completed high school. About 80 percent of municipal
police agencies required it (12 percent required some college, 12 percent a
two-year college degree, and 1 percent a four-year degree). These data vary
rather markedly among agencies.

Municipal police patrol is generally by car (87 percent) but occasionally
by motorcycle (5 percent), on foot (5 percent), bicycle (2 percent), or horse
(1 percent). In that car there is a lone officer nine times out of ten.

Figure 6.3 Average Percent of Sworn Employees, by Race, State, and Local Law Enforcement Agencies with 100 or More Officers, by Type of Agency, 1993

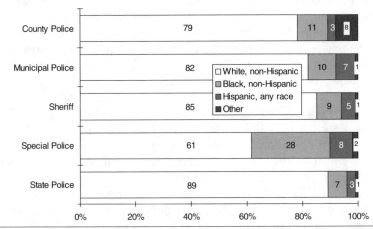

Source: data from Reaves, B. A., and Smith, P. Z. (1995). *Law Enforcement Management and Administrative Statistics, 1993: Data for Individual State and Local Agencies with 100 or More Officers*, Washington, D.C.: Bureau of Justice Statistics, *ix*.

Figure 6.4 Median Number of Training Hours Required for New Officers, State, and Local Law Enforcement Agencies with 100 or More Officers, by Type of Agency, 1993

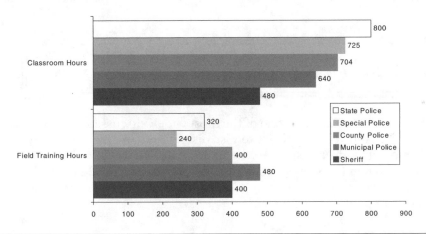

Source: data from Reaves, B. A., and Smith, P. Z. (1995). *Law Enforcement Management and Administrative Statistics, 1993: Data for Individual State and Local Agencies with 100 or More Officers*, Washington, D.C.: Bureau of Justice Statistics, *ix*.

Police and the Power of Arrest

Studies of calls to the police find that the vast majority of calls for assistance do not involve any crime.[13] The central feature of police work is dealing with a wide range of problems that have eluded alternative means of resolution.

In dealing with the interpersonal crises that result in police involvement, arrest is only one of many tools available for preserving order. It is the one that is least often used. Other police techniques that are used toward the goal of maintaining order include hospitalization, talk, traffic direction, physical presence, issuing an order to move on, and requesting that a radio be turned down. Each of these examples is aimed at restoring order.[14] Much evidence indicates that arrest is the tool of last resort.

Although the amount of time police spend in making arrests is small in relation to their other activities, the impact of these decisions affects the entire criminal justice system. The decision to make an arrest is a fundamental application of the power of the state, with extensive consequences for an accused person and for society as a whole. On whom, for what purposes, within what constraints this power is used are issues of much importance for the efficient, effective, and fair administration of justice. The next parts of this chapter focus on those critical decisions—decisions to make an arrest.

A scrutiny of the arrest decision allows us to examine the complexity of the police role and its ever controversial nature. Confronted daily by the conflicting demands of the community for safety and freedom, the police officer often must balance the decisions that must be made between community interest in vigorous crime control efforts and legal restraints on authority. Every decision is subject to criticism. Many may be physically dangerous for the officer. Failures to act by deciding to do nothing, as well as actions taken, may be subject to reprimand. But doing nothing may not be noticed and therefore may be neither punished nor rewarded. Laws may be unclear, resources may be limited. Literal enforcement of the law may be unnecessary or undesirable in terms of the problem solutions that are sought.

The police operate within the context of the familiar conflict that underlies the whole of the criminal justice system. We want the protection of the police, and we want minimal interference with our liberty. We require safety and demand freedom.

> *I'm not against the police; I'm just afraid of them.*
> *—Alfred Hitchcock*

The decision to arrest is one of the most widely discussed, argued about, and studied. And yet the police exercise discretion in many ways other than in deciding, in a given instance, whether to make an arrest. Whether to use force, how much to use, where and how to patrol, when and how to search, and whether to enforce a law at all are examples of areas of considerable discretion in police decision making.

Police Decisions to Arrest

We have seen, in our discussion of victims' decisions, that the victim of a crime is the main initiator of the criminal justice process. The crimes that come to the attention of the police do so mainly as a result of the initiative of citizens, usually victims. The police, like all subsequent actors in the criminal justice process, are dependent upon earlier decisions that to a large extent dictate their work. In this case, it usually is a decision by a citizen to call the police.

It has not always been recognized that the police have the discretionary power to decide whether the law should be enforced. In the past, both police administrators and scholars asserted that the police are not empowered to decide whether to enforce the law, regardless of the circumstances. Rather, they thought, the full enforcement of the law is not only desirable but a legal requirement. The letter of the law was to be followed: if circumstances fit the letter of the law, then an arrest must be made.

When police decide *not* to invoke the criminal law by making an arrest, the event is one of low visibility.[15] The event usually is not known publicly. As a result, there is no review on a regular basis to ensure that the discretion is not abused. Therefore, some who have studied the police have argued that within the constraints of the law (including legal restrictions on searches and arrests, for example) the police are authorized and expected to enforce the law and have not been delegated discretion in doing so. Thus, they have argued that the police must enforce the law in every case.

It is, however, unwise to hold police officers to unwavering enforcement of the law: "It is unrealistic, given the complexity and variability of behavior that, in any circumstances, can be considered criminal. It is ill advised because individualized judgment, taking account of the immediate circumstances of the behavior in question, is a necessary component of just decision making."[16]

Is Police Discretion Necessary?

After a neighbor called the police to report a loud argument at the house next door, police arrived to see a woman slap a man who then hit her with his fist. Should the police make an arrest? Of whom? Of both the woman and the man? Should they talk to each separately? Together? Should they offer counseling or advice? Should they issue a warning and leave? Should they refer the couple to professional counseling? Should they refer one party to the spouse abuse center? Does it matter that perhaps children are present? What if the man and the woman make up on the spot and no one wishes to issue a complaint? What if both the man and woman join in a verbal attack on the officers? What if one of the parties is armed with a knife? With a pistol? Do these elements of the situation matter? What if one of the parties turns to physically attack the officers?

These may all be called "domestic disturbances," but that term includes a wide range of events that may be clearly different from one another. The circumstances surrounding the event, as well as available alternatives, may have a lot to do with whether an arrest would be appropriate. The discretion of the police officers involved is a central and important feature of arrest decisions. It has been recognized increasingly that this discretion is both necessary and desirable and that, moreover, it should be "openly acknowledged, structured, and controlled."[17]

The growing recognition that full enforcement of the law *in every instance* is unrealistic, and that police discretion is necessary, by 1967 had led a presidential crime commission to assert that

> the police should openly acknowledge that, quite properly they do not arrest all, or even most, offenders they know of. Among the factors accounting for this exercise of discretion are the volume of offenses and the limited resources of the police, the ambiguity of and the public desire for nonenforcement of many statutes and ordinances, the reluctance of victims to complain, and, most important, an entirely proper conviction by policemen that the invocation of criminal sanctions is too drastic a response to many offenses.[18]

This does not mean that a police officer should always be free to decide without constraints. The officer should obey the law and should follow the rules. Although rational decision making is desired, it is the *system* that we should seek to make more rational, including the law and police policies that govern officer behavior. When the law and rules allow it, the officer should try to make decisions most likely to achieve the intended goals. It does not mean, either, that it is not desirable to fully enforce the law in specified instances. But in order to examine the goals and alternatives of their decisions we must put aside the "false pretense of full enforcement"[19] and acknowledge that the police do not blindly enforce the letter of the law but exercise much discretion in their everyday decision making.

Goals and Alternatives of Arrest Decisions

We can see each of the major criminal justice system goals of deserved punishment, incapacitation of offenders, treatment, and general deterrence in the purposes of police officers in deciding whether to arrest. Officers may have the goal also of acting so that justice is seen to be done. Identifying the goals of the decisions is made even more complicated, however, by practicality concerns, personal objectives and efficiency requirements. Wilson described the often conflicting goals and the difficult balancing act of the police officer as follows:

> [The] actual decision whether and how to intervene involves such questions as these: Has anyone been hurt or deprived? Will anyone be hurt or deprived if I do nothing? Will an arrest improve the situation or only make matters worse? Is a complaint more likely if there is no arrest, or if there is an arrest? What does the sergeant expect of me? Am I getting near the end of my tour of duty? Will I have to go to court on my day off? Will the charge stand up or will it be withdrawn or dismissed by the prosecutor? Will my partner think that an arrest shows I can handle things or that I can't handle things?[20]

Ignoring the personal aims of the officer at the moment of a decision, consider it in terms of the larger criminal justice system goals. The goal that justice is seen to be done may be involved in many officer decisions. The crime control goals of deterrence, incapacitation, and treatment and also the aim of punishment clearly are involved in many arrest decisions. Is an arrest required to protect a victim right now? Is an arrest needed as a warning to the offender? As a warning to others? Will an arrest lead to required treatment by the court? Will an arrest just make matters worse? Does the offender deserve a night in jail?

Wilson pointed out also that another question the officer may have is: What will the suspect do if released? This raises issues of the prediction of future behavior and perhaps the aim of incapacitation to prevent future crimes. If the suspect is not taken into custody, perhaps he or she will continue to do harm. The officer must make a prediction and decide whether the offender should be locked up for the protection of others. Consider again the domestic dispute discussed previously. A typical question posed for the officers responding to calls such as this is whether an arrest is required to prevent future or further assaults by the offender.

Consider the goal of treatment or rehabilitation. What if the officer's observation at the scene suggests that, rather than arrest, family counseling might offer a better chance of preventing future violence? Or, would an arrest

How these officers perceive their job may reflect their views of the purposes of the whole criminal justice system. Should they always enforce the law?

make a treatment intervention more likely, if ordered by the court or if arranged as part of a plea bargain? Will a talk with the family members involved in the dispute be sufficient to prevent future occurrences of fighting?

The aim of general deterrence—sometimes called general prevention—is fairly considered by many to be the dominant purpose of the criminal law. It refers to the prevention of crime by means of sanctions applied to offenders: when the guilty are punished, others are warned. It is clearly a purpose behind many arrest decisions. Examples abound: the officer arrests a youth in an area where vandalism is widespread but counsels and releases another in an area where such behavior is uncommon; the police "crack down" on drunk drivers on a holiday weekend. When it comes to serious crimes of violence and theft, general deterrence may be one goal in most arrests.

Most discussion of arrest decisions focuses on purposes of crime control but punishment that is seen as deserved is surely important. It may be argued that punishment is not up to the police, and certainly it is not for the police to decide on the innocence or guilt of a suspect. Yet, it must be acknowledged that an arrest is, in itself, a negative sanction. It deprives a person of liberty and freedom. It is unpleasant. It carries the stigma that the person's behavior was seen by the police as violating the law.

Thus, a concern for the criminal justice system goal of deserved punishment is reflected in the commonly accepted view that persons who do not deserve it are not, or should not be, arrested. Those whose behavior does not justify the deprivation of liberty and initiation of the criminal justice process caused by an arrest should not be arrested. This concern is apparent in the legal standards that must be met before an arrest can be made. "Probable cause" justifies the arrest partly on the basis of the behavior of the suspect.

This goal is also apparent when an arrest is *not* made. The officer may decide that the consequences of an arrest are more severe than warranted by the behavior. A remorseful young offender, admitting to shoplifting a small item but with no prior involvement with the police and a "good attitude," may well appear to the officer as a case for which an arrest and possible prosecution would be too severe a penalty for the relatively minor misbehavior. An alternative of counseling on the spot, warning, or more severely a report to the parents may be selected as a sanction more appropriate to the seriousness of the harm done. The man and woman fighting in the domestic dispute discussed previously may both be seen as blameworthy, but both may be regarded as victims as well as offenders. Perhaps the officer believes that in this circumstance neither deserves arrest, the most severe sanction he or she legally can apply.

The decision not to arrest is one major alternative for the arrest decision, but this choice of police officer options is more complex than that. The decision not to arrest may in fact involve doing nothing; referral to a private third party (such as parents); referral to another public agency (such as a social service agency); warning; mediation; issuing a citation; or driving a drunk home. Each alternative may involve a complex set of goals.

Various reasons are offered for not arresting. Maybe the legislature does not desire full enforcement. Perhaps enforcement resources are limited. It might be explained that the victim refuses to prosecute or that the victim also is involved in the misconduct. At other times, it may be acknowledged that the intent is to benefit other aspects of law enforcement, such as protection of the informant system. It may be argued that the harm caused to the offender or to the victim would outweigh the risk of inaction. [21]

In many jurisdictions, a lack of alternatives means that the police often are faced with arresting or doing nothing. In many situations, doing nothing is an appropriate choice—it is the best thing to do in the circumstance. For other situations, however, an arrest may be made when there are no alternatives, even though the criminal justice system provides only an inappropriate, or at best awkward, means of possible problem solution. "But in the absence of alternatives it is used, and often perverted in its use, in order to get things done."[22] It may be that arrests are made partly to increase public perceptions that justice is being done.

The complexity of the police officer's decision about arrest is apparent as soon as the variety of goals and alternatives is understood. As a result, the demands of the job are realized more clearly.

Many other circumstances may influence an officer's decision whether to arrest. The decision clearly must involve some assessment of the strength of the evidence bearing on the guilt of a suspect, an appraisal that often must be made quickly. It may make a difference if observers are present, and it may make a difference who they are. How the incident began may influence the decision: officers may be more likely to make an arrest when they themselves have brought about the circumstances, as in a drug raid.

Police Discretion and Arrest Decisions

Studies confirm that much discretion is indeed involved in arrest decisions. When the alleged offense is serious, not much discretion is found and may not be permitted. For more minor offenses, characteristics of the alleged offender, such as prior record and behavior, are influential. The legal seriousness of the alleged offense is strongly associated with the decision to arrest.[23] For less serious cases, however, the evidence indicates that the complainant's or victim's preference about arrest, the presence of evidence linking the suspect to the crime, and the suspect's degree of respect for the officer

are influential, at least with juvenile suspects. Black and Reiss found that
the very respectful and the very unrespectful were more likely to be arrested.
Within types of crimes, African American youths were more likely to be
arrested than were white youths. This was attributed not to prejudicial discrimination by the police but to differences in arrest preferences by complainants. Black and Reiss commented:

> In not one instance did the police arrest a juvenile when the complainant
> lobbied for leniency. When the complainant explicitly expresses a preference
> for an arrest, however, the tendency of the police to comply is also quite
> strong.[24]

Similar evidence about arrest decisions comes from an observational
study by Black of police encounters with adults. Again, the legal seriousness
of the alleged offense was found to be an important factor. The preference of
the complainant was again found to be related to the arrest decision. For
felonies, when police involvement was initiated by citizens, only 10 percent
resulted in an arrest when the complainant preferred no arrest, but 74 percent
resulted in arrests when that was preferred. Arrests were less likely when the
victim and suspect were known to one another than when they were strangers.[25] Other analyses have had similar results.[26] Arrests are more likely when
suspects are argumentative or when a victim wants a suspect arrested.

Some other factors are associated with arrests. If a police supervisor is
present or if the offense is a violent or property offense, arrest is more likely.
In cases of domestic assault, arrests are more often made when a woman
signs a complaint, both parties were present when the police arrived, the
man was drinking, or the man appeared disrespectful.[27] Similarly, in a study
of the likelihood of arrest in forcible sex offenses, the conclusion was that
"the two best predictors of arrest were legal variables: the victim's ability to
identify a suspect and her willingness to prosecute."[28]

The Police Filter

After victims, the police act as the next filter for screening out minor
offenders who will not, for one reason or another, be subject to full processing by the criminal justice system. The more serious the harm done by the
alleged offense, the more likely it is that a suspect will be arrested. As we
have seen previously, this factor also predicts victims' decisions whether to
report a crime to the police. Thus, these are two important filters for the
selection of offenders for processing in the criminal justice system: the more
serious the crime, the more likely it is that it will be reported. And, the more
serious the crime, the more likely it is that an arrest will be made.

We will later see that a similar screening by the factor of crime seriousness operates at each of the subsequent decision points in the criminal justice system. A similar filtering goes on at prosecution, sentencing, and
paroling. Over and over again, the seriousness of the crime is a dominant
influence on the decision.

The preference of the complainant or victim may be based largely on
the requirements of subsequent processing through the prosecutor's office
and at trial. Police know that the successful prosecution of an accused person requires the active participation of the complaining witness. When the
complainant prefers to drop the matter, ordinarily little is to be gained from
an arrest.

How the suspect behaves at the time of the first encounter may be important when the alleged offense is minor. For major crimes, there will be an arrest in any case, because the crime is serious. For less serious events, however, showing disrespect may tip the balance:[29]

> These studies confirm common sense. They indicate that if you are appre-hended committing a minor offense, being respectful to the police officer may get you off. If, on the other hand, you are apprehended for a minor violation and you talk tough to the "cop," the encounter will probably escalate into arrest. . . . if you are caught in a more serious crime—if, for example, you are found robbing a bank—being respectful to the police is not likely to keep you from being arrested.[30]

All arrests have in common that a suspect is taken into custody, but not every arrest is made with the aim of further processing by the criminal justice system in mind. Rather, the arrest may serve other purposes—such as an immediate objective of incapacitation in a domestic assault when the police believe that the violence will continue if the suspect is not restrained. The police may believe that the case will be dropped and the offender released, but arrest will solve the immediate problem. Thus, some suspects may pass through the arrest filter even though the officer knows that the arrest very likely will be the *only* sanction applied.

The legal standard for arrests—"probable cause" or "reasonable grounds to believe"—provides no guidance about the need for custody itself. Apart from initiating the criminal justice process, taking the suspect into custody may serve numerous other objectives. The issues here, as with arrest, are important for the perceptions of the public that justice is being done.

The aims of taking a person into custody may reflect functions that are: preventive, demonstrative, administrative, or social-medical:[31]

- *Preventive functions* may be involved when the objective is to make sure that the suspect will be available for later proceedings, and that he or she will not be able to commit further crimes. Or, prevention is the aim when an arrest is made for the specific purpose of stopping an ongoing victimization.

- *Demonstrative functions* are those aimed at specific deterrence—to impress the person arrested with the seriousness of the behavior and to warn that person of consequences if it continues.

- *Administrative and investigative functions* of taking a suspect into custody may involve a need to gather evidence, search, or conduct lineups.

- *Socio-medical functions* refer to the taking of a suspect into custody in order to provide treatment services or medical attention.

When an arrest is made in part to constrain the suspect by taking that person into custody, the officer makes predictions concerning the likely behavior of the alleged offender, or the expected outcomes of criminal justice processing. Little is known about the information used by officers in making such assessments, or about its validity. Such judgments typically are highly subjective and often are made with little policy guidance.

Some evidence about how these decisions are made comes from an observational study of arrest decisions by LaFave. Several criteria seemed to be prominent in the officer's determination of the need for custody. The seriousness of the offense again appeared to be influential. Those offenders facing more severe punishments were thought more likely to flee. The nature of the offense was another factor: numbers writers were thought to be good risks, for example. Residence in the community, prior criminal history, and the likelihood of conviction also seemed to be related to the officers' assessments of the need for custody.[32]

Police Diversion

Many programs have been developed with the aim of diverting the suspected offender from the criminal justice system by alternatives to arrest. Because arrests initiate the criminal justice process, various ways have been sought to handle a variety of problems without using arrest.

The goals of such programs are diverse. Some are aimed at crime reduction, based on the belief that processing through the system encourages crime. The familiar expression "schools for crime" reflects in part a common but mostly discredited belief that, rather than reducing repeated offending, the system increases it by undesirable labeling, making it impossible for people to avoid lives of crime by classifying them as "criminals." Many juvenile diversion programs have such a rationale. Other programs have been based on the concept that processing through the criminal justice system is simply an inappropriate response to many behaviors that bring the person into conflict with the law.

Medical, social welfare, family, or educational responses are more suited to dealing with many of the behaviors that might result in arrest. Many community treatment diversion programs aimed at alcoholic or other drug-dependent persons are based on this belief. A desire to reduce costs of traditional criminal justice system processing has led to the development of still other programs. It is argued that many diversion programs serve to economize resources if minor cases are not processed through the system, and more serious cases may then be dealt with more efficiently. Many police diversion programs involve a mixture of these purposes and conjectures, or guesses.

The word "conjecture" must be used here, because most of these programs have not set out their objectives clearly, have not measured the degree to which they have been attained by the program, or have used weak and inconclusive research methods for an intended evaluation. There is some evidence that many diversion programs, which have been developed more often for youthful offenders, become, in practice, extensions of the criminal justice system rather than an alternative to arrest, a phenomenon that has become known as "net widening" of the criminal justice system. Klein found, for example, that youths who would not normally be arrested (younger, minor offenders, and those without prior records) were the persons most likely to be selected for diversion:

> While there is clearly a desire in some police departments to divert juveniles from the system, the more common feeling is that referral should be used as an alternative to simple release. In short, the meaning of diversion has shifted from "diversion from" to "referral to." Ironically, one of the ramifications of this is that in contrast to such earlier cited rationales for diversion as reducing costs, caseload, and the purview of the justice system, diversion may in fact be extending the costs, caseload and system purview even further than had previously been the case.[33]

Experimental Study of Arrests

The lack of sound evaluations of police diversion programs to provide solid information about their degree of success or failure is a major problem, because such information is needed for improved police policy development. A study done by Sherman and Berk [34] of the relative effects of arrest and alternatives to it is an exception for its results and for its success as a well-designed experiment in the criminal justice system process. It is the first scientifically controlled test of the effects of arrest, and it received much attention from the law enforcement community (See Box 6.4 for comments by a leading police administrator). [35]

Box 6.4

Patrick Murphy: In His Own Words

No call for service is more familiar, challenging, and personally disheartening to a police officer than the summons to a domestic assault. Once again, two people living together are engaged in physical violence; once again, there are bruises, blood, and, perhaps, broken bones; once again, there has been an assault, and the officer fears that worse might occur. Often, terrified children witness the battle and pick up an early lesson that violence is somehow an appropriate way of dealing with problems and frustrations.

What does the officer do?

The common police tradition has been to do little. The battered partner in the typical domestic fight was unlikely to sign a complaint, the officer learned

from experience. So the officer restores a semblance of order, warns the assailant to behave, perhaps sends him out of the home, and goes on to the next call.

But on what could police rely if they sought to change their response to domestic violence? Hunch, supposition, tradition had been their guides and they seemed sufficient.

[T]he Police Foundation, through scientific inquiry, sought to supplant tradition with fact in resolving the question: How can the police deter future domestic violence? . . . the Minneapolis experiment makes substantial progress in suggesting how police can deter such violence.

—Patrick V. Murphy, former Police Commissioner, City of New York

---

With the cooperation of the Minneapolis police, three alternatives were used at random to deal with domestic assault cases. As used here, "at random" does not mean "haphazardly." It means that each member of a whole group of cases had an equal chance of being selected for the experimental treatment or condition—in this case, arrest—and that the absence of any case being included did not depend on the chance of any other. The alternatives available to the police were arrest, "advice," and "order to leave." The actions of the officers were determined by a lottery, seeking to ensure that there would be no differences among the three groups of suspects receiving the different police responses.

The researchers concluded that arrest was the most effective for reducing the numbers of repeated incidents of domestic violence. Sherman and Berk were suitably cautious in their interpretations, pointing out that the results should not be generalized to other jurisdictions or crimes. They urged that replications of the experiment be done in other jurisdictions. This means repeating the experiment in order to see whether the results would be the same. (This proved to be an important warning.) They pointed out, however, that they did present evidence that swift arrest and confinement may deter male offenders in domestic assault cases. The strength of this evidence came from the random nature of the assignments to the arrest, advice, and order to leave conditions.

Two measures of repeat violence in the six months after the incident were used. Police records were examined, and interviews were conducted with victims, who were asked whether there had been another incident with the same suspect. Some results of the experiment are shown in Figures 6.5 and 6.6. (The data shown are approximations and reflect statistical corrections for some problems such as a drop in victim cooperation for the interviews.) The results taken from police records of repeat violence are shown in Figure 6.5. When the suspect was sent away, there were two and a half times as many incidents of repeat violence as there were when the suspect was arrested. The "advise" condition was not distinguishable statistically from the other two actions. When the interview reports were examined, arrest still was found to be the most effective police action, as shown in Figure 6.6. The "advise" condition produced the worst results. Sending the suspect away gave results that could not be distinguished statistically from the other actions. Although the pictures in the two figures are somewhat different, arrest was found to work best in terms of repeat violence, whether measured by the police records or the interview reports.

For jurisdictions similar in their processing of domestic assault suspects, the authors of this study favored arrest but did not favor *requiring* it in all cases. They noted that arrest may work better for some kinds of offenders than others, and commented, "Equally important, it is widely recognized that discretion is inherent in police work. Simply to impose a requirement of arrest, irrespective of the features of the immediate situation, is to invite circumvention."[36]

The results of the Minneapolis study were highly publicized and prompted efforts to use arrest more often in domestic violence cases. The warning by the authors of the study, however, of the need for replication, or duplication of the experiment elsewhere, in other jurisdictions, proved to be wise. We should be careful in generalizing the results found in one study or jurisdiction to others. When this experiment was indeed repeated in other places, it was found that,

Figure 6.5 Percentage of Repeat Violence Over Six Months for Each Police Action (measured by official records)

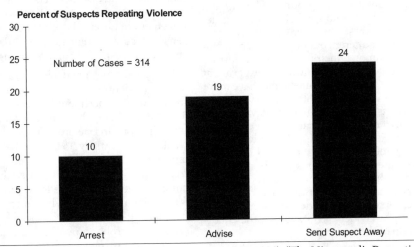

Source: adapted from Sherman, L. W., and Berk, R. A. (circa 1984). "The Minneapolis Domestic Violence Experiment," *Police Foundation Reports*. Washington, D.C.: The Police Foundation, 1.

Figure: 6.6 Percentage of Repeat Violence Over Six Months for Each Police Action (measured by victim interviews)

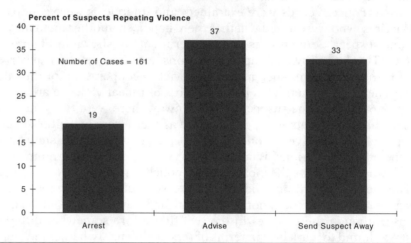

Source: adapted from Sherman, L. W., and Berk, R. A. (circa 1984). "The Minneapolis Domestic Violence Experiment," *Police Foundation Reports* Washington, D.C.: The Police Foundation, 6.

"Taken together with the Minneapolis results, three experiments now show evidence of a deterrent effect of arrest, while three others show evidence of a criminogenic [crime encouraging] effect." [37] Exact replication in field experiments of this sort is extremely difficult, and there were some differences at each site. See Box 6.5 for a summary and comments by one of the authors of the

---

Box 6.5

Lawrence Sherman: In His Own Words

Further analyses [of the arrest experiments] shed light on the different results. While there were no consistent differences *between* the two groups of experiments, there were consistent differences *within* at least four of them. In Milwaukee, Omaha, Dade County (Florida) and Colorado Springs, albeit to varying degrees, arrest consistently deterred employed batterers but increased repeat violence among unemployed men. A further reanalysis of the Milwaukee experiment suggests that this pattern may have more to do with the neighborhoods where the arrests are made than with individual employment status. That is, even employed people in neighborhoods of high unemployment tend to be deterred by arrest. Whatever the reasons for these results, they show that more arrests are no simple guarantee of less crime, as arrest advocates suggest. The effect of the arrest rate "pill" may depend heavily on the condition of the "patients."

Despite these findings about *domestic* crime, increasing the arrest rate may still be an effective strategy for preventing crimes against *strangers*. Arrest for minor public infractions by pedestrians and motorists, for example, shows a clear connection to robbery: the more police enforce traffic and disorderly conduct laws, the less robbery there is. High rates of enforcement in public places may convey a sense of control that generally deters street crime, especially among strangers.

This benefit may not depend on arrests as much as it does on intensive police patrol. A field experiment in San Diego found that when police cut back on field interrogations in one area, street crimes went up substantially. To be sure, field interrogations can easily become "provocative policing," and several blue ribbon commissions have blamed the practice for starting riots. A polite but formal police manner, however, may reduce the side effects of this robbery prevention strategy.

—Lawrence W. Sherman,
University of Maryland

Minneapolis study.[38]

The study demonstrated that arrest itself may act as a sanction, with important consequences for crime control. This raises questions also of the constraints on the arrest decision, the topic next to be considered. The controversies surrounding arrest provide another illustration of the pervasive conflict between our desires for both safety (including the control of crime) and freedom (including safety from unwarranted arrest).

Standards for Arrest

The Common Law Standard

The common law traditionally placed constraints on the police in making arrests without warrants, without an order of a court directing the police to make the arrest. The police could arrest without a warrant only if (1) the person committed a felony or misdemeanor in the presence of a police officer or (2) they had knowledge that a felony had been committed and had probable cause to believe that the person arrested committed it.

The Probable Cause Standard

An arrest means that a person has been deprived of liberty by a legal authority. It is a seizure of the person and therefore is subject to the Fourth Amendment and ordinarily requires probable cause. Probable cause means that a legal authority, usually a police officer, has made two decisions: that a crime has been committed and that the suspect probably is the person who did it. The U.S. Supreme Court has made it clear that the probable cause standard depends on "whether at that moment the facts and circumstances within [the officers'] knowledge and of which they [have] reasonably trust-

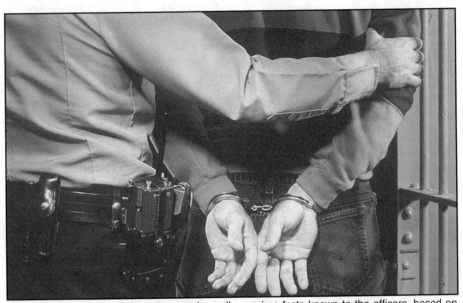

An arrest is a seizure of the person and usually requires facts known to the officers, based on reasonably trustworthy information, that are enough to enable a prudent person to believe the suspect has committed or was committing an offense. Should this standard be required in every case? —Photo courtesy of www.photostogo.com.

worthy information [are] sufficient to warrant a prudent man in believing that the [suspect] had committed or was committing an offense."[39] The Court has made it clear, further, that the Fourth Amendment protection is also required of the states.[40]

Exceptions to the Standard

The Supreme Court also has indicated, however, that there are exceptions to this otherwise minimal requirement for an arrest; not every arrest must be justified by probable cause. In *Terry v. Ohio*[41] (Box 6.6), the Court for the first time recognized an exception to the rule of the Fourth Amendment that probable cause was required for seizures of the person. In the *Terry* case, the suspects clearly were not free to leave. Probable cause for arrest clearly was absent. Notwithstanding, the Court said that the Fourth Amendment permits some stopping that is not an arrest. An officer may, on the basis of a *reasonable suspicion*, stop a person briefly to determine that person's identity or to conduct a "pat-down," "a carefully limited search of the outer clothing in an attempt to discover weapons which might be used to assault him."

Box 6.6

Terry v. Ohio

Detective Martin McFadden, in his 39th year as a policeman, had patrolled a downtown Cleveland neighborhood for shoplifters and pickpockets for three decades. Two men, Chilton and Terry, "didn't look right" to him. He later testified to watching their "elaborately casual and oft-repeated reconnaissance of a store window," his suspicion that they were "casing a job," and that he feared "they may have a gun." When the two men were joined by a third, the detective approached them, identified himself as a police officer, and asked their names. Receiving mumbles in reply, he grabbed Terry and patted down the outside of his clothing. He felt a pistol in Terry's overcoat pocket but was unable to remove it. He ordered all three men into a store, removed Terry's overcoat and its .38 caliber revolver and ordered all three men to face a wall. Patting down the other two men, he retrieved another revolver. He called for a wagon and took all three men to the station. Chilton and Terry were charged with carrying concealed weapons, and the court denied their motion to suppress. They were found guilty, the Court of Appeals confirmed the conviction, and the Supreme Court of Ohio dismissed their appeal. The Supreme Court of the United States considered whether the admission of the revolvers in evidence violated the defendants' rights under the Fourth Amendment, made applicable to the States by the Fourteenth (*Mapp v. Ohio*). The conviction was affirmed, the Court stating that "... where a police officer observes unusual conduct which leads him reasonably to conclude in light of his experience that criminal activity may be afoot and that the persons with whom he is dealing may be armed and presently dangerous, where in the course of investigating this behavior he identifies himself as a policeman and makes reasonable inquiries, and where nothing in the initial stages of the encounter serves to dispel his reasonable fear for his own or others' safety, he is entitled for the protection of himself and others in the area to conduct a carefully limited search of the outer clothing of such persons in an attempt to discover weapons which might be used to assault him. Such a search is a reasonable search under the Fourth Amendment, and any weapons seized may properly be introduced in evidence against the person from whom they were taken."

—392 U.S. 1 (1968)

In a later case, *Michigan v. Summers,* the Supreme Court, while reaffirming the probable cause standard for an arrest, noted, "Some seizures admittedly covered by the Fourth Amendment constitute such limited intrusions on the personal security of those detained and are justified by such substantial law enforcement interests that they may be made on less than probable cause, so long as the police have an articulable basis for suspecting criminal activity."[42] An "articulable basis" means that the police can explain the reason for their suspicions. A vague impression, unexplainable hunch, or "gut feeling" does not qualify. In this case, the police had a valid warrant for searching the suspect's house for narcotics, and they detained him while searching it. The Court noted a legitimate law enforcement interest in preventing flight and in minimizing potential harm to the police, and observed also that an orderly search might be facilitated if the occupants are present. Moreover, they noted that "a judicial officer has determined that police have a probable cause to believe that someone in the home is committing a crime."

The police may detain on reasonable suspicion for an investigation on the street, and they perhaps may detain a suspect briefly to obtain fingerprints.[43] "Reasonable suspicion" may be interpreted in terms of the "whole picture" as it would be viewed by trained law enforcement personnel.[44] They may detain an occupant while executing a valid search warrant.

Probable cause is needed for other detentions, including a trip to the station house for interrogation.[45] About compelling a suspect to be questioned at the station, the Court stated, "Detention for custodial interrogation—regardless of its label—intrudes so severely on interests protected by the Fourth Amendment as necessarily to trigger the traditional safeguards against illegal arrest."

Most arrests are made without a warrant. The Supreme Court has held that the police may make arrests in public places without a warrant, even without an emergency.[46] But, if there is no emergency, the police may not, without a warrant, arrest a suspect at home.[47] There may be exceptions even here if justified by an urgent necessity, such as a fire. A warrantless arrest in the home might be justified in cases of (1) a grave offense, (2) a reasonable belief that the suspect is armed, (3) a high degree of probable cause, (4) an especially strong reason to believe that the suspect is on the premises, (5) a likelihood that the suspect will escape if not apprehended quickly, and (6) a situation where the entry may be made peaceably.[48]

The common law entitled officers to break into a house to make an arrest only after identifying themselves and announcing their purpose. Now, the governing standards generally are set by statutes. Typically, an officer is allowed to break open a window or door if refused admittance, but only after announcing his or her authority and purpose.

> The police must obey the law while enforcing the law.
> —Chief Justice Earl Warren

Constraints on Searches

Just as there are legal requirements that restrict the decision to make an arrest, the law constrains the police decision to make a search. The main source is again the Fourth Amendment, as applied to the states through the due process clause of the Fourteenth Amendment. Others are state and federal statutes and municipal ordinances.

A guiding principle is that the police are required to obtain a warrant, issued by a magistrate upon demonstration of probable cause, except when it is not practical to do so. There are five main categories of circumstances in which a warrant is not required.[49] These are (1) a felony arrest; (2) a search incident to taking a suspect into custody; (3) a search of a car or other vehicle incident to a valid arrest made with probable cause; (4) the seizure of objects in "plain view" of an officer; (5) and entries of premises in order to make an arrest while in "hot pursuit." Warrants are not required, either, for searches at borders, by customs agents or immigration officials, when the party subject to the search provides "voluntary and intelligent consent," or in certain emergency situations.

After making an arrest, officers may search the person arrested, or the area under that person's immediate control. This can be justified by the need to protect the safety of the officer or to preserve evidence.

Seventy-five years ago, during prohibition, federal agents stopped a car that they had probable cause to believe contained liquor and searched it without a warrant. The Supreme Court held that no warrant was needed for the stop and search of an automobile upon probable cause, since the car could be long gone before a warrant could be obtained.[50] Later, the Court made it clear that a permitted search incident to an arrest extends to the entire car. Probable cause is required for the arrest and therefore for the search.

Police officers may seize items on probable cause when they are discovered in the ordinary and proper course of their work. At one time, only the "fruits and instrumentalities" of crime and contraband were permitted to be taken even if other incriminating items were found in plain view of an officer lawfully present. The seizure of items only for potential use by the government as evidence was prohibited. This rule was overturned by the Supreme Court, so now a police officer must decide whether an item is of sufficient value as evidence that its seizure is justified.

The police are not required to have a warrant to arrest a felon on probable cause in a public place.[51] And, when they are in hot pursuit of a person whom they have probable cause to arrest, they may enter the premises to which that person flees.[52] They may, if they have an arrest warrant, enter the suspect's premises to make an arrest upon probable cause to believe he is there.[53]

Box 6.7

A Warrant Is Not Required for

- A search in a felony arrest.

- A search in taking a suspect into custody.

- A search of a car or other vehicle, incident to a valid search.

- A seizure of objects "in plain view."

- Entry into a premise while in "hot pursuit."

- Some emergency situations, border searches, and searches with consent.

> *Those who would give up essential Liberty, to purchase a little temporary Safety, deserve neither Liberty or Safety.*
> —*Benjamin Franklin*

Over time, the laws governing searches and seizures have increasingly recognized privacy, as well as trespass, to be protected by the Fourth Amendment. In a famous case concerning the expectation of privacy, FBI agents had placed a bug (an electronic listening and recording device) outside a phone booth where Katz was expected to make calls from Los Angeles to Miami and Boston to do his bookmaking business. There was no physical trespass by the FBI agents, but the Court held that it was a Fourth Amendment intrusion requiring probable cause and a search warrant issued by a judicial officer was required. Although the petitioner to the Court had asked whether the booth was a "constitutionally protected area," the Court said that was the wrong question, adding ". . . the Fourth Amendment protects people, not places" and ". . . What a person knowingly exposes to the public, even in his own home or office, is not a subject of Fourth Amendment protection. . . . But what he seeks to preserve as private, even in an area accessible to the public, may be constitutionally protected." Justice Stewart, writing for the majority, went on to indicate that the requirement of ". . . advance authorization by a magistrate upon a showing of probable cause . . ." (that is, a warrant) does not vanish when the search is moved from a home to a telephone booth. He said, "Wherever a man may be, he is entitled to know that he will remain free from unreasonable searches and seizures." In a concurring opinion, Justice Harlan referred to a twofold requirement: first, that an actual, or subjective, expectation of privacy is exhibited, and, second, that the expectation is one that society is prepared to recognize as "reasonable."[54]

This case generated many other cases involving questions of the meaning of a "reasonable expectation of privacy," whether or not technology is involved. These questions may embrace such diverse issues as the use of binoculars, or night vision glasses, or parabolic microphones to pick up sounds at a great distance, or dogs trained to sniff out drugs, or "beepers" permitting trailing a car from a distance, or going through trash left at curbside, or transactions using passwords on the internet. Every case reflects the pervasive conflict between concerns for public safety and for liberty, including privacy.

The Exclusionary Rule

The legal requirements constraining searches are enforced by the "exclusionary rule," which refers to the exclusion of evidence from a criminal proceeding when it has been obtained improperly. The purpose, repeatedly made clear by the Supreme Court, is to control police behavior by deterring the police from acting illegally and to keep judges from allowing it. Evidence obtained by unlawful activity by law enforcement officers or their agents may be excluded from admission at a criminal trial. The rule is most often used to prevent violations of an individual's freedom ensured by the Fourth Amendment restriction on "unreasonable searches and seizures" and Fifth

Amendment restrictions on police interrogations. As a result of rulings by the Supreme Court, an arrested person cannot permissibly be questioned before being given the "Miranda warnings," that summarize some applicable rights of a suspect.

The exclusionary rule was established by the Supreme Court in *Weeks v. United States.* Police officers had searched Weeks's room and taken some papers and other possessions in order to use them later in a criminal trial against him. In violation of the Constitution, they had no search warrant or other legal justification. The Supreme Court ruled that the evidence seized should be excluded at trial, stating

> The tendency of those who execute the criminal laws of the country to obtain conviction by means of unlawful seizures and enforced confessions, the latter often obtained after subjecting accused persons to unwarranted practices destructive of rights secured by the Federal Constitution, should find no sanc-tion in the judgments of the courts which are charged at all times with the support of the Constitution and to which people of all conditions have a right to appeal for the maintenance of such fundamental rights. [55]

In 1914, the year of the *Weeks* decision, the exclusion of illegally obtained evidence applied only to the federal courts. Federal law enforcement officers could get around the rule by obtaining evidence in violation of the Constitution, then turning it over to a state prosecutor, as commonly was said, "on a silver platter," in states where there was no similar exclusionary rule. Prosecution in the state court then could proceed in utter disregard of the unconstitutionality of the seizure of the evidence by the federal agents. Not until 1960 was this practice held to be unconstitutional.[56] The next year, however, the misconduct of three Cleveland police officers led the Supreme Court to declare in *Mapp v. Ohio* that the exclusionary rule applies to proceedings in the state courts (see Box 6.8).

Box 6.8

Mapp v. Ohio

Mrs. Mapp's conviction of possessing pornographic materials was based on items "unlawfully seized during an unlawful search" of her home. Police had been searching for another person, for questioning about a bombing. Denied entrance without a warrant, the officers later broke in the back door and waved a paper claimed to be a warrant (although it apparently was not). Mrs. Mapp grabbed the "warrant" and placed it in her bosom. They struggled, the police came up with the paper, handcuffed Mrs. Mapp, and after more rough treatment proceeded to search the entire house. The obscene materials were found in a basement trunk. The State Supreme Court decided that the admission of evidence obtained by an unreasonable search and seizure was not forbidden and found the conviction to be valid. On appeal, the Supreme Court of the United States held that "the exclu-sionary rule is an essential part of the Fourth and Fourteenth Amendments." The Court said, "The ignoble shortcut to conviction [otherwise] left open to the States tends to destroy the entire system of constitutional restraints on which the liberties of the people rest." Reversing the Ohio judgment, the Court stated "Our decision . . . gives to the individual no more than that which the Constitution guarantees him, to the police officer no less than that to which honest law enforcement is entitled, and, to the courts, that judicial integrity so necessary in the true administration of justice." The Court concluded ". . . all evidence obtained by searches and seizures in violation of the Constitution is, by that same authority, inadmissible in a state court."

—367 U.S. 643 (1961)

Justice Tom Clark explained the Court's imposition of the exclusionary rule in this way:

> Since the Fourth Amendment's right of privacy has been declared enforceable against the States through the Due Process Clause of the Fourteenth, it is enforceable against them by the same sanction of exclusion as is used against the Federal Government. Were it otherwise, then just as without the *Weeks* rule the assurance against unreasonable federal searches and seizures would be a 'form of words,' valueless and undeserving of mention in a perpetual charter of inestimable human liberties, so too, without that rule the freedom from state invasions of privacy would be so ephemeral and so neatly severed from its conceptual nexus with the freedom from all brutish means of coerc - ing evidence as not to merit this Court's high regard as a freedom implicit in the concept of ordered liberty.[57]

He added that because the right to privacy embodied in the Fourth Amendment is of constitutional origin, ". . . we can no longer permit it to remain an empty promise, . . . revocable at the whim of any police officer who, in the name of law enforcement itself, chooses to suspend its enjoyment."

If the actions of a police officer or other agent of government are unconstitutional when evidence is seized, then evidence that is derived *indirectly* from the act, called "fruit of the poisonous tree," also is inadmissible in the prosecutor's case for guilt in criminal proceedings. For example:

> [I]f the police search someone's home illegally and seize his diary, thereby obtaining information that leads them to search someone else's home to look for evidence, whatever evidence they find at the second home is 'derivative' of the initial misconduct and is therefore, in Justice Felix Frankfurter's colorful phrase, 'fruit of the poisonous tree.' Such 'fruits' are inadmissible under the exclusionary rule, at least in a criminal trial against a defendant such as the diarist. . . .[58]

Evidence that has been obtained illegally, including both statements and physical evidence, that has been suppressed for the prosecutor's "case in chief" (the prosecutor's attempted direct proof of the defendant's guilt), may nevertheless become admissible at the same trial strictly for a purpose of impeachment. "Impeachment" means to challenge the truthfulness of a witness by offering evidence that shows he or she cannot be believed.

An exception to the exclusionary rule is called the "good faith exception." If there is a total absence of any intention to seek an unfair advantage and an honest and sincere intention to fulfill obligations, this is called "good faith."

Fifth, Fourteenth, and Sixth Amendment Rights

A few years after the *Mapp* decision, the Supreme Court in *Miranda v. Arizona* applied the exclusionary rule to statements made by a person interrogated by police while in custody without first having been warned about applicable constitutional rights (Box 6.9).[59] The Court, in the language quoted in the box, required specific warnings of the right to remain silent, of the possibility that statements made may be used against the suspect in a trial, and that the suspect has the right to the presence of an attorney. They said that the suspect could waive these rights, but that this must be made "voluntarily, knowingly, and intelligently." Moreover, they required that if the suspect indicates that an attorney is wanted before speaking, then all

Box 6.9

Miranda v. Arizona

"When an individual is taken into custody or otherwise deprived of his freedom by the authorities in any significant way and is subjected to questioning, the privilege against self-incrimination is jeopardized. Procedural safeguards must be employed to protect the privilege, and unless other fully effective means are adopted to notify the person of his right of silence and to assure that the exercise of this right will be scrupulously honored, the following measures are required."

"Prior to any questioning, the person must be warned that he has a right to remain silent, that any statements he does make may be used as evidence against him, and that he has a right to the presence of an attorney, either retained or appointed. The defendant may waive effectuation of these rights, provided the waiver is made voluntarily, knowingly and intelligently. If, however, he indicates in any manner and at any stage in the process that he wishes to consult with an attorney before speaking there can be no questioning. Likewise, if the individual is alone and indicates in any manner that he does not wish to be interrogated, the police may not question him."

—384 U.S. 436 (1966)

questioning must stop. In fact, they required that questioning a defendant who is alone stop if the suspect indicates in any way a desire not to be questioned. The *"Miranda* warning" now is well known to anyone who watches television, and Ernesto Miranda has the distinction of having had his name made into a commonly recognized legal procedure. When Miranda was killed in a bar fight 10 years after the Supreme Court decision, his suspected killer was "Mirandized."

The *Miranda* warnings must be given whenever two conditions are present: *custody* and *interrogation*. The suspect who has been arrested or who is significantly deprived of freedom has been taken into custody. There may be exceptions, such as when a requirement of public safety prohibits or delays the warning or the statement is voluntary as in the case cited in Box 6.10.[60] In general, the *Miranda* rights must be recited to the suspect in order that evidence not be excluded from the "case in chief" of the prosecutor at trial.

Box 6.10

Illinois v. Perkins

"An undercover government agent was placed in the cell of respondent Perkins, who was incarcerated on charges unrelated to the subject of the agent's investigation. Respondent made statements that implicated him in the crime that the agent sought to solve. Respondent claims that the statements should be inadmissible because he had not been given the *Miranda* warnings by the agent. We hold that the statements are admissible. *Miranda* warnings are not required when the subject is unaware that he is speaking to a law enforcement officer and gives a voluntary statement."

—496 U.S. 292 (1990)

After three young African American men were brutally tortured into confessing having committed a murder in Mississippi, for which they were convicted with no other evidence, the Supreme Court reversed the state supreme court which had upheld the conviction (Box 6.11).[61]

Box 6.11

Brown v. Mississippi

"The question in this case is whether convictions, which rest solely upon confessions shown to have been extorted by officers of the State by brutality and violence, are consistent with the due process of law required by the Fourteenth Amendment of the Constitution of the United States."

Early one Friday afternoon in 1934, the murder of Raymond Stewart was discovered. That night a deputy sheriff picked up Ellington, a black man, and took him to Stewart's home, where he was accused of the crime. A group of white men, including the deputy, hanged him (twice) by the neck to a tree. They also tied him to a tree and whipped him. Still he would not confess, and he was returned home in agony. The same deputy arrested him later. On the way to jail, Ellington again was whipped severely. He agreed to confess to a statement dictated by the deputy. Brown and Shields, the other black defendants, were whipped in jail until they confessed to every detail required of them. Within a week the defendants had been indicted, convicted, and sentenced to death.

There was no evidence against them other than the confessions which everybody, including the prosecutor and judge, knew to have been obtained by the torture described. The Supreme Court of the State, said Chief Justice Hughes for the majority of the Supreme Court of the United States, " . . . declined to enforce petitioners' constitutional right." The U.S. Supreme Court stated that the state court " . . . thus denied a federal right fully established and specially set up and claimed and the judgment [of the state court] must be reversed."

—297 U.S. 278 (1936)

" . . . nor shall [any person] be compelled in any criminal case to be a witness against himself . . ."
—Fifth Amendment to the U.S. Constitution

It was not only on the basis of the Fifth Amendment privilege against self-incrimination, however, that the Court overturned the conviction. Rather, it was mainly for the reason that the Constitution requires, by the Fourteenth Amendment, "due process of law." The whole trial was a sham—"a pretense of a trial." The Court said that due process requires "that state action . . . shall be consistent with the fundamental principles of liberty and justice which lie at the base of all our civil and political institutions, " and added, "It would be difficult to conceive of methods more revolting to the sense of justice than those taken to procure the confessions of these petitioners, and the use of the confessions thus obtained as the basis for conviction and sentence was a clear denial of due process."

In 1963, the right to counsel assured by the Sixth Amendment was made applicable to the states through the Fourteenth Amendment.[62] Later, the court assured the right to counsel in any accusation that could result in a deprivation of liberty (Box 6.12).[63]

Facts About Arrests

There has been a great deal of research on the decision to arrest, made within considerable police discretion but constrained by legal requirements.

Box 6.12

Gideon v. Wainwright

Mr. Gideon was charged with breaking and entering a poolroom with intent to commit a crime. He appeared in court with no money and no lawyer.

"The COURT: Mr. Gideon, I am very sorry, but I cannot appoint counsel to represent you in this case. Under the laws of the State of Florida, the only time the Court can appoint Counsel to represent a Defendant is when that person is charged with a capital offense. I am sorry, but I will have to deny your request to appoint Counsel to defend you in this case."

"The DEFENDANT: The United States Supreme Court says I am entitled to be represented by Counsel."

Defendant Gideon was not correct at that moment. Two decades before, the Supreme Court of the United States did *not* hold, in a very similar case, that that was required by the due process clause of the Fourteenth Amendment (*Betts vs. Brady*, 316 U.S. 455, 1942). But, the Court reconsidered in Gideon's case, and that judgment was reversed. The Court then stated, ". . . any person haled into court, who is too poor to hire a lawyer, cannot be assured a fair trial unless counsel is provided for him." The government hires prosecutors and persons with money hire defense lawyers. Considering this, the Court stated that the noble ideal of fair trials before impartial tribunals in which every defendant stands equal before the law " . . . cannot be realized if the poor man charged with crimes has to face his accusers without a lawyer to assist him." Ten years later, the Court make it clear that the rationale in Gideon "has relevance to any criminal trial, where an accused is deprived of his liberty." (*Argesinger v. Hamlin*, 407 U.S. 25, 1972). But, note that the defendant also has a right *not* to have a lawyer when he voluntarily and knowingly elects to conduct his own defense (See, *Faretta, California*, 422 U.S. 806, 1975). In the case cited, three justices dissented, stating "If there is any truth to the old proverb that '[o]ne who is his own lawyer has a fool for a client,' the Court by its opinion today now bestows a *constitutional* right on one to make a fool of himself."

—372 U.S. 335 (1963)

As a result, much now is known about this critical decision point in the criminal justice process. For example, it is known that:

- Arrest practices vary markedly by jurisdiction.

- The gravity of the harm done by an offense is strongly related to individual decisions whether to arrest.

- Citizens influence the arrest decision in two important ways:

  by deciding whether to call the police.

  by expressing their preferences concerning arrest.

- Among the less serious offenses, the decision whether to arrest may be influenced by:

  characteristics of the suspect such as age, sex, or race (arrest is more likely for youths, males, and minority group members).

  the demeanor of the suspect and his or her cooperation with police (a hostile attitude or lack of cooperation may mean more likely arrest).

- Some officers are much more likely than others to make arrests that result in conviction.

- The relationship of the victim and offender is an important factor in arrests as well as subsequent dismissals. (Suspects who are "strangers" are more apt to be arrested and less apt to have dismissals.)

- For a large share of persons arrested, the need for custody is slight.

- The quality of the evidence gathered at the scene of an arrest is important for later decisions.

These and many other facts found in studies of police decisions help guide policy decisions about policing in general, but much that would be desirable to know about the crime control effects of these decisions is yet unknown.

Some Information Needs

We have seen that the goals of police decisions to arrest may be identified, for particular decisions, as serving crime control purposes of the criminal justice system (such as deterrence, incapacitation, and treatment). We have seen that the purpose of deserved punishment might be served also by arrest. We have seen that the arrest decision alternatives are not limited to whether to arrest or to do nothing. Rather, alternatives of referral, citation, advising, sending the suspect away, or other means of dispute resolution often may be selected by an officer, particularly when the alleged offense is not an extremely serious one.

What we usually lack is solid information on how arrest decisions are related to goals. In addition to the need for the clear specification of objectives, we need the development of improved police information systems of a particular type. These systems would permit the tracking of cases beyond the arrest decision, whether or not the suspect was arrested, to determine what happened later. The purpose would be to see whether the objectives of the decision were, in fact, accomplished. Was the suspect convicted? If not, why not? Was the case dropped by the prosecutor? If the case was dropped, what was the reason? If the case was referred to another agency, what was the outcome in terms of the future offending by the suspect? Were the victims satisfied? Did the public believe that justice was done? Such questions can be answered only by a system of record keeping that keeps track of arrests and keeps score on the results of all the alternative choices made.

When such systems become available not only for the police but for later stages of the criminal justice process, much of the now obvious conflict among agencies may be reduced. It is common, for example, for police to complain that much of their work is to no avail because the prosecutor or judge dismisses so many suspects after their arrest. Most of the time, the prosecutor drops the case after an arrest. But, in most cases that are dropped, it may have been appropriate both for the police to make an arrest and for the prosecutor to dismiss it later. Differences in standards of proof, workloads, and resources may produce apparent conflict when a full accounting of the circumstances might show that none exists.

Information for Management Decisions

Just as information is required for individual *case* decisions by police officers, police administrators need information for many *policy* decisions. How much individual police officer discretion should be permitted, and when should attempts be made to guide decisions by directives? How much of the resources of a department should be devoted to patrol? Should patrol be dispersed evenly throughout a city or targeted on specific areas? Should patrol cars always have two officers? How much training is enough and how much can be afforded? How much force may be used in making an arrest and how much is "unnecessary" force? What will be the objectives and procedures for a recruitment effort? What resources can be provided for crime prevention efforts, and what programs will be initiated? The complexity of the police administrator's tasks is apparent as soon as it is realized that the police do not merely enforce the law but operate under public expectations that they serve a variety of other service functions.

These are not just "research questions." They also are matters of competent management. No organization may be expected to be productive in the absence of clear expectations for its workers. They also are important issues for formulation of police policy.

As described by Herman Goldstein:

> Recognition that the police do more than enforce the law and that they in fact have multiple functions poses a whole new series of perplexing ques-tions for the police administrator. With the competition for available per-sonnel and other resources, what should be the priorities of the agency? How much time and resources are to be devoted, respectively, to resolving domestic quarrels, controlling traffic, aiding the mentally ill, investigating robberies, and ferreting out large-scale dealers in narcotics? What does an administrator do when two or more functions are in conflict, for example, when a large number of demonstrators disrupt traffic? Which responsibility takes precedence—enforcing the law or protecting First Amendment rights?[64]

Another influential experiment was conducted in the early 1970s by the Kansas City, Missouri, police to test the effect of different patrol strategies on crime rates.[65] One group of areas was given more patrol coverage than usual, another group had no patrol except for answering calls for service, and another was left unchanged and exposed to normal patrol practice. No differences in crime rates were found among the groups. The results have been influential with police management. The study, like the Minneapolis domestic violence study, is important for showing that experimentation with policing policy is possible and provides an important means for improving management information.

An experiment often can provide the most rigorous test of the results of policy decisions. When an experiment is not feasible, there are other ways of learning from experience by observing the results of policy changes, including sophisticated statistical research designs that can come close to serving as experiments. Whatever the research methods used, the impor-tant thing is to examine the available evidence for help in formulating pol-icy.

One area where we do have information to guide police management concerns the effect of police presence on crime. In general, it can be said that much evidence indicates that what the police *do* is much more impor-tant than *how many* police do it. Adding officers, a politically popular con-cept often urged on the basis of a claimed crime reduction benefit, is not by itself apt to do much to reduce crime. This may be true particu-larly if the officers are assigned to patrol evenly throughout a city. Some of this evidence comes from observing the results of police strikes, of the effects of giving more attention to "hot spots" of crime, and of the conse-quences of police "crackdowns." Much of this evidence has been summa-rized by Sherman.[66]

Police Strikes

What would happen if we had no police? Available evidence from police strikes is that the police are indeed needed, even if it does not tell us how many.

> [I]n Boston and Liverpool in 1919, in Montreal in 1969, in Helsinki in 1973, and even in Nazi-occupied Copenhagen, the evidence is consistent: all Hell breaks loose. Robberies in particular show sudden increases, as well as fights and property crime. Hospital admissions for violent injuries in Hel-sinki rose substantially. In Montreal, the hourly burglary rate rose by 13,000 percent, and the hourly bank robbery rate rose by 50,000 percent. The evi-dence should leave no doubt that even homogeneous, well-educated, low crime societies need police to control crime. The argument is not over whether the medicine of policing is required but over what the dosage should be.[67]

Hot Spots and Crackdowns

Studies of the effects of police attention to specific areas of crime show how information can be obtained that has practical relevance to improved police management. Crime varies markedly over different places in a city, different days of the week, and different times of the day. Sherman pointed out that when patrol visibility is spread out evenly over space and time—every citizen getting a "fair share" of policing—policing is applied unevenly to crime. (This occurred in the Kansas City experiment.) It may be much more sensible to concentrate police visibility where most crime takes place in "hot spot" addresses or areas. An experiment in Minneapolis found that an unpredictable, intermittent police presence applied to randomly se-lected hot spots significantly, although modestly, reduced reported crime.[68]

Crackdowns are sudden, unexpected, substantial increases in police presence or activity. They have been reported to have produced substantial, temporary reductions in crime—drunk driving, robbery, drug dealing, pros-titution, and youthful disorder.[69] A concern often expressed is that crack-downs or increased attention to hot spots may simply "push" crime to another area, a phenomenon known as "displacement." After examining a variety of studies, Sherman concluded, while acknowledging that we can-not be sure, that the evidence is against it. His comments clearly show how research can improve information for police management decisions:

> The key to making crackdowns work is to keep them short and unpre-dictable. Long-term police crackdowns all show a "decay" in their deterrent effects over time. Short-term crackdowns, in contrast, show a free bonus of "residual deterrence" after the crackdown stops, while potential offenders slowly figure out that the cops are gone. Random rotation of high police visibility across different short term targets can accumulate free crime pre-vention bonuses and get the most value out of police visibility. Even if dis-placement to other hot spots occurs, the unpredictable increases in police presence at any hot spot may create generally higher deterrent effects from the same number of police officers.[70]

Policing Goals and Management Decisions

The clear identification of purposes and goals is essential for effective management of the police. Patterns of police behavior develop according to perceptions of important goals. For example, three decades ago James Q. Wilson described "styles" of management differing according to purposes and methods.[71] A *watchman* style emphasized order maintenance, with police allowed much discretion as to how that was accomplished. Perhaps a police officer, observing a drunk but not too disorderly person, causing no particular problems, would ignore the law violation. A *legalistic* style, aimed at strict law enforcement, would limit discretion, insist on enforcement, and otherwise avoid interventions. Perhaps the public drunk would be arrested, the officer enforcing the law strictly. A *service* style, aimed at community assistance, would help meet perceived community needs in a variety of ways rather than strictly enforce the law. Perhaps a person too drunk to drive or to be left alone would be transported home or to a shelter. As we have seen, the police are expected to do all these things; but where the emphasis is placed provides a policy context for individual police officer decisions.

Increasing concerns by managers about perceptions of the police by the community have led, since the mid-1950s, to the development of specific police community-relations programs intended to improve this image and to increase cooperation between the police and the rest of the community. As an outgrowth of this general movement, usually away from a strict enforcement orientation and towards a greater service frame of reference, a variety of programs have developed. Neighborhood watch programs, activities to encourage and assist in marking valuables for help in case of theft, police victim assistance programs, police visits for talks at schools about safety or drug use, and public education forums are examples.

Growing from the service orientation and increased community involvement also has been an important concept of "team policing." Officers have been assigned responsibility for a particular neighborhood. This has been expected to result in greater involvement, better understanding of community problems, and improved service.

Similarly, an emphasis on *problem-solving* or *problem-oriented* policing has emerged. From this perspective, police managers seek to discover the causes of disorder and crime, then find remedies. This may, like team policing, require greater community involvement and increased use of other community service agencies.

Community Policing

Many of these orientations, emphasizing proactive (initiative taking), problem solving, community-involved methods, now have come together in the concept of *community policing*. This viewpoint now is finding increased acceptance in many large police departments. The goals of policing, from this perspective, emphasize absence of crime and disorder rather than the detection and clearance of specific crimes. There is an emphasis on solving community problems more than greater efficiency in response to specific incidents, as in shortening response times or effectiveness in targeting specific offenses. Police should take the initiative to actively respond to general citizen concerns more than reactively responding to complaints about specific incidents. Proactive crime control and prevention is emphasized, with a value placed on increased interaction of police and community members collaboratively engaged in problem solving.

Despite widespread acceptance of these and related ideas, the general concept of community policing is not without its critics. Some place more value on the more traditional policing goals of order maintenance and enforcement and believe these may be neglected when too great an emphasis is placed on citizen concerns with the general quality of life. Thus, they regard a more general "public health" role for the police as much too broad and unrealistic.

Community Policing as Action Research

An important feature of community policing, with an emphasis on problem solving, is that it provides an "action research" model for the police. The action research model requires definition of a problem situation, specification of objectives that may help solve the problem, definition of methods for meeting those objectives, seeing whether the methods are carried out and whether the objectives were attained. All this is best done as a collaborative enterprise between the police and the community members concerned about the problem and its solution. See the comments by Herman Goldstein, sometimes called the "father" of problem-oriented policing, in Box 6.13.[72]

Box 6.13

Herman Goldstein: In His Own Words

[T]he major thrust in problem-oriented policing . . . was to try to redirect interest within policing away from just focusing on the organization and its personnel, and focus on the specific problems we confront in the community, what we're doing about those problems, and what careful analysis of them might produce in the way of new insights into how we deal with them in a more effective fashion. True problem-solving in the context of community policing focuses on the business of policing, and not on the endless number of other problems that arise in police operations and in our lives.

[W]e've seen as a result of the movement a tremendous amount of creative problem solving on the part of beat officers. If that is helpful, it is encouraging. But the original concept anticipated and hoped for a commitment to research and development at higher levels of an organization, which would look more systematically and rigorously at substantive pieces of police business and, after that analysis, provide the benefits to officers

on the street. So while I admire the problem-solving efforts of the officers and expect that if they get into that state of mind, and as they become leaders of policing, they will carry that up into higher levels of the organization, I would hope at the same time that we had a greater investment in research at the top of the agency that would look at citywide problems, expanding just beyond the beat.

Two other observations with regard to problem-solving. One is that, understandably when a movement like this gets going, some of the initial efforts are rather amateurish, rather awkward, but nevertheless to be commended just as one would commend a baby taking its first steps. But once we get going, I would hope that we could see much more in the way of rigor in the analysis, that we don't jump to conclusions as to how to deal with the problem differently, but instead invest much more in thinking through very critically what we're doing and what might be done differently, getting much more   ☞

☞ comfortable with the collection and use of relevant data and its analysis.

Finally, we need a major investment in developing methods to evaluate problem-solving. Because it's sort of the last stage, it's put off and it often gets short shrift. It's very uncomfortable to advo- cate new approaches without having any solid, rigorously developed support to assure us that what we are doing in lieu of past responses is indeed more effective.

—Herman Goldstein,
University of Wisconsin, Madison

Management Information Systems

For any police manager, regardless of the stance taken on the general issues of police as problem solvers and those that surround the concept of community policing, the clear identification of goals and objectives is of utmost importance. The information available to assist in management decisions must be related to those objectives if it is to provide useful guidance. By keeping track of the results of changes in practice and observing the results, the police administrator can learn from experience. Thus, the management information system of the police organization should do more than merely keep track of budgets, personnel, and arrests. It should include the following elements that are needed in order to keep track also of the results of policy decisions:

- A mission statement describing the general, overall goals of the police.

- A list of major specific objectives.

- For each objective, a list of police activities intended to assist in attaining them.

- For each objective, a description of how the achievement of the objective can be measured.

- Analyses, from experience, of whether each activity listed has been meeting its objectives as actually measured in practice.

This kind of information is needed for effective police management, because it is the only way the manager can discover what works for the jurisdiction for which that administrator is responsible.

Summary

The police are expected to maintain order, follow the law, and enforce it. In doing so, they exercise much discretion within legal and policy constraints.

Modern-day policing developed after police reforms in London. The unorganized policing of the American colonies gradually was replaced by more organized, full-time, paid officers. The police function always has been decentralized. Although we now have a variety of state and federal police, growing in numbers and scope of authority, most policing is done by municipal police and sheriff's departments. There now are about a half million local police and about 3,000 state and local law enforcement agencies.

Most calls to the police do not involve crime. Police deal with a wide range of problems when "something-is-happening-which-ought-not-to-be-happening-and-about-which-someone-had-better-do-something-now!"

Arrest is only one tool of the police for preserving order. It is a powerful tool but one of last resort. Police spend a small part of their time making arrests, but the impact of arrest decisions is large and pervasive, affecting the entire system of criminal justice.

The strain between our desires for both freedom and safety is nowhere more evident than in police decisions and in court decisions that both support and restrain them. Police must balance the decisions that must be made between community interests in vigorous crime control and legal constraints on their authority. We require safety and demand liberty.

The discretionary nature of decisions to arrest has been only recently recognized as necessary and desirable. There has been a growing acceptance of the view that the full enforcement of the law in every instance has been an unrealistic "false pretense."

The goals of arrest decisions include all the main criminal justice system goals of punishment, incapacitation, treatment, and general deterrence. The decision not to arrest is one main alternative to the arrest decision. It may involve doing nothing, but it may entail mediation, warning, citation, or other actions.

When the alleged offense is quite serious, the police are likely to arrest if there is probable cause. When it is minor, more discretion is used and characteristics of the suspect such as respect shown to the officer, and the preferences of the complainant are influential.

Arrests initiate the criminal justice process, and many "diversion" programs have been developed. They may be diversionary, or they may "widen the net" of social control. Rarely have they been evaluated rigorously.

Examples of the kind of careful evaluation that can guide police policies are given by the Minneapolis domestic violence experiment, the Kansas City patrol experiment, and other studies providing better information for management decisions.

An arrest is a seizure of the person subject to the Fourth Amendment and usually requires probable cause. "Probable cause" means that (1) a crime has been committed, and (2) the suspect probably did it. For the police officer, it means that the reasonably trustworthy facts he or she knows are enough for a prudent person to believe the suspect committed or is committing an offense. Officers may, however, "stop and frisk" on "reasonable suspicion."

Most arrests are made without a warrant. The police may do so in a public place. Although there are exceptions, the police may not ordinarily arrest a suspect at home without a warrant.

Constraints on searches are governed also by the Fourth Amendment, applicable to the states through the due process clause of the Fourteenth and often required by other statutes. The legal requirements are enforced by the "exclusionary rule," which means the excluding of evidence from a criminal proceeding when it has been obtained improperly.

The police must obtain a warrant, issued by a magistrate upon demonstration of probable cause, unless it is impractical to do so. A warrant is not required for a felony arrest, a search incident to taking a suspect into custody, a search of a vehicle upon probable cause for an arrest, the seizure of objects in plain view, or entries into premises in "hot pursuit." Warrants are not required for border searches by customs or immigration officials, or when voluntary and intelligent consent has been given, or in some emergencies. A search may be made after making an arrest.

The purpose of the exclusionary rule is to deter police and judicial misconduct. An arrested person cannot be questioned before being given the "*Miranda* warnings." When evidence seized illegally leads to other "derivative" evidence, the "fruit of the poisonous tree" may be inadmissible.

The Fifth Amendment dictates that no person shall be compelled to testify against himself in any criminal case. The Fourteenth Amendment requires "due process of law." The right to counsel, assured by the Sixth Amendment, applies to the states through the Fourteenth Amendment.

Concepts of team policing and problem-solving policing have emerged in the conception of community-oriented policing, with an emphasis on police and community collaboration in problem solving. This can be seen as an action research strategy for finding out what works best.

A critical need for police management and improvement of practices is for better specification of objectives and expected practices and for careful record keeping to track the results of decisions. This can provide information needed to ensure that the decisions taken are meeting the goals intended. Such information is needed for improvement of both individual case decisions and management decisions. Similar programs of record keeping and feedback are needed throughout the criminal justice system.

Notes

1. Packer, H. L. (1968). *The Limits of the Criminal Sanction*. Stanford, CA: Stanford University Press, 366.

2. Bittner, E. (1974). "Florence Nightingale in Pursuit of Willie Sutton: A Theory of the Police," in Jacob, H. (ed.). *The Potential for Reform in Criminal Justice*. Beverly Hills, CA: Sage, 18.

3. This discussion of the origins of police has been much informed by Bailey, D. H. (1983). "Police: History," in Kadish, S. H. (ed.). *Encyclopedia of Crime and Justice*, Vol. 3. New York: The Free Press, 1119–1125.

4. Ibid., 1122–1123.

5. Dobie, C. C. (1934). *San Francisco: A Pageant*. New York: Appleton-Century, 116–117.

6. Mason, D. (1955). "Constitutional History of California," in California State Senate (1955). *Constitution of the State of California*, 305–326.

7. Borkenstein, R. (1983). "State Police," in Kadish, S. H. (ed.). *Encyclopedia of Crime and Justice*, Vol. 2. New York: The Free Press, 1132.

8. Morgan, R. E. (1983). "Federal Bureau of Investigation: History," in Kadish, S. H. (ed.). *Encyclopedia of Crime and Justice*, Vol. 2. New York: The Free Press, 768.

9. Abrams, N. (1983). "Federal Criminal Law Enforcement," In Kadish, S. H. (ed.). *Encyclopedia of Crime and Justice*, Vol. 2. New York: The Free Press, 782–783.

10. Reaves, B. A. (1996). *Local Police Departments, 1993* Washington, DC: Bureau of Justice Statistics, 1; Federal Bureau of Investigation (1966). *Crime in the United States, 1995*, 278.

11. Reaves, B. A. (1996). *Local Police Departments, 1993: Executive Summary*. Washington, DC: Bureau of Justice Statistics, 1–2.

12. Reaves, B. A., and Smith, P. Z. (1995). *Law Enforcement Management and Administrative Statistics, 1993: Data for Individual State and Local Agencies with 100 or More Officers*. Washington, DC: Bureau of Justice Statistics.

13. Bercal, T. (1970). "Calls for Police Assistance: Consumer Demands for Governmental Service," *American Behavioral Scientist* 13:681; Cumming, E., Cumming, I., and Edel, L. (1965). "Policeman as Philosopher, Guide, and Friend," *Social Problems* 12:276; Wilson, J. Q. 1965. *Varieties of Police Behavior*. Cambridge, MA: Harvard University Press; Reiss, A. (1971). *The Police and the Public*. New Haven: Yale University Press.

14. Wilson, J. Q. (1965). *Varieties of Police Behavior*. Cambridge, MA: Harvard University Press

15. Goldstein, J. (1969). "Police Discretion Not to Invoke the Criminal Process: Low Visibility Decisions in the Administration of Justice," *Yale Law Journal* 69:543.

16. Gottfredson, M. R., and Gottfredson, D. M. (1988). *Decision Making in Criminal Justice: Toward the Rational Exercise of Discretion*. New York: Plenum Press, 51.

17. Goldstein, H. (1977). *Policing a Free Society*.Cambridge, MA: Ballinger, 94.

18. President's Commission on Law Enforcement and Administration of Justice. (1967). *The Challenge of Crime in a Free Society*. Washington, DC: U.S. GPO, 106.

19. Davis, K. (1975). *Police Discretion*. St. Paul: West Publishing.

20. Wilson, J. Q. (1965). *Varieties of Police Behavior*, p.84. Cambridge, MA: Harvard University Press.

21. LaFave, W. (1965). *Arrest: the Decision to Take a Suspect into Custody*. Boston: Little, Brown.

22. Goldstein, H. (1977). *Policing a Free Society*, p. 21. Cambridge, MA: Ballinger.

23. Piliavin, I., and Briar, S. (1964). "Police Encounters with Juveniles," *American Journal of Sociology* 70:206; Black and Reiss (1970). "Patterns of Behavior in Police and Citizen Transactions," in *Studies of Crime and Law Enforcement in Major Metropolitan Areas*. Washington, DC: U.S. GPO; Black, D. (1970). "Police Control of Juveniles," *American Sociological Review* 35:63.

24. Black and Reiss (1970). "Patterns of Behavior in Police and Citizen Transactions," in *Studies of Crime and Law Enforcement in Major Metropolitan Areas*, p. 71. Washington, DC.

25. Black, D. (1971). "The Social Organization of Arrest," *Stanford Law Review* 23:1087.

26. Friedrich, R. (1977). "The Impact of Organizational, Individual, and Situational Factors on Police Behavior." Ph.D. Dissertation, University of Michigan; Sykes, R., Fox, J., and Clarke, J. (1976). "A Socio-Legal Theory of Police Discretion," in Niederhoffer, A. and Blumberg, A., (eds.). *Determinants of Law Enforcement Policies*. Lexington, MA: Lexington; Lundman, R. (1974). "Routine Arrest Practices: A Commonweal Perspective," *Social Problems* 22:127; Lundman, R., Sykes, R., and Clarke, J. (1978). "Police Control of Juveniles: A Replication," *Journal of Research in Crime and Delinquency* 15:74.

27. Smith, D. (1984). "The Organizational Context of Legal Control," *Criminology* 22(1)19–38; Worden, R., and Pollitz, A. (1984). "Police Arrests in Domestic Disturbances: A Further Look," *Law and Society Review* 18(1): 103–119.

28. LaFree, G. (1981). "Official Reactions to Social Problems: Police Decisions in Sexual Assault Cases," *Social Problems* 28(5): 582–594.

29. Bittner, E. (1967). "The Police on Skid-Row: A Study of Peacekeeping," *American Sociological Review* 32:699.

30. Nettler, G. (1978). *Explaining Crime*, 2nd ed. New York: McGraw-Hill, 70.

30. Asher and Orleans. (1972). "Criminal Citation as a Post-Arrest Alternative to Custody for Certain Offenses." Paper cited in Berger, M., "Police Field Citations in New Haven." *Wisconsin Law Review* 2:382.

32. LaFave, W. (1965). *Arrest: the Decision to Take a Suspect into Custody*. Boston: Little, Brown.

33. Klein, M., Teilman, J., Styles, J. Lincoln, S. and Labin-Rosensweig (1976). "The Explosion in Police Diversion Programs: Evaluating the Structural Dimensions of a Social Fad," in Klein, M. (ed.). *The Juvenile Justice System*. Beverly Hills, CA: Sage, 10.

34. Sherman, L., and Berk, R. A. (1984a). "The Specific Deterrent Effects of Arrest for Domestic Assault," *American Sociological Review* 49 (2): 261.

35. Murphy, P. V. (circa 1984). In Sherman, L., and Berk, R. A. (circa 1984b). "The Minneapolis Domestic Violence Experiment," *Police Foundation Reports*. Washington, DC: The Police Foundation.

36. Sherman, L. W., and Berk, R. A. (circa 1984b). "The Minneapolis Domestic Violence Experiment," *Police Foundation Reports*. Washington, DC: The Police Foundation, 6.

37. Sherman, L. W. (1995). "The Police," in Wilson, J. Q., and Petersilia, J. (eds.). *Crime*. San Francisco: Institute of Contemporary Studies, 337.

38. Ibid., 337.

39. *Beck v. Ohio* (1964). 379 U.S. 89, 91.

40. *Wolf v. Colorado* (1949). 338 U.S. 25.

41. *Terry v. Ohio* (1968). 392 U. S. 1.

42. *Michigan v. Summers* (1981). 452 U.S. 692.

43. *Davis v. Mississippi* (1969. 394 U.S. 721.

44. *United States v. Cortez* (1981). 449 U.S. 411.

45. *Dunaway v. New York (1979). 442 U.S. 200.*

46. *United States v. Watson* (1976). 423 U.S. 411.

47. *Payton v. New York (1980). 445 U.S. 573.*

48. Whitebread, C. W. (1983). "Arrest and Stop," in Kadish, S. H. (ed.). *Encyclopedia of Crime and Justice*, Vol. 1. New York: The Free Press, 75, citing *Dorman v. United States* (1970). 435 F.2d 385, 392-393 (D.C. Cir. 1970).

49. White, J. B. (1983). "Search and Seizure," in Kadish, S. H. (ed.). *Encyclopedia of Crime and Justice*, Vol. 1. New York: The Free Press, 1417.

50. *Carroll v. United States* (1925). 267 U.S. 132.

51. *United States v. Watson* (1976). 423 U.S. 411

52. *Warden v. Hayden* (1967). 387 U.S. 294.

53. *Payton v. New York* (1980). 445 U.S. 573.

54. *Katz v. United States* (1967). 389 U.S. 347.

55. *Weeks v. United States* (1914). (232 U.S. 383, 392.

56. *Elkins v. United States* (1960). 364 U.S. 206.

57. *Mapp v. Ohio* (1961). 367 U.S. 643, 655.

58. Burkoff, J. M. (1983). "Exclusionary Rules," in Kadish, S. H. (ed.). *Encyclopedia of Crime and Justice*, Vol. 1. New York: The Free Press, 718.

59. *Miranda v. Arizona* (1966). 384 U. S. 436.

60. *Illinois v. Perkins* (1990). 496 U.S. 292.

61. *Brown v. Mississippi* (1936).

62. *Gideon v. Wainwright* (1963). 372 U. S. 335.

63. *Argesinger v. Hamlin* (1972). 407 U. S. 25.

64. Goldstein, H. (1983). "Police: Administration," in Kadish, S. H. (ed.). *Encyclopedia of Crime and Justice*, Vol. 2. New York: The Free Press, 782"783, 1128.

65. Kelling, G. L., Pate, T., Dieckman, D., and Brown, C. (1974). *The Kansas City Preventive Patrol Experiment*. Washington, DC: The Police Foundation.

66. Sherman, L. W. (1995), "The Police," in Wilson, J. Q., and Petersilia, J. (eds.). *Crime*. San Francisco: Institute of Contemporary Studies, 331–334.

67. Ibid., 331.

68. Ibid., 332–333.

69. Ibid., 332.

70. Ibid., 333.

71. Wilson, J. Q. (1968). *Varieties of Police Behavior: The Management of Law and Order in Eight Communities*. Cambridge, MA: Harvard University Press.

72. Rosen, M. S. (1997). "A LEN Interview with Professor Herman Goldstein, the 'Father' of Problem-oriented Policing." New York: John Jay College of Criminal Justice, Law Enforcement News, 23,461, 11.

CHAPTER SEVEN

The Prosecutor

Photo courtesy of www.photostogo.com.

Chapter Seven

After arrest, a decision must be made whether a suspect will be charged with a crime. In this chapter, the origins of the role of the prosecutor will be traced and the present duties will be examined. We will see that the decisions of prosecutors affect all other parts of the criminal justice system and are also influenced by the police, courts, and corrections. As with other central actors in the system, we will examine the goals, choices, and information needs of the prosecutor.

Questions to Think About

Where does the public prosecutor get the authority of that position?

Must the prosecutor file charges if a suspect has been arrested?

Can the police prosecute a suspect on their own? Can a victim do so?

Are most convicted persons found guilty by a jury?

What factors does the prosecutor take into account in deciding what charges to bring? What is considered in deciding whether to drop the charges?

Do prosecutors make their decisions following guidelines established by the legislature or the courts?

What are the goals of prosecutor decisions?

What alternatives does the prosecutor have for the charge decision?

Does the prosecutor ever dismiss charges when there is strong evidence to support a conviction?

Do you think plea bargaining should be permitted?

Does plea bargaining hinder or help the police? Does it hinder or help the courts? Does it hinder or help justice?

Prosecutors' Decisions

Consider the role of the prosecutor in the following cases. They are fairly typical examples of decisions made every day by prosecutors.

Tom

When in prison earlier, Tom described himself as a "fairly good writer of fairly good novels" and a "fairly good writer of fairly bad checks." He left town before the warrant was issued for his arrest. The bad checks totaled $80.00. When Tom was arrested in Hawaii, the deputy district attorney estimated the cost of his extradition (bringing him back to the state) as $2,800.00 and decided to drop the case.

Dick and Harry

Dick, 38, with two prior felony convictions for which he served time in prison, took Harry, 24, along on a burglary. Harry had never been in trouble with the law. They were arrested by two officers who were responding to a home alarm and noticed them driving erratically down the street a short distance from the crime scene. Dick had ten $100 bills in his pocket and $32 in his wallet. Harry had $18 in his wallet. Both were booked on charges of burglary in the first degree, grand theft, trespassing, reckless driving, and driving under the influence of alcohol.

The state's penalty for burglary in the first degree was 5 years to life in prison. With two prior felonies, the mandatory minimum was 30 years. Grand theft called for 1 to 20 years, and the other offenses were misdemeanors that could result in jail terms or fines up to $1,000.

The deputy district attorney reviewed the police report. Dick and Harry probably did the burglary, as the police thought, but the evidence for that crime was fairly weak. Certainly, there could be reasonable doubt. The $100 bills probably came from the home, but Dick told the police he had won the money at the races.

When the deputy public defender called, the prosecutor suggested that the charge against Harry might be dropped to trespassing if he agreed to testify against Dick, adding that "if he backs down, it will be 5 to life."

Harry and his attorney agreed to the arrangement, and the agreement was accepted by the judge. Dick went back to prison after trial and conviction on the strength of Harry's testimony. Harry plead guilty to trespassing and paid a $500 fine.

A Neighborly Fistfight

When two neighbors quarreled over the proper position for a fence one was building, the argument escalated into a minor fistfight. After a third neighbor called the police, the fighters were arrested for assault and disorderly conduct. The deputy prosecutor met with the men and their attorneys, secured from each a promise to apologize to the other and to pay half the cost of a survey to determine the correct boundary. The prosecutor warned each man that a record was made of the agreement and that a reoccurrence could result in serious charges. Then the prosecutor dropped the case.

Decision Making: An Important Role for the Prosecutor

These are but a few examples of the decisions made daily by prosecutors. It is up to the prosecutor to decide whether to charge, what to charge, and when to charge. The prosecutor must decide also how much of the resources of the office will be devoted to the case, whether for investigation or for trial. The cases above suggest only a few of the considerations that might be important for these decisions. The prosecutor's assessment of the seriousness of the matter and the potential threat to society, together with considerations of cost effectiveness of the operation, may have been important in the case of Tom, the writer. A similar concern with the seriousness of the offense may have been important for the case of Dick and Harry; but, in addition, the goals of incapacitation and possibly a judgment of greater culpability, hence deserved punishment, may have tipped the scales of justice in favor of locking up Dick and letting Harry go with a fine. The two neighbors essentially were kept out of the criminal justice system by negotiation. The prosecutor may have thought the case was settled reasonably without an unnecessary further involvement of the system. In each case, the prosecutor apparently had goals that commonly are represented in other discretionary decisions in criminal justice—efficiency, punishment in proportion to harm done, and crime control.

The Fourth Main Screen

If a victim of a crime does not call the police, no suspect ordinarily is arrested for that offense. Thus, the victim usually does the *first screening* of suspected offenders from the criminal justice system. If the police are called, and if the police investigation does not result in evidence sufficient for probable cause to believe that a crime was committed and a suspect did it, no one ordinarily is arrested. If the police for any reason decide not to arrest, it is usual that no suspect ever is arrested. Thus, the police provide a *second* screening of suspects out of the system. If the police decide to arrest but later drop the charges or the magistrate dismisses them at first appearance, the suspect goes no further into the criminal justice process. Thus, the police or the magistrate at the initial appearance do a *third screening*, filtering out more suspects. If the suspect is continued in the criminal justice process after these steps, the decision whether to prosecute must be made and, if so, for what crime or crimes. That is a *fourth main screening*, after which some suspects leave the criminal justice system (see Box 7.1).

Box 7.1

Criminal Justice System Filters

If

The **victim** does not report a crime, or
The **police** do not arrest, or
The **magistrate** dismisses the complaint, or
The **prosecutor** does not charge,

Then

The criminal justice system is not further involved.

In most American jurisdictions, the decision whether to charge is made by the district attorney (D.A., sometimes called the county attorney, or the state's attorney). In practice, it may be made by a deputy or assistant district attorney under the supervision of the D.A. Typically, prosecution for crimes against the state is organized by counties under the direction of an elected independent prosecutor. Only rarely is the prosecutor an employee of a state department of justice. Police departments typically are organized locally and they mainly enforce state laws. The county attorney thus is a major link between the legislature that writes the criminal code of the state, the judiciary, and the local police. It is the prosecutor's role in deciding whether charges should be filed or dismissed that is critical to this tie of local and state interests.[1]

Origins of Prosecution

As with so much of the American system of criminal justice, the role of the prosecutor has developed from its colonial beginnings, although some roots can be traced back thousands of years. In ancient Greece, there was a trial with a jury but no judge, defense attorneys, or public prosecutors (see Box 7.2).

Our prosecution procedures developed mainly from the English but were influenced also by Dutch settlers in "New Netherland"—now parts of Connecticut, New York, New Jersey, Pennsylvania, and Delaware. In England during the seventeenth and eighteenth centuries, the system was one of private prosecution. There was no public prosecutor. The attorney gen-

Box 7.2

The Prosecution of Socrates, 399 B.C.

Three Athenian citizens brought charges of impiety against Socrates. (There was no public prosecutor.) The Athenian law did not specify exactly the elements of such a crime, so the accusers had to convince the jurors that his acts were criminal. As usual in Athenian trials, there was no judge to rule on the admissibility of evidence or to interpret the law, no one to provide legal guidance to the jury. The accusers (the prosecutors) argued their case against Socrates before the 501 men over 30 years old drawn by lot from an eligible pool of jurors. They accused Socrates of not believing in the gods of the city-state and charged also that he had led the young men of Athens away from Athenian conventions and ideals. After the prosecutors presented their case, no attorney represented Socrates. As re-quired by legal procedure, he spoke in his own defense. According to Plato, Socrates did not rebut the charges or ask for sympathy, as jurors expected. Rather, he repeated his dedication to urging his fellow citizens to examine their own preconceptions in order to learn to live virtuous lives. They should care less about material possessions and more about making their souls as good as possible. He vowed to continue these admonishments no matter what the consequences to himself. [He was convicted by a narrow margin and sentenced to death.]

Adapted from Martin, Thomas, *Overview of Archaic & Classical Greek History.* http://www.perseus.tufts.edu/Secondary/TRM_Overview

eral, however, could dismiss any prosecution by filing a writ of *nolle prosequi* indicating his intention not to prosecute. It was entirely within the discretion of the attorney general. In England now, any citizen may still prosecute, although the attorney general may dismiss the charge; but most prosecutions are conducted by the local police.

Similarly, each of the American colonies had an attorney general who left criminal prosecution mainly to the victim. We can easily imagine the problems that followed, including victims discouraged by the difficulty and cost of pressing their accusations and prosecutions initiated as extortion, with innocent persons paying their accusers to stop (if they could afford it). Moreover, the courts were losing money that had been expected to be generated by fines. As a result, attorney generals themselves began prosecuting more often, and then, as work loads increased, county attorneys were appointed by county courts. They soon took over the prosecutorial function of the colony attorney general. In this way, public prosecution gradually replaced private prosecution in most of the colonies.

The Dutch settlers, however, brought their own system of public prosecution with them. This was later modified by the English, giving a prosecutorial role to the sheriff.

> In 1653, prosecutions were being conducted [in New Netherland] by an official called a *schout*. When the British took New York from the Dutch in 1664, criminal prosecution remained much as it had been under Dutch administration, except that the schout was replaced by a sheriff. In 1776, when two judges questioned the propriety of prosecutions by the sheriff . . ., the Governor's Council replied that he was authorized not only to apprehend offenders but to prosecute them as well.[2]

By the time of the American Revolution, local public prosecution had been established in each of the colonies. Often, county attorneys dealt with offenses against the state laws, and town prosecutors handled violations of local ordinances. This became the common practice in the states of the new nation.

A similar pattern was at first followed by the federal government. Under the 1789 Judiciary Act, the U.S. Attorney General was to prosecute in the U.S. Supreme Court all suits that involved the federal government. The authority for prosecution for federal crimes in the federal districts was given to United States Attorneys appointed by the President. In 1861, however, Congress gave the Attorney General direction of the U.S. Attorneys.

> *Of all the officers of the Government, those of the Department of Justice should be the most free from any suspicion of improper action on partisan or factional grounds, so that there shall be gradually a growth, even though a slow growth, in the knowledge that the Federal Courts and the representatives of the Federal Department of Justice insist on meting out even handed justice to all.*
> *—President Theodore Roosevelt*

Most local prosecutors now are elected. Originally minor judicial officials, prosecutors, along with judges, began to be elected in 1832, first in Mississippi. By 1912, nearly all states elected local prosecutors—although in a few states they are still appointed. The election of prosecutors continued after the practice of judicial elections was abandoned by some states. (Judges now often are appointed, although they are elected in most states.) The argument that there is a need for representation of the people, hence a need for elections, has prevailed in the case of the prosecutor. It now is commonly said that the prosecutor represents the people and the judge is impartial to both the people (the prosecution) and the defense (the defendant).

Currently in the United States, we may assume as a practical matter that the district attorney (or U.S. Attorney) has exclusive authority to initiate formal charges of crime. Neither citizens nor police may do so on their own any longer. Grand juries still might do so, but only in extraordinary circumstances, and even then the prosecutor might dismiss them.

This virtual monopoly on the decision to charge is enjoyed with an unusual degree of independence—from administrators in a statewide system, from judges, and from grand juries. As the local district attorney gained the authority to prosecute, the right of filing a writ of *nolle prosequi*—not to prosecute—remained. It is as if the rights and privileges of the attorney general of England had been inherited. Through this power, the prosecutor may dispose of cases without trial and without review. It is derived neither from constitutions nor legislation but only from tradition. It was assumed, from the right of *nolle prosequi*, that if the prosecutor could dismiss at will, then he "could initiate prosecution or not, as [the prosecutor] alone chose to do."[3]

Some forms of judicial control have developed along with the prosecutor's power. For example, prosecutors may be required to file motions for dismissal with courts that are authorized to grant or deny the motion. There generally has been, however, a judicial reluctance to interfere with the traditional power of the district attorney to dismiss or to substitute lesser charges. This may be due to concerns for avoiding administrative issues thought to be beyond the competence of the courts. It may be aimed at maintaining the constitutional separation of powers doctrine, which says that courts are not to interfere with the exercise of discretion by the executive branch of government. It probably is more closely related to the practice of plea bargaining, a process of negotiation by the prosecutor and the defendant, usually through that person's lawyer. The plea bargaining process is central to the prosecutor's role in the present system.

The prosecutor's discretion is a critical feature in the plea bargaining process that results in most criminal convictions. If courts were to begin evaluating the use of prosecutor discretion, plea bargaining, and guilty pleas, that procedure could have a major impact on the work of the courts and on the whole justice system. The courts have left the guilty plea, and the practices underlying it, mainly up to the prosecution and the defense.[4]

Plea Bargaining

Plea bargaining is "the process by which the defendant relinquishes his right to go to trial in exchange for a reduction in charge or sentence."[5] It is the usual practice used across the country. It is certainly often part of the decision whether to charge at all, and, if so, what crime or crimes to charge. It is a topic that has aroused, and continues to kindle, much controversy and debate. One national commission recommended stopping the practice, and several attempts have been made to abolish it.[6]

The vast majority of persons judged guilty of a crime are guilty because they *plead* guilty rather than being *found* guilty as a result of a trial. Many pleas are a result of negotiation or concessions. In a recent sample survey, more than 9 out of 10 convictions in state courts were a result of a plea of guilty (Figure 7.1). Persons convicted of murder (Figure 7.2) were the least likely to have plead guilty and the most likely to have been convicted by a jury. Most jury trials, however, are not for murder: in 1992, 44 percent were for violent crimes, and 56 percent were for nonviolent crimes. The single felony category most often decided by juries was trafficking in drugs—18 percent of all jury convictions.[7]

There is, however, a lot of variation among jurisdictions in the rates of guilty pleas. Surveys typically find the ratio of pleas to trials to range from as high as 20 to 1 to as low as 4 to 1.

Figure 7.1 Percent Type of Conviction for Felons Convicted in State Courts, 1992

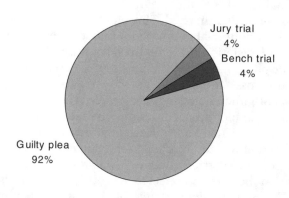

Source: data from Langan, P. A., and Graziadei, H. A. (1995). *Felony Sentences in State Courts, 1992.* Bureau of Justice Statistics Bulletin. Washington, D.C.: U.S. Department of Justice, 10.

Figure 7.2 Percent Type of Convictions for Murder and Negligent Manslaughter in the State Courts, 1992

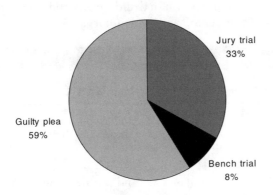

Source: data from Langan, P. A., and Graziadei, H. A. (1995). *Felony Sentences in State Courts, 1992.* Bureau of Justice Statistics Bulletin. Washington, D.C.: U.S. Department of Justice, 10.

The U.S. Supreme Court for the first time acknowledged the legitimacy of plea bargaining in 1970.[8] Brady had plead guilty to kidnapping and faced a possible penalty of death if a jury recommended it. He at first had plead not guilty but changed his plea after learning that his codefendant had confessed, would plead guilty, and would be available to testify against him. The judge had questioned him twice about the voluntariness of his guilty plea. He appealed on the grounds that his plea was coerced, that his lawyer pressured him to change his plea, and that his plea was influenced by promises of a reduction of sentence and clemency. The court found that "although Brady's plea of guilty may well have been motivated in part by a desire to avoid a possible death penalty, we are convinced that his plea was voluntarily and intelligently made and we have no reason to doubt that his solemn admission of guilt was truthful."

In discussion, the Court explained the issue as inherent in the criminal law and its administration because

> Guilty pleas are not constitutionally forbidden, because the criminal law characteristically extends to judge or jury a range of choice in setting the sentence in individual cases, and because both the State and the defendant often find it advantageous to preclude the possibility of the maximum penalty authorized by law. For a defendant who sees slight possibility of acquittal, the advantages of pleading guilty and limiting the probable penalty are obvious—his exposure is reduced, the correctional process can begin immediately, and the practical burdens of a trial are eliminated. For the State there are also advantages—the more promptly imposed punishment after an admission of guilt may more effectively attain the objectives of punishment; and with the avoidance of trial, scarce judicial and prosecutorial resources are conserved for those cases in which there is a substantial issue of the defendant's guilt or in which there is substantial doubt that the State can sustain its burden of proof. It is this mutuality of advantage that perhaps explains the fact that at present well over three-fourths of the criminal convictions in this country rest on pleas of guilty, a great many of them no doubt motivated at least in part by the hope or assurance of a lesser penalty than might be imposed if there were a guilty verdict after a trial to judge or jury. [9]

Debates surrounding the topic of plea bargaining are plentiful. There are arguments for abolishing it, for prohibiting parts of it, for judicial controls on it, and for guidelines, standards, or internal policy statements setting forth criteria for the exercise of discretion in deciding whether and what to charge. For some elements of the debate about plea bargaining, see Box 7.3.[10]

Box 7.3

Plea Bargaining: Pro and Con

Arguments in favor:

Essential to court system functioning.

Many courts could not sustain the burden of trying all cases.

If courts are overloaded, the quality of justice suffers.

Resources can be used better elsewhere.

Relieves both the defendant and the prosecution of the inevitable risks and uncertainties of trial.

Mitigates the harshness of mandatory sentencing provisions or offender registration requirements.

Allows fixing punishments more accurately to reflect the circumstances of the case.

Serves important law enforcement needs by agreements for leniency in exchange for information, assistance, and testimony.

Arguments against:

Danger that innocent persons will be convicted.

Underlying threat of harsher punishment if the defendant goes to trial.

Endangers the right to an accurate and fair determination of guilt or innocence.

Defense attorneys may encourage pleas primarily to expedite the movement of cases.

Defense attorneys may pressure clients into entering a plea.

May benefit older, more experienced defendants who "know the ropes."

"Last minute" plea bargaining makes efficient court scheduling difficult or impossible, wasting court and attorney time.

Results in leniency that reduces the deterrent impact of the law.

Makes the rehabilitation process more difficult.

May require the imposition of sentences inconsistent with correctional goals.

Increases offender cynicism of a process characterized by deception and hypocrisy.

A common criticism of the practice of plea bargaining is that some innocent persons may be induced to plead guilty by promises of leniency (a less harsh punishment). Another is that plea bargaining results in excessive leniency. In addition, it is argued that plea bargaining is impossible to control, that it shifts sentencing policy from the legislature and the judiciary to the prosecutor, and that it confuses the distinct features of the criminal process—the determination of guilt and of proper punishment. Yet, it may be argued that for the defendant it may reduce the likelihood of staying in jail awaiting trial, reduce financial costs, and result in a lesser penalty. For the state, it may reduce costs of prosecution and trials and speed up the process. Also, it may allow a greater focus on the most serious cases and avoid overwhelming the criminal courts with the huge numbers of cases that otherwise would be subject to full processing.

When attempts have been made to abolish plea bargaining, the rates of trials and of conviction have not changed much. After a change in Michigan's gun law prohibiting plea bargaining, trial rates stayed low, apparently because of the discovery of alternative methods for offering deals to those who plead guilty.[11] A study of the effects of a ban on plea bargaining by the attorney general of Alaska found that the court processes did not appear to be overwhelmed, the defendants seemed to plead guilty at about the same rate as before, and little change was detected in conviction rates.[12] It may be that defendants perceive an advantage to pleading guilty, hoping for a lighter sentence even though none is promised.

Despite the debates about plea bargaining, the necessity and validity of the discretion granted to prosecutors in pressing charges is generally accepted. Not all arrests should result in prosecution. There are many reasons for this. Some victims do not want prosecution. The police may make an arrest although never intending that the person will be prosecuted. There may be insufficient evidence to convict "beyond a reasonable doubt." The suspect may be innocent. There may be appropriate noncriminal alternatives. Full charging may be unrealistic in the light of available resources.

The President's Commission on Law Enforcement and Administration of Justice said in 1967:

> Among the types of cases in which thoughtful prosecutors commonly appear disinclined to seek criminal penalties are domestic disturbances; assaults and petty thefts in which victim and offender are in a family or social relationship; statutory rape when both boy and girl are young; first offense car thefts that involve teenagers taking a car for a short joyride; checks that are drawn upon insufficient funds; shoplifting by first offenders, particularly when restitution is made; and criminal acts that involve offenders suffering from emotional disorders short of legal insanity.[13]

The severest justice may not always be the best policy.
—Abraham Lincoln

Among the usual justifications for plea bargaining is that it is necessary because of heavy caseloads. It is argued that there simply is not enough time and resources to bring every case to trial. If a full court proceeding in every case were attempted, the system would quickly be overcome and grind to a halt. With plea bargaining, the case is more quickly disposed of. In the 1992 survey of state felony sentences, the median time between arrest and sentencing for felony cases was 231 days for jury trials, 171 days for bench trials, and 139 days for guilty pleas. Other pressures than that of caseload, however, are also at work.

It has been widely believed that persons who plead guilty get lighter sentences than do those who exercise their right to trial. This should not happen, but sometimes it does.[14] Studies show, however, that this usually may be more a matter of flawed perception than reality. Other factors such as the seriousness of the charge and the offender's prior record are much more important in determining how the penalty is set.[15]

Other benefits of plea bargaining have been claimed. It sometimes is argued that besides relieving caseload pressures, plea bargaining permits the individualizing of penalties by avoiding mandatory penalties, allows defendants to avoid publicity of a trial, and even allows a first step toward rehabilitation by permitting the defendant to admit guilt.[16]

A study of the perception of the defendant of the plea bargaining process found that most of the defendants represented by public defenders thought that their major opponent was neither the judge nor the prosecutor. Rather, it was usually the person who presented the "deal" to them—the public defender—who therefore was viewed as a surrogate of the prosecutor.[17]

The Decision to Charge

The decision to charge significantly changes the status of the accused person from a suspect into a defendant. It reflects the prosecutor's belief that the accused is guilty and should either bear the economic, social, and personal costs of a defense or plead guilty and suffer the legal and social consequences.

The charge itself is a sanction, even if usually not regarded or intended as one. It may forever damage the defendant's reputation, even if the person is acquitted later. It usually requires the defendant to provide bail money or other guarantees or to remain in jail—often for a long time—pending further action by the court. Charged defendants who are later acquitted suffer these consequences even though the charge was dismissed or they have been found not guilty.

The prosecutor's charging decisions are subject to two kinds of errors: a person who is not guilty may be wrongly charged, and one who is guilty may not be charged. Thus, not charging also has its consequences when the suspect is in fact guilty. Guilty persons who are not charged cannot be subject to the penalties of the criminal law.

Besides the profound consequences for the accused, the prosecutor's decisions greatly influence, and are affected by, other actors in the criminal justice system. The actions of the prosecutor notably affect the behavior of the police and judges. The actions of the police and judges substantially affect the behavior of prosecutors. If the prosecutor repeatedly declines to prosecute a certain type of crime, arrests for those offenses may go down as police come to regard them as futile. The evidence standards required by the prosecutor also may result in changes in evidence-gathering practices by the police. If more or stronger evidence is required, the police may seek it out or take more care in its preservation.

The prosecutor's policies also affect the courts. The charge usually limits the sentences set by trial judges. It sets boundaries on the judge's discretion. The prosecutor's use of provisions in the law for extended penalties or "sentence enhancements" limit the judge's decisions and also those of the parole board. Examples are charging prior felony or weapons offenses which, if proven, will result in much harsher sentences and will give little leeway to the sentencing judge. Other charges that may increase the penalty are those brought under habitual criminal statutes or mandatory sentencing provisions. If the prosecutor chooses to charge an offense that carries a mandatory sentence, this means that after conviction the judge will have no choice about the sentence.

Charging practices affect the implementation or revision of any sentencing guidelines. Sentencing guidelines may affect the practices of the prosecutor, and then the guidelines may be changed in response to the new prosecutorial practice.

The prosecutor is at the center of much action in the criminal justice system. As a result of the pervasive influence of prosecutor decisions on the rest of the criminal justice system, as well as its profound influence on the fate of the offender, it would be difficult to overestimate its importance in the American system of criminal justice. As suggested by Figure 7.3, the prosecutor influences, and is influenced by, all major parts of the criminal justice system. The discretionary power of the prosecutor to charge or to drop charges places the prosecutor in a position of influence perhaps unmatched in the entire system of criminal justice. These influences and interrelations provide a good example of why it is helpful to regard the criminal justice process as a single system.

Figure 7.3 Interrelation of Prosecutor Decisions and Other Criminal Justice Functions

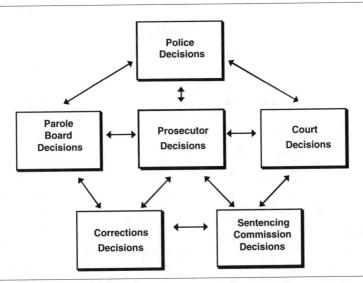

This influence has many other aspects as well. It includes, besides the charging decision and the negotiation of pleas, the trying of contested cases and investigation to discover crimes. The prosecutor not only investigates charges brought by the police but may initiate investigations of other crimes. Besides deciding on charging and conducting plea negotiations, the prosecutor must try cases in court. Charging decisions, however, more than any others made by the prosecutor, critically affect the lives of suspects and victims and the flow of cases through the criminal justice system.

The decision *not* to charge is the most invisible from public scrutiny of all the prosecutor's decisions. If these decisions are reviewed at all, it is within the prosecutor's office. There usually is no public or officially available record. They usually are not known to the public unless the case is a particularly newsworthy one.

Many arrests are rejected at an initial screening and others are dismissed later. Studies of the flow of cases after arrest, describing prosecutor decisions from arrest to conviction, are rare. One such study by Forst and his colleagues, published about 20 years ago, still is informative. Some results of their Washington, D.C. study are shown in Figure 7.4. Just half the arrested cases were dropped without formal charges. Common reasons for the prosecutor's decision to reject a case at an initial screening were that there was insufficient evidence or that there were problems with witnesses (Figure 7.5).

Figure 7.4 Outcomes of 100 'Typical' Arrests Brought to the Superior Court of Washington, D.C., in 1974. (based on the actual flow of 17,534 arrests)

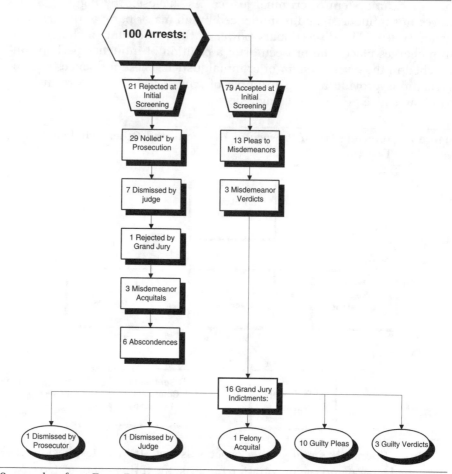

Source: data from Forst, B., Lucianovic, and Cox, S. (1977). "What Happens After Arrest?" *Institute for Law and Social Research*, Publication 4. Washington, D.C.: U.S. GPO.
Note: total does not agree due to rounding error. *Nolled by prosecutor means declined to prosecute.

Figure 7.5 Reasons Given by Prosecutors for Rejection at Initial Screening, Washington, D.C., 1974

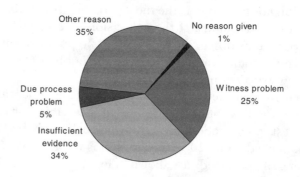

Source: data from Forst, B., Lucianovic, and Cox, S. (1977). "What Happens After Arrest?" *Institute for Law and Social Research*, Publication 4. Washington, D.C.: GPO.

A more visible part of the prosecutor's decision to charge, where much discretion is exercised, is the decision to charge fully or at a reduced level. Should a single offense or multiple offenses be charged? Many crimes can be charged under more than one offense category. For example, a burglary may also be charged as lesser offenses such as breaking and entering, theft, or trespassing. Many crimes encompass more than one offense. An embezzlement could involve fraud, theft by deception, forgery, and conspiracy to commit these offenses. Many crimes involve a number of acts, each of which might constitute a separate offense. A robbery might involve a car theft, an assault, and a kidnapping. Many serious crimes may be charged at the most serious level or at the level of a lesser but included offense. A homicide might be charged as either murder or manslaughter. A second assault with a handgun might be charged as an aggravated assault, as an assault with a deadly weapon, as an assault with prior conviction for assault, as a simple assault, as possession of a deadly weapon by an ex-felon, or as illegal possession of a firearm. Many crimes may also be charged either as felonies or as misdemeanors.

Goals of the Decision

At first, the purposes of charging a suspect with a crime seem straightforward: persons against whom there is enough evidence to sustain a court conviction should be charged, while cases lacking such evidence should not. Only the guilty should be charged, but all of them should be charged in order to maximize the proportion of offenders who are eventually convicted. It has been argued that conviction is itself the main goal of the charging decision and asserted "that the principle objective of the prosecutor is to convict offenders is well beyond dispute."[18]

The decision, however, is more complex than that. The prosecutor's ideal role is to seek justice. That, and some additional prosecutor goals, were described by Justice George Sutherland (in regard to federal prosecutors) as follows:

> The United States Attorney is the representative not of an ordinary party to a controversy, but of a sovereignty whose obligation to govern impartially is as compelling as its obligation to govern at all; and in whose interest, there-fore, in a criminal prosecution is not that it shall win a case, but that justice shall be done. As such, he is in a peculiar and very definite sense the servant of the law, the twofold aim of which is that guilt shall not escape nor innocence suffer. He may prosecute with earnestness and vigor—indeed, he should do so. But, while he may strike hard blows, he is not at liberty to strike foul ones. It is as much his duty to refrain from improper methods calculated to produce a wrongful conviction as it is to use every legitimate means to bring about a just one.[19]

It is better to risk saving a guilty man than to condemn an innocent one.
  —Voltaire

Thus the prosecutor may be concerned not only with the chances of conviction but also with the *desirability* of bringing charges. The concept that the prosecutor should impartially assess the justice of prosecution is consistent with the history of the office of prosecutor, since the English attorney general, particularly in exercising the right of the writ of *nolle prosequi*, did so as the principal means available for ending trivial, frivolous, or vengeful charges brought by citizens. The present role of the prosecutor in this respect is a distinctively American institution, developed in part to prevent overzealous charging by partisan victims of crime. It is believed, reasonably, that a person in a position of public trust could make decisions more impartially than could victims.[20]

The standard for charging is the same as for an arrest—"probable cause." The prosecutor may bring charges if this standard is met, just as a police officer may make an arrest based upon it. The prosecutor, however, must in practice look beyond this standard. That is, the prosecutor must look ahead to the higher standard for a criminal conviction; in order for a jury to convict a defendant, they must agree "beyond a reasonable doubt" that he or she is guilty. As a result, the decision to charge usually involves a *belief* on the part of the prosecutor that the suspect is guilty beyond a reasonable doubt (and that it can be proved in court).

The prosecutor is aware of limitations on resources. Also, prosecutors widely believe that it is unfair to charge a suspect who cannot be convicted. The prosecutor also must estimate the likelihood of winning. This may be based on an assessment of the strength of the evidence but also on an evaluation of the likelihood of being able to present it in court. If evidence is likely to be declared inadmissible by the court, or if witnesses are not likely to be available to testify, these circumstances will lower the prosecutor's estimate of the probability of conviction. This could be based partly on a police promise that additional evidence will be forthcoming.[21]

Besides concerns for convictability and justice in making charging decisions, prosecutors typically seek the reduction of crime. This goal may be expressed in many ways. For example, the prosecutor may select repeat offenders for prosecution, with less emphasis on charging first offenders. Or, specific charges may be selected choosing statutes that increase prison terms— such as habitual offender laws and "three strikes" statutes—or charging offenses with mandatory prison terms. These policies rest on the assumption that imprisonment is effective in reducing crime by deterring people from committing new crimes or by incapacitating potential offenders by confinement. Often they require the prosecutor's predictions that particular kinds of offenders are more likely to repeat their offenses.

A goal shared by prosecutors is the efficient utilization of scarce resources. Most jurisdic-

Prosecutors may charge on probable cause but must look forward to the challenge of proving the case beyond a reasonable doubt. Do you think these standards are too low, too high, or about right? Why?
—*Photo courtesy of www.photostogo.com*

tions lack the resources required for the prosecution of every case. The selection of which cases to prosecute often involve assessments of the seriousness of the crime and of the punishment deserved. In addition, they may require estimates of the effects to control crime that might be attained or lost by the decision whether to charge. The selection of cases to prosecute may be influenced by a shortage of jail or prison resources, because the prosecutor may seek to confine those offenders they perceive as the most serious or the most likely to do more harm.

Decisions may also be influenced by the prosecutor's perceptions of what is fair. This may mean that offenders should be selected for prosecution in relation to the harm done by the crime and that suspects should be treated equally.

The rehabilitation of the suspect might be a goal of the prosecutor, as recommended by the 1967 President's Commission on Law Enforcement and Administration of Justice. This may be more typically the case when the alleged offense is not a particularly serious one, or when the accused presents problems such as drug addiction or alcohol abuse. It may depend heavily on the treatment resources available in the jurisdiction. If there are no resources for treatment, or only meager ones, then the prosecutor does not have much choice even if rehabilitation is a goal.

Less often acknowledged may be political and personal goals. The position of prosecutor often is seen as a "stepping stone" to higher public office. Many judges and state governors previously were prosecutors. The political aims of publicly elected prosecutors undoubtedly direct or at least influence charging decisions, mainly shown in the desire to maintain a winning record and to be seen as "tough on crime." Here, it is convictions that count, and the more serious the charge of conviction the better. Such a record is an asset for re-election or for realizing aspirations for higher public office. It might also be reflected in public announcements, amid public outrage, of a "crack down" on particular kinds of offenses, or in selecting, with accompanying publicity, the most serious applicable charges in a case much in the news.

At times, constraints or opportunities given by aspects of the larger criminal justice system may lead to additional goals. The decision not to charge a suspect that otherwise could be charged may stem from a desire to support the police informant network. Charges may be dropped in exchange for information. Or, the decision to drop charges may originate in a desire for the successful prosecution of the "higher-ups" in a criminal conspiracy.[22]

Specific goals may underlie the development of policies of "nonprosecution."[23] That is, prosecutors may decide not to prosecute a particular kind of case at all (besides deciding that some kinds of cases should be given emphasis). In such a case, prosecutors have decided on their own not to enforce a particular statute. Such a decision might be made because of opposition from the community, difficulties in enforcing a statute in a legal manner, existence of an effective alternative, or the ability to prosecute the offender for another crime.

When there is no general formal or informal policy not to charge a particular kind of offense, the prosecutor still may make a decision not to charge in an individual case. Commonly, when this is done, the offense involves a minor crime, a crime with a consenting victim, or a crime for which there are conflicting community feelings about enforcement. According to Abrams:

> In particular jurisdictions, the incidence of no-charge decisions by the prosecutor is quite high. Most of these decisions result, however, from overly energetic police arrest policies or from poor police investigation and fact-gathering. The police sometimes bring cases to the prosecutor for decision knowing full well that they have insufficient evidence, but wanting the prosecutor to assume responsibility for the decision not to proceed. [24]

At trial, the prosecutor presents the "case in chief" in an opening statement, outlining the charges and the evidence expected to be presented to show the guilt of the defendant. In arriving at this stage, what goals do you think would be most important to the prosecutor? —*Photo courtesy of www.photostogo.com.*

Goals of the prosecutor's decisions may include those of winning cases, reducing crime, increasing efficiency, ensuring fairness, seeking justice, exacting deserved punishment, getting ahead in politics, and cooperation between and within various agencies (Box 7.4). Several goals may be involved in a given decision, and goals may even conflict with one another. The com-

Box 7.4
Prosecutor Goals

Winning cases	Getting ahead personally or politically
Reducing crime	
	Increasing interagency cooperation
Increasing efficiency	
	Protecting information sources or gaining information
Ensuring equity	
Seeking justice	Incapacitating offenders
Exacting punishment	Deterring others from crime

plexity of prosecutor goals is reflected in the criteria urged upon prosecutors by standard-setting bodies such as the American Bar Association, suggesting consideration of the following criteria besides the "weight of the evidence":

- The prosecutor's assessment of guilt.
- The extent of harm caused by the offense.
- The disproportion of the punishment to the harm caused by the offense.
- Possible improper motives for a complaint.
- Prolonged nonenforcement of a statute, with community consent.
- Reluctance of the victim to testify.
- Cooperation of the accused in the apprehension or conviction of others.
- The availability and likelihood of prosecution by another jurisdiction.[25]

What Influences the Prosecutor's Decision

When a former assistant U.S. Attorney discussed his personal experiences as a federal prosecutor, he reported that the first and most important factor influencing the decision to charge was the prosecutor's view of the guilt of the accused.[26] The prosecutor had to be convinced of guilt before filing charges, even if there was more than enough evidence to sustain them. Next considered was the question whether the case could result in conviction. In making that assessment, he indicated that both the record of convictions by the assistant prosecutor and the available resources were taken into account. He reported also that there were lower standards for the likelihood of conviction for serious cases, reflecting an intent to give some weight in the charging decision to the likelihood of future crimes by the accused. He noted that some accused were considered more valuable as witnesses than as defendants and therefore were not prosecuted so that their testimony could be used against others. He stressed also that a major factor in charging decisions was an assessment by the U.S. Attorney of the proportionality of the charge and potential penalty: Was the sanction for the charge too severe, given the nature and circumstances of the offense? Many of these factors have been confirmed by others.

Besides the first requirement that the prosecutor believe the accused to be guilty, several factors appear to be important in determining the prosecutor's decision not to charge (Box 7.5). The attitude of the victim, the cost to the system, undue harm to the suspect, the availability of alternative procedures, and the suspect's willingness to cooperate in achieving other law enforcement goals all may be important.[27] Thus, if the witness refuses to testify, if extradition (movement of the suspect) to another jurisdiction is possible, if the potential penalty is seen as too severe, if revocation of parole or an insanity commitment is preferable, or if the accused agrees to be a witness against more significant defendants, then the prosecutor may decide not to charge even though there is enough evidence to do so.

Other factors may influence the decision to charge when otherwise the prosecutor would not. These might include a public outcry about the offense or similar ones; clamor from the press about leniency generally or about the

Box 7.5

Factors Influencing Prosecutor Decisions

Belief in the guilt of the accused	Attitude of the victim
Strength of the evidence	Cost to the criminal justice system
Probability of winning	Availability of alternatives
Value of the suspect as a witness	Public outcry and public toleration
Proportionality of the charge and potential penalty (fairness)	Press clamor
	Police reactions

particular crime; protests by the police that the prosecutor does not follow through to seek convictions after all their efforts to arrest the accused; the perception by the prosecutor that a service for the suspect might be brought about by charging, since needed treatment might result; helping other investigations; the anticipation of new evidence in the case; or the desire to be rid of a suspect who is a particular nuisance.

Public tolerance of some offenses also may influence the decision:

> The public does not demand rigid enforcement of certain laws, and this is an important consideration in the decision not to prosecute. When the prosecutor feels that the community no longer considers criminal a pattern of behavior prohibited by statute, he either refuses to prosecute or strives to convince the complainant to drop charges.[28]

> *There are not enough jails, not enough policemen, not enough courts to enforce a law not supported by the people.*
> —*Hubert H. Humphrey*

Information for Prosecutor Decisions

Prosecution decisions should be guided by a general policy that provides a framework for consistent, fair decisions with adequate provision for necessary discretion. As described by Abrams:

> There is a competing tension between the need in prosecutorial decision making for certainty, consistency, and an absence of arbitrariness on the one hand, and the need for flexibility, sensitivity, and adaptability on the other. The problem is to design the system so as to reach an acceptable balance between the two sets of values. [29]

An important advance toward the development of clearer, more explicit policy and more consistency in information for charging decisions was made in the 1970s, using computerized case evaluation systems.[30] These were called the Prosecutors' Management Information System (PROMIS) of data collection for the prosecutors' decisions.[31] A prominent focus for development of this system was on the achievement of increased fairness and equal treatment.

One purpose of these systems is to indicate priorities for prosecution, with importance assigned on the basis of computer-generated scores providing evaluations of the seriousness of the crime, the criminal history of the suspect, and, in some cases, the weight of the evidence. Thus, each case is scored on the same factors in a consistent, objective manner. The policy is explicitly stated, as are the items of information to be used in the assessments and the weight given to them.

Such an explicit policy can be subject to a more informed debate and more subject to examination of consistency in practice. The clearly articulated policy made possible by the PROMIS system could be open to public scrutiny, critical examination, and improvement. Prosecutors, however, have been slow in adopting such systems. For an opinion on the needs for more explicit policy underlying prosecutor decisions, see the comments by Brian Forst, who has studied these decisions extensively (Box 7.6).

Box 7.6

Brian Forst: In His Own Words

When asked to explain the rationale behind the decisions, most prosecutors are inclined to say that case-handling decisions, like medical decisions, involve both science and craft, and that experienced prosecutors know how to blend the technical requirements of the law with the good judgment that comes from years of practice. Unfortunately, this tells us nothing about the underlying goals that influence their decision-making process. Nor do we know whether prosecutors consciously make case selection and handling decisions with such goals in mind. Most prosecutors argue that while justice, crime control, and speedy case processing are all worthy goals, each case is unique. Whether to accept the case, what charges to file, how much time to spend preparing it for a court proceeding, what charge or charges to allow the defendant to plead to in return for dropping other charges (or what sentence to recommend to the judge if the defendant pleads guilty to a particular charge) in any given case cannot be determined by pondering over abstract goals or resorting to a formula derived from such goals. Until a strong argument can be made for instituting a more explicit set of rules or guidelines for making case processing decisions based on well-established empirical links between the rules and such tangible goals as reduced case-processing time and crime control, decisions about individual cases are likely to continue to be made in a subjective and largely unpredictable manner.

Prosecutors may, however, be pushing the political, if not the lawful, limits of their discretion.

Prosecutors may disagree on the proper goals of prosecution, or on the best method of achieving a goal, but it is difficult to object to a more coherent and consistent basis for making case-processing decisions in a prosecutor's office. Prosecutors themselves can take the initiative in identifying those areas in which guidelines for more uniform practices are most needed and putting them in place, so that their work can be made both more explicit and more evenhanded. If they do not, others may do it for them.

—Brian Forst,
The American University

Summary

After arrest, a prosecutor typically must decide whether suspects will be charged, and if so, with what crimes. The district attorney (or county attorney) provides a link between the laws enacted by legislatures, the police, and the judiciary. Prosecutor decisions affect each of the other criminal justice system functions—decisions by the police, judges, and correction personnel —and are affected by them.

The traditional power of the prosecutor to dismiss cases or to substitute lesser charges is enormous. It is rarely open to public scrutiny or subject to controls by the legislature or the courts. The influence of the prosecutor on the criminal justice system has many aspects—charging, plea negotiation, trying cases, and investigation of crimes.

Plea bargaining is a process through which an accused trades the right to trial for a reduction in charges or sentences and a more certain outcome. Most convictions are a consequence of guilty pleas, many of which result from plea bargains. Plea bargaining is controversial, but courts have supported the practice when pleas have been made voluntarily and intelligently. At present, plea bargaining is an important feature of the American system of criminal justice.

The prosecutor's decision to charge changes the status of a suspect to that of a defendant. This change has profound personal consequences, regardless of the subsequent outcome of the case. If the accused is in fact not guilty, these consequences nevertheless may include financial loss, confinement, and reputation damage. If, however, guilty suspects are not charged, they are not subject to the penalties of the criminal law.

The goals of the prosecutor are complex: seek justice; win cases; use resources efficiently; reduce crime; ensure fairness; see that deserved punishment is exacted; support other agencies of justice; and get re-elected.

The prosecutor's decisions are influenced by a belief in the guilt of the accused, the weight of the evidence, the probability of winning at trial, and available resources. Other influences may concern the prosecutor's perceptions of fairness, victim attitudes, the availability of alternatives, and the value of the accused as a witness for other prosecutions. They may be influenced by community toleration or public outcry.

Procedures are available that more objectively and explicitly state prosecutorial policies. This could permit a more informed debate with greater public scrutiny, allow an easier examination of consistency in practice, and increase fairness. It could also allow testing the value of data used as information in seeking to achieve the goals of prosecutor decisions.

Notes

1. This section has been much informed by Goldstein, A. S. (1983). "Prosecution: History of the Public Prosecutor," in Kadish, S. H. (ed.). *Encyclopedia of Crime and Justice*, Vol. 3. New York: The Free Press, 1286–1290.

2. Ibid., 1286.

3. Ibid., 1289.

4. Heumann, M. (1975). "A Note on Plea Bargaining and Case Pressure," *Law and Society Review* 9:3:515.

5. National Advisory Commission on Criminal Justice Standards and Goals (1973). Washington, DC: GPO.

6. Daudistel, H. (1980). "On the Elimination of Plea Bargaining: The El Paso Experiment," In McDonald and Kramer, (eds.). *Plea Bargaining*. Lexington: D.C. Heath; Rubenstein, M., and White, T. (1980) "Alaska's Ban on Plea-Bargaining," In McDonald and Kramer, (eds.). *Plea Bargaining*. Lexington: D.C. Heath.

7. Langan, P. A., and Grazi, dei H. A. (1995). *Felony Sentences in State Courts, 1992*. Washington, DC: Bureau of Justice Statistics Bulletin, U.S. Department of Justice, 9.

8. Goldstein, A. S., (1983)"Prosecution: History of the Public Prosecutor," in Kadish, S. H. (ed.). *Encyclopedia of Crime and Justice*, Vol. 3. p.1289. New York: The Free Press.

9. *Brady v. United States* (1970). 397 U.S. 742; See also *North Carolina v. Alford* (1970). 400 U.S. 25; *Bordenkircher v. Hayes* (1978). 434 U.S. 357.

10. Adapted from National Advisory Commission on Criminal Justice Standards and Goals (1973). "The Negotiated Plea," in *Report on the Courts* 42–45, as cited in Snortum, J. R., and Hader, I. (eds.). (1978). *Criminal Justice: Allies and Adversaries*. Pacific Palisades, CA: Palisades Publishers, 144–149.

11. Huemann, M., and Loftin, C. (1979). "Mandatory Sentencing and the Abolition of Plea Bargaining," *Law and Society Review* 13: 393.

12. Rubenstein, M., and White, T. (1980). "Alaska's Ban on Plea Bargaining," in McDonald, W., and Cramer, J., (eds.). *Plea Bargaining*. Lexington: D.C. Heath.

13. President's Commission of Law Enforcement and Administration of Justice (1967). *The Challenge of Crime in a Free Society*. Washington, DC: GPO, 5.

14. Brereton D., and Casper, J. (1981–1982). "Does It Pay to Plead Guilty? Differential Sentencing and the Functioning of the Criminal Courts," *Law and Society Review* 16:1:45–70.

15. Eisenstein, J., and Jacob, H. (1977). *Felony Justice*. Boston: Little, Brown.

16. Casper, J. (1972). American Criminal Justice: The Defendant's Perspective. Englewood Cliffs, NJ: Prentice-Hall; Heumann, M. (1978). *Plea Bargaining*. Chicago: University of Chicago Press.

17. Ibid.

18. Forst, B., and Brosi, K. (1977). "A Theoretical and Empirical Analysis of the Prosecutor," *Journal of Legal Studies* 6:177, 65.

19. *Berger v. United States* (1935). 295 U.S. 78, 88.

20. Miller, F. (1970). *Prosecution: The Decision to Charge a Suspect with a Crime*. Boston: Little, Brown.

21. McIntyre, D. (ed.). (1967). *Law Enforcement in the Metropolis*. Chicago: American Bar Foundation.

22. Miller, F. (1970); Newman, D. (1966). *Conviction: The Determination of Guilt or Innocence Without Trial*. Boston: Little, Brown.

23. Abrams, N. (1975). "Prosecutorial Charge Decision Systems," *University of California Law Review* 21:1

24. Abrams, N. (1983). "Prosecution: Prosecutorial Discretion," in Kadish, S. H. (ed.). *Encyclopedia of Crime and Justice*, Vol. 3. New York: The Free Press, 1274.

25. American Bar Association. (1971). *Standards Relating to the Prosecution and the Defense Function*. Approved draft. New York: Institute for Judicial Administration.

26. Kaplan, J. (1965). "The Prosecutorial Discretion—A Comment," *Northwestern University Law Review*.

27. Miller, F. (1970). *Conviction: The Determination of Guilt or Innocence Without Trial*. Boston: Little, Brown.

28. McIntyre, D. (ed.). (1967) *Law Enforcement in the Metropolis*. Chicago: American Bar Foundation, 111.

29. Abrams, N. (1971). "Internal Policy: Guiding the Exercise of Prosecutorial Discretion," *UCLA Law Review* 19:1, 3–4.

30. Jacoby, J. (1977). *The Prosecutor's Charging Decision: A Policy Perspective*. Washington, DC: GPO.

31. Hamilton, W., and Work, C. (1973). "The Prosecutor's Role in the Urban Court System: The Case for Management Consciousness," *Journal of Criminal Law and Criminology* 64: 183; Jacoby, J. (1977); Institute for Law and Social Research. (1976). *Uniform Case Evaluation and Rating*. INSLAW Briefing Paper Number 3. Washington, D. C.: INSLAW.

CHAPTER EIGHT

The Courts

Photo courtesy of the California History Section, California State Library.

Chapter Eight

The victim may complain, the police may arrest, the prosecutor may charge, but the defendant is entitled to judgment by a court. This chapter explains the structure and functions of the criminal courts. This requires discussion of decisions whether to release an accused person before trial, the procedures of the trial courts, and the roles of the main actors at trials.

❏ Questions to Think About

❏ The Courts

❏ Court Structures

❏ Appeals Processes

❏ The Supreme Court of the United States

❏ The Lower Courts

❏ Pretrial Release

    Goals of the Pretrial Release Decision

    Alternatives for Pretrial Release Decisions

    Information for Pretrial Release Decisions

    Prediction of Decision Outcomes

    Kinds of Errors in Predictions

    What Influences the Bail Decision?

    Guidelines for Bail Decisions

❏ The Trial Courts

❏ The Trial

❏ Speedy Trials

❏ Public Trials

❏ The Jury

❏ Jury Selection

❏ Jury Nullification

❏ Pretrial Motions

❏ The Prosecutor's Case

❏ The Defense Case

❏ The Verdict

❏ Summary

How does the judicial branch of government differ from the administrative and legislative branches?

What kinds of courts do we have?

What is the purpose of bail?

Of all the people in jail, how many are not convicted but awaiting trial?

Can people be trusted to return to court when required?

What are the goals of bail decisions?

Can a judge keep accused persons in jail to prevent crimes?

What influences bail decisions?

What is the function of a grand jury?

What is meant by the adversary process?

Are there different kinds of trials?

How does a jury get selected?

How does a case get to the U.S. Supreme Court?

Can a lawyer exclude a potential juror without giving any reason?

If a jury finds a defendant not guilty, can the judge reverse its decision?

Can a prosecutor appeal a verdict of not guilty?

The Courts

Mrs. X was in deathly fear of a hostile alien from another planet. She had seen a mysterious car driving in front of her house, which she assumed was driven by the alien. She had trouble with her television—periodically getting nothing but static, which she thought probably was caused by the alien using some listening device connected to her home. When she searched for "alien" on the internet, her computer stalled, providing further evidence, she believed, that the alien was watching her every move and very much in control.

She had asked for help from the police, who said they couldn't do anything unless a crime had been committed and gave her the name of a mental health clinic. She tried to get help from the district attorney, to no avail. Finding no help anywhere else, she sought a hearing at court. She believed the alien presented a clear and present danger to herself and requested a judicial hearing to complain of a lack of protection.

She did not get a hearing. In order to have a case heard by the court, she would need to point to some violation of a specific and personal legal right. She might have had a case if she could specify the particular alien causing trouble and assert a legally protected right to be left alone. It is not likely that she could find a statute that imposes a nondiscretionary duty on some official to exterminate all hostile aliens from other planets. [1]

Mrs. X's hostile alien complaint cannot be satisfied by the court. There are two fundamental reasons:

- The courts, unlike administrators and legislatures, cannot initiate action. The judge cannot take off on his own to search out aliens, rescue people or protect them, order the *Enterprise* to do so, or make a rule that hostile aliens shall be eliminated. The judge must wait in court for someone to complain.

- The complainant must ask for a remedy that the court can grant.

There are many other ways that the process of the courts differs from administrative or legislative processes, including these:

- The court can legitimately hear only certain kinds of evidence.

- The court is required to follow particular procedures for receiving and weighing the evidence.

- All the evidence—oral, written, or physical—that the court may consider must be introduced in the presence of both sides of a dispute.

- Each side must have the same opportunities to present evidence and also to examine and rebut it.

- The judge cannot legitimately consider evidence denied to one side.

- The judge cannot base a decision on evidence not submitted in open court.

- Court proceedings are adversarial; they involve opposing sides. Attorneys for both sides of a controversy produce the evidence, define the issues to be considered, and present the arguments. The lawyers battle as equals with the judge as umpire for the adjudication of a dispute.

- The parties to the dispute may legitimately contact the judge or jury only under specific, structured circumstances.

> *A legislative, an executive, and a judicial power comprehend the whole of what is meant and understood by government. It is by balancing each of these powers against the other two, that the efforts in human nature toward tyranny can alone be checked and restrained, and any degree of freedom preserved in the constitution.*
> —*John Adams*

It often is said that legislatures make laws and the courts enforce them. This is true, but it is an oversimplification. Although the courts have functions that are distinct from those of legislatures, executives, or administrators, these functions overlap. The sources of authority for the criminal justice system are found in each part of government: executive, legislative, judicial, and administrative.[2] In the executive branch, presidents, governors, or mayors initiate legislation, appoint administrators, propose budgets, and may have other powers—such as those of presidents and governors to pardon offenders and commute sentences. Legislators define crimes. Appellate courts interpret the laws and may review laws for conformity to constitutions. Administrative agencies—such as police departments and sheriff's offices, prosecutor offices, probation departments, administrative offices of the courts, corrections agencies, and parole boards—enforce the laws, operate the criminal justice process, and make rules to do so. These parts of government together make and enforce rules, with varying degrees of authority.

The processes of the legislatures, administrative agencies, and the courts are better distinguished by their procedures.[3]

> It is impossible to draw a sharp line between legislating and adjudicating or between administering and the other two. . . . How can an executive enforce a law without interpreting it? When a policeman decides not to ticket a driver who is exceeding the speed limit by only five miles an hour, is the officer legislating, administering, or adjudicating? How can judges help but make law when they decide what a vaguely worded statute means in a situation that its drafters never foresaw?[4]

Court Structures

Because each state has a separate judicial system and the federal government has another, we have 51 court systems besides those of the territories. In another sense, we have as many court systems as we have counties, and therefore at least that many criminal justice systems. Prosecution for crimes defined by Congress are brought in federal courts. Those defined by state laws are prosecuted in state courts. State courts typically are operated by counties with state supervision for some aspects of the operation.

Every court system has both trial courts and appellate courts. The function of the trial courts is to hear the evidence in a dispute, determine how the law applies, and apply the law to the facts or else direct a jury to do so. The appellate court reviews the actions of the trial court for errors; it reviews appeals. It does not hold a hearing for examination of the evidence but reviews the trial court transcript.[5]

Some trial courts are specialized to deal only with certain kinds of legal issues but most are not, and criminal cases typically go to trial courts of general jurisdiction. Most state court systems are structured so that more minor cases are assigned to courts called magistrate courts and more serious cases to another court, the general trial court.

The courts of first instance—the court to which a criminal case will first be brought—for criminal justice are the magistrate courts, which are courts of limited jurisdiction. There is, however, no uniformity in the naming of these courts. They sometimes are called justice of the peace courts, municipal courts, district courts, police courts, or recorder's courts. These courts have jurisdiction over less serious offenses, sometimes all misdemeanors and sometimes only those that are punishable by more limited penalties, such as up to six months in jail. These courts also have a limited jurisdiction over many aspects of offenses beyond their *trial* jurisdiction—including issuing search and arrest warrants, handling the first appearance of an accused person, setting bail, appointment of counsel if the accused cannot afford an attorney, and determining at a preliminary hearing whether there is probable cause for the case to proceed to trial.

The general trial courts also are called by various names—superior court, circuit court, district court, or court of common pleas. (In New York, the general trial court is called the supreme court.) States usually are divided into districts, with at least one general trial court judge for each district. Commonly, the districts are the same as the counties. These courts may also hear appeals from cases in the magistrate courts, examining the record for possible errors.

Appeals Processes

About half the states have a single intermediate appellate court between the trial court and the highest state court. Sometimes there are more, with the state separated into divisions. A fairly typical structure is that of California, illustrated in Figure 8.1.

Figure 8.1 California Court Structure[6]

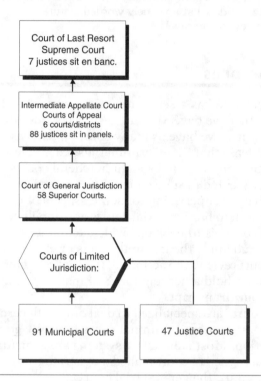

In about a dozen states, the highest appellate court—usually called the supreme court—is the first available appellate court for a defendant who has been convicted in a general trial court. When there is only one appellate court, the defendant usually has a right to appeal for a review in that court. When there is an intermediate level appellate court, then the state supreme court generally will grant only petitions that are decided to merit consideration beyond that of the intermediate court. In that case, the defendant typically will have a right to review in the intermediate court. (An exception is that a defendant sentenced to death usually has a right to review by the highest state court.)

Appellate courts usually sit in panels of three judges. The highest court—that is, the court of last resort for state cases, in matters of state law—typically is made up of five, seven, or nine justices, who usually sit *en banc*, that is, all together.

If the case involves a federal law, a further review can be sought from the U.S. Supreme Court. Accepting jurisdiction is generally discretionary with the Court—they do not have to take the case. It usually refuses to accept jurisdiction in cases coming from the state courts. Nevertheless, many of the most important cases affecting the criminal justice system have involved federal constitutional claims of defendants who had been convicted in state courts and had their objections rejected by the state appellate courts.

In the federal system, which does not have a magistrate court, each of the general trial courts, called U.S. District Courts, employs U.S. magistrates selected by the district court judges. The federal magistrates may try all misdemeanor cases, but a defendant may elect to be tried in the district court. As in state systems, these magistrates issue search and arrest warrants and preside for the first appearance. In felony cases, they hold preliminary hearings.

The general trial court is the district court. Each state has at least one, but there are 94 judicial districts. The district court has jurisdiction over all prosecutions brought under federal criminal law.

The federal district court influences the state criminal courts because a person tried and convicted in a state court for a violation of a state law may obtain relief in the federal district court if it can be shown that the conviction involved a violation of the convicted person's federal constitutional rights.

The federal system includes an intermediate court of appeals called the U.S. Court of Appeals. There are 13 appeals courts. Eleven of the courts each cover several states, while another is for the District of Columbia. Another appeals court has been called the Federal Circuit since 1982. It is located in Washington, D.C., but handles appeals in some specific matters and suits against the federal government from anywhere in the country. Cases decided by district courts may be appealed (as a matter of right) to the Court of Appeals for the circuit of which the district court is a part. Typically, appeals are heard by a panel of three judges of the circuit, but sometimes they are heard *en banc*.

The appellate court of last resort for the federal system is the Supreme Court of the United States. The Court is made up of nine justices, who hear all cases *en banc*. The justices can review any case decided by any of the Court of Appeals circuits, but appeal to the Court is not a matter of right. A person who has lost in the Court of Appeals may petition for review, but only a very small proportion of cases are accepted by the Supreme Court.

If a convicted defendant seeks to appeal the conviction on the basis that constitutional rights have been violated, and the state supreme court has rejected the appeal, the defendant may appeal to the U.S. Supreme Court. This is done by an application for a writ of *certiorari*. Such a writ directs a lower court (in this case the state supreme court) to send the records of the case to the higher court (here, the U.S. Supreme Court). Only relatively few such cases will be accepted by the Court—usually only those it decides involve substantial unresolved constitutional questions.

A defendant also can apply to the U.S. District Court for a writ of *habeas corpus*. The phrase *habeas corpus* means "you have the body of" and comes from the practice, in the common law of England, of a demand of a jailer to produce a prisoner for a judge in order to determine whether the prisoner was held lawfully. In the case of an alleged violation of constitutional rights, the federal district court could conduct a similar inquiry in order to determine whether the U.S. Constitution was violated in the defendant's trial. If the defendant's request is rejected by the district court, the defendant may appeal that decision to a U.S. Court of Appeal. If that court does not overrule the district court, application could be made to the Supreme Court. The Supreme Court, however, has held that the writ of *habeas corpus* is not available for Fourth Amendment search and seizure cases because the federal

courts cannot manage the huge caseload resulting from such applications.
The general process of appeals is illustrated in Figure 8.2.

Figure 8.2 Process of Appeals

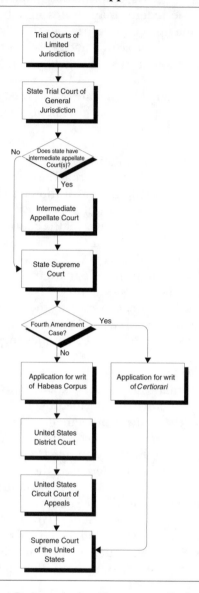

The Supreme Court of the United States

Besides its role in appeals, the U.S. Supreme Court, which has complete
authority over all U.S. courts, has original jurisdiction in cases in which a
public minister, ambassador, consul, or the United States government is a
party. Its jurisdiction extends to cases between governments or between citizens of different states.

The Chief Justice of the Supreme Court (now also called the Chief Justice
of the United States) and eight associate justices make up the Court. All are
appointed by the President, with the consent of the Senate, for life terms.
They can be removed only by resignation or impeachment. For most of its
history, there were no black Americans on the Court. Thurgood Marshall

was the first to be an associate justice of the Supreme Court, where he served for 24 years, after being appointed by President Johnson in 1967. For 191 years, all were men. President Reagan appointed Sandra Day O'Conner, the first woman justice, to the Court in 1981.

The Court reaches its decisions by majority vote, but any justice who disagrees can issue a dissenting opinion. It is up to the Executive Department to enforce the Court's decisions—which are called opinions.

Early in its history, the Supreme Court ruled that there were no common law crimes in the federal jurisdiction. That is, the usual common law crimes were the business of the states, not the federal government. Therefore, there could be no criminal prosecutions unless they were authorized by an act of Congress making some behavior a crime. This changed dramatically after the Civil War. Among the amendments to the Constitution then passed was the Fourteenth Amendment, which, as described earlier, has been the avenue for extending the application of most of the Bill of Rights to the states.

Then, in 1875, federal district courts were given jurisdiction over federal questions. This meant that cases involving claims of constitutional violation could be initiated in the federal courts. This was followed by a steady progression of increasing involvement of the federal courts in matters thought earlier to be concerns only of the states, including the civil rights laws enacted in the 1960s. Most recently, there has been a federalization of more and more crimes that previously were considered to be only state concerns. For an explanation of these changes by the Chief Justice of the United States, see Box 8.1. [7]

Although about 95 percent of the work of the courts is still done in the state courts, the present tendency of the Congress to make crimes federal offenses is increasing the involvement of the federal courts in criminal matters. More and more crimes once believed to be in the exclusive province of the states are being made into federal offenses.

Box 8.1

Chief Justice William H. Rehnquist: In His Own Words

Forty years ago when I began the practice of law in Arizona, there were not many federal criminal statutes on the books. There were some very esoteric crimes, but the staple of the criminal business of federal courts outside the metropolitan areas was confined to prosecutions for transporting a stolen car in interstate commerce, using the mails for interstate communications to commit fraud, and a very few other similar crimes.

But the landscape has entirely changed in the last forty years. Congress, understandably concerned with the increasing traffic in drugs and violence resulting from the use of guns, has legislated again and again to make what once were only state crimes federal offenses. . . . Congress has been of the opinion that even though these gun and drug crimes could be prosecuted under state law, the state penal systems were too lenient in paroling serious offenders after having served only a fraction of the time to which they were sentenced. So Congress has stepped in, prescribed very severe sentencing guidelines for federal crimes, and federalized crimes involving drugs and guns.

All of this means that in talking about the future of the federal courts, we must understand that Congress will probably continue to enact new legislation which provides new causes of action for litigants on the civil side of the docket, and new federal crimes to be prosecuted on the criminal side of the federal docket.

—Chief Justice William H. Rehnquist

The Lower Courts

Throughout the world, trial courts traditionally have been divided into lower and upper courts. Even Moses judged the larger matters but, on the advice of his father-in-law who saw that he was overworked, appointed assistants to handle the lesser cases.[8] His reason for the division into less and more serious cases was the workload. So it has been through history. Imperial administrations of the Roman Empire let local courts deal with petty matters but assumed authority over more serious ones. The magistrate courts in England originated in the local feudal courts of the 14th century and still are controlled locally. American courts grew from the early colonial courts as they were earlier imported from Great Britain, and the tradition continued.

It is not only tradition, however, that continues the division of our court system into lower and upper courts. Rather, the reason is still the workload. Of the vast numbers of cases coming to the criminal courts, relatively few involve very serious or politically sensitive charges. Much of the workload of the courts is done by the lower courts because much crime is relatively minor—petty theft, drunkenness, disorderly conduct, minor assaults, and prostitution.

In the early development of the lower courts, most states had locally elected justices of the peace, mayors, or police officials who had jurisdiction over a variety of petty offenses. In the cities, there were often justices of the peace, police courts, or magistrate courts to deal with these offenses. Those who presided usually had no legal training, often either were not paid or were paid a portion of the fines they imposed, and often worked part time. No record of the proceedings was required, jury trials were not permitted, and there were few formal procedures. Defendants usually were not represented by counsel. Sentences were usually warnings, fines, or short jail sentences. Defendants contesting the judge's decisions or wanting to be tried by a jury had to request a completely new trial in a higher court of record.[9]

Early in the present century, courts of no record such as police courts and justice of the peace courts began to be abolished, and now the lower courts are ordinarily courts of record in which criminal defendants have a right to trial by jury (prohibited in some states for minor offenses). Justice of the peace courts with substantial criminal jurisdiction are rare, but they continue in large numbers to deal with traffic cases and similar violations.

Feeley described the decision making process in most lower courts as follows:

> Decision-making in lower courts bears scant resemblance either to the popular image of trial courts portrayed in the media or to the practices of higher trial courts, which handle far fewer cases. As the general arraignment court for all criminal offenses, they are usually busy every morning (especially on Mondays), processing a batch of suspects who have been arrested the day (or weekend) before. These proceedings are usually fast-paced and highly routinized. Defendants are often herded before the bench in a group and informed of their rights *en masse*. Arraignments take place at a rapid pace. Unless they have been released prior to this first appearance or have retained a private attorney, it is unlikely that defendants will have consulted with a defense attorney prior to this appearance, and it is at this stage that defendants may make application for publicly appointed counsel.[10]

Typically, about half of the cases are disposed of at first appearance, mostly because prosecutors have dropped the charges–often at or just before arraignment—but sometimes because they are dismissed by the judge. If, however, the charges are not dropped or dismissed, a decision must be made as to whether the accused person will be released or kept in custody.

Pretrial Release

If an accused person has not been released by the police or if the case is not disposed of at first appearance, the judge must decide whether to release the person and, if so, under what conditions. A substantial portion of the accused persons are held in jail to await trial, having been denied bail, having been unable to meet the financial requirements for release, or having failed to be released on their own promise to return when required. A general picture of the extent of detention and of various forms of release is shown,

Figure 8.3 Type of Pretrial Release or Detention of Felony Defendants in 75 Largest Counties, 1992

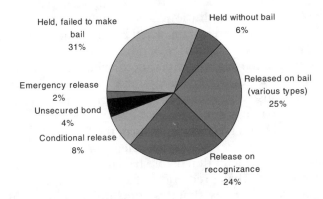

Source: data from Reaves, B. A., and Perez, J. (1994). *Pretrial Release of Felony Defendants, 1992.* Washington, D.C.: Bureau of Justice Statistics, 2.

Figure 8.4 Population of Philadelphia Prisons (Jails) 1980 (N = 2,695)

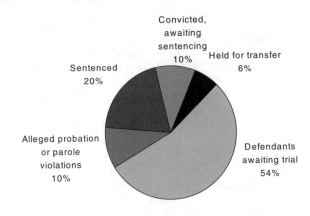

Source: data from Goldkamp, J. S., and Gottfredson, M. R. (1985). *Policy Guidelines for Bail: An Experiment in Court Reform.* Philadelphia: Temple University Press, 53.
Note: Held for transfer includes persons held for U.S. marshals and for the Commonwealth (state prison) and juveniles certified as adults.

for large counties, in Figure 8.3. It is typical that half or more of the population of jails is awaiting trial. Figure 8.4 provides an example of the composition of a jail at the time of a bail decision study discussed later in this chapter.

The original purpose of bail was the posting of money or other surety that would be kept by the court if the accused did not return for trial. The word surety shows this intention: the court wanted to be *sure* that the person would return to court when required. This continues to be a major purpose, but now there may be a second, more controversial, one of detention in order to prevent crimes that might occur if the accused person is released. That is, the person may be kept in jail not to ensure presence for the trial but to prevent him or her from doing crimes if released.

Often, the judge must decide only on the conditions of release, but the question of whether to release at all raises the often debated issue of whether there is a right to bail. At the basis of the debate is a more fundamental concern—the issue of punishment before trial.

Foote traced the origins of the clause in the Eighth Amendment that states "excessive bail shall not be required " through English common law to the framing of the U.S. Constitution.[11] He concluded that a right to bail was intended by the framers to be construed broadly, the view that certain offenses (capital crimes) were nonbailable notwithstanding. He argued that the specific language of the Eighth Amendment, which does not convey this precisely, was an inadvertence—just a mistake in writing. He maintained that at any rate the clause was intended to afford protection against pretrial imprisonment in a broad category of cases.

Foote argued further on grounds not only of the Eighth Amendment but also for three other reasons that preventive detention should not be allowed. Preventive detention is the detention before trial for the purpose of incapacitation. His reasons were that prediction of dangerousness is impossible without unacceptable error rates, that it is punishment before trial, and that it impairs a fair trial.

Foote's analysis of the purposes of pretrial decisions raised three questions that are still debated:

- Does the excessive bail clause impart a right to bail?

- Is the setting of money bail for the poor constitutional? Because many defendants cannot afford any bail, bail for them is equal in effect to pretrial detention. The question of constitutionality arises if this denies equal protection of the law to poor defendants.

- Are mechanisms other than money bail available that would ensure appearance at trial while avoiding pretrial detention and the discrimination against the poor inherent in money bail?

These and other complexities of the bail decision are easily overlooked by magistrates who routinely make many of their decisions in a hurry. The authors of an extensive study of the problem quoted one judge as saying

Judges don't know a thing about bail. They just do it. It's easy to do. [12]

The dilemmas posed by pretrial release decisions can be best considered in terms of the following questions:

- What are the legitimate purposes of bail?

- What decision alternatives are available to judges when this decision is made?

- Is appropriate information used for making the decisions?

- What are the consequences of the decisions for fairness, efficiency, and effectiveness of the criminal justice system?[13]

Goals of the Pretrial Release Decision

There is a consensus that a legitimate goal of the pretrial release decision is assuring the presence of the accused at trial. This is the traditional purpose of pretrial decisions, and it is widely accepted.

The U.S. Supreme Court in 1987 held that the purpose of protecting the community from dangerous crimes is also constitutionally permissible.[14] The Court upheld preventive detention resulting from the Bail Reform Act of 1984 as constitutional. Speaking for the majority, Chief Justice William Rehnquist stated, "We are unwilling to say that this congressional determination, based as it is upon that primary concern of every government—a concern for the safety and indeed the lives of its citizens—on its face violates either the Due Process Clause of the Fifth Amendment or the Excessive Bail Clause of the Eighth Amendment."

In a heated dissent, Justices Thurgood Marshall and William Brennan disagreed strongly, describing statutes such as the Bail Reform Act of 1984 and its authorization of preventive detention as "consistent with the usages of tyranny and the excesses of what bitter experience teaches us to call the police state, [and which] have long been thought incompatible with the fundamental human rights protected by our Constitution." After criticizing the logic of the majority's analysis, the dissenting Justices continued to say (in the 1987 decision cited):

> Throughout the world today there are men, women, and children interned indefinitely, awaiting trials which may never come or which may be a mockery of the word, because their governments believe them to be "dangerous." Our Constitution, whose construction began two centuries ago, can shelter us from the evils of such unchecked power. Over two hundred years it has slowly, through our efforts, grown more durable, more expansive, and more just. But it cannot protect us if we lack the courage, and the self-restraint, to protect ourselves. Today a majority of the Court applies itself to an ominous exercise in demolition. Theirs is truly a decision which will go forth without authority, and come back without respect.

The controversy about preventive detention is sure to continue, because of the basic conflict between the values of freedom and safety. The Supreme Court for now has made it clear that there is an "overwhelming" government interest in crime by arrestees and that the pursuit of that interest may involve *regulatory* (although not *punitive*) use of preventive detention. This means that although an accused person may not be kept in jail as punishment, he or she may be confined because of the government's interest in regulating—that is, controlling—crime.

Over the last several decades several trends have affected this issue. First, as exemplified by Foote, there were criticisms of illegal detention and of a punitive use of detention before trial. Later, debate focused on whether, besides the goal of ensuring the appearance of the accused at trial, judges could legitimately seek to base their decisions on the *threat* of crime.[15] Until the 1984 passage of the federal detention law and the *Salerno* decision, the practice, often not admitted by judges, of basing decisions on perceptions of dangerousness was highly controversial but now has become widely accepted in practice. Before the *Salerno* decision, no goals other than ensuring appearance at court were recognized in the law. Now, about 35 states, the federal government, and the District of Columbia have provisions in the law that are aimed at public safety as well as assuring presence for trial.[16]

Magistrates do not have free reign to jail accused persons on the basis of their belief that a suspect is dangerous. The use of preventive detention appears to be limited by the Supreme Court to serious crimes. Also, certain due process protections must accompany detention hearings.

Besides the two goals so far discussed—ensuring the presence of the accused when required in court and preventing crimes by incapacitation before the trial—several other goals have been suggested. Some argue that one function of pretrial detention is to protect the integrity of the trial process by preventing the accused from tampering with evidence or witnesses. To the extent that this is a legitimate goal, however, there may be alternatives of witness protection programs or restrictive release conditions such as house arrest.

It sometimes is argued also that pretrial detention is used explicitly for punishment. It is alleged that high bail is sometimes set, resulting in detention, in order to inflict punishment for an unproved offense. The magistrate can easily bring about detention in jail by setting the amount required beyond the means of the accused, without acknowledging the punitive intent. Landis, for example, interpreted the results of his study of bail setting in New York as suggesting that pretrial punishment may be a major rationale for the determination of the amount of bond.[17] That is, setting a high bond may be a vehicle for effecting punishment when there is doubt the accused will be punished after trial. Thus, in some jurisdictions, magistrates setting bail may believe that a "taste of the bars" would be a good thing for a defendant who is not likely to face confinement if convicted. Unlike the situation with the controversial goal of community safety, the goal of inflicting punishment by means of pretrial release decision making is unconstitutional. The magistrate who does this is breaking the law.

Setting a high bail also might force a guilty plea. Many defendants in minor cases, unable to afford the set bond, plead guilty, get a suspended sentence, and obtain their release. If this is the purpose of the magistrate, it is an unlawful one, not constitutionally permissible.

Alternatives for Pretrial Release Decisions

The use of money as bail has long been so common that most people think of bail as a sum of money deposited in order to secure release pending further criminal justice system proceedings. In medieval times, an accused person was "bailed" to another person—if the accused failed to appear when required that person was tried instead of the accused.[18] For many years, the main issue for the magistrate at initial appearance for suspects eligible for bail was how much money should be required for that person to secure a release from custody.[19] Over the last three decades, however, substantial changes have taken place, so that now, in some jurisdictions, the following alternatives to detention may be available:

- Release upon receipt by the court of the full money bail amount.

- Release upon securing a bond, from a bail bondsman, for a fee; (often, about 10 percent) to be promised to the court should the suspect flee.

- Release on "unsecured bail," with no money paid to the court but liability for the full amount if the defendant fails to appear for court proceedings.

- Release on recognizance (ROR), that is, on a promise to appear in court when required.

- Conditional release, that is, on the accused person's agreement to abide by conditions set by the court.

- Release to private third-party custody.

- Supervised release, that is, under supervision as required by the court.

- Release to a treatment program.

- Release upon deposit of a portion of the money bail amount (often, 10 percent).

- Citation release with arrested persons released until issued a written order by law enforcement personnel.

- Release with electronic monitoring (e.g., with "ankle bracelets" or other electronic devices).

- Release under "house arrest," that is, confined to home.

Box 8.2

Major Pretrial Decision Options

Financial Bond

Fully secured bail—the defendant posts the full amount of bail with the court.

Privately secured bail—a bonds-agent signs a promissory note to the court for the bail amount and charges the defendant a fee for the service (usually 10 percent of the bail amount). If the defendant fails to appear, the bonds-agent must pay the court the full amount. Frequently, the bondsagent requires the defendant to post collateral in addition to the fee.

Deposit bail—the courts allow the defendant to deposit a percentage (usually 10 percent) of the full bail with the court. The full amount of bail is required if the defendant fails to appear. The percentage bail is returned after disposition of the case, but the court often retains 1 percent for administrative costs.

Unsecured bail—the defendant pays no money to the court but is liable for the full amount should he or she fail to appear.

Alternative Release Options

Release on Recognizance (ROR)—the court releases the defendant on the promise that he or she will appear in court as required.

Conditional release—the court releases the defendant subject to specific conditions set by the court, such as attendance at drug treatment therapy or staying away from the complaining witness.

Third-party custody—the defendant is released into the custody of an individual or agency that promises to assure his or her appearance in court. No monetary transactions are involved in this type of release.

Citation release—arrestees are released pending their first court appearance on a written order issued by law enforcement personnel.

Emergency release—defendants are released only in response to a court order placing limits on a jail population because of overcrowding.

Of those who are not released by any of these procedures, many are held without bond or on very high bond because of outstanding warrants in other jurisdictions or for probation or parole violation allegations. The most common forms of financial sureties and alternative release procedures are summarized in Box 8.2.[20]

Release on own recognizance (ROR) now is a widely used alternative to bail, due largely to a pioneering bail reform innovation by the staff of the Vera Institute of Justice in New York City. ROR means a release upon the accused person's promise to appear, *in lieu* of bail. Usually, only the promise is required, but sometimes conditions may be set—such as remaining in the county.

About 70 years ago, Beeley studied the bail procedures in Chicago and concluded that a large proportion of defendants were detained needlessly. He thought that if data about the defendant's background, family ties, and

---

Box 8.3

How a Private Citizen Changed the Courts

In 1960, a chemical engineer-executive for a New York firm learned that accused persons were being held in jail for as long as 12 months because they could not afford the bail set. He knew nothing about legal proceedings but he was appalled. Together with a writer for a national boys' magazine, he toured one of the jails. He was more appalled. The two men decided to establish the Vera Foundation, with funds the executive could make available. The idea was to finance and administer a revolving fund to which indigents could apply in order to make bail that they could not afford.

When they presented the proposal to the chief magistrate of New York City and others, it was flatly rejected. The authorities emphasized that the state is not interested in the money but in ensuring appearance for trial. They believed that the revolving bail fund would only perpetuate the existing system. They suggested, though, that if a way were found to provide the magistrate with more information about the defendant's background, this might provide an adequate basis for release of the defendant on his own recognizance. They suggested that law students could be used to gather the needed information, which would be good for both the students and the system.

With this idea the circle of influential persons widened. Discussions included two U.S. Supreme Court Justices, a chief justice of the New York Supreme Court, and faculty of the New York University Law School. Staff of the National Council on Crime and Delinquency were keen on the project and provided personnel to formulate a program that could be adopted by the court.

The program that evolved had part-time law students interviewing defendants before arraignment, just outside the courtroom, to determine mainly whether the defendant had roots in the community—that is, family ties and a permanent address in the area. Information was to be verified by telephone through references provided by the defendant.

The business man turned reformer met with the mayor. He argued that the program could save the city money, families of defendants could be supported by the defendants rather than welfare, the jails were overflowing, two-thirds of the people detained eventually were found not guilty or dismissed, and pretrial imprisonment often exceeded the eventual sentence. The mayor ordered an experimental program, started in 1961. More objective criteria were sought, and interviewers made a recommendation to the magistrate either for release on the defendant's own recognizance or no recommendation at all. When defendants were released, the law school students followed up with a reminder of the court appearance to the defendant and to the reference. During the next three years, about 4 percent of defendants released in this way failed to appear for their court appearances. The program was presented at a national conference on bail in 1964, and since has spread in much the same form throughout the country.

reputation in the community were used, defendants could be rated as de-pendable or undependable in respect to the likelihood of appearing in court.[21] Decades passed before this concept was translated into action by a the Vera Institute of Justice.[22] The story of how this happened is told in Box 8.3.[23]

The Vera program included an interview with the defendant in order to obtain reliable data on employment, residence, and family ties in the area. Defendants were scored according to these variables and a recommendation about pretrial release was made to the court. Freed and Wald found that greater proportions of defendants were then released than was the case pre-viously. Programs modeled after the Vera program were implemented in many courts, beginning in the 1960s. By 1964, Freed and Wald reported:

> The Manhattan Bail Project and its progeny have demonstrated that a defen-dant with roots in the community is not likely to flee irrespective of his lack of prominence or ability to pay a bondsman. To date, these projects have produced remarkable results, with vast numbers of releases, few defaulters, and scarcely any commission of crimes [by persons released], in the interim between release and trial.[24]

By 1988 the Bureau of Justice Statistics reported that more than 300 pretrial service programs were operating throughout the United States. In the late 1960s, many states had passed laws that limited the role of bonds-agents, and some eliminated bail bonding for profit. As a result of these re-forms, the numbers of persons released before trial increased. Nevertheless, at least 85 percent of all defendants released pending trial appeared for all court sessions, and absconding (fleeing to avoid trial) or return of the defen-dant by force did not exceed 4 percent of all who were released. Rearrest rates ranged from about 1 to 2 persons out of 10, varying among jurisdictions. About half of those rearrested were convicted.[25]

A survey of felony defendants in 1992 found, for the most populous cit-ies, that about 63 percent were released before the disposition of their cases. About a third of the released defendants were either rearrested for a new offense, failed to appear, or had their pretrial release revoked for some other reason.[26] Some other highlights of this survey are shown in Box 8.4.

Box 8.4

Pretrial Release of Felony Defendants, 1992

Over all felony defendants, the pre-trial release rate is nearly two-thirds: 66 percent in 1988, 65 percent in 1990, and 63 percent in 1992.

The defendants least likely to be re-leased include: persons charged with murder, rape, robbery, or burglary, in that order, and persons with prior ar-rests or convictions. The more prior convictions, the more likely is deten-tion.

Six percent of all felony defendants were held without bail. Persons charged with murder were held without bail 40 percent of the time.

About three out of four felony de-fendants released before their case disposition made all scheduled court appearances. Two-thirds of those who did not were returned to the court dur-ing the next year after warrants were is-sued, and 8 percent remained fugitives.

Of all released felony defendants, 86 percent were not rearrested while on pretrial release; 10 percent were rear-rested on felony charges and 4 percent on misdemeanors.

Information for Pretrial Release Decisions

Whether the concern in pretrial release decisions is with ensuring appearance for trial, preventing new offenses, or protecting witnesses, the magistrate is faced with the task of forecasting the behavior of defendants. Each of the goals of the decision requires the judge to make predictions about what the defendant will do if released. In most jurisdictions, pretrial release decisions are made mainly on the basis of beliefs or hunches about variables thought related to the likelihood of appearance for trial or of new crimes if the defendant is not kept in jail. In many jurisdictions now, the limited data available to the magistrate is supplemented by data collected after the Vera model. An important question is whether the data used are actually predictive of either failure to appear or of new offenses during the time of release awaiting trial. The importance of this question is illustrated by an experimental study of decisions using the usual procedures of the court, including the Vera criteria, and release of a group not eligible for release by these procedures.[27] The study was designed, by an arrangement with the courts, to allow a comparison between subjectively chosen good and bad risks. A group of 201 defendants who were recommended by the ROR staff and approved by a judge were released on their own recognizance. Also, 328 persons not deemed eligible by the usual procedures were released.

Results were striking. Although there were differences between the two groups in rates of failure to appear, 85 percent of the recommended and approved group either appeared for trial or returned voluntarily, compared to 73 percent of the group that normally would not have been released. This means that some valid decision criteria were used by the judges. None of the items that made up the scale used in the Vera program however, were found to be related substantially to appearance or arrests. Most suspects appeared for trial, regardless of the magistrate's judgments about risk, and the Vera criteria were of little help in prediction. The study shows that beliefs about the relevance of data to decisions should be tested in order to determine whether the expected relations actually are found in practice. Otherwise, the decisions are made on untested hunches that may appear reasonable but nevertheless provide little useful information for the decision.

Studies of pretrial release decisions repeatedly have shown (as have investigations of other predictions in criminal justice) that we cannot predict the behavioral outcomes of defendants very well. This is true whether we rely on expert judgments or statistical predictions. That is not the same, however, as saying we cannot do it at all. There will always be errors in our predictions, regardless of the methods used to arrive at them, but some methods will result in fewer mistakes than will others. Many studies have shown that statistically developed prediction methods—relying on a systematic study of experience summarized by statistical methods—can be expected to do better than expert judgment alone.[28] We will discuss an example of this widespread decision problem and of the use of such methods in court efforts to improve decision policy in the next section.

Prediction of Decision Outcomes

The pretrial release decision provides an example of an often overlooked feature of the entire criminal justice system. It is a characteristic of criminal justice decisions that is present from arrest through final discharge. The universal feature is that the decisions are based on predictions. The magistrate seeks to predict the behavior of the defendant in appearing for trial and committing new offenses. Bail is an intervention intended to increase the rate of appearance at trial over that expected with outright release. Detention assures appearance, and bail provides some surety. In any case, the decision involves outcomes that are expected.

These predictions traditionally have been made at the pretrial processing stage, as at other points in the processing system, on the basis of beliefs or untested hunches by the responsible decision makers, using their judgment and relying on their own (possibly biased) experience. A case may be made that defendant characteristics such as community ties or employment stability could be expected to be predictive of appearance for trial—or absence of new crimes if the defendant is released. Many studies have shown, however, that plausibility is not enough; it is necessary to test whether such characteristics are actually predictive, as believed. The study of the Vera instrument showed that the relevance of various characteristics to appearance for trial was slight.

Many other studies show the difficulties of predicting "dangerousness."[29, 30] A National Bureau of Standards study found, for example, that of those defendants charged with crimes of violence 17 percent were rearrested during the pretrial period but only 5 percent were rearrested on violent offense charges.[31] The two groups could not be readily differentiated on the basis of background factors. Many other studies have had similar results.[32]

Goldkamp and Gottfredson studied a large sample of defendants in Philadelphia when they collaborated with judges there to develop guidelines for the pretrial release decision. Both failure to appear and new arrests were studied over a 90 day period after the pretrial release decision. They reached several important conclusions:

1. Although predictions of pretrial misconduct are difficult, statistical methods can greatly improve upon subjective judicial judgments.

2. The relation between pretrial crime (arrests) and failure to appear was significant, suggesting that *empirically* to predict one is to predict the other.

3. The vast majority of releases had no pretrial misconduct during the 90 day interval.

4. The amount of financial bond was not related to pretrial misconduct, once the risk of the defendant was taken into account.[33]

Not surprisingly, the length of time between arrest and trial is associated substantially with pretrial misconduct. One way to reduce rates of failure to appear and pretrial crime is to shorten the time between arrest and trial. This is hard to achieve, partly because diverse interests of both prosecution and defense are served by delay.[34]

These and similar studies illustrate the difficulties of achieving either of the main goals of the pretrial release decision—ensuring appearance in court when required and preventing new crimes in the community between arrest and trial. This does not mean that such predictions cannot be made more accurately than chance, nor does it mean that the use of better methods cannot improve over relatively uninformed judgments of magistrates. There are data reliably predicting both failure to appear and new arrests; these can be used to better inform the decision makers. The present state of the art is such that very large errors will be expected—no matter how the predictions are made.

Kinds of Errors in Predictions

Errors in pretrial predictions are of two kinds. When a defendant is predicted to fail but would in fact succeed, this is called a "false positive" error. When a person is predicted to succeed but in fact fails, it is called a "false negative" error. The only way to reduce these errors is to improve the prediction methods.

The costs associated with the two kinds of errors are different. The error of keeping a defendant in jail who would in fact succeed has obvious serious consequences for the defendant and for the defendant's family. The error of incorrectly predicting success may have even more serious consequences— or relatively minor ones. The error, for example, that permits the release of a child molester who repeats his offense has consequences gravely different from a similar error made about a check forger. Not only the *risk* (for example, of failure to appear or of new arrests) is involved but also the societal *stakes* are involved. Less is at stake if the expected new offense, should one occur, is a minor one. More is at stake also, from the point of view of the judge, when it seems clear that the defendant would likely threaten victims or witnesses or if there is strong community feeling against release of the defendant.

What Influences the Bail Decision?

Over and over again, studies have shown that the seriousness of the charge and the prior criminal record of the defendant are the main factors that influence the bail decision. Michael Gottfredson summarized the evidence as follows:

> The dominant influence of the criminal charge in bail setting is confirmed again and again in empirical research [citations given] as is the role of prior criminal record. When the charge is not serious and the defendant does not have a recent or extensive prior record, the defendant receives a less restric-tive release condition. Other factors matter to some degree, but these two dominate according to the research evidence.[35]

Guidelines for Bail Decisions

Over the last decade, research by Goldkamp and M. Gottfredson in collaboration with judges responsible for bail decisions in several jurisdictions have developed policy guidelines for these decisions. The goal of these projects was to improve the rationality, fairness, and visibility of the decisions and to improve the feedback to judges on the results of their decisions. In the first study, in Philadelphia, the developed guidelines were tested in an experiment with judges randomly assigned to two groups: one using the new guidelines and one using the traditional procedures.[36] M. Gottfredson summarized the results in part as follows:

1. Judges will voluntarily comply with policy guidelines and will give reasons when they depart, thus increasing visibility.

2. Policy guidelines greatly increase equity in decision making.

3. Evolutionary systems that permit decision makers to change policies as they learn from feedback are feasible—that is, change can be institutionalized with guidelines.[37]

After 17 years of experience with the Philadelphia pretrial release guidelines, it was found that the guidelines process had continued despite marked changes in the court setting and criminal justice system changes, including:

- Profound changes in administrative structure.

- Continued, increasing overcrowding in the jails.

- A resulting emergency release program.

- The acceptance by the U.S. Supreme Court of public safety as a legitimate concern for the pretrial release decision.

- A halt to jails admissions.

- Development of plans for alternatives to incarceration that would address conditions of confinement.

- A "skyrocketing" failure-to-appear rate as a result of emergency release procedures due to jail crowding.

- An increase in more serious and "high risk" cases.

- A Mayor's Task Force formed to redevelop and implement prerelease guidelines as a first step toward implementing the plan for alternatives to incarceration.[38]

The nature of the prerelease guidelines model as originally implemented in the Philadelphia court is shown in Figure 8.5, taken from the judicial worksheet used for the decision. The pretrial release policy is summarized by the matrix or grid shown. The matrix has two dimensions and is similar to those used for sentencing and paroling decisions discussed in Chapters 9 and 11 of this book. One dimension represents the main charge. Offenses are arranged by relative seriousness—from the least serious to most serious charges. Along the other dimension there is a point scale, developed empirically to measure risk differences among defendants according to their probability of either failure to appear or rearrest.

The guidelines were intended to be used in the following way. Staff of the pretrial services agency investigate the defendant's background and develop the information for the guidelines form. This includes determining both the risk category and classification of the offense seriousness. The form is given to the judge, along with the defendant's file for the bail hearing. The cell at the intersection of the charge and risk dimensions indicates the presumptive bail decision: ROR, ROR or a low cash bail range, or a cash bail range. Judges are expected to reach decisions for typical cases as indicated. They have the option, however, of departing from the guidelines' suggested decision to make decisions outside the guidelines. When they do, they are expected to indicate the reason for their decision. Not shown in Figure 8.5 but listed on the worksheet actually used are reasons that often might appear, such as outstanding warrants, likely interference with witnesses, or likelihood that prosecution will be withdrawn.

The risk classification sorts defendants into five categories using items based on the prediction studies. These studies showed that the most useful

Figure 8.5 Guidelines Matrix Used in the Bail Guidelines

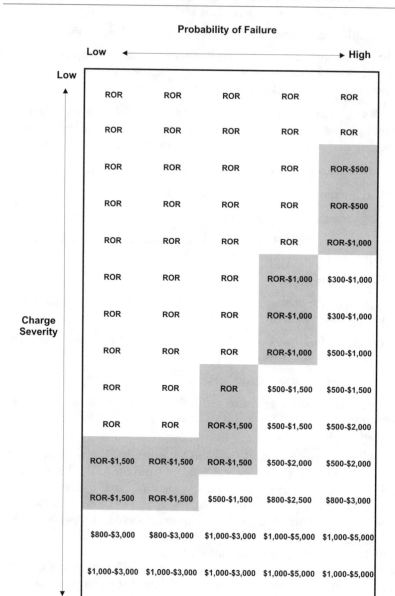

Probability of Failure

Low ←————————————————————→ High

Charge Severity				
ROR	ROR	ROR	ROR	ROR
ROR	ROR	ROR	ROR	ROR
ROR	ROR	ROR	ROR	ROR-$500
ROR	ROR	ROR	ROR	ROR-$500
ROR	ROR	ROR	ROR	ROR-$1,000
ROR	ROR	ROR	ROR-$1,000	$300-$1,000
ROR	ROR	ROR	ROR-$1,000	$300-$1,000
ROR	ROR	ROR	ROR-$1,000	$500-$1,000
ROR	ROR	ROR	$500-$1,500	$500-$1,500
ROR	ROR	ROR-$1,500	$500-$1,500	$500-$2,000
ROR-$1,500	ROR-$1,500	ROR-$1,500	$500-$2,000	$500-$2,000
ROR-$1,500	ROR-$1,500	$500-$1,500	$800-$2,500	$800-$3,000
$800-$3,000	$800-$3,000	$1,000-$3,000	$1,000-$5,000	$1,000-$5,000
$1,000-$3,000	$1,000-$3,000	$1,000-$3,000	$1,000-$5,000	$1,000-$5,000
$2,000-$7,500	$2,000-$7,500	$2,000-$7,500	$2,500-$7,500	$3,000-$7,500

Philadelphia Municipal Court

Source: adapted from Goldkamp, J. S., Gottfredson, M. R., Jones, P. B. and Weiland, D. (1995). *Personal Liberty and Community Safety: Pretrial Release in the Criminal Court.* New York: Plenum Press, 35.
Note: Shaded portion represents the judge's discretionary choice between ROR and money bail. Reasons need not be given for exercise of discretion within the dollar amounts shown.

information for predicting flight, crime, or both during pretrial release, for the Philadelphia sample, concerned age, the kind of offense, and aspects of the prior record. Defendants over 44 did better, except that a defendant over 44 who had a record of absconding (running away) was an especially high risk. Defendants who had a phone did better. Those who had a prior record of absconding, those whose charge occurred while the defendant already was on pretrial release, and those with prior arrests did worse. The kind of offense currently charged (rather than its seriousness) also was a help in the prediction. A person charged with a crime against another person was a lower risk generally, but such a person who also had a lengthy record of prior arrests was a high risk.[39]

The procedures for developing a risk instrument of this type can be complex, but the basic logic is simple. The steps followed in such a study for the purpose of developing a prediction instrument are shown in Box 8.5. The most important steps, regardless of procedures used, are the last two. These are testing the instrument to see how well it works in new samples from the jurisdiction in which it will be used and evaluating the usefulness of the instrument in reaching the goals of the decision.

Goldkamp and Gottfredson next undertook the study of three additional urban court systems in Boston, Massachusetts; Dade County, Florida; and

---

Box 8.5

Recipe For Developing a Risk Measure

Select: a representative sample for study. Example: a random sample.

Define: the behavior to be predicted. Example: "No failures to appear or no new arrests within one year."

Collect: data about defendants that may be related to the criteria. Examples: prior failure to appear, family ties in the community, pending charges.

Measure and Record: data about each defendant describing their outcomes. Example: Record whether each defendant appeared for all required court proceedings and whether there were any new arrests.

Enter: the data into a file that includes both the background data (potential predictor items) and the behavior to be predicted.

Calculate: the relation of each item of data to every other item, including the behavioral outcome.

Find: by using appropriate statistical methods, the best predictors and combine them into a scale.

Result: is an equation or classification method that fits the data well in this sample.

Test: how well the method works when applied to new samples.

Evaluate: the proof of the pudding is how well the method works in new samples. Example: in a new sample, how well does the method predict failure to appear and new arrests?

Maricopa County, Arizona, to see whether the lessons learned in Philadelphia could be applied to other jurisdictions. They found that the procedures in each jurisdiction were in some respects unique but also that they were in some ways similar. The procedures for the pretrial decision process in Maricopa County are depicted in Figure 8.6.[40] Some of the lessons learned from this extensive experience is summarized by the authors in their own words in Box 8.6.[41]

The days in jail are long for the innocent as well as the guilty, for those who have not yet had their day in court, and for those with and without financial resources to secure a release. The traditional presumption of innocence is highly valued because every citizen is entitled to liberty unless deprived of it by due process of law. Procedures that can help ensure those values deserve much more attention than so far has been given them. Across the country, magistrates still make these decisions on the basis of little information. That problem can be reduced by providing feedback to the judges about the results of their decisions and forming a rational decision making policy; and that can help improve pretrial release decisions.

Figure 8.6 Processing of Defendants in Maricopa County, Arizona

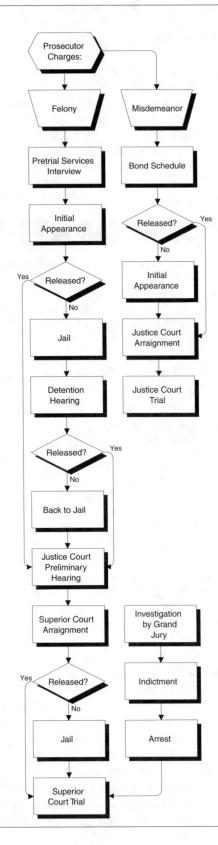

Box 8.6

John Goldkamp, Michael Gottfredson, Peter Jones, and Doris Weiland: In Their Own Words

Some Lessons from the Pretrial-Release Guidelines Experience

- Even after decades of bail reform, serious questions about the fairness and effectiveness of pretrial release in the United States have not been resolved.

- Continued reliance on financial bail as the currency of release decisions is a major reason. *Sub rosa* pretrial detention is the continued result, and the profiteering role of the bondsman still an unexplainable anachronism.

- Improvement in pretrial release and detention practices is in large part the responsibility of the judiciary. Chronic problems with pretrial release and detention in the United States will never be effectively addressed without judicial leadership and accountability in the pretrial release function.

- Either the judiciary will develop court-based approaches to improving management of the pretrial release function, or others (i.e., legislatures) will mandate their own versions of system improvements (and the history of such measures is not encouraging).

- The pretrial services mission is to "staff" the judicial pretrial release function and to provide the wherewithal to manage the fair and effective use of pretrial release and detention.

- As courts try to enter the information age, pretrial services agencies have a major responsibility to redefine their roles to serve as the gatekeepers of information for the criminal process as well as for pretrial-release and detention decisionmaking.

Given all this, the guidelines method appears to offer an important tool to criminal courts in their efforts to address pretrial release and detention problems.

—John Goldkamp, Peter Jones, and Doris Weiland are at Temple University. Michael Gottfredson is at the University of Arizona.

The Trial Courts

When a defendant accused of a felony has been bound over to a higher court by the judge at the preliminary hearing, the prosecutor has presented enough evidence against the defendant to establish a *prima facie* case. That means that at a first look the evidence is enough to support, although not to compel, a finding of guilt if there is no contradictory evidence. When the defendant is bound over to the higher court, it also means that the judge has decided not to dismiss the case, although the charges may have been changed and some may have been dropped.

The other way a defendant may be called to answer in a higher court is by means of a grand jury. This is a panel of lay persons, often 23 in number but ranging from 6 in Indiana to more than 23 in some states, who also have the function of determining whether an accused person should be tried. Whether by grand jury or judge, the standard to be met is probable cause to believe that a crime was committed and that the defendant did it. The grand jury, however, meets in secret, without the defendant or defense attorney— thus without rebuttal of the prosecutor's charges, confrontation of witnesses, or cross examination. The prosecutor presents an indictment (a formal written accusation) to the grand jury, charging one or more persons with a crime. The indictment is presented under oath by the prosecutor, and the grand jury has the task of deciding whether the accusation, if proved, would be enough to bring about a conviction of the accused. If they decide that it is, they issue a "true bill" and the indictment thus endorsed by the foreperson brings the defendant to arraignment in court.

A grand jury indictment or presentment is required for all felony prosecutions in 13 states, the federal courts, and the District of Columbia. A few jurisdictions require it only in capital or life imprisonment cases. In all states and the federal government, grand juries are responsible for criminal investigations. Often they are responsible for jail inspections or oversight of other correctional facilities and investigations of political corruption.[42]

The result of either the preliminary hearing or the grand jury indictment is that the charge is dropped or the defendant is brought to arraignment. The defendant is required to enter a plea. The defense counsel is appointed if the defendant cannot afford a lawyer. Most defendants plead guilty, often as a result of a plea bargain.

If the charge has been dropped at the preliminary hearing, the accused is not necessarily off the hook. The Fifth Amendment protection against double jeopardy does not prohibit the prosecutor from filing again or the grand jury from endorsing an indictment.[43] The provision against double jeopardy does not "attach," that is, come into play, until a trial starts—either by swearing in a jury or, in a bench trial, presenting evidence in court.

The Trial

A main feature of a criminal trial is that the charge—and every element of the crime alleged—must be proven beyond a reasonable doubt. The bur-

Every criminal trial is a drama, and the court room is its stage. The main actors are the judge as referee, the prosecutor and defense lawyer as adversaries, an accused defendant, witnesses, and sometimes a jury. How do you suppose the formalities and setting for a trial affect its course? —*Photo courtesy of www.photostogo.com.*

den of this proof is on the prosecutor. In a civil trial, the standard is very different: a preponderance of the evidence on one side of the issue is all that is needed in order to prevail. That is, in a civil case, the evidence on one side must be more convincing, tipping the scales—if only a bit—in favor of one side. The standard of beyond a reasonable doubt is a much higher burden of proof, and it is a heavy one. Moreover, it applies to every element of the charge. If there is reasonable doubt about any element, then the jury must return a verdict of not guilty.

The prosecution may present a convincing case, with evidence outweighing that provided by the defense, yet a jury is compelled to acquit the defendant if even seemingly implausible evidence leaves it with a reasonable doubt. The defense does not need to establish the defendant's innocence. It only needs to convince a jury that there is at least a reasonable doubt of that person's guilt in respect to any element of the crime.

The criminal trial is at the center of the entire criminal justice system. It affects not only the defendant in a particular case but reaches out to affect the behavior of police, prosecutor, and defense attorney outside the courtroom, and of course influences the correctional systems as well. As described by Kaplan and his colleagues:

> The criminal trial has an enormous importance in the operation of the whole criminal system. In some sense, it is the balance wheel of the entire process. Although . . . relatively few cases are disposed of after full trial, it is the threat of exclusion of evidence that is the basis of the exclusionary rule's effort to control the police; it is the projected result of a trial which influences the exercise of prosecutorial discretion and it is the chance of success at trial which determines the bargaining positions of the lawyers attempting to dispose of the case through negotiations for a guilty plea. [44]

Speedy Trials

The Sixth Amendment to the U.S. Constitution states:

> In all criminal prosecutions, the accused shall enjoy the right to a speedy and public trial, by an impartial jury of the State and district wherein the crime shall have been committed, which district shall have been previously ascertained by law, and to be informed of the nature and cause of the accusation; to be confronted with the witnesses against him; to have compulsory process for obtaining witnesses in his favor, and to have the assistance of Counsel for his defense.

> *Justice delayed is justice denied.*
> *—William Ewart Gladstone*

Although the Constitution directs that the defendant enjoy a speedy trial, a continuing criticism of the courts is their inability to dispose of cases in a timely manner. Blame has been placed on large caseloads, inadequate resources, scheduling problems, the necessity for pretrial hearings, and deliberate delay by prosecutors and defense lawyers.[45] Delay also may result from processes of investigation, as when evidence is gathered during an undercover operation and arrest would end the cover. Defendants free on bail or ROR but expecting to be found guilty may wish to avoid custody as long as they can. Delay may be necessary for preparation of an adequate defense, but generally a defendant is hindered by it, since it may affect his employment, education, and other opportunities. It is the defendant held in jail, however, who suffers most from delay, and prosecutors may bring it about in order to add pressure to accept a bargain requiring a guilty plea. Moreover, when long delay occurs, the perception of justice in the courts must suffer. As described by Katz,

> [T]he inability to provide for speedy trials tarnishes the image of the criminal justice system in the eyes of the community. The criminal law must not only implement justice, it must also appear to do so; even legitimate delay, if its purpose is misunderstood, detracts from public confidence. This, in turn, lessens the public's willingness to cooperate with the police and the court system.

Our right to a speedy trial goes back to the Magna Carta of 1215 in England. It became formalized for us in the Sixth Amendment. It is assured by every state constitution and has been held by the U.S. Supreme Court to be guaranteed in the federal courts. It has also been found to be binding upon the states by the Fourteenth Amendment.[46] The right is in operation at arrest or at formal charging, whichever comes first.

In the past, the U.S. Supreme Court has rejected either a fixed time rule or a rule that a defendant who does not demand a speedy trial forever waives that right.[47] Congress passed a Speedy Trial Act in 1974, however. It applies only to criminal trials in the federal courts. The act seeks to limit delays by three main provisions. It requires indictment of the defendant within a mandatory period of time. It limits the judge's discretion to grant continuances (postponements). It authorizes the imposition of sanctions on attorneys who cause delay unjustifiably.[48] The act requires that a trial begin within 100 days of the arrest, but some delays are excluded from the computation. Also, an indictment or an information must be filed within 30 days of arrest or summons. Trial must start within 70 days of the indictment or information or the first appearance, whichever is last.

A majority of states now have statutory provisions and court rules that require starting trials within a certain number of days after a specific event such as arrest, complaint filing, or the preliminary hearing. Some require the trial to begin within a fixed number of court terms after the arrest. Some leave it to the discretion of the trial court. Sometimes the trial court judge finds a creative way to speed things up (see Box 8.7).[49]

Box 8.7

One Judge's Speedy Trial Method

Attorneys warned U.S. Judge Lawrence Zatkoff that a pending trial would take months for them to call more than 100 witnesses. Three police officers were suing the city of Detroit in the federal court, claiming unfair suspension for their involvement in the beating death of Malice Green. The judge found his own solution for speeding up the trial.

He gave each side 60 hours to present their case, question witnesses, and make objections. Then he armed his law clerks with stopwatches to time every word uttered by attorneys and witnesses. The case was reported as running smoothly and faster than anticipated.

Public Trials

Besides addressing the issue of speed, the Sixth Amendment requires that trials be public. Members of the general public may go to the courtroom and observe the proceedings. The public nature of trials does not, however, necessarily extend to cameras and television equipment. This is a matter for legislative or judicial decisions. Cameras are permitted, though, in some courts in all states except Indiana and Mississippi. They are not allowed in the District of Columbia or in the federal courts when criminal cases are heard. Consent often is required, and in some states cameras are permitted only in appellate courts or the court of last resort. In Kentucky, Louisiana, and Wyoming, whether to allow them is up to the judge. In Missouri, recording and photographing are prohibited if a participant who is a victim, a police informant, an undercover agent, a relocated witness, or a juvenile requests it. In Oklahoma, consent of the accused is required. In Utah, only still photography is allowed in trial courts.[50]

There is a need for research to study the effects of cameras and television in the courtroom. How the behavior of courtroom participants is affected and whether any difference is made in the outcomes are topics of much speculation.

The judge must maintain order, settle disputes, give each side a fair hearing, mediate negotiations, and follow and enforce court rules and the law. What personal characteristics, education, experience, and training would you recommend for this job? —*Photos courtesy of www.photostogo.com.*

The Jury

One of the advantages of having a jury is that jurors may provide a check on each other's perceptions. Perception is selective, and it is influenced by individual personalities, emotion, and experiences. The perceptions of a group, after discussion, may be more accurate than those of its individual members. One writer commented:

I would rather trust twelve jurors with all their prejudices and biases than I would a judge. I think the reason democracy works is because as you multiply judgments, you reduce the incidence of errors.[51]

The Sixth Amendment specifies that the right to trial is not only to a speedy one in public but that it is a right to an impartial jury. The Supreme Court has held that this right applies to all criminal charges that could lead to imprisonment of six months or more. Some states (such as California) assure a jury trial to anyone facing criminal charges.[52]

The ordinary trial jury, as opposed to the grand jury, is called a petit jury, because the grand jury usually is larger. The grand jury (with as many as 23 or more people) determines whether the facts and accusations of the prosecutor warrant an indictment and eventual trial of an accused person. The function of the petit jury—the trial jury of 12 persons, typically—is quite different. It is to determine issues of fact and to reach a verdict based upon those findings.

Both the right to a jury trial and the independence of the jury are firmly established in the United States. The history of the jury system begins before the Magna Carta, for example with Henry II using citizen panels of 12 or more "lawful men" selected by the sheriff to accuse persons of crimes—a forerunner of the grand jury. The transformation of trial by jury into a right of the accused began, however, when the Magna Carta of 1215 extracted from King John the promise that "no free man shall be taken or imprisoned or [dispossessed] or outlawed or exiled or in any way destroyed . . . except by the lawful judgment of his peers and the law of the land."[53] A century later, the functions of the grand jury of deciding whether the evidence justifies bringing charges, and those of the trial jury in evaluating evidence were separate. But it was not until 1670 that the independence of the English jury became firmly established.

Both the prosecutor and the defense lawyer may present witnesses and cross examine those presented by the other side, while the jury listens. How does the jury system work in relation to the strain between needs for individual freedom and public safety? —*Photo courtesy of www.photostogo.com.*

Before that year, jurors could be fined or imprisoned, and their lands confiscated, if they brought an "erroneous" verdict. An "erroneous" verdict was one thought contrary to the interests of the Crown. When two young Quaker activists were accused of conducting an unlawful assembly in London, their jurors refused to bring a guilty verdict. The judge scolded the jurors, fined them, and put them in prison pending payment of the fines. After two and a half months, the Chief Judge and 10 other judges of the Court of Common Pleas freed the jurors and stated that jurors cannot be punished for their decisions.

It now is fully accepted in the United States that the jury must be a finder of facts with a great deal of autonomy. Otherwise, the jury would really be nothing more than a voice of the state.[54] The U.S. Supreme Court in 1968 explained that the right of trial by jury exists "in order to prevent oppression by the Government."[55] The Court stated:

> Those who wrote our constitutions knew from history and experience that it was necessary to protect against unfounded criminal charges brought to eliminate enemies and against judges too responsive to the voice of higher authority. . . . Providing an accused with the right to be tried by a jury of his peers gave him an inestimable safeguard against the corrupt or overzealous prosecutor and against the compliant, biased, or eccentric judge. . . . The deep commitment of the Nation to the right of jury trial in serious criminal cases as a defense against arbitrary law enforcement qualifies for protection under the Due Process Clause of the Fourteenth Amendment, and must there- fore be respected by the States.

The Constitution is not neutral. It was designed to take the government off the backs of the people.
—Justice William O. Douglas

All 13 of the colonies used juries. In addition to the Sixth Amendment, the U.S. Constitution provides, in Article III, Section 2, that "the Trial of all Crimes, except in Cases of Impeachment, shall be by Jury." The constitutions adopted by the original states guaranteed jury trials, and so have the constitutions of every other state entering the Union.

Jury Selection

Jurors are selected from lists compiled by court clerks. In most states clerks now select potential jurors from one or more lists such as voter lists or driver's license lists. Both lists are biased in terms of representativeness of society as a whole. After being called for duty, the judge may excuse some for various reasons. Then, others are excused after the competing attorneys challenge them. At each step, the representativeness of the panel (representing all the people without any bias) may be reduced.

Although it seems generally agreed that jury service is a duty and privilege of citizenship, it can be inconvenient, time consuming, and financially costly, and many people consider it a nuisance. In six states, the employer must continue to pay the salary of a juror, but in all other states and the federal government, this is not required. Jurors usually receive a small stipend, varying among states from nothing for the first five days in Connecticut through a minimum of $5.00 a day in California to $50.00 in Wyoming after the first four days. Payment of $10 or $15 a day is fairly typical.[56] When long jury service may be expected, about 60 percent of all whose names are drawn return their questionnaires asking to be excused.[57] The decisions made by jury commissioners, court clerks, and trial judges to these requests are important to the ultimate makeup of juries and also may affect the degree to which they are representative of the general population. Most likely to be excused are women with child-care duties, blue-collar workers whose employers may not pay them, young persons in school, and older persons with health or transportation problems.

States vary in factors that qualify or may exempt a person from jury duty. Exemptions often are based on age (for example, over 65 or 70) and occupation (such as judicial officers, police, public officials, physicians, attorneys, persons on active military service). There are none of these exemptions, however, in 16 states. Many have literacy and language qualifications. In most states, persons may be excused on the basis of factors such as undue hardship, extreme inconvenience, or public necessity.[58]

> *Jury: A group of twelve men who, having lied to the judge about their hearing, health and business engagements, have failed to fool him.*
> —*H. L. Mencken*

If the members of a selected juror panel have not yet been excused, either the prosecution or the defense may challenge a prospective juror "for cause." The persons may then be removed if the judge agrees that the potential juror has some bias or partiality that would interfere with a fair evaluation of the evidence. This need not be a specific bias, but may be a general prejudice. The right to question for a general bias was established in the 1807 trial of Aaron Burr for treason. Chief Justice John Marshall ruled that preconceived notions about the dispute were grounds for removal for cause and that prospective jurors therefore should be questioned to determine whether they had such ideas and could not be impartial. Since then such questioning has been permitted.[59]

Either the prosecution or the defense may also exercise a set of "peremptory" challenges, removing jurors thought unsympathetic to their side, without giving any reason whatever—but these challenges are limited in number. The allowed numbers vary among the states and also with whether the charge is a felony or a misdemeanor. For felony charges in courts of general jurisdiction, it varies from 3 for the state and 3 for the defense in Hawaii to 12 for the state and 20 for the defense in New Jersey.

If the defense can afford it, consultants sometimes are hired to advise on jury selection. Their effectiveness has not been evaluated in any systematic way.

In the South, before and for nearly a century after the Emancipation Proclamation, it was a rare jury list that included African Americans. After years of litigation, they finally were included, only to find that the prosecution often used its peremptory challenges to keep them off the jury. A series of Supreme Court cases dealt with this issue, and in 1986 the Court finally reversed the conviction of an African American petitioner who claimed he was denied equal protection by the prosecutor's use of peremptory challenges to exclude members of his race from the jury.

The prosecutor had used his peremptory challenges to exclude all four African American persons from the panel, leaving a jury composed only of white persons. The defense counsel moved to discharge the jury before it was sworn, on the ground that the prosecutor's removal of African Americans violated his client's rights under the Sixth and Fourteenth Amendments. Counsel for the defendant requested a hearing on the motion. The judge said that the parties were entitled to use their peremptory challenges to "strike anybody they want to."

The Supreme Court, in reversing the conviction, stated the peremptory challenge ". . . may be, and unfortunately at times has been, used to discriminate against black jurors. By requiring trial courts to be sensitive to the racially discriminatory use of peremptory challenges, our decision enforces the mandate of equal protection and furthers the ends of justice. . . . public respect for our criminal justice system and the rule of law will be strengthened if we ensure that no citizen is disqualified from jury service because of his race."[60] Justice Thurgood Marshall agreed with the opinion for the Court by Justice Lewis Powell.

Justice Marshall expressed the view that the racial discrimination that peremptories inject into the jury selection process can be ended only by eliminating peremptory challenges entirely. As it stands, peremptory challenges may not legally be used to exclude persons solely because of their race, but there remains doubt that such discrimination is thereby ended.

The process through which these challenges are made is called *voir dire*. This expression has been translated variously as "to speak the truth," "to see what is said," or, more literally, "to see and to speak." It is an examination by the court or the attorneys or both (variously among jurisdictions) to determine whether there is cause to excuse a prospective juror for bias and to elicit information for the peremptory challenges by both sides. In most states, it is conducted by the attorneys and the judge, but in seven states (Arizona, Illinois, Maine, Massachusetts, New Hampshire, New Jersey, and Pennsylvania) and in the District of Columbia, it may be done by the judge only. Usually, the judge may allow participation by the attorneys. In three states (Rhode Island, Texas, and Wyoming), it is done by the attorneys alone.[61]

> *A jury consists of 12 persons chosen to decide who has the better lawyer.*
> —Robert Frost

The size of the jury is usually 12 persons (in 46 states) for felony cases, but it can often be fewer for misdemeanors. According to the U.S. Supreme Court, this number is not required by the Constitution but is a "historical accident, wholly without significance except to mystics."[62] Practice varies among the states and territories. In Arizona it is 8 persons, unless it is a death penalty case or a sentence of 30 years or more, when it is 12. In Connecticut it is 6, except in capital cases, when the defendant can elect 12. It is 6 in Florida, but 12 in capital cases. Utah has 8 members on juries. Puerto Rico and the federal courts have 12.

The jury's decision must be unanimous, in all criminal cases, in all states but two. Oregon is an exception, requiring 10 of the 12 jurors to agree, except in murder trials, in which the verdict must be unanimous. Louisiana is the other, with similar rules. In 1972, the Supreme Court held these practices to be constitutional.[63]

Questions of both jury size and the requirement of unanimity for a verdict have been debated widely. The Supreme Court has made it clear that there need not be 12 members of the jury—although it has found that having fewer than 6 violate the guarantees of the Sixth and Fourteenth Amendments to an impartial jury and to equal protection.[64] Most states and the federal system nevertheless have maintained the 12-person jury. Similarly, states may use less than unanimous verdicts with juries of 12, but only Oregon and Louisiana do so. The jury of 12, with unanimity required for the verdict, is the norm.

Jury Nullification

A controversial aspect of jury trials concerns the power of a jury to acquit the defendant even when the evidence would justify a finding of guilty—called jury nullification. The traditional debate has not been about this power, but about whether juries should be told that they have it. In the eighteenth century, juries commonly were told that they had the power to judge inequities in the law as well as the facts of the case. The U.S. Supreme Court, however, in 1895 concluded that, since juries cannot increase penalties or make new laws, they should not be told that they have the power to reduce penalties or nullify laws.[65] The constitutions of two states, however—Indiana and Maryland—still provide for the jury to determine both the law and the facts. In these two states, juries are told they have this power.[66] Except in these states, the function of the jury is commonly said to be to determine the facts and then to apply the law as it is explained by the judge. The power of the jury to exercise their power, however, stems from the fact that a jury verdict of not guilty is not subject to reversal or review in any manner whatever.[67]

This means that in a criminal trial with a jury, the jury has the last word as to the finding of guilt. The jury need not explain any reasons for its finding. Its decision cannot be changed by the judge. It cannot be reviewed by any higher court. Regardless of any legal rules or any evidence others may see as justifying a verdict of guilty, the jury may acquit the defendant and the criminal case is over.

This power of the jury means that they can judge the justice of the law as well as the facts of the case. The right of the jury to hold laws invalid (in effect) by a finding of "not guilty" when a law is believed to be unjust or oppresive goes back to the 1215 Magna Carta and the English common law. The jury traditionally has had the right to judge the law as well as the facts.

The emphasis in the U.S. Constitution on the right to a jury trial reflected judgements about how the law should be administered in order to protect accused persons from oppression by the government. As a result, the U.S. Supreme Court often has upheld this power of the jury. Generally, judges do not advise juries that they have this power

Pretrial Motions

Some events that occur before the trial starts may be important—or even determining—of the outcome. These are associated with pretrial motions, which are objections raised by the defense. Motions may be oral or in writing. The most common are challenges to the sufficiency of the charging instrument, requests for discovery of the prosecutor's evidence, and requests for the holding back or suppression of evidence — that is, not allowing it to be used in court — allegedly obtained through means in violation of the law.

The pretrial motion most likely to result in a dismissal is the motion to suppress. If the motion is successful, it often is the case that the evidence remaining is not sufficient for the prosecution to continue. Nevertheless, only about 5 percent of felony cases (and probably fewer misdemeanors) are dismissed as a result of pretrial motions.[68] Other pretrial motions that might be made include motions to dismiss charges—for example, for lack of evidence, for a continuance (postponement), for a change of venue (move to a different court), and for determining whether the defendant is competent to stand trial. It might be asked that charges be dismissed when a motion to suppress evidence has been successful and the prosecutor's case is weakened. A continuance might be requested when the defense requests more time to find witnesses. A motion to determine competence raises the issue of whether the defendant is able to understand the proceedings and cooperate with the defense lawyer. A motion to determine present sanity might be made; a person cannot be tried while insane.

The Prosecutor's Case[69]

After a jury has been selected (if the right to a jury has not been waived by either the prosecution or the defense), the judge reads the charge or charges and a record is made that the defendant plead not guilty. All eyes will then be on the prosecutor, who begins the presentation of the state's case with an opening statement. This is a preview of the case that the prosecutor intends to present, including the evidence that will be offered.

The defendant (ordinarily, the defense lawyer) has the option of making an opening statement also, explaining in a similar way the evidence that will be presented. The defendant may, however, reserve making the opening statement until after the prosecution has finished presenting its case.

The prosecution then presents its "case in chief," which is all the evidence against the defendant except that which may be presented in rebuttal—in response to the defense case. Thereafter, the prosecution "rests."

The Defense Case

After the prosecution has rested, the defendant often will move for a dismissal of the charge or charges on the ground that the evidence can not establish the defendant's guilt beyond a reasonable doubt. If the court finds, after reviewing the evidence, that a jury could not properly find guilt beyond a reasonable doubt on the evidence presented, the case—or some of the charges will be dismissed. If, however, the court finds that the evidence meets a reasonable standard, then the charges are open for consideration by the jury (subject to the presentation of contradictory evidence by the defense).

The defense may introduce evidence contradicting that presented by the prosecutor, but is not required to do so. The defense may simply rest. The defendant is not required to testify, a right guaranteed by the Fifth Amendment, but has a right to do so. The defense also has a right to introduce additional evidence. For example, the defense may introduce evidence seeking to destroy the credibility of the prosecution witnesses. Or, evidence may be offered to convince the jury (or judge) that the defendant was elsewhere at the time of the crime—that is, the defendant has a valid alibi. The defense attorney may seek to establish a legal justification or excuse for any acts of the defendant or may seek to cast a reasonable doubt on any element of the crime.

After the defense has rested, the prosecution may introduce evidence that rebuts that presented by the defendant—but only that. Now the prosecuting attorney may seek to cast doubt on the reliability of witnesses introduced by the defense, try to rebut the evidence presented by the defense seeking to establish a justification or excuse, or otherwise discredit the case presented by the opposing side. New evidence, not initially presented and not brought up by the defense, may not be introduced.

After all the evidence has been presented by both the prosecution and the defense, each side may address the jury (or judge if there is no jury) to make a final argument or summation. Each may review the evidence presented and in addition argue its importance. The prosecutor, who has the burden of proof, has the last word.

After these summations, the judge instructs the jury about the law and may comment about the evidence. The judge usually instructs the jury that questions of fact, including the credibility and weight of the evidence introduced, are up to the jury to decide.

A central feature of this drama is its adversarial nature. Each side—prosecution and defense—is ethically responsible, respectively, for presenting the best case possible for the people and for the defendant. The judge is bound, on the other hand, to be impartial, to ensure that the law is followed, to see that each side is treated fairly, and to be evenhanded throughout.

The Verdict

A jury may return a verdict of acquittal (not guilty) or conviction (guilty) or none (deadlock). If the verdict is acquittal, that is the end of the story of the criminal case, because the state has no right of appeal from it. When the defendant has been found guilty, a judgment of conviction is entered on the record, and a date is set for sentencing. If the verdict is for conviction, the defendant may request a new trial on the grounds that either procedural errors were made or the evidence was not sufficient to sustain the verdict reached. If the judge declares a mistrial because the jury members cannot agree, then a new trial may be held. The decision whether to try again is up to the prosecutor. The decision may depend heavily on his or her assessment of the weight of the evidence. If the case is not strong, it may be dropped.

An acquittal in a criminal trial does not necessarily prevent a civil action. The defendant may be sued in a civil court despite a finding of not guilty in a criminal trial. Then the standard of proof is no longer "beyond a reasonable doubt," but the lower standard of "a preponderance of the evidence" is sufficient. Therefore, it is quite possible that a defendant found not guilty of a crime is held responsible in a civil court for the act alleged.

Summary

It may be said that the legislatures make the laws and the courts enforce them, but the various parts of government all contribute to rule making.

Courts cannot initiate action, can hear only certain kinds of evidence under set procedures, and must base decisions only on evidence presented in court. Court proceedings are adversarial; lawyers present evidence and argue, with the judge serving as referee.

Each state and the federal government has a separate court system. All have both trial and appellate courts.

Criminal cases are first brought to the magistrate courts, which are courts of limited jurisdiction—typically over all misdemeanor cases and less serious felonies. The general trial courts, courts of general jurisdiction, typically hear felony cases and review appeals from the magistrate courts. States have one or more appellate courts, and defendants usually have the right to review in the next higher court.

In the federal system, the trial courts are called U.S. District Courts. There are no magistrate courts but U.S. magistrates try misdemeanors. The federal system includes a U.S. Court of Appeals, which is divided into circuits. The appellate court of last resort is the U.S. Supreme Court, which has nine justices appointed by the President for life and who sit together *en banc*. Appeal to the Court is not a matter of right, but a defendant who has lost in the Court of Appeals can petition for review. A person who seeks an appeal based on an alleged violation of constitutional rights can, if a state's highest court has rejected the appeal, apply to the U.S. Supreme Court for a writ of *certiorari*. The Court accepts only few cases, usually those with substantial unresolved constitutional issues. If not a Fourth Amendment case, a defendant can apply to the District Court for a writ of *habeas corpus*. Besides its role as an appellate court, the U.S. Supreme Court has original jurisdiction over certain cases involving the U.S. government. The workload of the federal courts has increased markedly in recent years because Congress has made many offenses into federal crimes that were previously left to the states.

By tradition and because of workloads, courts are divided into lower and upper courts. Huge numbers of less serious crimes—disorderly conduct, drunkenness, prostitution, and minor thefts and assaults—are dealt with daily by the lower courts. About half are disposed of at first appearance, usually because the charges are dropped.

If an accused person has not been released already, the magistrate at first appearance must decide whether to release that person, and, if so, under what conditions. About half the people in a typical jail are not serving a sentence as punishment for conviction of any crime but are awaiting trial or are held for some other authorities. The Eighth Amendment states that excessive bail shall not be required, but high bail keeps many accused persons in jail.

The traditional and commonly accepted purpose of pretrial release decisions is to ensure that the defendant will be available for trial. Judges nevertheless typically have detained accused persons with a goal of preventing "further" crimes, despite the traditionally accepted presumption of innocence, while rarely admitting this on the record. The U.S. Supreme Court now has held that the purpose of community protection also is constitutionally permissible. The topic of preventive detention continues to be hotly debated.

The main alternatives to pretrial detention in jail are bail, release on recognizance (ROR), and conditional release. The use of ROR expanded greatly across the nation as a result of pioneering efforts of the Vera Institute of Justice, which developed programs for providing information to the court for pretrial release decisions.

The prediction of new offenses and of failure to appear is a central issue for pretrial release decisions. Judges usually make these predictions on the basis of untested hunches and beliefs. Methods are available for improving these predictions, keeping track of the decisions and keeping score on the results in order to devise a statistical prediction tool. Even when they are used, the validity of predictions is quite modest, but statistical prediction methods can be used to do better than expert judgment alone.

In Philadelphia and later in other jurisdictions, Goldkamp and Gottfredson developed guidelines for the decision, collaborating with judges to develop a policy model based on the seriousness of the charge and the risk of flight or new arrests. The procedures resulted in increased rationality, fairness, and visibility of the decisions and provide the judges with feedback on the results of their decisions so they can be improved.

Most defendants going to trial were bound over to the higher court at the preliminary hearing because the judge decided that the prosecutor had established a *prima facie* case. Some go to trial as a result of a grand jury indictment.

A central feature of a criminal trial is that every element of the alleged crime must be proven beyond a reasonable doubt. The burden of proof is on the prosecutor. The defense is not required to prove the defendant's innocence.

The criminal trial affects not just the defendant but the entire criminal justice system. The behavior of police, prosecutors, defense lawyers, and correctional agency personnel is influenced by what happens in court trials.

The Sixth Amendment provides for a trial that is speedy and public, by an impartial jury of the people from the place where the crime occurred. The defendant must be informed of the nature of the accusations, has the right to confront accusing witnesses, to obtain witnesses in his or her favor, and to have counsel for defense. Trials are public, but jurisdictions differ as to whether cameras are allowed. The right to a jury extends to all criminal charges that could result in imprisonment of six months or more; some states assure this right to all defendants. The jury is an independent finder of facts. Many factors influence the degree to which juries are representative of the general population.

In a further selection of jurors, a procedure called *voir dire* is used. The judge or attorneys examine prospective jurors for bias and to provide information for challenges by both sides. Either the prosecution or the defense may challenge "for cause" if it is believed that the potential juror is biased. If the judge agrees, that person may be removed. Both sides also have a limited, fixed number of "peremptory" challenges. These permit the lawyers on either side to bring about the removal of any prospective juror without giving any reason. Peremptory challenges have been used to systematically exclude persons on the basis of their race. That now is unconstitutional.

Juries of 12 persons, who must reach a unanimous verdict, are the norm. In nearly all states, the verdict must be unanimous, but that is not required by the U.S. Constitution. Juries can acquit a defendant even when the evidence would support a guilty verdict under the law, because a verdict of not guilty is not reversible.

Pretrial motions—such as for dismissal, exclusion of evidence, or continuance—can greatly influence the outcome of the prosecutor's charges. Only about 5 percent of felony cases, however, are dismissed as a result of pretrial motions.

The script for a trial begins with a reading of the charges, a plea, and an opening statement by the prosecutor. The defense then may make an opening statement also or reserve this for later. The prosecutor then presents the "case in chief." If a motion by the defense for dismissal is not granted, the defense case usually is next presented; but this is not required. After both sides have presented their evidence, each may make a final argument or summation. The jury may acquit, convict, or reach a deadlock. If there is an acquittal, the state has no right to appeal. If found guilty, the defendant may appeal. If there is a mistrial, a new one may be held.

Notes

1. Murphy, W. F., and Pritchett, C. H. (1986). *Courts, Judges, and Politics: An Introduction to the Judicial Process*, 4th ed. New York: McGraw-Hill, 34; the hypothetical case is adapted from these authors.

2. Newman, D. J. (1978). *Introduction to Criminal Justice*, 2nd ed. New York: J. B. Lippincott, 63.

3. Murphy, W. F., and Prichett, C. H. (1986), *Courts, Judges, and Politics: An Introduction to the Judicial Process*, 4th ed. New York: McGraw-Hill, 33.

4. Ibid., 33.

5. LaFave, W. R. (1983). "Organization of Courts," *Encyclopedia of Crime and Justice*, Vol. 1, Kadish, S. H. (ed.). New York: The Free Press, 292–294.

6. Rottman, D. B., Flango, C. R., and Lockley, R. S. (1995). *State Court Organization 1993*. Bureau of Justice Statistics, U.S. Department of Justice, Washington, DC: GPO, 352.

7. Rehnquist, W. H. (Chief Justice of the United States) (1996). Remarks of the Chief Justice, Washington College of Law Centennial Celebration, Plenary Academic Panes: The Future of the Federal Courts, American University. http://supct.law.corness.edu/supct/justices/rehnau96.htm, 2–3.

8. Exodus 18, 13–26.

9. Feeley, M. M. (1983). *Encyclopedia of Crime and Justice*, Vol. 1, Kadish, S. H. (ed.). New York: The Free Press, 413–415.

10. Ibid., 415.

11. Foote, C. (1965). "The Coming Constitutional Crisis in Bail," *University of Pennsylvania Law Review* 113: 959.

12. Goldkamp, J. S., and Gottfredson, M. R. (1985). *Policy Guidelines for Bail: An Experiment in Court Reform*. Philadelphia: Temple University Press, 3.

13. Goldkamp, J. S., Gottfredson, M. R., Jones, P. R., and Weiland, D. (1995). *Personal Liberty and Community Safety: Pretrial Release in a Criminal Court*. New York: Plenum, 5.

14. *U.S. v. Salerno* (1987). 481 U.S. 739.

15. Goldkamp, J. S. (1979). *Two Classes of Accused*. Cambridge, MA: Ballinger.

16. Goldkamp, J. S., Gottfredson, M. R., Jones, P.R., and Weiland, D. (1995). *Personal Liberty and Community Safety: Pretrial Release in the Criminal Court*. New York: Plenum, 17.

17. Landes, W. (1974). "Legality and Reality: Some Evidence on Criminal Procedure," *Journal of Legal Studies*. 3:287, 333.

18. Zawitz, M. W., Gaskins, C. K., Koppel, H., Greenfield, L. A., and Greenwood, P. (1988). "The Response to Crime," in *Report to the Nation on Crime and Justice*,

2nd ed. Washington, DC: Bureau of Justice Statistics, U.S. Department of Justice, 76.

19. Goldkamp, J. S. (1979); Thomas, W. (1976). *Bail Reform in America*. Berkeley: University of California Press; Feeley, M. (1983). *Court Reform on Trial: Why Simple Solutions Fail*. New York: Basic Books.

20. Zawitz, M. W., Gaskins, C. K., Koppel, H., Greenfield, L. A., and Greenwood, P. (1988), 76.

21. Beeley, A. (1927). *The Bail System in Chicago*. Chicago: University of Chicago Press.

22. Ares, C., Rankin, A., and Sturz, H. (1963) "The Manhattan Bail Project: An Interim Report on the Use of Pre-Trial Parole," *New York University Law Review* 38: 67.

23. Wilkins, L. T., and Gottfredson, D. M. (1969). *Research, Demonstration and Social Action*. Davis, CA: National Council on Crime and Delinquency, 82–86.

24. Freed, M. and Wald, P. (1964). *Bail in the United States: 1964*. Washington, DC: U.S. Department of Justice and the Vera Foundation, 62.

25. Zawitz, M. W., Gaskins, C. K., Koppel, H., Greenfield, L. A., and Greenwood, P. (1988), citing Pryor, D. E., and Smith, W. F. [1982]. "Significant Research Findings Concerning Pretrial Release," *Pretrial Issues*. Washington, DC: Pretrial Resource Center, 4, 1.

26. Reaves, B. A., and Perez, J. (1994). *Pretrial Release of Felony Defendants, 1992*. Washington, DC: Bureau of Justice Statistics.

27. Gottfredson, M. R. (1974). "An Empirical Analysis of Pre-Trial Release Decisions," *Journal of Criminal Justice* 2: 287.

28. Gottfredson, S. D. (1987). "Prediction: Methodological Issues," in Gottfredson, D. M., and Tonry, M. (eds.). *Prediction and Classification: Criminal Justice Decision Making*. Chicago: University of Chicago Press, 36-29.

29. Feeley, M., and McNaughton (1974). "The Pre-Trial Process in the Sixth Circuit." New Haven: Unpublished paper.

30. Clarke, S. (1974). *The Bail System in Charlotte: 1971-1973*. Chapel Hill, NC: Institute of Government.

31. Locke, J., Penn, R., Rock, R., Bunten, E. and Hare, G. (1970). *Compilation and Use of Criminal Court Data in Relation to Pretrial Release of Defendants: Pilot Study*. Washington, DC: GPO.

32. Gottfredson, M. R., and Gottfredson, D. M. (1988). *Decision Making in Criminal Justice: Toward the Rational Exercise of Discretion*, 2nd ed. New York: Plenum Press, 95–98.

33. Ibid., 97–98.

34. Feeley, M. (1983). *Court Reform on Trial: Why Simple Solutions Fail*. New York: Basic Books.

35. Gottfredson, M. R., and Gottfredson, D. M. (1988), *Decision Making in Criminal Justice: Toward the Rational Exercise of Discretion*, 2nd ed. New York: Plenum Press, 102–103.

36. Goldkamp, J. S., and Gottfredson, M. R. (1985). *Policy Guidelines for Bail: An Experiment in Court Reform*. Philadelphia: Temple University Press.

37. Gottfredson, M. R., and Gottfredson, D. M. (1988). *Decision Making in Criminal Justice: Toward the Rational Exercise of Discretion*, 2nd ed. New York: Plenum Press, 110.

38. Goldkamp, J. S., Gottfredson, M. R., Jones, P.R., and Weiland, D. (1995), *Personal Liberty and Community Safety: Pretrial Release in a Criminal Court*. New York: Plenum, 304–308.

39. Ibid.

40. Ibid.

41. Ibid., 307–308.

42. Rottman, D. B., Flango, C. R., and Lockley, R. S. (1995). *State Court Organization 1993*. Washington, DC: Bureau of Justice Statistics, U. S. Department of Justice, 280–282.

43. Anderson, G. L. (1983). "Preliminary Hearing," in Kadish, S.H. (ed.). *Encyclopedia of Crime and Justice*, Vol. 3. New York: The Free Press, 1180.

44. Kaplan, J., Skolnik, J. H., and Feeley, M. (1991), *Criminal Justice: Introductory Cases and Materials*. Westbury, NY: The Foundation Press, 390.

45. Katz, L. R. (1983). "Speedy Trial," in Kadish, S.H. (ed.). *Encyclopedia of Crime and Justice*, Vol. 3. New York: The Free Press, 1506.

46. Katz, L. R. (1983), 1507, citing *Beavers v. Haubert* (1905). 198 U.S. 77 and *Klopfer v. North Carolina* (1967). 386 U.S. 213 and *Dillingham v. United States* (1975). 423 U.S. 64.

47. Barker v. Wingo (1972). 407 U.S. 514.

48. Katz, L. R. (1983), "Speedy Trial," in Kadish, S.H. (ed.). *Encyclopedia of Crime and Justice*, Vol. 3. New York: The Free Press, 1509.

49. Josar, D. *The Detroit News*, November 5, 1995.

50. Rottman, D. B., Flango, C. R., and Lockley, R. S. (1995), *State Court Organization 1993*. Washington, DC: Bureau of Justice Statistics, U. S. Department of Justice, 232–249.

51. Nizer, L. 1978. *Chicago Tribune Magazine*.

52. Van Dyke, J. M. (1983) "Jury Trial," in Kadish, S.H. (ed.). *Encyclopedia of Crime and Justice*, Vol. 3. New York: The Free Press, 932.

53. Ibid., 933.

54. Ibid., 933.

55. *Duncan v. Louisiana* (1968). 391 U.S. 145.

56. Rottman, D. B., Flango, C. R., and Lockley, R. S. (1995), *State Court Organization 1993*. Washington, DC: Bureau of Justice Statistics, U. S. Department of Justice, 265–268.

57. Van Dyke, J. M. (1983), "Jury Trial," in Kadish, S.H. (ed.). *Encyclopedia of Crime and Justice*, Vol. 3. New York: The Free Press, 935.

58. Rottman, D. B., Flango, C. R., and Lockley, R. S. (1995), *State Court Organization 1993*. Washington, DC: Bureau of Justice Statistics, U. S. Department of Justice, 255–268.

59. Van Dyke, J. M. (1983), "Jury Trial," in Kadish, S.H. (ed.). *Encyclopedia of Crime and Justice*, Vol. 3. New York: The Free Press, 936.

60. *Batson v. Kentucky* (1986). 476 U.S. 79.

61. Rottman, D. B., Flango, C. R., and Lockley, R. S. (1995), *State Court Organization 1993*. Washington, DC: Bureau of Justice Statistics, U. S. Department of Justice, 269–273.

62. Van Dyke, J. M. (1983), citing *Williams v. Florida* (1970). 399 U.S. 78102.

63. *Johnson v. Louisiana* (1972). 406 U.S. 356; *Apodaca v. Oregon* (1972) 406 U.S. 404.

64. *Ballew v. Georgia* (1978). 435 U.S. 223.

65. *Sparf and Hansen v. United States* (1895). 156 U.S. 51.

66. Van Dyke, J. M. (1983), "Jury Trial," in Kadish, S.H. (ed.). *Encyclopedia of Crime and Justice*, Vol. 3. New York: The Free Press, 939–940.

67. LaFave, R., and Israel, J. H. (1985). *Criminal Procedure*. St. Paul, MN: West Publishing, 830–831.

68. Ibid., 16-17.

69. Hazard, G. C. (1983). "Criminal Justice System: Overview, in Kadish, S. H. (ed.). *Encyclopedia of Crime and Justice*. Vol. 1 New York: The Free Press, 463–464.

Sentencing

Photo courtesy of www.digitalstock.com.

Chapter Nine

After conviction, a decision about a sentence must be made. This decision by a judge is at the center of controversies about the basic purposes of the entire criminal justice system. The debates are about justice, fairness, and crime control.

Important topics include the proper goals of sentencing, the structure that can best provide a proper context for the decision making of judges, and appropriate sentencing alternatives. The purposes of sentencing are by no means agreed upon. How much choice should be left to the judge and how much discretion should be limited are questions that generate lively arguments. Methods of punishments, amounts of punishment, and the effects of punishment are topics that concern sentencing directly and affect the whole system of criminal justice.

In order to understand these debates, we must review the most commonly held theories of sentencing purposes and their philosophical underpinnings, explore the broad changes that have taken place over the last several decades, and then examine the most common sentencing structures, which differ markedly among jurisdictions.

❏ Questions to Think About
❏ The Hub of the Wheel
❏ Theories of Sentencing
❏ Two Views of the Ethics of Punishment
❏ Sentencing Goals
    General Deterrence
    Incapacitation
    Treatment
    Desert
❏ Specific Purposes of Judges
❏ Statistical Characteristics of Sentences
❏ Alternatives
❏ What Influences Sentencing Decisions?
❏ Sentencing Trends
❏ Determinate Sentencing
❏ Determinate Sentencing Effects
❏ Deserved Punishment
❏ Ethical and Scientific Views Intertwined
❏ Discretion and Disparity
❏ Sentencing Guidelines
❏ Sentencing Commissions
❏ Changes in Discretionary Sentencing
❏ The Sentence to Prison, Jail, or Probation
❏ Capital Punishment
    The Death Penalty in the United States
    The Death Penalty Debate
❏ Summary

Questions to Think About

What are the judge's goals?

Does the judge always have a choice in sentencing?

What information influences the sentencing decision?

What alternatives does the judge have at sentencing?

What theories of justice affect sentencing policy?

Do judges prefer certain sentences?

How does sentencing differ among jurisdictions?

What is an indeterminate sentence?

Do all states have parole boards?

Do all states supervise offenders after release from prison?

Are persons released from prison now more often supervised in the community?

Do all judges have sentencing guidelines?

What does a sentencing commission do?

How can unfair disparities in sentences be reduced?

How have sentencing policies increased prison populations?

Are you for or against capital punishment? Why?

The Hub of the Wheel

Judges' decisions are limited by laws that define penalties and sentencing structures, and sometimes by the rules of sentencing commissions that set additional limits on judges' decisions. Nevertheless, the judge typically still has much discretion in deciding on a penalty.

In choosing a sentence, the judge occupies a role of great influence on all other parts of the system. Sentencing decisions influence the roles and behaviors of police, prosecutors, and correctional authorities. Changes in sentencing law or policy have important consequences for law enforcement, courts, and corrections.[1]

Trends in the philosophy of sentencing address issues fundamental to criminal justice and have had a profound influence on the whole system. Broad changes have taken place over the last several decades that have had exceptional effects on sentencing. One trend involves increased emphasis on giving the offender the punishment deserved. There has been more focus also on restraining the offender for the purposes of crime control. Another trend concerns the amount of discretion that should be allowed judges in choosing punishments; there has been a decrease in choices allowed the judge in sentencing. Punishments have tended to be more harsh and more definite as the retributive purpose has been more accepted.

Theories of Sentencing

When legislators sit down to write or revise the laws that set the general policies under which sentences will be imposed on convicted offenders, they often fail to agree on basic purposes. They may not perceive that their purposes conflict with one another—but they may. Some people argue that criminals are not getting the punishment they deserve. Some emphasize increased punishment as a deterrent to crime. Others stress more confinement to keep offenders off the street. Others want to provide more rehabilitation services. Some simply demand harsher penalties. When increased penalties are proposed, politicians may feel no need to present any justification at all. As a result, each of the traditional aims of sentencing—retribution, general deterrence, incapacitation, and treatment—is thrown into the pot, highly seasoned with talk about getting tougher, giving criminals the punishment they deserve, and controlling crime. When stirred into an inconsistent mass, the resulting stew—concocted with something for everybody—is likely to please few persons, whether in the legislature, the courts, or the general public. Judges, faced with conflicting demands of inconsistent codes, perceived opinions of various publics, and their own convictions, must make sentencing decisions as best they can.

Sentencing theories are not divorced from either general sentencing policy or individual sentencing. Recently revised criminal codes in many states have resulted from intensive debate about purposes. Sentencing commissions have formulated sentencing rules intended to match their theories of sentencing, while individual judges make decisions based on their own theories and views of justice and crime control.

Two Views of the Ethics of Punishment

An important sanction already has been imposed before sentencing. This is the conviction itself. As described by Weiler, the conviction publicly, authoritatively, decisively, and enduringly certifies that the defendant is guilty of blameworthy conduct causing harm to an innocent victim. This stigmatization of the person inflicts "not only a damaging, but also one of the most enduring sanctions which the state can mete out."[2]

Yet the conviction actually is not the first sanction applied by the criminal justice system. As pointed out in previous sections of this book, the arrest, although not usually regarded as such, is itself a sanction. So is charging by the prosecutor. Both arrest and charging have serious consequences for the accused person. Now, however, with conviction, a clearly intended sanction is exercised by the public condemnation of the offender's behavior.

The conviction alone is rarely considered to be a sufficient sanction, however. Additional penalties usually are justified on one or the other—or both—of two basic views that are in conflict. The fundamental moral conflict is between utilitarianism and retributivism perspectives. The utilitarian perspective is committed to maximizing the general good; the retributive viewpoint is addressed to principles of justice, fairness, and equity. These basic differences have profound implications for sentencing policy and for the judge as an individual decision maker. The conflict was aptly summarized by Weiler:

The one view holds that criminal penalties can be justified if, but only if, they will reduce the level of crime within the community. The other responds that sanctions are justified if, but only if, the defendant has done something for which he merits their infliction. It is clear then that the arguments within the first perspective are focused forward in time, toward the future beneficial consequences of punishment; within the second the arguments look backward, to events which have already occurred, as the source of moral support.[3]

A central issue in sentencing is whether retributive and utilitarian objectives may both be achieved within a consistent ethical position. The philosophies that undergird these aims, reflecting moral (Kantian)[4] and utilitarian (Benthamite or Millsian)[5] views, contrast sharply and are inconsistent with one another. The debate has continued for more than 2,000 years.[6]

The sword of justice symbolizes punishment and the force of the law. An act is not a crime unless the law provides a punishment, and it is the duty of the judge to impose it. What purposes do you believe are served by punishment? —*Themis, Goddess of Justice, The Museum Company.*

The utilitarian orientation is one variety of consequentialism—the position that the rightness of an act should be judged by its consequences.[7] The utilitarian view includes the concepts of deterrence, treatment, and incapacitation. Each looks forward to some good to follow from punishment: to warn others, to rehabilitate offenders, or to isolate those likely to commit future crimes. Each seeks the reduction of crime. Utilitarianism is not concerned only with what is useful or works best to control crime. A more general view would be given by Locke's statement that "the end of government is the good of mankind."[8] The utilitarian theory is that the best course or act is the one that makes for the best whole (that results in the greatest good or the least dissatisfaction). Punishment, by definition a harm, must be avoided unless outweighed by the good to follow. This orientation relies on the concept of determinism and on the scientific method—behavior is determined (or caused) according to scientific laws.

The currently most popular retributive theory is called the theory of just desert. The desert theory, distinct from but related to retribution,[9] is not future-oriented. It looks only to the past harm done. Those who choose to do crimes are blameworthy and should be punished. Some of the philosophical foundations of this theory are in the writings of the eighteenth-century German philosopher Immanual Kant.

Kant's ethical objection to utilitarianism rests on his dictum that a human being never can be manipulated as a means to someone else's purposes. One must act so as to treat humanity always as an end and never as a means only.[10] Because people are responsible for their acts, on this theory, they ought to be given their just desert—that is, the punishment that is justly warranted. Following Kant rather than Beccaria [11] or the utilitarians, this theory emphasizes that punishment must be given if, but only if, it is deserved. Contemporary advocates of retributive theory [12] stress that punishment should be proportional to the gravity of the harm done and the culpability of the offender. This is Beccarian rather than Kantian, since Kant believed in *lex talionis* ("an eye for an eye"). Beccaria emphasized proportionality but also would impose the least severe sanction possible under the circumstances.

To the extent that an offender is to be punished according to the blameworthiness of his or her act—and only that—utilitarian objectives of crime control, treatment of the offender, incapacitation, or deterrence have no bearing. These aims have no standing whatever from the moral theory of deserved punishment. The fundamental flaw of utilitarian perspectives, from the Kantian viewpoint, is the failure to honor the principle that is stressed as the hallmark of moral behavior: one must act so as to treat persons always as ends and never as means only. The most offensive attribute of sentencing or correctional decision making in pursuit of utilitarian aims, it is argued, is a willingness to manipulate people as if they were objects, disrespecting their dignity, autonomy, and humanity in a manner starkly lacking in the humility that should characterize rendering judgments or power over other human beings.

Thus, from a few principles arise basic conflicts of ethical positions on sentencing. We must consider only the past harm done, and punish accordingly; yet, we must look to the future, to see what good may be done. Punishment must be based only on the crime, and never on one merely expected; but it must serve as an example to others, teach a lesson, and restrain the offender from future crimes. Punishment must be done; but it is forbidden unless necessary for a greater good. The person must not be used as a means to an end; but it may be necessary to punish the individual for the greater welfare of society. Punishment must be used to express society's condemnation; but punishment is never justified except by the prevention of harm. We may only look back to the crime for the justification of punishment; but since the past is gone, we must only look ahead.

Sentencing Goals

The ethical controversy finds expression in current debates about the four main sentencing goals: general deterrence, incapacitation, treatment, and deserved punishment (just desert). These are the principal goals of sentencing as now practiced in the criminal justice system.

General Deterrence

General deterrence is the concept that criminal acts in the general population can be prevented by means of punishment of persons convicted of crimes. It is called "general deterrence" to distinguish it from "specific" or "special" deterrence, which refers to the idea that an individual can be stopped from committing further crimes by punishment as a means of correction. For discussion in this book, specific deterrence is considered under the goal of treatment because, from that perspective, punishment is used in an effort to change the offender's behavior.

The theory of general deterrence is that the punishment given to a person or a class of persons convicted of crime serves the purpose of decreasing the probability that others will engage in criminal behavior. The validity of the theory is to be determined by the effect that a punishment has on the future criminality of those not punished.

> *Men are not hanged for stealing Horses, but that Horses may not be stolen.*
> *—1st Marquis of Halifax*

The deterrent aim is future-oriented. Its objective is to warn others or to persuade them not to commit crimes. Because the theory is that the punishment of offenders will decrease the likelihood of crime by others, general deterrence is sometimes called "general prevention."

In 1764 Beccaria cited criteria for the justification of punishment when he argued for general deterrence. In order for punishment to be acceptable, it must be, he said, public and prompt, necessary, lawful, proportional in severity to the seriousness of the crime, and the least severe sanction possible under the circumstances. The deterrence idea is common in our culture.

> *Pardon one offense and you encourage many.*
> *—Pubilius Syrus*

The aims of specific deterrence and general deterrence often have been combined as justifications for punishment. Together these two purposes may be thought to give at once a means of correction ("teaching a lesson") and a warning to others.

> *In revenges or punishments men ought not to look at the greatness of evil past, but at the greatness of the good to follow, whereby we are forbidden to inflict punishment with any other design than for the correction of the offender and the admonition of others.*
> *—Hobbes*

Incapacitation

Incapacitation is the sentencing aim of restraining the person being punished from committing further criminal acts. It sometimes is called "neutralization" or "isolation." Unlike a treatment orientation, attention is not focused on the offender's *propensity* for committing crimes. It is intended instead to control the offender in order to preclude the *opportunity* for criminal behavior, usually by confinement in a jail or prison.

This purpose, like that of general deterrence, is future-oriented. Like general deterrence, it is meant to prevent crime. While general deterrence seeks the prevention of crimes by others, incapacitation is aimed at the prevention of crime by the convicted offender. Its justification is not in what the offender has done but what he or she might do.

Two forms of incapacitation are commonly recognized: collective incapacitation and selective incapacitation. Based on the general idea of incapacitation, the two concepts differ in how the convicted offenders would be selected for restraint.

Under a collective strategy, all persons convicted of a designated offense would receive the same sentence. Recent "three strikes" type legislation—markedly increasing prison terms for repeated convictions in order to "keep offenders off the street"—could be regarded as a similar incapacitative strategy. It is based not only on the offense but on prior convictions. Blumstein noted that incapacitation effects can be expected under any policy that requires incarceration:

> A collective incapacitation effect occurs under any sentencing policy . . . as long as any of the offenders sentenced under the policy would have commit- ted crimes on the street during their period of confinement and those crimes would not be replaced on the street by others (as, for example, the drug sales of a sentenced drug dealer would be replaced by other dealers still on the street).[13]

Under a selective strategy, the sentence would be based at least in part on predictions that particular offenders would commit crimes at a high rate if not incarcerated. Thus, the strategy is to find high-risk offenders and sentence them to prison terms—or longer prison terms—because of their disproportionate risk of committing new crimes if not restrained. The flip side is not incarcerating offenders who are not likely to offend again. Its proponents have seen selective incapacitation as a means for simultaneously reducing prison populations and crime rates, simply by selecting high risks for incarceration decisions.[14]

Confinement in jail or prison is the most often used means when incapacitation is the aim, but other methods of restraint sometimes are used in sentencing. Examples are "ankle bracelets" for electronic monitoring and "house arrest" when offenders are confined to their homes.

The validity of the sentencing aim of incapacitation is to be determined by the crimes—which must be estimated by some means—that are avoided due to the restraint of the offender.

Treatment

Treatment purposes in sentencing are future-oriented, aimed at crime prevention, and focused on individual convicted offenders. The goal of treatment for a sentencing decision is to decrease the tendency of those offenders to commit crimes. The term "treatment," as used here, has a very broad meaning, encompassing anything done to, with, or for the offender with the objective of reducing the probability of new criminal acts by the individual. The many and diverse programs designed to achieve this goal seek rehabilitation of the offender, restoration, or reintegration into the community.

The term is widely used in other ways as well, including procedures designed to assist the person or to modify some state of the person in ways that are not necessarily related to crime reduction. It includes specific deterrence. It may include therapeutic communities, boot camps, counseling, group or individual therapy, vocational training, education programs, drug testing, or other correctional programs of supervision or intervention. Although usually focused on the offender, the word "treatment" as used here includes changes in the environment that are intended to change the behavior of the offender.

Desert

The only question to be answered under the deserved punishment theory of sentencing is, "What punishment is deserved in this case?" The purpose is to express disapproval or to exact retribution. It has no explicit aim to control crime. It differs from the other three purposes discussed by focusing exclusively on the past criminal behavior of the offender and is given only to express condemnation of that behavior.

The hallmark of the strict desert position is that as a result of the crime, the person convicted deserves a certain amount of punishment, and the severity of that punishment ought to be proportional to the seriousness of the harm done and the culpability of the offender. It has no crime control components. Past acts that the person has done are not relevant, nor are any likely future acts to be considered in determining the deserved punishment. (In some modern desert conceptions, some past acts may be considered.) The concept is as old as philosophy and is found repeatedly in literature.

> *Justice is the firm and continuous desire to render to everyone that which is his due.*
> —*Justinian*

Desert alone provides a legitimate and adequate basis for punishment, according to Kant, who described the penal law as a categorical imperative, a moral obligation, and added ". . . woe to him who rumbles around in the winding paths of a theory of happiness looking for some advantage to be gained by releasing the criminal from punishment or by reducing the amount of it. . . ." He gave this example:

> Even if a civil society resolved to dissolve itself by common agreement of all its members (for example, if the people inhabiting an island decided to sepa-rate and disperse themselves throughout the world) the last murderer re-maining in prison must first be executed so that everyone will duly receive what his actions are worth and so the bloodguilt thereof will not be fixed on the people because they failed to insist on carrying out the punishment; for if they fail to do so, they may be regarded as accomplices in this public vio-lation of legal justice.[15]

Desert as a purpose of sentencing, or of the criminal justice system as a whole, has nothing whatever to do with the utilitarian purposes of crime control, prevention, deterrence, incapacitation, rehabilitation, or any other crime reduction aim. The application of the concept may or may not have such effects, but whether there are such consequences is another question. The purpose of sentencing on the desert theory is satisfaction of a moral imperative. Rewards and punishments are means to the end of desert.

Specific Purposes of Judges

Individual judges might select any or all these purposes when choosing a sentence. Judges might differ in preferences for any purpose. One judge might usually emphasize retribution (desert) while another is more inclined to seek the rehabilitation of offenders; a third judge might stress incapacitation, and yet another may perceive general deterrence to be the most important sentencing goal.

Besides judges' individual inclinations toward certain purposes, a judge may, and typically does, consider different purposes—and perhaps even conflicting ones—when sentencing an individual convicted offender. This was illustrated in a study of sentencing in the Essex County, New Jersey, court in which 18 judges collaborated in a study of their judgments and dispositions.[16] The study was done 20 years ago, before changes in sentencing philosophy and practice—and in the criminal code in New Jersey—had taken place. At the time of the study, judges in New Jersey had wider discretion in sentencing than they now have.

The judges completed forms documenting their judgments on various factors at the time of sentencing nearly one thousand cases over about a year. A list of purposes was developed, by research workers in collaboration with the judges, at the start of the study. The judges recorded, among other judgments, the sentencing purposes they considered to be appropriate for each case. Purposes listed were retribution, incapacitation, special deterrence, rehabilitation, and "other" (including general deterrence). When each case was sentenced, the judges were asked to distribute 100 points among these items or to assign this value to any one item, provided only that the sums would be 100 points.

The judges usually distributed the 100 points among several purposes, rather than selecting only one purpose and giving it the whole 100 points. Of course, the way the question was asked may have suggested this; still, they did have the option of a single purpose, and occasionally they used it. When the purpose given the highest rating was considered to be the "main purpose," the most commonly identified aim was rehabilitation. That goal was given the most weight in more than a third of the sentences. If special deterrence, also a treatment purpose, is counted, then 45 percent of the sentences were classified as having a treatment aim according to the judge who imposed the sentence.

These judges were mainly utilitarians. When all forward-looking, crime prevention, or crime control aims were grouped together, then 83 percent of the sentences were included. The aim of retribution was not cited so frequently; it was noted as the main purpose in 17 percent of the sentences. The specific term "desert" (which is retribution) was not included on the list, since it was not suggested by any judge when the item was formulated for the study. The proportions of sentences for which purposes were give the largest weightings are shown in Figure 9.1.

These judges were more inclined to sentence with a retributive aim when the crime was seen as more serious than usual, when the convicted offender had a past record of convictions, and when the person was seen as a serious risk of doing harm. An analysis of differences between cases sentenced mainly for retribution and those sentenced principally for rehabilitation suggested that these judges tended to sentence offenders retributively rather than for rehabilitation under certain conditions. The judges, when retributive, appeared to be influenced by the following factors in the case: a serious conviction offense; an offender record of prior prison incarceration; the judge's expectation of recidivism—new offenses after release—particularly when the judge predicted a new offense against persons; and when the judge questioned the offender's social stability. When the opposite was true, the judges tended to see rehabilitation as an appropriate sentencing aim.

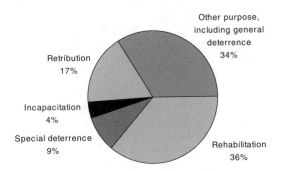

Source: Gottfredson, D. M. (1984). *The Effects of Criminal Sanctions.* Report to the National Institute of Justice, U.S. Department of Justice. Newark, NJ: Rutgers University School of Criminal Justice.

The strongest association of any item with the judges' choice of primary aim was their prediction of a new offense against persons. This suggests that the relatively rare selection of incapacitation as a main goal may be misleading. Judges may use this purpose without calling it incapacitation. Alternatively, it might indicate that for these judges utilitarian purposes may provide a partial justification for retribution.

The individual personality characteristics of judges are important in sentencing decisions. Hogarth, studying attitudes of judges in Canada, found that an important factor was "the degree to which an individual wishes to see offenders punished severely."[17] Judges with high scores on this attitude agreed that capital and corporal punishment are necessary, that prisons should be places of punishment, and that "the most important single consideration in determining the sentence to impose should be the nature and gravity of the offense."

Statistical Characteristics of Sentences

If sentencing were an exact science, one might expect that the penalty imposed would be precisely selected to achieve the specific objectives determined to be appropriate. The exactly right sentence might be, for example, imprisonment for 4 years, 3 months, and 15 days. Or, it might be 8 months in jail, with 3 months suspended to be served under probation supervision with drug testing once every 4 days and group counseling every day for the first 6 weeks. Of course, such precision is never expected; but it nevertheless is striking that an examination of sentence distributions invariably shows the nature of approximate justice that is found in reality.

Certain sentences seem to be preferred, for seemingly no particular reason. This is found in different places, at different times. In England in 1873, Sir Francis Galton studied the sentences of all males imprisoned that year. The frequencies of sentences in years are shown in Figure 9.2. Eighty-four years later, the sentences imposed by the Essex County court were those shown in Figure 9.3.

Figure 9.2 Number Chosen in Sentencing to Years in Prison, England, 1893

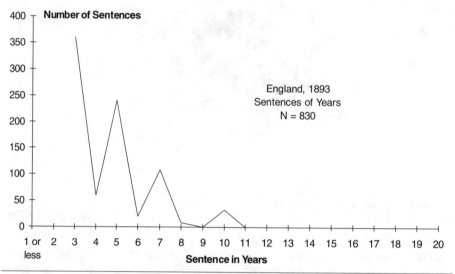

Source: data from Galton, as cited in Banks, E. (1964). "Reconviction of Young Offenders," *Current Legal Problems* 17:74, 74–76.

Figure 9.3 Number Chosen in Sentencing to Jail and Prison, Essex County Court, 1976–1977

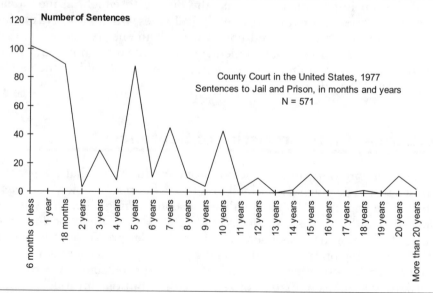

Source: Gottfredson, D. M. (1984). *The Effects of Criminal Sanctions.* Report to the National Institute of Justice, U.S. Department of Justice. Newark, NJ: Rutgers University School of Criminal Justice.

Galton wrote, about the sentences he observed:

It would be expected that the various terms of imprisonment . . . should fall in a continuous series. Such, however, is not the case. . . . The extreme irregularity of the frequency of the different terms of imprisonment forces itself on the attention . . . [and] it is impossible to believe that a judicial system is fair which allots only 20 sentences to six years, allots as many as 240 to five years, as few as 60 to four years and as many as 360 to three years. [18]

Sentences of 3, 5, 7, and 10 years appeared to be preferred to the values in between. The result was an irregular distribution with a series of spikes. Galton noted a similar phenomenon in the case of sentences to months. Although there were about 300 sentences to 18 months, there were none to 17 and only 20 to 19 months. He also noted rhythmical series of 3, 6, 9, 12, 15, and 18 months and 3, 5, 7, and 10 years. Galton interpreted his results as due to "the undoubted fact that almost all persons have a disposition to dwell on certain numbers, and an indisposition to use others." He added, "These trifles determine the choice of such widely different sentences as imprisonment for 3 or 5 years, 5 or 7, and of 7 or 10 for crimes whose penal deserts would otherwise be rated 4, 6, and 8 or 9 years respectively."

The sentences to confinement assigned by the New Jersey judges 84 years later are shown in Figure 9.3. There was a tendency to use sentences of 6, 12, or 18 months, and 3, 5, 7, 10, 15, and 20 years.[19]

The *shape* of the distributions (aside from its "spiked" nature) in both figures is also commonly found. They are "skewed to the right," which means that there is a long tail to the right. Less severe sentences are given commonly; and, as sentences become more severe, they are more rare. As a result, the median is a better representation of the typical sentence than is the usual average.

When Sir Francis Galton, a little over 100 years ago, collected the data cited, he suggested that comparison of different courts or judges might show that very different penalties were assigned for the same kinds of crimes. His expectation has been confirmed in many studies since then. Variation among courts and among individual judges contributes substantially to variations in sentences.

One of the earliest studies was an examination of sentences of more than 7,000 persons by six judges in a New Jersey court.[20] The number imprisoned ranged from 34 to 58 percent among judges. (The cases were assigned on a rotational basis, so it is plausible, although not demonstrated, that the cases were assigned evenly.) A later study of sentences in the federal courts found that the factors that appeared to determine who was sent to prison, as well as the length of stay, were different among the various district courts.[21]

Alternatives

The choices available to the judge at sentencing may be quite complex. Oversimplified, the main choices are whether confinement is ordered and, if so, for how long. The judge, however, may also make decisions about where the convicted offender will be confined (usually limited to a county jail or a state prison) and about probation length and conditions. Besides these choices, there may be a variety of alternative penalties that could be imposed. A fairly typical, simplified flow chart for the sentencing decision is that shown in Figure 9.4, which shows the main decisions for the Essex County court judges in 1977.

Figure 9.4 seems to depict an orderly process by which the judge first decides whether incarceration is necessary, then proceeds to determine

Figure 9.4 Simplified Flow Chart of Sentencing Decisions, Essex County Court, 1977

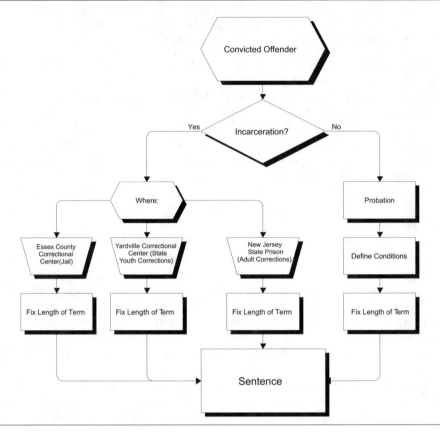

where (whether in jail, prison, or the state youth corrections facilities). Actually, we have no way of knowing whether this is justified. The judge may, for example, be torn between a short term in the youth facilities or a lengthy term of probation supervision. Or, the question of "how long" incarceration is to be required may help determine, thereafter, the choice of institutional setting.

The chart is simplified further because there are other decisions to be made at the time of sentencing. If probation is ordered, for example, special conditions may be required. If incarceration is decided upon, there is the possibility nevertheless of an order of probation as well—a decision called a "split sentence" under which the offender would first serve a time in jail, then be released under supervision. In addition, fines may be set, restitution may be required, community service may be demanded, or other programs may be ordered, usually as probation conditions. In the Essex County sample, for example, fines were imposed on about a fifth of all offenders sentenced. When probation conditions were specified, these included the requirement of participation in a drug treatment program in 6 percent of cases, urine monitoring in 3 percent, and alcohol treatment in 2 percent.

Another decision that must be made by the judge when the conviction is for more than one offense (or when the convicted offender was already serving a prior term at the time of sentence) is whether the offender will serve all sentences simultaneously or one after another. In the Essex County sample, 6 percent of cases sentenced were given multiple concurrent sentences, and a mix of concurrent and consecutive sentences was imposed on 5 percent.

What Influences Sentencing Decisions?

Many studies of sentencing have found consistently that two measures influence both the decision whether to incarcerate the offender and the length of term. These are measures of the seriousness of the offense and of the nature and gravity of the offender's prior criminal record. Although defined differently in different studies, it is clear that the type of behavior for which the person has been convicted not unexpectedly has a powerful influence on sentencing decisions. Similarly, although not found invariably, many studies indicate that the prior record is influential, though less so than the seriousness of the offense. There is considerable evidence also that the judge's expectation (prediction) of repeated offending by the offender often is of critical concern to the judge.

A thorough review of sentencing research by the National Academy of Sciences resulted in a similar conclusion about the seriousness of the offense and the extent of prior record:

> Using a variety of different indicators, offense seriousness and offender's prior record emerge consistently as the key determinants of sentences. The strength of this conclusion persists despite the potentially severe problems of pervasive biases arising from the difficulty of measuring—or even precisely defining—either of these complex variables. This finding is supported by a wide variety of studies using data of varying quality in different jurisdictions and with a diversity of measures of offense seriousness and prior record. [22]

These are broad, but remarkably consistent findings of sentencing research; other sources of influence are less clear-cut and may vary according to jurisdictions. There is some evidence that some of the variation in sentences is due to individual differences among judges—that is, to differences in attitudes or beliefs about the purposes of sentencing. There is some evidence also, although it is mixed, of "extra-legal" factors (such as race) that influence sentencing. The legal factors of offense and prior record, however, are—at least in the recent past—considerably more predictive of sentences.

Sentencing Trends

The major sentencing reform in the first part of the present century was the indeterminate sentence. The dominant characteristics were sentences of indefinite length (often having a possible range of zero to life) and (by the invention of parole) a removal of the time of release from the time of sentencing to a time later in the correctional process. [23]

Early in this century, sentencing and correctional structures were guided mainly by utilitarian principles, particularly the aim of rehabilitation. The indeterminate sentence was adopted increasingly in the early 1900s and became the general rule. The actual determination of the length of term was deferred when offenders were sent to prison until later in the term of confinement, when it was decided by a parole board. The premise was that the offender could be diagnosed and treated and should be released when ready to begin a law-abiding life. The treatment goal of sentencing—future-oriented, preventive in design, and focused on the individual offender—was most important.

Although intended as a means to individualize sentences to fit the needs of the particular offender, the indeterminate sentence has been criticized with increasing vigor over the last several decades. Major criticisms included:

- The uncertainty of the time of release is unfair and has an adverse psychological effect upon the offender.

- Sentences do not reflect the seriousness of offenses.

- The judiciary lacks specific criteria for the choice of sentence and as a result sentencing is arbitrary and unpredictable.

- Disparity in sentencing and parole — people guilty of the same crime receiving different punishment — has increased.

- Rehabilitation efforts have been unsuccessful, and in any event the state does not have a right to intervene for a purpose of rehabilitation.

> *The only purpose for which power can be rightfully exercised over any member of a civilized community, against his will, is to prevent harm to others. His own good, either physical or moral, is not a sufficient warrant.*
> —John Stuart Mill

As a result of widespread disenchantment with the concept of the indeterminate sentence and with the rehabilitative ideal linked to it, determinate sentences were urged. The indeterminate sentence should be abolished, many insisted, because changes were needed for a fair and just sentencing system. The dominant features of arguments for determinacy included these three main points:

- Specific standards, based wholly or mainly on the seriousness of the offense, are needed to establish the appropriate sanction, including both who is confined and the duration of confinement.

- An early determination of the time of release is required, either at the time of sentencing or early in the correctional process.

- A reduction in judicial discretion is necessary, in order to reduce unwarranted disparities in sentencing.

Variations in models of sentencing which could be alternatives to the indeterminate sentence were proposed. A first area of debate included different methods for determining the type and length of sentence. There were proposals for "flat time" sentences,[24] presumptive or commensurate sentences,[25] sentencing guidelines,[26] and sentencing commissions.[27] A flat time sentence is one with a fixed duration of punishment. A presumptive sentence implies a structure by which a fixed penalty is presumed to be given, although some deviation may be permitted by aggravating or mitigating factors. A commensurate sentence is one in which penalties are scaled in severity in relation to the seriousness of the offense. Sentencing guidelines may be established by law, usually by means of a sentencing commission, or they may be used by the judges voluntarily. Guidelines structure the sentencing decision process and indicate the usual sentences for offenses and offender characteristics. Typically, deviations are permitted when specific reasons are given. Sentencing commissions are typically bodies established by the legislature to determine the structure and standards within which sentences will be set—often through the use of guidelines.

There have been other areas of important debate. One concerns the legitimate use of mitigating and aggravating factors—characteristics of the offense or the blame worthiness of the offender that make the crime less or more serious—in determining the sentence. Another is the amount, if any, of "good time" that can be built up, reducing the period of confinement in custody for "good behavior." Good time may be a discretionary award—by correctional administration or a parole board—or by fixed "earned" amounts. Related to all these issues is the question of the existence of a parole board and its proper role, if any, in the release decision.

One important reason for the widespread tendency to discard the indeterminate sentence design was that many people perceived rehabilitation was ineffective in reducing crime. Increasingly it was argued that we do not have enough knowledge of diagnosis and treatment to make it work. The more fundamental challenge, however, rested on moral arguments about justice and fairness. Its basis was the desert perspective. Thus, a shift toward determinate sentencing and toward an emphasis on deserved punishment has occurred.

Determinate Sentencing

Besides the argument that the indeterminate sentencing model was ineffective in rehabilitating offenders, two arguments were especially influential: (1) criticisms of procedures on grounds of unfairness, and (2) the uncertainty felt by the prisoner was said to be unfair (or at any rate, counterproductive). Generally, it was said that both sentencing and paroling decisions were arbitrary, unpredictable, unfair and did not work. As a result, determinate sentencing legislation was passed in many states, the federal system also moved toward greater determinacy, and some parole boards were abolished.

By 1994, 20 states had some form of determinate sentencing, 16 states had sentencing guidelines, discretionary release by a paroling authority had been eliminated in 12 states, and all states and the District of Columbia had some form of mandatory minimum incarceration sentencing.[28]

Sentencing structures in the United States now provide a complex variety. Not everyone uses the terms "determinate," "indeterminate," "mandatory," or "presumptive" in just the same way. Austin and his colleagues used the definitions shown in Box 9.1 to classify the states by their sentence structures.

The variety of sentencing structures among states makes it difficult to classify them because the categories are not mutually exclusive. Some states have some elements of determinate sentencing along with some features of indeterminate sentencing. Wisconsin's guidelines, for example, have presumptive provisions for nonviolent property offenders. New Jersey, although classified as indeterminate, has some provisions for mandatory sentencing and a presumption of (discretionary) parole at first eligibility. The mandatory sentences in New Jersey have two forms. Some sentences allow the judge no discretion, calling for a prison sentence with a mandatory minimum time that must be served before parole consideration. Others have mandatory minimum terms only when the judge decides to impose them at sentencing. The classification of states shown in Box 9.2 is based on the Austin survey, with states classified first by whether they have sentencing guidelines. Those without guidelines then are classified as mainly determinate or mainly indeterminate. This can be a rough classification only. Many of the states shown as indeterminate have de-

Box 9.1

Terms Used in Describing Sentencing Structures

Determinate: sentences of incarceration in which the offender is given a fixed term that may be reduced by good time or earned time. There are usually explicit standards specifying the amount of punishment. There is a set release date for which there is no review by a parole board. Postincarceration supervision (parole) may or may not be a part of the sentence.

Indeterminate: a parole board has the authority to release the offender and to determine whether parole will be revoked for violations of the conditions of release. There are two forms of indeterminate sentencing structures:

1. The judge specifies only the maximum sentence length of incarceration. The associated minimum sentence is automatically implied but not within the judge's discretion.

2. In the more traditional form of indeterminate sentencing, the judge specifies a maximum and minimum sentence that is set by statute. The sentencing judge has discretion as to the minimum and maximum sentences.

Mandatory minimum: a minimum sentence of incarceration specified by statute. This may be applied for all convictions of a particular crime or a particular crime with special circumstances (e.g., robbery with a firearm, selling drugs to a minor within 1,000 feet of a school).

Presumptive sentencing guidelines: sentencing meets all the following conditions:

1. The appropriate sentence for offenders in individual cases is presumed to fall within a range of sentences authorized by sentencing guidelines. Sentencing judges are expected to sentence within the range or explain any departure.

2. The guidelines require written justification for departure.

3. The guidelines provide for some review, usually appellate, of the departure.

4. The guidelines were adopted by a legislatively created sentencing body, usually a sentencing commission. Presumptive guidelines may utilize determinate or indeterminate sentencing structures.

Voluntary/advisory sentencing guidelines: recommended sentencing policies are not required by law. They serve as a guide to judges and are usually based on past sentencing practices (i.e., are descriptive). The legislature has not mandated their use. Voluntary/advisory guidelines may utilize determinate or indeterminate sentencing structures.

---

terminate provisions for some offenses. So also do several of the states having guidelines.

All states now have some provision for mandatory sentencing. Typically, mandatory minimum incarceration sentences are required for repeat or habitual offenders (in 41 states) or for crimes involving possession of a deadly weapon (in 41 states). Mandatory minimum confinement provisions are found also in many states for drunk driving, drug offenses, possession of weapons, and sex offenses.

Major changes have taken place in some states concerning discretionary parole release and good time provisions. Parole boards have been eliminated or are in the process of being phased out in some states and in the federal system. Maine has fully abolished its parole board, and in other states the paroling authority has responsibility only for inmates sentenced under prior laws or for inmates serving life terms. Some states have kept postrelease supervision without the parole board. All states except Hawaii, Pennsylvania, and Utah have some form of good time provision. Box 9.3, also adapted

Box 9.2

Classification of States by Type of Sentencing Practice, 1994

Determinate Sentencing No Sentencing Guidelines	Indeterminate Sentencing No Sentencing Guidelines		Determinate or Indeterminate Sentencing Sentencing Guidelines	
			Voluntary/ Advisory	Presumptive
Arizona	Alabama*	Nevada	Arkansas	Delaware
California	Alaska*	New Jersey	Louisiana	Florida
Illinois	Colorado*	New York	Maryland	Kansas
Indiana	Connecticut*	New Mexico*	Michigan	Minnesota
Maine	District of Columbia	New Hampshire	Virginia	North Carolina*
	Georgia	North Dakota	Wisconsin*	Oregon
	Hawaii	Ohio		Pennsylvania*
	Idaho*	Oklahoma		Tennessee
	Iowa	Rhode Island		Utah
	Kentucky	South Carolina		Washington
	Massachusetts	South Dakota		
	Mississippi*	Texas*		
	Missouri*	Vermont		
	Montana	West Virginia		
	Nebraska	Wyoming		
5 States	29 States and the District of Columbia		6 states	10 states

*Partially determinate (may or may not have sentencing guidelines).

Source: modified from Austin, J., Jones, C., Kramer, J, and Renninger, P. (1995). *National Assessment of Structured Sentencing: Final Report.* Report to the Bureau of Justice Assistance, United States Department of Justice, January 31, 1995 (draft).

from the report by Austin and his colleagues, shows which states have discretionary release bodies (traditionally, parole boards) and which have some form of postrelease supervision (traditionally, parole supervision). Supervision after release still is usually called parole, as in California, but Delaware, Oregon, and Illinois have replaced parole with some form of postrelease supervision not called parole.

As dramatic as these changes have been, most states still have mainly indeterminate sentencing structures. Box 9.2 shows that, except for states with sentencing guidelines, 29 have mainly indeterminate sentencing structures while 5 have principally determinate sentencing. It is not shown in the box, but of the sentencing guideline states, Arkansas, Louisiana, Minnesota, Tennessee, and Washington may be classed as determinate sentencing states (Box 9.2) and Michigan, North Carolina, Pennsylvania, Utah, and Wisconsin could be said to have mainly indeterminate features in their sentencing structures. Despite the changes described, the indeterminate sentence is still a common feature of sentencing in the United States, even if it is not so dominant as it once was.

Not all states have good time provisions but most do. Not all have postrelease supervision, but that still is the most common form of release. Thus,

Box 9.3

Sentencing Guideline States, Discretionary Release by a Parole Board, and Use of Post-Release Supervision, 1994

State	Sentencing Guideline Commission	Discretionary Release	Post Release Supervision
Alabama	No	Yes	Yes
Alaska	No	Yes	Yes
Arizona	No	No	No
Arkansas	Yes 1994	Yes	Yes
California	No	No	Yes
Colorado	No	Yes	Yes
Connecticut	No	Yes	Yes
Delaware	Yes 1987	No	Yes
Florida	Yes 1983	No	No
Georgia	No	Yes	Yes
Hawaii	No	Yes	Yes
Idaho	No	Yes	Yes
Illinois	No	No	Yes
Indiana	No	No	Yes
Iowa	No	Yes	Yes
Kansas	Yes 1993	No	Yes
Kentucky	No	Yes	Yes
Louisiana	Yes 1992	Yes	Yes
Maine	No	No	No
Maryland	Yes 1983	Yes	Yes
Massachusetts	No	Yes	Yes
Michigan	Yes 1981	Yes	Yes
Minnesota	Yes 1980	No	Yes
Mississippi	No	Yes	Yes
Missouri	No	Yes	Yes
Montana	No	Yes	Yes
Nebraska	No	Yes	Yes
Nevada	No	Yes	Yes
New Hampshire	No	Yes	Yes
New Jersey	No	Yes	Yes
New Mexico	No	Yes	Yes
New York	No	Yes	Yes
North Carolina	Yes 1994	No	No
North Dakota	No	Yes	Yes
Ohio	No	Yes	Yes
Oklahoma	No	Yes	Yes
Oregon	Yes 1989	No	Yes
Pennsylvania	Yes 1982	Yes	Yes
Rhode Island	No	Yes	Yes
South Carolina	No	Yes	Yes
South Dakota	No	Yes	Yes
Tennessee	Yes 1989	Yes	Yes
Texas	No	Yes	Yes
Utah	Yes 1993	Yes	Yes
Vermont	No	Yes	Yes
Virginia	Yes 1991	Yes	Yes
Washington	Yes 1983	No	Yes
West Virginia	No	Yes	Yes
Wisconsin	Yes 1985	Yes	Yes
Wyoming	No	Yes	Yes
District of Columbia	No	Yes	Yes

both parole and good time still are important considerations in examining the sentencing process in most jurisdictions. Usually, the full meaning of a sentence imposed by a judge can be understood only in the context of provisions in the statutes about parole and good time.

What this means is that there now is much diversity in sentencing in the United States. Offenders convicted in different states for one kind of offense, such as armed robbery, may be sentenced under very different laws, procedures, and rules. In one state, with indeterminate sentencing, the armed robber will be sentenced to an uncertain term, perhaps with broad limits such as five years to life imprisonment. It will be up to a parole board to decide on a specific term and on whether or when the person will be released and under what conditions. In another state, robbery with a weapon may call for a mandatory prison term of, say, 10 years—with neither the judge or a parole board having any say in the matter. The statute may or may not require supervision after release. Such a sentence may or may not be reduced by earning good time credits or other credits awarded by prison administrators. In another state, after considering sentencing rules established by a state commission, the judge may sentence the same armed robber to five years in prison without giving any further reason—or to either more or less time if acceptable written justifications are given. In one state, the person might be sent to a county jail for a year, to be followed by a term of probationary supervision; in other states, the judge would not be allowed to impose any sentence other than the state prison. In one state but not in others, the judge could choose probation only. In still another state, the fixed penalty for robbery may be four years, to which must be added one year for the weapon—but only if both the robbery and the weapon are charged by the prosecutor and proven in court. Not only penalties but also who has discretion in decision making is different in different states.

Determinate Sentencing Effects

Some research has been aimed at assessing the effects of determinate sentencing. Good examples are a study of determinate sentences for gun offenses in Michigan and of the marked change, in California, from indeterminacy to determinacy.

The effects of the gun law were studied by Loftin and Heumann.[29] Michigan had added a mandatory two-year flat time sentence to the ordinary sentence for persons convicted of possession of a firearm in the commission of a felony. The effects of the law were evaluated in Detroit, because the prosecutor adopted a policy of charging under the law whenever the facts warranted it. This meant, for the researchers, that the data were "not affected by the common response to mandatory sentences, namely, a shift in discretionary decision making from the court to the prosecutor."[30] They found virtually no effect on either judges' dispositions or violent crime that could be attributed to the new law during the two years after its implementation. It appeared that sentences for the felony that involved gun use were systematically lowered to maintain the "going rate" for these crimes—that is, the usual sentences before the new law was passed.

> *Laws too gentle are seldom obeyed; too severe, seldom executed.*
> —*Benjamin Franklin*

In 1977 when California abolished the indeterminate sentence, it made sweeping changes in the law that, since 1944, had been thought by many to be a model of sentencing and corrections under a utilitarian philosophy. Under the determinate sentence law, the judge must set the prison term choosing only from a limited set of possibilities specified by the legislature, and discretionary release by a parole board was eliminated. There were many arguments for the new law along the lines already discussed. Some advocates sought a greater consistency in sentencing and more definite prison terms. Others wanted a greater proportion of offenders sent to prison and expected a lower crime rate as a result of tougher terms. Critics argued that the greater determinacy and consistency would not be forthcoming— particularly in view of the many "enhancements" to the sentence. Enhancements are increases in sentence terms provided for in the law because of aggravating factors that previously were matters of discretion for prosecutors and judges. It was argued also that the plea bargaining process would have the result that any discretion removed from judges would end up in the hands of the prosecutor.

Two important studies of the new law were done—one by Casper and his colleagues in three counties before and after its implementation and one by Utz in two counties.[31] The research showed that:

- Considerable discretion was exercised by prosecutors in charging enhancements.

- Once enhancements were charged and proven, judges did not differ much in imposing sentences with enhancements.

- The law had little effect on the number of charges filed.

- Plea bargaining was widespread after passage of the law and varied widely among counties.

- There were no changes in the rate of guilty pleas.

- Little impact on prison commitments was found.

- Some reduction in disparity of sentences seemed attributable to the new law.

Critics of legislatively based determinate sentencing have been numerous and vocal. Some of the more common criticisms were summarized aptly by von Hirsch:

> When called upon to write specific punishments for crimes, a legislative body has two major vulnerabilities. First, it has little time available; it cannot devote much effort and thought to developing a coherent rationale, comparing proposed penalties with one another for consistency and proportionality, projecting the new penalties' impact on sentencing practice and on the limited resources of the correctional system; and, once the penalties have gone into effect, reviewing the manner in which they have actually been administered. Second, legislatures are exposed to particularly strong and disruptive political pressures in the sentencing field. There are many voters who fear crime and criminals, and few convicted offenders who do (or even may) vote, making it tempting for legislators to adopt posturing stances of toughness. Under the traditional indeterminate sentence, such posturing did not make much difference: legislators inflated maximum sentences during election years, but those did not determine the times actually served by prisoners. However, the politics of legislative sentencing do matter when a legislature undertakes to prescribe actual durations of confinement.[32]

Deserved Punishment

Along with the trend toward increased determinacy in sentencing, there has been an increasing acceptance of desert as the main justification for punishment and the fundamental purpose of sentencing. Not only has it been urged that the sentence should be specified more precisely at the time of sentencing, but also that it should provide penalties commensurate with the seriousness of the conviction offense. The main arguments have not been made on scientific grounds. Nevertheless, a lack of scientific evidence on effects of rehabilitation programs often has been cited for good measure.

There are two main features of the desert argument. The first is that it is a fundamental requirement of justice that offenders with similar crimes and degree of guilt be punished similarly. Otherwise, sentencing is unfair. The second is the argument that the severity of the penalty should be proportional to the seriousness of the offense. Thus, the basic concepts of desert theory are closely related to the concept of equity or fairness. As a result, they are intertwined with the issue of sentence disparity, about which there has been wide concern among judges, other criminal justice professionals, and the general public.

Ethical and Scientific Views Intertwined

Conflicting views about ethics and morality do not exhaust the sources of conflicting advice given to those who would make sentencing policy. Claims are made also about the best means of achieving utilitarian (usually crime prevention) goals. These give rise to further ethical questions and issues of evidence and science.

As already discussed, the two major orientations are fundamentally opposed—the desert and utilitarian perspectives. Both perspectives lack enough scientific evidence of effectiveness to provide clear, definitive guides to policy formulation. A choice must be made on the basis of the ethical justifications for the contrasting philosophical foundations. The ethical debate, however, cannot be divorced wholly from the issues of effectiveness that surround the choices. It should be better informed by science.

The policymaker must be aware of the ethical choices available; moreover, there is a responsibility to be guided by the evidence when questions of fact are at issue. The central purpose of sentencing and corrections should be the reduction of harm, hence the reduction of crime; or else it should be the imposition of deserved punishment. Both positions can be better informed by science. It may be thought that scientific evidence is required only to inform the utilitarian perspectives by finding evidence of what works to reduce crime. The perspective of deserved punishment, however, also can be evaluated for its effectiveness in achieving the proportionality and equity concerns that are central to the position. This requires a more clear conceptualization and better measurement of the concepts of harm, culpability, fairnesss, and proportionality.

Discretion and Disparity

Besides the trends toward more definite sentencing and greater emphasis on deserved punishment, there has been over the last two decades another change in sentencing structures. This has been a trend toward a markedly reduced discretion by judges (and paroling authorities).

The word "discretion" has more than one meaning. It may mean being discrete in making distinctions—being prudent or careful. Judges are expected to make prudent distinctions. The word also may mean a freedom to make decisions. Debates about discretion focus on judges' discretion in the latter meaning, and when judges are criticized, the word discretion often is modified by words such as "unbridled," "unfettered," or "unrestrained."

Discretion in sentencing—a freedom to exercise judgment—may be justified in permitting an individual handling of each offender. If offenders and offenses are variable, then it should be expected that sentences too will be variable or disparate. The word "disparity" in sentencing, however, has come to be used in a negative sense, suggesting sentencing that is inequitable, hence, unfair and unjust. If some discretion is justified on grounds of individual differences in offenses or offenders, then some variation may be warranted. It is only "unwarranted" disparity that is a problem, perceived as resulting in inequities. Whether variation is unwarranted depends on the theory of justice accepted.

Three types of remedies for unwarranted disparity have been proposed, as already mentioned. As seen from the variety of sentencing structures now in place, each has been adopted in some jurisdictions. Each of these—including guidelines though to a lesser extent—reduces the discretion of the sentencing judge. First, there have been supporters of mandatory sentencing, with specific, unvarying penalties for specific crimes.[33] Second, have been the proposals for "presumptive" sentencing, according to which punishments would be set for the "normal" case within narrow bounds, usually allowing some deviation for aggravating or mitigating factors.[34] Third, systems of sentencing guidelines have been urged, with sentences determined according to an explicit policy intended to structure and control, but not eliminate, the exercise of discretion.[35]

With most sentencing guidelines, specific ranges of penalties are provided for combinations of offense and offender characteristics. Discretion is permitted within the prescribed range and also by provision for further exceptions or departures for specified reasons.

At one logical extreme, a fixed penalty would be imposed for every offender-offense combination, with no discretion. At the other extreme, a completely indeterminate sentencing structure would allow the judge complete freedom in selecting the penalty. Few persons actually urge that the judge should have no discretion, and few now argue that it should be unlimited. It is a complex task to cope with discretionary decision making and find a path to more evenhanded justice. Too much discretion without explicit goals and criteria for decisions produces inequitable decisions. Too little discretion under strict rules, which do not incorporate some flexibility for individual circumstances, leads to decisions that may provide equality in one or a few specific dimensions but result in inequities in others. The challenge is to provide an appropriate balance between the demands for consistency and for consideration of variability among individual cases. Remington and his colleagues summarized the problem:

> For every government decision there is an optimal point on the scale between the rule-of-law at one end and total discretion at the other end. The task . . . is to find that optimum point and to confine discretion to the degree which is feasible.[36]

The term "guidelines" is common in criminal justice jargon and in sentencing legislation, but two general meanings should be distinguished. The first use of the term is common in sentencing statutes, but often the "guidelines" are so vague that they are nearly useless. Such guidelines could not be expected to have much influence on judges' decisions. In the other meaning, guidelines provide rules that are more specific and precise, setting forth expected decisions for similarly situated convicted offenders but permitting (or even encouraging) noncompliance when special circumstances are present. Such guidelines are narrow enough to promote consistency in decisions but allow leeway for departures based on characteristics of the individual offense and offender.

Guidelines considered in this way were first used by Gottfredson, Wilkins, and Hoffman in a study of parole decision making done in collaboration with the U.S. Board of Parole (later the U.S. Parole Commission).[37] They, with others, also first applied the concept to sentencing in a study collaborating with judges.[38] The concept was developed as a mechanism for structuring the discretion of decision makers with several aims: increasing the fairness of decisions, that is, reducing uncertainty and unwanted disparity; bringing greater visibility to the decision-making process; enhancing the rationality of decisions; and providing a vehicle for describing decision policy and changing it if desirable.

In most guidelines, the offender is classified on two dimensions. The first is the seriousness of the offense. The second is a set of characteristics of the offender (such as the extent of the prior criminal record). Scores are assigned to each dimension. This provides a grid, with the intersection of the seriousness of the offense and the offender score providing the location of the guideline sentence. The guidelines thus provide a part of a statement of sentencing policy.

An example of guidelines is given by the first state sentencing guidelines adopted in Minnesota. A Sentencing Guidelines Commission was established by the legislature to create the guidelines, subject to approval by the legislature. Although the original sentencing guidelines developed by Gottfredson and colleagues were based first on a study of actual decision practices in the past, the Minnesota Sentencing Guidelines Commission decided to base their guidelines on theory. The theory chosen for emphasis was that of desert. Because they developed an offender score that gave some weight to the prior record of the offender (which is not in agreement with a strict desert theory), they called their theory one of "modified desert." The result, which is similar in structure to nearly all sentencing and paroling guidelines, is a two-dimensional grid, the cell values of which are presumptive sentences. The original Minnesota Guidelines are shown in Box 9.4.

As described by Knapp:

> The vertical dimension of the grid indicates the level of severity for the offense. The offenses listed in each category are the most frequently occurring offense(s) at each severity level. A measure of the offender's criminal history is provided with the horizontal dimension of the grid. The line running across the grid is the dispositional line—all cases that fall in cells below the dispositional line receive presumptive imprisonment sentences, and cases that fall in cells above the dispositional line receive presumptive nonimprisonment, unless a mandatory minimum sentence applies. The single number at the top of each cell is the presumptive duration of the sentence, in months, that should be stayed or executed.[39]

Box 9.4

Duration of Sentence in Months, According to the Minnesota Sentencing Guidelines Grid

CRIMINAL HISTORY SCORE

SEVERITY LEVELS OF CONVICTION OFFENSE		0	1	2	3	4	5	6 OR MORE
Unauthorized Use of Motor Vehicle Possession of Marijuana	I	12*	12*	12*	15	18	21	24 23-25
Theft Related Crimes ($150-$2500) Sale of Marijuana	II	12*	12*	14	17	20	23	27 25-29
Theft Crimes ($150-$2500)	III	12*	13	16	19	22 21-23	27 25-29	32 30-34
Burglary - Felony Intent Receiving Stolen Goods ($150-$2500)	IV	12*	15	18	21	25 24-26	32 30-34	41 37-45
Simple Robbery	V	18	23	27	30 29-31	38 36-40	46 43-49	54 50-58
Assault, 2nd Degree	VI	21	26	30	34 33-35	44 42-46	54 50-58	65 60-70
Aggravated Robbery	VII	24 23-25	32 30-34	41 38-44	49 45-53	65 60-70	81 75-87	97 90-104
Assault, 1st Degree Criminal Sexual Conduct, 1st Degree	VIII	43 41-45	54 50-58	65 60-70	76 71-81	95 89-101	113 106-120	132 124-140
Murder, 3rd Degree	IX	97 94-100	119 116-122	127 124-130	149 143-155	176 168-184	205 192-215	230 218-242
Murder, 2nd Degree	X	116 111-121	140 133-147	162 153-171	203 192-214	243 231-255	284 270-298	324 309-339

Cells below the heavy line receive a presumptive prison sentence; those cells above the heavy line receive a presumptive non-prison sentence (and the numbers in those cells refer only to the duration of confinement if probation is revoked). The asterisk (*) indicates one year and one day. First degree murder is excluded from guidelines by law and has a mandatory life sentence. (Modified from Minnesota Sentencing Guidelines Commission Report)

If the judge imposes a sentence within the range shown in the appropriate cell below the dark dispositional line, then this is considered consistent with the guidelines. Thus, the judge has some discretion within cells, even without stating any reasons. The judge can, however, set the sentence outside the range shown if written reasons are provided explaining the substantial and compelling reasons for the departure. The judge also can depart from the presumptive imprisonment or nonimprisonment specified by the dispositional line. Again, however, written reasons must be given, meeting the "substantial and compelling" standard. A short list of common aggravating and mitigating circumstances is contained in the guidelines, but judges can add others.[40] If the case is appealed, which may be done either by the defendant or the state, the adequacy of reasons for departure as applied to the individual case is decided by review by the appellate court.

A central feature of the legislation that established the Minnesota Sentencing Guidelines Commission is relevant to the problem of control of prison populations. The law required the Commission to consider prison capacity when developing the guidelines. The Commission decided to write the guidelines in such a way that they would not cause the currently rated capacity of the prisons to be exceeded. Furthermore, the Commission staff developed a computer simulation program enabling them to determine, for any contemplated change in the guidelines, the effect on prison populations. This linkage of sentencing guidelines with the problem of control of prison populations (although it is another departure from the desert perspective) is the central innovative idea of the Minnesota Sentencing Guidelines.

Most states, though not all, that have established sentencing guidelines have followed the example of Minnesota in directing that correctional resources be taken into account in formulating the guidelines. The language varies: Delaware required "due regard for resources and cost;" and Kansas, like Minnesota, required "substantial consideration." The U.S. Sentencing Commission is required to take correctional resources into account and to formulate guidelines that will minimize the likelihood that the federal prison population will exceed capacity. Some state commissions are merely required to assess the impact of guidelines on correctional resources (as in Arkansas and Tennessee). Washington state's commission "need not consider [correctional] capacity in arriving at its recommendations," but is required to provide an alternative plan if capacity will be exceeded, and is cautioned to make frugal use of the state's resources.[41]

The use of sentencing guidelines in Minnesota has resulted not only in a mechanism that can control prison populations, but has resulted in greater fairness. An initial assessment by the Commission reported three important results:

- There was a change in the types of offenders imprisoned—more person offenders and fewer property offenders went to prison.

- Unwarranted disparity in sentencing was reduced, as indicated by increased uniformity of sentences of persons similarly classified for the guidelines grid.

- An improved proportionality occurred, such that persons convicted of more serious offenses received more serious sanctions.[42]

> *Fairness is what justice really is.*
> *—Justice Potter Stewart*

After a few years, sentencing patterns shifted back toward those seen before the guidelines were implemented—toward imprisoning proportionately more property offenders and fewer person offenders. Knapp attributed this shift to changed prosecution practices, increased use by judges of departures for aggravating factors in property crime cases, and some defendants' preferences for a prison rather than a nonprison sentence.[43]

The changes in prosecutor behavior provide a good illustration of the interrelated nature of the criminal justice system. A change in one part of the system affects the other parts. Prosecutors apparently changed their charging practices in order to achieve their objectives of sending more persons to prison. By dropping fewer property crime charges, they could affect the offender's score on the "criminal history" dimension of the grid. This, in turn, affected the judges' dispositions by classifying the defendant into a category calling for a more severe sentence. The discretion previously in the hands of the judge was shifted to a degree to the province of the prosecutor.

Why would some offenders prefer prison to a nonprison sentence? Prison is ordinarily thought of as a more severe sanction. A short prison sentence, however, may be perceived by the convicted offender as less oppressive than the alternative. As explained by Knapp, a nonprison sentence in Minnesota "can include incarceration for up to a year in a local jail or workhouse, restitution, community service, treatment, and long periods of probationary supervision at the discretion of the judge." The case law in Minnesota supported the offenders' requests to have their sentences executed—that is, to be committed to prison.

The sentencing guidelines continued successfully to reduce disparities and to control the prison population. Despite the shifts described, later study still indicated a greater uniformity in sentencing. The use of guidelines with presumptive terms and a well worked out monitoring system seemed to ensure also that prison commitments did not exceed the capacity of the prisons.[44]

Sentencing Commissions

A trend distinct from but related to guidelines sentencing has been the development of sentencing commissions, as shown in Box 9.3. A jurisdiction may have sentencing guidelines without commissions and may have commissions without sentencing guidelines.

The increasing number of sentencing commissions established by legislatures was a result of the general disenchantment with the indeterminate sentence and its perceived ineffectiveness, unfairness, and unbridled discretion. The indeterminate sentence had grown in popularity ever since, in 1870, it was urged by the first congress of the American Prison Association (now the American Correctional Association) in its Declaration of Principles[45]. As acceptance of the utilitarian rehabilitative ideal increased, discretionary powers that resided with judges, though shared with prosecutors and defense lawyers, were distributed also to parole boards and, to a much lesser extent, to prison administrators. The resulting uncertainty of punishments, the growing skepticism about the effectiveness of the treatment ideal, criticisms of unwarranted disparities, disproportionalities in punishments, and lack of control of discretion all led directly to the concept of sentencing commissions.

An influential voice was that of a former law professor and federal judge, Marvin Frankel.[46] Frankel, who subtitled his book on sentencing "Law Without Order," declared that "the almost wholly unchecked and sweeping powers we give to judges in the fashioning of sentences are terrifying and intolerable for a society that professes devotion to the rule of law." He recommended the establishment of a permanent commission on sentencing. The proposal for a sentencing commission, and the arguments presented in support of its need, stimulated lively debate among judges, legislators, academics, and others. His book directly stimulated a Yale Law School work-

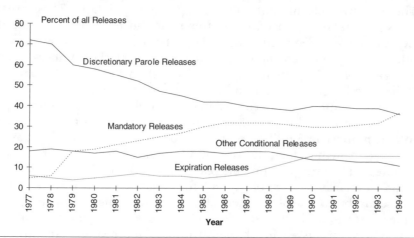

Source: Petersilia, J. (1997). "The Practice and Promise of Community Corrections," draft prepared for the *Oxford Criminology Handbook* edited by M. Tonry.

shop study of sentencing and paroling [47] that led to proposed legislation in the federal system—and ultimately to federal sentencing guidelines. When the movement toward sentencing commissions merged with the concept of sentencing guidelines, an important new sentencing structure emerged.

Changes in Discretionary Sentencing

Trends in sentencing philosophy and structures over the past two decades led to dramatic changes in the way convicted persons are sentenced in many jurisdictions. Along with this has been a change in the modes of release from prison confinement. When indeterminacy was a more common sentencing structure, most prisoners left prison by a discretionary release of a parole board. Now, more than half (53 percent) are released from prison either by the expiration of the sentence or by some form of mandatory release—that is, a release required by law. As seen in Figure 9.5, the percentage of inmates leaving prison by a discretionary act of a parole board has steadily declined since 1977, while mandatory releases, whether by expiration of sentences or by other required release provisions, have steadily increased.

The increase in release from prison at expiration of sentence, which increased gradually until the mid-1980s, then more sharply, means that fewer persons now are released under supervision. Not all mandatory releasees are supervised in the community, and none of those who have served their sentences fully are supervised. This means that as greater determinacy in sentencing has been called for and imposed, the criminal justice system's aims of providing post-release supervision, reintegration services, and prevention of repeated offenses have been less valued. Along with greater emphasis on deserved punishment and more definite sentences, there has been less emphasis on seeking community safety by providing supervision and treatment services in the community.

273

The Sentence to Prison, Jail, or Probation

There are two determinants of jail and prison populations. These are the numbers of person sentenced to confinement and the length of time the convicted offender is required to serve. There has been a substantial increase in both numbers confined and time served. As a result, the numbers in state and federal prisons have increased from fewer than 200,000 in 1970 to now more than a million, and a half million more are held in jails.

The major sentencing alternative in use is probation. If persons on probation or parole are included in the numbers under correctional supervision, the total is more than 5 million persons. Meanwhile, there has been an unprecedented growth in facilities required to house prisoners. In fiscal year 1995, state and federal governments planned $5.1 billion in new prison construction, at an average cost of $58,000 for a medium security cell.[48]

These are but a few of the facts about the consequences of sentencing decisions that will be discussed in later chapters. For convenience, jails and prisons will be discussed in Chapter 10 under the heading "institutional corrections." Alternatives to confinement—mainly probation but including other punishments and treatment programs—will be described in Chapter 11 as "community corrections." All are consequences of sentencing decisions, in which, as we have seen, legislators, police, prosecutors, and defense lawyers have all played a part along with the courts. Before turning to an exploration of corrections, we must consider sentences to punishment by death.

Figure 9.6 Methods of Executions and Numbers of Persons Executed in the United States, 1977–1995

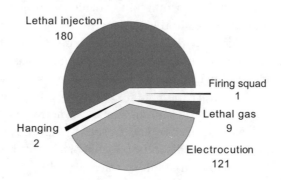

Source: data from Snell, T. L. (1996). *Capital Punishment 1995*. Washington, D.C.: U.S. Department of Justice, Office of Justice Programs, 16.

Capital Punishment

The Death Penalty in the United States

In the United States, some convicted offenders are sentenced to death. Of those, some are killed. The process that may hasten an offender's death involves all the actors in the criminal justice system drama.

More than half the countries of the world have done away with the death penalty, either in the law or in practice.[49] Twenty-eight European countries have done so. Great Britain abolished it, except for treason, in 1971. France (1981) and Canada (1976) have abolished it. The United States and most of its states, along with China, Iraq, Iran, South Africa, and the former Soviet Union have retained the penalty.[50]

Most commonly, those killed for their crimes in the United States are executed by lethal injection, authorized in 32 states. Often, they are executed by electrocution, permitted in 11 states. Sometimes the death is from lethal gas, as may be used in 7 states. Hanging is authorized in 4 states, and 3 states may use the firing squad. A number of states authorize more than one method.[51] The methods used for executions in the United States since 1977 are shown in Figure 9.6.

> *When I came back to Dublin I was court-martialed in my absence and sentenced to death in my absence, so I said they could shoot me in my absence.*
> —Brendan Behan

Methods of execution in history have shown a great deal more imagination than compassion. Colonial Americans preferred hanging—not for themselves, of course, but for others condemned for murder and for many other felonies. Two thousand years earlier, persons judged guilty were hanged, but only after they already were dead from stoning or burning. The hanging was just a further insult to the offender. Perhaps the public spectacle was thought to be an effective warning to others—a general deterrent. Maybe the purpose was to ensure no repetition of the crime by the offender— a clearly effective incapacitation. It may have been thought that death was deserved and that blameworthiness was enough justification.[52] Those three arguments are heard regularly today as debate over the use of capital punishment continues.

Death penalty laws were not always the same throughout the colonies. Perhaps the thief publicly flogged in one colony would have been hanged in another. The laws of the various states and the federal government today reflect a similar diversity.

Thirty-eight states and the federal government authorize the death penalty for some crimes. There is no death penalty in Alaska, the District of Columbia, Hawaii, Iowa, Maine, Massachusetts, Michigan, Minnesota, North Dakota, Rhode Island, Vermont, West Virginia, or Wisconsin. The death penalty is provided for one or more forms of murder in each jurisdiction that has that punishment. Some form of kidnapping with aggravating factors may be punished by death in four jurisdictions. Other offenses punishable by death in some states are train wrecking, treason, perjury causing execution, aircraft hijacking, some forms of rape, and assault by a life prisoner causing serious bodily injury.

A lengthy list of various forms of murder are federal offenses punishable by death. Examples are murder that is related to any of the following: smuggling illegal aliens; destruction of aircraft; a drug-related drive-by shooting; civil rights offenses; transportation of explosives; destruction of government property; intent to prevent (or retaliate for) testimony by a witness or informant; racketeering; train wrecking; bank robbery; carjacking; rape or child molestation; sexual exploitation of children; or a continuing criminal enterprise. Other federal death penalty laws provide for capital punishment for espionage and murder committed by use of a firearm during a crime of violence or a drug-trafficking crime. This does not exhaust the list of crimes, including many that at one time were left to the province of the states, that now are federal offenses for which the death penalty is authorized.[53]

Despite the long list of state and federal capital offenses, nearly all of which now involve some form of murder, relatively few persons convicted of these crimes are sentenced to death and executed. Of the many thousands of persons convicted of murder and other crimes potentially punishable by death from 1977 to 1995, a total of 5,237 were in prison under sentences of death. During that time, 313, or 6 percent, were executed, as seen in Figure 9.6. Between 1930 and 1995, however, 4,172 persons were executed in the United States.

Two departures from the common law have tended to limit the imposition of the death penalty. In the common law, all murders were punishable by death, and all such penalties were mandatory. As the laws developed in the various states, capital punishment increasingly was made discretionary, rather than required; and the concept of different degrees of murder was introduced. The U.S. Supreme Court in the 1970s declared the *mandatory* death penalty for murder unconstitutional because it was cruel and unusual punishment.[54] The introduction of differing degrees of murder, with capital punishment reserved for the most serious of those crimes, and the empowerment of the courts to impose lengthy prison terms instead of death have limited the use of the death penalty.

The numbers of persons in prison under sentences to death, which had steadily climbed in the 1960s (although the number executed declined to none in 1968) dropped abruptly in 1972. In that year, the U.S. Supreme Court ruled in *Furman v. Georgia* that the death penalty *as then administered* in trial courts was unconstitutional.[55] The reason was the lack of standards to govern the exercise of sentencing discretion, in violation of the Eighth and Fourteenth Amendments. This decision, in effect, abolished all death penalties in the United States. The vote of the Court was five to four, and all nine justices wrote opinions. Of the five voting that the death sentences considered were unconstitutional, Justices Brennan and Marshall said that capital punishment violated the Eighth Amendment prohibition against cruel and unusual punishment. Justices Douglas, Stewart, and White concurred with the finding of unconstitutionality on the basis that the penalty was applied arbitrarily.[56]

State legislatures soon reacted. They either passed new mandatory death sentence laws or enacted new statutes providing for a two-stage trial. In the bifurcated, or two-step trial, the first stage is for determination of guilt. The second stage is a postconviction hearing of evidence introduced specifically for the purpose of determining the sentence—that is, life imprisonment or death. Death sentences then typically are based on factors specified in the statutes that aggravate the offender's guilt, while life sentences are based on factors that mitigate it. Another typical requirement is an automatic review by the state supreme court.

The Supreme Court invalidated the first type of statute, deciding that mandatory death sentences were inconsistent with the kind of sentencing required by the *Furman* decision. The Court, however, held that the death penalty is not necessarily cruel and unusual punishment, and upheld state statutes incorporating guidance in the exercise of discretion and the two-stage trial procedure.[57]

Figure 9.7 Numbers of Persons Executed in the United States, 1977–1996

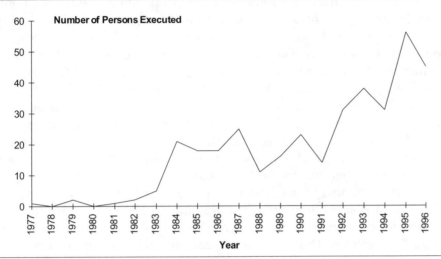

Source: data to 1995 from Snel, T. L. (1996). *Capital Punishment 1995*. Washington, D.C.: Office of Justice Programs, U.S. Department of Justice; data for 1996 from Amnesty International (http://www.oil.ca/amnesty/ailib/intcam/dp/dpfacts.htm#4).

Since the 1976 reinstatement of the death penalty by the Supreme Court, executions have increased (Figure 9.7). Two-thirds of the executions between 1977 and 1995 were carried out in 5 states: Texas (104), Florida (36), Virginia (29), Louisiana (22) and Georgia (20). (Texas and Georgia have jury sentencing. More commonly, the decision is made by the sentencing judge after a recommendation by a jury—as in Florida. In some states, the trial judge sets the sentence.) 56 prisoners were executed by 16 states in 1995: 33 whites; 22 African Americans; 1 Asian American; all men. They had been under a sentence of death for an average of 11 years and 2 months.

Most executions are carried out in a small number of countries. Except for those in the United States, they mainly are carried out by nondemocratic governments. In 1996, 45 persons were executed in the United States. In China, 3,500 executions were reported; in Ukraine, 167; in the Russian Federation, 140; and in Iran, 110. The executions in those countries accounted for more than 90 percent of the 4,272 known executions in 39 countries.[58]

The Death Penalty Debate

Arguments for and against the death penalty, other than religious arguments, are of two kinds. The religious arguments, discussions of which are beyond the scope of this book, include positions advanced both in favor of the penalty and opposed to it. The two types of secular arguments are appeals to justice, on one hand, and to utility on the other.

Among appeals to justice, there are arguments that focus on human rights, on unfairness, including racism and mistakes in the administration of the penalty, and on principles of retributive justice. The appeals based on utilitarian considerations focus on crime prevention—particularly on incapacitation and general deterrence. There are arguments advanced also about the cost of capital punishment in relation to alternative penalties.

Human Rights Arguments

At about the time of the founding of the United States, influential philosophers and legal scholars gave their support to the doctrine of the "rights of man" as the foundation for law and morality. John Locke, Jean-Jacques Rousseau, Cesare Beccaria, William Blackstone, Immanual Kant, and Thomas Jefferson agreed that a foremost right is "the right to life."[59] Nevertheless, except for Beccaria, they did not oppose the death penalty. It typically was argued that because a person has a right to life, murder is a violation of that right; and the execution of the murderer is not wrong because the offender has forfeited the right to life by committing the crime.

More recently, appeals typically have been made to three considerations of violation of other human rights in addition to the right to life. First, procedures for administration of the death penalty are inevitably arbitrary, unreliable, and violate offenders' rights. Second, executions done in error are impossible to reverse because they are violations of the right to life that cannot be corrected. Third, less severe, equally effective alternative punishments (such as long-term imprisonment) are available. It is part of the first argument that the death penalty as used in practice is inherently class- and race-biased, and therefore is unfair and inequitable in practice. This is an appeal to justice, in addition to the argument that human rights are violated.

Unfairness Arguments

Much evidence supports arguments that the administration of capital punishment laws has been biased according to race. It has been shown, for example, that in several states a person is more likely to receive a death sentence if the victim is white rather than nonwhite.[60] Earlier, it was shown that the application of the death penalty for rape, for mainly African American offenders with white victims, could be explained only by taking account of the race of the offender as well as of the victim.[61] In a more recent study in Georgia, race was found to be important in distinguishing offenders receiving a death sentence from those sentenced to life imprisonment. On the average, the probability that an African American defendant would get the death penalty was 12 percentage points higher than that for white offenders after taking account of culpability factors. When the victim was white, defendants also had a 12 percent higher likelihood of receiving a death sentence than the risk of that sentence when the victim was African American.[62] The U.S. General Accounting Office reviewed studies of racism and the death penalty, and reported to the Congress as follows:

> Our synthesis of the 28 studies shows a pattern of evidence indicating racial disparities in the charging, sentencing, and imposition of the death penalty after the Furman decision . . . [and] race of victim influence was found at all stages of the criminal justice system process.[63]

Bedau, who has studied the death penalty extensively, points out that "where the death penalty is involved, our criminal justice system essentially reserves the death penalty for murderers (regardless of their race) who kill white victims."[64] There is good evidence also that the administration of the death penalty is biased according to sex and class.[65] Bedau might have said the penalty is reserved mainly for male murderers who are poor and who kill white victims.

Mistake Arguments

An execution cannot be reversed, and there is substantial evidence that some innocent persons are convicted of crimes, including capital offenses, and have been wrongfully executed.[66]

Retributive Justice Arguments

Many death penalty advocates base their support for the death penalty on principles of retributive justice, arguing that only the sentence to death expresses sufficient moral condemnation of heinous acts such as murder. It typically is argued simply that the death penalty is deserved. All punishment—not just the death penalty—is retributive. Opponents of capital punishment rarely argue that convicted offenders do not deserve to be punished, or that the punishment for the most serious crimes should not be harsh, or that the severity of the punishment should not be proportional to the gravity of the harm done. Rather, it typically is argued that the principle of proportionality of harm and severity of punishment does not *require* the penalty of death. What the principle does require is that crimes other than murder be punished less severely than murder, or other especially heinous crimes, is punished. Most contemporary scholars advocating retributivism do not recommend the death penalty for any crimes.[67]

Incapacitation Arguments

Advocates of the death penalty often cite execution as the perfectly incapacitating punishment, and this is beyond dispute. Crimes that would have been committed by the executed person can never be known if an offender is executed. Therefore, the argument focuses on crimes done by persons who have been convicted of capital offenses, imprisoned, and later released. It is well established by many studies since the 1920s that paroled offenders convicted of murder do well generally on parole and rarely commit another murder or other violent crime.[68] Those arguing for the death penalty typically assert that it is unacceptable not to be *certain* that a convicted murderer cannot repeat the crime. Opponents of the punishment counter that the execution of all convicted murderers, thousands of which would be unnecessary for an incapacitive effect because so few repeat their crimes, would be worse. Moreover, it is argued, life imprisonment is also incapacitative so far as the community is concerned. Proponents of capital punishment counter that life imprisonment, even if the sentence is for life without possibility of parole, does not assure that the person will never be released.

General Deterrence Arguments

Perhaps the most frequent justification for the death penalty is the argument that it is necessary as a general deterrent to crimes such as murder. Perhaps no claim by advocates of the death penalty, however, has weaker empirical support. Careful studies by Thorsten Sellin compared murder rates in states before, during, and after abolition of the penalty, rates before and after executions, rates in adjacent states with and without capital punishment, and rates of the killing of police officers in jurisdictions with and without the death penalty. His results did not support the use of the death penalty for deterrence.[69] The panel of the National Academy of Sciences that studied the question found, after review of much available research, no useful evidence of a deterrent effect of capital punishment and expressed considerable skepticism that the execution of murderers deters murder.[70]

Cost

Proponents of the death penalty often argue that taxpayers should not have to pay the costs of life imprisonment and that these costs are saved by executions. Actually, studies generally show the larger costs to be the other way around: if all the relevant costs due to longer trials and litigation in capital cases are taken into account, having capital punishment on the books costs more. Estimates from such studies of the additional costs of capital punishment range from about double the cost of a life imprisonment sentence (in New York) to six times (in Florida).[71]

Summary

Judges typically have much discretion in sentencing, a decision that is at the center of controversies about basic purposes of the criminal justice system. These decisions are constrained by laws enacted by legislatures and, in an increasing number of states and the federal government, by guidelines written by sentencing commissions. Judges nevertheless have wide areas of discretion in most states.

Sentencing decisions influence law enforcement and corrections as well as other participants in the sentencing process, such as prosecutors and defense lawyers. Police behavior and workloads for both institutional and community corrections are affected directly.

At the heart of controversies about purposes of sentencing are two contrasting ethical views. One is that punishment must be given if and as it is deserved, proportionally to the blameworthiness of the offender. The other is that punishment may be administered only if it will result in some greater good. The conflict is between theories of desert and utility.

A public, authoritative conviction for crime is itself an enduring sanction, but it rarely is seen as enough. Further punishments are justified either as deserved or as necessary for the general welfare, including crime prevention and control.

The utilitarian view emphasizes the concepts of deterrence, treatment, and incapacitation. General deterrence is a warning to others. Treatment usually is aimed at rehabilitation. Incapacitation restrains the offender from further crimes. Each looks forward to some good to come from the sentence.

The desert orientation, which is retributive, stresses that those who choose to do crimes must be punished if they deserve to be. The punishment should be in proportion to the gravity of the harm done and the culpability of the offender. Persons never should be punished in order to achieve some other persons' purposes, as often is required in pursuit of utilitarian goals.

One view is directed toward future crime control. The other looks back to the harm done by the crime. General deterrence, incapacitation, and treatment (including specific deterrence) all have the sentencing goal of crime prevention or reduction. Each is focused on the future. On the other hand, the desert orientation is not aimed at crime control but is directed toward the past criminal behavior of the convicted offender only—in order to express condemnation of it and to penalize the offender.

Judges may differ in their emphasis on purposes, and they may have different goals in sentencing different offenders. Some may be more punitive than others, and they may differ in their emphasis on characteristics of the offense or of the offender. Nevertheless, the seriousness of the crime and the

prior record of the offender powerfully influence decisions whether to incarcerate, the length of terms of confinement, and the imposition of other
penalties.

The main sentencing reform in the early part of this century was the
indeterminate sentence. It was guided by utilitarian principles, especially
treatment. In recent decades, major criticisms of indeterminacy emerged.
These reflected concerns about fairness, proportionality of punishment and
crime seriousness, a lack of clear criteria for sentencing decisions, unwarranted disparities, and effectiveness.

Advocates of determinate sentencing urged specific standards for decisions, emphasized proportionality, and sought reductions of discretionary
powers of judges and parole boards. Flat, presumptive, commensurate, determinate, and mandatory sentencing structures, sentencing guidelines, and
sentencing commissions were all proposed and adopted in various jurisdictions.

Guidelines for decision making, developed first by researchers in collaboration with parole boards, were tried out for sentencing decisions. Minnesota established a sentencing guidelines commission in 1980 and 15 other
states and the federal government have followed suit with similar models.

Most sentencing guidelines include a grid placing measures of offense
seriousness and prior criminal record on two of its sides. This identifies a
relatively narrow range of penalties for usual cases. Typically, some discretion is available within the range. Also, it is common that departures may
be made within limits when written reasons are given, which may be subject
to appeal.

Often, states adopted determinate sentencing structures. An example is
California, which in 1977 abolished the indeterminate sentence (and the
parole board) and required the judge to choose the sentence from limited
options specified by the legislature. Now, 20 states have determinate sentencing, 16 have sentencing guidelines (voluntary or presumptive), 12 states
and the federal system no longer have discretionary parole board release,
and all states have some form of mandatory sentencing to incarceration for
some categories of offenders.

Proposals for reducing unwarranted sentencing disparities include
mandatory sentences, presumptive sentencing, and sentencing guidelines.
Each has been adopted in some jurisdictions. It generally is agreed that some
discretion is necessary in sentencing; how much, and the methods for its
control, are matters of dispute.

Ethical and scientific issues concerning sentencing are intertwined. Decisions should be informed by both a clear, internally consistent, ethical
theory of punishment and evidence about the validity and effectiveness of
the theory.

As a result of changes in sentencing philosophy and structures, most
prison inmates now return to the community not by a discretionary parole
decision but by mandatory provisions of the law. Some of these prisoners
who must be released according to the newer laws are supervised in the
community, as parolees traditionally have been. Many are not.

The two determinants of prison and jail populations are how many persons are sent to jail or prison and for how long. As a result of the changes
in sentencing policies in recent years, more persons have been sentenced to
confinement and they have been sentenced for longer terms. This has caused
confined populations to grow to more than 1.5 million persons. The main

alternatives to confinement have been parole and probation (community corrections). When parolees and probationers are included, the population under correctional supervision is now more than 5 million persons.

Capital punishment is an authorized sanction, mainly for murder, in most states. Although executions are rare in relation to the numbers of convictions for which the offender may be executed, 45 persons were put to death by the states in 1996.

The debate about capital punishment, besides religious arguments, focuses on principles of justice and on utilitarian concerns. Issues of justice include concerns about human rights, deserved punishment, and fairness, including racial and other biases in the administration of the penalty. They include also issues of mistake, causing innocent persons to be executed—an irreversible violation of human rights. Issues of utility include the aims of incapacitation and deterrence. Incapacitation is certain when the convicted offender is killed, but execution of all convicted of capital crimes is argued by many to be both unthinkable and unnecessary. Studies of a general deterrent effect of capital punishment have resulted in skepticism that there is any effect at all. Having the death penalty costs the taxpayer more than life terms. Worldwide trends are toward the abolition of capital punishment.

Notes

1. Ohlin, L. E., and Remington, F. (1958). "Sentencing Structure: Its Effects Upon Systems for the Administration of Criminal Justice," *Law and Contemporary Problems* 23:495.

2. Weiler, P. C. (1974). "The Reform of Punishment," in Law Reform Commission of Canada, *Studies on Sentencing*. Ottawa: Information Canada, 107.

3. Ibid., 107.

4. Kant, I. (1965). *The Metaphysical Elements of Justice: Part I of the Metaphysics of Morals*, translated by J. Ladd. Indianapolis, IN: Bobbs-Merrill, 100.

5. Mill, J. S. *Utilitarianism*. London: J. M. Dent and Sons, Everyman's Library, 1931, originally 1863; Hume, D., *An Enquiry Concerning the Principles of Morals*, in *Hume Selections*. Hendel, C. W., Jr. (ed.). New York: Charles Scribner's Sons, 1927, 194–252; Ryan, A. (1987). *Utilitarianism and Other Essays: J. S. Mill and Jeremy Bentham*. New York: Penguin Books.

6. Plato, *Laws II*, 984, as cited in Newman, G., (1978). *The Punishment Response*. New York: J. B. Lippincott, 201.

7. Smart, J. J. C. (1973). "An Outline of a System of Utilitarian Ethics," in *Utilitarianism: For and Against*. Cambridge: Cambridge University Press.

8. Lamprecht, S. P. (ed.). (1928). *Locke Selections*. New York: Charles Scribner's Sons, 79.

9. Some writers consider desert to be one variety of a class of positions called retributivism. Cottingham, J. G. (1979). "Varieties of Retribution," *Philosophical Quarterly* 29, as cited in Mackie, J. L. (1982). "Morality and the Retributive Emotions," *Criminal Justice Ethics* 3–10 lists nine theories of repayment, desert, penalty, minimalism, satisfaction, fair play, placation, annulment, and denunciation. Concepts of revenge and of retaliation also should be distinguished from all of these.

10. Kant, I. (1959). *Foundations of the Metaphysics of Morals*, translated by Lewis W. Beck, "Library of Liberal Arts," no. 113. New York: Liberal Arts Press, 39.

11. Beccaria, C. (1764/1963). *On Crimes and Punishments*. Reprint. Indianapolis, IN: Bobbs-Merrill.

12. von Hirsch, A. (1976). *Doing Justice: The Choice of Punishments*. New York: Hill and Wang.

13. Blumstein, A. (1984). "Sentencing Reforms: Impacts and Implications," *Judicature* 68:129, 134.

14. Greenwood, P. W., with A. Abrahamse. (1982, August). *Selective Incapacitation*. Santa Monica, CA: Rand Corporation.

15. Kant, I. (1797). *The Metaphysical Elements of Justice*. translated by J. Ladd (1965). Indianapolis: Bobbs-Merril, 100–102.

16. Gottfredson, D. M. (1984). *The Effects of Criminal Sanctions*. Report to the National Institute of Justice, U.S. Department of Justice. Newark, NJ: Rutgers University School of Criminal Justice; Gottfredson, D. M., Gottfredson, S. D., and Conly, C. H. (1984). "Stakes and Risk: Incapacitative Intent in Sentencing Decisions," *Behavioral Sciences and the Law*, 7, 1, 91–106.

17. Hogarth, J. (1971). *Sentencing as a Human Process*. Toronto: University of Toronto Press, 126.

18. Banks, E. (1964). "Reconviction of Young Offenders," *Current Legal Problems* 17:74, 74–76.

19. Gottfredson, D. M. (1984). *The Effects of Criminal Sanctions*. Report to the National Institute of Justice, U.S. Department of Justice. Newark, NJ: Rutgers University School of Criminal Justice.

20. Gaudet, F., Harris, G., and St. John, C. (1933). "Individual Differences in the Sentencing Tendencies of Judges," *Journal of Criminal Law and Criminology*, 23:811.

21. Sutton, L. (1978). *Variations in Federal Criminal Sentences: A Statistical Assessment at the National Level*. Washington, D.C.: National Criminal Justice Information and Statistics Service.

22. Blumstein, A., Cohen, J., Martin, S., and Tonry, M. (eds.). (1983). *Research on Sentencing: The Search for Reform*. Washington, D.C.: National Academy Press, 11.

23. O'Leary, V. O., Gottfredson, M.R., and Gelman A. (1975). "Contemporary Sentencing Proposals," *Criminal Law Bulletin* 11: 5, 560–566; Harris, M. K. (1975). "Disquisition on the Need for a New Model for Criminal Sanctioning Systems," *West Virginia Law Review* 77, 263–326; D'Esposito, J. (1969). "Sentencing Disparity: Causes and Cures," *Journal of Criminal Law, Criminology, and Police Science* 60, 182; Frankel, M. (1972). "Lawlessness in Sentencing," *University of Cincinnati Law Review* 41, 1; Frankel, M. (1973). *Law without Order*. New York: Hill and Wang.

24. Fogel, D. (1975). *We Are the Living Proof: The Justice Model for Corrections*. Cincinnati: W. H. Anderson.

25. von Hirsch, A. (1976); Morris, N. (1974). *The Future of Imprisonment*. Chicago: University of Chicago Press; Dershowitz, A. (1976) *Report of the Twentieth Century Fund Task Force on Criminal Sentencing: Fair and Certain Punishment*. New York: McGraw-Hill.

26. Gottfredson, D. M., Wilkins, L. T., and Hoffman, P. B. (1978). *Guidelines for Parole and Sentencing: A Policy Control Method*. Lexington, MA: Lexington Books; Wilkins, L. T. Kress, J. M., Gottfredson, D. M., Calpin, J. C., and Gelman, A. M. (1976) *Sentencing Guidelines: Structuring Judicial Discretion*. Albany, NY: Criminal Justice Research Center at the State University of New York at Albany.

27. Frankel, M. (1973). *Law without Order*. New York: Hill and Wang.

28. Austin, J., Jones, C., Kramer, J, and Renninger, P. (1995). National Assessment of Structured Sentencing: Final Report Report to the Bureau of Justice Assistance, U.S. Department of Justice, January 31, 1995 (unpublished manuscript).

29. Loftin, C., and Heumann, M. (1983). "Mandatory Sentencing and Firearms Violence: Evaluating One Alternative to Gun Control," *Law and Society Review* 17:2:287.

30. Ibid., 289.

31. Casper, J., Brereton, D., and Neal, (1982). *The Implementation of the California Determinate Sentencing Law*. Washington, D.C.: U.S. Department of Justice; Utz, P. (1983). "Determinate Sentencing in Two California Courts," cited by Cohen, J., and Tonry, M., "Sentencing Reforms and Their Impacts," in Blumstein, A. (ed.). Research on Sentencing: The Search for Reform, ch. 7. Washington, D.C.: National Academy Press, 1983.

32. von Hirsch, A. (1982). "Constructing Guidelines for Sentencing: The Critical Choices for the Minnesota Sentencing Guidelines Commission," *Hamline Law Review* 5:2: 164.

33. Fogel D. (1975). *We Are the Living Proof: The Justice Model for Corrections*. Cincinnati: W. H. Anderson.

34. Dershowitz, A. (1976). *Report of the Twentieth Century Fund Task Force on Criminal Sentencing: Fair and Certain Punishment*. New York: McGraw-Hill.

35. Gottfredson, D. M., Wilkins, L. T., and Hoffman, P. B. (1978); Gottfredson, D. M., Cosgrove, C. A., Wilkins, L. T., Wallerstein, J., and Rauh, C. (1978). *Classification for Parole Decision Policy*. Washington, D.C.: GPO; Wilkins, L. T. Kress, J. M., Gottfredson, D. M. Calpin, J. C., and Gelman, A. M. (1976); Gottfredson, M. R., and Gottfredson, D. M. (1980). *Decisionmaking in Criminal Justice: Toward the Rational Exercise of Discretion*. Cambridge, MA: Ballinger; Gottfredson, M. R., and Gottfredson, D. M. (1984) "Guidelines for Incarceration Decisions: A Partisan Review," *U. Ill. Law Review*, 2.

36. Remington, F., Newman, D., Kimball, E., Melli, M., and Goldstein, H. (1969). *Criminal Justice Administration*. Indianapolis, IN: Bobbs-Merrill, 889.

37. Gottfredson, D. M., Wilkins, L. T., and Hoffman, P. B. (1978).

38. Wilkins, L. T., Kress, J. M., Gottfredson, D. M., Calpin, J. C., and Gelman, A. M. (1976).

39. Knapp, K. A. (1984). "What Sentencing Reform in Minnesota Has and Not Accomplished," *Judicature* 68: 181, 185.

40. von Hirsch, A., Knapp, K. A., and Tonry, M. (1987) *The Sentencing Commission and Its Guidelines*. Boston: Northeastern University Press, 180–181.

41. Austin, J., Jones, C., Kramer, J, and Renninger, P. (1995).

42. Knapp, K. A. (1987) "Implementation of the Minnesota Guidelines: Can the Innovative Spirit Be Preserved?" in von Hirsch, A., Knapp, K. A., and Tonry, M. (1987), 127.

43. Ibid., 128–129.

44. Ibid., 129–130.

45. Lindsey, E. (1926). "Historical Sketch of the Indeterminate Sentence and Parole System," *Journal of Criminal Law, Criminology, and Police Science* 16: 17, 20.

46. Frankel, M. E. (1973). *Criminal Sentencing: Law without Order*. New York: Hill and Wang, 5.

47. O'Donnell, Churgin, M. J., and Curtis, D. E. (1977). *Toward a Just and Effective Sentencing System: Agenda for Legislative Reform*. New York: Praeger.

48. The Sentencing Project (1996). http://www.soros.org/lindsmith/sentence/tecsp.html.

49. Amnesty International (1997, August). http://www.amnesty.org/ailib/intcam/dp/abrelist.htm

50. Bedau, H. A. (1997). "The Case against the Death Penalty," Washington, D.C.: American Civil Liberties Union, http://www.dnai.com/~mwood/deathpen.html.

51. Snell, T. L. (1996). *Capital Punishment 1995*. U.S. Department of Justice, Office of Justice Programs, 5.

52. Portions of this section are based substantially on Bedau, H. A. (1983). "Capital Punishment," in Kadish, S. H. (ed.). *Encyclopedia of Crime and Justice*, Vol. 1. New York: The Free Press, 133–142, and Bedau, H. A. (1997).

53. Snell, T. L. (1996), *Capital Punishment 1995*. U.S. Department of Justice, Office of Justice Programs, 3–12.

54. Bedau, H. A. (1983), citing *Woodson v. North Carolina* (1976). 428 U.S. 280 and *Roberts v. Louisiana* (1977). 431 U.S. 633.

55. *Furman v. Georgia* (1972). 408 U.S. 238.

56. Weinreb, L. L. (1975). *Criminal Law: Cases, Comments, Questions*, 2nd ed. Mineola, NY: The Foundation Press, 616.

57. Bedau, H. A. (1983), 136, citing *Gregg v. Georgia* (1976). 428 U.S. 153; *Jurek v. Texas* (1976). 428 U. S. 262; and *Proffitt v. Florida* (1976). 428 U.S. 242.

58. American Civil Liberties Union (1997). *The Death Penalty*. (http://www.aclu.org/library/pbp8.html) 17.

59. Bedau, H. A. (1983), "Capital Punishment," in Kadish, S. H. (ed.). *Encyclopedia of Crime and Justice*, Vol. 1. New York: The Free Press, 139.

60. Bowers, W. J., and Pierce, G. L. (1980). "Arbitrariness and Discrimination under Post-Furman Capital Statutes," *Crime and Delinquency* 26, 563–635.

61. Wolfgang, M. E., and Reidel, M. (1973). "Race, Judicial Discretion, and the Death Penalty," *Annals of the American Academy of Political and Social Science*, 407, 119–133.

62. Baldus, D. C., Woodworth, G., and Pulaski, C. A., Jr. (1990). *Equal Justice and the Death Penalty: A Legal and Empirical Analysis*. Boston: Northeastern University Press.

63. U.S. General Accounting Office (1990). *Death Penalty and Sentencing*, 5–6, as quoted in Bedau, H. A. (1997), 6.

64. Bedau, H. A., (1997), "The Case against the Death Penalty," Washington, D.C.: American Civil Liberties Union, 7,http://www.dnai.com/~mwood/deathpen.html.

65. Ibid., 7.

66. Ibid., 8.

67. Hirsch, A. von, (1976).

68. Gottfredson, D. M., and Tonry, M. (eds.). (1987). *Prediction and Classification: Criminal Justice Decision Making* Chicago: University of Chicago Press; Gottfredson, S. D., and Gottfredson, D. M. (1986). "The Accuracy of Prediction Models," in *Research in Criminal Careers and "Career Criminals,"* Vol 2, edited by Blumstein, A., Cohen, J., Roth, J. A. and Visher, C. A. Washington, D.C.: National Academy Press.

69. Sellin, T.(1959). *The Death Penalty: A Report for the Model Penal Code Project of the American Law Institute*. Philadelphia: American Law Institute; Sellin, T. (1980). *The Penalty of Death*. Beverly Hills, CA: Sage.

70. Blumstein, A., Cohen, J., and Nagin, D. (eds.). (1978). *Deterrence and Incapacitation: Estimating the Effects of Criminal Sanctions on Crime Rates*. National Research Council, Panel on Research on Deterrent and Incapacitative Effects. Washington, D.C.: National Academy Press.

71. Bedau, H. A. (1997), 13.

Institutional Corrections: Jails and Prisons

Photo courtesy of the California History Section, California State Library.

Chapter Ten

The story of an offender's conviction does not end when the judge announces the sentence. A large portion of the criminal justice system is that part called corrections. In this chapter, we will discuss jails and prisons—institutional corrections. We will examine how our present system has evolved, including major changes in attitudes and beliefs about the proper functions of confinement. In Chapter 11, we will explore community corrections—probation and parole.

Questions to Think About

True or False?

Queen Elizabeth I introduced galley slavery in order to make punishments more severe. T F

Penitentiaries were introduced so that convicts would learn good work habits. T F

Those who started reformatories believed punishment to be more powerful than reward for reforming criminals. T F

The number of persons in prisons and jails has decreased every year for the last ten years. T F

Most prisoners are in jails. T F

Most jail inmates are white non-Hispanics. T F

The number of persons under correctional supervision is steadily declining. T F

Nearly all jail inmates have been convicted of a crime. T F

A majority of prison inmates were unemployed before arrest. T F

Research has proved that rehabilitation does not work. T F

Women in the 1990s most often go to prison for robbery. T F

Prisoners under sentence of death are about evenly distributed among the states. T F

All are false.

Origins of Jails and Prisons

Once upon a time, a man was accused of having stolen a pig from his neighbor, and he was thrown into a deep, dank pit to await his fate. The sides were steep and slippery. There was nothing to do but await his accusers, judgment, and punishment. A woman in a nearby village fared little better. Accused of heresy (holding beliefs that were not approved), she was tied securely to a tree to await, night and day, in sun and darkness, the decision of the authorities and probable burning or hanging. A few hundred years later, in pre-Norman England, the two, both accused of crimes punishable by death, may have been detained in a fortress dungeon or placed on a ledge outside a high castle wall; or they may have been held instead in the dark, damp cellar of one of the town's buildings. The tenth-century gaol, with its dual function of detaining persons awaiting trial and those convicted but still awaiting punishment, was not yet invented. The prototype of modern jails as a local government institution was not created in England until 1166, when King Henry II ordered their construction.[1]

> *The degree of civilization in a society can be judged by entering its prisons.*
> —*Fyodor Dostoevsky (attrib.)*

The Gaol

The sheriff, representing the King, had among other duties the control of the gaol. Together with the justice of the peace, the sheriff was responsible for constructing and maintaining it. Typically, he appointed a keeper, at no salary, who either purchased the position or was given the post as payment for prior services. Costs, including the income of the sheriff, were paid by fees that the prisoner paid from personal funds, donations of friends, or begging. Charges included those for admission to the gaol and for discharge, even after prisoners were acquitted at trial. Until the 18th century, instruments of torture such as the thumbscrew were used to exact the fees. The irons attached to the legs were heavy unless the prisoner paid for lighter ones. Flogging was common.[2]

As with so many of our criminal justice institutions and practices, the jail was continued in the colonies. In Boston in 1632, the construction of a "people pen" was ordered.[3] Until the end of the 18th century, the jails kept their limited function of detaining people who were awaiting trial, convicted persons not yet sentenced, and debtors who could not pay. Jails were not seen as instruments of punishment or correction.[4] The use of the jail as a punishment for crime was not yet invented.

Early Punishments

Most punishment was corporal (inflicting of bodily harm): death by hanging, physical mutilation, branding, and whipping were usual for the more serious offenses. Public ridicule and humiliation (the whipping stocks, the pillory, the public cage, and the ducking stool) were common for lesser offenses. Fines and banishment sometimes were used.

The idea of imprisonment as punishment, rather than merely a place to hold the accused until otherwise punished, did not arise until the early part of the nineteenth century. In early days in England, there was no thought of imposing a term of confinement for the purpose of punishment. Felons were killed, mutilated, or, through the twelfth century, sold as slaves. Banishment was common, as were severe physical punishments: death by hanging, beheading, drowning, burning or stoning; castration, flogging, bodily mutilation, or branding. In the thirteenth century, breaking an offender's body on the wheel was common for treason; in the sixteenth century, the law authorized prisoners to be boiled alive. The penalty for treason, heresy, murder of a husband by a wife, or of a master by a servant was burning (lawful until 1790). As a kindness, women were strangled before they were burned.

Until the middle of the nineteenth century, both men and women were whipped in public. More serious misdemeanants were placed on display in a pillory (not abolished in England until 1817), with head, arms, and feet protruding from the apparatus and perhaps with ears nailed to it, the hapless offender was readily available for ridicule or stoning.[5]

Getting Rid of Convicts

Beginning in the seventeenth century, England adopted two other ways of dealing with felons. One was consignment to a galley, a low, flat ship pulled by banks of oars manned by chained convicts. The other was transportation, meaning deportation and exile as punishment. The main goal was a benefit to the state; and getting rid of convicts without execution provided a rationalization of the punishment as more merciful than killing. As reported by Orland,

> In 1602, Elizabeth I appointed a commission to establish a system of involuntary galley servitude for the condemned as an alternative to death. The Elizabethan scheme permitted prisoners, "except when convicted of wilful Murther, Rape and Burglarye," to be reprieved and sent to the galleys, "wherein as in all things, our desire is that justice may be tempered with clemency and mercy . . . and the offenders to be in such sort corrected and punished that even in their punishment they may yield some profitable service to the Common Welth."[6]

When sailing ships replaced boats pulled by oars in the late sixteenth century, convicts were no longer needed for galleys. With gaol populations rising and cheap labor needed in the American colonies, the Crown began to conditionally pardon felons who were transported to America—an estimated 50,000 of them. The shipment of convicts to the colonies began in 1618 and was encouraged by legislation that granted land to colonists who imported convicts. The convict then assumed the status of an indentured servant—a person required to work as punishment. At the end of a term of servitude determined by the colonial legislatures, the servant was freed, customarily given tools, and occasionally, land.[7]

Transportation to America terminated abruptly with the American Revolution. England turned to Australia (recently discovered by Captain Cook). Now felons were transported in chains to Australia, but the program was quite different: penal colonies were established, separate from the free settlers. In eight years after the start of the program in 1787, an estimated 135,000 convicts had been shipped to Australia under inhuman conditions of chains, close confinement, starvation, and sickness.[8]

Birth of the Penitentiary

As the American colonists began to question and to reject some practices of the government in England, two widely distributed documents were influential: Blackstone's *Commentaries on the Laws of England* and Beccaria's *On Crimes and Punishments*. Blackstone pronounced that "crimes are more effectively prevented by the *certainty* than the *severity* of the punishment," because "excessive severity of the law" hinders law enforcement.[9] This idea echoed Beccaria, who believed that the severity of punishment itself increases crime, because criminals are driven to commit more crimes in order to avoid the punishment for a first one. Quaker reformers in Pennsylvania, appalled by the current brutal treatment of offenders, acted on such advice, and by May of 1787 Benjamin Franklin and William Rush organized the Philadelphia Society for Alleviating the Miseries of Public Prisoners. Moderate punishments, enforced strictly, were to be substituted for corporal punishments, particularly execution.

This organization and its work led to the first penitentiary for housing convicted felons. Urged by Beccaria's concepts of penal reform and influenced by Quaker doctrines of the efficacy of prayer and solitude for the reformation of the soul, solitary confinement and hard labor were the hallmarks of the reform. Penitence—being sorry for wrongdoing and wishing to make amends—was regarded as the means to the goal of reformation, and the instrument for its attainment was named the penitentiary. The premise was not questioned, and evidence was not sought; it was accepted as a matter of faith.

The penitentiary movement spread quickly to New York, Connecticut, Massachusetts, Maryland, and New Jersey. During the first half of the nineteenth century, there was much debate—not about whether the goals and methods were correct, but only over the degree of solitude that ought to be required. Total isolation around the clock was insisted upon in the "Pennsylvania system," while working in groups during the day with no talking allowed but isolated at night were advocated according to the "Auburn system." Enforcement of the intended total isolation of the prisoner from the outside world and even fellow inmates was rigorous. Compliance was exacted by some of the very methods the Quaker reformers had found repulsive: placement in a dark cell with less food; whipping; use of chains and the ball and chain; and starvation.[10]

From the Penitentiary to Contemporary Corrections

Imagine Benjamin Franklin's amazement today if he could learn that the philosophy underlying the penitentiary system begun at Philadelphia's Walnut Street jail was later replaced by the concept of the reformatory, with emphasis on rewards for good behavior and on reformation of the convict. Picture his astonishment in realizing the prisons next were named correctional institutions to reflect their use for diagnosis and treatment for rehabilitation. Envision his wonder at the later shift from changing the offender, to restraint and isolation from the community— not for repentance but for the prevention of crimes and the application of deserved punishment. This has been the course of events over a mere 200 years, as illustrated by Figure 10.1.

Interior of a cell block in Folsom Prison (California), constructed in 1878-1882. Across the United States, many prisons built more than a century ago are still in use. What do you expect are the main problems associated with the use of old prisons? —*Photo courtesy of the California History Section, California State Library.*

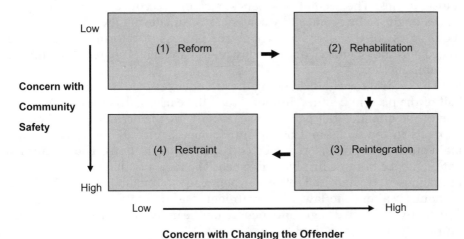

Note: Follow the arrows that show changing orientations over time.

1. The reform orientation of the early penitentiaries was minimally concerned with community safety and only tangentially aimed at changing the offender through contemplation and prayer.

2. Concern for changing the offender increased with the establishment of late nineteenth-century reformatories and the early twentieth-century focus on rehabilitation.

3. As emphasis on changing the offender increased with realization of needs for community involvement for reintegration of the offender, in the middle part of the present century, this reflected an increased focus on community protection.

4. With the collapse of the importance placed on rehabilitation and reintegration, emphasis was given increasingly in recent decades to public safety, thought to be achieved by punishment, deterrence, and incapacitation. The resulting politically popular "get tough" policies have resulted in dramatic increases in numbers of persons in jails and prisons, and a decline of emphasis on changing the offender.

The figure contrasts two differing viewpoints. The first is community safety and protection; the second is the changing of the offender's behavior. The pendulum has swung from isolation and reformation to rehabilitation and community involvement and back to isolation and restraint. It may yet swing back to an emphasis on public safety that includes, as required for increased protection, the reintegration of the offender back into society in a condition presenting less danger to the community.

The reformatory was the result of a new movement that arose in the wake of the Civil War. The establishment of a reformatory at Elmira in New York was based on the central concept of reform of the offender. It was seen also as a reform of the *system*: programs for the reform of criminals would replace those regarded as providing nothing but vindictive suffering. The new reformatory models were based substantially on the ideas of Crofton and Maconochie, discussed in the next chapter of this book, on concepts of the power of rewards for good behavior, and on education and the development of good work habits. This was an increased emphasis on changing the behavior of the offender. Two enduring results of this era are "good time" credits and the indeterminate sentence and parole. The first is a survivor of the system of "marks" earned for industry and good behavior initiated in the reformatories. The second is a persistence of the concept that fixed sentences ought to be replaced by sentences of indeterminate length, so that the progress of the offender through the process of reformation could be traced and the offender conditionally released when prepared to assume a law-abiding life.

The central focus on changing the offender reached its peak in the first half of the present century. Influenced by the earlier advocates of reformation of the offender, but persuaded especially by the driving force of developments in the social and behavioral sciences, rehabilitation became the main purpose of prisons, renamed correctional institutions. The indeterminate sentence became firmly established. The idea was that prisoners could be diagnosed, treated, and released when ready to remain in the community without breaking the law. The treatment goal of sentencing—future-oriented, preventive in design, and focused on the individual offender—was the ultimate goal of corrections.

Most prisoners are released into the community at some time, and there was an increasing recognition that community protection, and the more complete rehabilitation of the offender, required programs of supervision in the community and increased efforts to integrate the released offender back into that community by strengthening such programs. The reintegration of the offender back into the community came to be stressed as in the best interest of that community.

The rehabilitative balloon that had risen so quickly in the first half of the century burst in the second half. There were two main reasons. First, it was seen as unfair. Second, it was regarded as clearly ineffective. The fundamental challenge was from the desert perspective. As we have seen in our discussion of sentencing, issues concerning equity, proportionality in sentencing, and the fundamental purposes of punishment led to a pronounced shift toward determinate sentencing and emphasis on deserved punishment. Along with this shift, an increased public and political concern with crime and public safety

Folsom State Prison in the early 1900s. The stripes are gone, but the walls remain. How does this prison reflect the changes in policies shown in Figure 10.1? —*Photo courtesy of the California History Section, California State Library.*

leading to "get tough" rhetoric has led to an increased focus on incapacitation and resulting dramatic increases in jail and prison populations. The predominant orientation now popular is one of restraint of the offender, with a substantial collapse of the rehabilitative ideal.

The tide definitely has turned. Candidates for public office need not now explain why they support more punishment, longer terms in prison, and mandatory minimum sentences. In one recent election, candidates for governor argued over who was *more* in favor of capital punishment.

The illustration of Figure 10.1 oversimplifies these changes. In any correctional institution today, an overlapping of these concepts may be perceived; and among both institutions and individuals, the orientations may differ. When differences in emphasis are present, however, it is reasonable to believe that these are reflected in the decision making of the correctional personnel. For example, some correctional staff may place a strong emphasis on seeking to strengthen the inmate's work habits and on following the rules—concepts akin to those of the reformatory model. Others may stress counseling and personal development of the offender, as in the rehabilitative orientation. Still others may value the maintenance of family ties and preparation for later integration back into the community. Others may perceive the job as mainly maintaining control of the institution, providing the societal protection afforded by isolation of the inmate from the community. Chances are that each of these perspectives could be found today in any jail or prison.

The Rehabilitative Goal

In recent years, it has become popular among academics, politicians, and some correctional personnel to express disenchantment with the rehabilitative ideal that undergirded correctional reforms in the earlier part of this century. It has become unpopular to advocate rehabilitation as a sentencing aim. This abandonment of hope that prisoners could be helped to become more law-abiding was based in large on a series of widely cited reviews of evaluations of correctional treatments in the late 1960s and early 1970s.[11] Thus, the marked change in attitudes has been attributed to science, and many people now seem to believe that it has been demonstrated that nothing works. The evidence from evaluation research does not, however, support a policy of abandoning it. We will return to this topic in the last chapter of this book.

State and Federal Prisons Today

From its early beginnings in America, the system of jails and prisons has grown to a huge enterprise. Prisons are mostly operated by the states, but there is also a large federal system. Jails continue to be operated mainly by local jurisdictions. By 1995, the states operated 1,375 confinement facilities (such as prisons, prison hospitals, prison farms, boot camps, reception centers, and alcohol or drug treatment units) and community-based facilities (such as halfway houses or work release centers). The federal system had 125 such facilities. Eighty percent of all these institutions confined the prisoners around the clock; the other 20 percent were facilities in the community in which half or more of the residents were allowed to leave the premises unaccompanied. All but 3 percent of all inmates, however, were housed in confinement facilities.

These correctional institutions had nearly 350,000 employees. Two-thirds of the correctional staff were in custody or security positions. Others were engaged in professional, technical, or educational positions (56,000), clerical positions (27,000), maintenance or food service (24,000), or administration (9,500). About a third of all correctional staff were women. 71 percent were classified by the government as white, 20 percent as black, 6 percent as Hispanics. The proportions of employees who were members of minority groups had increased substantially in the prior 5 years.

As prisons became more and more crowded, the courts abandoned their previous "hands off" policy of noninterference with prison administration. Federal judges began to find prisons often operated under conditions not permitted by the U.S. Constitution. More than a fourth of state facilities in 1995 were operating under court orders or consent decrees requiring improvement in specific conditions, population limits, or both. Crowding was the most frequently cited specific condition that courts sought to remedy. Other conditions involved medical facilities, library services, and staffing.

A movement toward "privatization" of correctional facilities had grown by 1995 to the extent that 110 facilities were operating under contract with states or the federal government. There were 16,426 inmates in private institutions. Some of these were secure institutions, but nearly three out of four of the private institutions operated community-based programs.[12] This movement is controversial, particularly concerning the operation of confinement facilities. Objections are made that private individuals should not profit from the punishment system and that the seeking of such profits is inconsistent with the provision of needed improvements in services. Proponents counter that private industry can operate the needed facilities and programs in a more cost-effective manner than can governments and therefore can provide more efficient and effective programs.

Despite state and local control, jails and prisons now are often operating under court orders to meet constitutional standards, due mostly to crowded conditions. Confronted with rapid growth in the last two decades, correctional

Old prisons gradually are being replaced by modern facilities such as this unit of the New Jersey Department of Corrections. How would prison programs be affected by the design of the prison? Would you design the prison first and then the program, or the other way around? —*Photo courtesy of the New Jersey Department of Corrections.*

institutions now emphasize restraint of the offender as a central purpose; but they nevertheless continue to seek goals of rehabilitation and community reintegration. Although the main business is holding inmates serving sentences as punishment, the correctional apparatus operates a wide variety of programs: large prison industries of many kinds; school and vocational programs; hospitals; psychiatric facilities; specialized units for young inmates and elderly ones; counseling programs; therapeutic communities; boot camps; halfway houses; reception-diagnostic centers; institutions for men, for women, and for men and women; narcotics addiction treatment units; alcohol treatment programs; work release programs; and restitution and community service programs.

Jail and Prison Populations

An alarming growth in jail and prison populations now has taken place along with the changes in sentencing and correctional policies already described. Two measures of jail and prison populations provide our best source for the national data. These are the National Prisoner Statistics Program and the Annual Survey of Jails, both operated by the Bureau of Justice Statistics of the U.S. Department of Justice (Box 10.1).[13]

Box 10.1

Measures of Prisoner Populations

The National Prisoner Statistics Program of the U.S. Bureau of Justice Statistics, collaborating with the Bureau of the Census, has conducted an annual count of prisoners since 1926. Year-end and mid-year counts are obtained from departments of corrections in each state, the District of Columbia, and the Federal Bureau of Prisons. Prisoners in custody are distinguished from those under the jurisdiction of the corrections agency. A person in custody is held in one of the agency's facilities. Jurisdiction means that the government entity has legal authority over the prisoner. Prisoners in a state's jurisdiction, for example, may be held in a local jail, a prison of another state, or some other correctional facility.

The Annual Survey of Jails is another program of the Bureau of Justice Statistics. Each year between the full census done every four years, a survey of jails is done to estimate characteristics of inmates of jails. The most recent survey, in 1995, was the eleventh such survey since the program started in 1982. National estimates are based on samples designed to represent the total.

The number of persons in jails and prisons has increased so substantially in the last two decades that by mid-1996 there were 1,630,940 inmates in custody of prisons and jails. At year's end, well over a million—1,182,169—persons were prisoners in the jurisdictions of federal or state prisons and more than a half million persons were held in local jails.[14]

Prison population *numbers* have doubled in the last 10 years. The *rate* of incarceration in prisons, which has increased, was 427 sentenced inmates per 100,000 U.S. residents in 1996. One out of every 118 men and one in every 1,818 women were prisoners of the state or federal governments.[15] The rates of incarceration, as well as the numbers confined, differed among the states. Table 10.1 shows the top 10 and lowest 10 for both numbers of prisoners and rates of incarceration. The District of Columbia, an urban area which has prisons and jails as one integrated system, is not included in the table. The rate of incarceration of prisoners with sentences of more than a year was 1,609 per 100,000 residents in the District.[16]

Table 10.1 Numbers of Prisoners and Incarceration Rates of Selected Jurisdictions, 1996

Ten Highest			
Jurisdictions	Number of prisoners	Jurisdictions	Incarceration rate
California	147,712	Texas	686
Texas	132,383	Louisiana	615
Federal	105,544	Oklahoma	591
New York	69,707	South Carolina	532
Florida	63,763	Nevada	502
Ohio	46,174	Mississippi	498
Michigan	42,349	Alabama	492
Illinois	38,852	Arizona	481
Georgia	35,139	Georgia	462
Pennsylvania	34,537	California	451
Ten Lowest			
North Dakota	722	North Dakota	101
Vermont	1,125	Minnesota	110
Maine	1,476	Maine	112
Wyoming	1,483	Vermont	137
South Dakota	2,064	West Virginia	150
New Hampshire	2,071	New Hampshire	177
Montana	2,073	Nebraska	194
West Virginia	2,754	Utah	194
Rhode Island	3,271	Rhode Island	205
Nebraska	3,275	Iowa	222

Source: adapted from Mumola, C. J. and Beck, A. J. (1997). *Prisoners in 1996*. Washington, D.C.: U.S. Department of Justice, Office of Justice Programs, 5.
Note: numbers of prisoners are persons with a sentence of more than one year. Incarceration rates are numbers of sentenced prisoners per 100,000 residents. The Federal Bureau of Prisons and the District of Columbia are excluded from the calculation of rates.

The steady increase in *numbers* is reflected in Figure 10.2, which shows the rise in jail, parole, probation, and prison populations since 1980, when these populations already had increased substantially over prior records. The figure reflects the fact that in 1995 an estimated 5.1 million adults were under some form of correctional supervision. Not only prison populations have increased. The rate at which adults are supervised in the criminal justice system—in prison but also in jails, on probation, or on parole—more than doubled in 10 years. About 2.7 percent of the adult resident population were under correctional supervision in 1995—confined or supervised in the community—an increase from 1.1 percent in 1980. If the incarceration rate is calculated to include persons in both prisons and jails in relation to the resident population, it was 615 persons per 100,000 residents in 1996.[17] More than a million persons were in prison. More than a half million were in jail (Box 10.2).[18]

Figure 10.2 Estimated Correctional Populations, 1980–1995

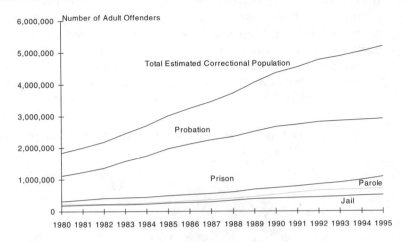

Sources: Bureau of Justice Statistics, *Prisoners in 1994* August, 1995; *Correctional Populations in the United States* April, 1995; *Correctional Populations in the United States 1994*, July, 1996; *Prison and Jail Inmates, 1995* August, 1996. Washington D.C.: U.S. Department of Justice.
Note: data for prison populations are year-end estimates; data for jail populations are for midyear. Data are for inmates in custody, not total jurisdiction. Probation and parole data for 1995 are extrapolated. Confined military populations and U.S. territories are excluded; in 1994, all services combined held 2,782 prisoners (*Correctional Populations in the United States, 1994* 3) and U.S. territories held 12,807 persons in prison (*Prison and Jail Inmates, 1995*).

Box 10.2

Prisons and Jails Held About 1.6 Million Inmates in 1995

At the end of the year—

- 1,127,132 prisoners were under the jurisdiction of the 50 states and the District of Columbia (together holding 1,026,882) and the federal government (100,250).

- The increase was about 7 percent over the year before.

- State prison systems were between 14 and 25 percent over their reported capacities; the Federal system was 26 percent over reported capacity.

- Nearly 30 percent of all prisoners were incarcerated in California (135,646), Texas (127,766) and New York (68,484).

On June 30—

- 541,913 persons were held in or supervised by local jails.

- The increase was about 4 percent from the year before.

- About 6 percent of these persons were in community supervision programs such as electronic monitoring, house detention, and day reporting.

- About 8,000 juveniles (under 18) were held in adult jails, up 17 percent from the previous year, with more than three out of four tried or awaiting trial as adults.

- About 6 percent were state prisoners held in jail because of prison crowding. In Louisiana, this was more than a third of state prisoners. It was 18 percent in Mississippi, 16 percent in New Jersey, 13 percent in Virginia.

- 6 percent of all state and federal prisoners, and 8 percent of jail inmates, were women.

- A majority of jail inmates were black or Hispanic. Forty percent were white non-Hispanics, 44 percent were black, 15 percent were Hispanics.

About two-thirds of these prisoners were in the custody of the states, the federal government, or the District of Columbia—the remainder were in local jails (Figure 10.3). Most prisons and jails were crowded, with populations often dangerously and miserably exceeding their rated capacities. In many prisons, tents and trailers were used, and classrooms, recreational areas, hallways, and chapels had been converted into bed space for housing in cramped quarters. About 6 percent of persons sentenced to prison were still in jail because the prison was too crowded to be able to accept them.

Figure 10.3 Prisoners in Custody in Prisons and Jails in the United States, December 1995

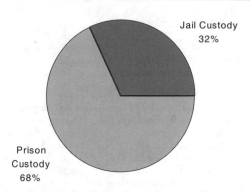

Source: Gilliard, D. K. and Beck, A. J. (1996) *Prison and Jail Inmates, 1995* Washington, D.C.: Bureau of Justice Statistics, 1–2.

Note: Prison custody means the custody of the 50 states, the District of Columbia, and the federal government; jail custody means the custody of local jails.

Who Is in Jail and Prison?

Jails have continued to serve their original function of detention before trial, but now they also serve a punishment function for sentenced offenders. Among prisoners held in jails, however, more than half typically have not been convicted but are awaiting trial (Figure 10.4).

Some jail prisoners are held on the basis of violations of probation or parole conditions, others are charged with bail bond violations, some are held in protective custody, including some witnesses, and some are held awaiting transfer to other jurisdictions (Box 10.3).

The populations of jails and prisons include members of minority groups far out of proportion to their representation in the general population. In 1994, 60 percent of the jail populations were minority group members—44 percent were black non-Hispanics, and 15 percent were Hispanics (Figure 10.5). In prisons, 51 percent were blacks.

The prison incarceration rates for all races, both men and women, have increased in the last decade. The rates have grown more rapidly for black and Hispanic males, for women, and for drug offenders. In the 10 years before 1995, the numbers of drug offenders in state prisons increased from 38,900 in 1985 to 224,900 in 1995. As described by the Department of Justice:

> Between 1985 and 1995 the number of prisoners with sentences of more than one year rose by over 600,000. The number of white males increased by 103 percent, the number of black males by 143 percent, the number of white females by 194 percent, and the number of black females by 204 percent. . . .

Figure 10.4 Conviction Status of Adult Jail Inmates, Midyear 1995

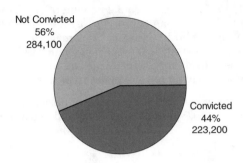

Source: Gilliard, D. K. and Beck, A. J. (1996). *Prison and Jail Inmates, 1995* Washington, D.C.: Bureau of Justice Statistics, 11.
Note: the number of convicted inmates may be undercounted because some jail records do not show this status. Data were available for 96 percent; totals were estimated and rounded to the nearest 100.

Box 10.3

Jails

- **Receive** persons pending arraignment and hold them awaiting trial, conviction, or sentencing.

- **Receive** persons with alleged probation, parole, and bail bond violations.

- **Detain** juveniles pending transfer to juvenile authorities.

- **Hold** mentally ill persons pending placement in other facilities.

- **Hold** persons for the military, for protective custody, for contempt of court, and for the courts as witnesses.

- **Hold** inmates for federal, state, and other authorities because of crowding of their facilities.

- **Operate** community programs as alternatives to incarceration.

Figure 10.5 Jail Populations by Race/Hispanic Composition, 1994

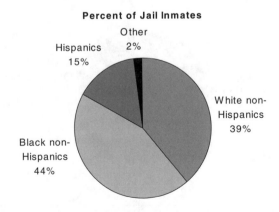

Source: Perkins, C. A., Stephan, J. J., and Beck, A. J. (1995). *Jails and Jail Inmates 1993–94* Washington, D.C.: Bureau of Justice Statistics, 1.

At year end 1995 (the latest available data), there were more black males in State or Federal prisons (510,900) than white males (493,700).

On December 31, 1995, an estimated 3.2 percent of all black males were in prison, compared with less than half of 1 percent of all white males. While the incarceration rates of both white and black males have risen since 1985, the rate for black males has grown more rapidly. In 1985 black males were about 6.3 times more likely than white males to be in prison; by 1995 they were 7.0 times more likely than white males to be in prison.

Hispanics . . . represent the fastest growing minority group being imprisoned, increasing from 10.9 percent of all State and Federal inmates in 1985 to 15.5 percent in 1995. . . . During this period the number of Hispanics in prison rose by 219 percent.[19]

Some states are not able to report data on Hispanic origin, provide only estimates, or report incomplete counts. Therefore, the numbers of Hispanic inmates may be larger.

Prisoners in Community Programs

The distinction between corrections in the community and corrections in institutions has become increasingly blurred in recent years. The use of community programs run by jails as alternatives to confinement has expanded. Thus, in 1995, about 6 percent of jail inmates were under jail supervision but supervised outside the confines of the jail (Figure 10.6). Similarly, prison programs such as work or education release and halfway houses also make distinctions between institutional and community corrections somewhat less distinct.

These alternative programs will be discussed further in the next chapter. They included jail prisoners in work programs, weekend confinement, and community service (Figure 10.7). Prisoners in jails may be at home in house arrest, often with supervision using electronic monitoring. Some may be at work but required to report daily to a center organized for that purpose.

Figure 10.6 Persons Under Jail Supervision by Confinement Status, Midyear 1995

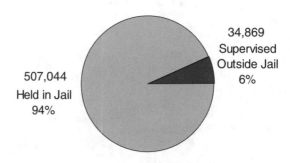

34,869
Supervised
Outside Jail
6%

507,044
Held in Jail
94%

Source: Gilliard, D. K. and Beck, A. J. (1996). *Prison and Jail Inmates, 1995* Washington, D.C.: Bureau of Justice Statistics, 9.
Note: excludes persons under supervision by probation or parole agencies.

Characteristics of Prison Inmates

Prison inmates tend to be young male minority group members who have never been married or are separated or divorced, who often have little education and few skills, and many of whom have poor work histories. Many

Figure 10.7 Persons Under Jail Supervision but Supervised Outside the Jail Facility, by Type of Program, 1995

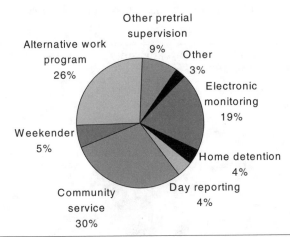

Source: Gilliard, D. K. and Beck, A. J. (1996). *Prison and Jail Inmates, 1995*. Washington, D.C.: Bureau of Justice Statistics, 9.
Note: persons supervised by a probation or parole agency are excluded. Home detention includes only those without electronic monitoring. Work programs include work release, work crews, and other work programs administered by jails.

have been in prison before, and some have long histories of repeated contacts with both juvenile and adult courts.

Young men are most likely to commit crimes, and this is reflected in the composition of prison populations (Figure 10.8). Nearly half are in their late

Figure 10.8 Ages of State Prison Inmates as a Percent of Prison Populations, 1991

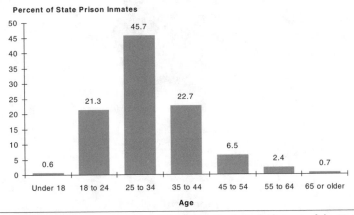

Source: as cited in *The American Almanac, 1995–1996: Statistical Abstract of the United States*. Austin, TX: The Reference Press, 217 1995; data were based on the Bureau of Justice Statistics' Survey of State Prison Inmates, 1991.

twenties and early thirties. Although only about 3 inmates in 100 are 55 or older, this proportion is changing as longer sentences are imposed and longer time is served before release. An increasing strain on correctional management is the obligation to care for the elderly. Increasingly, "geriatric prisons" must be planned. More than half of all state prison inmates have never married. About a fourth are separated or divorced (Figure 10.9). Many prison inmates have poor work records, although two-thirds say they were employed at the time of arrest for the charge for which they were convicted (Figure 10.10). About half of the unemployed reported that they were looking for work. About two out of five have less than 12 years of school (Figure 10.11).

Figure 10.9 Marital Status of State Prison Inmates as a Percent of Prison Populations, 1991

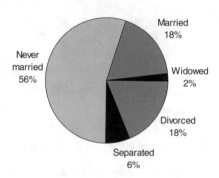

Source: as cited in *The American Almanac, 1995–1996: Statistical Abstract of the United States.* Austin, TX: The Reference Press, 217, 1995; data were based on the Bureau of Justice Statistics' Survey of State Prison Inmates, 1991.

Figure 10.10 Pre-Arrest Employment Status of State Prison Inmates, 1991

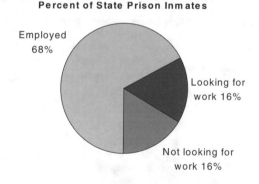

Source: as cited in *The American Almanac, 1995–1996: Statistical Abstract of the United States.* Austin, TX: The Reference Press, 217, 1995; data were based on the Bureau of Justice Statistics' Survey of State Prison Inmates, 1991.

There has been an increase in recent years in the proportion of minority group members under correctional supervision, whether in confinement or under supervision in the community. At present, a third of all black men in their twenties are under some kind of supervision by correctional authorities (Figure 10.12). Increases in proportions, particularly of black men, have

Figure 10.11 Educational History of State Prison Inmates, 1991

Percent of State Prison Inmates

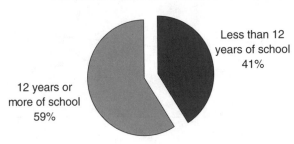

12 years or
more of school
59%

Less than 12
years of school
41%

Source: as cited in *The American Almanac, 1995–1996: Statistical Abstract of the United States.*
Austin, TX: The Reference Press, 217, 1995; data were based on the Bureau of Justice Statistics'
Survey of State Prison Inmates, 1991.

Figure 10.12 Young Black Men Under Correctional Supervision, 1994

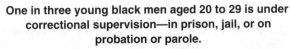

**One in three young black men aged 20 to 29 is under
correctional supervision—in prison, jail, or on
probation or parole.**

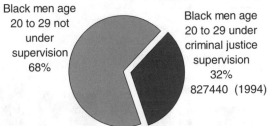

Black men age
20 to 29 not
under
supervision
68%

Black men age
20 to 29 under
criminal justice
supervision
32%
827440 (1994)

Source: *Overcrowded Times*, 6, 6, December 1995, 1.

occurred in both jails and prisons (Figures 10.13 and 10.14). In the past few years, prisons have held more black males than white males, and nearly one in five prisoners is of Hispanic origin (Figure 10.15). The increased minority representation in institutions is due in large part to increased penalties for drug offenses. The ethnic composition of an institution results from who is sent there and how long they stay. An increased number of drug offenders, more often than not minorities, are being sent to institutions (Figure 10.16) and they are staying longer. Although the proportions of new admissions to prison for violent crimes has declined, persons convicted of such crimes serve longer times. As a result, prisons now have an increasing number of offenders who are serving time for violence or drugs.

Men in Prison

Men are in state prisons most commonly for drug offenses, robbery, burglary, and murder, in that order. The percentage in prison for drug of-

Figure 10.13 Trends in Numbers of Jail Inmates by Selected Population Characteristics, 1988–1994

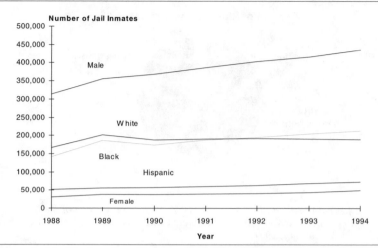

Source: as cited in *The American Almanac, 1995–1996: Statistical Abstract of the United States*. Austin, TX: The Reference Press, 217 1995; Bureau of Justice Statistics (1995 and 1996) *Correctional Populations in the United States*, 1993 and 1994; African American and white data for 1993 estimated by the author.

Figure 10.14 Numbers of White and Black Male Prisoners Under State and Federal Jurisdiction, 1990–1993.

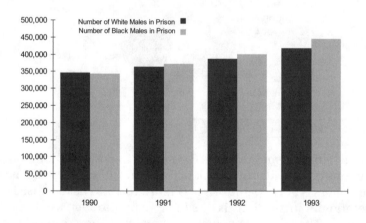

Source: Beck, A. J. and Gilliard, D. K. (1995). *Prisoners in 1994*. Washington, D.C.: Bureau of Justice Statistics, 8.

fenses has increased markedly in the last ten years and now about a fourth of all prisoners are confined for drug offenses. Many more than that have drug abuse problems that may be related to their offenses. During that time, the proportion of persons with violent crime convictions has decreased, as has the percentage with property offenses. Proportionately more men now in prison have been sentenced for a public order offense—for example, one involving weapons, drunk driving, escape, obstruction of justice, morals charges, or liquor law violations.

Figure 10.15 Race/Hispanic Origin of Inmates of State and Federal Prisons on December 31, 1993

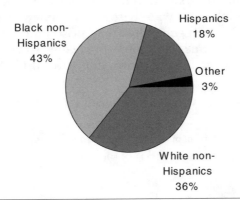

Source: Beck, A. J. and Gilliard, D. K. (1995). *Prisoners in 1994.* Washington, D.C.: Bureau of Justice Statistics, 9.
Note: data were estimated from population counts and 1991 inmate surveys. "Other" includes Asian Americans, Pacific Islanders, Native Americans, and Alaska Natives.

Figure 10.16 Percent of New State Prison Admissions Convicted of Violent Crimes and Drug Crimes, 1985–1992

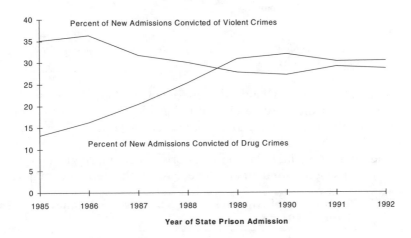

Source: Beck, A. J. and Gilliard, D. K. (1995). *Prisoners in 1994.* Washington, D.C.: Bureau of Justice Statistics, 10–11.
Note: these data are for new admissions to prison. Changes in the makeup of the prison populations are a different matter, because some categories of prisoners, of course, serve longer than others. From 1980 to 1993, the distribution of offense categories in state and federal prisons changed markedly because of changes in sentencing practices. The percent of violent offenders fell from 57 percent in 1980 to 45 percent in 1993. The percent of property offenders decreased from 30 percent to 22 percent. The percent of drug offenders increased from 8 percent to 22 percent and public order offenders increased from 5 percent to 7 percent. The increase in drug offenders, proportionately to the total number of persons confined, was greatest among federal inmate populations. In the federal prisons, inmates sentenced for drug violations made up 60 percent of the total, up from 25 percent in 1980. The growth in prison populations is associated with the increasing numbers of inmates in prison for violent and drug offenses. In state prisons, nearly ten times as many inmates were serving time in state prisons for drug offenses in 1993 as in 1980. Despite the decline in admissions of violent offenders as a percent of all new admissions, in absolute numbers of persons in state prisons, the increase of persons in prison for violent offenses increased markedly. Thus, the bottom line is that prisons now have proportionately more violent offenders and more drug offenders.

Women in Prison

The survey of state prison inmates done by the Bureau of Justice Statistics provides information about the characteristics of women in prison. The data from their sample survey are based on interviews with about 1 in 11 women in prisons. Women generally are in prison for a drug offense (one-third of all), a violent crime (one-third), or stealing (most of the remaining third). Offenses of conviction are shown in Figure 10.17. About 1 woman in

Figure 10.17 Most Serious Offenses of Women Prison Inmates, 1991

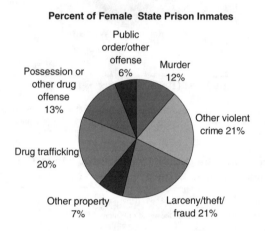

Percent of Female State Prison Inmates

Source: Snell, T. L. and Morton, D. C. (1994). *Women in Prison: Survey of State Prison Inmates, 1991*. Washington, D.C.: Bureau of Justice Statistics, 3.

10 is in prison for murder. One-third of those women killed a spouse or other person with whom there was a close relationship. The victim in about another third of the homicides was a relative or close acquaintance (Figure 10.18).

Women in prison tend to be young, poorly educated, single, members of minority groups, and often unemployed. As with men, the majority of

Figure 10.18 Relationship of Women Serving a Sentence for Homicide to Their Victims, 1991

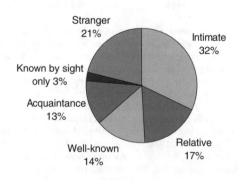

Source: Snell, T. L. and Morton, D. C. 1(994). *Women in Prison: Survey of State Prison Inmates, 1991*. Washington, D.C.: Bureau of Justice Statistics, 3.

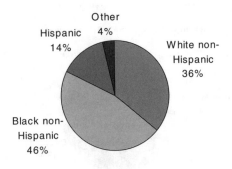

Source: Snell, T. L. and Morton, D. C. (1994). *Women in Prison: Survey of State Prison Inmates, 1991*. Washington, D.C.: Bureau of Justice Statistics, 2.

women prisoners are either black or Hispanic (Figure 10.19). Only a little more than a third are white non-Hispanics. Half are in their late twenties or early thirties (Figure 10.20). About three out of four were never married or are separated or divorced (Figure 10.21). The majority did not finish high school (Figure 10.22). Nearly half the women in prison, according to their interview reports, were working full- or part-time at the time of their arrest. About two-thirds of those not employed were not looking for work (Figure 10.23).

Figure 10.20 Ages of Female State Prison Inmates as a Percent of Prison Populations, 1991

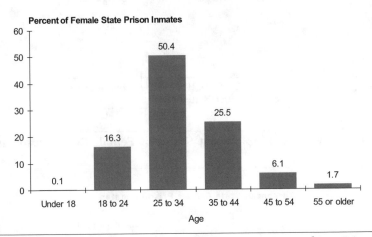

Source: Snell, T. L. and Morton, D. C. (1994). *Women in Prison: Survey of State Prison Inmates, 1991*. Washington, D.C.: Bureau of Justice Statistics, 2.

Prisoner Offenses and Race

Most prisoners, regardless of race, are in prison for violent crimes, property crimes, and drug offenses. The distributions of offenses are similar, but somewhat different, for white and black offenders, as shown in Figure 10.24. Many more black offenders are confined for drug offenses than are white offenders. More white offenders are serving time for property crimes. (Comparable data are not available for Hispanic offenders.)

Figure 10.21 Marital Status of Female State Prison Inmates as a Percent of Prison Populations, 1991

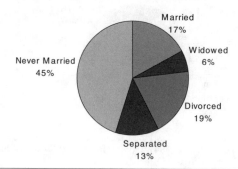

Percent of State Female Prison Inmates

Source: Snell, T. L. and Morton, D. C. (1994). *Women in Prison: Survey of State Prison Inmates, 1991*. Washington, D.C.: Bureau of Justice Statistics, 2.

Figure 10.22 Educational History of Female State Prison Inmates, 1991

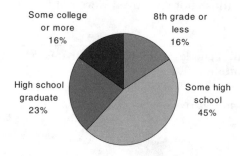

Percent of Female State Prison Inmates

Source: Snell, T. L. and Morton, D. C. (1994). *Women in Prison: Survey of State Prison Inmates, 1991*. Washington, D.C.: Bureau of Justice Statistics, 2.

Figure 10.23 Pre-arrest Employment Status of Female State Prison Inmates, 1991

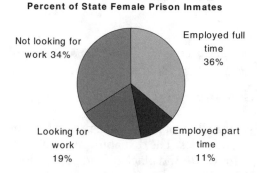

Percent of State Female Prison Inmates

Source: Snell, T. L. and Morton, D. C. (1994). *Women in Prison: Survey of State Prison Inmates, 1991*. Washington, D.C.: Bureau of Justice Statistics, 2.

Figure 10.24   Offenses and Estimated Numbers of Black and White State Prisoners, 1995

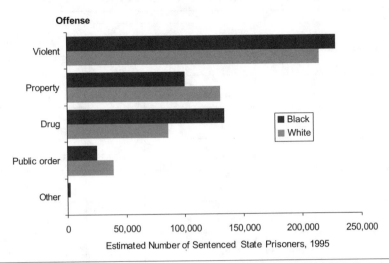

Source: data from Mumola, C. J. and Beck, A. J. (1997). *Prisoners in 1996*. U.S. Department of Justice, Office of Justice Programs, 10.
Note: offense classification is for the most serious offense. Violent includes murder, manslaughter, rape, other sexual assault, robbery, assault, and other offenses; property includes burglary, larceny, motor vehicle theft, fraud, and other offenses; drug offenses include possession and sale.

Prisoners on Death Row

In 1995, all 310 prisoners under death sentences received that year by state and federal prisons had been convicted of murder. The number of persons in prison under sentence of death has increased sharply since 1976, when the U.S. Supreme Court upheld state capital punishment laws.

Since the 1976 ruling, when fewer than 500 persons were on death rows, the numbers have grown to more than 3,000 in 1995 (Box 10.4). Forty-eight were women.[20] Fifty-seven percent were white, 42 percent were black. Twenty-two persons were Native American, 19 were Asian American, and 8 were classified as "other race." The 237 Hispanic inmates accounted for 8.5 percent of the inmates whose ethnicity was known.

The minimum age at which capital punishment is authorized differs among the states. Frequently (in 13 states and the federal jurisdiction) it is 18, but often (in 16 states) youths under 18 may be executed. The minimum age is 14 in Arkansas and Virginia, and 16 in 10 states. Eight states specify no minimum age. The average age at arrest of prisoners on death row in 1995 was 28. It ranged from 17 or younger to 60 or older. The average age of death row inmates was 36. The youngest was 18; the oldest was 80.

Decision Making in Correctional Institutions

The broad goals of jails and prisons are those already discussed: reform, rehabilitation, reintegration, and restraint. Within these aims, correctional agencies have goals of security, treatment, incapacitation, and organizational maintenance. These goals are related closely to the sentencing aims

Box 10.4

Status of the Death Penalty, December 31, 1995

Executions During 1995		Number of Prisoners Under Sentence of Death		Jurisdictions Without a Death Penalty
Texas	19	California	420	Alaska
Missouri	6	Texas	404	District of Columbia
Illinois	5	Florida	362	Hawaii
Virginia	5	Pennsylvania	196	Iowa
Florida	3	Ohio	155	Maine
Oklahoma	3	Illinois	154	Massachusetts
Alabama	2	Alabama	143	Michigan
Arkansas	2	North Carolina	139	Minnesota
Georgia	2	Oklahoma	129	North Dakota
North Carolina	2	Arizona	117	Rhode Island
Pennsylvania	2	Georgia	98	Vermont
Arizona	1	Tennessee	96	West Virginia
Delaware	1	Missouri	92	Wisconsin
Louisiana	1	22 other jurisdictions	549	
Montana	1			
South Carolina	1			
Total	**56**	**Total**	**3,054**	

discussed previously, but the context of decision making in correctional institutions differs substantially from that of the sentencing judge.

Burnham described this context of decision making in correctional institutions as follows:

> First . . . there is the very strong effect of system constraints and requirements. All prisons are, in several senses, run by their inmates, and a regular supply of these to essential jobs, such as kitchen and the laundry, must be maintained. Thus there are two types of decisions usually collapsed into one. (1) "What is the appropriate disposition for that particular inmate?" (in terms of which institution, which work assignment, which training program, etc., is the most suitable for him), and (2) "Which inmates are to be used to provide

the manpower for the following essential tasks?" The problem emerges . . . as (3) "Is this inmate suitable for what he requests, and does it suit system requirements for him to be so allocated?" or more simply (4) "Can we allow him to do what he wants?" In version (4), the factors involved in "allowing" refer to both the personal qualities of the inmate (e.g., offense, violence record, intelligence, aptitude test scores) and vacancies either open to be filled or which must be filled.

Second, the sheer number of decisions is different. For each passage through the system, each inmate usually is arrested once, tried once, sentenced once, paroled once, and so on. In the correctional stage, he is subject to frequent decisions which affect where he lives, what he does, and other issues which matter deeply to him. Thus, in one respect correctional decision making impinges more on an inmate's life. But in a more important way, it matters less—for most of these decisions are reversed with relative ease; and thus, as well as having less far-reaching implications for the subsequent system career path of the individual, they are not so final.

The third main difference is in the amount and type of information available to the decisionmaker. The arresting police officer, the district attorney or whoever brings the charge, the court which tries, and the judge or jury who sentence will often have, or probably feel they have, a shortage of data upon which to base a decision. But what they have is significant. Once an individual is in the correctional system, however, data about him are accumulated very rapidly, so that a great deal is known, but much of it seemingly trivial and uninformative with regard to the particular decisions required.[21]

The context of decision making in institutional corrections systems has changed with the unprecedented growth of prisons in the last two decades. The rapid expansion of prisons is disruptive in many ways. Administrators must turn attention from programs to focus on simply housing larger and larger numbers of inmates, maintaining control of the population, and meeting the prime function of keeping their charges behind walls or fences. In this context, the development of programs of education, counseling, work, or other items on the rehabilitation agenda are likely to get much less attention. Similarly, programs for individual assignments of inmates for custody and treatment may be disrupted, because these assignments may be more influenced by housing availabilities than by the risks and needs presented by the offender. The orderly process of planning and implementation of programs may be disrupted. Dramatic increases in the sheer numbers of inmates may push a greater emphasis on restraint and control functions, with less emphasis on rehabilitative aims.

Safety of Persons, Institutions, and the Community

Decisions that must be made very early in both prisons and jails concern safety. There are three concerns for safety: protection of the staff and inmates in the institution, protection of the community, and protection of each individual inmate. These decisions must be made in the context of the goal of institutional maintenance. Not only the individual and the population of inmates, but also the institution itself is at risk. Thus, important decisions must be made quickly, often with little information, about the risk presented by the inmate for escape, for suicide, and for assault on others—both inmates and staff. Decisions must be made also about inmate needs for protective custody. Sometimes the decision is literally a matter of life and death.

Inmate Classification

Correctional managers have two top priorities. One is providing a safe environment for both staff and inmates. Another is the protection of the community outside the walls or fences. Both goals require valid methods for classification and assignment of prisoners.

The process of inmate classification has two main functions. These often are called "classification for treatment" and "classification for custody." The first concerns program assignments such as work, training, and educational programs, or programs of treatment intended to meet special needs. In this case, the attempt is made to match the needs of the inmate with institutional needs and resources. The other classification function, which establishes constraints within which the decisions about programs must be made, depends on assessments about the threat posed by the inmate to the safety of the institution and the outside community. Those who are considered likely to seek to attempt escape or to present serious misconduct problems are placed in physically more secure settings or in environments with more supervision. Those who are expected to serve their terms without serious misconduct are placed in less secure or less supervised environments. The latter may mean more freedom within an institution or placement in forestry camps, work programs, or other settings with less surveillance and direct supervision.

Decisions about classification and assignment are made by correctional staff—who are sometimes well trained, sometimes not. They often are made by a classification committee, sometimes by an individual. Many are made entirely subjectively, and many have little basis in objective study to determine whether the information used actually is relevant to the decisions.

In recent years there has been an increase in efforts in correctional institutions to make these decisions more fairly and effectively, based on more objective information about the inmate that is related to the goals of the classification and assignment process. As with discretionary decisions throughout the criminal justice system, there is a great potential for unwarranted disparities in classification decisions, decision makers typically receive little systematic feedback about the results of their decisions, and no formal mechanism exists for learning in order to improve the decision-making process.

Classification for Custody and Security

There is a distinction between classification for custody and for security. Custody refers to the level of supervision in the institution to be assigned, and it refers to the need for protection of staff and other inmates. Security refers to the need for protection of the outside community and concerns the potential that the inmate will escape and do harm if that occurs. The two goals are related but not the same, and different information may be required for effective classification for the two purposes. Information about inmates may not predict both a tendency to attempt escape and to violate other rules of the institution.

It is common, for example, that an older inmate, never in trouble before, serving time for murder, can be expected to be a "model prisoner," following the rules and causing no trouble in the institution. Such a person poses little threat to staff or inmates. Nevertheless, when received in prison, the potential for escape may be seen by classification staff to be relatively high, because the inmate faces a long term in prison. As a result, the inmate is apt to start the prison term in a secure environment. Custody needs are low but security needs are perceived to be high. On the other hand, a young, rebellious troublemaker sometimes involved in minor incidents in the institution, serving time for theft, with a long history of institutional confinement without running away, may present no particular risk of escape or apparent danger to the community. Needs for supervision (custody) are relatively high, but community protection (security) concerns are relatively low.

In deciding on custody classification, correction administrators must balance concerns for community protection and the aims of correctional programs. Working outside the fence requires minimum custody status. How would you decide which inmates could be allowed to work outside?
—*Photo courtesy of the New Jersey Department of Corrections.*

Control Within the Institution

It is common in correctional institutions that several degrees of custodial control are recognized. There may be several degrees of minimum custody, with varying degrees of intensity of supervision, but each with fairly minimal confinement and observation, perhaps with some restriction of approved movements inside a fence. Next in degree of control is usually called medium custody, ordinarily with considerable freedom of movement within the walls of the institution. A more strict control is expected of close custody, with the inmate under constant surveillance and more restricted confinement—perhaps to a cell block with segregation from the general institutional population. Maximum custody provides yet closer restrictions and more surveillance and may require isolation.

Institutions often are designated according to the custody levels that predominate in them, but ordinarily all or most degrees of custody may be found in a single large institution. Even in maximum custody prisons, some minimum custody inmates are needed to operate the institution. Or, a minimum custody inmate may be placed in a maximum institution on the basis of treatment concerns, to be nearer family, or for a vocational program.

Control as Community Protection

Methods for custody and security classification that are more objective and reliable than those from traditional subjective judgments make use of known or believed relations between inmate characteristics and behavior in the institution. Examples of factors often used in inmate classification for custody assignments are shown in Box 10.5. [22] To be most useful, the validity of the items used should be investigated, in order to ensure that they are in fact related to the behavior that is sought to be predicted.

An example of more objective classification decisions is given by the procedures of the New Jersey Department of Corrections, similar to those

---

Box 10.5

Factors Often Used in Inmate Classification for Custody

Age

- Younger inmates usually have higher rates of disciplinary infractions.

Marital status

- Inmates who have never married have higher rates of disciplinary problems (but note that marital status is related to age).

Job stability

- A history of steady employment is related to low violation scores.

Drug and alcohol use

- Research results are mixed, but being young and using drugs may be related to high infraction rates.

Stability of residence

- This factor often is used, but its relation to institutional misconduct is inconsistent or weak.

Criminal history

- Different aspects of criminal history have different relations to disciplinary problems. For example, persons with extensive involvement in delinquency as a youth may have higher rates of misconduct; but persons with lengthy criminal histories as adults may not pose higher custodial risks.

Past violent offenses

- Often included in classification systems, this factor nevertheless may have only a weak or inconsistent relation to custody requirements. For example, persons convicted of murder often are good custody risks, while persons convicted of other violent crimes may have higher misconduct rates.

---

now used in many states, for determining the custody level to which the inmate will be assigned.[23] Inmates are given ratings in areas traditionally believed useful in assigning custody classifications. Examples are the seriousness of the commitment offense (which ordinarily is related to the length of sentence), the assaultive offense history of the inmate, the history of escapes or attempted escapes in the most recent three years of incarceration, and any history of violence in either jail or prison (also during the last three years of confinement). The scores for these ratings are added to provide a "maximum custody score." Inmates scoring higher than a selected "cutting score" are assigned to an initial status of maximum custody. An exception (called an "override") may be made by the classification committee with reasons given for it.

If not assigned to maximum custody initially by this process, further ratings are completed. Items considered are the balance of the term to be served, a rating of alcohol or drug abuse history, whether there is a current detainer if the inmate is wanted by another jurisdiction or whether additional charges are pending, the number of prior felony convictions, age, educational achievement, and employment history. Custody classifications are determined by cutting scores, placing inmates in maximum, medium, or minimum custody according to their scores, unless "overridden" with reasons given. Overrides may be due to specific administrative code provisions or to provide protective custody.

Classification for placements with security in mind may be based on some similar and some different items of information.[24] Some factors commonly used are shown in Box 10.6.

Box 10.6

Factors Often Used in Inmate Classification for Security

Prior criminal behavior

- Prior criminal histories are important factors for predicting future crimes.

Age

- Younger offenders are often the most serious public risks.

Socioeconomic status and unemployment

- Unemployment may be predictive, but as with other social factors, many political, legal, and ethical concerns complicate their use in security classifications.

Drug and alcohol use

- Substance abuse is related to offending, and the use of both alcohol and drugs may be an even better predictor of future crimes.

Time to be served

- Persons facing unusually long sentences are often believed to present risks of escape.

History of escape or attempted escape

- People tend to do what they last did in the same situation. Persons who have tried before are more likely to try again.

Classification for Treatment

To the extent that rehabilitation is a correctional goal, the classification of offenders for treatment is important. Unless all offenders are to be treated alike, or all are to be assigned to programs haphazardly, some classification for treatment is necessary.

Classification for treatment in correctional institutions means, in most prisons and jails, the selection of inmates for assignment to programs of education, training, counseling, or specialized treatment aimed at changing behavior. Often it is done subjectively, by an individual classification officer or by a classification committee. In jails, there often is little information to help other than the arrest report, the criminal history record, and an interview. In prisons, there may be added the investigation report prepared by the probation officer before sentencing. Besides usually providing the judge with a social history, some record of education and employment, family circumstances, and another description of the offense (partly from the offender's own account), this document is a primary source of data for institutional corrections decisions. Other important additions typically are the observations by the treatment and correctional officer staff of the inmate's behavior in the institution.

Group counseling session in a California prison in the late 1950s, when the most prominent aim of corrections was said to be rehabilitation. Should such counseling be offered to prison inmates?

In both jails and prisons, there often is insufficient study of individual needs and potentials. This differs substantially among jurisdictions, and in larger, more sophisticated institutions there may be a careful assessment by social workers, psychologists, medical personnel, vocational counselors, custody staff, and others intended to be of help in placement decisions.

Limitations due to custody decisions and the availability of housing in program placements restrict the program choices, because those thought most desirable from a treatment perspective may not be available in the settings required for custody. In most cases, the program choices are limited to placements in programs of school, vocational training, work in correctional industries, counseling, recommendations for attendance at drug or alcohol treatment programs, or selection for specialized units such as psychiatric hospital facilities.

The treatment aim has been the topic of much research, with conflicting results and uncertainty about effectiveness in the achievement of treatment goals. In some, though not all institutions, there is an extraordinary diversity of treatments offered, despite the general decline in emphasis and support for this orientation. Procedures for reliable and valid classification of inmates for program assignments may be useful to promote a match between characteristics and needs of the inmate with the program resources of the institutions.

Despite the importance of classification for treatment in institutional corrections, the necessary research to establish classification systems that are clearly and consistently useful for program assignments affecting later offender behavior remains mainly to be done. If the rehabilitative aim of corrections is valued, the problems of effective classification for treatment remain as central unresolved issues for correctional systems.

The goals of the drafters of the Declaration of Principles, at the first meeting of what is now the American Correctional Association, for classification and treatment under indeterminate sentencing, have not yet been achieved (Box 10.7).

Box 10.7

Declaration of Principles
American Prison Association (1870)

I. Crime is an intentional violation of duties imposed by law, which inflicts injury upon others. Criminals are persons convicted by competent courts. Punishment is suffering inflicted on the criminal for the wrongdoing done by him, with a special view to secure his reformation.

II. The treatment of criminals by society is for the protection of society. But since such treatment is directed to the criminal rather than the crime, its great object should be his moral regeneration. Hence the supreme aim of prison discipline is the reformation of criminals, not the infliction of vindictive suffering.

III. The progressive classification of prisoners based on characteristics and worked on some well-established mark system, should be established in all prisons above the common jail.

IV. Since hope is a more potent agent than fear, it should be made an ever present force in the minds of prisoners, by a well devised and skillfully applied system of rewards for good conduct, industry and attention to learning. Rewards, more than punishments, are essential to every good prison system.

V. The prisoner's destiny should be placed, measurably, in his own hands: he must be put into circumstances where he will be able, through his own exertions, to continually better his own condition. A regulated self-interest must be brought into play and made constantly operative.

VI. Peremptory sentences ought to be replaced by those of indeterminate length. Sentences limited only by satisfactory proof of reformation should be substituted for those measured by mere lapse of time.

Reclassification

Custody and treatment classifications may be changed after periodic reviews. For the committee meeting to consider reclassification, the original ratings of offense and assaultive or escape history are augmented by others concerning disciplinary reports, infractions that are rated for seriousness, and program participation. Again, when objective procedures are used, it is typical that the committee may override the usual decision as indicated by the score, giving reasons.

Well designed vocational programs, as in this construction trades class, may help increase an inmate's chances for a law abiding life after release. Would you favor offering vocational counseling in prisons? —*Photo courtesy of the New Jersey Department of Corrections.*

Reclassification is used as a means to control the inmate population, by providing a system of sanctions. Assignment to a lower classification—with more freedom—is used as a reward. Assignment to a higher level of control and supervision (or continuation of it) is used as a punishment. In addition, however, a gradually increasing freedom may help achieve the rehabilitative aims of the institution.

Decreasing Control Over Time

An idealized model for gradually decreasing custody levels and control over the offender's life as the institutional stay progresses is shown in Figure 10.25.

Such a concept is implied by the concepts of classification, repeated reclassification, placement in the community under parole supervision, and eventual discharge. Of course, many inmates will have repeated changes in custody, repeated denials of parole, and changes in supervision levels in the community as well. Nevertheless, the general concept is one that fits well with idealized rehabilitative, reintegrative, or restorative models—according to which an inmate would progress through stages to progressively more independence and freedom.

Ensuring Effectiveness and Fairness

As is the case with many areas of decision making in criminal justice, there is a need for careful follow-up study of such procedures to ensure that the right factors are used in the instruments and that they are used both fairly and effectively. Very often, such needed study has not been done, and reliance must be placed on the subjective judgments and experience of the decision makers, with resulting unreliability, bias, and unfairness.

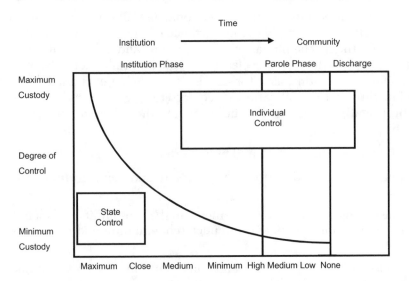

The Variety of Institutional Decisions

Besides the decision about initial custody, many other important decisions must be made early in an inmate's period of confinement. Usually, it must be decided in which of several institutions the inmate should be housed initially. Even within a single state, there is ordinarily a great deal of difference among various prisons. Often, there is much difference among parts of a single institution. Populations of various institutions tend to be different: some tend to have older, more experienced offenders, with longer prior records of convictions. Some institutions may be specialized—for example, they may be more equipped to deal with physically or mentally ill inmates. Others may have better facilities of education, vocational training, or work in correctional industries.

The classification committee may see the geographical location of the institution as relevant, either facilitating visits and continued family ties, or in effect cutting these off by placement in a remote location. A classification committee would likely consider this concern within the context of other perceived needs for the inmate's program: Should the inmate be placed in school or in a vocational program? Is there a need for counseling or psychotherapy? Should the person be given the opportunity for drug or alcohol abuse treatment programs? Is there a need to ensure some protection for this inmate from older or stronger predators? Is there a need in a correctional industries unit for the type of skills possessed by the inmate? These and many other concerns are those often considered in inmate classification early after arrival in prison and at later reclassification.

There remains a need for research aimed at determining how inmates should best be classified for both the custody and the treatment purposes of the institution. Reliable, objective classification using data that are clearly relevant to these placement decisions can provide the foundation for effective programming.

The Importance of Institutional Classification

The central importance of the correctional institution's goals of security, custody, and treatment imply the importance of the procedures used in efforts to reach them. The management of prisons and jails requires careful classification procedures, using clearly reliable and valid methods, in order to meet many of the administrator's goals. Brennan has explained the many roles of institutional classification as required to meet a variety of objectives of institutional management.[25] These include the following objectives or functions:

- Protecting inmate, staff, and public safety.

- Classifying offenders for rehabilitation and reintegration programs.

- Classifying offenders for placements in the community, balancing goals of public safety and offender rehabilitation and reintegration.

- Improving equity, fairness, and consistency in decisions by minimizing subjectivity, bias, and prejudice.

- Providing appropriate service by identifying the vocational, physical, and mental health needs of inmates.

- Improving efficiency and rationality in resource utilization, avoiding waste by a correct matching of agency resources and inmates.

- Improving management planning by forecasting levels of need for different resources or services.

- Maintaining social control and discipline by the distribution of rewards and punishments.

- Making inmate movement, housing, and transfers more predictable and consistent, contributing to institutional order by decreasing arbitrary or biased decision making.

- Assisting communication among staff and inmates by procedures that provide a sense of predictability.

- Monitoring and recording goal attainment to see whether goals are being achieved.

- Protecting jail and prison personnel from liability. Good classification procedures properly implemented can help jail and prison personnel avoid public embarrassment, maintain good public relations, and avoid costly litigation. Valid classification can help avoid devastating placement errors; and it can provide justification for decisions, providing protection against litigation.

About Time

The Effect of Prison Time Served on Recidivism

Besides other goals of imprisonment, it may be hoped or expected that the length of time served is related to the probability of new crimes or to success or failure on parole. "Specific deterrence" may include two ideas:

imprisonment itself may "teach the offender a lesson" and the longer the sentence the greater the deterrence effect.

Research does not support the expectation that the length of time served in prison is related to recidivism (repeated offending), particularly when relevant offender characteristics are taken into account.

In an early study of the federal prison system, "success rates" were studied in relation to the time served before release for different categories of offenders. Generally, there were little differences in outcomes by offender risk group associated with the length of time served. Older inmates without previous incarceration were found to be good risks regardless of how long they were confined. Younger inmates without prior incarceration who were released late were worse risks than those released early. For inmates with prior incarceration, postrelease failure was also greatest for those who were confined the longest.[26] These results, from study during the time that most release decisions were made by a parole board, are consistent with a use of longer terms for those with rules violations or who were progressing poorly in programs.

The experience in several states shows a similar result. In 1958, the state of Washington made a policy decision to reduce the overall average time served in prison. A 10-month reduction over a three-year period produced no appreciable reduction in recidivism rates.[27] In California, two matched groups on parole were selected after having committed misdemeanors while under supervision. One group was jailed locally and then continued on parole while the parole of persons in the other was revoked and they were returned to prison. There was no difference in the recidivism rates of the two groups, despite the fact that the jail group served 7 months in confinement on the average and the prison group 20 months.[28]

Other studies in California have had similar results. An extensive review by the California Assembly Committee on Criminal Procedure concluded that "no evidence can be found to support extended incarceration as a determinate element in the deterrence of crime." Criticizing California's policy of lengthy time served, the Committee stated further that " . . . there is no evidence that the California prisoner's average stay of 30 months has contributed to his rehabilitation more than would a stay of 20, 12, or 6 months."[29] Another study for the Assembly Select Committee on the Administration of Justice reviewed the results of a number of extensive studies of parole releases and concluded that recidivism rates for offenders were not related to time served. From a later study it was concluded similarly that "the length of time served by California prisoners has no relationship to their performance after release."[30]

The most comprehensive study on the topic was done on the basis of individual parolee data from a national parole reporting program—a statistical reporting program no longer maintained. Its value for this study was in its individual time served and parole outcome data for a large national sample—104,182 offenders. The data were submitted by all 50 states and the District of Columbia. All offenders studied were paroled for the first time by a discretionary release by a paroling authority between the years 1965 and 1970. Thus, the study involved only the amount of time served on the charge for which the offender was confined before the decision by the parole board to release that person initially on parole. The behavior of the parolees was followed by a parole officer for a year, or until discharged from parole. This is the only study using national data and a very large sample collected under fairly rigorously controlled conditions. Moreover, the study controlled statistically for differences in offense, age, and prior record, each of which is known to be related to parole outcomes. It concluded:

> [A]lthough some differences are found in parole outcome according to the time offenders serve in prison, the differences are relatively small . . . and not of an order to justify any but the most cautious statements about parole policy.

And, although some differences among states were observed, it concluded:

> With infrequent exception those offenders who serve the longest terms in prison tend to do less favorably on parole than those who serve the shortest terms before first release. . . . Differences in parole performance by those in short time categories and those in long time categories are neither consistent nor large. The data lend some support to the idea that parolees who served longer terms do less well under supervision. [31]

Results of a similar study in Ohio were consistent with the national study. There was no large positive relation between the time served in prison and parole outcome.[32]

Many of the studies were done when parole boards generally had considerable discretion about release and the studies do not take account of subjective risk judgments by paroling authorities. That is, those kept longer probably were relatively poor risks. Nevertheless, these studies show that the arguments of those who perceive increasing or decreasing prison time as a ready means to reducing repeat offending must be viewed with a healthy dose of skepticism.

Sentence Lengths and Time Served

The median maximum sentences imposed by state courts in 1992 are shown in Figure 10.26. The ranking of medians corresponds generally to most ratings of seriousness of offenses, reflecting the strong impact of that variable on sentencing. The mean of times actually served during the era of greater indeterminacy and more recently are shown in Figure 10.27.

Growth in Jails and Prisons

The alarming growth of prison and jail populations since 1980 is reflected in Figure 10.28. The numbers in prison have markedly increased, due to a higher rate of incarceration and longer terms. More persons are being sent to prison for a longer time. The increased rate of incarceration is due substantially to a greater use of imprisonment for drug offenses, which also has increased the confinement of members of minority groups. Prison growth has been due to changes in the general level of punishment demanded, changes in sentencing philosophy and structures discussed previously, and the imprisonment of increasing numbers of drug offenders. For one expert's view on increased rationality in the use of prisons, to be discussed further in the last chapter of this book, see Box 10.8.[33]

Figure 10.26   Median Maximum Sentences Imposed by State Courts, 1992

Most Serious Conviction

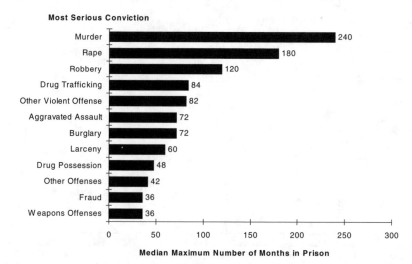

Source: adapted from Maguire, K. and Pastore, A. L. (1996). *Sourcebook of Criminal Justice Statistics—1995*. Washington, D.C.: Bureau of Justice Statistics, 505.

Note: murder includes nonnegligent manslaughter and excludes cases sentenced to death or life in prison. "Other violent offense" includes crimes such as negligent manslaughter, sexual assault, and kidnapping. Larceny includes vehicle theft. Fraud includes forgery and embezzlement. "Other Offenses" includes nonviolent crimes such as receiving stolen property and vandalism. The median is the point at or below which half the cases fall.

Figure 10.27   Average (Mean) Time Served in State Prisons in 1965–1970 and Estimated to Be Served in 1990 (First Releases for Selected Offenses)

Most Serious Conviction Offense

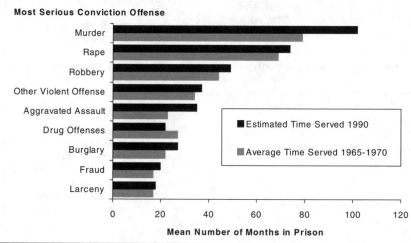

Sources: data for 1965–1970 are for persons paroled for the first time and are from Gottfredson, D. M., Neithercutt, G., Nuffield, J., and O'Leary, V. (1973). Davis, CA: National Council on Crime and Delinquency Research Center. Data for 1990 are for first releases, whether paroled or discharged, with estimates from average sentence lengths and percents of sentences served in the various jurisdictions, from Maguire, K., and Pastore, A. L. (1995). *Sourcebook of Criminal Justice Statistics—1994*. Washington, D.C.: Bureau of Justice Statistics, 491.

Note: estimated average months to be served in 1990, for drug offenses, were 14 months for possession and 26 months for trafficking; the breakdown is not available for the earlier period. More recent comparable data are not available. The mean is the sum of all time served divided by the number of offenders.

Figure 10.28 Estimated Jail and Prison Populations, 1980 to 1995

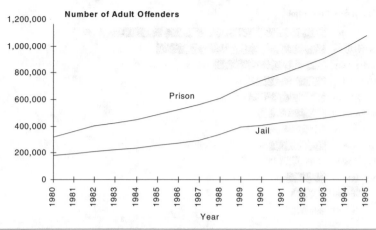

Sources: Bureau of Justice Statistics, *Prisoners in 1994* August, 1995; *Correctional Populations in the United States,* April 1995; *Correctional Populations in the United States 1994,* July 1996; *Prison and Jail Inmates, 1995* August 1996. Washington D.C.: United States Department of Justice. Note: see notes for Figure 10.2. These data for prison and jail populations are the same, with the scale changed to show the trends more clearly.

Box 10.8

Alfred Blumstein: In His Own Words

Any development of a rational strategy regarding prisons must recognize several key facts:

- There has been a massive growth in prison populations between the mid-1970s and the mid-1990s, with no demonstrable strong effect on crime rates.

- There has been a major growth in the use of imprisonment for drug offenders, and prison is demonstrably ineffective for diminishing drug selling or drug abuse, except for being able to coerce drug treatment.

- Prisons are expensive, costing about $20,000 per year per prisoner to operate, and these funds are diverted from other needs (such as education or economic development, or even juvenile institutions, where rehabilitation is most likely with the right programs and resources applied) which might have some possibility of diminishing the future calls for prison.

- Prisons are generally ineffective for rehabilitation of adults.

- While the threat of a lengthy prison term is undoubtedly very effective at deterring white collar crimes that tend to be committed by middle class individuals, [it is] probably far less effective in deterring the crimes committed by underclass individuals, who are the primary occupants of prisons, and for whom the increment of pain associated with prison time may be far less severe than it would be for those ensconced in a comfortable job.

- Incapacitation through imprisonment is probably the only effective means of restraining the violent crimes that are committed by some individuals otherwise out of social control, and so incarceration of these people should be a high priority for the use of limited prison capacity.

- It is important to find ways to remove prison policy from a primarily political agenda that reacts to the crime of the moment, and to develop a coherent schedule and process of imposing punishment and controlling offenders.

—Alfred Blumstein,
Carnegie-Mellon University

Many of the 1.5 million persons now in confinement in the United States live under extremely grim conditions. Despite a flurry of building in recent years to keep up with population growth, about a fourth of all confinement facilities are more than 50 years old, and 41 institutions are 100 years old or older. More than half of those are maximum security facilities.[34]

For the first half of the present century, courts did not intervene even in the face of devastating conditions of some prisons and many jails—small, inadequate cells, crowded conditions, buildings in disrepair, inadequate ventilation, leaking plumbing and sewage problems, rodent infestation, lack of food standards for health and safety, inadequate medical care, and other shocking conditions. Prison administrators were free to punish inmates by solitary confinement, or other punitive segregation, without any of the safeguards provided ordinary citizens when accused of wrongdoing. The "hands-off" doctrine prevailed, with the courts unwilling to interfere with the performance of the executive branch of government in performing its role. In an early case concerning rights of prisoners, the court declared the prisoner is a "slave of the state" and had no rights.[35]

This did not begin to change until the 1960s, but there were earlier signs that the courts might ultimately take on a stronger role. In 1944, a federal court judge declared that "a prisoner retains all the rights of an ordinary citizen except those expressly or by necessary implication, taken from him by law. While the law does take his liberty and imposes a duty of servitude and observance of discipline for his regulation and that of other prisoners, it does not deny his right to personal security against unlawful invasion."[36] As late as 1958, however, the U.S. Supreme Court held that it had no power to intervene in the domain of prison administration.[37]

In the late 1960s and early 1970s, the courts began to intervene actively. The change was associated with the civil rights movement stressing the rights of minorities and heightened public attention to the conditions in prisons. As the Civil Rights Act of 1871 [38] was used increasingly in the 1960s to enforce federally protected rights, it began to be used also to address claims by prisoners. The hands-off doctrine came to an end, and a series of court cases dramatically changed the previous understandings of the rights of prisoners.

The Court found in 1964 that prisoners may bring civil suits under the Civil Rights Act of 1871.[39] Subsequent cases addressed issues of the First, Fourth, Sixth, Eighth, and Fourteenth Amendments. Kranz described the important principles that emerged from these decisions as follows:

1. Prisoners retain certain constitutional rights in spite of conviction and incarceration;

2. Detainees [accused but not convicted persons awaiting trial] retain even greater constitutional protections;

3. Many existing practices in prisons and jails abridge those retained rights and protections;

4. Correctional officials bear the burden of justifying the restriction of constitutional rights;

5. The Civil Rights Act is an appropriate tool for protecting and enforcing the constitutional rights of prisoners and detainees.[40]

Examples of the movement within the federal courts are given by cases in the U.S. Supreme Court and in the federal district courts in the late 1960s and early 1970s. The Supreme Court found, in 1968, that racial segregation in prison (unless there is a compelling state interest) violated the Fourteenth Amendment equal protection clause.[41] The next year, the Court decided that an inmate cannot be prevented from serving as a "jail house lawyer" to other prisoners unless the state provided alternative legal assistance.[42] The district court decisions were especially far reaching in their implications. A political activist and black Muslim brought a civil rights action after being held in solitary confinement for a year for possessing literature described as political and refusing to reveal its source. The judge held that a prisoner cannot be placed in punitive segregation without certain protections:

- [The prisoner has a right to] prior procedural due process safeguards such as written notice, a hearing, the right to present witnesses, the right to cross-examine adverse witnesses, the right to retain counsel or counsel substitute, and a written record of the hearing and reasons for the decision reached.

- The prisoner has First Amendment rights to freedom of political thought and expression, limited only by reasonable rules and regulations necessary to maintain prison discipline.

- The Eighth Amendment prohibition against cruel and unusual punishment is violated if the prisoner is held in punitive segregation for more than 15 days.[43]

Another case, a class action suit by prisoners at prison farms in Arkansas raised the argument that the conditions at these institutions were so bad that they constituted cruel and unusual punishment. There were three major divisions to the institution at Tucker, one of the two institutions, with three dormitories corresponding to the three classifications of prisoners there (in addition to one block of cells). The three inmate classifications were called "Trustee," "Do-pop" and "Rank." The Trustees carried guns and supervised the Rank inmates working on the farm. The Do-pop inmates were in an intermediate classification, neither carrying guns nor required to work at the farming. (The classification, pronounced "dough-pop," was said to be derived from a traditional work assignment of opening and closing doors). Most supervision was done by the Trustee inmates. For example, one inmate was designated "Sheriff" and patrolled the perimeter of the farm at night in a pickup truck. Inmate trustees with rifles were in the guard towers. Personnel who were not serving sentences, called "free world" people, were often entirely absent from the institution. Stories of brutal punishments and torture were widespread in the institution. [44] The arrangement, including the supervision by inmates, was justified by the prison authorities on the basis that the state could not afford more typical supervision and confinement. The court agreed with the prisoners' cruel and unusual punishment argument, ordered elimination of the barracks, the trustee system, other changes, and held that a lack of funds is not a defense to running an unconstitutional prison system.[45]

The prisoners' rights movement received a dramatic boost through much publicized prison riots calling attention to poor conditions in many prisons. One was a 1971 uprising at Attica prison in New York, during which a group of prisoners took over the institution and held 14 correctional officers hostage. In a subsequent attack by the state police, 43 persons were killed. Other riots in the same decade also called attention to prison conditions, and prisoners' rights became a controversial public issue. Many of the prisoners' demands, at Attica and riots elsewhere, were for rights that are addressed by the First, Sixth, Eighth, and Fourteenth Amendments. The results of a flood of petitions to the courts that ensued can be seen in some court decisions related to the Bill of Rights.

First Amendment Rights

After inmates challenged mail censorship in a Rhode Island institution, the court held in 1970 that the First Amendment freedom of speech and expression clause applies to prisoners. The court ruled that some inspection or censorship may be necessary, but it required that prison administrators use every legitimate means to provide the least restrictive alternative method for accomplishing it. [46] In 1974, the court held that mail may be censored only when there is a substantial government interest in maintaining security.[47]

In the 1960s and more often in the 1970s, courts held that prisoners cannot be denied their rights to pursuing their religious beliefs unless prison administrators could prove that the activities were not really based in religious beliefs or constituted a clear and present danger to the institution.[48] In the same year, the Supreme Court found that the denial to Buddhist inmates of the opportunity to practice their faith was discriminatory and in violation of their First Amendment right.[49]

Sixth Amendment Rights

After the case already mentioned concerning "jail house lawyers," many court decisions have established standards that expand, but also limit, legal assistance to prisoners. Generally, prisoners have a right to meet with their lawyers for a reasonable amount of time.[50] The court, however, might permit the conversation to be monitored. It could be expected, nonetheless, to prohibit the use in court of any evidence obtained in this way.[51] Inmates may have a right to correspond with their lawyers, but the prison personnel may be allowed to open letters to check for unpermitted objects; nevertheless, they may not be allowed to read them.[52] Courts have a duty to help inmates prepare and file legal papers; [53] but access could be provided by trained personnel or law libraries in each institution. In such ways, courts have sought to provide access to legal assistance while still protecting the prison administrations' abilities to carry out precautions for security and custody concerns.

Eighth Amendment Rights

The prohibition against cruel and inhuman punishment was the basis for a federal court ruling in 1968 that whipping prisoners "offends contemporary concepts of decency and human dignity and precepts of civilization which we profess to possess." [54] Prisoners soon raised many claims of cruel and unusual punishment, and the courts supported some, rejected others. Many suits brought by inmates cite this prohibition, along with the Fourteenth Amendment's due process and equal protection provisions. After the declaration of the Arkansas prison system as unconstitutional, and as

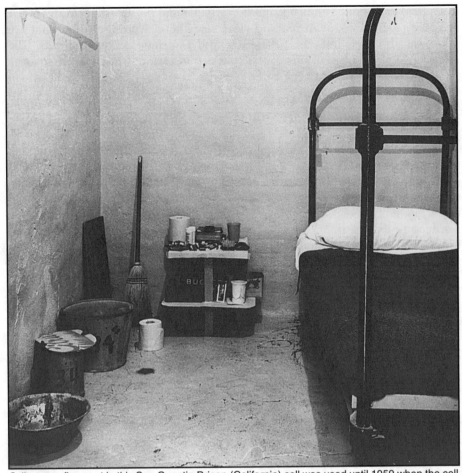

Solitary confinement in this San Quentin Prison (California) cell was used until 1959 when the cell was demolished. Beginning in the late 1940s, California became a national leader in advocating rehabilitation as the main purpose of corrections. Do you believe this is still an important purpose of prisons? —*Photo courtesy of the California History Section, California State Library.*

crowding in prisons became worse, courts intervened in many other states. By 1975 Alabama, with a prison population more than double the rated capacity, was prevented from accepting any more prisoners. Specific standards were spelled out, which had to be met before the state accepted additional inmates. These included guidelines on living space, staffing, visiting privileges, the racial composition of staff, and food service changes.[55]

Prison crowding alone does not automatically lead the courts to conclude that the punishment provided is cruel and unusual. Prisoners in an Ohio maximum security prison claimed that double bunking of prisoners serving long terms is cruel and unusual. They complained that the prison population was far above its design capacity, that cell sizes were below standards, and that prisoners spent too much time in their cells. The federal district court agreed,[56] and so did the Court of Appeals.[57] The Supreme Court, however, reversed the finding and said that the claims fell far short of establishing cruel and unusual punishment. In order to succeed in such a claim, the Court said, the prisoners must demonstrate that the punishment either "inflicts unnecessary or wanton pain" or is "grossly disproportionate to the severity of the crime warranting punishment."[58] It must be determined that the crowding results in deprivation of basic human needs, resulting in "wanton pain."

Not all "cruel and unusual punishment" arguments have been rejected by the courts. A deliberate indifference to prisoners' medical needs is cruel and unusual punishment.[59] Confinement in a segregation cell for an extended period of time may be cruel and unusual punishment.[60] Use of excessive force by guards may be cruel and unusual punishment even if it does not result in serious injury.[61]

Fourteenth Amendment Rights

Most litigation in the 1970s focused on the procedural due process rights of prisoners. Traditionally, prison officials regularly made decisions on punishments for rules infractions without any clear standards. A Supreme Court precedent in a nonprison case in 1970 influenced later cases, extending procedural safeguards to prison discipline. The Court ruled that benefits to welfare recipients could not be simply revoked, holding that, when a grievous loss is at stake, certain minimum due process requirements exist. These include, said the court, the following: a timely and adequate notice of the charge; an opportunity to be heard; a right to confront and cross-examine adverse witnesses; the right to retain an attorney; an impartial decision maker; and a statement of reasons for the determination and an indication of evidence relied upon.[62] Some federal district courts used this ruling as a basis for finding that prisoners cannot be disciplined severely or transferred to other institutions; but most did not.[63]

The Supreme Court has been reluctant to impose restrictions on prison officials. It concluded, in a case brought by an inmate who had had "good time" credits taken away because of rule infractions, that certain due process protections applied. This did not include, however, all those formulated in the case of the welfare recipients even when the prisoners were deprived of liberty through solitary confinement or loss of good time. As summarized by Kranz, the Court:

> limited the procedural rights of prisoners to the right to written notice of an alleged violation; the right to call witnesses and present documentary evidence unless prison officials concluded that this would be unduly hazardous to institutional safety or correctional goals; and the right to a written statement of the fact finders as to the evidence relied upon and the reasons for the disciplinary action taken. The Court stressed that prisons and prisoners are dangerous and that the prison environment is replete with tension, frustration, resentment, and despair, and concluded that more extensive safeguards would jeopardize "valid correctional goals." Two years later . . . the Court refused to apply even these limited safeguards to transfers from one prison to another.[64]

Despite these limitations, the Court established in this case a number of procedures to which prisoners now are entitled at disciplinary hearings.

Summary

The use of jails and prisons as punishments began in America only after the revolutionary war. Appalled by brutally severe corporal punishments, reformers established penitentiaries in which isolation and solitude, strictly enforced, was expected to lead to the repentance of the offender. This movement was replaced by a reformatory movement. Institutions would not provide merely vindictive suffering but would reform criminals through education and development of good work habits. Sentences became indeterminate, with the offender to be released when ready to be law-abiding. This concept was reinforced and modified with the advent of the social sciences and support of the idea that the offender should be diagnosed, treated, and conditionally released at the best time for successful adjustment in the community without law violations. As the use of this model reached its peak in the 1950s and 1960s, more emphasis was placed on the reintegration of the offender back into the community. This was followed, however, by increased emphasis on deserved punishment and incapacitation as sentencing goals, with less importance given to rehabilitation and reintegration.

Goals of corrections have changed in emphasis from penitence and reform to rehabilitation and reintegration and then to restraint. The decline in stress on rehabilitation was due to perceptions of ineffectiveness of treatment and of indeterminate sentencing, increased political "get tough" rhetoric, concerns about fairness, and more emphasis on concepts of deserved punishment and deterrence. The goals of reformation, rehabilitation and reintegration—in addition to restraint—nevertheless continue to guide correctional practice, even if to a lesser degree.

One result of these changes has been an alarming growth of jail and prison populations, particularly of minority group members, drug offenders, serious offenders, and women. More offenders convicted of violent crimes now are in prison, despite recent decreases in admissions of these offenders. The mix of prison populations differs from that at admissions, because it is affected by lengths of sentences. Because of the sharp rise in inmate populations, due to increases in both rates of imprisonment and length of sentences, many jails and prisons are crowded beyond capacity, and many more are under court orders because of constitutional violations.

Goals of institutional corrections include security, treatment, incapacitation, and organizational maintenance. Decisions by correctional staff related to these goals are many, frequent, and complex. Some of the most important ones are those related to classification and assignment for security, custody, and treatment.

Until recently, information for inmate classification in most jurisdictions has been limited to the subjective judgments of staff, with accompanying unreliability, ineffectiveness, and questionable fairness. Many institutions now use more objective and reliable procedures for many of these decisions. Methods of classification, using information intended to provide means for more rational and effective decisions, are of central importance to correctional management.

The length of time served in prison often is thought to have a specific deterrent effect. This is not supported by the studies available which show that time served has little relation to repeated offending.

Traditionally, courts maintained a "hands-off" policy about prison administration. That changed in the late 1960s and 1970s, with the prisoners' rights movement and intervention by the courts. Many of the protections of the Bill of Rights now apply to prisoners, but courts still have been reluctant to impose requirements on prison administrators that restrict their ability to maintain security and custody.

Alternatives to punishment by confinement in jails and prisons already are in place to some degree with persons under the jurisdiction of jails and prisons. About 6 percent of jail inmates are supervised in the community on work or educational release or another community program, and many prison programs include work furloughs for some minimum custody inmates. Most such programs, however, are operated as part of probation or parole programs, considered in the next chapter.

Notes

1. Flynn, E. E. (1983). "Jails," in Kadish, S. H., (ed.). *Encyclopedia of Crime and Justice*, Vol. 3. New York: The Free Press, 915, citing Barnes, H. E., and Teeters, N. K. (1959). *New Horizons in Criminology*, 3rd ed. Englewood Cliffs, NJ: Prentice-Hall, 460.

2. Flynn, E. E. (1983), 915; Orland, L. (1975). *Prisons: Houses of Darkness*. New York: The Free Press, 17.

3. Flynn, E. E. (1983), citing Jordan, P. D. (1970). "The Close and Stinking Jail," in *Frontier Law and Order: Ten Essays*. Lincoln: University of Nebraska Press, 140–154.

4. Flynn, E. E. (1983), citing Rothman, D. J. (1971). *The Discovery of the Asylum: Social Order and Disorder in the New Republic*. Boston: Little, Brown.

5. Orland, L. (1975). *Prisons: Houses of Darkness*. New York: The Free Press, 14–15.

6. Orland, L. (1975), 17, citing Rymer, *De Commissione Speciali pro Condempnatis ad Galleas Transferendis*, tom. XVI, at 446.

7. Orland, L. (1975), *Prisons: Houses of Darkness*. New York: The Free Press, 18.

8. Ibid., 19.

9. Orland, L. (1975), 21, citing IV Blackstone, *Commentaries* 753 (1892).

10. Orland, L. (1975), *Prisons: Houses of Darkness*. New York: The Free Press, 21–33.

11. Bailey, W. C. (1966). "Correctional Outcome: An Evaluation of 100 Reports," *Journal of Criminal Law, Criminology, and Police Science* 57:153–160; Kassebaum, G., Ward, A., and Wilner, D. M. (1971). *Prison Treatment and Parole Survival*. New York: Wiley; Lipton, D., Martinson, R., and Wilks, J. (1975). *The Effectiveness of Correctional Treatment: A Survey of Evaluation Studies*. New York: Praeger; Martinson, R. (1974). "What Works? Questions and Answers about Prison Reform," *The Public Interest* 35:22; McCord, J. (1978). "A Thirty Year Follow-Up of Treatment Effects," *American Psychologist* 33:284.

12. Stephan, J. J. (1997). *Census of State and Federal Correctional Facilities, 1995*. Washington, DC: U.S. Department of Justice, Office of Justice Programs, 1–20.

13. Stephan, J. J. and Snell, T. L. (1996). *Capital Punishment 1994*. Washington, DC: Bureau of Justice Statistics.

14. Mumola, C. J. and Beck, A. J. (1997). *Prisoners in 1996*. U.S. Department of Justice, Office of Justice Programs, 1–2.

15. Ibid., 1.

16. Ibid., 3.

17. Ibid., 2.

18. Gilliard, D. K. and Beck, A. J. (1996). *Prison and Jail Inmates, 1995*. Washington, DC: Bureau of Justice Statistics, 13.

19. Mumola, C. J. and Beck, A. J. (1997), *Prisoners in 1996*. U.S. Department of Justice, Office of Justice Programs, 9–10.

20. Snell, T. L. (1996). *Capital Punishment 1995*. Washington, D.C.: Bureau of Justice Statistics, 1.

21. Burnham, R. W. (1975). "Modern Decision Theory and Corrections," in Gottfredson, D. M., (ed.) *Decision-Making in the Criminal Justice System: Reviews and Essays*, ch. 7. Washington, DC: GPO, 93–94.

22. Brennan, T. (1987). "Classification for Control in Jails and Prisons," in Gottfredson, D. M., and Tonry, M., (eds.). *Prediction and Classification: Criminal Justice Decision Making*. Chicago: University of Chicago Press, 340–342.

23. Stan Repko, Director, New Jersey Department of Corrections, personal communication, August 1996.

24. Brennan, T. (1987), "Classification for Control in Jails and Prisons," in Gottfredson, D. M., and Tonry, M., (eds.). *Prediction and Classification: Criminal Justice Decision Making*. Chicago: University of Chicago Press, 343–344.

25. Ibid., 325–330.

26. Glaser, D. (1964). *The Effectiveness of a Prison and Parole System*. New York: Bobbs-Merril, 302–303.

27. Department of Institutions, State of Washington (1967). *Research Monograph No. 27*. Olympia: Department of Institutions, State of Washington.

28. Department of Corrections, State of California (1967). *Long Jail Terms and Parole Outcome*. Sacramento: Department of Corrections, State of California.

29. Assembly Committee on Criminal Procedure (1968). Sacramento: Assembly of the State of California, 32.

30. Kolodney, S. (1970). *Parole Board Reform in California: Order out of Chaos: Report to the Select Committee on the Administration of Justice*. Sacramento: Assembly of the State of California.

31. Gottfredson, D. M., Neithercutt, Nuffield, J., and O'Leary, V. (1973). *Four Thousand Lifetimes: A Study of Time Served in Prison and Parole Outcomes*. Davis, CA: National Council on Crime and Delinquency.

32. Gottfredson, D. M., Gottfredson, M. R., and Garafalo. (1977). "Time Served in Prison and Parole Outcomes among Parolee Risk Categories," *Journal of Criminal Justice* 5, 1.

33. Blumstein, Alfred. (1995). "Prisons," in Wilson, James Q. and Petersilia, J. (eds.). *Crime*. San Francisco: Institute for Contemporary Studies, 416–417.

34. Stephan, J. J. (1995), *Census of State and Federal Correctional Facilities, 1995*. Washington, DC: U.S. Department of Justice, Office of Justice Programs, 7.

35. *Ruffin v. Commonwealth* (1871), 62 VA, (21 Gratt.) 790, 796 as cited by Kranz, S. (1983) "Legal Rights of Prisoners," in Kadish, S. H. (1983), 1191.

36. *Coffin v. Reichard* (1944). 143 F. 2nd 443 (6th Cir.) as cited by Kranz, S. (1983), 1191.

37. *Gore v. United States* (1958) 357 U.S. 386.

38. Civil Rights Act of 1871, 42 U.S.C. Sec 1983 (1976 & Supp. iv 1980).

39. *Cooper v. Pate* (1964). 378 U.S. 546.

40. Kranz, S. (1983), "Legal Rights of Prisoners." In Kadish, S.H. (1983) *Encyclopedia of Crime and Justice*, vol. 3, p. 1192. New York: The Free Press.

41. *Lee v. Washington* (1968). 390 U.S. 333.

42. *Johnson v. Avery* (1969) 393 U.S. 483.

43. Kranz, S. (1983), "Legal Rights of Prisoners." In Kadish, S.H. (1983) *Encyclopedia of Crime and Justice*, vol. 3, p. 1192. New York: The Free Press.

44. Gottfredson, D. M., personal observation (circa 1970).

45. *Holt v. Sarver* (1970). 309 F. Supp. 362 (E. D. Ark. 1970), aff'd, 442 F. 2nd 304 (8th Cir.) 1971.

46. *Palmigiano v. Travisono* (1970) 317 F. Supp. 776 (D.R.I. 1970.

47. *Procunier v. Martinez* (1974). 416 U.S. 396.

48. *Theriault v. Carlson* (1972) 339 F. Supp. 375 (N. D. Ga. vacated, 495 F. 2nd 390 (5th Cir.) 1974.

49. *Cruz v. Beto* (1972). 405 U.S. 319.

50. *In re Harrell* (1970) 87 Cal. Rptr. 504, 470 p. 2nd 640.

51. *O'Brien v. United States* (1967) 386 U.S. 345; *Weatherford v. Bursey* (1977) 429 U.S. 545.

52. *Taylor v. Sterrett* (1976) 532 F. 2nd. 462 (5th Cir.).

53. *Bounds v. Smith* (1977) 430 U. S. 817, 821.

54. *Jackson v. Bishop* (1968). 404 F. 2nd 571 (8th Cir.).

55. Schmalleger, F. (1994). *Criminal Justice: A Brief Introduction,* 2nd ed. Upper Saddle River, NJ: Prentice-Hall, 390–391.

56. *Chapman v. Rhodes* (1977). 434 F. Supp. 1007 (S. D. Ohio).

57. *Chapman v. Rhodes* (1980). 624 F. 2nd 1099 (6th Cir.).

58. *Rhodes v. Chapman* (1981). 452 U.S. 337.

59. *Estelle v. Gamble* (1976). 429 U.S. 97.

60. *Hutto v. Finney* (1978). 437 U.S. 678.

61. *Hudson v. McMillian (1992). 112 S. Ct. 995, 117 L. Ed. 2nd 156.*

62. *Goldberg v. Kelly* (1970). 397 U.S. 254 as summarized by Kranz, S., 1193–1194.

63. Kranz, S. (1983), "Legal Rights of Prisoners." In Kadish, S.H. (1983) *Encyclopedia of Crime and Justice*, vol. 3, p. 1194. New York: The Free Press.

64. Ibid., 1194.

Corrections in the Community: Probation and Parole

Themis, Goddess of Justice.

Chapter Eleven

Most convicted and sentenced offenders are not in jails or prisons. Rather, they are on probation or parole. How this came about, and how community corrections is changing, are topics discussed in this chapter. The goals, choices, and information needs of judges, parole boards, and probation and parole staff will be examined. Because of criticisms, many changes in sentencing and in probation and paroling procedures have taken place. Other changes, including an increased use of intermediate punishments—between probation and prison in severity—are now taking place.

Does parole shorten a sentence?

Is parole leniency?

Do most probationers successfully complete their sentences?

What are the goals of probation and of parole?

What alternative probation programs are available to the judge?

What is the optimal probation or parole caseload size?

Can a probation officer revoke probation? Can a parole officer revoke parole?

What influences a judge considering probation?

What are the goals of parole boards?

Would parole boards ever knowingly parole prisoners they see as poor risks?

What have been the main criticisms of parole boards?

How should parole boards be evaluated?

What are the goals of probation and parole supervision?

Should offenders be classified for different kinds of community supervision?

Does community supervision work?

What is meant by "intermediate sanctions"?

The judge made a curious demand of the prisoner. He was asked to read the 51st Psalm. The time was the thirteenth century, the place was England, the crime was theft. Unable to read, the convicted felon recited the psalm from memory, saying in part: "Have mercy on me, O God, . . . For I acknowledge my transgressions, and my sin is ever before me. . . . Create in me a clean heart. . . . Then I will teach transgressors thy ways; and sinners shall be converted unto thee." He had memorized the passage as if his life depended on it—it did.

A plea for forgiveness and mercy, an admission of wrongdoing, and a promise to do better were contained in the passage. It became known as the "neck verse," because those who could read or recite it were excused from their crimes by "benefit of clergy." In the time of William the Conqueror, churches had been given the authority to try members of the ordained clergy who had violated the criminal law. Lay citizens soon discovered they could become honorary church functionaries, thereby taking advantage of the greater leniency of ecclesiastic justice than that current in the King's courts. Benefit of clergy later was extended to all who could read the passage. Those thereby excused, however, were branded on their thumbs in order that the privilege could be granted only once. One strike and you're out.

The practice of benefit of clergy was later granted routinely to all, and it persisted in both England and the colonies until about 1827. It was abandoned only when the state established its clear preeminence over the church in the criminal law jurisdiction.[1]

The link of this practice to present-day probation and parole is weak, but the early American statutes authorizing the suspension of sentences if the convicted offender demonstrated good behavior may stem in part from this and related precedents. Probation developed with a clearly rehabilitative aim in early days in New England, and parole followed with the advent of the indeterminate sentence and the reformatory movement.

Probation and Parole

The concepts of probation and parole, which cover most of what now is called community corrections, are distinctly different yet often confused. Probation is traditionally a conditional release from custody without incarceration, and parole typically is a mode of conditional release from prison.[2]

Probation is a term that comes from the Latin *"probatus"* (meaning tested or proved) and refers to a procedure by which a convicted person is released, without imprisonment and usually without jail confinement, subject to conditions imposed by the court. Typically, the placement on probation occurs after imposition of a sentence to prison, but the sentence is suspended. The decision is made by the sentencing judge.

The conditions imposed, which must be agreed to by the offender, usually include supervision (surveillance, counseling, or other services) in the community by a probation officer. Violation of the conditions can lead to the execution by the court of the sentence of confinement imposed earlier. Thus, probation is a part of the decision made by the judge at the time of sentencing. This does not necessarily mean that the prisoner will not be confined at all; a condition permitted in most jurisdictions is that some time must be served in jail (called a "split sentence"). Probation is a judicial stay of sentence, a program placement with imposed supervision, and a conditional release into the community.

Parole is a word that derives from the French *"parole d'honneuer"* (meaning word of honor). It refers traditionally to a conditional release from prison by a discretionary act of a parole board and to imposed supervision in the community.

The conditions are agreed to by the prisoner. Thus, the paroled offender is allowed to serve out the remainder of his or her term under supervision in the community and outside the prison if the specified conditions are met. Otherwise, the person can be returned to prison by the paroling authority after it has received and reviewed reports from the supervising parole officers.

Both probation and parole are terms sometimes confused also with related concepts: pardon, reprieve, clemency, and commutation. These have different meanings in the criminal law and refer to discretionary powers of a chief executive (a president or governor). A pardon relieves the person of punishment, or of further punishment. A reprieve merely postpones the execution of a sentence. Clemency forgives the person from criminal liability. Commutation shortens or lessens a sentence.

Usually, probation is an alternative to confinement in jail or prison, and parole is a release from prison under supervision. There are many differences, however, among jurisdictions in the legal structures and practices of probation and parole. As a result, exceptions to nearly any general definitions may be found. Sometimes probation is imposed by an informal agreement by which prosecution is suspended with the understanding that if probation is completed successfully, the charges will be dropped. In some jurisdictions, the judge may suspend the imposition (the announcing) of the sentence, although the more usual practice is to suspend its execution (carrying it out).

In the case of both probation and parole, any line between institutional and community corrections is blurred by the use of confinement in halfway houses, by periodic short-term confinement in jail or prisons during probation or parole supervision, by the occasional placement of state prisoners on probation, and (rarely) by parole from jail by local authorities.

Probation

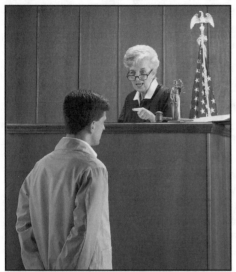

Here, a judge suspends a sentence to prison, placing the convicted offender on probation. If he violates the law or other conditions of probation the judge may execute the prison sentence. What do you expect are the main reasons for the judge's decisions in such situations? —*Photo courtesy of www.digitalstock.com.*

Probation as now practiced is traced to the volunteer work of a shoemaker in Boston with a habit of attending court. In August of 1841, he asked the judge to let him take care of a drunken misdemeanant about to be jailed. Three weeks later, John Augustus was back in court with the offender, whose apparent reformation impressed the judge to the extent that he fined him one cent and let him go. For the next 18 years, Augustus voluntarily supervised more than 2,000 persons.[3]

The volunteer work of Augustus and others led in 1878 to the passage in Massachusetts of the first probation law.[4] The concept of probation spread with the creation of the juvenile court in Chicago in 1899; and by 1900 six states had passed probation statutes. By 1940 all states had similar procedures for juvenile offenders and all but six had statutes permitting probation for adults.[5] By the early 1980s, all states and the federal government had probation for at least some kinds of offenders.

More than two-thirds of the convicted offenders under correctional supervision were on probation or parole in 1994 (Box 11.1). There were 2.8 million persons on probation. About 20 percent were women. About two-thirds of adults on probation were white, and 32 percent were black. Six out of 10 persons discharged from probation had completed their sentences without having been declared probation violators.[6]

Box 11.1
Community Corrections Facts

- More than two-thirds of offenders under correctional supervision are on probation or parole.

- There are nearly 3 million persons on probation.

- Most probationers are white males.

- Most persons discharged from probation have completed their sentences without being declared violators.

Parole

Walter Crofton, a speaker at the 1870 meeting of what now is the American Correctional Association, had been in charge of the Irish prison system.[7] He advocated reform of the individual as a purpose of imprisonment, with release dependent upon progress in reformation. He went even farther by urging that "tickets of leave" be given to those prisoners who showed a change in attitude. A prisoner given a ticket of leave was released under supervision in the community. Those released by a ticket of leave were supervised either by police or, in Dublin, by an inspector of released prisoners who had the duty of finding them work. Thus, parole at its beginning was tied to the concepts of offender reformation and the indeterminate sentence. Tickets of leave had been originated by Alexander Maconochie, who was in charge of an English penal colony in Australia, Norfolk Island. They were first used in 1840 in the program of transporting prisoners from England to Australia, where they were part of a plan for steadily decreasing supervision and control as the convicted person progressed through the sentence: imprisonment, then chain gangs, then freedom within a limited area, next a ticket of leave, and finally full restoration of liberty.

In Ireland's prisons, prisoners received marks for good conduct and achievement in education and industry. As early as 1832 in Ireland, there had been advocates of a fully indeterminate sentence, arguing that prisoners "should not be turned loose upon society again until they had given some indication that they are prepared to live without a repetition of their offenses."[8]

The "Declaration of Principles" adopted by the prison administrators attending the 1870 meeting of the American Correctional Association reflected the concepts of the progressive classification of prisoners. The ticket of leave evolved gradually into the concept of parole. In the next half century or so, all the states and the federal government adopted it.

By the end of 1979, there were nearly 200,000 parolees released from prison by discretionary decisions of paroling authorities in all of the states, the federal system, the District of Columbia, Puerto Rico, and the American Virgin Islands. Until the late 1970s, the use of parole as a mode of release from prison steadily increased. For example, it rose during 1965 to 1977 from about 60 percent to 72 percent of all released prisoners. Thereafter, it decreased because of the growth of determinate sentencing and conditional releases that were not results

---

Box 11.2

Facts about Paroling

- All states, the federal government, Puerto Rico, and the American Virgin Islands until recently had parole boards with discretionary release authority.

- Most states still have parole boards and discretionary parole release, but a substantial number do not, including the federal system. Parole boards in 12 states and the U.S. Parole Commission have been abolished.

- About 700,000 persons are on parole.

- Many people now under parole supervision have not been released by a parole board's decision.

- About half the persons on parole were released from prison by a discretionary act of a parole board. The others were required to be released under supervision.

of discretionary acts by parole boards.[9]

As we have seen, a dozen states and the federal government no longer have parole as a discretionary release decision, although the postrelease supervision function has been retained in all but four states. Despite this decline in numbers of jurisdictions with discretionary release by a paroling authority, there still were an estimated 690,000 persons on parole at the end of 1994, which was an increase of 2 percent from the year before. The number of adults on parole had tripled from 1980 to 1984. About half the entries to parole were based on a discretionary parole board decision; the rest were required to be released from prison under supervision (see Box 11.2).[10]

Probation and Parole Structures

The governmental organizations for probation and parole are different. Parole board decisions, and parole supervision, are generally state functions. Probation placement decisions are made by judges and supervision is typically a county function. Parole supervision agencies are usually a part of a department of corrections; probation supervision agencies are arms of the court. Probation is usually a local court supervision program, while parole typically is a state corrections supervision operation. Because the decision-making structures are different, we will first look at an overview for probation, then for parole, even though the general goals, alternatives, and information needs are similar. Then we will discuss a variety of community programs that are used with either structure.

Goals of Probation Placements

The use of probation began as an alternative to confinement justified occasionally on economic grounds but mainly by the prospect of the offender's reformation. Later, it was justified also on the grounds that prisons failed to accomplish their stated purpose of rehabilitation and that long sentences produced prison crowding and, consequently, security and disciplinary problems. Now it is more often justified also by high costs of incarceration and lack of prison resources. Some argue that it is more effective in crime prevention.

The aim of probation always has been utilitarian, with two main purposes aimed at crime reduction. The first is to reform the offender, thus reducing crime. The second is to refer violators back to the court for possible incarceration, thus possibly preventing crime.

This mix of treatment and control functions—of counseling and other services along with surveillance and rule enforcement—is inherently filled with conflict, which has plagued probation throughout much of its history.[11] The question often asked is whether a supervisor can be effective as "part cop and part social worker." The probation or parole officer traditionally has functions of both control and treatment.

The behavior of the probationer or parolee is expected to be monitored, and this role of the supervisor is similar to that of police. Probation and parole officers can and do respond to reports of crime and calls for assistance, investigate crimes, make unannounced visits for surveillance, make arrests or work with police in this role, seize illegal weapons and contraband, assist witnesses, appear in court to testify, enforce court orders concerning their charges, and perform many other law enforcement duties. Following established rules or at their own discretion, they may refer probationers back to court or parolees back to the parole board for consideration of revocation of the probation or parole status.

Parole and probation officers also can and do provide individual counseling services directly. They also make referrals to treatment programs and other services, conduct group counseling sessions, give assistance in obtaining employment, provide help in obtaining financial aid, and render or arrange many other services to probationers and parolees.

That the main aim of probation and parole is in crime prevention does not mean there is no punishment. Probation involves a restriction of liberty and may include a variety of required activities, some of which may seem a more harsh punishment to the offender than confinement. This is true especially of some intensive supervision programs today, which may have demanding requirements. Punishment, however, has not traditionally been a purpose. The general aim of probation has always been crime reduction rather than retribution.

The concept of prediction is central to the idea of probation, because an emphasis traditionally has been placed on the selection of "good risks" for assignment to probation. When a judge chooses probation, it usually means that the judge believes the offender can stay in the community under supervision without law violations, and that supervision is expected to further increase the likelihood that the offender will not offend again. The placement of a person on probation may reflect any of the general aims of sentencing—general deterrence, incapacitation, treatment, or just desert—but writings on probation since its beginnings suggest mainly the goal of treatment for offenders who are seen as good prospects for rehabilitation.

The goal of crime reduction is to be achieved not only through rehabilitation efforts but also by the prevention of new offenses by the incapacitation of the violator when probation is revoked. The main perceived objective of probation has been to decrease the probability of further offending. This is to be accomplished by counseling and other services to the probationer. Providing treatment and services only is not regarded as adequately protecting the community, however; and supervision is intended also to have a control function. This is evident in the attention given to surveillance. Thus, if rule violations are demonstrated, then the court may impose the sentence suspended earlier and imprison the violator. Alternatively, the court may change the conditions of probation and may require a short stay in jail, impose other punishments, or add other requirements.

Probation Conditions

When a judge places a convicted offender on probation, there always are general conditions that apply to all probationers, and the judge also may add special or specific conditions. The offender must agree to abide by the conditions set by the judge. If the court finds that the conditions were not met, the sentence previously suspended may be executed.

General conditions typically include rules such as obeying all laws, not possessing weapons, remaining in the county, reporting to the probation officer as required, maintaining steady employment, notifying the probation officer of any change in employment or residence, and similar conditions that apply to all probationers.

Special conditions may be tailored by the judge to the individual case. The court may require, for example, that the probationer submit to warrantless searches of the person, residence, or car, prohibit the use of alcohol or nonprescription drugs, or submit to tests for alcohol or drug use. Other frequent conditions are payments of restitution or fines, completion of community service orders, or participation in specific counseling, drug or alcohol abuse programs, and other treatments. Another requirement may be that part of the probationary period will be spent in jail, boot camp, or house arrest.

Goals of Probation Supervision

After the offender has been placed on probation, what are the goals of probation supervision? Most important are treatment, control, and organizational maintenance. The first two are the same as the goals of the sentencing judge. The treatment aim has been a basic purpose since John Augustus, more than a century and a half ago, first persuaded the court to release offenders to him. The control function is reflected in the attention given to surveillance. It is seen also in recommendations to the court that probation be revoked or conditions changed when thought necessary by the probation officer. A third goal, as with all organizations, is continuing or enhancing the organization.

Alternatives to Probation

The main alternative to the selection of probation by the judge is incarceration—usually in a state prison, sometimes in a county jail. Under current laws, there are other alternatives to confinement in many jurisdictions, although most are but rarely used. A notable alternative, besides a simple suspension of the sentence, is the fine. Others are community service orders, house arrest, electronic monitoring programs, intermittent (part-time) incarceration, and restitution.

Because placement on probation is a result of a judicial decision at the time of sentencing, knowledge of the factors influencing that decision comes from studies of sentencing. Probation usually is one alternative at the sentencing hearing. Increasingly, with more frequent passage by legislators of requirements of mandatory sentencing to prison for specific kinds of convictions, the judge's discretion to grant probation is reduced. Legislatures often have decided that probation may not be granted for some specific offenses.

There are differences among jurisdictions in how probation is used. For example, in some places, probation may be a state-run program, at least for intensive supervision. Programs intended to provide other alternatives to confinement, such as restitution or community service, may sometimes be the sole sentence imposed by the court. In others, it can be used only with probation supervision. These programs or penalties—as well as required drug testing, attendance at narcotics or alcohol treatment programs, or other requirements—typically are made special conditions of probation. That is the usual procedure in most jurisdictions.

Probation Supervision Alternatives

After an offender has been placed on probation by a judge, probation officers must make decisions about control and treatment. First, the extent and intensity of supervision and surveillance must be established; second, the kind of supervision or treatment must be decided. Most probation departments have classifications of control ranging from minimum through medium and intensive, with corresponding differences in frequency of expected contacts and sizes of caseloads—the number of offenders to be supervised by an officer. For treatment, requirements of drug testing, drug and alcohol treatment programs, and counseling are common.

Because there are broad differences in administrative structures, government subdivision, geography, economics, and legal frameworks of probation supervision programs, the resources available to probation administrators vary widely. Nevertheless, some issues of classification and assignment of probationers are important everywhere. They have received much attention nationally and now are regarded as essential for improving the effectiveness and efficiency of probation management.

One of those issues is the size of caseloads to which probationers (or parolees) should be assigned. A related concern is that of different classifications for varying levels of supervision. The first question is whether there is an optimal caseload size for probation supervision. The second, discussed later in this chapter, is whether differing levels of intensity of supervision are appropriate for differing classifications of probationers or parolees.

Caseload Size

Whether the size of the caseload of probation or parole officers affects the later success or failure of the persons supervised has been examined in many studies. Authoritative pronouncements however often have been made about the optimal or required caseload size—on the basis of no evidence whatever. Examples are influential early statements since the 1920s that no probation officer should have more than 50 cases, the inclusion of this standard in the 1954 Manual of Correctional Standards of the American Correctional Association, and its endorsement in 1962 by the National Council on Crime and Delinquency. The President's Commission of Law Enforcement and Administration of Justice in 1967 reduced this value to an average of 35. Other prestigious groups have similarly pronounced standards on the basis of absolutely no evidence of effectiveness.

Such pronouncements provide good examples of how public policy is sought to be shaped by claims made with no basis in evidence. They serve political purposes—for example, by helping managers obtain resources to improve programs. They have some basis in management experience, however; officers obviously cannot do the jobs expected if caseloads are too large. Any specific caseload size, however, cannot be justified as definitely required for more effective practice.

Two assertions may be made with confidence. First, no optimal caseload size has been demonstrated. Second, no clear evidence of reduced crime, simply from reduced caseload size, has been found.[12]

Placement on probation results from a decision by a judge, but other actors in the criminal justice system contribute to it. Given the extensive use of plea and sentence bargaining, as we have seen in previous chapters, the roles of the prosecutor and of the defense attorney in shaping the judge's decision cannot be ignored. Probation staff may be influential also; the judge often is informed of details of the offense, prior criminal record, social history, and other data about the offense and offender by a presentence investigation report completed by the probation service. This is another important part of the probation officer's role. The report is customary in felony cases but rare for misdemeanants. Jurisdictions differ in the presentence services available, and the extent and quality of the information provided is apt to be different from one place to another. In large jurisdictions, there often is a specialized unit for the preparation of the presentence reports, and probation officers may be assigned full-time to this activity. In other places, each probation officer may have, as part of the job of supervision, the investigation, interviewing, and writing that is required for these reports.

One study of the relation between the probation officer's recommendations and the decisions of judges about probation found that when probation was recommended, it usually was granted.[13] It may be that the probation officers and the judges were using similar information to arrive at similar conclusions, but there was considerable variation in proportions of persons granted probation by different courts, and this seemed to be associated with differences among the probation officers.

In research on sentencing decisions, two factors have emerged as most important for the decision whether probation will be granted: the seriousness of the crime and the nature and gravity of the offender's prior criminal record. The judge's estimate of the likelihood of repeated offending by the offender also plays a part.[14]

Box 11.3

Factors Influencing Judges' Placement on Probation

- The seriousness of the crime.

- The extent of the prior criminal record.

- The seriousness of the prior criminal record.

- The perceived risk of new crimes by the offender.

When a probation officer reports to the court with an allegation of probation violation, the judge must decide whether to revoke the probation order and execute the sentence suspended earlier—imposing the term of confinement—or to continue the offender on probation, perhaps with other or additional conditions or brief jail confinement. Given the importance of the probation revocation decision, it is unfortunate that there are few studies to inform us about how these decisions are made. The criteria used are not the same across various jurisdictions and they may differ even among judges in the same court system. Similarly, the conditions specified at the time of placement on probation may differ widely among jurisdictions. They may result from judges' seeking to match specific conditions to the individual features of individual offenders or offenses.

Because of the prominence of prediction in probation decision making, both in selecting those fit for probation and in revoking probation with the aim of preventing crime, it is surprising that there have been so few studies of probation prediction—research aimed at predicting which offenders will succeed or fail on probation. Most of the relevant literature, which has a long history, deals with parole prediction. When studies have been done, it generally has been found that information on the nature of the offense, the prior criminal record, the offender's age, and a few other items may be combined to provide classifications of persons with different probabilities of probation success. Such probation prediction measures have been used only rarely in making probation decisions, which continue to rely mainly on the subjective predictions by judges.

Parole Board Goals

As with probation decisions, the utilitarian aims of treatment and incapacitation have been the primary goals of parole decision making. These clearly have not been the only goals, however. All the objectives of sentencing have been involved also in deciding whether a prisoner will be released on parole. Besides the usual goals of the sentencing decision, the decision whether to parole may involve consideration of the control of the prison and the parole system. It may reflect a somewhat different perspective on fairness and equity in punishment. Although paroling often has been criticized as mere leniency, the paroling decision actually emphasizes crime reduction through incapacitation, general deterrence, rehabilitation, and prison control.

Further insight into the goals of paroling decisions and their complexity was provided in O'Leary's six "frames of reference" or value systems commonly demonstrated by parole decision makers.[15] These six types of concerns differ among jurisdictions and among individual parole board members within a single jurisdiction, but they may be important to all paroling authorities in varying degrees. An individual board member may of course have all these concerns, but one or more may be emphasized. The first two value systems reflect concerns related to the desert aims of punishment; the other four reflect utilitarian goals and perceived expectations of the public. The frames of reference are as follows:

- The **jurist** value system is related to parole board members' concerns with due process, rules of evidence, impartiality, fairness, and equity.

- The **sanctioner** value system reflects a concern that the severity of an assigned penalty is proportional to the seriousness of the crime.

- The **treater** orientation is concerned that the offender be dealt with in a manner that lessens that person's propensity to commit crimes.

- The **controller** frame of reference addresses the risk that a paroled prisoner will commit new crimes.

- The **citizen** orientation focuses on the expectations of the citizenry regarding the appropriate handling of offenders.

- The **regulator** value system is sensitive to the potential impact of paroling decisions on the prison and parole system.

Besides specific aims consistent with the sentencing goals of retribution, incapacitation, deterrence, and rehabilitation, parole decision making often has various "latent functions" or unofficial goals. Three of these have to do with equity and control of prisons. The equity concern is to reduce differences in sentencing seen as unwarranted—that is, to reduce unfairness in sentencing by the courts. The prison control functions have two aspects. One is the control of inmate behavior, and the other is the control of institutional population sizes.

Observation of parole hearings and discussions with parole board members show that parole board members often value the role of the parole board in correcting unwarranted disparities in court sentencing. Examples of sources of such disparities often include differences between rural and urban reactions to some similar offenses; differences in reactions by different judges; and variations in the success of plea bargaining for a reduction in charges by the prosecution. Parole authorities often claim that the board is in a unique position to correct such inequities, because the board regularly reviews the results of sentencing by the full variety of judges throughout the state. Moreover, it is argued, the board can take account of all aspects of the offense behavior in addition to the legal offense of conviction. For example, although a pistol was used in a theft, the crime may, as a result of plea bargaining, be classified at conviction as larceny. The conviction for larceny rather than robbery may make a difference in the constraints on the decision by the parole board. The board may be able to release earlier and may be prohibited from holding the offender for as long. But within the legal constraints, the parole board will treat the offense as a robbery.

The potential provided by the parole process in controlling behavior in institutions often is argued to be an important function. Although procedures vary among jurisdictions, parole boards often play a role in the awarding or withholding of "good time." The withholding of parole often is seen as an important sanction without which prison management would be made more difficult.

The paroling function also may be important as a "safety valve" to help control the levels of prison populations in relation to capacities and thus to avoid the dangers and costs of crowding. In some jurisdictions, boards have been directed by courts to speed up parole for some offenders in order to relieve prison crowding. A state governor may hint strongly to the politically appointed board that the prison population should be reduced. In other places, programs of early parole for selected offenders have been designed with the explicit aim of avoiding additional prison construction. In still other cases, legislatures have enacted "emergency release" procedures that may be triggered when the prison population reaches a certain point above the capacity of the prisons.

Paroling Decisions

The procedures used by paroling authorities in different jurisdictions are quite varied, as are the legal and administrative structures that provide the context for decisions. The legal constraints range from a presumption of parole at first eligibility (for example, at expiration of a fixed portion of the sentence) to a very wide allowance for discretion under indeterminate sentencing systems. In indeterminate systems, the parole board may establish rules for determining the date of the first parole consideration hearing.

A state parole board typically consists of three to seven members appointed by the governor. (Members of the United States Parole Commission, now eliminated with the enactment of the federal provisions for a sentencing guidelines commission, were appointed by the President of the United States.) Parole board members usually have term appointments, often of four or six years. They may not be removed without cause or for political reasons. Some statutes set vague requirements for these appointments, usually expressed in broad general terms such as "one must be an attorney, one widely experienced in corrections, one knowledgeable of the social sciences." As a practical matter, these are political appointments usually rewarding political support, and, as a result, parole boards across the United States include members quite diverse in relevant experience and competence. Like judges, they rarely have training specific to the decision-making task required.

The styles of decision making adopted by boards are equally varied. Most boards require an interview with the inmate, although not always for all decisions. The parole hearing may be held before the full board, before panels of the members, or before hearing officers whose recommendations then are made to the board. Others—including lawyers, victims, or the inmate's family—may or may not be present, depending on the law of the state and the board's own rules.

Parole hearings usually include a review of the inmate's file, an interview, a discussion after the inmate has left the room, and a vote or consensus of the board. Different rules prevail in different jurisdictions. The case file typically includes accounts by criminal justice officials and by the inmate of the following areas: the offense of conviction; sociological and psychological assessments, noting employment history and personal problems such as alcohol and drug abuse; details of any prior history of offenses; and descriptions of institutional program assignments and progress, including prison disciplinary infractions. Much of this information typically comes from the report prepared by the probation officer before sentencing. These materials often are summarized, with a description of the inmate's plans for parole, in a report prepared by correctional staff for the board hearing.

The extent and quality of the information in the case files varies dramatically among jurisdictions and from case to case. The interview typically is conducted by one member or hearing officer, followed by questions from other members. The demeanor and attitudes of the inmate, as perceived by the board members, may strongly influence the board's decision. Usually, the inmate then is asked to leave, while his or her fate is decided and then is called back into the room to learn the decision. A denial of parole usually is in the form of a continuance; parole consideration is postponed, often for a year. It may, however, be decided that there will be "no further parole consideration" unless that is prohibited by statute or the board's rules.

Parole revocation hearings are conducted in a similar manner. Added to the materials already described is the report of the parole officer, summarizing the activities of the parolee and specifying the charges and evidence of rules violations. Since 1972, the parolee has had a right to procedural safeguards not usually provided before. These include a preliminary hearing for the determination of probable cause, written notice of alleged violations, disclosure of evidence, opportunity for defense, including the calling of witnesses, and a right to cross-examine witnesses.[16] (In 1973, these protections were extended to probationers at violation hearings.)[17]

The parole decision-making process is complicated by the diversity of legal and administrative structures that prevail. Many influences other than the parole board's decisions affect how long offenders serve in prison and whether they are paroled. Legislative, judicial, and administrative decisions all interact in a complex system in finally resolving this question. Moreover, the aims of the parole authorities in different jurisdictions may differ markedly.

Various options and constraints affect parole decisions. These depend on who has discretion and authority (within the legislature, the judiciary, prison officials, or the parole board) concerning minimum and maximum terms, mandatory terms, the system for awarding good time credits, the degree of discretion allowed for amending decisions, and the administrative rules adopted by the board itself. The results of decisions at parole board hearings may include, for example, fixing the date for first parole consideration or for subsequent hearings, fixing minimum terms, denying any further parole consideration, awarding good time credits, fixing the length of sentence to be served in prison and on parole, or setting the conditions of parole.

As with probation revocation decisions, there has been but little study of the bases for parole revocation decisions or of their results. This decision involves "in part, a penalty and, in part, a prediction."[18] Despite evident inconsistencies in judgments by parole agents and substantial differences in recommendations among parole offices and over time, there has been little effort to learn systematically from revocation experience. This experience has been described accurately as "recorded in fragments, separated into case folders, stuffed into filing cabinets, and eventually burned."[19] Both probation and parole revocation decisions are central issues for community corrections, and it is astounding that so little effort has been spent in determining their consequences.

Paroling Controversies

Until the 1970s, sentencing, correctional, and paroling structures were guided mainly by utilitarian principles. Since rehabilitation was the ideal, indeterminate sentencing was most often used. Actual terms of confinement were determined not only by the court at the time of sentencing but later by a parole board. Although still the model in most states, this has changed in many jurisdictions as a result of shifts in the philosophy of sentencing, including parole. As described already, these shifts have been toward determinate sentencing, just desert punishment, general deterrence, and incapacitation. There also has been an assertion of a right *not* to be treated— that is, through required participation in rehabilitative programs.[20] Along with those changes came increasing concerns with unwarranted disparities in sentences, resulting in a movement to remove or reduce sentencing and paroling discretion and increased use of mandatory or presumptive sentencing. Debates were more often heard about the desirability of having a parole system at all.[21] Strong criticisms of parole, always an undercurrent to its operation, became a flood in the 1970s.

The emerging criticisms of parole in the 1970s were well summarized by Harris:

> Many critics focus on procedural failings, contending that present parole procedures lack the safeguards necessary for fair and accurate decisionmaking. Other critics believe that the present parole system creates a level of anxiety and frustration among confined populations that is counterproductive in terms of institutional management and the correctional process. A smaller, but growing, number of critics are questioning the wisdom of having a parole system at all, contending that the system is not, and perhaps cannot be, effective in achieving its stated goals.[22]

The first concern mentioned by Harris focused on issues of procedural safeguards and the lack of explicit rules and criteria for both initial decision making and administrative review. It included issues of fairness and equity—that is, the problems of unwarranted disparities in punishment. The second asserted that the parole system "epitomized for most inmates a system of whim, caprice, inequity, and nerve-wracking uncertainty."[23] The third criticism concerned the complex issue of the effectiveness of treatment—that is, of the rehabilitation model.

A related criticism, pertinent also to judicial sentencing decisions, including the probation option, had to do with judges' or paroling authorities' subjective estimates of the risk that an offender will commit new crimes. Such subjective judgments are notoriously unreliable and have questionable validity.

The accuracy of risk assessments can be improved by the use of prediction methods based on experience. These can estimate the probability of success on probation or parole for various groups.[24] Although the predictive validity achieved will be modest, the evidence supports the belief that it will be better than subjective judgments.

Estimates of risk raise an important ethical issue. The ethical question may be posed in relation to the just desert theory of sentencing. Is it fair to punish not for what the person has done but for what he or she *may* do? The desert theorist would claim that it is not, because punishment is justified only if it is deserved and proportional to the harm done, taking into account the culpability of the offender.

Even if the aims of deterrence, incapacitation, and treatment are seen as justified, there is a further problem—that the predictions made will always be imperfect. This leads to decision errors of two kinds: wrongly anticipating failures and wrongly expecting successes for those who in fact fail. The errors of the first kind, sometimes called "false positives," may lead to unnecessary confinement. The errors of the second kind, called "false negatives," lead to releasing an offender who may do harm to additional victims. Because of the centrality of prediction in probation and parole decision making, this issue continues to be a point of fundamental dispute.

Three types of structural changes have emerged in response to these criticisms, and each has been adopted in various jurisdictions. The first two have been mentioned already: mandatory sentencing (penalties are fixed either by the legislature or by the courts) and presumptive sentencing (punishments must be set by the courts within much narrower bounds than had been customary under the concept of sentence indeterminacy and parole). The third structural variation has been the development and use of guidelines that limit parole decisions or sentences within a specific and narrow range of discretion, according to an explicit policy. Each of these three models reduces the discretion of the parole authorities.

Parole Decision Guidelines

As noted in our discussions of sentencing and of pretrial decision making, recent attention has been given to developing guidelines aimed at providing flexible methods for structuring discretion in criminal justice decisions. The development of such models began in the field of parole.[25]

The studies leading to parole guidelines were developed and implemented by research workers in collaboration with the U.S. Parole Commission (then the U.S. Parole Board) in the early 1970s. Previously, the board had no written general policy providing a framework within which its individual case decisions could be made. The guidelines were developed by a study of the decisions of the board in prior years. They were intended to structure and control, but not to eliminate, the board's discretion.

The guidelines used by the parole commission were in the form of a two-dimensional chart, similar to that later used in sentencing and pretrial release guidelines. On one dimension, the seriousness of the offender's commitment offense was considered. Six categories of offense seriousness were designated, and for each the commission listed examples of common offense behaviors for that category (arrived at by consensus judgments of the commission members). On the other dimension, four categories of "risk" of parole violation were defined. These classifications of offenders were established by a parole prediction device called a "salient factor score."

At each intersection of the two dimensions, a decision range was indicated. This decision range specified the usual paroling policy in terms of the number of months to be served before release (subject to the limitations of the judge's imposed sentence) assuming the prisoner had demonstrated good institutional behavior. After the offender was classified according to both the seriousness of the offense and the risk of parole violation if released, the parole board member or hearing examiner checked the grid to determine the expected decision. When the decision was made outside the expected range, reasons were required.

The system was designed to be changed as needed, and it was intended to reduce inmate uncertainty about their terms. The board established procedures for examining, updating, or modifying the guidelines in periodic reviews. Inmates were informed early in the process of the time they could expect to serve.

A major advantage of this type of decision-making system, as in the case of sentencing and other areas of central criminal justice decision making, is that its development requires the explicit statement of policy for the decisions. Hence, it is open for public review and criticism. Another central feature of the system is its provision for repeated review and revision. This allows for, and indeed invites, rigorous scrutiny of the parole decision-making criteria used. The ethical issues can be better informed and debated more readily, and matters of effectiveness of the decisions can more easily be tested.

The concept of paroling guidelines caught on quickly in some of the states, and 14 states, the District of Columbia, as well as the federal system had similar parole guidelines by 1983. It is ironic that the arguments of the U.S. Parole Commission in support of its decision making reforms were apparently so persuasive to Congress that its members decided that when similar procedures were in place for sentencing there would be no need for the parole board, which they eliminated.

The originators of the guidelines system argued that one latent function of parole boards is the reduction of unwarranted disparity. This had been proposed by numerous authorities. For example, the National Advisory Commission of Criminal Justice Standards and Goals stated:

> Though it is seldom stated openly, parole boards are concerned with supporting a system of appropriate and equitable sanctions. This concern is reflected in several ways, depending upon a jurisdiction's sentencing system. One of the most common is through decisions seeking to equalize penalties for offenders who have similar backgrounds and have committed the same offense but who have received different sentences.[26]

The evidence suggests that guidelines can indeed serve a function of disparity reduction. As Cohen and Tonry summarized the evidence:

> All of the studies reviewed that assessed the impact of parole guidelines on disparity found evidence that the guidelines reduced sentencing disparity. Thus, it appears that well-managed parole guideline systems can operate to reduce sentence disparity among persons imprisoned.[27]

Evaluations of Parole Boards

To many citizens relatively uninformed about parole decision making, the answer to the question, "How should the performance of a parole board be evaluated?" seems obvious and straightforward. It is often assumed that paroled persons who subsequently commit new crimes or are returned to prison for violations of parole rules may be counted as "failures," and these measure the mistakes of the board in granting parole. Frequent criticisms of parole boards appear in the press when offenses by parolees occur, especially when particularly heinous crimes are involved.

The problem of parole board evaluation, however, is not that simple. The different rules governing parole in different places, and the different goals of different parole boards, add complexities to the apparently simple question. As a result, the question of how effective parole boards are, over all parole boards—or *overall* in terms of a single board's multiple goals—is almost meaningless.

Recall that in some jurisdictions nearly all persons who leave prison do so as a result of placement on parole, whereas in others relatively few are released in that way. Although nearly all who are sent to prison are released sometime, the mode of release varies. The prisoner must be discharged when the sentence has expired, and, in some jurisdictions, the person must be released to supervision when certain criteria have been met. Since the parole decision often does not involve *whether* to release so much as *when* to release and *under what circumstances* to release, the measure of repeat offense may provide little information on the effectiveness of parole.

Parole board decisions are only one type of the many decisions that influence the length of sentences. The legislature, the judiciary, and correctional administrative decisions all play a role, even under indeterminate sentencing structures. All these decisions interact in a complex system to

determine the time that inmates actually serve in prison. When we recall the
diversity of objectives of parole decisions implied by the "frames of reference" of parole board members, it is apparent that the assessment of risk for incapacitative purposes is only one of the aims of parole boards.

The simple criterion of recidivism has shortcomings for evaluation of effectiveness even if only the aim of incapacitation is considered. Decisions by a parole board to parole are not merely decisions about release, or even only about how long the inmate should serve in prison. Rather, they are placement decisions. In many jurisdictions, parole release is linked to supervision in the community that otherwise would not be provided. The parole board member may prefer to release poor parole risks under supervision rather than to deny parole with the result that the inmate will otherwise be released a little later without any supervision and control.

It often has been assumed that one function of the parole decision-making and supervision process is to permit return to prison if parole rules are violated and the offender is seen as likely to commit new offenses. That is, there is assumed to be a crime prevention function of parole supervision. From this perspective, the return of a technical parole violator may—if new crimes were prevented—be a success of the system rather than a failure. (Demonstrating that new crimes were prevented is, of course, a different matter. Another related but different question is that of fairness, since under this strategy some "false positive" errors will occur.)

Because parole decision making may reflect legislative, judicial, and correctional staff decisions as well as those of the board, it is difficult to identify those factors of parole decision making that may be attributed to the parole boards alone. The nature and seriousness of the offense, the prior criminal record of the prisoner, the estimated risk of parole violation, and the offender's behavior in prison clearly are important in making the decision (Box 11.4).[28]

Box 11.4

Factors Influencing Parole Board Decisions

- nature of the offense
- seriousness of the offense
- prior criminal record
- institutional disciplinary record

- perceived program participation and progress
- estimated risk of parole violation
- perceived need for supervision in the community upon release

---

Evaluation of parole board decisions should also involve review of how well the sanctioning, treater, citizen, jurist, and regulator aims of parole board decision making are achieved. Raising the question in this way points to the complexity of the problem of parole decision evaluation. The decisions of parole board members, like those of judges, prosecutors, and police, may involve the aims of the whole of the criminal justice system.

Evaluation of Changes in Probation and Parole

The increased emphasis on deserved punishment is a shift from the traditional utilitarian crime control aims of rehabilitation and control that have been fundamental to probation and parole since their creation. If principles of just desert, equity, and fairness are to be emphasized, then the system may be made more fair. To the degree, however, that the utilitarian aims of prevention, crime reduction, and effective treatment of the offender are abandoned in the process, then the system may be emptied of hope. The changes that are occurring have been directed at increasing fairness, with some justification; but the traditional utilitarian aim of treatment to reduce or prevent future criminal behavior may not merely be neglected but rejected in the process.

These trends were noted by Rothman, as they emerged, as a more general social movement when he remarked, "A new generation of reformers . . . is challenging the ideal of the state as parent; or put another way, is pitting rights against needs."[29] Under the indeterminate sentencing model of the rehabilitation era, with wide discretion by probation and parole staff and by paroling authorities, reformers were confident that the treaters and the treated were on the same side. Later reformers, however, have argued that benevolent purposes do not suffice, that state paternalism is not to be trusted, and that discretionary authority—the limitation of which was not seen previously as necessary or desirable—must be restricted sharply.

The actual consequences of these shifts in decision-making structures and practice should be examined carefully. It is not yet clear what the results will be. The fundamental challenges to probation and parole are profound: How can justice and fairness be emphasized and improved, the rights of offenders be better protected, and unwarranted disparity in sentencing lessened while preserving and enhancing the aims of prevention, crime reduction, rehabilitation, and restoration? How can all this be done without lessening efforts to identify effective placements in community treatment and control programs, without depriving offenders of helpful services that may assist them and better protect the community, and without making jails and prisons more crowded and less humane?

Probation and Parole Supervision

The history of probation and parole supervision is best understood as a part of the changes in penology (the study, theory, and practice of prison management and offender rehabilitation) through the penitentiary, reformatory, rehabilitation, and restraint phases already described. The two traditional functions of community supervision—control and rehabilitation—represent concerns with public safety and with services designed to assist the offender to remain law-abiding. The built-in conflict between these two functions is a result of how the supervision of probationers and parolees developed from beginnings in the use of transportation as a penalty.[30]

During the 250 years that England transported prisoners to America, Africa, and Australia, parole permitted convicts to be released from confinement earlier by working. In 1853, England passed the Penal Servitude Act that ended transportation and made imprisonment the main criminal sanction. It legalized "tickets of leave" and authorized wardens to grant them. Supervision expanded in Ireland, with an emphasis on public safety. Later, government subsidized "aftercare societies" developed, mainly to provide assistance in securing employment, with parolees required to file regular reports on their activities. By 1864, parole and supervision had become synonymous, and supervision had both public safety and rehabilitation functions.

This development was paralleled in America and took hold particularly with the establishment of the best known of the new reformatories at Elmira, in New York, opened in 1877. With reformation emphasized—through work, training, and education—inmates with 12 months of good behavior, a postrelease job, and a supervising guardian could be paroled. By 1900, 20 states and the federal government had parole statutes. Parole supervision agents monitored the behavior of parolees, who were expected not only to obey the law but to live in a manner that conformed to community norms.

Probation also appeared during the reformatory period, and supervision stressed reform. With the introduction of the rehabilitation model, parole was increasingly seen as a continuation of treatment. Probation also saw its biggest gains during the rehabilitation movement, and it gained further with the emergence of stress on the concept of reintegration, reintroducing and restoring the inmate to society.

Both probation and parole agencies now have both control and treatment functions. In the federal system, supervision of parolees and probationers have been combined. The roles are similar, except that a substantial part of the work of a probation officer in many jurisdictions is in doing presentence investigations and reports. Caseloads may range from about 30 to 300 cases. The growth in numbers on probation and parole, and the often huge caseloads of persons to be supervised, emphasize the importance of programs of supervision in the community and underscore the problems of classification and differential supervision for more efficient and effective use of resources.

Classification and Community Supervision

Classification in community corrections began with the development of measures of risk violations. Different supervision models or work loads were used for different classifications of parolees. Later, differential supervision models were extended to probation.

The earliest use of risk measures for classification for assignment to supervision levels was in California in the early 1960s. Minimal supervision caseloads were established for both male and female parolees. Persons classified as having a high probability of successful completion of parole received only minimal supervision. A careful follow-up study showed that these persons could be given less supervision with no increase in parole violations. In this way, parole agent time was focused on cases with greater risk of parole failure.[31] The different levels of supervision, combined with a program that selected good parole risks for earlier parole consideration, resulted in substantial cost savings with no increase in parole violations. In the case of the program for women, it made building a new prison for women unnecessary.[32]

By 1969, the California Department of Corrections had assignment systems for parolees with three classes of supervision, based on risk classifications. The department reported a substantial decrease in prison returns for new crimes and violations of parole rules and concluded that the cost savings from men kept in the community rather than in prison was the equivalent cost of the entire population of an average size major prison.[33]

It was another decade before the concept of classification of probationers and parolee supervision caught on across the country. In the early 1980s, the National Institute of Corrections developed a classification-workload system that has been widely put into effect.[34] Besides classification for "risk," these models also score offenders for "needs." The risk classification is focused on surveillance and community protection. The needs classification is intended to identify needs for rehabilitative and reintegrative help. Many probation departments, and some parole departments, have developed similar programs using a management system based on both risk and needs.

As described by Clear and Braga, the "model" system of caseload management has three main parts:

- Supervision classification using standardized risk and needs assessment criteria;

- Written and systematic strategies for supervision planning;

- Workload accounting based on studies of the amount of time it takes to supervise a case.[35]

They summarized the model as follows:

Classification involves the use of a standardized scale to assess individual clients in terms of risk to the community and need for assistance. Probation ers are differentiated into levels (minimum, medium, maximum) based on scores. Clients who have the highest scores for risk or need receive the maxi mum available supervision.[36]

Each probation officer is responsible for a certain number of "work units," and each case has been assigned a work unit value based on the time needed for supervision, based on time studies.

The original applications based on both risk and needs were based on time studies of supervision and more structured classification procedures in Wisconsin.[37] The National Institute of Corrections model system has been well received by community corrections agencies, so much so that by 1985 those without classification-workload systems were described as "probation dinosaurs."[38]

Effectiveness of Community Supervision

Some regard community programs as the best current hope of corrections, while others regard them as relatively useless. When positions on the effectiveness of community corrections programs are taken, they may reflect mere opinion, hope, or wish; or they may be based on a careful analysis of the evidence about the effects of these programs in terms of either community crime control or of rehabilitation. Just as opinions may be offered without supporting evidence of the effectiveness of the deserved punishment model in attaining goals of justice and fairness, there is unfortunately little conclusive evidence from careful analysis on success in attaining community corrections goals.

There has been little study of the effects of probation and parole in terms of crimes avoided through incapacitation of offenders who violate the conditions of their release and are then confined. There is somewhat more information from research on the rehabilitation effects, but that too is fairly limited. The influential survey by Lipton, Martinson, and Wilkes, often cited

Parole officers have the dual tasks of surveillance and counseling—of crime control and enforcement and of service provision. Do you believe a parole officer can be effective as both "cop and counselor?"

as showing that rehabilitation efforts do not work, was based on review of 251 studies of correctional rehabilitation, but only five of these were studies of adult probation.[39] Later, Gottfredson, Finckenauer, and Rauh reviewed about 130 studies of various aspects of probation and its effects.[40] Although much was learned in these studies, problems of research methods often reduced the confidence one could have in the results and in generalizations that might be made. A later summary stated:

> If we ask whether probation is more effective as a rehabilitative treatment than is imprisonment, we must respond that the necessary research has not been done.

> If we ask whether the personal characteristics of offenders are more impor-tant than the form of treatment in determining future recidivism, we must answer that the evidence tends to support this conjecture.

> If we ask whether the size of the caseload makes any difference to results in terms of recidivism, we must answer that the evidence is mixed. From limited evidence, it appears that intensive supervision may result in more technical violations known and acted upon and also in fewer new offense convictions.

> If we ask who succeeds and who fails on probation supervision, we may reply that a useful technology for development and validation of prediction instru-ments is available, that there is some information on the question (for some jurisdictions), that attempts to develop such instruments for probationers have been rare, and that these attempts have been put to relatively little use.

> If we ask what works, out of interest in discovering what forms of treatment and supervision provide more effective results when applied to probationers generally or to any particular classification of offenders, we must reply that there is limited evidence and it is mixed. [41]

Probation and parole programs are on trial, with increasing demands for evidence of effectiveness. All the evidence, however, has not yet been provided to a jury of informed decision makers. Much of the presentation of both the prosecution and the defense must be regarded as scientifically inadmissible.

Demands for change and programming decisions are more often made on the basis of guess, hope, or despair than on sound evidence. Methods are available to provide the needed evidence in systematic management information programs, but they have not yet been used to the extent needed to provide the needed, more informed, judgments.

Drug and Alcohol Abuse Programs

There is accumulating evidence about the effectiveness of specialized programs, including those for drug and alcohol abuse. More recent studies have focused also on specialized community corrections programs that have been seen as "alternatives to confinement," "alternative punishments" "intermediate punishments," or sentences "between prison and probation."[42]

Many substance-abusing offenders, including alcohol, narcotics, and stimulant drug abusers, cycle through the criminal justice system repeatedly. Higher priority recently has been given to breaking this cycle of substance abuse, crime, and incarceration—for addressing not only the problem of growth of prison populations but that of crime in general.

In the last two decades, nationally, corrections administrators have increased the enrollment of prison inmates in programs for substance abuse treatment. By 1987, Chaiken estimated 11 percent of inmates across the country were enrolled in such treatment programs.[43] The numbers enrolled in such treatment, however, are far smaller than the apparent need. Most substance abusing offenders are, instead, confined without drug treatment.

Holden and coworkers reviewed more than 1,000 books, articles, and papers on drug treatment since the late 19th century. Their review suggested a need for increased support of substance abuse programming and closer links of these programs between prison and community supervision.[44] Based on their extensive review, these authors concluded:

> The majority of evaluations of drug treatment outcomes show positive indications of reduced drug use and criminality for those individuals who remain in treatment for several months. The literature also indicates that the use of compulsory treatment can be a valuable tool in inducing addicted offenders into treatment.

> State and local policymakers should be encouraged to provide adequate drug treatment programs for drug-dependent offenders in conjunction with the appropriate criminal sanctions, which may include incarceration. Most states report that drug treatment services in many of their facilities are inadequate. Treatment services for drug-dependent offenders also are limited in many communities.

Few prison programs have done careful evaluations of the results of their programs for drug-abuse offenders. The review by Chaiken analyzed four programs that collected evaluation information on their programs and reported relatively low rates of repeated offending.

There is a gradual increase in the availability of these programs in prison and in the community, because of the increase in drug-related crimes and the sharply increasing use of confinement for these offenders, a need to treat intravenous drug users to prevent the spread of the AIDS virus, long waiting lists of users needing treatment, and the lower relative costs of treatment compared to incarceration. Nevertheless, the general quality of treatment programs for criminal offenders, including drug treatments, remains low.

An irresistible compulsion to use drugs must be expected to continue without treatment.

The potential cost benefits of treatment often have been cited as a reason for increasing support for treatment. A 1987 estimate of costs for needle-using drug abusers indicated that methadone maintenance treatment costs an average $3,000, outpatient drug treatment $2,300, and residential drug treatment $14,600.[45] A more detailed cost benefit analysis in California concluded that, on average, benefits of drug treatment programs exceed the costs of these programs by 11 ½ times. Benefits were estimated on the basis of reduced arrest and court costs, reduced incarceration costs, and reduced property crime.[46]

The U.S. Department of Justice has supported and endorsed programs across the country known as TASC (Treatment Alternatives to Street Crime). The Bureau of Justice Assistance has claimed that the program, with more than 125 TASC sites in 27 states, has reduced recidivism, improved treatment participation, and provided a cost-effective alternative to the criminal justice system.[47]

A decade or so ago, practitioners and research workers were pessimistic about whether drug treatment programs "worked." Now, there is more optimism that some programs can be helpful and cost-effective. Most evaluations show reduced drug use and criminality for individuals remaining in treatment for several months. There is strong evidence for the cost effectiveness of drug treatment programs, but much of the result depends on having well-planned and well-managed programs.

Intermediate Punishments

During the last decade as politicians continued to push "get tough" policies and as the populations in prison and on probation and parole continued to rise, a new phrase was heard as a substitute for "alternatives to incarceration." The new catch phrase was "intermediate punishments." The phrase "alternative to incarceration" seemed to many to reflect a too liberal, soft-on-crime attitude. Probation as ordinarily practiced was seen widely as letting the offender off—the "slap on the wrist." Prison was expensive, but intermediate punishments were possible. These exist "between prison and probation," as indicated by Morris and Tonry's influential book on the subject.[48]

The increasing popularity of intermediate punishments and growth in their use (Box 11.5)[49] was attributable to the harmony of the concept with the political tenor of the times. As described by Cullen and his colleagues:

> . . . intermediate *punishments* or community *controls* "made sense" because the rhetoric of this reform resonated with the prevailing politics of crime. By the 1980s, the legacy of the Great Society programs and "doing good" in corrections was in disrepute, and it was a rare politician—liberal or conservative—who did not blame lenient punishments for the U.S. crime problem and promise if elected to toughen up criminal sentences. In this context, intermediate punishments drew their appeal from the often-repeated belief that whether exercised in the prison or in the community, threats of punishment and enhanced surveillance were the keys to deterring criminality. It made little difference that, when first proposed, there was little theoretical or empirical basis in the criminological literature for believing that these programs would be effective.[50]

Box 11.5

Growing Popularity of Intermediate Punishments

- More than 70 percent of states use intensive *probation* supervision, with a total caseload of about 60,000 offenders.

- More than 60 percent of states use intensive *parole* supervision, with a caseload of more than 63,000 offenders.

- Many states use electronic monitoring for probationers or parolees, with about 10,000 offenders monitored at any one time.

- In 48 states and the federal system, probationers are tested for drug use. A study of adult felons on probation indicated that 31 percent had received drug testing.

- In 45 jurisdictions and the federal system, parolees are tested for drug use.

- More than half the states have at least one boot camp, and five more have plans to implement a boot camp program.

Figure 11.1 Estimated Annual Costs of Incarceration, Halfway Houses, Home Confinement, and Probation

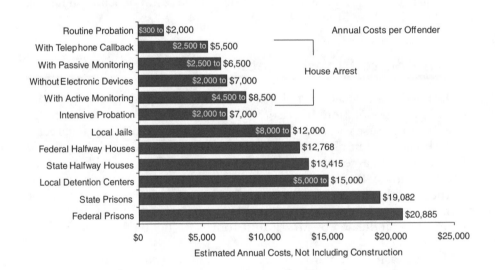

Source: adapted from National Committee on Community Corrections (1994). *A Proposal for Action*. Washington, D.C.: National Committee on Community Corrections, 14–15.
Note: when a range is given, the upper bound of the estimated average costs is shown by the figure; for prisons and halfway houses, the amount is an estimated average. Costs differ widely among jurisdictions, vendors, and types of electronic surveillance systems. See text for definitions of active and passive electronic monitoring.

Many programs have been supported as alternatives to incarceration, thereby providing a potential for relief from the crowded facilities and institution building boom recently experienced. When programs are developed with the intention of providing alternatives to confinement, however it is possible that although the level of punishment may be increased, jail or prison population growth may not be reduced. That often happens because these options simply may be used as penalties additional to—rather than instead of— probation. If the interest is in stemming the growth of jail and prison populations, it is essential that these programs contribute to population reductions and not merely to an escalation in severity of sanctions imposed as conditions of probation.

Programs of intermediate punishments have become increasingly popular (Box 11.5) because they may serve two quite different masters. Supporters of their use as alternatives to confinement often cite the high costs of incarceration (Figure 11.1) as compared with the substantially lower costs of programs such as home confinement or intensive supervision. Other supporters of their use, more inclined to increase rather than to decrease penalties, argue that probation or parole supervision as usually practiced does nothing either to control crime or to change the offender for the better; and "tougher" measures are needed for those now placed on regular supervision. Thus, both "liberal" and "conservative" views may be accommodated.

Alternatives to Confinement

Some of these programs that might reduce the use of incarceration may be regarded as sentencing options—"front door" options for reducing prison or jail populations. Others are "back door" options, dealing with choices after confinement—usually requiring decisions by correctional staff or paroling authorities. "Side door" options—with placement decisions taken after sentencing but before usual parole procedures—are also possible. Finally, some release procedures have been developed as emergency mechanisms as required to deal with crowding (sometimes in response to court orders to reduce populations). These could be called "trap door" options.

Front Door Options

Examples of such programs are the following:

- **Community service orders:** This is an intermediate sanction between straight probation and confinement. It can be one distinct sentence or imposed as a condition of probation. In at least one jurisdiction (Manhattan), "prison bound" accused are selected as candidates for this program, with a community service order recommended to the court. Offenders are required to provide labor, usually for a public agency or not-for-profit service organization, as a penalty. Offenders might be found in many communities picking up litter on the roadways, painting public buildings, landscaping parks, building playgrounds, or doing other work that benefits the community. Arguments in favor of this sanction, besides the avoidance of incarceration, are that a useful service is performed, it is more appropriate than a fine for poor offenders, and it may be a useful treatment by changing offender attitudes and giving a sense of accomplishment. The latter would be just a bonus; the main arguments are avoidance of costly confinement while providing a benefit. It is most often used with relatively minor offenders, typically misdemeanants, occasionally felons—often combined with other penalties.

- **Monetary penalties:** Fines can be used as the only sanction or in combination with others in order to reduce the use of confinement (or, of course, to increase the severity of punishment). Financial penalties can be substantial punishments.[51] Other financial penalties can include the payment of court costs and fees for services—including those of public defenders, alcohol or drug testing, and probation supervision. Although fines typically are the sanction used for traffic offenses, the fine often is combined with jail for alcohol- or drug-related offenses; and in the case of repeated offenses of this type, with prison. A currently popular idea is that of "day fines," with the judge setting the amount of fine in relation to the daily earnings of the offender. This may make up for income differences among offenders and therefore is arguably more fair. Forfeitures also are used as penalties, often in the case of drug offenders, when automobiles, boats, and other property may be seized. Restitution is required compensation to the victim for losses suffered because of the crime. Unlike victim compensation, in which case the state makes a payment to the victim, restitution requires that the offender pay or repay the victim. Restitution often is used in combination with other penalties.

- **Probation:** Strengthening the role of probation officers, for example by providing smaller caseloads, may lead to the greater use of probation—as intended originally—as an alternative to confinement. Many probation leaders describe current intensive supervision programs as probation run the way it ought to be for all offenders. When judges perceive the available probation programs as weak or ineffective due to large caseloads, they are less prone to use it. Investing money in probation might save higher jail and prison costs.

- **Intensive supervision diversion:** In Georgia, a program is aimed at diverting offenders from prison, with intensive supervision by both a surveillance officer and a counselor. Evidence is that probation is strengthened for some who otherwise would be on probation anyway. Others would be in prison if the program were not available to the courts.[52] The program may provide a true diversion program for some offenders, while for others, who might have been on probation even if the program were not available, are subjected to increased surveillance and supervision.

- **House arrest (home confinement):** This may be used in conjunction with intensive supervision programs, with or without electronic monitoring devices (Box 11.6)[53] to confine offenders to their homes. Three degrees of severity of the sanction may be recognized: *curfew*, *detention*, and *incarceration*. Curfews require an offender to be at home at specific times, usually at night. Detention requires that the offender stay at home unless working, seeking medical care, attending religious services, or performing community service. Home incarceration means the offender is prohibited from working, shopping, or perhaps even from entering his or her own back yard.[54] House arrest may be used in the more limited way of detention or it may be used as confinement as extensive as jail.

- **Electronic monitoring:** These systems differ in complexity and cost. At one end are passive systems which include telephone systems programmed to call at predetermined or random times in order to verify the offender's presence at home. The offender must call back within a specified period of time. This may be combined with a voice recognition system in order to verify that it is the offender who returns the call. Active systems provide constant

Box 11.6

Electronic Monitoring

Home confinement programs often use electronic monitoring devices along with other elements of supervision in the community. These were first used in 1984. More than 42 states have adopted some form of electronic monitoring system. The devices vary in capabilities, cost, and reliability. Some have automatic dialers that call the offender's home to verify his or her presence there. Others are electronic shackles (ankle bracelets) that emit a signal over a 200-foot radius that can be detected by receivers placed in offenders' homes. Devices available include a video phone that requires the offender to show his or her face and transmitters that can track an offender's movement throughout an entire city.

monitoring. The "ankle bracelet" is a transmitter that may send a continuous signal to a central computer or portable receiver kept by the supervisor. Sometimes there is a modem installed in the home, requiring the insertion of a computer chip in a wrist band worn by the offender in order to enable verification of presence in the house. The use of these systems has increased dramatically in many states in the last 10 years.

- **Day reporting centers:** Offenders must report daily to a central location for supervision, with whereabouts and activities monitored closely at all times. These programs often are combined with monitoring for substance abuse and used to ensure compliance with community service orders or other conditions of probation.

- **Specialized probation caseloads:** It often is plausible that judges and paroling authorities can be convinced that offenders can reside in the community if they will be supervised in well-managed, specialized probation or parole caseloads. Examples are specialized caseloads for restitution, community service, alcohol and drug abuse, drinking drivers, and domestic violence cases.

- **Shock incarceration:** This means short-term confinement, often as a condition of probation. Its name implies an intended specific deterrent effect. Supporters believe a "taste of the bars" has the effect of "teaching a lesson" by impressing on the offender the seriousness of the criminal act and providing a sample of that which is in store for repeated offending.

- **Boot camps:** This is a currently popular program of harsh regimental discipline, usually followed by probation supervision. Some such programs emphasize substance abuse recognition, prevention, and treatment (e.g., in Nevada). Programs differ in many ways, but all emphasize strict discipline and close order drill. These programs are used only for young offenders.

- **Weekend sentences:** This is often discussed as an option for sentencing that could reduce confined populations. The offender may continue working, supporting a family, and maintaining social ties. This is the most commonly used form of intermittent incarceration.

- **Community housing:** Pregnant women inmates may be removed to secure facilities in the community.

- **Short-term treatment and confinement facilities:** Private companies have developed therapeutic community programs as an alternative to probation or confinement.

- **Short-term violator confinement:** Facilities may be provided for the relatively brief confinement of probation or parole technical violators instead of probation or parole revocation and imprisonment. Such facilities may be operated by probation, parole, or prison departments.

- **Offender-specific planning:** Programs that avoid confinement can be developed specifically in relation to the needs of individual offenders and victims. These programs typically require a careful study of the offender, development of a detailed treatment plan, and presentation of a convincing case to the judge that placement in the program is preferable to confinement for the particular case.

Back Door Options

Although it may appear that postsentencing options would have little potential for impact on prison populations, this is not the case. Strong programs of community supervision and postrelease treatment may lead the paroling authority to release some offenders otherwise denied parole and to release others earlier. Moreover, paroling authorities may elect to release offenders viewed as "poor risks" to programs of supervision rather than letting prison terms expire resulting in release of prisoners to the community with no supervision. Examples are as follows:

- **Work and education furloughs:** Prisoners may be released to structured programs in the community while still serving time in jail or prison. In some jurisdictions, this may be done by decisions of the corrections staff; in other places, the approval of the parole board may be required.

- **Work release:** Prisoners may be released to employment to serve a remaining portion of the sentence under controlled conditions such as house arrest, electronic monitoring, or frequent supervision contacts.

- **Halfway houses:** Facilities may be designed for preparole programs in the community, transitional to the regular parole program. Prisoners may be released during the day for educational or work programs. These programs date to at least the 1850s, when Crofton designed the "Irish system" with confinement, an "intermediate stage," or halfway house, and the "ticket of leave," the precursor of parole.[55]

- **Prerelease centers and restitution centers:** Minimum security facilities or camps may be used to house inmates shortly before release on parole, with programs designed to assist in the transition to the community. Some centers are specialized to permit work and enable restitution to victims.

- **Outpatient clinics:** These may be appropriate community-based facilities for the treatment of substance abuse or psychological treatment.

- **Intensive probation and parole supervision programs:** Intensive surveillance, sometimes combined with house arrest, electronic monitoring, and substance abuse testing may allow the appropriate release of offenders who otherwise would be in prison or, if in prison, discharged later without any supervision.

Side Door Options

- **Intensive supervision diversion:** A second model of diversion with intensive supervision is in place in New Jersey. Offenders already in prison apply to a judicial panel for placement in this community program. Prison beds clearly are freed up; the offenders were in prison before release into this program—and if not accepted for it would continue in prison custody. (See Box 11.7.)[56]

Box 11.7

Intensive Supervision Diversion: The New Jersey Intensive Supervision Program

This program was started by the judiciary specifically with the goal of reducing the numbers of offenders in prison by developing a program of punishment and surveillance in the community that would permit prison inmates to be resentenced to this intermediate form of punishment. The program was described by the courts as having these features:

- It permits selected prison inmates to serve the remainder of their sentences in the community rather than in prison.

- It is a highly structured and rigorous form of community supervision. It involves extensive offender contact, surveillance, a restrictive curfew, and urine monitoring for alcohol and drugs.

- Full-time employment, onerous community service, maintenance of a budget and a diary, payment of all court-ordered financial obligations, and payment toward child support and the cost of the program are required.

- The application screening process selects only those inmates who have the potential to succeed in the program and will not jeopardize community safety.

- The application assessment process seeks input from the sentencing judges, prosecutors, police, victims, presentence report writers, and probation and parole officers.

Applicants accepted for review may be resentenced by a panel of judges. Reviews by the court and by an independent assessment have been very favorable to the program in terms of its goals, cost benefits, and recidivism.

Trap Door Options

- Procedures for the emergency relief of prison crowding may be developed, for example (as in some states) giving the governor special authority when a certain level of crowding occurs. The selections for release may involve sentence reductions resulting in earlier parole eligibility for some inmates (as in Michigan), or the awarding of additional good time credits by corrections administrators (as in Illinois). The federal system, the District of Columbia, and all but four states have some provision for administrative reduction of time served in prison. Some programs have included "rolling back" parole dates already set.[57] The procedures among jurisdictions are quite varied, but generally seem to be based on some concept of release of the "most deserving"—that is, on ideas similar to those of the just desert theory of sentencing. A proposed alternative, from a utilitarian, crime control perspective, would allow only the demonstrably "best risk" offenders to be released.[58]

Effects of Intermediate Punishments

In the case of intermediate punishments, as in that of probation and parole supervision programs generally, when the question, "What works?" is asked, we still must answer that the data are not yet all in to provide an adequate answer. A recent informative review of available studies of intensive supervision, home confinement and electronic monitoring, drug testing under community supervision, and boot camps or shock incarceration mainly emphasized recidivism—committing further crimes—as the outcome criterion for evaluation. The authors offered six provisional conclusions on the basis of their review, as follows:

> Control in the community will not resolve the correctional crisis in the United States.

> More correctional control in the community will mean that more offenders will be detected committing crimes and, especially, violating conditions of their supervision.

> The success in detecting technical violations is inconsistent with the need to reduce prison crowding and the concomitant fiscal crisis.

> Intermediate punishments are unlikely to deter criminal behavior more effectively than regular probation or prison placements.

> Intermediate punishments appear to be more effective if coupled with treatment interventions.

> Without more evaluation research using [better, more rigorous research designs] it will be difficult to reach more definitive conclusions about the effectiveness of intermediate sanctions.[59]

Other conclusions from extensive study of the topic are offered in Box 11.8.[60]

Box 11.8

Joan Petersilia: In Her Own Words

[S]everal recent reviews of intermediate sanction programs [ISPs] . . . have produced rather consistent findings. The most important are:

- Most ISPs have been probation-*enhancement* programs rather than prison or jail diversion programs. They seek a "tougher" probation to replace traditional methods, and they target the "toughest" probation cases. This approach can reduce crowding and related costs only by substantial reductions in failure rates compared to traditional probation. But the stringent conditions and strict enforcement associated with most ISP programs means they actually produce a *higher* failure rate of technical violations. As a result, most ISPs implemented to date have

not saved money—since the intermediate sanction is usually more expensive than the routine probation program they would have participated in.

- Well implemented ISPs *do* restore credibility to the justice system, and provide a much-needed spectrum of punishments to match the spectrum of risk posed by criminals. Policy-makers, judges, corrections practitioners and the public strongly support intermediate sanctions for non-violent offenders. Offenders judge certain ISP programs as more punitive than short incarceration terms. This is particularly true in ISPs which include mandatory work and drug testing requirements.

- For offenders who do not present unacceptable risks of violence, ☞

☞ well-managed intermediate sanctions offer a cost-effective way to keep them in the community at less cost than imprisonment and with no worse prospect for criminality.

• Intermediate sanctions may offer promise as a way to get and keep offenders in drug and other treatment programs. With drug treatment programs, at least, there is evidence that coerced treatment programs can reduce both later drug use and later crimes, and there is evidence in the ISP and boot camp literature that these programs can increase treatment participation.

• The most important finding from the intermediate sanctions literature is that programs must deliver high "doses" of *both* treatment and surveillance to assure public safety and reduce recidivism. "Treatment" alone is not enough, nor is "surveillance" by itself adequate. Programs that can increase offender-to-officer contacts *and* provide treatment have reduced recidivism. And offenders who received drug counseling, held jobs, paid restitution and did community service were arrested at rates 10 to 20 percent lower than others.

—Joan Petersilia,
University of California at Irvine

Summary

Community corrections refers to correctional programs outside jails and prisons. Most convicted offenders are not in jail or prison but are on probation or parole.

If a person is on probation, this usually means that a sentence to prison has been suspended and the person has been released conditionally under supervision. If the conditions are not followed, the probation may be revoked by the court and the sentence that was suspended may be executed. The probation violator goes to prison.

If a person is on parole, this usually means that he or she has been serving time in prison but has been released conditionally to serve a part of the sentence in the community under supervision. Until recently, most persons on parole had been released by a discretionary decision of a parole board; now, about half are. If the conditions are not followed, the person may be returned to prison by administrative authority or by the parole board.

Probation began and grew as an alternative to confinement, with the principle purpose of rehabilitation. Parole began and grew as part of the idea that state control and supervision of the offender should be decreased progressively as a process of reformation progressed.

As the concept of the indeterminate sentence took hold in the late 1800s, the use of parole grew with it. By the late 1970s, parole was used by all states. This changed substantially in recent years along with moves toward more definite sentences and the accompanying decrease in discretion allowed both judges and parole boards. Most states still have parole boards, although the federal system does not. Nearly all, including the federal system, have kept parole supervision.

As both probation and parole evolved, the two main functions have been utilitarian. The purpose is to reduce crime, in two ways. The first is by reforming the offender, thus reducing crime. The second is by sending violators back to the court or the parole board for possible incarceration, thus preventing crime. The first function requires counseling and other services to the offender. The second demands surveillance and control.

Although the main alternative to probation or parole is incarceration, there are many choices left to the judge, parole board, or staff in selecting assignments or programs within community corrections. Examples are community service orders, restitution requirements, house arrest, drug testing, or attendance at substance-abuse treatment programs.

The selection of offenders for probation by judges and the placement of prison inmates on parole by parole boards both are influenced by the nature and seriousness of the crime, the prior criminal record of the offender, and estimates of the risk of future offending. Both kinds of decisions are based substantially on subjective judgments by the decision makers, who are usually untrained specifically for making these decisions.

Parole board goals are complex, involving jurist, sanctioner, treater, controller, citizen, and regulator functions. Procedures and decision alternatives are varied across the country, because legal and administrative structures including sentencing laws differ markedly from place to place. The information provided to assist in the parole decision also varies widely.

Often, the decision whether to parole a prisoner is not so much a decision to release the inmate or not as it is a decision about when, how, and under what conditions to release that person. Evaluations of parole boards are complicated by the diversity of parole board goals and also by the two expected functions of rehabilitation and crime control.

Increasing criticisms of indeterminacy in sentencing generally and paroling particularly mounted in the 1970s. Critics assailed paroling for procedural failings, for a process seen as counterproductive to rehabilitative aims, and for alleged ineffectiveness of the model imbedded in the indeterminate sentencing structure. As a result, three kinds of structural changes have taken place: (1) mandatory sentencing, (2) presumptive sentencing, and (3) development of parole decision guidelines.

Parole guidelines are procedures intended to structure and control discretion but not to eliminate it. They require explicit statements of paroling decision policy, specify the usual decisions for different offender circumstances, require reasons for exceptions to usual decisions, and procedures for periodic examination and revision of policy. Although guidelines were first developed by the federal paroling authority, a substantial number of states now have similar systems. Evidence is that the use of well-managed guidelines results in reduced unwarranted disparities and greater fairness.

Probation and parole supervision agencies have both control and treatment functions. Questions about the degree of effectiveness of agencies in achieving either control or treatment aims are very difficult to resolve because they are so complex. Much of the needed research has not been done.

Many substance-abusing offenders cycle repeatedly through the criminal justice system. Programs of treatment have increased, though not yet to the extent needed. Evidence is that well-managed programs can be effective is increasing, and cost benefits as well as reductions in offending now appear to be realistic aims.

The use of "intermediate punishments" has grown recently. This is partly in response to the costs of incarceration and partly as a result of increasing "get tough" attitudes. These programs can divert offenders from confinement but also can increase punishment and control of probationers and parolees without such diversion. Thus, sometimes these programs are "enhancements" to regular community supervision, sometimes alternatives to confinement. The effects of these programs are not yet understood fully.

1. Bloch, H. A. and Geis, G. (1962). *Man, Crime, and Society: The Forms of Criminal Behavior*. New York: Random House, 543.

2. Gottfredson, D. M. (1983). "Probation and Parole: Release and Revocation," in *Encyclopedia of Crime and Justice*, Vol. 3. Kadish, S. H. (ed.). New York: The Free Press, 1247–1255.

3. Bloch, H. A. and Geis, G. (1962), 545–546; Barnes, H. E. and Teeters, N. K. (1959). *New Horizons in Criminology*, 3rd ed. Englewood Cliffs, NJ: Prentice-Hall.

4. 1878 Mass. Acts, Ch. 198.

5. Barnes, H. E. and Teeters, N. K. (1959). *New Horizons in Criminology*. Englewood Cliffs: Prentice Hall, 375.

6. Bureau of Justice Statistics (1996). *Correctional Populations in the United States, 1994*. Washington, DC: Bureau of Justice Statistics, 1.

7. Gottfredson, D. M. and Gottfredson, M. R. (1980). *Decision Making in Criminal Justice: Toward the Rational Exercise of Discretion*. Cambridge, MA: Ballinger, 281–372.

8. Lindsey, E. (1925). "Historical Sketch of the Indeterminate Sentence and Parole System," *Journal of Criminal Law, Criminology, and Police Science* 16, 9–69.

9. National Council on Crime and Delinquency (annual). *Parole in the United States*. Washington, DC: U.S. Department of Justice, Law Enforcement Assistance Administration, National Criminal Justice and Statistics Service.

10. Bureau of Justice Statistics (1996). *Correctional Populations in the United States, 1994*. Washington, DC: Bureau of Justice Statistics, 2.

11. Studt, E. (1972). *Surveillance and Service in Parole: A Report of the Parole Action Study*. Los Angeles: University of California at Los Angeles, Institute of Government and Public Affairs.

12. Neithercutt, M. G. and Gottfredson, D. M. (1973). *Caseload Size Variation and Difference in Probation/Parole Performance*. Pittsburgh: National Center for Juvenile Justice.

13. Carter, R. M. and Wilkins, L. T. (1967). "Some Factors in Sentencing Policy," *Journal of Criminal Law, Criminology, and Police Science* 58, 503–514.

14. Gottfredson, M. R. and Gottfredson, D. M. (1980). *Decision Making in Criminal Justice: Toward the Rational Exercise of Discretion*. Cambridge, MA: Ballinger.

15. O'Leary, V. and Hall, J. (1976). "Frames of Reference in Parole." Mimeographed. Hackensack, NJ: National Council on Crime and Delinquency.

16. *Morrissey v. Brewer* (1972). 408 U.S. 471.

17. *Gagnon v. Scarpelli* (1973). 411 U.S. 778.

18. Robison, J. and Takagi, P. T. (1976). "The Parole Violator as an Organizational Reject," in *Probation, Parole, and Community Corrections*, 2nd ed. Carter, R. M. and Wilkins, L. T. (eds.). New York: Wiley, 365.

19. Robison, J. and Takagi, P. T. (1976), 367.

20. von Hirsch, A. (1976). *Doing Justice: The Choice of Punishments*. Preface by C. E. Goodell. Introduction by W. Gaylin and D. Rothman. New York: Hill and Wang; Harris, M. K. (1975). "Disquisition on the Need for a New Model for Criminal Sanctioning Systems," *West Virginia Law Review* 77, 263–326; Kittrie, N. N. (1971) *The Right to Be Different: Deviance and Enforced Therapy*. Baltimore: The Johns Hopkins University Press.

21. von Hirsch, A. and Hanrahan, K. J. (1979). *The Question of Parole: Retention, Reform, or Abolition?* Introduction by S. Messinger. Cambridge, MA: Ballinger.

22. Harris, M. K. (1975), "Disquisition on the Need for a New Model for Criminal Sanctioning Systems," *West Virginia Law Review* 77, 326.

23. Kastenmeier, R. W. and Eglit, H. C. (1973). "Parole Release Decisionmaking: Reha-bilitation, Expertise, and the Demise of Mythology, *American University Law Review*, 22, 477–525.

24. Gottfredson, D. M. and Tonry, M. (eds.) (1987). *Prediction and Classification: Criminal Justice Decision Making*. Chicago: The University of Chicago Press.

25. Gottfredson, D. M., Wilkins, L. T., and Hoffman, P. B. (1978). Guidelines for Parole and Sentencing: A Policy Control Method. Lexington, MA: Lexington Books; Gottfredson, Cosgrove, C. A., Wilkins, L. T., Wallerstein, J., and Rauh, C. (1978). *Classification for Parole Decision Policy*. Washington, DC: GPO.

26. National Advisory Commission on Criminal Justice Standards and Goals (1973). *Corrections*. Washington, DC: GPO.

27. Cohen, J. and Tonry, M. (1983). "Sentencing Reforms and Their Impacts," in A. Blum-stein, et al, *Research on Sentencing*. Washington, DC: National Academy Press, 438.

28. Gottfredson, M. R. and Gottfredson, D. M. (1980). *Decision Making in Criminal Justice: Toward the Rational Exercise of Discretion*. Cambridge, MA: Ballinger.

29. Rothman, D. J. (1978). "Unto Others, But . . . " *New York Times*, March 7, 35.

30. McCleary, R. (1983). "Probation and Parole: Supervision," in *Encyclopedia of Crime and Justice*, vol. 3, Kadish, S. H. (ed.). New York: The Free Press, 1255–1259.

31. Havel, J. (1963). *Special Intensive Parole Unit, Phase IV: A High Base Expectancy Study*. Sacramento, CA: California Department of Corrections.

32. Gottfredson, M. R. and Gottfredson, D. M. (1988). *Decision Making in Criminal Justice: Toward the Rational Exercise of Discretion*. New York: Plenum Press, 180–181.

33. Parole and Community Services division (1969). *The Work Unit Parole Program: 1969*. Sacramento, CA: California Department of Corrections.

34. Baird, S. (1981). "Probation and Parole Classification: The Wisconsin Model," *Corrections Today* 43: 36–41.

35. National Institute of Corrections (1981). *Model Probation and Parole Management Project Handbook*. Washington, DC: National Institute of Corrections.

36. Clear, T. and Braga, A. A. (1995). "Community Corrections," in Wilson, J. Q. and Petersilia, J. (eds.). *Crime*. San Francisco: Institute for Contemporary Studies.

37. Baird, S., Heinz, R., and Bemus, B. (1979). *The Wisconsin Case Classification/Staff Deployment Project: A Two Year Follow-Up Report*. Madison, WI: Wisconsin Department of Health and Human Services.

38. Clear, T. and Gallagher, K. (1985). "Probation and Parole Supervision: A Review of Current Classification Practices," *Crime and Delinquency* 31: 423–443.

39. Lipton, D., Martinson, R., and Wilkes, J. (1975). *The Effectiveness of Correctional Treatment: A Survey of Evaluation Studies*. New York: Praeger.

40. Gottfredson, D. M., Finckenauer, J. O., and Rauh, C. (1977). *Probation on Trial*. New-ark, NJ: School of Criminal Justice, Rutgers University.

41. Gottfredson, M. R. and Gottfredson, D. M. (1988). *Decision Making in Criminal Justice: Toward the Rational Exercise of Discretion*. New York: Plenum Press, 198–199.

42. Morris, N. and Tonry, M. (1990). *Between Prison and Probation: Intermediate Punishments in a Rational Sentencing System*. New York: Oxford University Press.

43. Chaiken, M. R. (1989). *In Prison Programs for Drug Involved Offenders*. Washington, DC: National Institute of Justice, vii.

44. Holden, H., Wakefield, P., and Shapiro, S. J. (1990). *Treatment Options for Drug-De-pendent Offenders: A Review of the Literature for State and Local Decisionmakers*. Washington, DC: National Institute of Justice.

45. Johnson, B., Lipton, D., and Wish, E. D. (1986). *Facts about the Criminality of Heroin and Cocaine Abusers and Some New Alternatives to Incarceration*. Washington, DC: National Institute of Justice.

46. Tabbush, V. (1986). *The Effectiveness and Efficiency of Publicly Funded Drug Abuse Treatment and Prevention Programs in California: A Benefit-Cost Analysis*. California Association of County Drug Program Administrators.

47. Bureau of Justice Assistance (1989). *Treatment Alternatives to Street Crime (TASC): Resource Catalog, 1989*. Washington, DC: Bureau of Justice Assistance.

48. Morris, N. and Tonry, M. (1990). *Between Prison and Probation: Intermediate Punishments in a Rational Sentencing System*. New York: Oxford University Press.

49. Cullen, F. T., Wright, J. P., and Applegate, B. K. "Control in the Community: The Limits of Reform?" in Harland, A. (ed.). (1996). *Choosing Correctional Options that Work*. Thousand Oaks, CA: Sage, 73–74.

50. Ibid., 71–72.

51. Hillsman, S. and Greene, J. (1992). "The Use of Fines as an Intermediate Sanction." In *Smart Sentencing: The Emergence of Intermediate Sanctions*. Byrne, J., Lurigo, A., and Petersilia, J. (eds.). Newbury Park, CA: Sage; von Hirsch, A., Wasik, A. M., and Greene, J. (1984). "Punishments in the Community and the Principles of Desert," *Rutgers Law Journal* 20: 595–618.

52. Georgia Department of Corrections (circa 1989). *Probation's Role in a Balanced Approach to Corrections*. Atlanta, GA: Georgia Department of Corrections.

53. National Committee on Community Corrections (1994), *A Proposal for Action*. Washington, DC: National Committee on Community Corrections, 9.

54. National Committee on Community Corrections (1994), 7–9.

55. National Committee on Community Corrections (1994), 6.

56. Lipsher, R. D. and Goldstein, H. M. (1990). *New Jersey Intensive Supervision Program: Progress Report*. Trenton, NJ: Administrative Office of the Courts; Pearson, F. S. and Harper, A. G. (1990). "Contingent Intermediate Sentences: New Jersey's Intensive Supervision Program," *Crime and Delinquency* 36: 1, 75–86.

57. Gottfredson, M. R. and Gottfredson, D. M. (1984). "Guidelines for Incarceration Decisions: A Partisan Review," *University of Illinois Law Review* 2, 311–312.

58. Gottfredson, S. D. and Gottfredson, D. M. (1985). "Selective Incapacitation?" *Annals of the American Academy of Political and Social Science* 478:135–149.

59. Cullen, F. T., Wright, J. P., and Applegate, B. K. (1996), "Control in the Community: The Limits of Reform?" in Harland, A. (ed.). (1996). *Choosing Correctional Options that Work*. Thousand Oaks, CA: Sage, 113–115.

60. Petersilia, J. (1997). "The Practice and Promise of Community Corrections," in Tonry, M. (ed.). *Oxford Criminology Handbook*. In preparation.

The Juvenile Justice System

Photo courtesy of the New Jersey Department of Corrections.

Chapter Twelve

Each generation views the behavior of its youths with alarm. How can we know whether delinquency and crime by young people is actually getting worse, as many people now believe? For how much crime are juveniles responsible? How do structures for dealing with youth crime differ from those designed for adults? How are they changing? What decisions are made about youths involved in the juvenile justice system, and by whom? In this chapter we will examine the nature and extent of delinquency and youth crime, structures and functions of the juvenile justice system, the nature of juvenile justice decisions, and some information needs for better management in the juvenile justice system.

❏ Questions to Think About
❏ Juvenile Justice
❏ The Juvenile Court
   Problems of Focusing on Law Violations in Exploring the Juvenile Courts
   The Court as Parent
❏ Change in the Juvenile Courts
❏ The Supreme Court Intervenes: Kent, Gault, and Winship
❏ Juvenile Court Jurisdiction
❏ Getting Tougher
❏ Decisions in the Juvenile Justice System
   Intake
   Prosecution
   Juvenile Court
❏ Formal and Informal Dispositions in Juvenile Courts
❏ The Nature and Extent of Delinquency and Youth Crime
   Self Report Studies
   Juvenile Arrests
   Juvenile Responsibility for Crime
   Youth Involvement in the Juvenile Justice System
   Victim Reports
   Cases Handled by the Juvenile Courts
   Juveniles Transferred to the Adult Criminal Courts
❏ Goals, Alternatives, and Information Needs in Juvenile Justice
   Goals
   Alternatives
   Information for Decisions
❏ Examples of Factors Influencing Decisions
   Factors Influencing Informal vs. Formal Processing
   Factors Influencing Program Selection in Informal Processing
   Factors Influencing Outcomes to Informal Processing
   Factors Influencing Judicial Dispositions
   Factors Influencing Outcomes to Formal Processing (Judicial Dispositions)
❏ Summary

1 . Most juveniles who are arrested are charged with
   a . a violent crime.
   b . a nonviolent crime.

2 . Petitions for status offenses most often charge
   a . truancy.
   b . running away.

3 . The offense most often cleared by arrest of a juvenile is
   a . motor vehicle theft.
   b . arson.

4 . Juveniles are responsible for
   a . most reported crime.
   b . less reported crime than are adults.

5 . Juvenile courts are getting more and more
   a . tough.
   b . lenient.

6 . The race in most delinquency cases is
   a . white.
   b . African American.

7 . Most youths in detention have been charged with
   a . property offenses.
   b . drug violations.

8 . Most delinquency cases processed in the juvenile courts involve
   a . assault.
   b . stealing.

9 . In delinquency matters, the state must prove its case
   a . beyond a reasonable doubt.
   b . by a preponderance of the evidence.

10 . In a given year, what percent of juveniles are arrested for a
   violent crime?
   a . 5 percent or more.
   b . less than one-half of 1 percent.

Answers: 1, b; 2, a; 3, b; 4. b; 5, a; 6. a; 7, a; 8, b; 9, a; 10, b.

Juvenile Justice

The term "juvenile justice" refers most directly to the work of the juvenile courts, but it includes that of other institutions and their personnel that also have responsibilities for and make decisions about the control and treatment of children and youths who violate the laws. Included are the police, the staff of the juvenile court including probation personnel, prosecuting and defense attorneys, detention center personnel, staff of juvenile correctional facilities, "aftercare" or parole boards, and parole supervision staff. The schools, public and private welfare agencies, and mental health institutions and agencies should be included also, because personnel of such agencies also make decisions that affect whether and how the juvenile system deals with youthful offenders. Far more decisions about these youths are made by school personnel, although they are not defined as a part of the juvenile justice system. Legislators, of course, make laws that provide a context for these decisions.

Despite the variety of agencies involved in juvenile justice, the juvenile court is both its symbol and its focus within the justice system. When the juvenile court was invented, a new way of handling children in trouble with the law, with their parents, or with others was initiated—and it differed markedly from the ways of the criminal courts.[1]

For more than a hundred years in the history of the United States, young persons alleged to have committed crimes were treated little differently than were adults. Very young children—usually under the age of 7 but sometimes 12—were presumed unable to commit crimes because they were thought to be "below the age of responsibility." Teenagers—most official delinquents—were processed and punished by the criminal justice system just as were adults.

The Juvenile Court

The juvenile court system was created about a century ago. The first was in Cook County, Illinois, in 1899. In a mere 20 years, juvenile courts became established in nearly all jurisdictions.[2] Now all states have courts with juvenile jurisdiction, although in most states they are not actually called juvenile courts. With variation among states, courts with juvenile jurisdiction may be found in district, superior, circuit, family, or probate court structures. These courts usually have jurisdiction over delinquency, status offenses (violations not considered crimes if committed by an adult), and abuse and neglect matters. They may have jurisdiction also in matters of adoption, termination of parental rights, and emancipation of minors. Whatever their names, courts with juvenile jurisdiction usually are called juvenile courts.[3] Who is considered an adult and who is not depends mainly on age—but may include other considerations—and differs among the states.

Problems of Focusing on Law Violations in Exploring the Juvenile Courts

Much of the work of the juvenile courts is ignored in this chapter, because the focus of this book is on the adult criminal justice system. A substantial part of the work of the juvenile courts concerns children who are abused or neglected, and it is that part that is not discussed. This presents major problems for providing a balanced view of the delinquency jurisdiction of the juvenile courts for two main reasons. First, the court was created precisely because children are not adults and it was believed that they are in need of protection. The second problem is that there is a large overlap between issues of neglect and of law violations by young persons. In many ways, the distinction between the delinquency jurisdiction of the courts and the abuse and neglect jurisdiction is in name only: the delinquent child often is a neglected child, and the neglected child is in danger of becoming a delinquent child (Box 12.1). In reality, the issues of neglect and of delinquency are interrelated. This chapter focuses on the delinquency side, and the juvenile courts are focused substantially on the neglect side as well—with a prominent goal of protecting the welfare of the child. The juvenile court is not a criminal court, but we will discuss the procedures used in

Box 12.1

Bobby

Bobby was sent to the school office for insubordination after he refused to remain in his seat. The assistant principal sent Bobby home with a note saying that he was to return to school in the company of a parent or guardian. Bobby was absent from school for the next 67 days.

Bobby's teachers, a little relieved not to have him in class, dutifully recorded these absences. Eventually, a computer listing of chronic absentees was run by the assistant principal's staff and sent to the school social worker. For two weeks the social worker repeatedly tried to call the home. Usually there was no answer. Twice someone answered but appeared to be incoherent. Afraid to go alone to Bobby's neighborhood, the social worker visited his home with an assistant.

The mother eventually answered the door, partly clothed and apparently drunk. She said that Bobby had left the county with his uncle, who would not bring the boy back because he feared arrest on an outstanding warrant. She said she had no transportation herself. She asked that the social worker not report Bobby's absence, because she was afraid that her welfare benefits would be taken away. She promised (unbelievably to the social worker) to have Bobby in school the following week.

After Bobby had been absent 117 days, the assistant principal reported his truancy to the local police. The police were unable to find anyone at home and turned to matters that seemed more pressing.

Bobby turned up at school the next year. After attending for two days, he stopped at a convenience store on the way home and tried to rob the clerk with a BB gun. He was arrested and taken by police to the intake unit of the juvenile court.

relation to law violations to the neglect of those aimed mainly at the protection of the child.

The Court as Parent

The idea of probation, a central aspect of juvenile courts to this day, had begun to take hold a half century before the first juvenile courts, as discussed in the previous chapter. John Augustus had been "bailing" youths for the purpose of their rehabilitation since the mid-1800s (Box 12.2).[4]

With the development of the juvenile courts, delinquency was distinguished from adult crime by the establishment of separate court and correctional systems for youths. The purposes of treatment and rehabilitation

Box 12.2

John Augustus, 1847: In His Own Words

I bailed 19 boys, from seven to fifteen years of age, and in bailing them it was understood, and agreed by the court, that their cases should be continued from term to term for several months, as a season of probation; thus each month at the calling of the docket, I would appear in court, make my report, and thus the cases would pass on for five or six months. At the expiration of this term, 12 of the boys were brought into court at one time, and the scene formed a striking and highly pleasing contrast with their appearance when first arraigned. The judge expressed much pleasure as well as surprise at their appearance, and remarked, that the object of the law had been accomplished and expressed his cordial approval of my plan to save and reform.

—John Augustus, the shoemaker who started probation.

were emphasized rather than either punishment or deterrence. Indeed, punishment was not a purpose. The state was to act *in the interest of* the child rather than to engage in a proceeding *against* the child. The system was to be beneficent. Its main characteristic was to be an attentive concern for the welfare of children and youths. As described by Schlossman,

> In juvenile court, children were never to stand accused of specific crimes, no matter what objectionable acts had brought them into court in the first place. Children were not to be formally accused of anything particular at all; instead, they were assumed to require the court's intervention, guidance, and supervision. A child might be officially recorded as dependent, neglected, or delinquent in order to provide a patina of procedural regularity. But it was a child's "status" or "condition"—literally, his life story—that was of principal concern. Juvenile courts were to respond as surrogate parents to children presumed to be in need, and to be so solicitous of their well-being that the courtroom process itself would become therapeutic. [5]

The legal foundation for the juvenile courts was in the civil, rather than the criminal, law. Its basis was the concept of *parens patriae* (meaning state as parent), which, from English medieval times, had authorized the right of the Crown to intervene or supplement family relations when the welfare of the child was threatened—to stand in the place of the parents. The application of the *parens patriae* doctrine was well established before the juvenile court came into existence.[6]

This doctrine and the benevolent purposes of the juvenile courts led to the extension of their jurisdiction to conduct not considered to be criminal if committed by an adult. These are the so-called "status offenses." Youths could be considered delinquent for truancy, for behavior defying correction or control—delinquency called "incorrigibility"—, and for other acts or conditions as well as for acts that would be considered to be criminal if committed by an adult. When youths were accused of delinquencies, their identity was to be withheld from the public in order to avoid stigma. Even for serious offenses, usual sentencing procedures did not apply, and the child was to be held in custody or under court control until no longer a minor.

For the first part of the twentieth century, there was wide acceptance of the philosophy, design, and methods of the juvenile courts. The premises and procedures of the courts were not often questioned.

Change in the Juvenile Courts

Despite a widespread early acceptance, there were some critics. Judge Edward Lindsey presented legal challenges: the procedures of the juvenile court conflicted with guarantees of the Bill of Rights; there were class biases in the application of the *parens patriae* doctrine; status offenders were punished under the guise of delinquency prevention; and no child should be placed in a reformatory without a formal conviction for a specific crime. The law now has caught up with many of his objections, but began to do so only decades later. Other early critics, such as the psychiatrist William Healy, though generally sympathetic, questioned some of the then current assumptions of the juvenile court and demanded their empirical study (see Box 12.3).[7] His plea for careful study to determine the results of the programs of the court is valid today.

Few argued, however, that the system should be scrapped. Children in need or in trouble with the law should be provided humane, individualized

treatment by a benevolent, paternalistic state.[8] This now has changed somewhat in emphasis, but it still is the dominant philosophy for most juvenile
courts, and for most youths under their jurisdiction. The court is to act in
the best interests of the child.

Box 12.3

Healy and Bronner, 1926: In Their Own Words

It is amazing that modern civilization, with all its frank devotion to conceptions of efficiency, has not yet undertaken thoroughly critical studies of what really are the results of its dealings with delinquency and crime. Despite the tremendous equipment and expenditure for protection, detection, apprehending, for courts, jails and prisons, reformatory education, probation, little or nothing is spent to ascertain with care what is or is not accomplished. In industry, business or active science such an inquiry into results is regarded as absolutely fundamental.

—William Healy and Augusta Bronner, psychiatrists who were influential in delinquency study.

Criticisms increased sharply in the 1960s, with the view that children in
need and in trouble often had to be protected from intervention by the supposedly benevolent state into their personal and family lives. A series of
decisions by the U.S. Supreme Court (Box 12.4), as well as the growing
criticism, changed the character of the juvenile courts while nevertheless
maintaining much that was fundamental to the original reforms.

Concerns about rising rates of delinquency and serious crime by youth,
accompanied and reinforced by media reports, also have led to changes that

---

Box 12.4

Decisions of the U.S. Supreme Court That Changed the Nature of the Juvenile Courts

1966	*Kent v. United States:* Courts must provide the "essentials of due process and fair treatment" when transferring juveniles to the adult criminal courts. 383 U.S. 541 (1966)
1967	*In re* **Gault**: Juveniles have rights to notice and counsel, to question witnesses, and to protection against self-incrimination in hearings that could result in commitment to an institution. 387 U.S. 1 (1967)
1970	*In re* **Winship**: In delinquency matters, the State must prove its case beyond a reasonable doubt. 397 U.S. 358 (1970)
1971	*McKeiver v. Pennsylvania:* Jury trials are not constitutionally required in juvenile court hearings. 403 U.S. 528 (1971)
1975	*Breed v. Jones:* Waiver of a juvenile to a criminal court after adjudication in juvenile court constitutes double jeopardy. 421 U.S. 519 (1975)
1977	*Oklahoma Publishing Co. v. District Court in and for Oklahoma City:* A court order prohibiting the press from reporting the name and photograph of a youth in juvenile court, which it legally obtained elsewhere, was an unconstitutional infringement of freedom of the press. 480 U.S. 308 (1977) ☞

☞ 1979	**Smith v. Daily Mail Publishing Co.:** The press may report information lawfully obtained independent of the court about juvenile court proceedings. 443 U.S. 97 (1979)
1984	**Schall v. Martin:** "Pretrial" preventive detention of juveniles is allowable under certain circumstances. 467 U.S. 253 (1984)

Adapted from Snyder, H. N. and Sickmund, M. (1995). *Juvenile Offenders and Victims: A National Report.* Washington, DC: Office of Juvenile Justice and Delinquency Prevention, 80–82.

are generally making the juvenile courts more like the adult criminal courts. Consider this prediction, written about 20 years ago:

> . . . the national media has been concentrating on stories of juvenile violence, and a crime wave mentality is evident in many legislative committees. It may be that the response to this perceived crisis will be major modification of the juvenile justice system toward a much more punitive stance. [9]

The Supreme Court Intervenes: Kent, Gault, and Winship

The changing conceptions of children's rights in court were reflected in three major decisions of the U.S. Supreme Court. Each concerned the due process clause of the Fourteenth Amendment to the U.S. Constitution, and taken together they transformed the juvenile court into a court of law. They supported the rights of children to basic procedural safeguards and to the same standard of proof of guilt that is required in adult criminal trials.

The first case concerned a 16-year-old boy, Morris Kent, whose Washington, D.C., case was transferred to the adult criminal court without a hearing. Such a transfer typically is made by a "waiver" of jurisdiction by the juvenile court—hence, the terms "waiver" and "transfer" often are used as synonyms.

In the criminal court, Kent was convicted of six counts of housebreaking and robbery and sentenced to 30 to 90 years in prison. Although his attorney had requested a hearing on the matter of the transfer, the judge held no hearing and waived jurisdiction, stating he did so "after a full investigation." This was not good enough for the Supreme Court, which noted that such a waiver of jurisdiction is a critically important stage in the juvenile process and ruled that it must be attended by the essentials of due process and fair treatment. This requires a hearing on the waiver if that is considered by the juvenile court, representation by counsel at that hearing, access by the youth's attorney to the social records of the youth, and, if the youth is transferred, a statement of reasons in support of the order.

The case of Morris Kent is also notable because the Court raised a potential challenge to the *parens patriae* doctrine that lies at the foundation of the juvenile court. Previously, the Court had held that less due process might be provided if there was a compensating benefit. The juvenile courts theoretically, while providing less due process, had a greater concern for the interests of the youth. But the Court said that such a compensating benefit may not exist in reality. If not, the youth may receive "neither the protection accorded to adults nor the solicitous care and regenerative treatment postulated for children."[10]

The second case was that of 15-year-old Gerald Gault, on probation in Arizona for a minor property offense and accused of making an obscene phone call to an adult neighbor. When the victim did not appear at the adjudicatory hearing (the hearing for the judge's determination whether Gerald was delinquent), the court did not resolve the issue of whether the boy made the allegedly obscene remarks. Nevertheless, he was committed to the training school until age 21 (although the maximum sentence for a convicted adult would have been a $50 fine or two months in jail). Three years after his arrest, the Supreme Court ruled that, in hearings that could result in commitment to an institution, juveniles have the right to notice, to counsel, to question witnesses, and to protection against self-incrimination. Gerald was being punished, not helped. The court declared the concept of *parens patriae* was murky and of dubious historical relevance. The Fourth Amendment rights of Gerald Gault had been violated.[11]

The third case concerned 12-year-old Samuel Winship, accused of stealing $112 from a woman's purse. Although Winship's attorney elicited from the court agreement that there was reasonable doubt about guilt, the court's ruling that adjudicated Winship delinquent was based on the standard of a "preponderance of the evidence." The New York juvenile courts operated under this lower standard of proof, as is required typically in civil courts. Winship was sent to the training school.

The question for the Supreme Court was whether the higher standard of proof of "beyond a reasonable doubt," as required for adults, should be required in adjudications of delinquency. The court ruled that the "reasonable doubt" standard should be required.[12] Thus the court insisted on the same standard of proof as is required for the conviction of adults in a criminal trial.

Juvenile Court Jurisdiction

Determination of whether a youth accused of a crime or referred to a court will be dealt with by a juvenile or criminal court is determined by state statutes, which differ among the states. The definition of original juvenile court jurisdiction typically is based mainly on age. In most states and the District of Columbia, the oldest age of original jurisdiction in delinquency matters is 17. In those places, persons charged with an offense, or arrested, or referred to the court before the age of 18 are in the jurisdiction of the juvenile court. In some states, the age criterion is 16, and in a few it is 15 (Box 12.5).[13] There are, however, exceptions in many states to the simple age criterion.

In some states, a combination of age, the offense alleged, and sometimes the prior court history may place the youth under the original jurisdiction of the criminal court. In other states, the circumstances of age, offense alleged, and prior record put the youth under the jurisdiction of both the juvenile and criminal courts (called concurrent jurisdiction). In that case, the choice of the court—the decision whether a petition will be filed with the juvenile court alleging delinquency or the youth will be tried for a crime in an adult court—is made by the prosecutor.

Box 12.5

Oldest Age for Original Juvenile Court Jurisdiction in Delinquency Matters

15	16	17		
Connecticut	Georgia	Alabama	Kansas	Ohio
New York	Illinois	Alaska	Kentucky	Oklahoma
North Carolina	Louisiana	Arkansas	Maine	Oregon
	Massachusetts	California	Maryland	Pennsylvania
	Michigan	Colorado	Minnesota	Rhode Island
	Missouri	Delaware	Mississippi	South Dakota
	South Carolina	District of Columbia	Montana	Tennessee
	Texas	Florida	Nebraska	Utah
		Hawaii	Nevada	Vermont*
		Idaho	New Hampshire	Virginia
		Indiana	New Jersey	Washington
		Iowa	New Mexico	West Virginia
			North Dakota	Wisconsin
				Wyoming

- Many states have higher upper ages of juvenile court jurisdiction in status offense, abuse, neglect, or dependency matters—often through age 20.

- In many states, the juvenile court has jurisdiction over young adults who committed offenses while juveniles.

- Several states also have minimum ages of juvenile court jurisdiction in delin‑ quency matters—ranging from 6 to 12.

* In Vermont, the juvenile and criminal courts have concurrent jurisdiction over all 16- and 17-year-olds.

Typically, the jurisdiction of the juvenile court extends beyond the upper age of original jurisdiction to age 20. In some states, however, it is as young as 17. In a few states, it is older than 20, and in some it is until the full term of the juvenile court's disposition order has expired.[14]

There are three ways a juvenile may come to be tried as an adult in a criminal court. The first is by a decision of the juvenile court judge who waives jurisdiction of the juvenile court. This is possible in most states (other than Nebraska and New York). The result is a transfer to the jurisdiction of the criminal court. Or, a youth whose case is in concurrent jurisdiction of both the juvenile and criminal courts may be tried in a criminal court if the prosecutor decides to bring charges there. The third way the youth can end up in criminal court is a result of decisions by legislators. In that case, legislatures have enacted statutes that exclude some otherwise eligible alleged offenders from the jurisdiction of the juvenile court. These exclusion criteria usually include some combination of age and the seriousness of the alleged offense. The state statutes governing jurisdiction are varied and complex, and exceptions may be found to most general statements about it.

Getting Tougher

Traditionally, transfers to the adult courts were made in the first way—by discretionary decisions of juvenile court judges. Since the 1970s, however, along with the other trends associated with politically popular "get tougher" attitudes, statutes increasingly have excluded some youths from the juvenile court jurisdiction. Now, in half the states, some offense allegations exclude the accused from the juvenile court, and some states recently have added others to the offenses already excluded. By statutory exclusion, legislators have "transferred" many cases from the juvenile to the criminal courts; this now is how the largest number of juveniles are tried in adult courts. In a fourth of the states, prosecutors have been given the discretion to charge some offenses in either the juvenile or the criminal court.[15] Thus, for some classifications of accused youths, the legislators have taken the discretionary decision from the judges and have given it to prosecutors.

Across the country, states in recent years have taken action to respond to concerns about presumably increasing violent crimes by juveniles. Typically, legislative or executive action has been aimed at violent crimes—often in reaction to an isolated incident with much accompanying publicity. The net result, however, has been an increase in the severity of sanctions for juveniles generally—not only for those accused of serious crimes. In many cases, states are incarcerating more youths for longer times and treating more and more as adults.[16] Increasingly, legislatures are changing the rules

---

Box 12.6

States Are Changing to "Get Tougher" on Serious Crime by Juveniles

- Change is everywhere:

Since 1942, 47 of the 50 state legislatures and the District of Columbia have made substantive changes to their laws targeting juveniles who commit violent or other serious crimes.

- Change is consistent:

Offender accountability, punishment, and incarceration have replaced traditional notions of individualized justice.

- Change in decision-making roles:

Juvenile court judges have significantly less authority to make decisions regarding the venue for, and the disposition of, cases involving violent or other serious crimes than they did in 1992.

- Change is not tested:

Most of the changes *have not* been based on evidence that demonstrates their efficacy.

- Change will impact the number of minority juveniles:

Because minorities are already overrepresented in targeted crime categories, new laws will have a disproportionate impact on minorities in jails and state prisons.

—Patricia Torbet,
National Center for Juvenile Justice

about the jurisdiction of the juvenile courts. A result is that more youths are subject to the criminal law reserved for adults and therefore are exposed to lengthy sentences to confinement or the death penalty. For summary statements, see Boxes 12.6[17] and 12.7.[18]

Box 12.7

State Responses to Serious and Violent Juvenile Crime

- Since 1992, all but ten states adopted or modified laws making it easier to prosecute juveniles in adult court.

- New laws have had a dramatic impact on sentencing, including the imposition of mandatory minimums and "blended sentences."*

- Juvenile and adult corrections administrators are under pressure to develop new institutional programs.

- States have increasingly called for a resumption of open proceedings,

the release of offenders' names, and sharing of information.

- All of the states and the District of Columbia now have legislation explicitly addressing the rights of victims of juvenile crime.

—Patricia Torbet,
National Center for Juvenile Justice

---

*"Blended sentences" are combinations of increased sanctions by either the juvenile or criminal court.

Decisions in the Juvenile Justice System

Just as in the case of adult criminal processing, the juvenile justice system may be considered to be a series of decisions—in this case, decisions made about youths alleged to be delinquent or otherwise in need of the intervention of the state. As in the case of adults, these decisions typically are made within wide areas of discretion. Similarly, the goals, alternatives, and information needs of decision makers in the juvenile justice system may be examined.

We will consider the flow of cases through the juvenile justice system in terms of three phases: (1) referral and intake into the system, (2) prosecution, and (3) the courts. Actually, it is a continuous process and these steps may overlap, but it is easier to view it in these stages.

Intake

A youth's involvement in the juvenile justice system typically begins when he or she allegedly commits a delinquent or incorrigible act or has been neglected or abused. This event may be observed either by police or any other citizen. If it is not observed, the juvenile justice system is not invoked. If it is observed by police, the child can be taken into custody immediately. Then the police officer will conduct an investigation into the incident while the child is being held at the police station. The investigating police officer fills out a report and, if he or she concludes that there is probable cause to believe a crime was committed and that the youth did it, a complaint (or referral) on the incident is completed.

In all jurisdictions, the juvenile justice system is initiated when an alleged delinquent act or state of need of a child is observed by the police or others. Obviously, if a delinquent act occurs but is not observed by anyone, no record is made of it and the juvenile justice system does not become involved. This calls attention to the fact that we can never know with precision and certainty the extent of delinquency or neglect or abuse—just as we can never know completely and accurately the full extent of adult crime.

Most cases that are referred to the juvenile courts are, by far, referred by the police. For person, property, and drug offense allegations, it is about 90 percent. General categories of offenses alleged in these referrals by police are shown in Figure 12.1. Other cases, referred by schools, parents, neighbors, welfare agencies, or others, more typically are for truancy, neglect, or running away.

Figure 12.1 Youths Referred by Law Enforcement, 1993, by Offenses Alleged

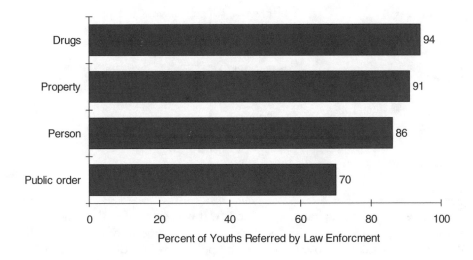

Source: data in Butts, J. , Snyder, H. N., Finnegan, T. A., Aughenbaugh, A. L., and Poole, R. S. (1996). *Juvenile Court Statistics 1993*. Washington, D.C.: Office of Juvenile Justice and Delinquency Prevention, 6.

If police observe the act or acts, they must decide whether there is probable cause to believe that an offense or offenses occurred. Next, it must be decided that there is probable cause to believe that the youth did it. If either of these questions is decided in the negative, nothing will be done. Similarly, nothing will be done if the officer decides to ignore the event. Often, the officer may decide to counsel or reprimand the youth, talk with the parents, or otherwise seek to bring about a resolution of the situation short of taking the youth into custody. The situation is similar to that found in the case of adults—the police operate within a wide range of discretionary decision making.

If a police officer decides to take a youth into custody, the police themselves may have a police lockup—a temporary holding facility run by the police. In 1990, the year of the most recent national survey, 29 percent of

Figure 12.2 Juvenile Justice System Intake Decisions

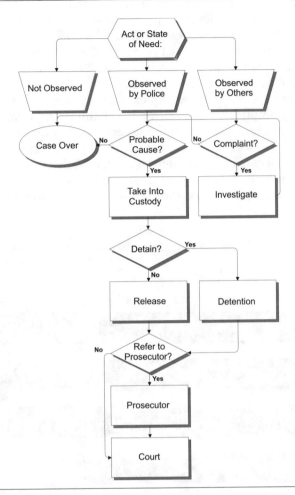

local police departments had such a facility. It was estimated that about 750 youths were admitted to police lockups on a given day in that year. About a third of youths taken into custody by the police are handled by the police department and released, usually with a warning and usually to parents. About two thirds are referred to the intake units of the juvenile courts or (for 7 percent in 1992) to the adult criminal courts for prosecution.[19]

The decision to take a youth into custody is based on whether the charge is a felony, misdemeanor, or incorrigibility. The more serious the charge, the more likely will be the detention of the child. Police must contact the child's parents whether or not the child is detained.

A next important decision is whether the detained youth will be released. If not, it must be decided whether the complaint will be referred to the court or submitted to the prosecutor. About 30 percent are warned and released, usually to parents, other relatives, or friends. This sometimes is called "station adjustment." A few may be diverted from the juvenile justice system through programs operated by the police, including referrals to other agencies. About two out of three, however, are referred to the court intake process. Of these, most—more than nine out of ten—are referred to the juvenile court or probation department. The rest (7 percent) are referred to the county attorney for possible prosecution in the criminal courts as adults.[20]

Figure 12.3 Prosecution Decisions

Chapter 12

▲ ▲ ▲ ▲ ▲ ▲

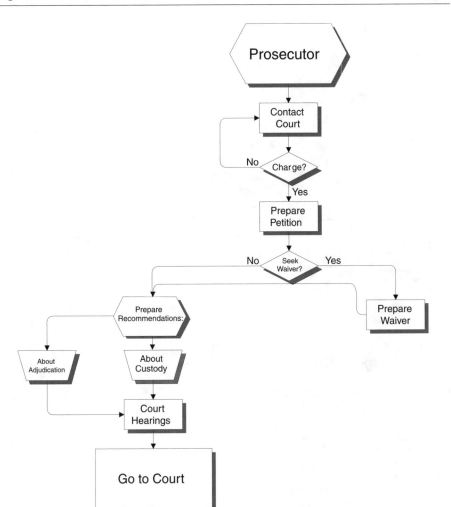

If the alleged misbehavior was not observed by the police, it may have been observed by others. This may have been a parent, a teacher, a neighbor, or anyone else. If there is no complaint to the police, usually nothing will be done. If, however, the police receive a complaint, they may or may not decide to investigate further. If they do not simply drop the matter but decide to investigate, they again have the decisions as to probable cause, detention, release, and referral—just as if they had observed the act.

Prosecution

If the case is referred to the prosecutor by the police (or, later, by the court), then the prosecutor must decide whether to charge. Usually the court has discretion regarding a referral, but legislatures may require referral to the prosecutor for specific kinds of repeated or more serious cases. The prosecutor's job then is to decide whether or not to file a petition with the court alleging that the juvenile is delinquent or otherwise in need of the supervision of the court. The basis for the decision often is said to be "legal sufficiency," referring to the strength of the evidence and estimated prob-

Figure 12.4 Court Decisions

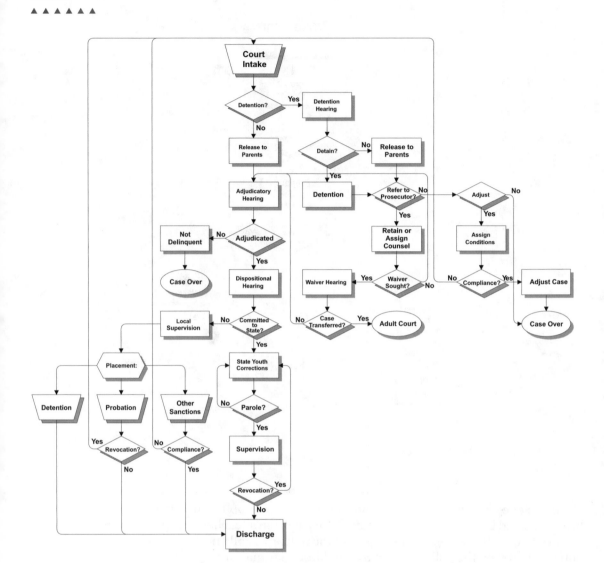

ability of obtaining an delinquency adjudication (similar to conviction). The prosecutor may decide not to file also if the case is deemed relatively non-serious.

If a petition is to be filed, the prosecutor also must decide, in most jurisdictions, whether to request a waiver—that is, transfer—to the adult court. The prosecutor also must decide, typically, what recommendation to make to the court concerning custody or disposition. The prosecutor's choice whether to file a petition is critical, because it determines whether the youth will be formally charged and prosecuted in the juvenile court, with a judge deciding whether the youth is delinquent, and, if so, what should be done within the alternatives available to the court. Otherwise, the case will be dropped or else, as is much more common, dealt with informally within the court's probation system.

This youth has been placed in detention while he awaits a decision whether he will be prosecuted as a juvenile or an adult. Under what circumstances do you believe he should go to the adult court? —*Photo courtesy of www.photostogo.com.*

In cases of misdemeanors and incorrigibility (behavior resisting correction), the police in some jurisdictions may refer the child to "intake services," a department of probation separate and distinct from the intake screening workers at the juvenile court. In these cases, the child and family will be interviewed, the child will be asked to accept guilt, and "consequences" will be explained to the child by the probation officer, without the child ever attending a formal court hearing. This involves the intake officer "adjusting" the complaint, in which case the probation officer establishes specific conditions the juvenile must fulfill before the complaint may be adjusted. Adjustment of the complaint by the intake officer may involve several alternatives: family or individual counseling, special education programs, work hours, restitution, community service, or some similar resolution. If the child does not acknowledge responsibility for the offense or does not agree to the consequences, then the case may be referred to the prosecutor for the possible filing of a petition. This process is somewhat akin to plea bargaining, because the usual alternative to adjustment for the youth is referral to the prosecutor with a recommendation that a petition be filed.

If police do not transport the juvenile to the intake services or directly to the juvenile court, he or she is released to the parents and is contacted later by a probation officer about the charge and date of an advisory hearing. This hearing for nondetained juveniles usually is intended to be held fairly soon, such as within 30 days of taking the child into custody. If the child does not hire counsel, an attorney is provided.

Once taken to the juvenile court, the court's intake screening staff conduct a brief investigation, usually including a prior records check and sometimes an assessment of risk of further delinquency and needs for supervision and treatment, to assist them in making a decision whether the child shall be detained. Intake screening staff also decide whether the charge should be referred to the prosecutor. If the staff agree with police that the child should be detained, an advisory hearing is set, usually for the next day. Most detained juveniles either have counsel assigned or obtain counsel on the day of the advisory hearing.

If we ask "Which youths are detained?" the answer depends on whether the question means "Who is most likely to be detained?" or "Who is in detention?" When we consider only general categories of alleged offenses, the most *likely* to be detained are youths accused of drug law violations, but

**Figure 12.5 Percent of Delinquency Cases Detained, by Category of Offense,
1993**

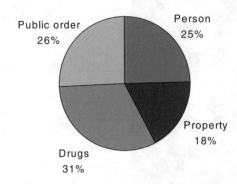

Source: data in Butts, J., Snyder, H. N., Finnegan, T. A., Aughenbaugh, A. L., and Poole, R. S.
(1996). *Juvenile Court Statistics, 1993*. Washington, D.C.: Office of Juvenile Justice and
Delinquency Prevention, 7.

those with alleged person and public order offenses often are detained as
well (Figure 12.5). If we ask a different question, namely, "What are the main
categories of alleged offenses for youth who are detained?" we get a very
different answer, as shown in Figure 12.6. Now we see that most children
and youth who are detained are those accused of property offenses, because
this is such a common kind of offense for juveniles.

When the case is referred to the prosecutor, attorneys review the complaint and decide whether to file a petition. Alternatively, the prosecutor may
seek various noncourt dispositions for the child. The prosecutor may, for
example, in some jurisdictions, choose to file a petition for a social evaluation by the juvenile court. The probation field services then may recommend alternative treatment or supervision plans.

If the prosecutor wishes to seek transfer of the juvenile to the adult court,
he or she must do so before the child's adjudicatory hearing. Otherwise, the
juvenile can not be tried in the criminal court, because this would constitute
double jeopardy. Transfer decisions are made only at formal court proceedings presided over by judges.

At the advisory hearing, the juvenile is advised of the charges, informed
of his or her legal rights, and, in the case of contested petitions, scheduled
for an adjudication or formal hearing. If the child admits the charges at the
advisory hearing, an adjudicatory hearing is not required, and the child can
be judged delinquent at that moment. Most juvenile cases are disposed of
in this manner. A disposition hearing (similar to sentencing) is then scheduled. Alternatively, the hearing officer could dismiss the petition at this
point. If the child contests the charges, but later admits them, the adjudicatory hearing is also skipped.

The prosecutor argues contested petitions at the adjudication hearing,
which is an adversarial proceeding where the juvenile is represented by
counsel. At this hearing, the judge (or, often a commissioner or other officer)
decides whether to dismiss the case or whether to adjudicate the youth delinquent or incorrigible. Once a child is adjudicated delinquent or incorrigible, a disposition hearing is set.

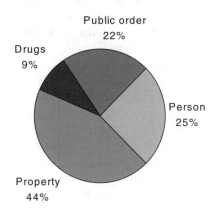

Source: data in Butts, J., Snyder, H. N., Finnegan, T. A., Aughenbaugh, A. L., and Poole, R. S. (1996). *Juvenile Court Statistics 1993*. Washington, D.C.: Office of Juvenile Justice and Delinquency Prevention, 7.
Note: although detention was least likely in property offense cases, they accounted for 44 percent of all delinquency cases detained, because property offenses represent the largest share of juvenile court caseloads.

Before the disposition hearing, a juvenile probation officer usually conducts a detailed social history of the child. The data gathered are compiled in a report known as the predisposition report. At the disposition hearing, the probation officer, defense counsel, and prosecuting attorney typically make recommendations to the judge regarding the child's program placement, penalties, or other sanctions. The disposition hearing resembles sentencing in the adult courts.

The judge typically has four basic choices of dispositions for the child: (1) probation only, (2) residential treatment in the community, normally accompanied by probation, (3) an intensive supervision program when available, and (4) the state department of youth corrections for placement in one of its secure facilities. Some conditions of probation may involve restitution, fines and community service, placement in a foster home, and/or day support programs. The judge also can impose penalties such as fines or community service with or without having a probation officer follow the case.

The child's disposition typically is reviewed periodically by the juvenile court judge if the child is placed on intensive probation; otherwise, juveniles are followed by juvenile probation officers but often do not receive review hearings unless triggered by some critical event, such as allegation of probation violation. Once a child is committed to the state corrections agency, the state has complete decision making jurisdiction regarding his or her treatment plan, level of custody, release date, and supervision after release. The juvenile may be released from state custody after going before a committee or paroling authority, depending on the requirements of the jurisdiction.

Formal and Informal Dispositions in Juvenile Courts

Roughly half the cases referred to the juvenile courts are handled informally—that is, without either adjudication or referral to the adult courts.

The typical flow of cases through major decision points for 1,000 cases is shown in Figure 12.7. When cases are handled formally, most (except those that are transferred to the adult criminal court) have adjudication hearings. Many, however, are not adjudicated delinquent. When handled informally, many are dismissed, and a substantial portion are placed on "informal" probation, or have other dispositions.

Since Figure 12.7 deals only with major events, much important detail is lacking. Many of those cases that were dismissed may have been assigned that outcome only after completing requirements imposed by informal agreement, such as completing community service requirements, making restitution, attending counseling or educational programs about drug or alcohol abuse, or satisfying other conditions. Often in such cases, the youth is required to accept responsibility for the alleged misbehavior as well as to accept the consequences assigned in order to avoid adjudication and possibly harsher penalties. This whole process often is handled by probation staff, with little or no direct involvement of a juvenile court judge.

Figure 12.7   Typical Flow of 1,000 Cases through the Juvenile Courts, 1992

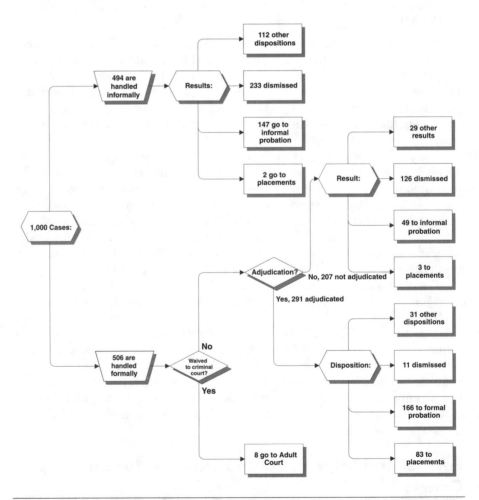

Source: adapted from Snyder, H. N. and Sickmund, M. (1995). *Juvenile Offenders and Victims: A National Report*. Washington, D.C.: Office of Juvenile Justice and Delinquency Prevention, 126 (from data in Butts, J., et al [1995] *Juvenile Court Statistics 1992*).

The Nature and Extent of Delinquency and Youth Crime

As with measures of adult crime, there are three main ways to assess the amount of crime attributable to youth: (1) ask them about their offending (self-report surveys), (2) ask victims of crime about the age of offenders, and (3) measure crimes cleared by arrests, noting the age of the person arrested. Another informative resource for learning about the nature of delinquency is examination of the workloads of the juvenile courts—that is, observation of the numbers and kinds of cases referred. Thus, useful information on juvenile offending comes from self-reports, from the National Victim Survey data, from the Uniform Crime Reports, and from juvenile court statistics. Each has some strengths and some limitations—as described in Chapter 2—as measures of the nature and extent of juvenile crime.

> *The children now love luxury. They have bad manners, contempt for authority, they show disrespect to their elders, love chatter in place of exercise. They no longer rise when their elders enter the room. They contradict their parents, chatter before company, gobble up dainties at the table, cross their legs, and tyrannize over their teachers.*
> —Socrates, Fifth Century, B.C. (attrib)

Self-Report Studies

An advantage of self-report studies is that behavior that never came to the attention of juvenile justice agencies nevertheless may be reported. Such studies typically find a much higher proportion of youths involved in delinquency than that indicated by official records. They indicate, for example,

These youths in an engine repair class in a corrections facility have been handled formally, adjudicated delinquent, and placed in a state facility (see figure 12.7). Do you believe that all cases should be handled formally through adjudication and disposition, or agree with the informal processing of some youths? —*Photo courtesy of the New Jersey Department of Corrections.*

that 90 percent or more of males and about two-thirds of females report committing a delinquent act before age 18. And, a national youth survey found that by their 18th birthday, 30 percent of males and 10 percent of females reported that they committed at least three violent offenses within a one-year period. Disadvantages, besides those of interviewing children on a topic that may be intrusive, include the expense of interviewing large enough samples to adequately measure relatively rare events, such as the most serious crimes.[21]

Most of our information on the extent of youth crime comes from official records. Despite their limitations, these data do provide good indications of the workload of the juvenile justice system.

Juvenile Arrests

Because there is so much concern with youth crime, it is informative to ask what proportion of all youths and how many are arrested for any offense, and for a violent offense, in a given year. More than one in four Americans— 69 million—are under age 18. For many reasons—because more than one in five of these children and youths live in poverty, because fewer children now than in the past live with both parents, [22] or because the newspapers and television report serious crimes by juveniles with alarming regularity— it might be expected that a large percentage of youths will be arrested in any specific year.

By far, however, most youths do *not* get into trouble with the law in a given year. Examine Figure 12.8, which shows that 95 percent of juveniles were not arrested for any offense in 1992. It shows also that less that one-half of 1 percent were arrested for a violent crime. Surely 5 percent arrested is too many, and one-half of 1 percent arrested for violent crimes is deplorable. But it nevertheless should be remembered that the great majority of youths are not represented in these numbers.

Figure 12.8 Percent of Youths Aged 10 to 17 in the United States Arrested in 1992

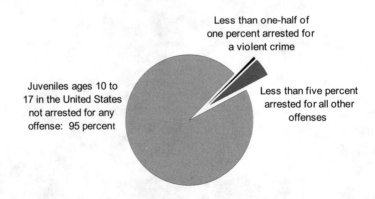

Source: adapted from Snyder, H. N. and Sickmund, M. (1995). *Juvenile Offenders and Victims: A National Report.* Washington, D.C.: Office of Juvenile Justice and Delinquency Prevention, 51 (based on Crime in the United States, 1992).

Juvenile Responsibility for Crime

Unfortunately, however, a substantial share of crime is committed by juveniles. When we examine offenses known to the police and cleared by arrests, we find that noteworthy contributions to the extent of crime are made by youths in all major categories of offenses. Youths are responsible for 40 percent of arsons. They steal, committing about one out of five reported larcenies, motor vehicle thefts, and burglaries. They are assaultive, responsible for perhaps one in 10 or more of reported assaults, rapes, and murders (Figure 12.9). But most reported crime by far is attributable to adults beyond the age of the juvenile court jurisdiction.

In examining the figures in this section, we must be clear about what is being measured. Arrest statistics and crime clearance statistics measure different things and, thus they answer different questions. If we ask "How much crime is done by juveniles?" the clearance data (as in Figures 12.9 and 12.10) give the better answer, because the count is of *crimes*, not *persons* arrested. If we ask "How many youth are involved in the juvenile justice system?" then the arrest data are more informative, because *persons*, not *crimes*, are counted. Both measures are based only on offenses reported to the police. As a result, self-report data may be more informative on both counts because youths may report on the offenses they have committed besides others that involve them with the system.

Figure 12.9 Juvenile and Adult Responsibility for Crime, as Measured by Offenses Cleared by Arrest, 1991

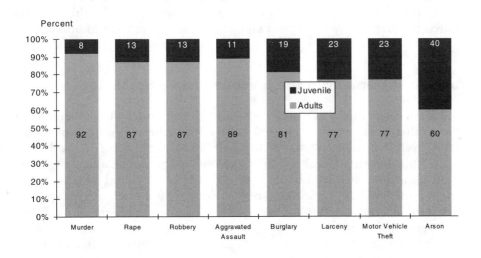

Source: adapted from Snyder, H. N. and Sickmund, M. (1995). *Juvenile Offenders and Victims: A National Report*. Washington, D.C.: Office of Juvenile Justice and Delinquency Prevention, 48 (based on data from Federal Bureau of Investigation [1992] *Crime in the United States, 1991*).

The crime clearance data are thus the most informative about the amount of serious crime done by juveniles.[23] These data, shown in Figures 12.9 and 12.10, show the responsibility of youths to the serious "felony" categories of crime when these are counted by the police as cleared. It is clear from Figure 12.9 that most crimes by far, when they are cleared by arrest, have been cleared by the arrest of one or more adults. Figure 12.10

Figure 12.10 Percent of Cleared Offenses That Involved Juveniles, 1992

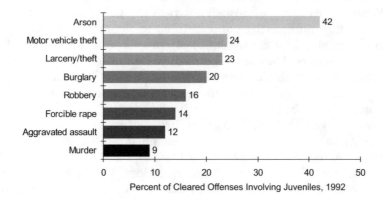

Source: adapted from Snyder, H. N. and Sickmund, M. (1995). *Juvenile Offenders and Victims: A National Report.* Washington, D.C.: Office of Juvenile Justice and Delinquency Prevention, 101 (based on Crime in the United States, 1992).

shows also that crimes cleared by the arrest of juveniles differ according to the type of crime. Arsons, when cleared, are often cleared by juvenile arrests. Personal crimes are much less often cleared by arrests of youths. The data for two different years show the consistency of the results from year to year. Juveniles are responsible for about 10 or 12 percent of personal crimes cleared and for a somewhat larger percentage of property crimes. They are responsible for nearly a fourth of reported larcenies and vehicle thefts cleared by the police with arrests and about one in five cleared burglaries.

Youth Involvement in the Juvenile Justice System

Classifying crimes in a different way—determining the percentage of *arrests* rather than of crimes cleared—also reflects the involvement of youths in the juvenile justice system for different kinds of offenses (Figure 12.11), but is more informative about the workload of the police and the courts. About a third are involved because of property crimes, and 18 percent for violent crimes. When we want to know the proportion of arrests for specific offenses that involve juveniles, the results are shown in Figure 12.12. These data may overestimate the contribution of juveniles to crime, because youths are more likely than are adults to commit offenses in groups.

Victim Reports

The National Crime Victimization Survey provides data on offenders' ages as reported by victims who are themselves age 12 or older. From these data, based on the 1991 survey, we would conclude, for example, that persons most likely to be victimized by juveniles are other juveniles, and juveniles are seldom the offenders against older victims.[24] The victim surveys give another way of obtaining some data about the nature and extent of crime by youths.

Figure 12.11 Percent of Arrests Involving Juveniles, 1992, by General Type of Crime

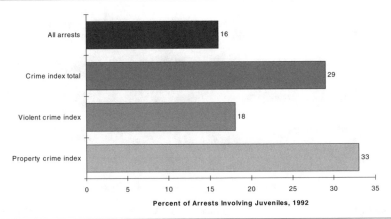

Percent of Arrests Involving Juveniles, 1992

Source: adapted from Snyder, H. N. and Sickmund, M. (1995). *Juvenile Offenders and Victims: A National Report.* Washington, D.C.: Office of Juvenile Justice and Delinquency Prevention, 101.

Figure 12.12 Percent of Arrests Involving Juveniles in 1992

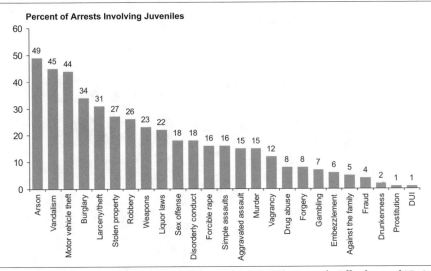

Source: adapted from Snyder, H. N. and Sickmund, M. (1995). *Juvenile Offenders and Victims: A National Report.* Washington, D.C.: Office of Juvenile Justice and Delinquency Prevention, 101 (based on *Crime in the United States, 1992*).
Note: the percents shown are percents of arrests, not of offenses. For example, the chart shows that 49 percent of all persons arrested for arson were juveniles, not that juveniles committed 49 percent of the arsons. Compare with Figure 12.9, based on crimes cleared. Crimes with larger discrepancies in the comparison may be those crimes for which the act is more often committed in groups.

Cases Handled by the Juvenile Courts

Differences in youth characteristics found in the delinquency caseloads of the juvenile courts also are informative about which youths are involved. Most are boys and young men, but girls and young women make up a substantial share (Figure 12.13). About one in five public order, property, and person offense cases handled by the juvenile courts are those of females. Among those with drug violations, the proportions of females is more like

Figure 12.13 Percent of Delinquency Cases Involving Males and Females, 1993

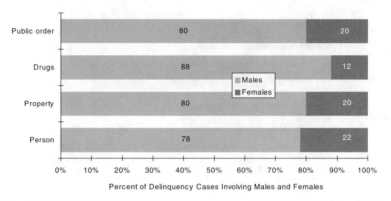

Percent of Delinquency Cases Involving Males and Females

Source: data in Butts, J., Snyder, H. N., Finnegan, T. A., Aughenbaugh, A. L., and Poole, R. S. (1996). *Juvenile Court Statistics 1993*. Washington, D.C.: Office of Juvenile Justice and Delinquency Prevention, 20.

one in ten. About two-thirds of all delinquency cases in the juvenile courts involve white offenders (Figure 12.14).

Figure 12.14 Race Group Membership by Offense Types for Delinquency Cases, 1993

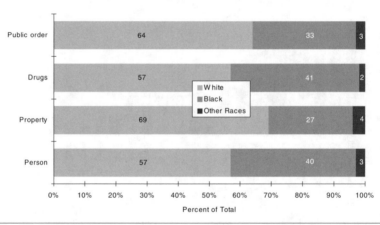

Percent of Total

Source: data in Butts, J., Snyder, H. N., Finnegan, T. A., Aughenbaugh, A. L., and Poole, R. S. (1996). *Juvenile Court Statistics 1993*. Washington, D.C.: Office of Juvenile Justice and Delinquency Prevention, 26.

The *rates* of delinquency vary substantially with age. Figure 12.15 shows the ages at referral of male and female cases in the juvenile courts. As young men and young women get older, the rates of referral to the juvenile courts increase. The leveling off at age 17 shown in the figure is due to the definitions and variations in age of juvenile court jurisdiction. Many 17-year-olds have gone to the criminal courts to be tried as adults.

The increase in delinquency with age is found for all categories of offenses, as seen in Figure 12.16. The drops in the curve again are observed only for the 17-year-old category, when many are tried as adults.

The juvenile courts deal not only with cases of alleged crimes, but also with the "status offense" behaviors that would not be considered crimes if

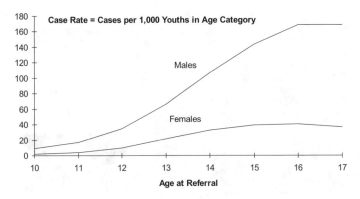

Source: data in Butts, J., Snyder, H. N., Finnegan, T. A., Aughenbaugh, A. L., and Poole, R. S. (1996). *Juvenile Court Statistics 1993*. Washington, D.C.: Office of Juvenile Justice and Delinquency Prevention, 21.

committed by an adult. Each year, the juvenile courts handle more than 100,000 petitioned status offense cases (Figure 12.17). Most common are truancy, liquor law violations, running away, and "ungovernable" (also called "incorrigible") classifications of status offenses.

Figure 12.16 Delinquency Case Rates by Age at Referral and Offense Category, 1993

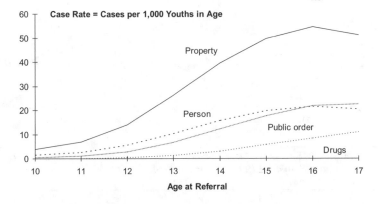

Source: data in Butts, J., Snyder, H. N., Finnegan, T. A., Aughenbaugh, A. L., and Poole, R. S. (1996). *Juvenile Court Statistics 1993*. Washington, D.C.: Office of Juvenile Justice and Delinquency Prevention, 17.

The delinquency case *rates* for these categories differ for male and female young people. For example, runaway rates are higher for females who are petitioned (Figure 12.18). They are higher for boys petitioned for liquor law violations, especially among 16- and 17-year-olds. They are about the same for truancy and ungovernability.[25]

More than half the cases in the juvenile courts involve alleged property offenses (Figure 12.19). One in five, however, are classed as person offenses. Thus, the cases involved in the juvenile courts most often involve stealing or assaultive behavior. The largest number of cases in the juvenile courts is that for property offenses (Figure 12.20). When we make a detailed classifi-

**Figure 12.17 Numbers of Petitioned Status Offense Cases in the Juvenile
Courts, 1993**

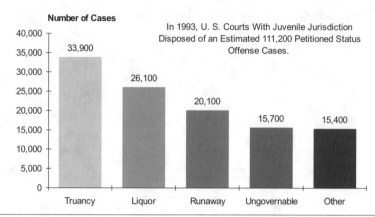

Number of Cases

In 1993, U. S. Courts With Juvenile Jurisdiction
Disposed of an Estimated 111,200 Petitioned Status
Offense Cases.

Truancy 33,900 · Liquor 26,100 · Runaway 20,100 · Ungovernable 15,700 · Other 15,400

Source: data in Butts, J., Snyder, H. N., Finnegan, T. A., Aughenbaugh, A. L., and Poole, R. S.
(1996). *Juvenile Court Statistics 1993*. Washington, D.C.: Office of Juvenile Justice and
Delinquency Prevention, 33.

Figure 12.18 Petitioned Male and Female Runaways, by Age at Referral, 1993

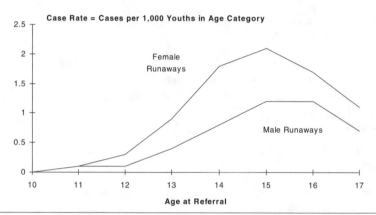

Case Rate = Cases per 1,000 Youths in Age Category

Female Runaways

Male Runaways

Age at Referral

Source: data in Butts, J., Snyder, H. N., Finnegan, T. A., Aughenbaugh, A. L., and Poole, R. S.
(1996). *Juvenile Court Statistics 1993*. Washington, D.C.: Office of Juvenile Justice and
Delinquency Prevention, 43.

cation of the most common offenses, we see that larceny/theft is the largest
single category of the most serious offense alleged (Figure 12.21) and that
other kinds of stealing are prominent as well, burglary, for example. Assaults, however, are common, as are vandalism and drug law violations.

Minority group members, particularly blacks, are represented in the juvenile justice system markedly disproportionately to their numbers in the
general population (Figure 12.22). This is especially so for drug and person
offenses. Most delinquency cases, however, involve white youths.

Juveniles Transferred to the Adult Criminal Courts

Increasing numbers of cases of juveniles are being transferred—the juvenile court having waived or lost jurisdiction—to the adult courts for trial.

Figure 12.19 Percent of Delinquency Cases Charged with Person, Property, Drug, and Public Order Offenses in 1993

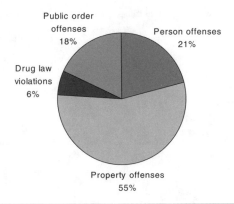

Source: data in Butts, J., Snyder, H. N., Finnegan, T. A., Aughenbaugh, A. L., and Poole, R. S. (1996). *Juvenile Court Statistics 1993*. Washington, D.C.: Office of Juvenile Justice and Delinquency Prevention, 6.

Figure 12.20 Estimated Number of Delinquency Cases in Courts with Juvenile Jurisdiction, by General Category of Most Serious Offense, 1993

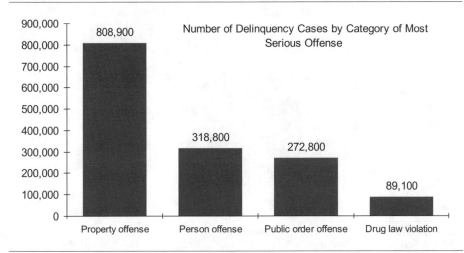

Source: data in Butts, J., Snyder, H. N., Finnegan, T. A., Aughenbaugh, A. L., and Poole, R. S. (1996). *Juvenile Court Statistics 1993*. Washington, D.C.: Office of Juvenile Justice and Delinquency Prevention, 5.
Note: delinquency offenses are acts by juveniles that could result in criminal prosecution when committed by an adult.

For a five-year period, the numbers are depicted in Figure 12.23. Youths accused of person offenses are now more likely to be transferred than was the case in earlier years (Figure 12.24). The largest share of transferred cases is that of person offenses, but more than a third of transferred cases in 1993 were youths accused of property crimes (Figure 12.25).

Figure 12.21 Estimated Number of Delinquency Cases in Courts with Juvenile Jurisdiction, by Most Serious Offense, 1993

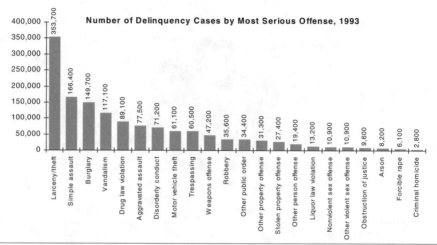

Number of Delinquency Cases by Most Serious Offense, 1993

Source: data in Butts, J., Snyder, H. N., Finnegan, T. A., Aughenbaugh, A. L., and Poole, R. S. (1996). *Juvenile Court Statistics 1993*. Washington, D.C.: Office of Juvenile Justice and Delinquency Prevention, 5.

Note: delinquency offenses are acts by juveniles that could result in criminal prosecution when committed by an adult.

Figure 12.22 Race Group Membership for Delinquency Cases, 1993

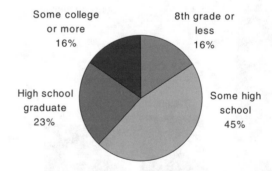

Some college or more 16%

8th grade or less 16%

High school graduate 23%

Some high school 45%

Source: data in Butts, J., Snyder, H. N., Finnegan, T. A., Aughenbaugh, A. L., and Poole, R. S. (1996). *Juvenile Court Statistics 1993*. Washington, D.C.: Office of Juvenile Justice and Delinquency Prevention, 26.

Goals, Alternatives, and Information Needs in Juvenile Justice

Goals

If there is a general mission of the juvenile justice system—and surely there would be some disagreements in emphasis among different jurisdictions—it is the protection of both the child and the community. This goal is

Figure 12.23 Numbers of Cases Judicially Waived to Adult Courts, 1989 and 1993, by Most Serious Offense

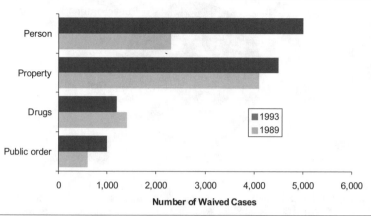

Source: data in Butts, J., Snyder, H. N., Finnegan, T. A., Aughenbaugh, A. L., and Poole, R. S. (1996). *Juvenile Court Statistics 1993*. Washington, D.C.: Office of Juvenile Justice and Delinquency Prevention, 13.

Figure 12.24 Percent of Petitioned Delinquency Cases Waived to the Adult Courts, 1988–1993

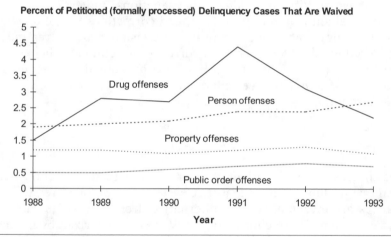

Sources: data in Snyder, H. N. and Sickmund, M. (1995). *Juvenile Offenders and Victims: A National Report*. Washington, D.C.: Office of Juvenile Justice and Delinquency Prevention, 154; and in Butts, J., Snyder, H. N., Finnegan, T. A., Aughenbaugh, A. L., and Poole, R. S. (1996). *Juvenile Court Statistics 1993*. Washington, D.C.: Office of Juvenile Justice and Delinquency Prevention, 13.

to be served in part by the reduction of delinquent behavior. Abuse and neglect cases often are not reported at all, but when they are, the welfare of the child is clearly the main focus of attention. In the case of delinquency, however, the protection of the child often is clearly secondary to objectives of delinquency prevention and control. A common belief is that preventing delinquency is in the best interests of the child, and measures designed to reduce it are therefore consistent with concern for the child's welfare.

The general missions of the various agencies related to the juvenile justice system vary. Schools emphasize education. Welfare agencies emphasize

Figure 12.25 Most Serious Offense of Judicially Waived Cases in 1993

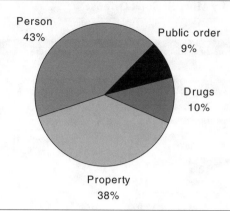

Source: data in Butts, J., Snyder, H. N., Finnegan, T. A., Aughenbaugh, A. L., and Poole, R. S. (1996). *Juvenile Court Statistics 1993*. Washington, D.C.: Office of Juvenile Justice and Delinquency Prevention, 13.
Note: 1993 was the first year in recent years in which the largest proportion of cases transferred to the adult courts was that of person offenses. Earlier, the largest percent typically was that for property offenses.

the protection of the child. Mental health workers might stress development and adjustment. Police and prosecutors perhaps pursue prevention and containment, while social agency workers and defense counsel often seek the least restrictive and intrusive alternative sanctions. Judges try to provide both individual and community justice, and corrections workers, whether in institutions or engaged in community supervision, provide treatment intended to reduce the likelihood of recurrence of delinquent behavior. All have in common— sometimes as a first priority, sometimes secondary to major aims—a desire to reduce delinquent acts as a service to both the child and the community.

Alternatives

The choices along the path of decisions that markedly affect the lives of children involved in the juvenile justice system are complex. Yet, until new alternatives are invented, specific alternative decision choices can be defined at each step. These choices typically are characterized by much discretion exercised by the individual decision maker. All the problems of discretionary decision making in human affairs thus come into play. In the juvenile justice system, these require attention to problems of fairness and equity of treatment; but they also involve the problems of the efficient and rational use of data to provide information relevant to the aims of protection of the child and the community.

The decision choices available depend upon the specific stage of processing in the juvenile justice system. A major choice, however, which relies substantially upon discretion and is involved in many of the decisions early in processing, is whether the case will be processed informally or formally. Whether the case will avoid full processing, which includes petitioning by the prosecutor and adjudication by the juvenile court, or whether it will be dealt with in a less formal fashion is a question that is raised at numerous decision points. These choices typically involve the discretionary decision making of probation officers and the prosecuting attorney.

Vocational education often is emphasized in correctional facilities for youths. This young man is receiving instruction in metal shop work. What role should offender classifications play in determining program placements? — *Photo courtesy of the New Jersey Department of Corrections.*

Whether or not the youth is diverted from full processing, important decisions have to do with placement in various treatment programs. For example, options may include consequences such as community service, restitution, attendance at alcohol or drug abuse educational programs, or participation in counseling. Or, they might include changes in living arrangements, such as placement in a residential treatment program.

When the case goes forward to the adjudication stage and the youth is adjudicated delinquent, the juvenile court judge typically has four basic choices:

1. Placement on probation.
2. Placement in a different living arrangement.
3. Placement in a specialized probation program such as intensive probation supervision.
4. Commitment to the state corrections authority.

When the decision outcome is to place the youth on probation, the judge usually has a number of choices concerning the specific conditions to be required. When it is commitment to the state, the judge usually has no further control over the case. A decision process similar to that already described for adult institutions follows.

Information for Decisions

Information helpful to decision makers in achieving their goals is, as we have seen in earlier chapters, of two kinds—that needed for general management decisions and that required for individual decisions. In juvenile justice systems generally, decision makers may find much more information from existing systems for *management decisions* than for *individual case* decisions. When it comes to the latter, the expression "much data, little information" fairly characterizes the state of affairs. That is because the necessary analytical work to provide guidance for deciding the best alternatives for various classifications of youth in order to meet the aims of the system has not yet been done. There are many data available, but little information to guide the decision maker in the critical individual case decisions that are made within wide areas of discretion every day. Subjective decisions, made on the basis of limited information, is the general rule.

Factors Influencing Decisions

Some examples of how information influences decisions in juvenile justice, and of the kinds of analyses that can help determine the effectiveness of programs, come from studies in Arizona,[26] where useful management information systems have been developed.[27]

Factors Influencing Informal vs. Formal Processing

Youths in Arizona that are processed informally are generally younger, tend more often to be enrolled in school, and have fewer complaints involving drug use. Females are more likely to be processed informally. Those youths who have complaints of more serious offenses and who have more prior petitions to the court are more likely to be subject to formal processing. In terms of all variables that differentiate the groups formally and informally processed, the groups overlap; there is no one youth characteristic that distinguishes the youths given formal and informal processing.[28]

The two groups do differ on measures of the risk of new referrals to the court—that is, of the likelihood of additional complaints of delinquency later. Those subjected to formal processing, including adjudication by the court, tend to be poorer risks.[29]

Measures of risk of new complaints were found in Arizona to include youth characteristics typically found to be predictive, such as age, prior record, and the type of offense involved in the complaint. The best predictors were the number of prior counts of delinquent offenses previously alleged, the age at the referral, and the number of prior referrals. Age was inversely related to new referrals; as is found typically, older youths tended to have fewer new referrals. A more extensive prior record, measured by prior counts and petitions, also was associated with later new referrals. Factors apparently influencing the informal vs. formal processing decisions were the seriousness of the referral offense, the number of prior referrals to the juvenile court, the seriousness of the previously alleged offenses, a history of drug abuse, prior instances of formal processing with adjudications of delinquency or incorrigibility, and prior instances of informal processing.[30]

Factors Influencing Program Selection in Informal Processing

For cases processed informally, an important decision is that of the probation staff in selecting the program placements of the youths—the assigned consequences. The information influencing these decisions again includes the

Figure 12.26 Percents Assigned to Consequence Groups

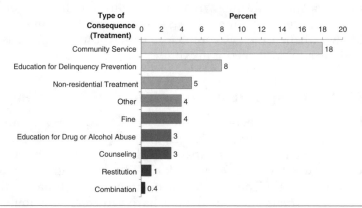

Source: Gottfredson, D. M. and Gottfredson, S. D. (1995).
Note: these data are based on all youths assigned these consequences, regardless of whether they were processed formally or informally. Most were processed informally.

seriousness of the offense, the history of drug abuse, the number of prior counts of offenses and of prior petitions, and other case characteristics.[31]

The main alternatives used in Arizona when cases are processed informally are shown in Figure 12.26. The figure is based on all cases—processed formally as well as informally—but relatively few cases were assigned these alternatives after adjudication by the court. They are used mainly for those youths who are assigned consequences by informal agreement, without adjudication. Community service is most often assigned. Programs of education for delinquency prevention often are also used, as is nonresidential treatment. Other major

Figure 12.27 Percent Compliance for Types of Consequences

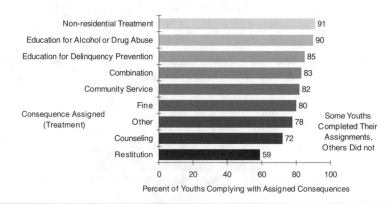

Source: Gottfredson, D. M. and Gottfredson, S. D. (1995).
Note: these data are based on all youths assigned these consequences, regardless of whether they were processed formally or informally. Most were processed informally.

programs are named in the figure.

An important question is whether, after agreeing to accept a specific program rather than formal processing, youths actually complete the assignments of community service, counseling, education, or other consequences. Compliance can be measured, of course, only if a monitoring system is in place in order to keep track of whether the youths did complete the program.

Since procedures are in place in Arizona to do that, we can observe the percentage of compliance for each program, as shown in Figure 12.27. As we can see, compliance was most frequent for education for alcohol or drug abuse and nonresidential treatment. It was lower for restitution and counseling. It is not known whether the low compliance with restitution orders is related to the economic circumstances of the youths with such orders.

Factors Influencing Outcomes to Informal Processing

Now we can ask whether either the choice of program assignments or compliance makes any difference in terms of the goal of preventing further delinquency. We can obtain that answer if the court information systems keep track of new referrals and can link the files for treatment with those indicating return to the court with new complaints. Fortunately, this also can be done in Arizona, since all counties have agreed to contribute data to a common system.

Since the youths were not assigned to the different consequences in an experiment, with equivalent groups selected for each, the analysis must take account of differences among the groups that bias the comparison. Therefore, statistical corrections were made for (1) measured risk before treatment, (2) selection by the probation staff, and (3) the time each youth was free in the community (not in detention).

After these corrections were made, two informative results appeared. Both program placement and compliance were found to be important. Differences in new referrals associated with program placement and also with compliance were found that could not be explained by risk before treatment, selection, or time in the community.

The type of consequence assigned did make a difference in whether there was a later delinquency referral. Youths placed in the education for drug or alcohol abuse and in the nonresidential treatment programs had fewer new referrals than expected without the placements. Figure 12.28 shows the percentages of youths with new referrals, with the required statistical adjust-

---

Figure 12.28 Percents With New Referrals, by Consequence Groups, Adjusted for Time at Risk, Risk, and Selection

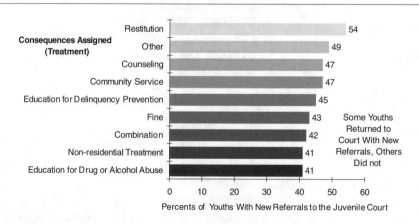

Source: Gottfredson, D. M. and Gottfredson, S. D. (1995).
Note: These data are based on all youths assigned these consequences, regardless of whether they were processed formally or informally. Most were processed informally.

ments. The Administrative Office of the Courts provided the following summary descriptions of the programs of education about drug or alcohol use and of nonresidential treatment, which seemed to be the programs that worked best:

- **Delinquency Prevention (Education for Drug or Alcohol Abuse):** This service is for juveniles who have a specific educational need pertaining directly to the reason for their referral. This service is usually provided as an educational program in either singular or multiple episodes which build upon one another. It may include other outpatient counseling services. The service intent is to educate the client by providing necessary skills, tools, and knowledge which can be utilized to make responsible choices and to discontinue behaviors that instigated court involvement.

- **Evening Support Service (Nonresidential Treatment):** This service provides a minimum of 3 hours (excluding meals and transportation) of supplemental services to youth who may attend daytime school. Services often include supplemental education, tutoring, GED study, pre-vocational and/or vocational instruction, individual living skills development, general counseling activities, substance abuse counseling, social and/or recreational activities. Structure and supervision may be moderate to intensive with flexibility to accommodate changes in individual needs. Programming may take place at a provider location, and/or in various community locales.[32]

Compliance (program completion) with the assigned consequences also affected the percentages with new referrals (Figure 12.29). The youths who complied with the assigned consequences had fewer new referrals. This was true after taking account of biasing factors of risk, selection, and time in the community regardless of the county.

We cannot tell for sure from this analysis whether the fact of compliance or some characteristics of the youths associated with a tendency to comply with the agreement (not included in the available data) is responsible for the effect. While this poses a new research question, it nevertheless may reason-

Figure 12.29 Percents of Informally Processed Youths With New Referrals After Compliance or Noncompliance With Assigned Consequences

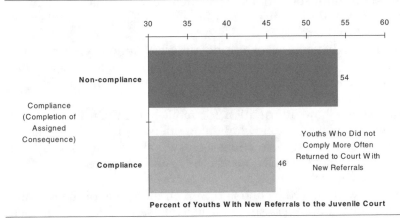

Percent of Youths With New Referrals to the Juvenile Court

Source: Gottfredson, D. M. and Gottfredson, S. D. (1995).
Note: the percents with new referrals are corrected for time at risk, risk, selection of consequences, and county. Most were processed informally.

ably stimulate management efforts to improve monitoring efforts for increased compliance.

Factors Influencing Judicial Dispositions

In Maricopa County, Arizona, the case dispositions ordered by the judges after adjudications of delinquency (that is, in formal processing) were studied. A number of youth characteristics were found to be influential in the discretionary selection among the four main alternatives for the judge: probation, intensive supervision probation, residential placement, and commitment to the state corrections department.[33] Notably, various measures of the previous delinquency history were important: the number of prior counts of offenses, the number of prior referrals, the numbers of prior person and property offenses, and previous probation violations. If there were additional petitions pending, that too was important. These variables appeared to influence the decision for placement of probation vs. commitment to the state youth corrections facilities.

In the context of the prior delinquency history, the age of the youth, the age that the youth first was referred to the juvenile court, and the relative seriousness of the offense appeared to influence the choice of residential placement. The decision to place the youth in the intensive probation supervision program was influenced by drug offending and school attendance.

Factors Influencing Outcomes to Formal Processing (Judicial Dispositions)

In the study cited, the new referrals to the courts were studied, as in the case of the informal program assignments. With statistical controls for risk, judicial selection, and time at risk (which are the main sources of bias), the youths assigned to the three programs within the court jurisdiction—probation, intensive probation supervision, and residential placement—were returned to court with new complaints at the rate expected regardless of the placement. There were no differences that could be attributed to the placement. It was not possible to determine the outcomes for those youths committed to the state youth corrections department, because that department did not have a system for keeping track of the later delinquency and crime of the youths sent to them.

As surprising as that may seem, it is not unusual. Although it is possible to learn from experience by keeping track of program assignments and implementations and keeping score on the results, many juvenile (and criminal) justice agencies do not yet have that capability.

The study shows how information for management can be provided when a system is in place for following up on offenders treated differently. In the case of the state youth corrections agency, it shows also that without such procedures it is not possible to learn the results of discretionary decisions taken earlier in the process.

Although the welfare of the child is the preeminent goal of the juvenile courts, there has been even less study of the effects of the juvenile justice system operations on the overall well-being of children and youths. The systems for following up to determine the outcomes of the different treatments of children should provide other measures of the welfare of the child besides the records of further involvement with the juvenile or criminal justice systems.

Chapter 12
▲ ▲ ▲ ▲ ▲ ▲

Summary

The juvenile justice system is composed of the work of the police, prosecutors, juvenile courts, and youth corrections agency staff. It often is affected by the work of representatives of schools, welfare agencies, and other organizations that often work with justice agencies. It focuses on the juvenile courts and closely related law enforcement and corrections personnel such as probation staff but also involves others in the community.

For nearly half the history of the United States, young persons other than very young children who were accused of crimes were dealt with in the same way as adults. It sometimes is said that they were hanged from the same tree.

This changed with the invention of the juvenile court system. Now the state was to act benevolently, in place of the parents, when it was thought that a young person was in need of guidance, intervention, or supervision. Now, all states have courts with juvenile jurisdiction, so there are separate courts and correctional systems for youths.

The doctrine of *parens patriae* and the benevolent purpose of the juvenile courts led to the extension of their jurisdiction to "status" offenses—behavior not considered crimes if done by adults. Youths could be adjudicated delinquent or incorrigible for such behavior as truancy or running away.

Despite some complaints, the philosophy of the juvenile court was widely accepted until criticism increased in the 1960s. Increasingly it was argued that children and youths need protections from the supposedly benevolent interventions by the state. A series of decisions by the U.S. Supreme Court began to change the character of the juvenile courts. Youths accused of crime now are protected by various Fourteenth Amendment rights, and the adjudication of delinquency requires the state to prove guilt beyond a reasonable doubt. Along with increasing concerns and media attention about serious crime by youths, these developments have changed the juvenile courts in the direction of the procedures, protections, and punishments of the adult courts.

Laws governing juvenile court jurisdiction vary among the states. Commonly, the upper age is seventeen. Some combinations of offense, age, and sometimes prior record place the youth under concurrent jurisdiction, in some places. The decision about jurisdiction then is discretionary with the prosecutor, not the judge.

An accused juvenile may end up in criminal court in one of three ways: through a discretionary decision by a judge, by a prosecutor's decision, or through "transfer" by exclusionary statute. The first, judicial discretion, is the traditional way, but youths increasingly are being excluded by statute.

Decisions throughout the juvenile justice system, like those in counterpart agencies for adults, are made within wide areas of discretion. Police, probation staff, prosecutors, and judges have a great deal of choice in handling a particular case.

Entry into the juvenile justice system usually begins with the police. As with arrests of adults, choices often are available—ranging from ignoring the trigger event through detention and referral to the court or the prosecutor. If the case is referred to the juvenile court, a further series of decisions is initiated—to detain or release, refer to prosecutor or not, or to "adjust" the case informally. If referral is made to the prosecutor, he or she makes a discretionary decision whether to file a petition. The prosecutor also may have the choice of seeking transfer of the case to the criminal court. Such decisions usually are made by the juvenile court judge, but now in some circumstances in some jurisdictions, it is made by the prosecutor.

If a petition is filed and contested, an adversary proceeding called an adjudicatory hearing is held. If the juvenile is adjudicated delinquent or incorrigible, a dispositional hearing comes next. At this stage, the judge usually has only the choices of probation, residential treatment, or commitment to the state corrections agency. Many differing conditions of probation, however, can be used, including intensive supervision programs, restitution, fines, community service, educational programs concerning drug and alcohol abuse, counseling, foster home placements, and day support programs. (Many of the same programs and penalties are used when the case is processed informally.) If the youth is sent to the state system, a new sequence of decision making is initiated. Corrections personnel will decide on custody and security classifications, institutional program assignments, release, release conditions, and postrelease supervision. About half the cases referred to the juvenile courts are handled informally and do not go through the full program of a petition, adjudication, and disposition.

Most of our information about the extent of crime by juveniles comes from official records. Although many youths get into trouble with the law, in a given year fewer than 5 percent are arrested. Less than one-half of 1 percent are arrested for a violent crime.

Juvenile offenders do contribute substantially to crime—some crimes more than others. At one extreme, 40 percent of arsons that are cleared are solved by the arrest of a juvenile. At the other extreme, about one in 10 solved murders and aggravated assaults are cleared by juvenile arrests. Most crime is attributable to adults. Persons victimized by juveniles are most likely other juveniles.

The cases handled by the juvenile courts are mostly boys and young men. The majority are white, but minority youths are represented out of proportion to their share of the general population. This is the case especially for those accused of drug and person offenses. The rates of delinquency increase with age and differ for males and females. More than half the cases handled by the juvenile courts involve alleged property offenses.

Increasing numbers of juveniles now are being transferred to the adult criminal courts for trial—especially youths arrested for person offenses, but also many accused of property crimes.

The general mission of the juvenile justice system in its delinquency jurisdiction is the protection of both the child and the community. This goal is intended to be served by the reduction of delinquency behavior.

The familiar theme of conflict between desires for safety and for freedom are present at every step. In the juvenile justice system, an added strain results from desires to nurture and protect children and youths but punish their transgressions, incapacitate offenders, and deter other youths from doing harm.

The alternative decision choices along the tree of juvenile justice decisions are complex. Yet, the available choices can be defined at each step. These choices typically are characterized by substantial discretion exercised by individual decision makers. All the problems of discretionary decision making in human affairs thus come into play. In the juvenile justice system, these require attention to problems of fairness and equity of treatment; but they involve also the problems of the efficient and rational use of data to provide information relevant to the aims of protecting the child and the community.

The necessary analytical work to provide information for guiding decision makers to the best alternatives for achieving the aims of the system has not yet been done to the extent that it is needed. Little information typically is provided to guide the decision maker in individual case decisions because there still are few studies of the effectiveness of the juvenile justice system design or of its many parts. Procedures are available to provide better information for management, including the results of the discretionary decisions made throughout the juvenile justice process, but so far they have been little used. Most juvenile justice agencies do not have adequate management information systems for providing guidance about what works best for which youths.

Notes

1. Rosenheim, M. K. (1983). "Juvenile Justice: Organization and Process," in Kadish, S. H. (ed.). *Encyclopedia of Crime and Justice*, Vol. 3. New York: The Free Press, 969–970.

2. Newman, D. J. (1978). *Introduction to Criminal Justice*, 2nd ed. New York: J. B. Lippincott, 422.

3. Snyder, H. N. and Sickmund, M. (1995). *Juvenile Offenders and Victims: A National Report*. Washington, DC: Office of Juvenile Justice and Delinquency Prevention, 79.

4. Moreland, D. (1941). "History and Prophesy: John Augustus and His Successors," *National Probation Association Yearbook,* as cited in Snyder, H. N. and Sickmund, M. (1995). *Juvenile Offenders and Victims: A National Report*. Washington, D.C: Office of Juvenile Justice and Delinquency Prevention, 70.

5. Schlossman, S. L. (1983). "Juvenile Justice: History and Philosophy," in Kadish, S. H. (ed.). *Encyclopedia of Crime and Justice*, Vol. 3. New York: The Free Press, 962.

6. Ibid., 963.

7. Healy, W. and Bronner, A. F. (1926). *Delinquents and Criminals: Their Making and Unmaking*." New York: Macmillan, 3.

8. Schlossman, S. L. (1983), "Juvenile Justice: History and Philosophy," in Kadish, S. H. (ed.). *Encyclopedia of Crime and Justice*, Vol. 3. New York: The Free Press, 966–968.

9. Newman, D. J. (1978), *Introduction to Criminal Justice*, 2nd ed. New York: J. B. Lippincott, 423.

10. *Kent v. United States* (1966). 383 U.S. 541.

11. *In re* Gault (1967). 387 U.S.

12. *In re* Winship (1970). 397 U.S. 358.

13. Snyder, H. N. and Sickmund, M. (1995). *Juvenile Offenders and Victims: A National Report*. Washington, DC: Office of Juvenile Justice and Delinquency Prevention, based on Szymanski, L. (1995). *Upper Age of Juvenile Court Jurisdiction Statutes Analysis* (1994 Update) and (1995) *Lower Age of Juvenile Court Jurisdiction (1994 Update)*.

14. Snyder, H. N. and Sickmund, M. (1995), *Juvenile Offenders and Victims: A National Report*. Washington, DC: Office of Juvenile Justice and Delinquency Prevention, 73.

15. Ibid., 85–89.

16. Torbet, P. "States Respond to Violent Juvenile Crime: System Impact." (1997). *NCJJ in Brief*, 1. Pittsburgh, PA: National Center for Juvenile Justice, 1.

17. Ibid., 1.

18. Ibid., 1.

19. Snyder, H. N. and Sickmund, M. (1995), *Juvenile Offenders and Victims: A National Report*. Washington, DC: Office of Juvenile Justice and Delinquency Prevention, 121.

20. Ibid., 121.

21. Ibid., 46–49.

22. Ibid.,, 2–13.

23. Ibid., 99.

24. Ibid., 47.

25. Butts, J., Snyder, H. N., Finnegan, T. A., Aughenbaugh, A. L., and Poole, R. S. (1996). *Juvenile Court Statistics 1993*. Washington, DC: Office of Juvenile Justice and Delinquency Prevention, 43.

26. Gottfredson, D. M., Gottfredson, M. R., Gottfredson, S. D., Etten, T. J., and Petrone, R. F. (1994a). *Improving Information for Rational Decision Making in Juvenile Justice: A Notebook*. Sacramento, CA: Justice Policy Research Corporation.

27. Maricopa County Juvenile Court Center (no date). *Computer System Documentation*. Phoenix, AZ: Research and Planning Division, 3125 W. Durango, Phoenix, AZ 85009; Gottfredson, Don M., Gottfredson, Michael R., Gottfredson, Stephen D., Etten, Tamryn J., and Petrone, Robert F. (1994b). *Needs for System Development in the Maricopa County Juvenile Justice System*. Sacramento, CA: Justice Policy Research Corporation.

28. Gottfredson, D. M. and Gottfredson, S. D. (1995). *Empirical Evaluation of the Progressively Increasing Consequences Act Program*. Phoenix, AZ: Administrative Office of the Courts, Supreme Court of Arizona, 43–46.

29. Ibid., 48–50.

30. Ibid., 51–52.

31. Ibid., 56.

32. Ibid., 57–58.

33. Gottfredson, D. M., Gottfredson, M. R., Gottfredson, S. D., Etten, T. J., and Petrone, R. F. (1994a). *Improving Information for Rational Decision Making in Juvenile Justice: A Notebook*. Sacramento, CA: Justice Policy Research Corporation.

CHAPTER THIRTEEN

Justice With Eyes Open

Photo courtesy of the Comstock Historic District Commission, Department of Museums, Library and Arts, State of Nevada

Chapter Thirteen

We have considered the criminal justice system by examining each of the main points of decision making and by looking at some of the evidence about the goals, alternatives, and information needs of those decisions. The premise for this review was that the criminal justice system is a series of decisions that are constrained by the law and procedural rules but nevertheless made within wide areas of discretion. Questions were raised about these constraints and about the nature of these decisions by the police, magistrates, prosecutors, judges, corrections staff, and others that together make up the criminal justice system. We have examined some of what is known about decision making at each step in the process. At each stage, we have observed the tension between conflicting desires for both safety and freedom. We have seen how this strain is represented in decisions throughout the system—in law enforcement, the courts, and correctional programs. Now we may consider the system as a whole in a similar way. This means again examining questions of purposes, choices, and needed information. We will examine the evidence that may provide informed answers. If we ask the right questions, the available evidence may help us understand how the criminal justice system is doing in meeting its goals of punishment and crime control. It may also help us see how it can be improved.

❏ Questions to Think About
❏ Asking About Goal Attainment
❏ Evidence About What Works
    Deterrence
    Incapacitation
    Rehabilitation
    Punishment Severity
❏ Another Look at Deterrence
❏ Another Look at Incapacitation
    Do Rising Prison Populations Provide a False Comfort?
❏ Another Look at Treatment
❏ Another Look at Retribution
    Kinds of Retributive Theory
❏ Another Look at the Problem of Prediction
    Informal vs. Formal Predictions
    Improving Risk Assessments
❏ Prevention
❏ Management Information Systems
    Horse and Buggy vs. Space Travel
    Needs for Feedback
    Turning Data Into Information
❏ Making Decisions With Eyes Open
    Structured Decision Making
    Guidelines for Guidelines
❏ Stumbling Toward Justice

True or False?

The evidence shows clearly that crime is decreased by more severe punishment. T F

The crime rate has been going up while the prison population has been going down. T F

The theory of just desert prescribes increasing punishment. T F

Because retribution is a moral justification for punishment, it does not raise scientific questions. T F

When a released prisoner is arrested again, it usually is for the type of offense that led to prison in the first place. T F

Modern "state of the art" information systems are now available to most criminal justice agency administrators. T F

Offenders usually progress in their criminal careers from less serious to more serious crimes. T F

Persons who commit the most crimes tend to be the most serious offenders. T F

Experienced judges can predict recidivism best without using statistical prediction methods. T F

Opportunities for experimentation in criminal justice are rare. T F

All are false.

How we ask questions is often important. We can ask questions about the criminal justice system in many ways. One of the best ways is asking questions that can be answered by looking at the observable facts. This is the empirical attitude that sets the investigative orientation apart from others. The best questions often are *empirical* questions. These are questions that can be answered by making observations—by formulating hypotheses that can be tested by examining the evidence. Not all questions about criminal justice are empirical questions. Some are questions of morality and ethics. In criminal justice, these questions are often interwoven, but both are important. In this chapter, we will examine some questions of both kinds.

Smoking and Praying

So frequently, it's the way the proposition is stated. My Master reminded me of the story of the two priests arguing whether it is proper to smoke and to pray at the same time. To settle the disagreement they decided to write the Archbishop. Two weeks later they met again, each claiming support from the same high authority. After some perplexity, one finally asked the other, "What did you ask the Archbishop?"

The second priest replied, "I asked whether it was proper to smoke while praying; and the Archbishop answered, 'Certainly not, praying is a holy affair and tolerates no frivolous distractions.' And what did you ask?"

"Well," said the other, "I asked whether it was proper to pray while smoking, and the Archbishop answered, 'Certainly, prayer is always in order.'"

—R. G. H. Siu

We will begin by looking further at the most general goals of the criminal justice system. The purposes of punishment and crime control have endured over centuries, but we have seen that the ways of seeking these goals have changed in emphasis in recent decades.

Asking About Goal Attainment

How can we know whether, or to what degree, the general crime control goals of the criminal justice system are met? If decisions are made throughout the system in pursuit of these goals, improving those decisions requires assessment of the broad theories of deterrence, incapacitation, and treatment on which they rely. These are the means to the goals of the criminal justice system that look forward to some good to follow from decisions made about offenders. As a result, to ask whether deterrence, incapacitation, or treatment work to reduce crime are questions that we should be able to answer by looking at the evidence, if we ask the questions in the right way.

The Horse's Mouth

Over three centuries ago, Francis Bacon told of a heated argument among friars over the number of teeth in the mouth of a horse. Despite exhaustive searches of the theological literature, following traditional methods, they found no answer, and the quarrel continued. When a young and evidently inexperienced friar suggested that they find a horse, look into his mouth, and count his teeth, his colleagues became so angry that they beat him and banished him from the group. It probably seemed quite obvious to them that only the devil could have put this undignified, unprofessional, and unholy idea into the young man's head. They returned to argument and their search of the literature. Still no answer was found, and they concluded that because historical and theological evidence was lacking, the question was unanswerable.
—C. E. Mees

The other important perspective affecting decisions, as we have seen, is that of retribution or deserved punishment. The theory of deserved punishment relies basically on a perspective in moral philosophy for its justification of inflicting punishment by the state. Nevertheless, it too raises questions that can be answered only by looking at the evidence. The fact that the desert theorist does not argue for the justification of punishment on the basis of expected consequences does not mean that there are none. In addition, there are questions about the use of the desert theory: How can we assess whether it leads to more justice and greater fairness, as proponents claim?

We can raise questions about both the utilitarian—crime control—and retributive—desert—perspectives, and these questions can be answered by examining the evidence. We have seen that in the last two decades there has been a dramatic escalation of punishments, increased reliance on deterrence and incapacitation, and less interest in rehabilitation. Let's examine each of these most prominent means for achieving criminal justice goals in terms of some of the evidence about them that was available when those trends began. One question is whether the changes were based on knowledge derived from examining the evidence. Another question is whether the evidence of what has happened since the changes took place is in accord with the goals or ethical presumptions of the authors of the reform.

Chapter 13
▲ ▲ ▲ ▲ ▲ ▲

Evidence About What Works

Nearly 20 years ago, as the trends toward increased punishment, more emphasis on deterrence and incapacitation, and decreased stress on treatment were gaining momentum, two panels of the National Research Council of the National Academy of Science examined the scientific evidence on the effects of deterrence, incapacitation, and rehabilitation.[1] After their searching inquiry, the scientists reached informative conclusions on the effectiveness of each of these major traditional means for seeking crime control.

Deterrence

For the panel on deterrence, Nagin reviewed more than 20 analyses directed at testing the deterrence hypothesis for noncapital sanctions. Then he cautioned:

> [D]espite the intensiveness of the research effort, the empirical evidence is still not sufficient for providing a rigorous confirmation of the existence of a deterrent effect. Perhaps most important, the evidence is woefully inadequate for providing a good estimate of the magnitude of whatever effect may exist. . . . This is in stark contrast to some of the presentations in public discussions that have unequivocally concluded that sanctions deter and that have made sweeping suggestions that sanctioning practices be changed to take advantage of the presumed deterrent effect. . . . Policy makers in the criminal justice system are done a disservice if they are left with the impression that the empirical evidence, which they themselves are frequently unable to evaluate, strongly supports the deterrence hypothesis.[2]

The National Research Council panel as a whole offered a similar caution:

> In summary . . . we cannot yet assert that the evidence warrants an affirmative conclusion regarding deterrence. We believe scientific caution must be exercised in interpreting the limited validity of the available evidence and the number of competing explanations for the results. Our reluctance to draw stronger conclusions does not imply support for a position that deterrence does not exist, since the evidence certainly favors a proposition supporting deterrence more than it favors one asserting that deterrence is absent. The major challenge for future research is to estimate the magnitude of the effects of different sanctions on various crime types, an issue on which none of the evidence available thus far provides very useful guidance.[3]

We cannot prove it, yet, the panel said, but deterrence *may* work to some degree. With whom, under what circumstances, with what degree of effect, we cannot tell. Certainly, in the scientific literature, there was no strong policy guidance for an escalation of punishments in order to reduce crime by general deterrence.

Incapacitation

The scientists were somewhat more positive about incapacitation effects—the crime control effects of confinement. On this topic also, however, they were cautious about making recommendations for changing policies:

Models exist for estimating the incapacitative effect, but they rest on a num-ber of important, and as yet untested, assumptions. Using the models re-quires adequate estimates of critical, but largely unknown, [measures] that characterize individual criminal careers. [4]

Because estimating the effects of incapacitation required knowledge not yet available, the panel did not offer strong policy guidance about its use as a criminal justice goal.

Later, the more selective use of incapacitation described in Chapter 9 was proposed, with promises of simultaneously decreasing the rate of seri-ous crimes and prison overcrowding.[5] The proposal was that prison terms for some types of crimes should be set on the basis of how much crime the offender is predicted to commit if not in prison. High risk offenders would be kept in prison longer, while low risk offenders would have lesser penalties. This controversial suggestion generated criticisms on the basis of both the ethical issues involved and the scientific ones.[6]

As noted in Chapter 9, the concept of collective incapacitation has been distinguished from that of selective incapacitation.[7] Under collective strate-gies, all persons convicted of a designated offense would receive the same sentence. Under selective strategies, the prescribed sentence would be based at least in part upon predictions that particular offenders would commit serious crimes at a high rate if not incarcerated. The resulting criticisms pointed out that persons would be punished for offenses that are expected but might never occur and that offenders convicted of similar crimes could be punished quite differently.

The evidence from investigations of projected incapacitation effects—whether selective or collective—did not justify setting policy on the basis of crime control gains to be expected on the basis of research. Cohen summa-rized the evidence on both selective and collective incapacitation in these terms:

> Collective incapacitation policies have only modest impacts on crime but can cause enormous increases in prison populations. Selective incapacitation strategies offer the possibility of achieving greater reductions in crime at considerably smaller costs in prison resources, but their success depends critically on the ability to identify high-rate offenders early in their careers and prospectively. As yet, this has not been accomplished. [8]

Thus, when the increased reliance on incapacitation began, the existing evidence was not sufficient to justify using these rationales as a basis for policy formulation. Moreover, the evidence of effects that did exist did not support the effectiveness of longer terms or other harsher sanctions. Deter-rent effects seemed to be tied more strongly to the certainty of sanctions than to their severity. Besides, the relative benefits of incapacitative effects from incarceration seemed to drop markedly as terms were extended.[9]

Thus, as was seen to be the case with deterrence, no clear policy guid-ance was available from the scientific evidence for a sentencing strategy that emphasized incapacitation when the now-increased acceptance of that per-spective began its course.

> *Get out of the way of Justice. She is blind.*
> —*Stanislaw Lee*

It has become popular to talk about the "demise of the rehabilitative ideal," and quite unpopular to continue to support rehabilitation as a general aim of the criminal justice system. Much of this marked change in attitudes and, indeed, in values has been attributed to findings of science. Many people seem to believe that it now has been demonstrated that, when it comes to rehabilitating offenders, "nothing works." But the evidence available when that conclusion was reached by many influential policymakers did not support the notion that treatment programs or even alternatives to incarceration had been tried and found totally unproductive.[10]

The attack on the rehabilitative ideal came from two main sources. The first was a set of complaints about unfairness and coercive treatment. A Working Party of the American Friends Service Committee referred, in their influential 1971 report, to the "crime of treatment,"—a combination of contradictory ideas and hypocrisy which resulted in many unacceptable features of prisons in America.[11] These included the broad and unstructured indeterminacy in sentencing, a frequently extended incarceration of persons for purposes of "treatment," the maintenance of coercive and punitive prison programs under a guise of "rehabilitation," and many pathetic prison programs served up under that name.

The second assault was the series of widely known reviews and extensive research projects, which summarized the generally negative evidence about the effectiveness of rehabilitation efforts.[12] These reports were followed by a report of a 30-year follow-up study of the Cambridge-Summerville Youth Project summarizing the evidence that the treated group did *worse* than the untreated control group, not better.[13]

Enthusiasm for rehabilitation was lost. This no doubt contributed to the increased acceptance of the idea of deserved punishment as the fundamental, if not the *only*, aim of the criminal sanctioning system. Those in favor of retribution, deterrence, and incapacitation were quick to cite the reported, generally negative, evidence on rehabilitative effects.

With this urging of a return to a single-minded purpose of making the punishment fit the crime, policymakers may have concluded that rehabilitation—a nice idea once—should be either ignored as a purpose of sentencing and corrections or else actively discouraged. A scientist, however, after examining the evidence from evaluation research, would not have concluded that it supported a policy of abandoning it.

The 1979 report of the National Academy of Sciences' National Research Council on Research on Rehabilitative Techniques concluded:

> There is not now in the scientific literature any basis for any policy recommendations regarding rehabilitation of criminal offenders. The data available do not present any consistent evidence of efficacy that would lead to such recommendations.

The panel, however, also concluded:

> The quality of the work that has been done and the narrow range of options explored militate against any policy reflecting a final pessimism. . . . The magnitude of the task of reforming criminal offenders has been consistently underestimated.

One member of the panel stated:

> Because there is so little evidence that credible treatments have been implemented with fidelity, and because so much of the evaluation research done

so far has been inefficient or defective in other ways, we have no compelling experimental evidence for the contention that powerful, theoretically defensible, and faithfully executed interventions hold no promise. . . . Good evaluation research does not focus solely on the outcomes of programs, strategies, or reforms. It should assess also the operation and implementation of the program or reform. If the rehabilitative ideal has failed, it is in a failure to *implement* interventions with realistic prospects of preventing future delinquent or criminal behavior. Feeble, ineffectual interventions would not be expected to work; and there is little evidence that potent interventions have been tested.[14]

Thus, the scientific evidence on the effectiveness of the three main utilitarian purposes of sentencing and corrections—deterrence, incapacitation, and treatment—was in each case insufficient to provide clear guides to policy formulation when the sweeping changes began. The profound changes that have taken place cannot be attributed to a rational response to the evidence about crime control effects.

Punishment Severity

Some may think that the theory of just desert, emphasizing as it does that punishment must be inflicted if it is deserved, is responsible for the escalation in the level of punishment that has been observed. But the desert theory did not call for that. Contemporary versions of this retributive theory do not address the issue of the general *severity* of punishment that is to be administered. For example, von Hirsch, an advocate of desert theory, in his influential book *Doing Justice*, wrote of hopes for the implementation of desert principles:

> Penalties will be scaled down substantially. Incarceration will be restricted to offenses that are serious—and most prison sentences kept relatively short.[15]

These hopes have not been fulfilled. The political process involved in implementing sentencing reforms may make reductions in penalties difficult to accomplish. Discretion, sought to be controlled and more fairly exercised, may slip and slide from one system decision maker to another when attempts are made to limit it. What is hoped for does not always come to pass. Strategies for reform are not always implemented as intended. That which is implemented may have consequences other than those envisioned.

Even though the theory of just desert has become the main justification for punishment that has risen in acceptance (or returned to increased popularity) in the last two decades, it did not call for making punishments more severe.

The emphasis of desert theory on proportionality and fairness have shaped sanctioning in other ways. The desert orientation is perhaps best known as a justification for punishment, but three other central features of the perspective have been influential. One is an emphasis on proportionality of punishment and the harm done (taking account also of culpability). Another is a stress on fairness, meaning that similar punishments ought to be given for similarly situated offenders. The third is on the principle that a person ought to be punished for the harm done in the past, but ought *not* to be punished for crimes that may or may not occur in the future.

It is so easy to agree with this last principle that it is often overlooked that incarceration for crimes that have not yet occurred is precisely the point of incapacitation. Thus, it is important that, from the perspective of deserved punishment, a person may not be punished for crimes not done and which might never be done.

Two decades of change in perspectives on how to best achieve criminal justice goals could not be justified either by the then-available scientific evidence or the rising popularity of the desert theory. The evidence did not support sweeping policy changes. The most popular punishment theory did not call for more punishment but for more fair punishment. Let's take another, more contemporary look at each of these issues.

Another Look at Deterrence

Asking simply whether deterrence works is an example of asking the right question in the wrong way. The issue is more complex than that. Better questions are raised by asking whether different levels of *severity* of punishment, different levels of *certainty* of punishment, or different *kinds* of punishment prevent crime or achieve other specific aims. No one seems to doubt that some traffic offenses are deterred by prohibitions enforced by fines or other penalties. It is doubtful that the death penalty for overparking would promptly open up more parking spaces because it would not likely be enforced. Penalties that are not implemented are unlikely to have any effect. Few people seem to doubt that some people do not require a deterrence system in order to avoid crime; they would not commit crimes anyway. No one seems to doubt that the presence of the criminal law and the criminal justice system as a whole does exercise some deterrent effect for some people much of the time. The more important policy question—an empirical one—is whether an increase in the level of certainty or severity of punishment for specific crimes decreases the crime rate.

When research workers posed the question in this way, they found mixed results, indicating again that deterrence sometimes seems to work in some specific situations. Generally, however, research continues to support the contention that the certainty of punishment is a more important consideration than is the level of severity. For example, Blumstein states,

> Research on deterrence has consistently supported the position that sentence 'severity' (that is, the time served) has less of a deterrent effect than sentence 'certainty' (the probability of going to prison) [citation]. Thus, from the deterrence consideration, there is a clear preference for increasing certainty, even if it becomes necessary to do so at the expense of severity. [16]

There appears to be little or no serious debate among criminologists about the degree to which the recent change in severity of punishment has affected the crime rate—which probably can be said to be very little or not at all.

Yet, the changes in punishment policy that have been described have been advocated on the basis of deterrence as well as a claimed incapacitation benefit. We may ask whether this agrees with what we know best about the nature of criminal behavior.

Does what is known about the nature and extent of crime support a policy of increasing incarceration for its deterrent effects? If most offenders are focused, as they seem to be, on short-term, immediate gratification, we would not expect legislative changes in the criminal code that increase penalties or make harsher punishments mandatory to have much, if any, effect. So far, the evidence supports this view. We have seen that most crime is stealing and assault, that many assaults grow out of intent to steal, and that most crimes, including violent ones, may be characterized as impulsive behaviors by persons lacking in foresight and ability to look ahead beyond the immediate gratification of the moment.

Another Look at Incapacitation

With evidence concerning the effectiveness of deterrence and rehabilitation widely reported as disappointing, the incapacitation of criminal offenders has tended to dominate criminal justice policy choices in the last two decades. It has tended to be highly praised in the public press since the early 1980s,[17] and in political campaigns for the last two decades as well. A close look at the facts about offender behavior that would best support policies of incapacitation, however, should give the policymaker (or honest political candidate) pause.

The concept of incapacitation, and particularly the idea of *collective* incapacitation, has been used to mean any crime-reducing effects of changes in the use of incarceration or other restraints regardless of the nature of the changes.[18] Any punishment strategy that restrains the potential offender might have crime-reducing effects, and the term "collective incapacitation" may be used and understood in this sense. For example, Cohen notes that "collective incapacitation refers to the benefits in reduced crime that accompany a sentencing policy without invoking any explicit predictions of the future criminality of particular individuals."[19] There is no doubt that while an offender is incarcerated that person cannot commit crimes in the community.

Many recent changes in laws that govern sentencing—such as mandatory penalties, mandatory minimum terms, increased sentences, and "three strikes" type laws—have been advocated on the basis of a somewhat different concept of incapacitation. As traditionally conceived, that concept was well defined by Packer, who considered incapacitation to be:

> the simplest justification for any punishment that involves the use of physical restraint [because] for its duration the person on whom it is being inflicted loses entirely or nearly so the capacity to commit further crimes. . . . [It] rests on a prediction that a person who commits a certain kind of crime is likely to commit either more crimes of the same sort or other crimes of other sorts. This latter prediction does not seem to figure largely in the justification for incapacitation as a mode of prevention. To the extent that we lock up burglars because we fear that they will commit further offenses, our prediction is not that they will if left unchecked violate the antitrust laws, or cheat on their income taxes, or embezzle money from their employers; it is that they will commit further burglaries, or other crimes associated with burglary. . . . The premise is that the person may have a tendency to commit further crimes like the one for which he is now being punished and that punishing him will restrain him from doing so.
>
> Incapacitation, then, is a mode of punishment that uses the fact that a person has committed a crime of a particular sort as the basis for assessing his personality and then predicting that he will commit further crimes of that sort. It is an empirical question in every case whether the prediction is a valid one.[20]

This concept is simple and intuitively appealing: if we restrain people through imprisonment, they cannot repeat their crimes. It is based on an assumption about our ability to predict criminal behavior. We predict that an offender will continue breaking laws if not restrained from doing so. Also, we predict that burglars will continue doing burglaries, robbers robbery, and assaulters assault. Such predictions are used to justify many mandatory sentencing statutes, "habitual offender" laws, and the recent wave of "three strikes" initiatives.

Most public policymakers are familiar with the fact that a small number of offenders commit a vastly disproportionate number of crimes.[21] By identifying and restraining this group of offenders, policymakers hope to have a significant impact on crime. But they may not know that the studies uncovering this important fact were all *retrospective* in nature: the small groups of offenders responsible for large numbers of crimes all were identified after the fact—that is, after they had accumulated long criminal records. Incapacitation policies, however, are *predictive* in nature. In order to be successful, they require that likely persons be identified before they have had a chance to commit numerous crimes. Unfortunately, we do not really know how to do that very well.

Incapacitation strategies also could be supported if some of the supposed "common wisdom" about criminal behavior were true. Three important common beliefs, however, have been shown by research to be more false than true.[22]

First, it is commonly believed that offenders tend to specialize in certain types of crimes. By confining a violent offender, we expect a decrease in the number of violent crimes committed. By locking up a person convicted of robbery, we expect to prevent robberies. There is some evidence for consistency in offending, but the overwhelming weight of evidence is that offenders are quite versatile in their choices of crimes. Offenders tend to be opportunistic "generalists" rather than "specialists" in, say, burglary or robbery, and there is no evidence that such "patterning" increases as a "criminal career" progresses.

Second, it is commonly believed that offenders progress from less serious to more serious offenses and to more and more crime as their "careers" advance. If this were so, restraining "career criminals" not only should cut the number of crimes committed but also should diminish the number of serious crimes. But, there is little evidence that offenders tend to progress from less serious to more serious offenses. Moreover, the number of offenses that an individual commits declines with age in adulthood. Not only the *tendency* to offend but also the *rate* of offending decreases as people get older.

Third, it is often believed that the people committing the most crimes are the most serious offenders, and therefore are most in need of restraint. Actually, those who commit the most crimes are far more likely to be committing minor, rather than major, offenses—for example, disorderly conduct or being intoxicated in public rather than robbery or rape.

Can we identify ahead of time those offenders who will continue to break laws? The answer is "yes, to a degree." If we can predict correctly at all, that always will be the correct answer, because we cannot expect to achieve perfection in prediction. We cannot expect to write biographies in advance, but by following methods already described, we can develop useful prediction instruments. We can, however, predict only modestly well. That means we will have relatively high rates of error. We "predict" that many offenders need restraint who are never again convicted of a crime. Money spent on confining those persons for that purpose is wasted (except, of course for those who offend but are not caught and convicted, about whom we do not know).

Similarly, we "predict" that some offenders do not need to be imprisoned who do offend again. Those errors are costly in terms of harm done to the community through crimes that might have been prevented. When offenders have been confined needlessly for an incapacitative purpose, it never is learned that they would not have, in fact, offended if released. The error of releasing an offender who is predicted not to offend, however, is quite noticeable when the culprit is again arrested. In combination, the two types of errors perpetuate the false beliefs that support the selective incapacitation strategy. Both types of errors are very costly—measured in both human and monetary terms.

Because they ignore much scientific evidence, "three strikes" and similar mandatory sentencing laws are based on extremely crude "predictions" that are full of error. They can be expected to increase the prison overpopulation problem without changing the crime rate appreciably.

Does what we know about the nature and extent of crime support a policy of increasing use of incapacitation? As we have seen, most crime is stealing of some sort. Many assaults grow out of stealing attempts that go wrong, as when a burglary attempt is thwarted by the unexpected presence of a victim, or a mugging victim does not come up with the cash. More serious crimes such as assaults, rapes, and murder are extremely difficult to predict. It is firmly established that "specialization" in types of crimes is rare, and it is known that the most likely next crime by a released prisoner, if one occurs, is a minor offense—a crime of the "nuisance" variety.[23] Most of the crime prevented by incapacitation is that of a relatively minor nature, and efforts to select and restrain only the most serious offenders, expected to do much harm if released, is to base a policy on a presumed ability, which we do not yet have, to select those offenders.

Because selective incapacitation is now the basis for many current policies and recent changes in the law, it is especially important to examine the evidence about "criminal careers." Some important facts about the subsequent behavior of men paroled from prison come from a recent study. It was based in part on examination of their criminal records over the 26 years after their releases. Important considerations for incapacitation are:

- Desistence of crime by parolees (some stop committing crimes).

- The likelihood that parolees who commit crimes will commit minor offenses.

- The lack of "specialization" in types of crime committed.[24]

The point is not that these offenders did not commit new crimes after release. More often than not, they did. The 6,310 men were arrested more than 30,000 times in the 26 years after their release from prison. Of course, they were charged with many more crimes than that, because a person may, and often is, charged with more than one crime for any arrest.

The point is not, either, that these offenders did not commit many serious crimes. They did. Although, as shown in Figure 13.1, minor "nuisance" offenses predominated, these men were charged with 184 homicides, 2,084 assaults, 126 kidnappings, 144 rapes, 2,756 burglaries, 655 auto thefts, and 1,193 robberies. After their release 26 years earlier, they were charged with almost 10,000 serious offenses. Many more crimes may not have been detected.

The point is not that this tally of new offenses was for arrests and charges, not convictions, although it was. Many resulted in acquittals or

Figure 13.1 Most Serious Charge in Arrests of Paroled Prisoners in the Next 26 Years after Release

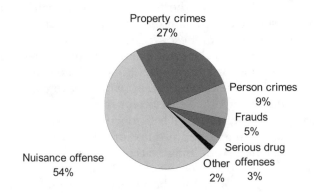

Property crimes
27%

Person crimes
9%

Frauds
5%

Serious drug offenses
3%

Other
2%

Nuisance offense
54%

Source: data from Gottfredson, S. D. and Gottfredson, D. M. (1994). "Behavioral Prediction and the Problem of Incapacitation," *Criminology* 32, 3, 451.

Note: Nuisance offenses include offenses such as parole and probation rules violations, drunk driving, possession or use of drugs, disorderly conduct, and gambling. Property crimes include, typically, burglaries, robberies and attempts without assault or physical harm, larcenies and attempts, and auto theft. Person crimes include illegal homicides, assaults, rape, and robberies with assault or physical harm. Frauds include forgery and bad checks, as well as other frauds. Serious drug offenses include the sale or manufacture of large quantities of illegal substances.

dismissals. For example, their first arrests after release from prison resulted in 56 percent being convicted, but a fourth were acquitted, dismissed, or (for 2 percent) subject to some other action such as transfer to another jurisdiction. (The disposition could not be discerned from the records for about 19 percent.)

The point is not that these men stayed out of jail and prison. They did not. Although almost a third never were incarcerated again, two-thirds did additional time in jail or prison. Nearly one man in five was confined again at least six times. Many cycled in and out of prison and jail. The record was held by one offender who was locked up 28 times during the 26 year period of follow up. The imaginary "typical" released prisoner was locked up again 1.68 times, which was the median.

So, what is the point? It is that, in various ways, the evidence from this study provided little support for the justification for incapacitation as preventing repeated serious crimes, and little support for collective incapacitation as commonly understood. An emphasis on either *selective* or *collective* incapacitation strategies turns out to be inconsistent with what we know about crime. Incapacitation "works," but the crimes prevented are mostly relatively minor, and incapacitation is very costly. We do not yet know how to use incapacitation efficiently and effectively to prevent the most serious crimes.

The selective incapacitation strategy is burdened with problems because we cannot—nor can judges or parole boards—predict very well. We can predict fairly well which offenders will be in some sort of trouble with the law again; we cannot, however, predict at all well which offenders will commit more serious crimes. In addition, knowledge of the conviction offense does not tell us the nature of the most likely next offense—we know only that it can be expected to most likely be a minor one. Strategies such as "three strikes" laws are based on the mistaken belief that the most serious criminal behavior can be predicted from knowledge of the crime of conviction or past convictions.

The collective incapacitation strategy also can be assessed by the evidence from this study. If none of these men ever had been released from prison, the crimes associated with their more than 30,000 arrests would have been prevented. Almost 10,000 of these arrests were for serious crimes which would have been prevented by the total incapacitation of these men. Since these are only the number of arrests, it is quite possible that they in fact committed many more crimes than that. All would have been prevented if all these prisoners had been kept in prison for the 26 years.

It is also true, however, that nearly a fourth of these men were never arrested after release. Setting aside any question about whether life in prison for all felons would be deserved, imagine that all were kept for life without parole. The lifetime commitment of these 1,413 nonrepeat offenders *for the purpose of incapacitation* would have been very costly, and, except for any crimes not detected, would have been a mistake. (Of course, there might have been *other* purposes.) In addition, the subsequent offenses at arrest of those charged with committing additional law violations were far more likely, by more than three to one, to be minor offenses than serious crimes.

In considering any selective incapacitation strategy, we must remember that there are four potential consequences to any predictive selection decision. We will have two types of errors and two types of correct predictions:

- We will predict that some persons will fail by committing new crimes who, in fact, will succeed. These errors usually are called "false positives."

- We will predict that some persons will succeed who, in fact, will fail. These errors are usually called "false negatives."

- We will predict that some persons will fail who will fail— a correct prediction.

- We will predict that some persons will succeed who will succeed— a correct prediction.

For a given failure rate, the total *number* of errors, both false positives and false negatives, will be the same with any particular method of prediction, whether we predict that a smaller or a larger group will fail. We may have fewer or more of either type of error by changing the proportion predicted to fail. For example, if we select fewer persons to fail, we will make fewer false positive mistakes, but more false negatives. Thus, by changing the proportions selected for incapacitation, we can increase or decrease either false positives or false negatives, but this *always* is at the expense of more errors of the other kind. The *total number* of errors cannot be manipulated in this way; only the relative proportions of the two kinds of errors may be changed. The only way to change the *total number* of errors is to increase the accuracy of the prediction method. There is no other way around the problem.

There are only two ways to increase the accuracy of the prediction method. The first is to increase the dependability of the prediction measure by finding information that improves prediction. The other is to increase the dependability of the criterion measure, the measure of new crimes, by more careful definition, better record keeping, or more efficient law enforcement.

Because we can predict only modestly well with data that now are collected, any presently available method of prediction will result in large numbers of false positive and false negative errors. This is true whether the prediction is made by human judgment, such as by a judge, or by using an objective, empirically derived prediction device. False positives—representing those persons kept in confinement because of a mistaken prediction of failure—would be criticized by philosophers from the ethics of desert, by inmates treated unfairly, by correctional administrators dealing with overcrowded prisons, and by economists for the waste of money. False negatives—representing those persons released because of a mistaken prediction of success who do in fact commit new crimes—would be criticized by philosophers from the ethics of utility, by members of the press, by the general public, and certainly by the citizen who had no wish to be set upon by a false negative.

Because we can never expect to be able to predict perfectly, the utility of incapacitation as a crime control strategy always will be constrained by our ability to predict. Improving that ability is important, but it never will be perfect, so we always can expect the two kinds of errors.

Besides the scientific evidence, there are ethical reasons—pointed out in the desert theory—to be wary of the current emphasis on incapacitation. When a person is punished out of proportion to the harm done in order to restrain that person from crimes that he or she has not done and might not do, that is not only costly, but from the perspective of deserved punishment, it is also unfair.

Do Rising Prison Populations Provide a False Comfort?

When we are confining more people than ever before for a wide variety of crimes and keeping them longer, we ought to ask, "Have these costly policies really made our lives safer?" As we have seen in previous sections of this book, persons imprisoned for drug offenses and offenses against the public order have increased—dramatically, for drug offenses. Our current policies thus favor imprisonment of an increasing proportion of people convicted of relatively less serious offenses. Policies designed to simply incarcerate more people have a limited capacity to actually make us safer.

Changes in public policy that have little support from evidence about reducing crime are responsible for the increases in prison populations. The prison populations depend entirely on how many persons are sent to prison and for how long. These are matters of public policy that are largely decided by our elected representatives, and that policy is limiting the ability of criminal justice personnel to make decisions.

Getting tougher on crime by sending more people to prison and keeping them longer appears to many to be a big help by increasing the safety of society. Unfortunately, as believed by many others, the *appearance* of help by a remarkably increased use of prisons in an effort to lower the crime rate may be a false comfort given by a public policy not supported by what we know about crime.

Recall that one of the most firmly established facts about crime has to do with its age distribution. As we have seen, the age distribution of crime peaks in late adolescence or early adulthood at around age 17–22 and declines sharply and continuously from that peak. That is true whatever the form of crime or how it is measured, whatever the time period studied, whatever the society, and whatever the subgroup of society. Our nation does have one of the highest crime rates in the world, but that rate has been declining for several years and this is due substantially to decreases in the proportion of teenagers and young adults in the population. Research has shown that the relative size of the crime-prone age group does a better job of predicting crime rates than does anything else.[25] When the group was large during the 1960s and 1970s, the crime rate increased. When the group decreased, as it has since 1980, so did crime rates.

As pointed out by Blumstein, demographic factors profiling the population are, of course, not the only factors influencing crime rates:

> Even though crime rates in the early 1980s followed demographic influences, other factors assumed much greater importance in the late 1980s, particularly the crack cocaine epidemic that began in the mid-1980s and continued to be a focus of intense law enforcement activity.

The changes in age composition that were associated with the lessening of crime rates in the early 1980s contributed at the same time to growth in the prison populations, not to a decrease. As explained by Blumstein,

> This seeming paradox results from the difference in the peak crime ages and the peak imprisonment ages. . . . Arrest rates peak between the ages of sixteen and eighteen. In contrast, the peak imprisonment ages are the late twenties, with a median age of prisoners close to thirty. The difference results mainly from the fact that very few people under eighteen are sent to prisons, which are intended primarily for adults . . . [and the use of probation for persons with minimal prior records and less serious crimes]. As a result, even though crimes were expected to decline, prison populations were expected to increase over the 1980s as the bulge of the baby boom (with a peak at about the 1960 cohort) continued to flow through the high imprisonment ages. But it was also expected that by the early 1990s, those cohorts would be past the peak imprisonment ages, and so prison populations were expected to decline—at least based on these considerations of the age composition of the population.[26]

Pointing out that unforeseen developments can of course affect the accuracy of all such projections, Blumstein added, "The emergence of the crack epidemic of the late 1980s was an important factor in the reversal of the anticipated decline in crime rates. Also, the changing policy environment surrounding crime and punishment during the 1980s could override any influence of demographics alone."

Generally, the crime rate has been decreasing while the prison population has been growing. To many people who do not carefully examine the relevant evidence, the interpretation of these facts seems simple and direct: since more criminals are incapacitated through imprisonment, the crime rate has dropped. Others may argue that increasing the use of imprisonment has had a deterrent effect. But the changes are best accounted for by the changes in the crime-prone age groups, the prison-prone age groups, and the changes in policy related to drug use.

Because the crime rate has been falling recently while the incarceration rate and severity of punishment have been rising, some politicians have been quick to claim that the "get tough" policies they have publicly supported should be credited. Usually overlooked, however, are the more likely explanations we have discussed, particularly the facts of the age distribution of crime. This provides a good example of what systems analysts call "forced fittings" of the evidence to the proposition favored, as in the following example:

Forced Fittings

There are a million and one influences—some explicit, some perceivable, some submerged, some unknown—that effect the final answer. The fact that many transformations have to be made among disparate factors gives much room for forced fittings, particularly if there's something to be gained personally for the individual concerned. One of the best examples of forced fittings I have come across is an algorithm for success. It has been advanced as the secret of success for overzealous young systems analysts on the rising slope of the gamesmanship curve. It goes like this: To obtain success from zero to zero plus delta success Monte Carlo the third partial derivative involving the conjugate of the skew-Hermitian matrix, divided by the fourth moment about the mean in dimensionless form, as adjusted by the Bayes estimator, and add the entire quotient to what the boss wants to hear at the moment.

—R. G. H. Siu

Many persons believe that, over the next decade, current "get tough" policies are going to be tougher on taxpayers than on crime. At the same time, it may be expected that crime rates will increase substantially as the proportion of teenagers and young adults begins to climb again. From this perspective it is argued that we should change the familiar slogan, "Lock 'em up and throw away the key" to "Lock 'em up and throw away your money."

Another Look at Treatment

We have seen that the demise of the rehabilitative ideal was not really justified by sound and convincing evidence that rehabilitation efforts are useless. The decline in popularity of that design for sentencing and corrections may have had as much to do with increased acceptance of retribution, increased severity of punishments, and increasing popularity of the deterrence and incapacitative orientations as with the evidence about "what works." (For one inmate's view, see Box 13.1.)[27] Nevertheless, we may ask what the evidence *now* shows about the effectiveness of treatment.

Asking whether treatment works is another right question asked in the wrong way. The helpful questions must be more specific. We need to know what works in what respect with what group of offenders under what circumstances.

Asking what works *in what respect* reminds us that the goals of decisions throughout the criminal justice system are multiple and complex. It is possible, for example, that a treatment program may reduce new crimes, reduce the seriousness of crimes, delay the commission of crimes, reduce the incidence of illegal drug or alcohol abuse, lower the rate of parole or probation violations, or result in fewer failures to appear at court. Or, a treatment program may have benefits other than crime control: it may increase the earnings of offenders in the community, provide services to the community, reduce reliance of offender dependents on welfare, or achieve any number of other objectives that may be believed to be attained by the program.

Asking what works *with what group of offenders* reminds us that all offenders are not alike but nevertheless may be classified to good advantage for assignments to treatment programs. What works for one kind of offenders does not necessarily work with another.

Box 13.1

Evan D. Hopkins: In His Own Words

When I was sent to the State Penitentiary, in 1981, I was twenty-six—the quintessential angry young black male. However, there was a very different attitude toward rehabilitation at that time, particularly as regards education. I was able to take college courses for a number of years on a Pell grant. Vocational training was available, and literacy (or at least enrollment in school) was encouraged and increased one's chances for making parole.

In the late seventies, there was a growing recognition that rehabilitation programs paid off in lower rates of recidivism. But things began to change a few years later. First, the highly publicized violence of the crack epidemic encouraged mandatory minimum sentencing.

The throw-away-the-key fever really took off in 1988, when George Bush's Presidential campaign hit the Willie Horton hot button, and sparked the tough-on-crime political climate that continues to this day. The transformation was nearly complete when President Clinton endorsed the concept of "three strikes you're out" in his 1994 State of the Union address. And when Congress outlawed Pell grants for prisoners later that year the message became clear: We really don't give a damn if you change or not.

—Evans D. Hopkins,
Nottoway Correctional Center, Virginia

Asking what works *under what circumstances* reminds us that there are three important issues that should be considered in evaluations of programs. These are called program integrity, program fidelity, and program strength. Programs that do not correspond to the theory underlying their development or are not faithful to the program design, or are not strong enough to be reasonably believed to make a difference should not be expected to work. Also, it reminds us that we must be wary of applying results found in one jurisdiction to others without assessing whether the observed facts can be generalized to other times and other places. Rigorous evaluations of well-thought-out treatment programs that are carefully and faithfully implemented according to a sound plan and match services to carefully assessed treatment needs may find that the programs do work.

Despite a widespread current belief that treatment programs for offenders do not work, clinicians and research workers have continued to study the effectiveness of programs aimed at rehabilitation. Results do not always support the common negative opinion made popular by the reviews already cited. They do tend to support the view that some well-planned and implemented programs work in respect to some goals for some offenders under some circumstances.

A substantial literature on treatment effectiveness studies shows that treatment programs can and often do reduce recidivism.[28] If the evidence is summarized by surveying studies that meet specific criteria for inclusion, to ensure that acceptable research conditions were met in the studies included, then a useful way to summarize the products of research is provided. From this perspective, Gendreau, Cullen, and Bonta summarized two general findings as follows:

> First, if one surveys all the treatment studies that had control group comparisons, as Mark Lipsey [citation] did for 443 studies, 64 percent of the studies reported reductions in favor of the treatment group. The average reduction in recidivism summed across the 443 studies was 10 percent. Secondly, ac-

cording to Lipsey, when the results were broken down by the general type of
program (e.g., employment), reductions in recidivism ranged from 10 to 18
percent.[29]

Chapter 13
▲ ▲ ▲ ▲ ▲ ▲

Based on their reviews, Gendreau, Cullen, and Bonta listed features of
the most effective and ineffective programs. Characteristics of programs that
reduced recidivism included the following:

- Intensive services aimed at modifying behavior are provided to higher-risk offenders.

- The goal of treatment is to reduce criminogenic needs.

- The style and mode of treatment is matched to the offender.

- Program rules are enforced in a firm but fair manner.

- Therapists relate to offenders in interpersonally sensitive and constructive ways and are trained and supervised appropriately.

- The program structure and activities should disrupt the criminal network.

Characteristics of programs that did *not* appear to reduce recidivism included the following:

- Programs that target low-risk offenders.

- Programs that target offender need factors that are not predictive of criminal behavior (such as anxiety, depression, self-esteem).

- Traditional therapies based on psychoanalytic or nondirective counseling theories.

- Traditional medical approaches such as diet change, pharmacological treatments (such as testosterone suppressants for sex offenders), plastic surgery (which may increase self-esteem).

- Programs based on other theories such as those seeking to provide legitimate opportunities only, diversion from the stigmatization of the criminal justice system, or use of less severe punishments while avoiding coercive treatment.

- Deterrence strategies, such as intensive supervision programs emphasizing control and surveillance without features of rehabilitative services. Examples are bootcamps, electronic monitoring, and shock incarceration used without treatment services.

Another Look at Retribution

Retributive theories are moral theories, not scientific ones. But in criminal justice, ethics and science are inextricably intertwined. It is valuable to consider the just desert theory in the context of retributive theories more generally. We already saw that the desert theory does not require or even suggest an escalation in the level of severity of punishment. It does, however, require an insistence on proportionality and on fairness. From these two concerns, the theory suggests, a fixed penalty within narrow boundaries should apply and these *must* be provided in every case. This justification often is used for fixed, flat, or mandatory sentences.

The word "must" in the sentence above is a moral judgment. The moral philosophers who have written about retribution, however, have not been in agreement about this part of retributive theory.

Kinds of Retributive Theory

The just desert orientation that has risen in popularity in the United States in recent years is one variant of the more general class of positions called retributivism.[30] Mackie calls attention to three types of retributive principles: (1) negative retributivism, (2) positive retributivism, and (3) permissive retributivism.

The first asserts that one who is not guilty *must not* be punished. The second states that one who is guilty *ought* to be punished. The third posits that one who is guilty *may* be punished. In these principles, the words "must not," "ought," and "may" express moral judgments.

We may think that *negative* retributivism is noncontroversial. No one proposes that a person found not guilty should be punished. Yet, as we have seen, it is precisely one point of criticism of some proposed incapacitative sentencing strategies that some persons *expected* to do crimes will be punished for offenses not yet done and which might not ever be done.

Permissive retributivism has considerable appeal for those whose moral views are based on the consequences of acts. It gives room for seeking aims that might be defeated by punishment. An example is a sentence requiring a treatment program that would provide services to an offender that would not be possible or would be hindered by the imposition of confinement. It appeals also to those who wish to support concepts of forgiveness or mercy. It may have some appeal also to those who, with Morris, would regard deserved punishment only as a "limiting" principle.[31] The punishment dictated in the law for a crime may provide only an upper, but not a lower, limit for the penalty. If the punishment thought to be deserved is specified as "not to exceed" a certain penalty, then retribution may be served by a lesser one than the maximum allowed. In that case, less oppressive punishments thought to serve utilitarian aims could be permitted. This would mean that retribution as a principle only limits the amount or severity of punishment.

It is the second principle, *positive* retributivism, that is the most controversial. It is particularly so when correlative, or related, principles are added, as in desert theory. The first correlate, that even a guilty person must not be punished out of proportion to the harm done and degree of culpability, puts a limit on incapacitation. What is more at issue is the assertion that one who is guilty ought to be punished in proportion to that guilt. This requirement is a rejection of the alternative permissive principle. In the theory of just desert, the reason is that otherwise the principles of equity and of proportionality may be violated. This view has appeal for those who place a high value on the idea of equal punishment for equal crimes. It may appeal also to those who view any reduction in punishment as undesirable leniency.

The retributive goal of criminal justice has persisted for centuries. But we are still left to decide the *type* of retributive ethic—negative, positive, or permissive—that should be incorporated into a sanctioning scheme. If negative retributivism is accepted, then incapacitation as a purpose is out because it is not seen as legitimate. If positive retributivism is accepted, then every offender should receive the penalty deserved, never more and never less. This would eliminate much of the exercise of discretion by a prosecutor, judge, or jury, and it would require perfect efficiency by the police, the prosecutor, and the finders of facts. If permissive retributivism is accepted, then judges and parole boards may provide a lesser penalty than that ordinarily imposed, for example by imposing alternative sanctions that may be less severe as punishments but perceived as more appropriate from the rehabilitation perspective.

If retribution is primary, and if desert sets limits only—with an upper and lower bound—then the utilitarian purposes of incapacitation and treatment may be sought within those limits without violating retributive principles. How wide such bounds should be is the question of how much discretion should be allowed.

If utility, including crime prevention, is primary, crime control objectives set limits within which deserved punishment may be exacted. The amount of discretion to be allowed in punishment must be determined.

Different *types* of punishments might be equally severe. If so, the desert theory does not specify any preference. That theory, a positive retributivism, requires that punishments for similar persons in similar circumstances be given punishments similar in their severity. If the severity of two punishments were measured and found to be the same, the theory of deserved punishment would be silent on any preference. Imagine, for example, that house arrest with electronic monitoring for six months with periodic random drug testing and required attendance at counseling were found to be equally oppressive as a sentence to confinement in jail for, say, 30 days. Because the punishments are equal in severity, the desert theorist would not object to the judge's imposition of the sentence with expected rehabilitation value or, to the jail term. We cannot measure either harms or sanction severity with the precision required for such comparisons, but we can make rough comparisons of that sort. Prosecutors and judges often make them.

Can the criminal laws define crimes well enough to permit an appropriate amount of punishment deserved? How is the amount of harm to be measured? How can the quantity of pain delivered by the punishment be assessed? Is placement in minimum prison custody equally punishing as placement in maximum? How much punishment is delivered by house arrest, or drug testing, or jail days, or days in San Quentin? What is the meaning of proportionality? Should punishment be proportional in equal measures of pain to harm done or as some other function of crime seriousness? Should the ratio of pain to harm differ as harm increases? How is culpability to be defined well enough to permit its reliable measurement? If neither harm nor punishment can be measured reliably, how can equity be assessed? How can errors in the assessments required in order to determine the punishment deserved be avoided or reduced? Why do we require demonstrations of effectiveness of incapacitation, rehabilitation, and deterrence without equally demanding assessments of attempted implementations of the theory of deserved punishment?

Another Look at the Problem of Prediction

We have seen that the problem of predicting criminal behavior is present in decisions made throughout the criminal justice system. It is not only the currently popular incapacitation strategy that relies on a presumed ability to predict. Prediction is central to the decisions made about bail and preventive detention. It is part of police decision making, as when particular groups are targeted for surveillance. It is involved in prosecutor decisions to crack down on repeat offenders. It is critical to sentencing, as seen by judges' reliance on their estimates of likelihood of continued criminal behavior. It is reflected in the shift that has been described in corrections toward a greater emphasis on restraint—an incapacitative attitude. It is a strong feature of parole decision making. It is central to many modern programs in corrections. Both probation and parole programs rely on predictions for the assignment of offenders to various levels of supervision. Thus, how well such predictions can be made, how they should be made, and the information needed to improve them are critical questions for the entire criminal justice system.

Informal vs. Formal Predictions

Nearly 70 years ago, Burgess studied 3,000 parolees in Illinois, carefully gathering data from case records of both characteristics of the offender and the outcomes after release on parole. He combined 21 factors to make a parole prediction scale, using items such as age, the nature of the crime, and the number of prior offenses. Then he could examine the relation of the scores to the parole outcomes. As part of the study, three prison psychiatrists made subjective judgments about probable parole success. Burgess found that the objective method was clearly superior to the psychiatric judgments in predicting the outcomes of parole.[32]

This may have been the first comparison ever of the main two methods available to us for classifying persons for prediction. These two methods are an informal, subjective, impressionistic conclusion by a human judge and a formal, objective (usually derived from experience) method using an equation, formula, graph, or table to forecast an expected value of some outcome. The informal prediction method—the subjective, impressionistic one—is the most widely used in making decisions in the criminal justice system. Police, bail magistrates, prosecutors, probation staff, correctional managers, and parole authorities use the informal method in thousands of important decisions daily. The formal prediction method sometimes is used, as has been described in this book, for bail decision making, sentencing, paroling, institutional decisions about security and custody, and placement in probation and parole community supervision programs.

In the 70 years that have passed since Burgess's comparison of his more mechanical, objective method with the clinical judgments of the psychiatrists, there have been 617 distinct comparisons of the two basic methods of prediction in 136 studies.[33] The more objective, mechanical method was shown to be equal to or superior to the clinical, subjective method. These studies were not all in the criminal justice arena, by any means, although some were. They included a wide range of predictive criteria, such as medical and mental health diagnoses and prognoses, treatment outcomes, success in training or employment, adjustment to institutional life (such as prison or military service), parole violation, and violence. Similar findings have been reported in such areas as predicting freshman academic grades by comparing counselor judgments with an equation using only college aptitude test score and high school grade record.[34] In criminal justice decisions and in all these other areas, the evidence clearly shows that the objective methods do better.

Improving Risk Assessments

Despite the evidence from research, most professionals in criminal justice and many others continue to rely on subjective judgments when making predictive decisions. The evidence against doing so is substantial, varied, and consistent. If the objective prediction method is properly done (such as following the "recipe" presented in Chapter 8), then it must be expected to do a better job of prediction than the magistrate, judge, probation officer, or district attorney. Meehl, who has studied this issue extensively, claims, "All policymakers should know that a practitioner who claims not to need any statistical or experimental studies but relies solely on clinical experience as adequate justification, by that very claim is shown to be a nonscientifically minded person whose professional judgments are not to be trusted."[35] It is clear that the development of improved classification devices for the predictive element in criminal justice decisions throughout the system is an important way that criminal justice decision making can be made more efficient and effective.

Prevention

How much emphasis in the adoption of criminal justice system goals should be given to "secondary prevention" and how much to "primary prevention"? Primary prevention refers to efforts to stop crimes from occurring in the first place, while secondary prevention refers to the reduction of repeated offending. The goals of incapacitation and treatment are secondary prevention purposes.

The primary prevention of crime is a large topic. When we ask how crime can be prevented, however, the best short answer may be, "Start earlier." Remember the age distribution of crime and the fact that young adults are by far the most prone to crime. Remember the nature of most delinquency and crime—thoughtless, impulsive, spur-of-the-moment acts by bumblers lacking in foresight, concern for others, and self-control. From these simple, well-known facts, a society with eyes open will determine the best answer: start 15 years earlier to help children and young adults avoid the juvenile and criminal justice systems as wards or inmates. Help them through the schools. In order to reduce crime in the next decade, we need to begin doing whatever is required now to help children develop their full potentials for positive contributions to our society. That is called primary crime prevention, and it involves caring families, responsible child rearing, good schools, and other agencies outside the juvenile and criminal justice systems.

> It is curious to reflect how history repeats itself the world over. Why, I remember the same thing [reducing funding for public education] was done when I was a boy on the Mississippi River. There was a proposition in a township there to discontinue public schools because they were too expensive. An old farmer spoke up and said if they stopped the schools they would not save anything, because every time a school was closed a jail had to be built. It's like feeding a dog on his own tail. He'll never get fat. I believe it is better to support schools than jails.
> —Mark Twain, 1900

Management Information Systems

Horse and Buggy vs. Space Travel

The information systems of the police, the courts, and correctional institutions have yet to take advantage of the information age. Most management information systems in criminal justice do little more than keep track of current cases, record some of the decisions made, maintain financial data for budget spending and planning, provide for workload estimation, and create voluminous files never used for examination of the successes and failures of their work. Without investigation of successes and failures, police managers, judges, or correctional personnel cannot learn what works.

Computer science now has progressed to the point that routine assessments of the results of decisions—both individual and management decisions—could be economically and efficiently addressed in a timely manner to systematically improve decisions. The necessary elements for such systems are suggested by the variety of decision objectives, alternatives, and information availabilities discussed throughout this book. Systems to study and improve decisions require the following:

- Explicit identification of decision objectives;

- Specification of the information used in making the decisions;

- Measurement of the decision outcomes in terms of the objectives sought;

- Clerical, organizational, psychometric (behavioral measurement), statistical, legal, and behavioral science expertise.

When data on objectives and outcomes are collected, the power of modern computers allows the required statistical analyses, which only a few decades ago could be done only occasionally and at considerable expense, to be done easily, quickly, and efficiently.

Computer power is not yet used effectively in criminal justice management. If you send a package across country overnight, you can track it to its destination from your desktop computer, through each major point of transition from truck to airplane to holding area to truck to doorstep. If you seek an airline reservation for tomorrow or next month, go to your desktop and see whether there are any seats on the flight you select. If you want a rare book that you have not been able to find, go to the internet and find it, perhaps in North Dakota. But if a judge tries to find out from a court information system how many persons sentenced to X, having Y characteristics, were released after Z months and rearrested before N months, the answer, if it can be found, may be obtained only after days or months of staff work.

If, on the other hand, the court could obtain such data quickly and easily, and if the court were motivated to learn the results of its sentencing practices, such data could be extremely valuable in informing future decisions. Given such data, powerful statistical designs are available to permit fair comparisons with the results of other choices at the time of sentencing. Similarly, magistrates could be informed about the results of bail decisions, police managers could be advised about the effects of policy changes concerning patrol, probation staff could be informed about the results of classification for differential supervision, and prison administrators could tell

Sophisticated systems are used to control prison populations but modern technology is yet little used to provide better information for decisions. The central control booth in this photo has "state of the art" electronic equipment to control movement throughout the institution. Can other technologies be used to improve management in criminal justice agencies? *—Photo courtesy of the New Jersey Department of Corrections.*

better whether they were placing the right inmates in the right programs and facilities.

The obstacles to management information systems of this sort are not found in a lack of the available technology. They more often are found in a lack of a questioning attitude, a failure to demand the evidence, a lack of qualified research personnel, and the absence of an insistence on studying the effects of decisions in order to improve them.

Needs for Feedback

The information needs of the criminal justice system are not limited to those of any particular agency. The victim should be advised, or at least should be able to find out, what happened after the complaint. The police should be advised, or be able to learn, what happened after the arrest. The prosecutor should know systematically, for various kinds of cases, not only the dispositions but also the actual sentences as finally imposed and executed. Victims and the police deserve this information. The judge should be informed, systematically, about the ultimate outcomes of sentencing decisions in terms of sentencing goals.

At each step in the criminal justice process, decisions are made in pursuit of objectives; but whether the objectives are attained may never be discovered unless a suitable information system is in place. In order that decision makers receive feedback on the results of their decisions, systems for tracking offenders through the subsequent steps of criminal justice processing are required. Once the information is available, then better procedures are needed for providing feedback to other parts of the system.

Turning Data into Information

Criminal justice agencies collect much data about offenders, the decisions made, and often about relevant decision outcomes. But data by themselves are not *information* in the sense of data that will inform or shape future decision making for more rational decisions.

We have two basic methods for turning data into information, two basic procedures for discovering information about the consequences of decisions that will help in reaching the goals specified for the decision. As we have seen, these are experiments and statistical designs. We have seen how both methods can improve information for decisions. The opportunities for turning data into information by both of these methods abound in the criminal justice system. They should be used as a routine part of a modern management information system.

Experiments—with comparisons of effects of an intervention applied to one group while not using it with another *equivalent* group—are the strongest research designs, and they could be used much more often. Experiments could be used effectively when a new program is tried but resources do not permit using it with all eligible persons. Many other opportunities arise when there is a question about which program or practice will produce the most benefit.

What is sought is not mere data but information that is related to the desired outcomes of the decision. The right questions, asked in the right way, often involve the evaluation of programs.

Program evaluations are investigations designed to answer two important questions: What was done, and with what effects? Well-done evaluations can contribute to the formation of the program by helping to specify the goals clearly, define how program elements and program events will be measured, and monitor progress. A detailed description of what was done is needed, because it is essential that what is being tested is clearly established. Then the program's results can be analyzed to find out whether the program worked the way it was envisioned.

Making Decisions With Eyes Open

Structured Decision Making

The topic of structured decision making is closely related to the problem of information development for criminal justice decisions. We have seen how, in many criminal and juvenile justice arenas, decision makers are moving—either voluntarily or through legislative mandate—toward an increased use of explicit decision making standards. The trends toward mandatory, fixed, or presumptive sentencing are examples of this, as is the increasing tendency for legislatures to provide for mandatory transfers of jurisdiction to adult courts for certain offenses or for youths of certain ages.

We have seen throughout this book that discretionary decisions are made at every step in the criminal and juvenile justice processes. We have seen that many of these are predictive in nature, at least in part. We have seen that the objectives of these decisions are rarely stated explicitly and the information used for the decisions is rarely clearly defined. We have seen that empirically tested instruments or rules for decision making have many advantages over subjective "made in the head" decisions, which are subject to unreliability, low validity, bias, and much variability among decision makers. Thus, the topic of guidelines that may be used for more systematic and rational decision making deserves a further look.

Correctional agencies, like others of the criminal justice system, maintain extensive data systems but often fail to examine these data in relation to their goals. These prison inmates are working in a data processing unit of the correctional system. How can data about offenders and their treatment be better used to improve decisions?—*Photo courtesy of the New Jersey Department of Corrections.*

Some methods and procedures for structured decision making may be recommended over others.[36] They can be of use in making decisions at key points throughout the juvenile and criminal justice systems, wherever discretion is exercised. As already described, some guideline procedures are in use in some jurisdictions for bail decisions, sentencing, and paroling. Other, similar procedures could be developed for police decisions, prosecutorial decisions, correctional institution classification decisions, community corrections placement decisions, and juvenile justice system decisions. The method and the principles are general and can be applied wherever important policy and case decisions are made.

Perhaps no topic has become more controversial among criminal justice decision makers than the idea of guidelines. Many structured decision systems travel under the name of guidelines, from legislatively constructed sentencing codes, to presumptive sentencing aids constructed by sentencing commissions, to broad and essentially meaningless statements of purpose for disposition decisions. What we will discuss here, under the heading of guidelines, is specific. It is a system for decision making with the following critical features:

- The distinction between policy and case decisions is recognized.

- Discretion is valued but structured, in order that similar cases will be treated alike but cases that are different will be treated differently.

- Consistency in decision making is examined and fostered by facilitating comparisons among decision makers in a particular setting.

- Visibility is promoted by providing those outside the system with a set of explicit purposes and rules that govern decision making.

- Explicit attention is given to the main goals for the decision and information is gathered systematically about performance in order to increase the efficiency and effectiveness of the decisions.

- The capacity to improve the system is built in as part of the system.

- It will actually be used by the decision makers whom it is designed to help.

Not all structured decision making systems that are advocated currently fit well into these requirements. Perhaps the best current example of decision systems far removed from these characteristics are those mandated by legislatures. They are inflexible, designed to treat all cases alike without regard for individual differences, contemptuous of any need for discretion, and likely to be undermined by practitioners.

Guidelines for Guidelines

What then are the essential features of a structured decision-making system that would include the characteristics that are desirable for guidelines? The "guidelines for guidelines" in Box 13.2 are offered as appropriate for many criminal justice system decisions.[37]

The essential aspects of guidelines as a general policy control method include the following:

1. A general policy for making a particular decision, including a statement of the goals sought, articulated in explicit terms, within which individual case decisions are made.

2. Explicitly defined criteria for decision making, with the specific weights to be given to these criteria, also explicitly defined.

3. Within the general policy model, guidelines in the form of a chart (matrix or grid) typically are used in the process of arriving at a particular decision. The most important policy concerns, decided by those responsible of the decision-making policy, are reflected in the dimensions of the grid. Usually, there is a small number of main dimensions—often only two or three. In most models with two dimensions, one axis reflects the seriousness of the offense and the other reflects characteristics of the offender. The intersection of the appropriate columns and rows for the two axes provides an expected decision for cases possessing the attributes used in classifications for the chart.

4. The guidelines grid is intended to structure the use of discretion but not eliminate it. There are two ways in which discretionary judgments are required of the decision maker:

    a. Some discretion must be exercised within the cells of the two-dimensional grid. For example, a range of sentence durations may be suggested within which a choice may be made.

    b. Considering the facts of each case, the decision maker is expected sometimes to reach a decision that is an exception from the suggested decision outcome.

5. When departures are made, the decision maker must provide explicit reasons for the exception from the usual decision for offenders or accused persons in the classification that applies.

6. There is an established system of monitoring to provide periodic feedback to the authorities responsible for the decision policy, giving the percentage of decisions falling outside each guideline category and the reasons given for these decisions.

7. The authorities may modify the guidelines at any time.

8. The general policy, including the guidelines incorporated within it, is not regarded as a "once and for all" statement of a "right" policy; rather, the policy statement and the procedures are designed to facilitate an evolutionary system of policy development changing in response to experience, resulting learning, and social change.

9. The policy in general, and the guidelines specifically, are open and available for public review, criticism, and debate.

Jurisdictions have approached the task of creating such guidelines in a variety of ways. Some have based their guidelines on empirical study of recent practice. A model of recent decision making is created through the study of a large number of cases, and the main factors emerging from such modeling are used to establish initial assumptions. These are subject to modification as determined to be desirable by the persons responsible for policy. Others have engaged in debate, for example, about the proper manner to scale seriousness of offenses and the appropriate elements of an offender score. Still others have been linked to prison capacity, examining the effect of changes considered according to the available space in existing prisons. Whatever the mechanism by which they are created, the two-dimensional form (one dimension reflecting offense seriousness and the other risk or prior involvement) is remarkably general in its application.[38] Two examples of working guidelines models have been presented in previous chapters. One was an example from bail setting and the other from sentencing.

The development of guideline structures can be incorporated into a modern management system making full use of available technology. This can provide a basis for the development of better information for decisions through a wider use of both experiments and statistical approximations. Such a system is more readily envisioned and described than developed and implemented in practice, but there are enough examples to show that it could be done more widely.

Stumbling Toward Justice

The delicate balancing of desires for safety and insistence on freedom goes on, sometimes shifting to the right, sometimes to the left. The criminal justice system continues to provide both protection and liberty, yet it continues to struggle with these competing demands.

In the Old Supreme Court Chamber, first used by the Supreme Court of the United States in 1819, there is a plaster relief sculpted by Carlo Franzoni in 1817. Justice is seated with a pair of scales in her left hand, with her right hand resting on the hilt of an unsheathed sword. She wears no blindfold.[39]

Justice with eyes open can see that the criminal justice system is plagued by problems. Yet, promising developments in law enforcement, the courts, and correctional programs continue to encourage efforts toward more efficient, effective, fair, and humane administration of the criminal law. In each of these three areas of criminal justice, advances have come in part through application of the scientific method. Its greater use promises a greater return.

Each of the main, traditional crime control means—deterrence, incapacitation, and treatment—may work to some extent, some of the time. Certainly, they do not provide any crime control cure-all. We are likely to continue to rely on them, but decisions throughout the system of criminal justice can be improved by better using what is now known about the nature and extent of delinquency and crime and about how the system works. The scientific method can better help determine when, how, and with whom they can be used to best effect to reduce crime.

Similarly, the traditional purpose of retribution is apt to continue to be demanded as a major function of the system. The application of punishment for the retributive purpose also can be made more fair—with punishments more proportional to harm and more fairly distributed—by application of methods for improving decisions that have been described in this book.

Opening the eyes of justice requires the questioning attitude and search for the evidence that is needed for the improvement of decisions and programs throughout the criminal justice system, including those that address the punishment purpose. Although a blind justice may be desired to ensure impartial treatment, it must be recognized that justice must open her eyes to the evidence and procedures that can help ensure fairness. Criminal justice on the information superhighway can mean that a blind justice makes the same mistakes, only faster. Alternatively—aided by more attention to clarity of ethical concerns and increased use of methods of science—it can help toward both more justice and more crime control.

Opening the eyes of justice must mean a greater clarity of purposes and methods, better identification of the goals, development of alternative choices, and improvement of information on which decisions can be based. It must mean less reliance on unrealistic solutions and "forced fittings," even though popular, and more reliance on what we know about crime and the system. In these ways, the criminal justice system can be made more rational, more effective, and more fair.

> It is well to recall the words of the Emperor of China, many centuries ago, who wandered in his garden and found a beautiful, strong, gigantic oak. Returning to the palace, he called his trusted advisors together and explained that he wanted a giant oak like the one he had seen—and he wanted it in the middle of the palace courtyard. His advisors looked at one another in disbelief, and one finally asked, with all due deference and respect, "Emperor, do you know how long it takes to grow a tree like that?" "No," replied the Emperor, "How long?"
>
> "Centuries!" was the answer.
>
> The Emperor pondered, then replied, "Then we had better plant it right away."
>
> —Vincent O'Leary[40]

1. Blumstein, A., Cohen, J., and Nagin, D. (eds.). (1978) *Deterrence and Incapacitation: Estimating the Effects of Criminal Sanctions on Crime Rates*. Washington, DC: National Academy of Sciences; Sechrest, L., White, S. O., and Brown, E. D. (eds.). (1979). *The Rehabilitation of Criminal Offenders: Problems and Prospects*. Washington, DC: National Academy of Sciences.

2. Nagin, D. (1978). "General Deterrence: A Review of the Empirical Evidence," in Blumstein, A., Cohen, J., and Nagin, D. (eds.). (1978).

3. Blumstein, A., Cohen, J., and Nagin, D. (eds). (1978). *Deterrence and Incapacitation: Estimating the Effects of Criminal Sanctions on Crime Rates*. Washington, DC: National Academy of Sciences.

4. Ibid.

5. Greenwood, P. W., with Abrahamse, A. (1982). *Selective Incapacitation* Santa Monica, CA: Rand Corporation.

6. von Hirsch, A. and Gottfredson, D. M. (1983–1984). "Selective Incapacitation: Some Queries about Research Design and Equity," *New York Review of Law and Social Change* 1, 12, 1; Cohen, J. "Incapacitation as a Strategy for Crime Control: Possibilities and Pitfalls," in Tonry, M. and Morris, N. (eds). (1983). *Crime and Justice: An Annual Review of Research* 1, Vol. V. Chicago: University of Chicago Press, 18; Gottfredson, S. D. and Gottfredson, D. M., "Selective Incapacitation?" in *Annals of the American Academy of Political and Social Science*.

7. Cohen, J. (1973). "Incapacitating Criminals: Recent Research Findings," *Research in Brief*. Washington, DC: National Institute of Justice; Cohen, J. (1978). "The Incapacitative Effect of Imprisonment: A Critical Review of the Literature," in *Deterrence and Incapacitation*, in Blumstein, A., Cohen, J., and Nagin, D. (eds.). (1978).

8. Cohen, J. (1983). "Incapacitation as a Strategy for Crime Control: Possibilities and Pitfalls," in Tonry, M. and Morris, N. (eds).

9. See generally, Blumstein, A., et al, (1978) and Cohen's article therein.

10. Sechrest, L., White, S. O., and Brown, E. D. (eds.). (1979); the discussion in this section is adapted by permission from Gottfredson, G. D., in "Penal Policy and the Evaluation of Rehabilitation," remarks prepared for a symposium titled Evaluating the Rehabilitation of Criminal Offenders, meeting of the American Society of Criminology, November, 1979.

11. American Friends Service Committee (1971). *Struggle for Justice: A Report on Crime and Punishment in America*. New York: Hill and Wang.

12. Notable and often cited examples were Bailey, W. C. (1966). "Correctional Outcome: An Evaluation of 100 Reports," *Journal of Criminal Law, Criminology, and Police Science*, 57, 153–160; Kassebaum, G., Ward, D. A., and Wilner, D. M., (1971). *Prison Treatment and Parole Survival*. New York: Wiley; Lipton, D., Martinson, R., and Wilks, J. (1975). *The Effectiveness of Correctional Treatment: A Survey of Treatment Evaluation Studies*. New York: Praeger; Martinson, R. (1974) "What Works? Questions and Answers about Prison Reform," *Public Interest*: 10, 180–191.

13. McCord, J. (1978). "A Thirty Year Follow Up of Treatment Effects," *American Psychologist*, 33, 284–289.

14. Gottfredson, G. D. (1979). "Penal Policy and the Evaluation of Rehabilitation," remarks prepared for a symposium titled Evaluating the Rehabilitation of Criminal Offenders, meeting of the American Society of Criminology, November, 1979.

15. von Hirsch, A. (1976). *Doing Justice: The Choice of Punishments*. New York: Hill and Wang, 140.

16. Blumstein, A. (1995). In *Crime*, Wilson, J. Q. and Petersilia, J. (eds.). San Francisco: Institute for Contemporary Studies, 408–409.

17. Newsweek (November 15, 1982). "To Catch a Career Criminal," 77; *The New York Times* (October 6, 1982). "Cutting Crime Tied to the Busiest Criminals;" *U.S. News and World Report* (October, 1982). "Key to Criminals' Future: Their Past;" *The New York Times* (November 14, 1982). "Making Punishment Fit Future Crimes," E-9.

18. Greenberg, D. F. (1975). "The Incapacitative Effect of Imprisonment: Some Estimates." *Law and Society Review* 9, 541–580; Cohen, J. (1978). "The Incapacitative Effect of Imprisonment: A Critical Review of the Literature," in Blumstein, A., Cohen, J., and Nagin, D. (eds.). *Deterrence and Incapacitation: Estimating the Effects of Criminal Sanctions on Crime Rates* Washington, DC: National Academy Press; Blumstein, A., Cohen, J., Roth, J., and Visher, C. (eds.). (1986). *Criminal Careers and "Career Criminals."* Washington, DC: National Academy of Sciences.

19. Cohen, J. (1978), "The Incapacitative Effect of Imprisonment: A Critical Review of the Literature," in Blumstein, A., Cohen, J., and Nagin, D. (eds.) 189.

20. Packer, H. L. (1968). *The Limits of the Criminal Sanction*. Stanford: Stanford University Press, 48–49.

21. Wolfgang, M., Figlio, R., and Sellin, T. (1972). *Delinquency in a Birth Cohort*. Chicago: University of Chicago Press.

22. Gottfredson, S. D. and Gottfredson, D. M. (1994). "Behavioral Prediction and the Problem of Incapacitation," *Criminology* 32, 3, 441–474; Gottfredson, S. D. and Gottfredson, D. M. (1992). *Incapacitation Strategies and the Criminal Career*. Sacramento, CA: California Department of Justice. Portions of this section were adapted by permission from S. D. Gottfredson, "Fighting Crime at the Expense of the Colleges," *The Chronicle of Higher Education*, January 20, 1995.

23. Gottfredson, S. D. and Gottfredson, D. M. (1994). "Behavioral Prediction and the Problem of Incapacitation," *Criminology* 32, 3, 441–474; Gottfredson, S. D. and Gottfredson, D. M. (1992). *Incapacitation Strategies and the Criminal Career*. Sacramento, CA: California Department of Justice.

24. Ibid.

25. Blumstein, A., Cohen, J., and Miller, H. (1980). "Demographically Disaggragated Projections of Prison Populations," *Journal of Criminal Justice* 8, 1–26; Blumstein, A. (1995). "Prisons," in Wilson, J. Q. and Petersilia, J. (eds.). *Crime*. San Francisco: Institute for Contemporary Studies, 392–395.

26. Blumstein, A. (1995), "Prisons," in Wilson, J. Q. and Petersilia, J. (eds.). *Crime*. San Francisco: Institute for Contemporary Studies, 395.

27. Hopkins, E. D. (1997). "Lockdown: Life Inside Is Getting Harder." *The New Yorker*, February 24 and March 3, 70.

28. Andrews, D. A. and Bonta, J. (1994). *The Psychology of Criminal Conduct*. Cincinnati, OH: Anderson; Andrews, D. A., Bonta, J., and Hoge, R. D. (1990). "Classification for Effective Rehabilitation: Rediscovering Psychology," *Criminal Justice and Behavior*, 17, 19–52; Cullen, F. T. and Gendreau, P. (1989). "The Effectiveness of Correctional Rehabilitation: Reconsidering the 'Nothing Works' Debate," in Goodstein, L. and MacKenzie (eds.). *American Prisons: Issues in Research and Policy*. New York: Plenum Press, 23–44; Garrett, C. J. (1985). "Effects of Residential Treatment on Adjudicated Delinquents: A Meta-analysis," *Journal of Research in Crime and Delinquency* 22, 287–308; Gendreau, P. and Andrews, D. A. (1990). "Tertiary Prevention: What the Meta-analysis of the Offender Treatment Literature Tells Us about What Works," *Canadian Journal of Criminology*, 32, 173–184; Gendreau, P. and Ross, R. R. (1979). "Effective Correctional Treatment: Bibliotherapy for Cynics," *Crime and Delinquency*, 25, 463–489; Gottschalk, R., Davidson, W. S., Mayer, J., and Gensheimer, R. (1987). "Behavioral Approaches with Juvenile Offenders: A Meta-analysis of Long-term Treatment Efficacy," in Morris, E. K. and Braukman, C. J. (eds.). *Behavioral Approaches to Crime and Delinquency: A Handbook of Application, Research, and Concepts*. New York: Plenum Press, 399–422; Izzo, R. and Ross, R. R. (1990). "Meta-analysis of Rehabilitation Programs for Juvenile Delinquents: A Brief Report," *Criminal Justice and*

Behavior 17, 134–142; Lipsey, M. W. (1992). "Juvenile Delinquency Treatment: A Meta-analytic Inquiry into the Variability of Effects," in Cook, T. D., Cooper, H., Cordray, D. S., Hartmann, L. V., Hedges, L. V., Light, R. J., Louis, T. A., and Mosteller, F. (eds.). *Meta-analysis for Explanation*. New York: Russell Sage Foundation, 83–127; Palmer, T. (1992). *The Re-emergence of Correctional Intervention*. Newbury Park, CA: Sage.

29. Gendreau, P., Cullen, F. T., and Bonta, J. (1994). "Intensive Rehabilitation Supervision: The Next Generation in Community Corrections?" *Federal Probation* 58, 1, 75.

30. Cottingham, J. G. (1979). "Varieties of Retribution," *Philosophical Quarterly* 29, as cited in Mackie, J. L. (1982). "Morality and the Retributive Emotions," *Criminal Justice Ethics*, Winter/Spring, 3–10.

31. Morris, N. (1976). "Punishment, Desert, and Rehabilitation," in U.S. Department of Justice, *Equal Justice under the Law*, Bicentennial Lecture Series, Washington, DC: GPO.

32. Burgess, E. W. (1928). "Factors Determining Success or Failure on Parole." In Bruce, A. A. (ed.). *The Workings of the Indeterminate Sentence Law and the Parole System in Illinois*. S205–249. Springfield, IL: Illinois Committee on Indeterminate-Sentence Law and Parole.

33. Meehl, P. E. and Grove, W. M. (1996). "Comparative Efficiency of Informal (Subjective, Impressionistic) and Formal (Mechanical, Algorithmic) Prediction Procedures: The Clinical-Statistical Controversy," *Psychology, Public Policy, and Law* 2, 2, 293–323.

34. Sarbin, T. R. (1943). "A Contribution to the Study of Actuarial and Individual Methods of Predictions," *American Journal of Sociology* 48, 593–602.

35. Meehl, P. E. and Grove, W. M. (1996), 320, citing Meehl, P. E., "Credentialed Persons, Credentialed Knowledge," *Clinical Psychology: Science and Practice* in press.

36. Recommendations about the development of guidelines for decisions and justifications for the recommendations presented here are presented elsewhere. For the original statement of guidelines, see Gottfredson, D., Wilkins, L., and Hoffman, P. (1978). *Guidelines for Parole and Sentencing*. Lexington, MA: Lexington Books. Further discussion of the justification for guidelines and examples may be found in Gottfredson, M. R. and Gottfredson, D. M. (1984). "Guidelines for Incarceration Decisions: A Partisan Review," *University of Illinois Law Review* 2, 801–827, and in Gottfredson, M. R. and Gottfredson, D. M. (1988). *Decisionmaking in Criminal Justice: Toward the Rational Exercise of Discretion*. New York: Plenum Press, and in Goldkamp, J. and Gottfredson, M. R. (1985). *Policy Guidelines for Bail: An Experiment in Court Reform*. Philadelphia: Temple University Press.

37. Gottfredson, M. R. and Gottfredson, D. M. (1984). "Guidelines for Incarceration Decisions: A Partisan Review." *University of Illinois Review*, 2, p. 801–827.

38. For discussion and illustration of alternative models, including sequential decision tree models and use of more than two dimensions, see Gottfredson, D. M., Cosgrove, C., Wilkins, L. T., Wallerstein, J., and Rauh, C. (1978). *Classification for Parole Decision Policy*. Washington, DC: National Institute of Law Enforcement and Criminal Justice.

39. http://www.aoc.gov/rooms/oldsuprc.htm

40. O'Leary, V., State University of New York at Albany, personal communication.

Glossary

Photo Courtesy of the New Jersey Department of Corrections.

Absconding running away or leaving to avoid the laws or rules.

Accused a person against whom a criminal proceeding is initiated.

Acquittal judicial discharge from a criminal charge after a finding of not guilty.

Actus reas the criminal act; the deed of crime.

Adjudication the method used by the courts for peaceful resolution of conflicts in which adversaries present, to a neutral third party, arguments and evidence for a decision in their favor according to established procedures and rules of law.

Adjudicatory hearing an adversary hearing by a juvenile court judge to determine whether a youth is delinquent, similar to a trial in a criminal court.

Adversarial persons or groups contending against each other, as in a contest.

Advisory hearing a hearing by a juvenile court judge or other judicial officer to determine whether a case may be resolved informally or should proceed to an adjudicatory hearing; similar to an arraignment in a criminal court.

Aggravated assault assault with serious bodily injury or with a dangerous or deadly weapon, or an assult done intentionally along with another crime.

Aggravating factors offense or offender characteristics that may increase the severity of a penalty.

Alarm reaction a response to stress characterized by extreme anxiety and disorganization, often with feelings of fear, humiliation, depression, anger, and guilt.

Alcades in California under Mexico, judicial officers appointed by the Governor, who were responsible for maintaining order.

Alleged asserted or claimed but not proven.

Appeal a resort to a higher court seeking a review of the lower court's decision and a reversal of its judgment.

Appellate courts courts with jurisdiction to review and examine the judgments of a trial court for errors of law.

Arraignment a court appearance at which an accused person is requested to plead to formal charges. It is sometimes combined with the initial appearance. The accused must be given a copy of the complaint and informed of constitutional rights. It is sometimes called "an arraignment on the warrant (or complaint)."

Arrest a deprivation, by legal authority, of a person's liberty; the seizure of an alleged or suspected offender to answer for a crime.

Arrest warrant a written order by a court directing a seizure of a person; see Warrant.

Arson willful and malicious burning of a house or other structure, motor vehicle, or aircraft.

Articulable basis an explainable reason.

Assault an attempt to inflict bodily injury on another person.

Attorney General the chief legal officer of each state and the federal government.

Back door options sanctions that may be used after confinement that may reduce prison or jail populations. They include work and education furloughs, work release, halfway houses, pre-release centers, restitution centers, outpatient clinics, and intensive probation and parole supervision programs.

Bail security given to ensure re-appearance of a defendant when required at every stage of criminal proceedings; given to obtain release from confinement.

Bench trial a trial by a judge without a jury, which may only occur after both the prosecution and defense have waived any rights to a trial by jury.

Bill of attainder in common law, legislative acts inflicting punishments without a hearing or judicial trial.

Bill of Rights the first ten amendments to the Constitution of the United States, now largely incorporated into the due process clause of the Fourteenth Amendment and thus made applicable to the states.

Bobbies nickname of the London Metropolitan police, after their originator, Sir Robert Peel.

Bond written promise of a surety.

Bondsagent persons (paid by defendants) who post a required amount with the court in order to obtain the release of a defendant from confinement.

Booking registration of an arrest.

Boot camp sanction involving a program of regimental discipline, usually followed by probation supervision.

Bow Street Runners a forerunner of the London police; a small group of professional police created in the mid-eighteenth century by John and Henry Fielding.

Burden of proof the duty of one party in a dispute to substantiate an allegation, either to avoid a dismissal or convince the judge or jury as to the truth of a claim in order to prevail.

Bureau of Justice Statistics part of the Department of Justice charged with collecting, analyzing, and reporting data on crime.

Burglary entering or being in a building with intent to steal property or commit another crime.

Capital offense a crime punishable by death.

Capital punishment the penalty of death.

Case in chief the main case presented by the prosecutor in a criminal trial, attempting to prove the guilt of the defendant beyond a reasonable doubt.

Challenge for cause in the selection of a jury, each side has the right to a certain number of challenges to the seating of jurors based on evidence that the potential juror may have a bias that could affect the decisions required. If the court agrees, the potential juror is excused.

Charge the offense contained in an accusation or indictment; the instructions by a judge to a jury, explaining the law applicable to the case.

Civil suit an action in court to protect a private right or compel a civil remedy (as opposed to a criminal prosecution).

Classical school of criminology early criminologists including Bentham and Beccaria who were influenced by British empiricist and utilitarian philosophers. Persons have free will and seek pleasure and avoidance of pain. To reduce crime, punishment should be certain, just severe enough but no more so, and swift.

Classification as commonly used in corrections, the process of assignment of inmates to security and custody levels, to educational, vocational, and other treatment programs, and to work. More generally, classification refers to the process of assignment of individuals to groups that are similar to one another but different from other groups.

Collective incapacitation the confinement of all persons guilty of a specific offense in order to restrain that group.

Commensurate sentences penalties scaled in severity in proportion to the seriousness of the crime.

Common law unwritten laws that developed in England on the basis of tradition and court decisions (precedents) rather than legislative enactments.

Community corrections sanctions ordered by a court requiring any of a variety of programs allowing the offender to remain in the community rather than to be incarcerated in a jail or prison. It includes probation and parole, but also various other penalties not requiring confinement in traditional jails or prisons. Most are non-custodial sentences, but some programs require custody in the community—for example, house arrest.

Community housing confinement in the community, sometimes used for pregnant women inmates.

Community policing proactive, problem-solving, community-involved police methods emphasizing goals of absence of crime and disorder and the solving of community problems through police–community collaboration in planning and assessment.

Community service order sanction requiring the offender to perform work benefitting the community.

Commutation a substitution of a lesser punishment for a greater one, such as changing a death sentence to life or shortening the period of required confinement.

Competency a legal concept for whether a defendant understands the charges and proceedings and is presently able to cooperate with a defense attorney with a reasonable degree of understanding.

Concurrent jurisdiction jurisdiction by more than one court, as by both the juvenile and criminal courts.

Concurrent sentences penalties to run together, that is, to be served at the same time.

Conditional release a discretionary release from confinement subject to rules established by authorities, such as a court or a parole board, such that violation of the rules may result in incarceration; or a mandatory release from prison with supervision in the community and possible return to prison if conditions of the release are not met.

Confession an admission of guilt made by an accused person. A confession is not admissible against a defendant at trial unlesss the prosecution demonstrates that it was made voluntarily, which must be established at least by a preponderance of the evidence, or, in some jurisdictions, beyond a reasonable doubt.

Consecutive sentences penalties to be served one after the other; sentences that are accumulative or sequential.

Consequentialism the position that the rightness of an act should be judged only in terms of its expected or actual consequences (effects).

Continuance postponement.

Conviction a determination by the court of guilt of the crime charged, based on a plea of guilty or a verdict of guilty and judgement of conviction.

Correctional officers persons employed by correctional agencies who are authorized to use physical force to maintain institutional order and safety.

Corrections general term, including institutional (e.g., jail, prison, reformatory, detention) and community (e.g., probation, parole) facilities and programs for offenders.

Counsel lawyer; attorney at law.

Court the branch of government responsible for resolving disputes under the laws of the government.

Court of record court which preserves a history of its cases.

Crackdown sudden, unexpected, substantial increases in police presence or activity.

Crime an intentional act committed without excuse or justification, causing harm that a government has determined to be injurious to the public and prosecutable in a criminal proceeding that may result in punishment.

Crime index the sum of the numbers of four common crimes against persons plus the numbers of three common property crimes plus the number of arsons; an index to the number of crimes in which the crimes included are given equal weight.

Crime rate the number of crimes in relation to some other number; for example, the ratio of the number of index offenses to 100,000 inhabitants.

Crimes against the social order crimes committed by an agent or agency in power.

Crimes of strict liability *malum prohibitum* crimes that do not require specific *mens rea*. There is liability without a showing of fault.

Criminal courts courts that hear cases under the criminal laws.

Criminal homicide a killing of one person by another when it is not justified or excused.

Criminogenic causing crime.

Culpability blameworthiness; fault; deserving of blame; intentional wrong-doing.

Custody restraint and physical control over a person, depriving that person of freedom; the level of supervision and surveillance assigned to an inmate for protection of the inmates and staff of an institution.

Day fine monetary penalty with the amount set in relation to the offender's daily earnings.

Day reporting sanction requiring offenders to report daily to a central location for supervision.

Defense a denial, answer, or plea opposing the truth or validity of an accusation.

Defense attorney the lawyer representing a defendant or accused person; the counsel for the defendant in a criminal proceeding.

Delinquency adjudication judgment by a juvenile court that a youth is delinquent or incorrigible; similar to a conviction in a criminal court.

Delinquent/delinquency terms used to describe minors who have committed an offense usually punishable if committed by adults but who are under the statutory age of criminal responsibility.

Desert reward or punishment according to merit; just desert; deserved punishment.

Detention restraint of a person, as in holding a person in jail before trial.

Determinate sentence penalties that are fixed at the time of sentencing (except perhaps they may be reduced by "good time" or "earned time").

Deterrence stopping or preventing crime by warning of the consequences.

Differential supervision provision of different supervision styles or programs of control or service for different classifications of probationers or parolees.

Directed verdict a verdict by the court in a jury trial, entered without consideration by the jury because the facts and law make it clear that it is the only one that reasonably could be returned. There may be a directed verdict of acquittal, but not of conviction, because the defendant has a constitutional right to the determination by a jury of the verdict of guilty or not.

Discharge termination of a proceeding; acquittal; release from custody.

Discretion choice or latitude in decision making.

Disparity differences; variation. When sentencing variation is associated with inequities, it is "unwarranted disparity." The term disparity by itself often now is used with this pejorative meaning.

Displacement movement of criminal activity to another area when opportunity is decreased or crime is otherwise deterred in one place.

Disposition the sentence received by a defendant.

Disposition hearing a hearing by a juvenile court judge to determine the placement or penalty to be required of a youth adjudicated delinquent or incorrigible at an adjudicatory hearing; similar to a sentencing hearing in a criminal court.

District attorney an officer of a government with the duty to prosecute persons accused of crimes; sometimes called the state's attorney or the county attorney; in the federal government, the United States Attorney.

Diversion methods of response by police or others intended to move a suspect out of the criminal justice system to another more appropriate agency.

Double jeopardy a provision of the Fifth Amendment to the Constitution of the United States is that no person shall twice be put in jeopardy of life or limb for the same offense. It generally prevents a second prosecution, regardless of the outcome of the first trial. It applies only after "jeopardy attaches" by the swearing in of the jury or, in a bench trial, after the judge has received the first evidence presented. It bars double punishments as well as double prosecution.

Ducking stool a stool or chair on which a prisoner was tied, as part of an apparatus permitting easy submersion in water, along with other public humiliation and abuse.

Due process of law this phrase of the Fifth and 14th Amendments to the Constitution does not have a fixed meaning, but its fundamental mandate that no person shall be deprived of life, liberty, or property without reasonable, lawful procedures is elaborated by changing judicial attitudes about fundamental fairness.

Education release program allowing an inmate to leave a correctional institution briefly for the purpose of education.

Electronic monitoring sanction involving computer assisted or telephonic checks on the whereabouts of offenders whose movements are restricted; using a device usually attached to the ankles ("ankle bracelets"); the movements of an offender may be tracked, or compliance with house arrest can be monitored.

Elements of a crime the parts of a criminal offense (acts and mental state) that a statute defines as composing a crime.

Emergency relief provisions statutes permitting or requiring the release of prison inmates when crowding reaches some specified level.

Empirical data observations derived from experience.

Empirical question a question that can be answered by observation.

En banc the full court, rather than panels, parts, or divisions.

Ex post facto **law** a law that makes an act that was done prior to passing the law punishable (or subject to more severe punishment) or changes the rules of evidence after the act in order to convict.

Exclusionary rule a constitutional rule of law that prohibits the admission of otherwise admissible evidence in a criminal trial if it was the product of illegal conduct by the police.

Exclusivity the requirement of classification that the categories used be mutually exclusive, that is, that a particular case cannot be put into more than one class.

Excuse defense negating the existence of a crime because there is no *actus reas* concurring with *mens rea*.

Exigency urgent necessity; an emergency situation calling for immediate action such that there is no time to obtain a search warrant.

Experiment classical experimental research plan by which equivalent groups are compared with and without the introduction of a variable being tested in order to determine its effects.

False negative an error in prediction in which a predicted success actually is a failure.

False positive an error in prediction in which a predicted failure actually is a success.

Federal Bureau of Investigation part of the Department of Justice charged with law enforcement functions including the collection, analysis, and reporting of crime statistics from the **Uniform Crime Reports (UCR)** published annually in *Crime in the United States*.

Felony a serious crime, as distinguished from a misdemeanor, often defined as an offense punishable by death or imprisonment for a year or more.

Felony murder an unlawful homicide occurring in the commission of a felony; a criminal homicide caused unintentionally by intentional participation in a felony; a killing of another while intending to do that person serious bodily harm. Felony murder usually is a category of First Degree Murder.

Fine monetary penalty.

First appearance an arrested person must be brought before a magistrate within a reasonable time for bail consideration; also called "initial appearance."

Flat time sentences penalties with fixed duration of punishment.

Forfeiture sanction requiring the seizure of property.

Formal prediction methods procedures for making predictions using tools, such as equations, tables, or charts, usually empirically derived, to forecast the expected value of some outcome.

Fraud crimes of deception; intentional deception resulting in loss of the property of another person.

Front door options sanctions that may be used at the time of sentencing that may reduce prison or jail populations. They include community service orders, monetary penalties, probation, forfeitures, restitution, fines, intensive supervision, house arrest, day reporting, assignment to specialized probation programs, shock incarceration, boot camps, intermittent sentences, community housing, placement in short term treatment or confinement facilities, and offender-specific planning.

Fruit of the poisonous tree the doctrine that all evidence that is the result of illegal conduct by an official is not admissible in a criminal trial against the victim of that misconduct. Once the tree is poisoned (primary illegally obtained evidence), then all the fruit of the tree (secondary or derivative evidence) is poisoned or tainted also and may not be used. Such evidence may be used, however, to impeach the testimony of the defendant who takes the stand in his or her own defense.

Galley a low, flat ship pulled by banks of oars manned by chained slaves or convicts.

Gaol jail in England that held persons accused of crimes or awaiting punishment.

General deterrence the prevention of crimes by warning the general public through punishing offenders; also called "general prevention."

General theory of crime the theory of Michael Gottfredson and Travis Hirschi explaining the propensity to crime, based in part on the nature of common crimes.

Good faith exception if there is a total absence of any intention to seek an unfair advantage and an honest and sincere intention to fulfill obligations, this is called "good faith." When evidence was obtained by police acting in good faith with a search warrant, the evidence may be admissible at trial even though the warrant later was found to be invalid. This is known as the good faith exception to the exclusionary rule.

Good time time off for good behavior.

Grand jury a group of citizens, often 23 in number, serving as a part of a criminal court, formed to investigate crimes and to accuse persons of crimes when it has discovered sufficient evidence to support holding a person for trial. When a Grand Jury determines that a prosecutor's accusation in a **indictment**, if proved, would be sufficient to bring about a conviction, the indictment is endorsed by the foreman as a **True Bill**. An **Indictment** is a written accusation by a prosecutor submitted to a grand jury, charging a person (or persons) with a crime. The grand jury is distinguished from a **petit jury** (petty jury) in a criminal trial, traditionally made up of 12 persons who are the finders of facts.

Guilty found to have committed a crime charged or a lesser included one. A finding of guilt requires that the evidence indicates beyond a reasonable doubt that the defendant committed the crime.

Halfway house correctional facility providing, in part, confinement and in part, release into the community for work or education; institutions with partly custodial and partly non-custodial programs. Such facilities may house offenders as an alternative to sentences to full custodial programs such as prisons, or they may operate as pre-parole programs.

Harm an injury or damage done to another.

Home confinement house arrest.

Homicide a killing of one person by another. Criminal homicide is such a killing when not justified or excused.

Hot pursuit exception to the general requirement of a valid search warrant to authorize a search and seizure. Police may engage in a search and seizure without a warrant if they are in immediate pursuit of a suspect believed to be dangerous, or they may enter a suspect's home in hot pursuit if they have reason to believe that the suspect is there.

Hot spots areas of a community where most crimes take place.

House arrest sanction requiring confinement to home instead of jail or prison.

Hypothesis a statement that can be confirmed or not by examining the evidence that would or would not support it; a tentative, testable conjecture.

Impeachment an attempt, by either the prosecution or defense attorney in a criminal trial, to challenge the truthfulness of a witness by showing evidence that he or she cannot be believed.

Implementing carrying out activities or programs planned.

Incapacitation the prevention of crime by restraint of a potential offender, usually through confinement.

Incarceration imprisonment; confinement in a jail, prison, penitentiary, or other correctional facility.

Inclusivity the requirement of classification that the classes established include all the elements of the population of interest, that is, that none are left out.

Incorrigible a legal term meaning uncorrectable or ungovernable; a juvenile whose behavior cannot be made to conform to legal standards.

Indentured servant a person bound by a contract to provide services, required as a punishment for a period of time fixed by colonial legislatures.

Indeterminate sentence a penalty of indefinite term or length, the actual and ultimate nature of which is to be determined later. Most indeterminate sentences actually are "quasi-indeterminate" with a lower and upper bound but still providing a wide range of discretion, usually by a paroling authority.

Indictment a formal written accusation submitted to a grand jury by a prosecutor, charging one or more persons with a crime. The prosecutor presents the indictment under oath to the grand jury, who must determine whether the accusation, if proved, would be enough to bring about the conviction of the accused person; if the jury decides that is the case, then the indictment is endorsed by the foreperson as a true bill.

Informal prediction methods procedures for making predictions subjectively, impressionistically, or "in the head."

Information data that demonstrably reduce the uncertainty in a decision; data that are related to the objectives of a policy or individual decision; in law, formal charges brought by a prosecutor to a Grand Jury in an indictment, or, more usually, to a court, including a statement of specific charges and evidence in their support.

Inmate a person committed to an institution such as a jail or prison.

Insanity a legal term meaning a mental disorder that relieves the person of criminal responsibility for an act.

Intensive supervision strict supervision, often with requirements such as drug testing, curfew, or other restrictions, with more frequent contact and surveillance by probation or parole officers; there is no standard or agreed upon definition.

Intensive supervision diversion program of close supervision on probation or parole designed to divert offenders from prison; or, a program under which offenders already in prison are re-sentenced to intensive supervision in the community.

Intermediate punishments sanctions more severe than routine probation but less so than traditional incarceration in jail or prison.

Intermittent incarceration repeated confinement with intervals of freedom from custody, as in week-end jail sentences.

Interrogation process of rigorous questioning by police.

Investigation an inquiry into the question whether a crime has occurred and, if so, the identification of the offender or offenders. The investigation is essential to establishment of probable cause for an arrest, for prosecutor decisions, and for collection and preservation of evidence for court.

Involuntary manslaughter unintentionally causing death by reckless disregard of a substantial risk to the life of another.

ISP see **intensive supervision** program.

Jail a correctional facility, usually operated by a county or municipal government, in which persons are held awaiting trial or to which convicted persons are generally sentenced to a year or less in confinement.

Judge the person who presides over a court of justice for the purpose of settling controversies between opposing parties in a dispute.

Judicial precedent a case decided earlier, which then becomes recognized as authority for deciding later cases.

Jurisdiction the power to hear and adjudicate a case; also, particular legal systems.

Jury nullification the power of a jury to acquit even when the evidence would justify a finding of guilt, stemming from the fact that a jury finding of not guilty is not subject to reversal or review.

Jury trial the trial of an issue of fact before a jury, guaranteed by the Sixth Amendment to accused persons in all criminal prosecutions other than petty offenses for which punishment may not exceed six months imprisonment. The jury must be impartial and must be chosen from a cross section of the community and may not discriminate against any class of potential jurors.

Just desert the position that punishment must be inflicted in proportion to the harm done by a crime, considering also the culpability of the offender.

Justice of the Peace in the early Southwest, a judicial officer assisting an alcade by hearing less serious cases; now, a judicial officer of a lower local or municipal court of limited jurisdiction.

Justification defense negating the existence of a crime because the act is not prohibited.

Juvenile court general name for a court with jurisdiction over delinquency, status offenses, and matters of abuse and neglect (and often over adoption, parental rights, and emancipation of minors).

Labeling putting persons in a certain class, often with accompanying stigma.

Larceny stealing; taking another person's property without permission.

Legalistic style police management mode of strict law enforcement with limited discretion and avoidance of other interventions.

Lex talionis the position that punishment inflicted for a crime must be identical to the harm it caused, or as nearly so as possible, as in "an eye for an eye . . ."

Litigation seeking legal rights to be determined and enforced by a civil court action.

M'Naghten rule a rule of law that a person was not responsible for a crime if, because of mental disease or defect, he did not know what he was doing or that it was wrong, or he was deluded and thought he was acting in self defense.

Magistrate judicial officer of the lower courts such as a justice of the peace or judge of a municipal court.

Magna Carta the "great charter" that King John of England was forced to grant in 1215, guaranteeing certain liberties to the English people.

Malum in se a "natural wrong" that would be thought evil by the community even without a specific prohibition.

Malum prohibitum wrong because it is prohibited and made unlawful by the state.

Mandatory release a mode of release from prison, by which a prisoner who has served a required sentence, often shortened by credits for work or lack of disciplinary infractions, must be released.

Mandatory sentence a term or portion of a term that must be served.

Mean average; the number obtained by adding the scores for each case and dividing by the number of cases; also called the arithmetic average.

Median in a frequency distribution, the point above and below which half the cases fall; the 50th percentile; the mid-point of the distribution.

Mens rea the mental state accompanying a forbidden act; a guilty mind.

Miranda warning before any questioning, a suspect must be warned of the right to remain silent, that any statement made may be used against him or her, that he or she has a right to an attorney, and that an attorney may be retained or will be appointed.

Misdemeanor a less serious crime, usually distinguished from a felony by the place of confinement (jail rather than prison) or duration of punishment (usually less than a year) or type of punishment (e.g., fines, community service).

Mistake an act due to ignorance or misconception of the law or of facts.

Mitigating factors offense or offender characteristics that may lessen the severity of a penalty.

Monetary penalty fine, payment of court costs, fees for services, or other sanctions requiring money payments.

Moratorium a delay, as required in an emergency.

Murder intentional killing of one person by another, without justification or excuse.

Murder in the First Degree premeditated, deliberate, killing; by statute, some other killings even without deliberation.

Murder in the Second Degree killing with intent to cause death, without premeditation and deliberation.

National Crime Victimization Survey the national representative sample survey of victimizations of persons at least 12 years old conducted for the Bureau of Justice Statistics, based on interviews by Census Bureau personnel.

Negative retributivism the position that a person who is not guilty must not be punished.

Net widening practices intended to divert offenders from the criminal justice system but have instead the effect of extending it.

NIBRS National Incident Based Reporting System; a program for the improvement and enhancement of the UCR program now in the process of implementation by the Federal Bureau of Investigation and the Bureau of Justice Statistics.

Nolle prosequi a writ, used in England since the 16th century, that could be filed by the Attorney General of England to dismiss charges brought by private prosecution. The writ was used in early America, but now it has been replaced by the prosecutor's power to decline to charge or to file motions for dismissal with the court.

Nolo contendere a plea to a criminal charge indicating that the defendant will not contest it. It is equivalent to a plea of guilty for that criminal matter, accepted only at the discretion of the court. The court must be satisfied that it is voluntarily and intelligently made and that there is a factual basis for it. It cannot be used elsewhere as an admission of guilt.

Nuisance offenses a category of crimes generally viewed as relatively non-serious.

Offender-specific planning program developed in relation to individual offender and victim needs as an alternative to confinement.

Outcomes all the consequences of a decision that concern the person making the decision (or the institution represented).

Outpatient clinic community based facility for psychological or substance abuse treatment.

Pardon an exercise of the sovereign prerogative of mercy, relieving a person of punishment, further punishment, or other legal liabilities for a crime.

Parens patriae literally, "state as parent;" the doctrine that the state may assume the role of guardian when parents are determined to be incapable or unworthy.

Parole traditionally, a conditional release from prison, usually as a result of a discretionary decision by a parole board, enabling a prisoner to serve the remainder of a term of imprisonment in the community under supervision. If the conditions set by the parole board are violated, the parolee may be returned to prison by the parole board. It now also may mean any placement under imposed supervision in the community after incarceration.

Parole board group of officials appointed by state governors to establish rules and make discretionary decisions about the conditional release of prisoners to the community under supervision and with decision making authority for return of parolees to prison for violations of conditions of release.

Parole guidelines policy governing the exercise of discretion in parole decision making, prescribing usual decisions for similarly classified offenders but allowing alternative choices when specific written reasons are given.

Parole officer an employee of a government charged with supervision of persons on parole.

Parole revocation order by a parole board, after finding that a parolee has violated the conditions of parole, that the offender be returned to prison, either to finish the term originally imposed by the court or with a new sentence by the court for a crime while on parole.

Pat down a carefully limited search of the outer clothing of a suspect in order to discover concealed weapons; a "frisk."

Penitence profound regret and sorrow with a determination to make amends for a wrong.

Penitentiary prisons named for their purpose of reforming the offender through penitence.

Penology the study of punishment; the study of prisons.

Peremptory challenge in the selection of a jury, each side has the right to a certain number of challenges to the seating of jurors without giving a reason; the word peremptory means "absolute, conclusive, final, and not subject to appeal."

Permissive retributivism the position that a person who is guilty may be punished.

Personal offenses crimes including physical assault, personal harm, and interpersonal confrontations, generally seen as most serious.

Petit jury a trial jury; a group of people summoned and sworn to determine issues of fact and to reach a verdict concerning those findings.

Pillory wooden framework on a post, with holes to hold the head and hands, in order that a person could be punished further by public ridicule and abuse.

Plain view exception to the general requirement of a valid search warrant to authorize a search and seizure. Observing that which is open to view is not a search. The exception may be limited in areas where the person has a reasonable exception of privacy, and in all cases there must be a legal justification for being in a position to observe the seized property.

Plea a defendant's answer at arraignment of "guilty," "not guilty" or in some jurisdictions *"nolo contendere" (no contest)*.

Plea bargaining a process by which the accused (usually through a defense attorney) and a prosecutor negotiate a mutually agreed upon disposition of criminal charges. The negotiations can focus on a plea of guilty by the defendant to a lesser offense or to only one of the charges that the prosecutor might bring. The defendant seeks in return a reduction in the counts charged, lesser charges, or a reduced severity of the sentence. The judge has discretion whether to accept the resulting plea, but, if it is accepted, then the state must keep the bargain. Most persons found guilty of a crime are convicted after a plea of guilty rather that after a trial. Many are the result of plea bargains.

Police persons employed by a government who are authorized to use physical force to maintain public order and safety; an organized civil force for maintaining order, detecting and preventing crime, and enforcing the law.

Positive retributivism the position that a person who is guilty ought to be punished.

Positivist school of criminology early criminologists, including Lombroso, who sought to identify individual correlates of crime based on an empirical, scientific approach.

Posse comitatus persons called to assist the 12th century sheriff who, once summoned, had police powers equivalent to the sheriff.

Pre-release center minimum security correctional facility with programs for offenders shortly before release on parole.

Pre-sentence report a report to the court providing information to assist with sentencing, prepared by a probation officer, typically presenting the facts of the case, data on the person's prior criminal record, various social history data, and sentencing recommendations.

Pre-trial motions applications to the court by the prosecution or defense before a trial begins, such as for discovery of evidence not disclosed, postponement, or suppression of evidence claimed to have been illegally collected. Motions may be addressed to issues that are discretionary with the judge or are a matter of law.

Preliminary hearing a court proceeding for the purpose of determining whether probable cause existed for the arrest of a person. It must be decided whether there is enough evidence to warrant the accused person's detention or continued detention and the continuance of the criminal justice process.

Preponderance superiority in weight or number; more on one side than on the other.

Presumption a rule of law requiring the assumption of a fact from another fact or facts.

Presumption of innocence the principle that a person is innocent of a crime until proven guilty. The principle is not contained in the Constitution but traditionally has been accepted as part of our system of criminal justice and is shown in the constitutional requirement that the guilt of a defendant must be shown by the prosecution to be beyond a reasonable doubt.

Presumptive sentences penalties presumed to be fixed but which may be modified by aggravating or mitigating factors.

Preventive detention confinement for the purpose of incapacitation, that is, to prevent future crimes by the accused person.

Prima facie **case** a case in which evidence is "sufficient on its face" to support but not compel a conclusion.

Primary prevention avoidance of delinquency or crime in the first instance (as opposed to stopping repeated offending).

Prison a correctional facility, usually operated by a state or the federal government, to which convicted persons are generally sentenced to a year or more in confinement.

Privatization movement toward operation of correctional services and institutions by private industry under contracts with governments.

Proactive taking action based on looking ahead rather than merely reacting to complaints or emergencies.

Probable cause on the basis of available information, it is believed reasonably that a crime has been committed by a particular person.

Probation a procedure by which a convicted person is released, usually without imprisonment, subject to conditions imposed by the court. Also, it is a judicial stay of sentence, a program placement with imposed supervision, and a conditional release. The person then is supervised in the community under the specified conditions. If the conditions are violated, the probation may be revoked by the court and an original sentence to custody may be executed.

Probation officer an employee of a court charged with supervision of persons on probation.

Probation revocation an order by the court, after finding that probation conditions have been violated, resulting in execution of a sentence previously suspended. This usually means confinement in jail or prison.

Problem solving policing a search by police for the causes and remedies of crime and disorder.

Procedural due process assures the fairness of procedures by which the government would deprive a person of property or liberty.

Program evaluation investigations designed to describe interventions and their effects.

Program fidelity the degree to which a program is implemented with faithfulness to the program design, that is, to the program planning.

Program integrity the degree to which a program corresponds to the theory underlying its development.

Program strength the intensity of an intervention or program effort ("dosage" of a treatment).

Propensity inclination or tendency

Property offenses crimes involving theft or property damage, without serious physical harm or assault.

Prosecutor a person who investigates alleged or suspected crimes and prepares and conducts prosecutions of persons accused of crimes. State prosecutors usually are called district (or county) attorneys. The federal prosecutor is called the United States Attorney for a particular federal district. The role of the prosecutor, who is charged with the duty to see that the law is faithfully executed and enforced, is to seek justice.

Protective custody classification for custody intended to safeguard an inmate or witness from harm by others.

Psychometric measurement of mental states or activities; measurement of behavior.

Public defender a defense attorney hired by the government, often appointed by the court, to represent accused persons who are unable or unwilling to hire an attorney.

Punishment sanctions imposed as a result of conviction for a crime.

Random method of selecting members of one group from a larger group such that every member of the larger group has the same likelihood of being selected for the smaller group. Random selection often is used in an experiment in order that the groups to be compared can be considered equivalent in all respects other than the variable being studied for its effects.

Rape usually, sexual intercourse with a female without consent, by force, fear, or threat; in some jurisdictions, renamed sexual assault, with gender neutral provisions and elimination of previous marital exemption. Statutory rape usually means sexual intercourse with a female who is under a statutory age of consent, regardless of her willingness.

Rational decision a decision choice among the available alternatives that, on the basis of information available, maximizes the likelihood of attainment of the purposes of the decision.

Reasonable suspicion a sensible belief, short of probable cause, that a crime has occurred and a specific person did it. This standard, lesser than the probable cause standard, is sufficient for stopping a person who is reasonably suspected of criminal activity. In order to "frisk" or "pat down" the person, the officer must have a reasonable suspicion that the suspect has weapons that might be used to assault him.

Rebuttal refutation by evidence or argument.

Recidivism repeated offenses by a person after conviction and sentencing for a crime. A convicted felon or misdemeanant who returns to criminality including rearrest, reconviction and renincarceration.

Reclassification review of inmate custody and treatment assignments with a view to changing them.

Reformatory prisons named for their purpose of reforming the offender through rewards for education and good work habits.

Rehabilitation restoration of a person to good repute or accepted responsibility, after disrepute.

Reintegration recombination of the person and community into a harmonious whole.

Reliability the degree to which a measurement is consistent, for example, the degree of agreement in repeated measures using the same methods or procedures; the degree to which a measure is free of unwanted variability.

Replication repetition of an experiment in order to see whether the results are again observed.

Restitution sanction requiring compensation to a victim to be paid by the offender.

Restitution center minimum security correctional facility with programs of work and victim payments by the offender.

Restorative justice concept of reparation rather than retribution as a goal of the justice system, restoring the victim to the community, emphasizing victim-offender mediation, restitution, community service, and community sanctions rather than confinement; a general framework for criminal justice planning and policy emphasizing repairing the harms caused by crime.

Retribution punishment for a harm done.

Retributivism the position that a person who is blameworthy *must* be punished. (This is also called positive retributivism. Negative retributivism is the position that a person not blameworthy must *not* be punished. Permissive retributivism is the position that a person who is blameworthy *may be, but need not be* punished.)

Right to counsel an accused person has the right to the assistance of a defense attorney, as assured by the Sixth amendment, applicable to the states through the 14th amendment, in any accusation that could result in a deprivation of liberty.

Robbery taking another person's property by force or threat.

ROR release on recognizance—release of a suspect from custody on the person's own promise to appear in court when required.

Sanction a penalty or reward imposed on persons in order to enforce the law.

Search an inspection or examination of a person or place in order to find and take evidence useful in investigation and prosecution of a crime.

Search and seizure searches and seizures are limited constitutionally by the Fourth and Fourteenth Amendments to the Constitution of the United States and by provisions of various state constitutions, statutes, and court rules. They must be reasonable, usually requiring probable cause. Usually, a search **warrant** is required, but that may not be the case for searches incident to an arrest, frisks done as part of an investigative stop (limited to a "pat down,") seizures of items in plain view, seizures of abandoned property, searches and seizures in exigent circumstances (**exigencies**) in which it would be impossible or unwise to obtain a warrant, searches for which proper consent has been given, and searches at international borders. If the search is unreasonable or otherwise unconsitutional, the evidence seized is excluded at any criminal proceeding in which the defendant has standing to object to its introduction. Moreover, all fruits of the illegal search are excluded. Victims of an illegal search also may bring a civil tort suit against the officers who conducted the search for violation of their civil right of privacy.

Secondary prevention avoidance of repeated offending.

Security the level of supervision and surveillance assigned to an inmate for the protection of the outside community.

Seizure the forcible dispossession of property from its owner, under presumed or actual authority of law. A seizure of the person is an arrest.

Selective incapacitation the confinement of groups of persons predicted to do crimes at a high rate if not restrained.

Selective incorporation a process by which the Supreme Court of the United States, by a series of court decisions, has determined that most of the provisions in the Bill of Rights apply not only to the federal government but also to the states.

Self-incrimination the giving of testimony against oneself. The Fifth Amendment to the Constitution of the United States, applicable to the states through the 14th Amendment, assures the right to refuse to answer questions or otherwise give testimony against oneself that have a substantial likelihood of criminal incrimination.

Sentence execution the carrying out of the sentence by the court.

Sentence imposition the announcing of the sentence by the court.

Sentencing assignment of the punishment ordered by a court to be inflicted upon a person convicted of a crime.

Sentencing commissions legislatively established bodies for the purpose of prescribing the structure and standards for fixing sentences, often through the use of sentencing guidelines.

Sentencing guidelines procedures that structure the sentencing decision process by indicating the usually expected sentence for combinations of offense and offender characteristics, typically with departures expected but requiring that specific reasons be given for such exceptions.

Serious drug offenses crimes of selling or manufacturing heroin, hallucinogens, cocaine, barbiturates, and amphetamines.

Service style police management type aimed more at community assistance, with less emphasis on strict law enforcement.

Shire-reeve sheriff, who, by royal authority, governed groups of shires (hundreds of households).

Shock incarceration short-term confinement intended to have a specific deterrent effect.

Short-term treatment and confinement facilities sanction combining a therapeutic community program and confinement.

Side door options sanctions that may be used after sentencing but before usual parole procedures that may reduce prison or jail populations. An example is the intensive supervision diversion program in New Jersey.

Specific deterrence the prevention of further crime by an offender by punishing that person.

Split sentence a common sentencing disposition in which a period of confinement in jail is combined with supervision on probation after the prisoner is released.

Standing mute refusing to plea; equivalent to a plea of not guilty.

Status offense an act by a juvenile that would not be a crime if committed by an adult but which is a violation of the juvenile law.

Statute an act of the legislature which becomes law.

Stocks apparatus for punishment, with holes to hold the prisoner's ankles and sometimes wrists in order to expose the person to public ridicule and abuse.

Substantive due process requires that legislation must be reasonably related to the furtherance of legitimate governmental objectives.

Surety security against loss or damage; a pledge or bond.

Surveillance oversight; watching (observation of) a person under supervision or suspicion.

Suspended sentence a sentence, the imposition or execution of which has been withheld by the court under specified terms and conditions.

Team policing assignment of teams of officers to a particular neighborhood or area in order to provide a better understanding of community problems and a better service.

Testimony a statement of a witness under oath, usually in court.

Tort a private or civil wrong or injury resulting from a breach of a legal duty, for which an injured person may have a right to recover damages.

Transportation deportation and exile as punishment.

Trap door options emergency release procedures in some states that may be initiated when prison populations exceed a specified amount of crowding.

Treatment anything done to, with, or for the offender or the environment with the aim of changing behavior to prevent new crimes.

Trial an examination before a court, based on established procedures, to judge the facts and the law about an issue, for the purpose of settling it.

Trial courts courts of general jurisdiction over all cases involving civil or criminal law.

UCR see **Uniform Crime Reports**

Unconstitutional conflicting with a provision of a constitution, usually the United States Constitution; a finding that a statute is unconstitutional voids the statute (as if it never had been enacted).

Uniform Crime Reports annual reports of the Federal Bureau of Investigation based on voluntary reports from law enforcement agencies, including statistics on crimes known to the police, arrests, crimes cleared by arrests, and on trends, rates, and other information about the extent of crime; UCR.

United States Attorney the district attorney in the federal government.

United States Supreme Court the final authority in interpreting federal law; the ultimate authority in interpreting the United States Constitution as it applies to federal and state law.

Utilitarianism the moral theory that we ought always to do that which will produce the greatest good.

Validity the degree to which a method of measurement measures what it is intended to measure or allows correct inferences of some specific nature.

Victim compensation money awarded by the state to victims in order to make up for losses.

Victim impact statements written statements by victims expressing to the court the economic, physical, or psychological losses suffered because of a crime.

Victimization a harm.

Victim-offender mediation programs using a third party to help negotiate an agreement between victims and offenders in order to resolve a criminal incident.

Vigilantes informal groups of citizens acting on their own initiative to "take the law into their own hands"—sometimes convicting and sentencing an accused person on the spot.

Vigiles public police in ancient Rome.

Voir dire examination by the court or by the attorneys for the prosecution and defense to determine whether there is cause for challenge (see **Challenge for Cause**) and to provide information to the attorneys for their exercise of **peremptory challenges**; also, the phrase may refer to a hearing required to be held without the jurors.

Voluntary manslaughter an intentional killing without malice, as in the heat of passion; unintentional killing resulting from unreasonable and grossly negligent conduct.

Waiver voluntary surrender of jurisdiction by the juvenile court; transfer to the criminal court by a discretionary decision of the juvenile court judge.

Warrant a search warrant is an order issued by a judge directing law enforcement officers to conduct a search of specified premises for specific things or persons and to bring them before the court. They are issued only after probable cause is shown that the described item is located in the place designated and was involved in the planning or commission of a crime, supported by sworn allegations particularly describing the place to be searched and the person or things to be seized. An important exception to the requirement of a warrant is that of a search of the person and the area under his or her control when the search is incident to a valid arrest (a seizure of the person made upon probable cause). There are other exceptions; see text. Only a judicial officer can issue a warrant.

▲ ▲ ▲ ▲ ▲ ▲ ▲ **Watchman style** police management type emphasizing order maintenance, with broad police discretion.

Week-end confinement a person is confined to jail on weekends only, enabling the person to remain at home and continue working in the community.

Week-end sentence sanction requiring confinement on week-ends; a common form of intermittent incarceration.

Work release program allowing an inmate to leave a correctional institution briefly for the purpose of work.

Writ of *certiorari* a means of gaining review by an appellate court; a demand for the record in a particular case, made by a superior court to one of inferior jurisdiction, in order that the court issuing the writ may examine the proceedings in order to determine whether there were any irregularities. In the Supreme Court of the United States, the writ is discretionary but will be issued if at least four justices vote to hear the case.

Writ of *habeas corpus* a procedure for obtaining a judicial determination of the legality of holding a person in custody. Known as the "great writ," it means "you have the body of." It brings a petitioner before the court in order that the court may determine the legality of the person's confinement. The federal writ is used to test the constitutionality of a state criminal conviction.

Subject
and
Author

Subject Index

T

U

Author Index